Alex Mitchell · Mirjam Vosmeer (Eds.)

# Interactive Storytelling

14th International Conference
on Interactive Digital Storytelling, ICIDS 2021
Tallinn, Estonia, December 7–10, 2021
Proceedings

Springer

*Editors*
Alex Mitchell ⓘ
National University of Singapore
Singapore, Singapore

Mirjam Vosmeer
Amsterdam University of Applied Sciences
Amsterdam, The Netherlands

ISSN 0302-9743          ISSN 1611-3349 (electronic)
Lecture Notes in Computer Science
ISBN 978-3-030-92299-3          ISBN 978-3-030-92300-6 (eBook)
https://doi.org/10.1007/978-3-030-92300-6

LNCS Sublibrary: SL3 – Information Systems and Applications, incl. Internet/Web, and HCI

This Springer imprint is published by the registered company Springer Nature Switzerland AG
The registered company address is: Gewerbestrasse 11, 6330 Cham, Switzerland

# Lecture Notes in Computer Science 13138

More information about this subseries at https://link.springer.com/bookseries/7409

# Preface

This volume constitutes the proceedings of the 14th International Conference on Interactive Digital Storytelling (ICIDS 2021). ICIDS is the premier conference for researchers and practitioners concerned with studying digital interactive forms of narrative from a variety of perspectives, including theoretical, technological, and applied design lenses. The annual conference is an interdisciplinary gathering that combines technology-focused approaches with humanities-inspired theoretical inquiry, empirical research, and artistic expression.

This year's conference was built around the central theme of "Interconnectedness and Social Impact". This theme was intended both to reflect the ways in which we are increasingly interconnected with each other and with the world around us, and the ways in which the challenges of recent years are forcing us to find ways to reconnect as we are increasingly in danger of becoming disconnected. We hoped that this theme would help us to explore the ways in which Interactive Digital Narrative, as an academic discipline, represents an interconnection of multiple fields of study while at the same time is developing into a unique, independent discipline, with its own methods, approaches, and rich history. Finally, in the spirit of acknowledging the interconnectedness of our actions with the world around us, we hoped that this theme would encourage a reflection on the ways in which our research and practice can provide positive social impact.

These proceedings represent the latest work from a wide range of researchers, with representation from around the world. Authors of submitted papers represent 29 different countries, with a similar range of representation in terms of the Program Committee. The program was divided into four main areas: Narrative Systems (covering technological research from narrative AI to authoring tools), Interactive Narrative Theory (exploring topics such as narratological models, literary approaches, aesthetics, and critical readings), Interactive Narrative Impact and Applications (describing the impact of interactive narrative on society, ethical, moral, social, and policy issues, and novel applications), and Interactive Narrative Research Discipline and Contemporary Practice (presenting new philosophies and methodologies for research and teaching).

Although ICIDS 2021 was hosted at Tallinn University, Estonia, due to the ongoing COVID-19 pandemic, the conference was organized as a hybrid event, with participants either attending on-site or joining the conference remotely through a number of different online platforms. Care was taken to ensure that all aspects of the program, from the workshops and paper sessions through to the posters, demos, and art exhibition, were equally accessible to those who were attending physically and virtually.

This year, we received 99 paper submissions (71 full papers, 20 short papers, and 8 posters/demos). Following the review process, the Program Committee accepted 18 full papers, 17 short papers, and 17 posters/demos, including full or short papers which were resubmitted in the short paper or the poster/demo category. The acceptance rate for full papers was 25.35%.

As part of our ongoing efforts to improve the review process, some changes were made this year. As in the past, the review process was strictly double-blind, used a structured and detailed review form, and included an extended discussion phase between the reviewers, steered by our area chairs, to attempt to build a consensus opinion. A minimum of three reviews per paper were requested before the decision, with additional reviews solicited on the recommendations of reviewers, or in the light of their discussions. In addition, we included a rebuttal phase, and final decisions were made at a virtual program chairs meeting, which included all the area chairs. We believe that including a virtual program chair meeting as part of the process helps to improve the transparency of the review process. We welcome feedback from both the authors and reviewers to help us continue to refine and strengthen the way that we run the conference. We want to thank our area chairs for their hard work and participation in the meta-reviews process: Ben Samuel, Boyang "Albert" Li, Frank Nack, Ruth Aylett, Vincenzo Lombardo, Cristina Sylla, Christian Roth, and Lissa Holloway-Attaway.

Finally we want to thank the members of the ICIDS community who have served as reviewers this year, particularly given the ongoing difficult and changing circumstances around the world. The commitment of our reviewers to provide high-quality reviews and constructive and insightful discussions is a credit to our community, and helps to maintain the rigour and integrity of our ongoing development of this exciting and growing field.

December 2021                                                      Alex Mitchell
                                                                Mirjam Vosmeer

# ARDIN, the Association for Research in Digital Interactive Narratives

ARDIN's purpose is to support research in Interactive Digital Narratives (IDN), in a wide range of forms, be that video and computer games, interactive documentaries and fiction, journalistic interactives, art projects, educational titles, transmedia, virtual reality and augmented reality titles, or any emerging novel forms of IDN.

ARDIN provides a home for an interdisciplinary community and for various activities that connect, support, grow, and validate said community. The long-term vision for the suite of activities hosted by ARDIN includes membership services such as a community platform, newsletters, job postings, and support for local gatherings, but also conferences, publication opportunities, research fellowships, and academic/professional awards. ARDIN holds monthly online socials, where both established researchers and graduate students share their ongoing work in an informal setting. There are also several committees and task forces, which are listed on the following page.

ICIDS is the main academic conference of ARDIN. Additional international and local conferences are welcome to join the organization. The Zip-Scene conference, focused on eastern Europe, is the first associated conference.

Diversity is important to ARDIN. The organization will strive towards gender balance and the representation of different people from different origins. Diversity also means to represent scholars at different levels of their careers.

No ARDIN member shall discriminate against any other ARDIN member or others outside of the organization in any way, including but not limited to gender, nationality, race, religion, sexuality, or ability. Discrimination against these principles will not be tolerated and membership in ARDIN can be withdrawn based on evidence of such behavior.

The association is incorporated as a legal entity in Amsterdam, the Netherlands. First proposed during the ICIDS 2017 conference in Madeira, Portugal, the association was officially announced at ICIDS 2018 in Dublin, Ireland. During its foundational year, members of the former ICIDS Steering Committee continued to serve as the ARDIN board as approved by the first general assembly at ICIDS 2018. The current board structure and membership were approved at the second general assembly at ICIDS 2019 in Utah, USA, and as of October 2021 ARDIN has more than 190 members.

More information about ARDIN can be found at https://ardin.online/. ARDIN is also on Facebook https://www.facebook.com/ARDINassociation, Twitter @ARDIN_online, and Discord https://discord.gg/jNg5b5dWP4.

## Committees

Diversity and Inclusion committee – chaired by Theresa (Tess) Tanenbaum and including Rebecca Rouse. This committee will work to further inclusivity and equity within our community and the discipline at large. Projects to tackle will be determined by a needs assessment of the community members, but one initiative already underway focuses on trans-inclusive publishing practices in terms of facilitating author name changes. Please reach out to Tess directly if you are interested in working together (tess.tanen at gmail.com). Come join us and let's make a difference together!

Graduate Research committee – led by Sarah Brown. This task force puts a focus on research by graduate students (Masters and PhD) to further exchange, provide support, and offer a forum for early career researchers. Contact Sarah Brown to join the committee (sarah.brown at ufl.edu).

Promotion and Advancement committee – led by Hartmut Koenitz and Josh Fisher and including Luis Bruni and Colette Daiute. The aim of this committee is to create a tenure equivalency document and recruit a team of expert reviewers for tenure and examination. Those interested should reach out to Hartmut Koenitz (hkoenitz at gmail.com).

IDN in Education committee – led by Jonathon Barbara. This committee will be looking into how IDN can become a part of school (K-12) curricula and will be producing a white paper with recommendations. Students are also welcome to join as task force members! Those interested should reach out to Jonathon Barbara (barbaraj at tcd.ie).

## Task Forces

Task Force on Inclusive Pricing Structure – led by Agnes Bakk. This task force will be looking into how to adjust registration for membership and conference registration according to GDP. Those interested should reach out to Agnes Bakk (bakk at mome. hu).

Task Force on ARDIN Outreach – led by Maria Cecilia Reyes. Aims of this task force are to create awareness about Interactive Digital Narratives and around ARDIN, and to build partnerships with industry, art, and educational institutions, among other key stakeholders. Contact Maria Cecilia Reyes (mariaceciliareyesr at gmail.com) for further information.

# Organization

## Organization Committee

### General Chairs

| | |
|---|---|
| Michael Mateas | UC Santa Cruz, USA |
| David Lamas | Tallinn University, Estonia |

### Program Committee Chairs

| | |
|---|---|
| Alex Mitchell | National University of Singapore, Singapore |
| Mirjam Vosmeer | Amsterdam University of Applied Sciences, The Netherlands |

### Art Exhibits Chairs

| | |
|---|---|
| Lynda Clark | University of Dundee, UK |
| Raivo Kelomees | Estonian Academy of Arts, Estonia |

### Workshop Chair

| | |
|---|---|
| Mirjam Vosmeer | Amsterdam University of Applied Sciences, The Netherlands |

### Doctoral Consortium Chairs

| | |
|---|---|
| Sylvia Rothe | University of Munich, Germany |
| Hartmut Koenitz | Södertörn University, Sweden |

### Virtual Chairs

| | |
|---|---|
| María Cecilia Reyes | Akademie Schloss Solitude, Germany |
| Joshua Fisher | Columbia College Chicago, USA |

### Logistics Chairs

| | |
|---|---|
| Annegret Kiivit | Tallinn University, Estonia |
| Sirli Peda | Tallinn University, Estonia |

## ARDIN Officers and Board

### Executive Board

| | |
|---|---|
| Hartmut Koenitz | President, Södertörn University, Sweden |
| Frank Nack | Treasurer, University of Amsterdam, The Netherlands |
| Lissa Holloway-Attaway | University of Skövde, Sweden |
| Alex Mitchell | National University of Singapore, Singapore |
| Rebecca Rouse | University of Skövde, Sweden |

## General Board

| | |
|---|---|
| Ágnes Bakk | Moholy-Nagy University of Art and Design, Hungaria |
| Luis Bruni | Aalborg University, Denmark |
| Clara Fernandez-Vara | New York University, USA |
| Josh Fisher | Columbia College Chicago, USA |
| Andrew Gordon | University of Southern California, USA |
| Mads Haahr | Trinity College Dublin, Ireland |
| Michael Mateas | University of California, Santa Cruz, USA |
| Valentina Nisi | University of Madeira, Portugal, and Carnegie Mellon University, USA |
| Mirjam Palosaari Eladhari | Södertörn University, Sweden |
| Tess Tanenbaum | University of California Irvine, USA |
| David Thue | Carleton University, Canada, and Reykjavik University, Iceland |

## Program Committee Area Chairs

### Narrative Systems

| | |
|---|---|
| Ben Samuel | University of New Orleans, USA |
| Boyang "Albert" Li | Nanyang Technological University, Singapore |

### Interactive Narrative Theory

| | |
|---|---|
| Frank Nack | University of Amsterdam, The Netherlands |
| Ruth Aylett | Heriot-Watt University, UK |

### Interactive Narrative Impact and Applications

| | |
|---|---|
| Vincenzo Lombardo | Università degli Studi di Torino, Italy |
| Cristina Sylla | University of Minho and ITI/LARSyS, Portugal |

### The Interactive Narrative Research Discipline and Contemporary Practice

| | |
|---|---|
| Christian Roth | HKU University of the Arts Utrecht, The Netherlands |
| Lissa Holloway-Attaway | University of Skövde, Sweden |

## Program Committee

| | |
|---|---|
| Panos Amelidis | Bournemouth University, UK |
| Sasha Azad | North Carolina State University, USA |
| Julio Bahamon | University of North Carolina at Charlotte, USA |
| Ágnes Karolina Bakk | Moholy-Nagy University of Art and Design Budapest, Hungary |
| Paulo Bala | Universidade Nova de Lisboa and ITI/LARSyS, Portugal |
| Jonathan Barbara | Saint Martin's Institute of Higher Education, UK |
| Marguerite Barry | University College Dublin, Ireland |

| | |
|---|---|
| Nicole Basaraba | Maastricht University, The Netherlands |
| Mark Bernstein | Eastgate Systems, Inc, USA |
| Rafael Bidarra | Delft University of Technology, The Netherlands |
| Tom Blount | University of Southampton, UK |
| Kevin Bowden | University of California, Santa Cruz, USA |
| Wolfgang Broll | Ilmenau University of Technology, Germany |
| Luis Emilio Bruni | Aalborg University, Denmark |
| Beth Cardier | Griffith University, Australia |
| Elin Carstensdottir | University of California, Santa Cruz, USA |
| Miguel Carvalhais | INESC TEC and Universidade do Porto, Portugal |
| Marc Cavazza | University of Greenwich, UK |
| Chiara Ceccarini | University of Bologna, Italy |
| Vanessa Cesário | Técnico Lisboa and ITI/LARSyS, Portugal |
| Ronan Champagnat | L3i, Universite de La Rochelle, France |
| Fanfan Chen | National Taipei University of Business, Taiwan |
| Yun-Gyung Cheong | Sungkyunkwan University, South Korea |
| Colette Daiute | City University of New York, USA |
| Rossana Damiano | Università di Torino, Italy |
| Pierre De Loor | Lab-STICC and ENIB, France |
| Jan de Wit | Tilburg University, The Netherlands |
| Melanie Dickinson | University of California, Santa Cruz, USA |
| Mara Dionisio | Madeira Interactive Technologies Institute, Portugal |
| Markus Eger | Cal Poly Pomona, USA |
| Sergio Estupiñán | University of Geneva, Switzerland |
| Clara Fernandez Vara | New York University, USA |
| Maria José Ferreira | Universidade de Lisboa, Portugal |
| Joshua Fisher | Columbia College Chicago, USA |
| Christos Gatzidis | Bournemouth University, UK |
| Elizabeth Goins | Rochester Institute of Technology, USA |
| Andrew Gordon | University of Southern California, USA |
| Mads Haahr | Trinity College Dublin, Ireland |
| Chris Hales | RISEBA University Riga, Latvia |
| Charlie Hargood | Bournemouth University, UK |
| Sarah Harmon | Bowdoin College, USA |
| Brent Harrison | University of Kentucky, USA |
| Clare J. Hooper | Independent, Canada |
| Ryan House | University of Wisconsin Milwaukee, USA |
| Ido Aharon Iurgel | Hochschule Rhein-Waal, Germany |
| Akrivi Katifori | University of Athens, Greece |
| Geoff Kaufman | Carnegie Mellon University, USA |
| Sofia Kitromili | University of Southampton, UK |
| Erica Kleinman | University of California, Santa Cruz, USA |
| Andrew Klobucar | New Jersey Institute of Technology, USA |
| Vincent Koeman | Vrije Universiteit Amsterdam, The Netherlands |
| Hartmut Koenitz | Södertörn University, Sweden |
| Max Kreminski | University of California, Santa Cruz, USA |

Hui-Yin Wu                Inria and Université Côte d'Azur, France
Nelson Zagalo             University of Aveiro, Portugal
Massimo Zancanaro         University of Trento, Italy
Huiwen Zhao               Bournemouth University, UK

# Contents

## Narrative Systems

## Interactive Narrative Theory

## Interactive Narrative Impact and Applications

**The Interactive Narrative Research Discipline
and Contemporary Practice**

# Narrative Systems

# *Who Am I that Acts?* The Use of Voice in Virtual Reality Interactive Narratives

Jonathan Barbara[1,2]([✉]) [iD] and Mads Haahr[2] [iD]

[1] Saint Martin's Institute of Higher Education, Hamrun, Malta
jbarbara@stmartins.edu
[2] School of Computer Science and Statistics, Trinity College Dublin, Dublin, Ireland
haahrm@tcd.ie

**Abstract.** Self-identification is a key factor for the immersion of the VR interactive narrative player. Diegetic non-protagonist narrators, touched-up heterodiegetic narrations with internal focalization, and casting the player in a 'virtual sidekick' role are suggested by the literature to support self-identification. This paper analyses the use of second-person voice and level of interactivity in two VR productions. In one, minimal use of the second person to address the player and negligible agency results in limited telepresence in a 360-video VR tour of a concentration camp accompanying a Holocaust survivor. In the second, use of a touched-up heterodiegetic narration with internal focalization heightens immersion levels but self-identification of the player as sidekick suffers as the narrative's forward drive shifts between narrator, protagonist and antagonist. Future empirical work should explore the impact of second-person voice and interaction on the resultant self-identification and immersion.

**Keywords:** Virtual reality · Second-person · Immersion · Interactive narrative

## 1 Introduction

While visual discrimination between non-diegetic user interfaces and diegetic elements of a virtual world seen through a Virtual Reality (VR) headset is aided by depth perception, the aural dimension presents a challenge for the player to assess whether a sound is diegetic or not. Building on Bernstein's [1] analysis of audio in terms of what information sounds provide the player, Ekman classifies sounds in relationship to the diegesis of their referent as 'the thing being told by the sound' [2]. She presents two approaches to such an assessment: (i) whether its apparent source is itself diegetic; or (ii) whether the non-player inhabitants of the virtual world react to the sound. Both approaches are dependent on a non-guaranteed relationship between the sound and its potential source's visual representation or lack thereof. The ambiguity is compounded by the layers of information carried by audio signals: frequency, timbre, and semantics [3] and its exaggerated use to compensate for visual shortcomings [4] such as the use of the 'menacing zombie drone for brains' [5] in *Zombies, Run!* [6].

© Springer Nature Switzerland AG 2021
A. Mitchell and M. Vosmeer (Eds.): ICIDS 2021, LNCS 13138, pp. 3–12, 2021.
https://doi.org/10.1007/978-3-030-92300-6_1

These multiple levels of aurally delivered meanings offer a challenge of understanding to the listener as they acclimatize and give meaning to the virtual space. Due to sound's higher reflective nature compared to light, we often hear objects before they become visible, causing players to speculate and build expectations as to what is to come [5]. This behavior is re-enforced in films where, when an off-screen sound calls for attention, the shot cuts to reveal the source of the sound [7]. Should these expectations fail to manifest themselves, such as when a voice is heard by the player but no speaker is seen or no reactions to it come from diegetic characters, the player's understanding of the virtual space is challenged, undermining narrative engagement [8]. Following Ekman [2], this disembodied voice is thus perceived to be non-diegetic, which negatively influences the VR player's immersion, as they are reminded of their non-diegetic existence. Embodied speech, on the other hand, supports the player's (tele)presence, especially through the use of the second-person 'you' which helps create the feeling of being addressed through aesthetic-reflexive involvement [9] and thus present in the virtual world, which in turn increases immersion [10–12].

Given the ambiguous diegetic nature of sound and its influence on presence as immersion [13], the aim of this paper is to explore the role of disembodied voice in VR interactive narratives and its effect on presence through self-identification. To this end, we begin with voice as disembodied speech in VR: 'Who speaks?' We then shift to the VR player's voice: 'Who am I that speaks?' and interaction: 'Who am I that acts?' Two close readings of VR interactive narratives explore different implementations of voice and perspective, and a consideration of the elicited self-identification is used to compare its effect between the different uses. Subsequently, the concepts touched upon in the first part of the study are considered in the context of these two experiences.

## 2   Voice in Narratives: Who Speaks?

In his essay on Narrative Discourse, Genette [14] uses Vendryes's definition of voice as used in his *Traité d'accentuation grecque* (Treaty of Greek Accentuation): "the mode of action of the verb considered for its relation to the subject" ([15] as cited in [14]). Thus, voice determines "who speaks?" where the subject of the action includes the narrator and the narratee(s). In the context of fiction, the narrator is a fictional character invented by the author, thereby separating the act of narration from the author's writing and indeed from the author being in the narrative [14]. This frees the author from narrating in the diegetic first-person (*homodiegetic narration)*, and gives the option to narrate in the non-diegetic third-person (*heterodiegetic narration)* [14], which in turn results in new options for narrating the protagonist's experience of the plot: as the protagonist (*autodiegetic narrator*), as a non-protagonist character diegetic to the story (*homodiegetic narrator*), or as a non-diegetic, unrepresented, character (*heterodiegetic narrator*).

Aare [16] clearly distinguishes between the voice (who speaks) and the perspective (who sees). Genette categorises perspective into three forms: (i) in *Internal focalization,* knowledge is bound to one character, usually the protagonist-narrator; (ii) in *External focalization,* knowledge about the protagonist is limited to a third-person's perspective; and (iii) in *Non-focalization,* the knowledge would not be limited to the perspective of a single character. This could suggest the existence of a non-diegetic implied author [14] or an impersonal voice of the narrative, linked to no one character in particular [17] and comparable to a third-person heterodiegetic narration.

Narration has been an important counterpart to mimesis in theatre [18] when, in prologues and epilogues, the presence of narrators on stage present a prolepsis (what is yet to be mimetically shown) and, in some non-Western drama, such as Japanese plays, the importance of the narrator is as much as that of the main characters in terms of lines and time on stage. In games, prologues find their equivalent in tutorial missions. Due to their interactive nature, games most often use tutorials to guide the player-narratees in their participation of the narration through their gameplay. Such players are addressed using voices whose diegesis depends on the game's genre. Non-diegetic narration serves to direct the mimetic gameplay, giving motivation and justification for the player's in-game actions, similar to 'generative narrators,' whose narration instantiates action [18]. Diegetic voice, situated inside the virtual environment via spatialisation effects and the Barthesian concept of 'voice grain' to assist in matching the aural dimension with the visual representation of the source, needs to be loaded with emotional semantics in order to help deliver the narrative and cohere it with the gameplay [4].

## 3 "Who Am I that Speaks?" in Virtual Reality

VR marries theatrical mimetic performance with gameplay as, rather than pushing keys or buttons, the player virtually embodies the action-triggering performance. The question "Who speaks?" is pertinent to the VR player who, sensorially immersed in the virtual world, will attempt to seek out a diegetic owner of the voice and understand the perspective and focalisation of this voice. A non-focalised owner would have access to information beyond one's knowledge which may confuse the player and lessen realism. Non-diegesis, or even trans-diegesis, would lessen the VR player's immersion, because they are reminded of their physical self's role as an external audience. Diegetic voices presenting an external focalisation, on the other hand, would represent a realistic character's perspective and thus heighten immersion [19]. Once the characters behind the voices around the player and their nature are identified and, especially, when addressed directly by these characters, the next question for the player is self-identification: 'who am I that speaks?' or rather, due to the affordable strong literal interaction [20] of VR, 'who am I that acts?' What is the player's avatar's relationship to those around them in the virtual world? How are they expected to behave?

### 3.1  Second Person Voice and Self-identification in VR

When the audience is addressed in the second person 'you' in a narrative, their presence in the virtual space is acknowledged and reaffirmed [21], whether they have no visible impact upon the narrative or its space, or they are given a role as co-creators [22], giving them a share in the responsibility of decision-making [23]. In digital interactive experiences such as first-person perspective games and interactive documentaries (i-docs), this responsibility demands knowledge of who they are relative to the storyworld and the characters within it. Following Bell and Ensslin [21], answering the question '*who am I that acts?*' in VR demands sensitivity to media-specific affordances, specifically having the player entering the virtual world through the aural and visual senses of a virtual character diegetic to the storyworld and demanding an interactive role in the virtual space. So, who could this character be?

In traditional narratives (e.g., novels or films) the narratee may identify as: (1) the narrator, who may or may not be the protagonist of the story; (2) the protagonist of a story, told by a third-party narrator; or (3) an onlooker to a protagonist's story, narrated by the protagonist or a third party [24]. These identities are now considered in a VR context:

The first identity has the player identify as the narrator by assigning a voice to the player's avatar that mismatches the player's own voice breaks immersion [25], and thus using the player's own voice for commands or reading out choices may be considered instead, as used successfully in the game In Verbis Virtus [26]. Using the player's own voice would allow us to address the original question, 'who am I that speaks?' and would also help further immerse the player through 'ludonarrative consonance' by matching voice with action [4]. Higher presence can be achieved if the voice is augmented with real-time echoes to model the spatialisation effects of the virtual space being inhabited. Such effects suggest that the source of the sound is diegetically situated in the virtual space, and since the source of that sound is the player him/herself, then this supports the experience of telepresence [27].

The second identity has the player identify as the protagonist [28], which is akin to the use of second-person voice in Choose Your Own Adventure (CYOA) books, where players have a say in the narration of the story through the interaction afforded by the narrative device. The reader is addressed with a "you" as the main protagonist within the narrative (*intradiegetic narration*) but also as the decision-maker in charge of the non-diegetic interaction (extradiegetic narration), causing the narratee to shift alternately between the two [24]. Interactive Fiction, offline text adventure games, Multiuser Dungeons (MUDs), and their object-oriented variations (MOOs), as digital adaptations of CYOA books, also employ second-person voice as they address the player in the role of a character – the same player who writes textual commands to guide the narrative in their role as co-author [25]. In the case of the digital game *The Stanley Parable* [29], the player's actions cause Stanley to behave differently from the narrator's description, as the role of the player from narratee to protagonist slowly reveals itself to the narrator.

In the context of VR interactive narratives, however, having the player inhabit the avatar's visual and aural senses may minimise the separation between intradiegetic and extradiegetic narration by embedding their interaction into their diegetic agency and may thus augment their feeling of presence in the interactive narrative's storyworld. This may cause tension between the authorial control of the narrative and the agency provided to the player, known as 'ludonarrative dissonance' [30]. For the third identity of the player as an onlooker, Larsen [31] suggests a solution in the use of second-person point-of-view that allows viewers to participate as sidekicks (diegetic observers) to the protagonist without the ability to modify the narrative structure. This solution lets the audience tackle side quests alongside the main narrative, while still allowing the main narrative to progress resolutely, irrespective of player action. Larsen's approach also suggests a preference for non-protagonist roles of the VR player in order to support 'ludonarrative consonance'. Thus, the character may be a bystander who perceives the protagonist as Other, as they suffer the narrative (narratee≠protagonist). Whether the audience are passive observers or active sidekicks will depend on the agency afforded to the player [31].

# 4 Case Studies

We now consider the use of voice in a close reading of two VR documentaries. Both are situated during World War II, but our interest is in their use of voice, rather than their setting or subject matter. Both case studies project the viewer as a non-protagonist non-narrating character, but they use second-person voice differently and provoke different levels of self-identification through the provided agency.

## 4.1 Case Study #1: The Last Goodbye (2017)

Pinchas Gutter is an 89-year-old Polish Jew who survived the concentration camps of Nazi Germany. A series of interviews were held with Gutter in order to capture his memories and give evidence of the Holocaust atrocities perpetuated against the Jewish communities in Europe. There were four recorded narrations of Gutter about his experiences: two video interviews held during the 1990s, a collection of video-recorded replies used for an interactive interview [32] and a voice-over for the first ever Holocaust VR film entitled *The Last Goodbye* [33], in which the player accompanies Gutter on a visit to the Majdanek concentration camp through a 360 camera. The visit is narrated by Gutter: as a guide explaining the function of the place and his memories of it and as a voice-over in the opening and closing scenes, as well as during the visit to the crematorium, which brings him back memories that are too emotional for him to revisit.

While he never addresses the player with an absolute "you", he often acknowledges the player's virtual presence by breaking the fourth wall and looking at the camera, rather than at the objects he is describing. The effect is to help the player focus on the subject. The experience offers no interaction with the objects except for room-scale movement and observation, which sometimes leads to the 'Swayze effect' [25]. The illusion of presence is further broken by the penultimate scene when the camera drone's shadow, cast on the grass as we accompany Gutter, is revealed by the sun. The single use of a derivative of "you" is left until the final scene. We are beside Gutter, who is seated on a bench. A young boy, possibly Gutter's nephew, comes along on a scooter and talks with him inaudibly. The boy goes away on his scooter and Gutter, in a voice-over narration, tells us that he expects better times for all of us in the future: "not in my lifetime, but maybe in yours…" Our unacknowledged, intangible presence as Gutter looks away, the very recent presence of the young boy, and the suggestion that we are listening to his thoughts through the use of voice-over rather than being addressed directly, makes us wonder whose future Gutter was referring to: the implied player's or the young boy's.

## 4.2 Case Study #2: The Book of Distance (2020)

Randall Okita is the nephew of Yonezo Okita, a Japanese immigrant to pre-WW2 Canada who left behind his family in Hiroshima to seek a new life amongst other Japanese immigrants. Randall serves as the embodied narrator who takes the VR player along an imagined journey of his grandfather Yonezo in the VR short documentary[1] entitled *The Book of Distance* [34]. In the experience, Yonezo is presented through original photographs, digitized and made virtually available for picking up for close-up inspection, during which Randall's voice explains who is who in the photos. A game of horseshoes – which serves as a connection between Yonezo and his nephew as evidenced by one of the photos – is presented to the player as an ice-breaker into the interactive narrative, empowering the player with agency and bringing out Randall's character. Playing on the lack of ambient light, Randall often moves off into the shadows, shifting the player's attention to the unfolding story that his off-screen voice narrates. Members of Yonezo's family, such as Randall's father, are presented through their Japanese cartoon representation as well as the playback of recorded vocal interactions. Yonezo's family in Hiroshima, including his younger sister, are presented through animated coloured silhouettes but are not given a voice, reflecting the narrator's lack of familiarity with them.

Throughout the first part of the experience, the player acts as a sidekick to Randall's grandfather, helping him pack his clothes and photographic camera into his luggage for his voyage to Canada, responding to his family and future wife's waving whilst on the ship, having his passport stamped at the Canadian customs, taking photos of his house-building activities, giving a hand in clearing up the land, building the house, sowing the strawberries and serving them at the dinner table. All this ends abruptly as World War II starts and Yonezo's family are taken away by Canadian military to an internment camp for the Japanese. All their possessions are taken away: the camera, the house, the strawberry business, and likewise the player's narrative agency is greatly reduced.

Yonezo eventually returned to freedom, but it was hard earned and he never spoke about it to his nephew. Randall's lack of familiarity with this part of the story is reflected in the narrative's shift of focus away from the grandfather onto the father, and in the player's lack of agency, distancing them from the storyworld. The photographic camera is back in post-war Yonezo's hands as he takes photos of his growing children, photos that the player had seen at the beginning of the story. These are now brought back to the player's scrutiny with the addition of more recent, colourful photos of the grown characters. The story ends with the player looking through photos of Randall's father's childhood while, in the background, Randall discusses them with his father, seeking to further understand the last years of his grandfather's life in Canada.

## 5 Discussion

The two case studies provide contrasting examples of the use of second-person voice and its effect on self-identification from the viewer's behalf. With respect to the Holocaust VR film *The Last Goodbye*, Zalewska [33] reports that the subject of the VR film is the *player's* experience of the Majdanek camp rather than that of Gutter's. Doubts are also cast on the perceived fidelity of the experience due to the scripted narration making the experience more of a documentary than a testimony. While Gutter imparts his painful

---

[1] https://www.youtube.com/watch?v=b9DDoeeQq6g.

experience of the concentration camp and his turmoil in remembering nothing about his twin sister except her golden braid, there is no requirement or incentive for the player to identify themselves with Gutter or with any other relevant character. The player is offered no meaningful agency except linear narrative progression. Thus while it is clear that Gutter is the one 'who speaks', there is no self-identification for the player.

*The Book of Distance* tackles the VR player's self-identity very differently. The player is immediately given agency through a book presented in front of them with instructions to turn the page – reminiscent of CYOA books. From the beginning, the player is addressed with the second-person voice: "To You, the Time Traveller" and, as soon as Randall (the narrator) makes an entrance, he addresses the player directly, teaching them how to throw the horseshoe. This second-person address of the player continues throughout the journey of discovery, with the narrator's voice (who speaks?) embodied by Randall's character explicitly represented in the scene or implied to be hiding in the shadows around the player.

*The Book of Distance* makes use of mechanics and structures frequently used in games and traditional films, even though the experience itself is neither. The empowerment of the player's agency and its subsequent reduction is a common technique used to challenge the player by limiting his/her skills. In *The Book of Distance*, however, the effect is not a feeling of increased challenge but a sense of loss of freedom, of identity. It starts with a prologue where modern-day Randall presents his grandfather, whose story we explore together throughout the rest of the experience, until we reunite with his father for the story's epilogue. We are then told exactly how Randall knows of his grandfather's life: through the photos, his father's testimony, and the letters received from the Canadian government, to name a few. The experience uses touched-up heterodiegetic narration, attempting an internal focalisation as the nephew tries his best to understand his grandfather's experience of his life as a Japanese immigrant in war-time Canada.

Self-identification suffers, however, as the actual role of the VR player is indeterminate. Observation of Randall's exploration of his grandfather's story through his photo album evolves into active participation as he starts recounting his grandfather's story. As players, we become active sidekicks to the grandfather, helping him paint, write letters, prepare the luggage for his voyage to Canada, and making him aware of his family waving him off. But as the experience progresses, it is not clear whose sidekicks we are: Randall's or his grandfather's. As we help the latter build his house, sow his fields, serve the strawberries on the table, the question begs to be asked: who am I that acts? A friend of the family perhaps? This becomes even less clear when, as Yonezo is separated from his family and taken away to a field, it is the player who gets to raise the lever that traps the Japanese farmer inside the internment camp. Are we now sidekicks of the Canadian government? It appears to be impossible to reconcile these three different roles: chronologically separate sidekicks to the nephew and to the grandpa and morally separate sidekicks to the grandpa and to the Canadian military, and it raises the question: Whose side is the sidekick on? As a result, the player identifies with none of these diegetic roles, but instead the experience constructs a non-diegetic player role whose responsibility is to push the narrative forward. By not sticking to a specific persona, the virtual character that is embodied becomes transient across time and actions, such that the question, 'who am I that acts', does not resolve to a specific characterisation, leaving the player with themselves as enactors of the experience. This was a design choice with the player only identifying themselves as 'a part of the story' [34].

Thus, neither of the two experiences manages to successfully assist in self-identification. *The Last Goodbye*, through its limited agency and non-address of the player only serves to inform of the terrible loss of Pinchas Gutter at the hands of the Nazi regime. *The Book of Distance* makes it a point to continuously address the player and to provide agency that serves LudoNarrative Coherence as the gameplay contributes to the progression of the narrative while the empowerment and reduction of agency progresses with the narrative. However, as the experience follows a prologue/interlude/epilogue structure pertinent to theatre and film, the diegetic identity of the player transcends time, and the fruitful agency of the player's character places them on the same diegetic space as the younger grandfather and his family to which the nephew seems to have no access, except as an observer. The already fragile link between the two trans-chronological personas is further disconnected with the entrapment action that results in Yonezo Okita's confinement in the internment camp, the character's body language showing as much disbelief at the player's traitorous act as his introvert self could afford.

## 6    Conclusion

Providing enough information to allow the VR player to self-identify is an important factor in their immersion into a virtual world. Narrative theory on fiction and Genettian focalization identify possible relationships between the narrator, the protagonist and the narratee, helping the VR player to answer the question, 'Who am I that acts?' Having the VR player as a 'virtual sidekick' [31], acknowledged and addressed by the diegetic characters, facilitates self-identification and improves immersion.

Both case studies underserve self-identification. *The Last Goodbye* does not address the player, resulting in reduced telepresence and minimal self-identification, while *The Book of Distance*, while empowering the player through meaningful agency, leaves self-identification vague as the narrative is driven forward by different characters.

In the light of the above, future work can improve upon the work by Vosmeer et al. [25] and explore any causal relationships that the combined use of second-person voice to address the VR player and the afforded interactivity may have on self-identification.

## References

1. Bernstein, D.: Creating an interactive audio environment. Gamasutra **1**, 2013 (1997)
2. Ekman, I.: Meaningful noise: understanding sound effects in computer games. Proc. Digit. Arts Cult. **17** (2005)
3. Wallmark, Z., Kendall, R.A.: Describing sound: the cognitive linguistics of timbre. In: The Oxford Handbook of Timbre, p. 14. Oxford University Press, New York (2018). https://doi.org/10.1093/oxfordhb/9780190637224.013
4. Ward, M.: Voice, videogames, and the technologies of immersion, p. 15 (2010)
5. Gardner, K.: Braaiinnsss!: zombie-technology, play and sound. In: Technologies of the Gothic in Literature and Culture, pp. 81–93. Routledge, New York (2015).
6. Guerilla Bandit: Zombies, Run! (2012)

7. Barker, J.M.: The Tactile Eye: Touch and the Cinematic Experience. University of California Press (2009)
8. Busselle, R., Bilandzic, H.: Measuring narrative engagement. Media Psychol. **12**, 321–347 (2009). https://doi.org/10.1080/15213260903287259
9. Mildorf, J.: Reconsidering second-person narration and involvement. Lang. Lit. **25**, 145–158 (2016)
10. McMahan, A.: Immersion, engagement, and presence: a method for analyzing 3-D video games. In: The Video Game Theory Reader, pp. 89–108. Routledge (2013)
11. Brown, E., Cairns, P.: A grounded investigation of game immersion. In: CHI 2004 Extended Abstracts on Human Factors in Computing Systems, pp. 1297–1300. ACM, Vienna (2004)
12. Lombard, M., Ditton, T.: At the heart of it all: The concept of presence. J. Comput.-Mediat. Commun. **3**, JCMC321 (1997)
13. Nordahl, R., Nilsson, N.C.: The sound of being there: presence and interactive audio in immersive virtual reality. In: The Oxford Handbook of Interactive Audio. Oxford University Press, United Kingdom (2014). https://doi.org/10.1093/oxfordhb/9780199797226.013.013
14. Genette, G.: Narrative Discourse: An Essay in Method. Cornell University Press, Ithaca (1983)
15. Vendryes, J.: Traité d'accentuation grecque. C. Klincksieck (1904)
16. Aare, C.: A narratological approach to literary journalism: how an interplay between voice and point of view create empathy with the other, p. 34 (2016)
17. Nielsen, H.S.: The impersonal voice in first-person narrative fiction. Narrative **12**, 133–150 (2004)
18. Richardson, B.: Point of view in drama: diegetic monologue, unreliable narrators, and the author's voice on stage. Comp. Drama **22**, 193–214 (1988). https://doi.org/10.1353/cdr.1988.0017
19. Barreda-Ángeles, M., Aleix-Guillaume, S., Pereda-Baños, A.: An "empathy machine" or a "just-for-the-fun-of-it" machine? Effects of immersion in nonfiction 360-video stories on empathy and enjoyment. Cyberpsychol. Behav. Soc. Netw. **23**, 683–688 (2020)
20. Ryan, M.-L.: Immersion vs. interactivity: virtual reality and literary theory. SubStance **28**, 110–137 (1999)
21. Bell, A., Ensslin, A.: "I know what it was. You know what it was": second-person narration in hypertext fiction. Narrative **19**, 311–329 (2011)
22. Walmsley, B.: Co-creating theatre: authentic engagement or inter-legitimation? Cult. Trends. **22**, 108–118 (2013)
23. Ciancio, G.: Active spectatorship, changes and novelties in the performing arts sector. In: Bonet, L. and Négrier, E. (eds.) Breaking the Fourth Wall: Proactive Audiences in the Performing Arts, pp. 90–96 (2018)
24. DelConte, M.: Why you can't speak: second-person narration, voice, and a new model for understanding narrative. Style **37**, 204–219 (2003)
25. Vosmeer, M., Roth, C., Koenitz, H.: Who are you? Voice-over perspective in surround video. In: Nunes, N., Oakley, I., Nisi, V. (eds.) ICIDS 2017. LNCS, vol. 10690, pp. 221–232. Springer, Cham (2017). https://doi.org/10.1007/978-3-319-71027-3_18
26. Ferrari, M.: In verbis virtus. Presented at the (2015). https://doi.org/10.1007/978-3-319-05326-4_18
27. Johansson, M.: VR for your ears: dynamic 3D audio is key to the immersive experience by mathias johansson· illustration by Eddie guy. IEEE Spectr. **56**, 24–29 (2019)
28. Fludernik, M.: Second person fiction: Narrative "you" as addressee and/or protagonist. AAA - Arb. Aus Angl. Am. **18**(2), 217–247 (1993)
29. Wreden, D., Pugh, W.: Stanley parable (2011)
30. Hocking, C.: Ludonarrative Dissonance in Bioshock. http://clicknothing.typepad.com/click_nothing/2007/10/ludonarrative-d.html. Accessed 24 Jan 2016

31. Larsen, M.: Virtual sidekick: second-person POV in narrative VR. J. Screenwrit. **9**, 73–83 (2018). https://doi.org/10.1386/josc.9.1.73_1
32. Traum, D., et al.: New dimensions in testimony: digitally preserving a holocaust survivor's interactive storytelling. In: Schoenau-Fog, H., Bruni, L., Louchart, S., Baceviciute, S. (eds.) ICIDS 2015. LNCS, vol. 9445, pp. 269–281. Springer, Cham (2015). https://doi.org/10.1007/978-3-319-27036-4_26
33. Zalewska, M.: The last goodbye (2017): virtualizing witness testimonies of the holocaust, p. 8 (2017)
34. Oppenheim, D., Okita, R.L.: The book of distance: personal storytelling in VR. In: ACM SIGGRAPH 2020 Immersive Pavilion, pp. 1–2. ACM, Virtual Event USA (2020). https://doi.org/10.1145/3388536.3407896

# A Synset-Based Recommender Method for Mixed-Initiative Narrative World Creation

Mijael R. Bueno Perez<sup>(✉)</sup>, Elmar Eisemann, and Rafael Bidarra

Delft University of Technology, Delft, The Netherlands
{M.R.BuenoPerez,E.Eisemann,R.Bidarra}@tudelft.nl

**Abstract.** A narrative world (NW) is an environment which supports enacting a given story. Manually creating virtual NWs (e.g. for games and films) requires considerable creative and technical skills, in addition to a deep understanding of the story in question. Procedural generation methods, in turn, generally lack in creativity and have a hard time coping with the numerous degrees of freedom left open by a story. In contrast, mixed-initiative approaches offer a promising path to solve this tension. We propose a mixed-initiative approach assisting an NW designer in choosing plausible entities for the locations, where the story takes place. Our approach is based on a recommender method that uses common and novel associations to narrative locations, actions and entities. Our method builds upon a large dataset of co-occurrences of disambiguated terms that we retrieved from photo captions. Building on this knowledge, our solution deploys entity (un)relatedness, offers clusters of semantically and contextually related entities, and highlights novelty of recommended content, thus effectively supporting the designer's creative task, while helping to stay consistent with the story. We demonstrate our method via an interactive prototype called TALEFORGE. Designers can obtain meaningful entity suggestions for their NWs, which enables guided exploration, while preserving creative freedom. We present an example of the interactive workflow of our method, and illustrate its usefulness.

**Keywords:** Narrative world · Recommender method · Authoring tool · Mixed initiative · Synset vectors

## 1 Introduction

Narrative Worlds (NW) are environments designed to support enacting a given story [2]. In the fast-paced industry of games and films, NWs are becoming more realistic and complex in nature. NW designers need new techniques and workflows to rapidly explore their creative ideas while preserving story consistency and integrity. Tools such as the game engines *Unity* or *Unreal Engine* have become increasingly popular for the creation of virtual worlds in form of game levels or virtual film production. Yet, these tools lack any narrative understanding and leave designers with full creative responsibility.

© Springer Nature Switzerland AG 2021
A. Mitchell and M. Vosmeer (Eds.): ICIDS 2021, LNCS 13138, pp. 13–28, 2021.
https://doi.org/10.1007/978-3-030-92300-6_2

*Procedural content generation* (PCG) techniques support designers in automating the generation of specific types of content [29]. PCG methods often involve a trial and error process due to their stochastic nature, and their frequent lack of intuitive control [1]. Also, most PCG methods fail to accurately capture the creative intent of a designer, as well as to properly combine and harmonize their generative process with other types of content [14], e.g., a story. In contrast, *mixed-initiative approaches* have proven to support designer creativity in different domains [7]. Mixed-initiative methods combine the strengths of PCG approaches with the input of a human designer, often in an iterative process. Thus, rather than randomly generating content, mixed-initiative methods try to adapt to the creative intent and methodology of a designer, following their chosen directions, preferences and choices.

Due to the complexity of NWs and their strong dependency on a story, a mixed-initiative approach can use both the story and choices of a designer to provide suggestions throughout the creation process. In this paper, we propose a mixed-initiative approach to assist a designer in choosing appropriate entities for an NW. Our approach is based on a recommender method that uses the story and designer guidance to suggest entities based on learned real-world associations. Our method takes into account narrative locations and actions as well as additional entities chosen by the designer.

At its core, our method relies on an embedding of synset vectors. A synset is a set of synonyms that share a common meaning. The embedding encodes their contextual associations. This representation is similar to word vectors but instead of using words, we use previously disambiguated terms annotated with synsets from WORDNET[1]. We learned these synset vectors by extracting the co-occurrences of synsets found in photo captions obtained from *Shutterstock* and by using the unsupervised learning algorithm GLOVE [20]. A vector representation allows us to perform several operations such as relatedness/similarity search, vector negation for unrelatedness and hierarchical clustering. In addition, a synset representation allow us to take advantage of WORDNET's semantic knowledge for categorization and highlighting novelty over the recommended content. With our solution TALEFORGE, designers can easily populate NWs with relevant entities with little effort, while maintaining creative control.

## 2   Related Work

In this section, we examine mixed-initiative approaches, as well as strategies to encode contextual associations, as they form the basis of our solution.

**Mixed-Initiative Content Creation.** A mixed-initiative approach is based on a human-computer collaboration paradigm; a creative dialogue to co-create content [7,27,34]. SKETCHAWORLD facilitates non-technical users to create complete 3D worlds through the integration of procedural techniques [30]. TANAGRA uses human-computer collaboration to produce levels of a 2D platformer

---

[1] WORDNET is an open lexical database of synsets, wordnet.princeton.edu.

by respecting user-specified constraints [31]. SENTIENT SKETCHBOOK assists in the creation of maps for strategy or roguelike games by providing suggestions to a designer and improving upon their choices with novelty search [15]. ROPOSSUM helps users to create and test puzzle levels by using grammatical evolution [26]. Linden et al. generate dungeons that fulfill high-level designer-specified gameplay requirements [16].

Other work has focused on mixed-initiative story authoring. WIDE RULED is an interactive interface that generates stories based on author's specified story world and goals [28]. WRITINGBUDDY aims to help authors with the generation of story beats and actions by using the social simulation engine ENSEMBLE [24]. TALEBOX is a game that supports players to collaboratively create stories [5]. It uses GLUNET, a semantic knowledge base that integrates several lexical databases for commonsense reasoning of narratives [12].

Only little work has focused on using a story as a basis for assisting an NW designer [13], and no solution has examined our goal: suggesting and supporting the exploration of suitable entities for an NW. GAMEFORGE is a PCG method that helps a designer to create NWs for computer role-playing games by using a genetic algorithm that balances story requirements, designer control and player preferences [10]. The designer controls the algorithm by setting adjacency probabilities between narrative locations. SCRIPTVIZ assists writers by executing their screenplays in real time with computer graphics [17]. It conveys a scene, with a location, camera position, characters and their poses.

**Word Vectors for Contextual Associations.** Hand-crafted semantic knowledge has been extensively used for expanding story-world domains [21,22]. In this paper, we extract semantic knowledge from automatically learned contextual associations among locations, objects and actions described in photo captions, which allows us to support a designer in their task of choosing NW content. Fortunately, word vector models have been effectively used for learning these associations. OBJ-GLOVE bridged language and vision by learning word vectors for common visual objects [33]. VICO learned visual co-occurrences between objects and attributes in annotated photos [9] and vis-w2v learned co-occurrences of visual cues (e.g., objects, actions) from abstract scenes [11]. In addition, some models provide novel associations due to their ability to capture high-order relations (e.g., *frisbee* related to *ball*, due to *frisbee* to *dog* and *dog* to *ball*) [25].

## 3   Mixed-Initiative Approach

In this section, we describe the basis of our mixed-initiative approach, as well as its interactive workflow, both illustrated in Fig. 1.

First, assume that an NW designer has a working space (e.g., game engine or level editor) that allows to create virtual locations for an NW; we refer to this as NW *canvas*. We improve the designer's workflow with a recommender method, which also supports exploration. Our method suggests plausible entities for an NW based on common and novel associations to narrative locations, actions and other entities. Similar to a screenplay, the designer first selects a

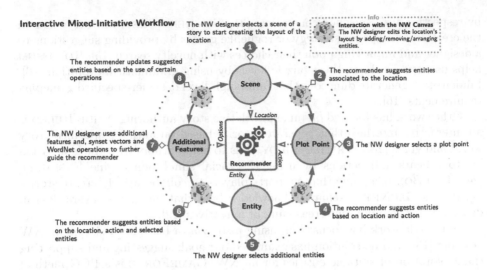

**Fig. 1.** A proposed interactive workflow for our mixed-initiative approach. We arbitrarily chose the steps shown in this illustration.

particular scene of the story and an NW canvas is shown with the location's layout of the scene; the recommender then suggests entities associated only to the location. The designer iteratively adds, removes and arranges entities by exploring recommendations or searching for specific content. The designer walks through each plot point or selects entities to further guide the recommender. At this point, the recommendations are based on the location, action and selected entities. The designer can select additional features to guide the exploration process. In the following subsections, we describe in detail the main components of our approach.

### 3.1    Story Elements, Structure and Representation

Our approach focuses on representing the lexical elements (terms in a vocabulary) and structure of a story. In a broad sense, a story can be seen as a sequence of events involving particular entities and their relations. We use the concept of *entity* to refer to the lexical and physical elements specified in the story and existing in the NW. An *entity* can be *abstract* (e.g., love) or *concrete* (e.g., desk). In addition, we adopted the hierarchy of two basic elements of a screenplay: *scene* and *action*. A *scene* is a story unit describing the particular *location* and sequence of actions at a specific *time*. A *location* refers to the particular space of the scene; it can be the *interior* or *exterior* of a *room* (e.g., bedroom), *natural area* (e.g., lake), or other. The *time* describes the point of the day (e.g., day, night, etc.) that hints about, for example, the potential illumination required for the location during the scene. An *action* describes what a character does in a given moment of the scene, as well as the involved entities. It can refer to a character (e.g., man) performing a certain activity (e.g., play tennis) and interacting with certain physical objects (e.g., racquet) and other characters (e.g., boy).

We represent an action and its involved entities by means of a *plot point* ($pp$); a semantically-coherent structure which describes an important event of a story. The argument structure of a plot point is determined by the verb of an action (e.g., eat, give) and involved entities, each slot denoted by a *semantic role* (SR). SR names can be customized to provide clarity about the role an entity has in the plot point. A general structure of the plot point representation with $N$ slots is as follows:

$$[\text{SLOT-0}]_{\text{SR}_0} \underset{\text{Verb}}{[\text{SLOT-VERB}]} \underset{\text{Direct Object}}{[\text{SLOT-1}]_{\text{SR}_1}} ... \underset{...}{[\text{SLOT-N}]_{\text{SR}_n}}$$

The number of slots and their corresponding SRs depend on the common argument structure of a verb. In our approach, we used the argument structure of verbs and SRs already provided by the hand-crafted lexical-semantic resource VERBATLAS[2] [8]. To illustrate our representation, consider a story with a scene happening in a *living room* in the *evening*, with this sequence of two plot points:

$$S_1. \underset{\text{Space}}{[\text{INT.}]} \underset{\text{Location}}{[\text{LIVING ROOM}]} - \underset{\text{Time}}{[\text{EVENING}]}$$
$$pp_1. \underset{\text{Subject}}{[\text{Bob}]_{\text{AGENT}}} \underset{\text{Verb}}{[\text{Give}]} \underset{\text{Direct Object}}{[\text{Pizza}]_{\text{THEME}}} \underset{\text{Indirect Object}}{[\text{Sally}]_{\text{RECIPIENT}}}$$
$$pp_2. \underset{\text{Subject}}{[\text{Sally}]_{\text{AGENT}}} \underset{\text{Verb}}{[\text{Eat}]} \underset{\text{Direct Object}}{[\text{Pizza}]_{\text{PATIENT}}}$$

The first line is a scene description $S_1$, followed by the two plot points, $pp_1$ and $pp_2$. In $pp_1$, *give* is used as a transitive verb of three argument slots: the subject *Bob* is the AGENT who initiates the action, the direct object *Sally* is the RECIPIENT, and the indirect object *pizza* is the thing being transferred as THEME. In $pp_2$, *eat* is used as a transitive verb of two argument slots; the subject *Sally* is the AGENT who performs the action, and the direct object *pizza* is the thing affected as PATIENT.

## 3.2   Narrative World Content

An NW can have several locations, each of them decorated with physical entities that are coherent with associations suggested by a story [2]. We identify two types of NW content: *explicit content* and *plausible content*. The *explicit content* consists of every entity specified in a plot point. For example, in *"Bob drinks coffee"*, *coffee* must exist in the location to support the action *drink*. In contrast, *plausible content* is every entity that potentially fits in the location, but their implicit nature is more of an open question. These entities might be required or only serve as decoration for the location. Traditionally, designers determine plausible content based on their own creative experience. Our method assists designers with suggestions based on the following learned associations:

- *Location-centric associations.* The entities associated to a location, e.g., *bed*, *closet* and *alarm clock* are commonly found in a *bedroom*.

---

[2] VERBATLAS provides semantically coherent structures of verbs, see verbatlas.org.

- *Action-centric associations.* The entities associated to an action/activity, e.g., *tv* and *popcorn* found when *watching a movie.*
- *Object-centric associations.* The entities associated with an object, e.g., *pen* to *paper, tennis racquet* to *tennis ball,* etc.
- *Character-centric associations.* The entities stereotypically associated to a character, like *film director* to *movie camera, doctor* to *stethoscope,* etc.

Plausible content can vary depending on the combination of location, action and even other entities involved. For example, entities during *sleep* vary if the location is a *mountain* or *bedroom.* On a *mountain, sleep* might suggest *tent* and *sleeping bag.* In contrast, *sleep* in a *bedroom,* might result in *bed* and *mattress.*

### 3.3   Learning Synset Vectors

Learning common and novel associations for recommending NW content given narrative locations, actions and entities is a challenging problem. If we assume that these associations resemble what co-occurs in the real world, then we can rely on many exemplars to cover the vast number of cases. To address this, we looked into textual knowledge found on the web, assuming that co-occurrence data within photo captions are a good basis for learning the aforementioned associations. We represented this co-occurrence data as an embedding of synset vectors, which allowed several vector operations for suggesting NW content.

**Photo Captions Dataset.** We created a dataset based on the photo captions and keywords provided by users of stock photography services. We found that in this way we could include a vast number of real-world associations. We extracted 99.7 million photo captions by using the *Shutterstock* API service[3].

**Synset Representation.** We identify entities as synsets instead of as words. A synset is a set of synonyms with shared meaning. Lexical databases such as WORDNET and BABELNET, contain a rich glossary of synsets and semantic knowledge for defining their meaning [18,19]. We used WORDNET and identified a synset entry with a WORDNET ID, composed of a letter for *part of speech* (e.g., *n* for noun) followed by 8 digits (e.g., n02958343 for a *car* synset).

**Dataset Preprocessing.** We preprocessed the dataset by removing or replacing characters that were not alphanumeric, tokenizing single-word (e.g., cat) and multi-word (e.g., tennis ball) expressions, and tagging words with a WORDNET ID by using the *adapted lesk algorithm* for word sense disambiguation [3]. This algorithm compares the context (a photo caption) of a target word with WORD-NET's semantic knowledge of candidate synsets to determine a plausible synset for the word. Then, we extracted a *dependency tree* of each caption by using python's *spaCy*[4]. A *dependency tree* is a hierarchic representation of the syntactic structure of a sentence. From this, we captured verb and direct object as a

---

[3] see api.shutterstock.com
[4] spaCy has pre-trained models, which perform many NLP tasks (see spacy.io).

bigram term of an action/activity, e.g., *play tennis* is tagged with WORDNET IDs of *play* and *tennis* separated by a semicolon   v01072949:n00482298. In total, we tagged 3.75 billion tokens (an average of 38 tokens per caption).

**Vocabulary and Co-occurrences.** We extracted a vocabulary of all synsets $V$ available in the dataset and kept only synsets that occur over 10 times. Our vocabulary contains 470,577 terms: 78,400 unigram WORDNET IDs and 392,177 bigram WORDNET IDs for actions/activities. Then, we aggregated the pairwise co-occurrences of all synsets within each photo caption to the global co-occurrences counts $X_{ij}$. We captured 457.2 million of such co-occurrence pairs.

**GloVe Formulation.** GLOVE is a widely used unsupervised learning algorithm for learning word vectors [20]. It uses a log-bilinear model to optimize the $d$-dimensional embeddings $w_i \in \mathbb{R}^d$ by using the non-zero co-occurrence counts $X_{ij}$ in the following objective:

$$J = \sum_{i,j=1}^{V} f(X_{ij})(w_i^T w_j + b_i + b_j - \log X_{ij})^2 \tag{1}$$

We optimized a single embedding layer for both $w_i$ and $w_j$ instead of an additional embedding layer for the context vectors $\tilde{w}_j$. This should not make a difference due to the symmetry in the objective, ideally both embeddings should be identical [9]. In addition, the original formulation [20] uses a weighting function $f(X_{ij})$, but offers just an empirical motivation for it; instead, we use $f(X_{ij}) = 1$. With these simplifications, we did not observe any impact on the quality of our synset vectors. We learned and tested synset vectors of different $d$-dimensions: 50, 100, 200 and 300 dimensions.

### 3.4   The Recommender Method

Our mixed-initiative approach is powered by a recommender method able to compute and deploy related entities by using several vector and WORDNET operations. In this subsection, we discuss the different components of the recommender, such as input/output and operations (see Fig. 2).

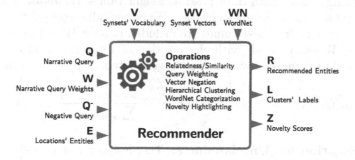

**Fig. 2.** Schematic of inputs/outputs of the recommender.

**The Narrative Query.** We define a *narrative query* as a set of synsets $Q = \{q_1, q_2, ..., q_n\}$ that prompt the recommender to output a set of $k$ most related synsets $R = \{r_1, r_2, ..., r_k\}$. The argument $k$ is set by the designer to control the number of results. A narrative query is formed by extracting the synsets of location, action and designer-selected entities (e.g. in the plot point or already placed in the NW canvas). If the plot point involves a direct object, the narrative query includes a combined term for verb and direct object; if, however, the combined term does not exist in our vocabulary, only the verb is included in $Q$.

**Relatedness/Similarity Search.** This search operation is based on the assumption that similar or related terms appear closer together for a certain distance metric in a semantic vector space. We use the *cosine similarity score* $\cos(\vec{A}, \vec{B})$ as a quantifiable measure of similarity between two synset vectors with values between 1 (similar directions) and $-1$ (opposite directions). Then, we compute the *angular cosine distance* $\varphi_{dist}$ of values from 0 to 1 to respect the notion of similarity based on closeness:

$$\varphi_{dist}(\vec{A}, \vec{B}) = \frac{\arccos(\cos(\vec{A}, \vec{B}))}{\pi} \quad \cos(\vec{A}, \vec{B}) = \frac{\vec{A} \cdot \vec{B}}{\|\vec{A}\|\|\vec{B}\|} \tag{2}$$

We obtain a set of related entities $R$ by computing the average angular distance $\bar{\varphi}$ of each synset vector $\vec{v_j}$ in the vocabulary $V$ to every synset vector $\vec{q_i}$ in the narrative query $Q$:

$$\bar{\varphi}_{dists}(Q, V) = \{\bar{\varphi} \in \mathbb{R} : \bar{\varphi} = \frac{1}{|Q|} \sum_{\vec{q_i} \in Q} \varphi_{dist}(\vec{q_i}, \vec{v_j}), \forall \vec{v_j} \in V\} \tag{3}$$

Then, we sort the result according to the average angular distances $\bar{\varphi}_{dists}$ and select the $k$ entities with the smallest distances.

**Narrative Query Weighting.** We determined that computing related entities by considering narrative query terms $q_i$ of equal importance is not an optimal approach. The designer might be interested in controlling the association strength of location, action or selected entities. Thus, we propose a controllable weighting scheme with three possible weight values: the *location weight* $w_l$, *action weight* $w_a$ and *selection weight* $w_e$. We empirically set $w_l = 0.5$, $w_a = 0.7$ and $w_e = 1$ by default. These values are included in a set $W = \{w_1, w_2, ..., w_n\}$, where $w_i \in W$ corresponds with the position of its query term $q_i \in Q$. We expand Eq. (3) to compute weighted averaged distances $\bar{\varphi}_w$ with $W$ as follows:

$$\bar{\varphi}_{dists}(Q, W, V) = \{\bar{\varphi}_w \in \mathbb{R} : \bar{\varphi}_w = \frac{\sum_{i=1}^{n} w_i \, \varphi_{dist}(\vec{q_i}, \vec{v_j})}{\sum_{i=1}^{n} w_i}, \forall \vec{v_j} \in V\} \tag{4}$$

**Vector Negation for Unrelatedness.** The designer can provide a *negative query* as a set of synsets $Q^- = \{q_1^-, q_2^-, ..., q_n^-\}$ that must appear unrelated to the results, analogous to a boolean NOT query (e.g. *animal* NOT *bird*). Thus, we perform *vector negation* as $Q$ NOT $Q^-$ to extract a subspace $Q^+$ of vectors that has no features in common with $Q^-$ [32]. We obtain $\vec{q_i}^+ \in Q^+$ by subtracting the vector projections of all synset vectors $\vec{q_j^-} \in Q^-$ on each $\vec{q_i} \in Q$:

$$Q^+ = \{\vec{q_i}^+ \in Q^+ : \vec{q_i}^+ = \vec{q_i} - \sum_{\vec{q_j^-} \in Q^-} \frac{\vec{q_i} \cdot \vec{q_j^-}}{||\vec{q_j^-}||^2} \vec{q_j^-}, \forall \vec{q_i} \in Q\} \tag{5}$$

We replace $Q$ for $Q^+$ in Eq. (4) as $\bar{\varphi}_{dists}(Q^+, W, V)$ and retrieve the top $k$ entities with shortest distance. Interestingly, this feature can be used to neutralize common human subjective biases (e.g., gender and cultural biases) prone to be found in models learned from text corpora [4].

**Hierarchical Clustering.** We observed that recommended entities belong to meaningful clusters, which reflect similarity or contextual relatedness; for example, several types of animals for a forest. To this extent, we present the recommended content clustered, using a set of labels $L = \{l_1, l_2, ..., l_n\}$ that associate a cluster number to each recommended entity $r_i \in R$. To determine clusters, we used the *agglomerative clustering algorithm* to iteratively fuse clusters (starting from clusters containing a single entity) based on a distance measure (linkage) between clusters [6]. We chose the *complete-linkage*[5] criterion; the distance between two clusters is the maximum pairwise distance between their entities:

$$\varphi_{dist}(C_a, C_b) = \max\{\varphi_{dist}(\vec{a_i}, \vec{b_j}) : \vec{a_i} \in C_a, \vec{b_j} \in C_b\} \tag{6}$$

We chose this criterion due to the tendency to form smaller, compact clusters. The optimal clusters are determined via the *silhouette coefficient* [23]: a value from $-1$ (bad fit) to 1 (good fit) which measures the quality of the clusters in terms of how good each entity fits in its own cluster. Given the mean intra-cluster distance $a_i$ and the mean nearest-cluster distance $b_i$, we compute the coefficient $s_i$ for each entity and the average coefficient $\bar{s}$ as follows:

$$s_i = \frac{\bar{b_i} - \bar{a_i}}{\max(\bar{a_i}, \bar{b_i})} \qquad \bar{s} = \frac{1}{|R|} \sum_{i=1}^{|R|} s_i \tag{7}$$

We further constrain clusters by only considering the steps where their size is below the maximum threshold $T_{max} = 3$ to ensure compact clusters. For convenience, we sort clusters in ascending order by the average of the score obtained with Eq. (4) for entities $\vec{c_j}$ in each cluster $C_k \in C$:

$$\bar{\varphi}_{cdists}(Q, W, C) = \{\varphi_c \in \mathbb{R} : \varphi_c = \frac{1}{|C_k|} \sum_{\vec{c_j} \in C_k} \bar{\varphi}_{dists}(Q, W, C_k), \forall C_k \in C\} \tag{8}$$

---

[5] For hierarchical clustering visit nlp.stanford.edu/IR-book/completelink.html

**WordNet Categorization.** The designer might be interested in exploring certain categories of entities (e.g., *plants* for *forest*, *furniture* for *bedroom*, etc.). Fortunately, WORDNET allows us to create custom sets of synsets $V_c \subset V$ based on *lexnames* and *hyponyms* of synsets. A *lexname* is one of 45 tags for each synset in WORDNET (e.g., noun.animal, noun.plant, etc.) and *hyponyms* are less generic synsets below a synset's semantic tree, for example, *car* and *motorcycle* are hyponyms of *vehicle*. We can perform any previous operation with a custom set $V_c$ instead of the whole vocabulary $V$. To showcase this feature, we created custom sets for *artifact, tool, furniture, food, substance, plant,* etc.

**Novelty Highlighting.** We highlight novelty of a recommended entity based on a novelty score that measures how new the entity is for the current location. First, we compute a dictionary of counts $X : H \to V$ of WORDNET's *hypernyms* and *hyponyms* $H$ of all synsets of entities $e_i \in E$ placed in the location. Then, we obtain $g_i \in G$ as the $\log_{10}$ of sum of counts $X(h)$ of only intersecting hypernyms and hyponyms $h \in (H_i \cap H)$ of the synset of a recommended entity $r_i \in R$. We use $\log_{10}$ to smooth out the influence of large counts. Lastly, we calculate a novelty score $z_i \in Z$ with min-max normalization in reverse order of $G$ to get values from 0 (least novel) to 1 (most novel):

$$G = \{g_i \in \mathbb{R} : g_i = \log_{10} \sum_{h \in (H_i \cap H)} X(h)\} \quad Z = \{z_i \in \mathbb{R} : z_i = \frac{\max(G) - g_i}{\max(G) - \min(G)}, \, g_i \in G\}$$

$$(9)$$

## 4   Interactive Prototype

We implemented TALEFORGE, an interactive prototype to showcase our mixed-initiative approach. For this, we use a story of three scenes in three locations: a *forest, beach,* and *tavern*; see Fig. 3. The story is about a *pirate* stranded in an uninhabited island. The *pirate* performs several actions to survive, and finds a *treasure* while trying to repair his *ship*. Eventually, he ends up celebrating in a *tavern*, plays a game against the *barkeeper* and gives his *treasure* away. Assume that a designer is looking for inspiration to further design an NW for this story.

| $S_1$ [EXT.] [FOREST] - [EVENING] | $S_2$ [EXT.] [BEACH] - [MORNING] | $S_3$ [INT.] [TAVERN] - [NIGHT] |
|---|---|---|
| Space Location     Time | Space Location     Time | Space Location     Time |
| $pp_1$. [Pirate] [Look_for] [Food]<br>AGENT    Verb    THEME<br>Subj              DObj | $pp_4$. [Pirate] [Cut]  [Tree]<br>AGENT  Verb  PATIENT<br>Subj             DObj | $pp_7$. [Pirate] [Buy] [Drink] [Barkeeper]<br>AGENT  Verb  THEME  SOURCE<br>Subj         DObj     IObj |
| $pp_2$. [Pirate] [Make] [Fire]<br>AGENT  Verb  PATIENT<br>Subj             DObj | $pp_5$. [Pirate] [Repair] [Ship]<br>AGENT  Verb  PATIENT<br>Subj             DObj | $pp_8$. [Pirate] [Play] [Game] [Barkeeper]<br>AGENT  Verb  THEME  Co-AGENT<br>Subj         DObj |
| $pp_3$. [Pirate] [Prepare] [Food]<br>AGENT  Verb  PATIENT<br>Subj             DObj | $pp_6$. [Pirate] [Find] [Treasure]<br>AGENT  Verb  THEME<br>Subj             DObj | $pp_9$. [Pirate] [Give] [Treasure] [Barkeeper]<br>AGENT  Verb  THEME  RECIPIENT<br>Subj         DObj     IObj |

**Fig. 3.** The story *"Once upon a time, a pirate..."*: with 3 plot point per scene/location.

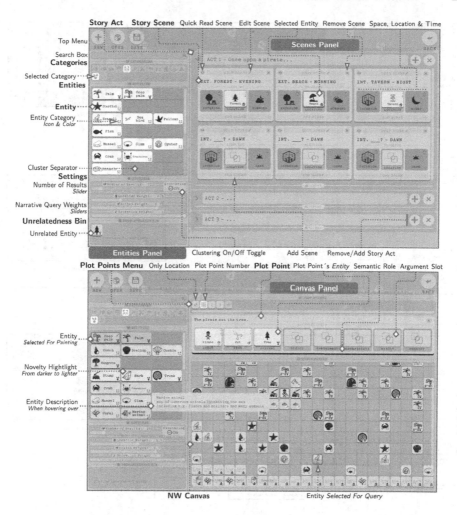

**Fig. 4.** TALEFORGE, an interactive prototype of our mixed-initiative approach.

In Fig. 4, we show three main panels of TALEFORGE: the *entities panel*, *scenes panel* and *canvas panel*. In the *entities panel*, the designer searches for entities, obtains recommendations and configures the recommender by setting categories, weights, number of results, clustering and an unrelatedness bin for NOT queries. An entity appears with a name, icon[6], category color and description when hovering over it. The novelty of a recommended entity is visualized as a lighter (more novel) to darker (least novel) background. In the *scenes panel*, the designer sees every scene of the story and selects one for editing the location's layout. In the *canvas panel*, the designer creates a location by placing entities into cells of the canvas. The designer can select individual plot points and entities to guide

---

[6] Entities' icons are populated automatically from thenounproject.com

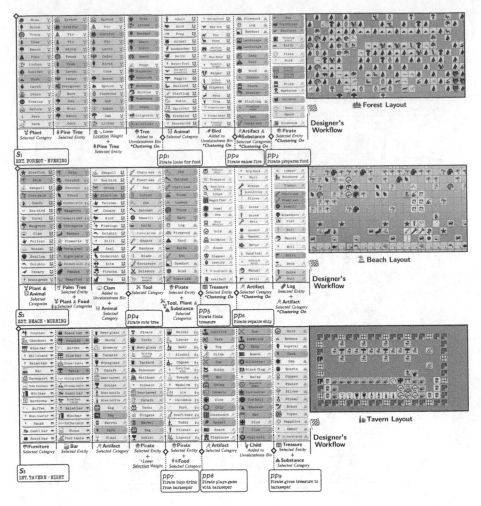

**Fig. 5.** Designer's workflow while creating an NW for *"Once upon a time, a pirate…"*.

the recommender. The front end of TALEFORGE was implemented in *Unity*, and the recommender method is served by a Python's *flask* API.

In Fig. 5, we show the recommender's output at various steps of the designer's workflow, together with the final layouts of the locations for our showcase story. To explain the designer's workflow, consider the first scene $S_1$ as an example. Here, the designer creates a layout for a *forest*. When selecting this scene, a plot points menu (top) and an empty NW canvas (bottom) is shown. The designer adds entities by searching for them and dragging/dropping them. Further, it is possible to *paint* on the canvas, e.g., to place several trees, by selecting the object and moving the mouse over the canvas, while holding the mouse button pressed. The recommender is prompted when interacting with any element. At first, it only considers entities related to the location (the *forest*). The designer selects the category *plant* ❦ and adds recommended entities like *pine trees* and *bushes*. When entities are added to the canvas, the novelty scores are updated, thus, recommended entities such as *bark*, *trunk* and *lichen* appear lighter (more novel). The designer can enforce a different output of the recommender by changing the narrative query weights or using the unrelatedness bin. The designer prompts the recommender by selecting a *pine tree* and lowers the weight of the location to put more emphasis on the selected object, causing *pinecone* to appear in the top results. Next, the designer might be interested in entities that are not related to *tree*, so the designer drags and drops *tree* into the unrelatedness bin and activates clustering. Consequently, the recommender suggests and groups different types of *mushrooms*.

The designer selects a plot point to consider the influence of an action. In $pp_1$, the designer selects the category *animal* 🐼 to add animals in the location for *finding food*. The output shows different *birds* which might not be interesting for the designer. Thus, the designer drags and drops *bird* to the unrelatedness bin and activates clustering to obtain groups of animals unrelated to *bird*, like *chipmunk*, *squirrel*, *deer*, and so on. In $pp_2$, the designer selects the category *artifact* 🔧 and *substance* ▲ to find entities related to *making a fire*, such as *wood*, *firewood*, *axe*, and others. In $pp_3$, the recommender outputs entities for *preparing food*, however, these are common cooking utensils and might not be interesting enough for a story, where a *pirate* is involved. Thus, the designer selects *pirate* from the plot point and discovers *caldron* in the recommendations.

Figure 5 presents similar designer workflows for Scenes $S_2$ and $S_3$.

## 5  Conclusion

We have introduced a novel mixed-initiative approach based on a recommender method that assists designers throughout the creation of a narrative world (NW) for a given story. Our method discovers and suggests NW content based on previously-learned common and novel associations to current narrative locations, actions and entities. Our method provides several vector and WORDNET operations that further expand the creative exploration of a designer. In addition, we have shown the usefulness of our approach through TALEFORGE, an interactive prototype that assists a designer with recommendations of entities for an NW.

Bringing mixed-initiative approaches into the workflows of NW designers can significantly improve the consistency between stories and NWs. The design of procedural tools to simplify artistic and technical tasks, as well as solutions to enhance designers exploration, are considered very important and challenging endeavours. However, there is a strong lack of research work on using a computational narrative as a basis for assisting NW designers. We believe this work provides a valuable step to a more complete NW authoring tool.

# References

1. Amato, A.: Procedural content generation in the game industry. In: Korn, O., Lee, N. (eds.) Game Dynamics, pp. 15–25. Springer, Cham (2017). https://doi.org/10. 1007/978-3-319-53088-8_2
2. Balint, J.T., Bidarra, R.: Procedural generation of narrative worlds (2021). Submitted for publication
3. Banerjee, S., Pedersen, T.: An adapted Lesk algorithm for word sense disambiguation using WordNet. In: Gelbukh, A. (ed.) CICLing 2002. LNCS, vol. 2276, pp. 136–145. Springer, Heidelberg (2002). https://doi.org/10.1007/3-540-45715-1_11
4. Caliskan, A., Bryson, J.J., Narayanan, A.: Semantics derived automatically from language corpora contain human-like biases. Science **356**(6334), 183–186 (2017). https://arxiv.org/abs/1608.07187
5. Castaño, O., Kybartas, B., Bidarra, R.: Talebox-a mobile game for mixed-initiative story creation. In: Proceedings of DiGRA-FDG (2016). https://graphics.tudelft.nl/ Publications-new/2016/CKB16/
6. Day, W.H., Edelsbrunner, H.: Efficient algorithms for agglomerative hierarchical clustering methods. J. Classif. **1**(1), 7–24 (1984). https://doi.org/10.1007/ BF01890115
7. Deterding, S., et al.: Mixed-initiative creative interfaces. In: Proceedings of the 2017 CHI Conference Extended Abstracts on Human Factors in Computing Systems, pp. 628–635 (2017). https://doi.org/10.1145/3027063.3027072
8. Di Fabio, A., Conia, S., Navigli, R.: VerbAtlas: a novel large-scale verbal semantic resource and its application to semantic role labeling. In: Proceedings of the 2019 Conference on Empirical Methods in Natural Language Processing and the 9th International Joint Conference on Natural Language Processing (EMNLP-IJCNLP), pp. 627–637 (2019). https://doi.org/10.18653/v1/D19-1058
9. Gupta, T., Schwing, A., Hoiem, D.: ViCo: word embeddings from visual co-occurrences. In: Proceedings of the IEEE/CVF International Conference on Computer Vision, pp. 7425–7434 (2019). https://arxiv.org/abs/1908.08527
10. Hartsook, K., Zook, A., Das, S., Riedl, M.O.: Toward supporting stories with procedurally generated game worlds. In: 2011 IEEE Conference on Computational Intelligence and Games (CIG 2011), pp. 297–304. IEEE (2011). https://doi.org/ 10.1109/CIG.2011.6032020
11. Kottur, S., Vedantam, R., Moura, J.M., Parikh, D.: Visual word2vec (vis-w2v): learning visually grounded word embeddings using abstract scenes. In: Proceedings of the IEEE Conference on Computer Vision and Pattern Recognition, pp. 4985–4994 (2016). https://arxiv.org/abs/1511.07067
12. Kybartas, B., Bidarra, R.: A semantic foundation for mixed-initiative computational storytelling. In: Schoenau-Fog, H., Bruni, L.E., Louchart, S., Baceviciute, S. (eds.) ICIDS 2015. LNCS, vol. 9445, pp. 162–169. Springer, Cham (2015). https:// doi.org/10.1007/978-3-319-27036-4_15
13. Kybartas, B., Bidarra, R.: A survey on story generation techniques for authoring computational narratives. IEEE Trans. Comput. Intell. AI Games **9**(3), 239–253 (2016). https://doi.org/10.1109/TCIAIG.2016.2546063
14. Liapis, A., Yannakakis, G.N., Nelson, M.J., Preuss, M., Bidarra, R.: Orchestrating game generation. IEEE Trans. Games **11**(1), 48–68 (2018). https://doi.org/10. 1109/TG.2018.2870876
15. Liapis, A., Yannakakis, G.N., Togelius, J.: Sentient sketchbook: computer-aided game level authoring. In: FDG, pp. 213–220 (2013). http://julian.togelius.com/ Liapis2013Sentient.pdf

16. Linden, R.V.D., Lopes, R., Bidarra, R.: Designing procedurally generated levels. In: Proceedings of the second AIIDE workshop on Artificial Intelligence in the Game Design Process, November 2013
17. Liu, Z.Q., Leung, K.M.: Script visualization (ScriptViz): a smart system that makes writing fun. Soft. Comput. **10**(1), 34–40 (2006). https://doi.org/10.1007/s00500-005-0461-4
18. Miller, G.A.: WordNet: An Electronic Lexical Database. MIT Press, Cambridge (1998). https://doi.org/10.7551/mitpress/7287.001.0001
19. Navigli, R., Ponzetto, S.P.: BabelNet: the automatic construction, evaluation and application of a wide-coverage multilingual semantic network. Artif. Intell. **193**, 217–250 (2012). https://doi.org/10.1016/j.artint.2012.07.001
20. Pennington, J., Socher, R., Manning, C.D.: GloVe: global vectors for word representation. In: Proceedings of the 2014 Conference on Empirical Methods in Natural Language Processing (EMNLP), pp. 1532–1543 (2014). https://doi.org/10.3115/v1/D14-1162
21. Porteous, J., Ferreira, J.F., Lindsay, A., Cavazza, M.: Extending narrative planning domains with linguistic resources. In: Proceedings of the 19th International Conference on Autonomous Agents and Multiagent Systems (AAMAS 2020), pp. 1081–1089. International Foundation for Autonomous Agents and Multiagent Systems (IFAAMAS) (2020). https://dl.acm.org/doi/abs/10.5555/3398761.3398887
22. Porteous, J., Lindsay, A., Read, J., Truran, M., Cavazza, M.: Automated extension of narrative planning domains with antonymic operators. In: Proceedings of the 14th International Conference on Autonomous Agents and Multiagent Systems (AAMAS 2015), May 2015. https://doi.org/10.5555/2772879.2773349
23. Rousseeuw, P.J.: Silhouettes: a graphical aid to the interpretation and validation of cluster analysis. J. Comput. Appl. Math. **20**, 53–65 (1987). https://doi.org/10.1016/0377-0427(87)90125-7
24. Samuel, B., Mateas, M., Wardrip-Fruin, N.: The design of writing buddy: a mixed-initiative approach towards computational story collaboration. In: Nack, F., Gordon, A.S. (eds.) ICIDS 2016. LNCS, vol. 10045, pp. 388–396. Springer, Cham (2016). https://doi.org/10.1007/978-3-319-48279-8_34
25. Schlechtweg, D., Oguz, C., Walde, S.S.I.: Second-order co-occurrence sensitivity of skip-gram with negative sampling. arXiv preprint arXiv:1906.02479 (2019). https://arxiv.org/abs/1906.02479
26. Shaker, N., Shaker, M., Togelius, J.: Ropossum: an authoring tool for designing, optimizing and solving cut the rope levels. In: Ninth Artificial Intelligence and Interactive Digital Entertainment Conference (2013). https://ojs.aaai.org/index.php/AIIDE/article/view/12611
27. Shaker, N., Togelius, J., Nelson, M.J.: Procedural Content Generation in Games. Springer, Heidelberg (2016). https://doi.org/10.1007/978-3-319-42716-4
28. Skorupski, J., Jayapalan, L., Marquez, S., Mateas, M.: Wide ruled: a friendly interface to author-goal based story generation. In: Cavazza, M., Donikian, S. (eds.) ICVS 2007. LNCS, vol. 4871, pp. 26–37. Springer, Heidelberg (2007). https://doi.org/10.1007/978-3-540-77039-8_3
29. Smelik, R.M., Tutenel, T., Bidarra, R., Benes, B.: A survey on procedural modelling for virtual worlds. Comput. Graph. Forum **33**(6), 31–50 (2014). https://doi.org/10.1111/cgf.12276
30. Smelik, R.M., Tutenel, T., de Kraker, K.J., Bidarra, R.: Interactive creation of virtual worlds using procedural sketching. In: Eurographics (Short papers), pp. 29–32 (2010). https://doi.org/10.2312/egsh.20101040

31. Smith, G., Whitehead, J., Mateas, M.: Tanagra: a mixed-initiative level design tool. In: Proceedings of the Fifth International Conference on the Foundations of Digital Games, pp. 209–216. ACM (2010). https://doi.org/10.1145/1822348.1822376

32. Widdows, D.: Orthogonal negation in vector spaces for modelling word-meanings and document retrieval. In: Proceedings of the 41st Annual Meeting of the Association for Computational Linguistics, pp. 136–143 (2003). https://doi.org/10.3115/1075096.1075114

33. Xu, C., Chen, Z., Li, C.: Obj-GloVe: scene-based contextual object embedding. arXiv preprint arXiv:1907.01478 (2019). https://arxiv.org/abs/1907.01478

34. Yannakakis, G.N., Liapis, A., Alexopoulos, C.: Mixed-initiative co-creativity. In: FDG (2014). https://www.um.edu.mt/library/oar/handle/123456789/29459

# Ressaca and Dispersão: Experiments in Non-linear Cinema

Bruno Caldas Vianna(✉) iD

Uniarts Helsinki, Helsinki, Finland
bruno.caldas@uniarts.fi

**Abstract.** Two interactive, non-linear, fictional, movie theater projects are described. The first, Ressaca, was released in 2008. A live-editing interface sits between the audience and the main screen. It is usually manipulated by the director, who creates a new improvised ordering of the sequences in each screening. The second one, Dispersão, was not yet launched. The interaction device is provided by the mobile phones of the audience: viewers may use an app which simulates a social network used by the movie characters. The engagement of the audience will interfere with the unfolding of the story. Agencies, syuzhets and algorithms for both experiences are discussed. Finally the article locates these projects as belonging to the field of interactive digital narratives specific to the movie theater, and also part of poorly charted tradition of interactive media from developing countries.

**Keywords:** Interactive cinema · Combinatory narratives · Storytelling · Non-linearity · Agency

## 1 Introduction

This demo paper describes two interactive cinema experiences created by the author, namely Ressaca (Hangover) and Dispersão (Dispersion). Both are meant for movie theaters, have feature film length (between 75 and 120 min) and portray fictional stories based in local historical events. They also share a collective device of agency and a non-branching narrative based on audiovisual lexia [8] which are the movie sequences. We will describe narrative, interactive and technical aspects and situate them in the context of interactive visual storytelling.

## 2 Ressaca

The movie follows the puberty and teenage years of a middle-class Brazilian during the turbulent times of re-democratization in the 80's and 90's. During that period, the country faced economic crisis, hyperinflation, dead and impeached presidents.

The project's interaction device is a 1-m round touch screen that stands between the main screen and the audience. The device (Fig. 1), baptized as

© Springer Nature Switzerland AG 2021
A. Mitchell and M. Vosmeer (Eds.): ICIDS 2021, LNCS 13138, pp. 29–33, 2021.
https://doi.org/10.1007/978-3-030-92300-6_3

Engrenagem (Sprocket) was developed and programmed by Maíra Sala [2], and is inspired by the musical interface named Reactable [5]. It is manipulated any one person with sufficient knowledge of the material and interface. It works effectively as an editing tool, allowing the user to create an order for the pre-edited sequences and even the individual shots of the film in real time. The usual session starts with 5–10 sequences overhead, and subsequent lexia were added impromptu, according to the will of the editor, which could be influenced by the reaction of the audience, his or her mood, or a specific goal like focusing on one of the stories. The movie has 128 sequences in total [6], and a session could use anything between fifty to eighty from them.

**Fig. 1.** The director between the main theater screen and the Engrenagem interface

Ressaca was released in 2008 and exhibited in several festivals and venues throughout the world until 2011. It won four awards, including Best Film in Cinesquemanovo 2009 [7], in Porto Alegre, Brazil. This was the only festival in which it took part of the competition. In others, the project was shown in non-competitive screenings.

The goal of the project was to offer a non-linear experience that didn't disrupt the immersive cinema experience by asking the audience to make choices. The "editor" – the director himself, most of the times – assumes a role of representing the audience [9]. At the same time, the imposing presence of the interface and the movements of the person manipulating it introduce an element of risk. There is tension in building the storyline. Any mistakes in the operation can be noticed by the public. In other words, Ressaca brings elements of live performances, which are the rule in theater representations, to the cinematic experience.

The storytelling device does not offer a branching, tree-like structure: topology-wise it could be considered arbitrary [10], although the term doesn't take into account the fact that the decisions made by the editor are not arbitrary, but based on several factors. There is not a predefined path, and any random trajectory might result in interesting concatenations. The structure is inspired by the strategy used by novelist Cortázar in Hopscotch: some syuzhets [1] are suggested, but the reader is also welcome to explore the chapters freely and created his or her own experience. There are paths to follow, and some of the lexia are better connected to a small set of others. It is a navigation that yields better results when the agent has familiarity with these features. I call this particular strategy a *narrative landscape*: previous knowledge of the ground leads to satisfying routes, but random walkabouts will also take the viewer to unexpected corners with surprising shortcuts. The naming also serves as a nod to Jeffrey Shaw pioneering cinema work.

## 3   Dispersão

In 2018, we started a new project continuing our research on cinema and non-linear narratives. Dispersão (Dispersion) [3] is also a feature-length experience created for movie theaters, and offers a collective narrative agency. But instead of relying on a representative to decide on the storytelling route, this project puts the structuring of the sequences on the hands of viewers.

The audience of the film receives information on the story and characters through two different streams: the first and more visible is the big theater screen, where live action scenes take place. And the other is the mobile phone of each viewer. A social network app was created specially for the project, again by creative developer Maíra Sala. This software imitates the mechanism of a micro-blogging platform, except that its participants are not the moviegoers, but the characters of the movie. Thus, events on the main story told on the theater screen might trigger some posts and comments inside the app.

Even though the spectators cannot make posts, they can interact with the app by reacting to them. And that is exactly the interactive strategy for storytelling: the system will choose the next sequences depending on the engagement with each post. The rationale here follows the logic of existing commercial social networks. If a posts provokes more engagement it means that the audience is interested in the character, and/or the plot around it. In the case of a platform like Twitter, this would make the post be shown to a greater number of users (as it proves to be more popular) and would also bring up more posts related to it to the particular user who "liked" it. And in the case of the collective audience of Dispersão in the movie theater, this would have the effect of guiding the stories towards that plot and/or character, by selecting specific sequences.

The algorithm behind it includes a classification of each sequence according to the plot, character and "ideal" position in the movie. This position is related to the narrative structure, but it is not necessarily dictated by a chronological order: some sequences might work well both in the beginning and the end of the movie, for instance. A modified logistic function is used, taking as parameter the distance to the ideal position. The result is used as a weight in random selection of the next scene.

The story also evolves around the effects of politics in the lives of characters, and is set around 2011–2016, during the crisis of the left wing government in Brazil. The project was delayed by the COVID pandemic and is now expected to be released in the beginning of 2022. Even though the software development and post-production phases are finished, live tests could not yet be made.

The topology of the lexia in Dispersão was created after the experiences in Ressaca. It is a mix of hardwiring some connections and leaving enough room for chance and audience control through the algorithm described above. Again, it is difficult to classify the narrative algorithm based on the topology. The proposed category of narrative landscape still applies to the method, as it has simply been partially fixed into software. The devices used – mobile phones – are nonetheless intrusive and might create disruptions. Their use during sessions, no matter how much a widespread habit it is, is still frowned upon. It remains to be seen how much of a liability or a benefit this will be for the cinematic experience.

## 4   Conclusion

When discussing the future of the Interactive Digital Narratives field, Murray proposes this image of a kaleidoscope of multiple taxonomies and artifacts [4]. The projects described here are to be found in a very specific branch of this looking glass, the one dedicated to collective interactive experiences that take place inside the movie theater. But even within this small field, they belong to a more exotic leaf which aggregates the ones produced in the periphery of the western world - in developing countries.

It is hard to claim novelty on such projects when there isn't even a reference frame to discuss them in the same language. A quick lookup on an academic search engine reveals three pages of articles dedicated to the project Ressaca written in Portuguese or Spanish, and not one single document in English, even after more than a decade from its inception.

Practitioners from the global south are used to being subject to "discoveries", specially if their practice is performed in non hegemonic languages. This demo proposes to fill a gap in the documentation of such practice. By opening a small crack in this wall, I hope that new projects - like "Dispersão" - can find a voice of their own, free from a colonialist perspective.

# References

1. Bordwell, D.: Narration in the Fiction Film. Routledge, Abingdon (2013)
2. Coutinho, E.L., Pinto, I.: A participação do espectador no filme Ressaca (2011)
3. Dispersão website. https://web.archive.org/web/20190710073406/, http:// dispersao.net/. Accessed 11 Oct 2021
4. Murray, J.H.: Research into interactive digital narrative: a kaleidoscopic view. In: Rouse, R., Koenitz, H., Haahr, M. (eds.) ICIDS 2018. LNCS, vol. 11318, pp. 3–17. Springer, Cham (2018). https://doi.org/10.1007/978-3-030-04028-4_1
5. Reactable. https://en.wikipedia.org/wiki/Reactable. Accessed 11 Oct 2021
6. Ressaca edited scenes. https://archive.org/details/ressaca. Accessed 11 Oct 2021
7. Ressaca wins Cinemaesquemanovo Festival. https://web.archive.org/web/20091029191702/https://g1.globo.com/Noticias/Cinema/0,,MUL1354133-7086,00.html. Accessed 11 Oct 2021
8. Ross, C.: Hypertext 2.0: The Convergence of Contemporary Critical Theory (1999)
9. Rodrigues, A.C.: Live Cinema: Autoria Coletiva em Narrativas Objetivas e Subjetivas (2015)
10. van Dyke Parunak, H.: Hypermedia topologies and user navigation. In: Proceedings of the Second Annual ACM Conference on Hypertext, pp. 43–50 (1989). https:// doi.org/10.1145/74224.74228

# Pedagogical Challenges in Social Physics Authoring

Daniel DeKerlegand[1]([✉]), Ben Samuel[1], and Mike Treanor[2]

[1] University of New Orleans, New Orleans, LA 70148, USA
`dldekerl@my.uno.edu`, `bsamuel@cs.uno.edu`
[2] American University, Washington, DC 20016, USA
`treanor@american.edu`

**Abstract.** Authoring interactive narrative content for AI engines can be a difficult task, and as our work on collaborative social-physics based projects like *VESPACE* and *Vox Populi: The Ustradian Games* has revealed, there exist numerous key difficulties in training content authors. Despite the prevalence of these setbacks over years of training new authors, no comprehensive survey, analysis, or codification of pedagogical challenges has heretofore been completed. In order to formalize this knowledge, we have conducted an analysis of experiential results from previous workshops and collaborations as well as from written participant feedback and reflections. Our primary research objective has been to analyze these pedagogical challenges and their origins, including conflicting paradigms, unfamiliarity with computer science concepts, difficulty visualizing and managing authored content, and unresponsive feedback loops. Lastly, we introduce a design and prototype of a tutorial game which will train users in the authoring of content for the Ensemble social physics engine. The game's design is a response to the challenges revealed in our analysis and will be one of open-ended freedom of play, leveraging the playful experimentation of the engine and guiding players to an intuitive understanding of the engine's underlying mechanisms as they create and explore.

**Keywords:** Emergent narrative · Authoring tools · Pedagogy

## 1 Introduction

Emergent narratives are narrative structures which are not predefined but rather generated by users through interactions and choices [2,13]. These narratives have exponentially larger spaces of possible playthroughs as compared to more traditional narrative experiences, including modern video games using branching narrative logic [26]. Social physics engines like Comme il Faut (CiF) [20] and its spiritual successor Ensemble [27] offer one approach to the creation of emergent narratives by leveraging concepts relevant to the broader domain of social physics, including network theory and predicate logic. Social physics games can

© Springer Nature Switzerland AG 2021
A. Mitchell and M. Vosmeer (Eds.): ICIDS 2021, LNCS 13138, pp. 34–47, 2021.
https://doi.org/10.1007/978-3-030-92300-6_4

take the form of social puzzles [17], where players must try to anticipate the potential social effects of their actions [18], considering, for example, the range of likely emotional responses by non-player characters [12]. Social physics systems in the CiF family have been implemented in mods to AAA games such as *Skyrim* and *Conan Exiles*, with user studies suggesting that players prefer and gravitate toward NPCs guided by such engines [10,11,23].

Unlike pre-written narratives, however, the authoring of content for the CiF and Ensemble engines requires the composition of predicate logic defining the logical structures and rules of the interactive world, including the realm of possible truths and states–known as a schema–as well as the individual rules which govern social behaviors and the range of actions that players and NPCs can take. Previous research has identified general challenges in the field of interactive digital narrative storytelling [14], surveyed issues presented by existing interactive narrative authoring tools [9], and examined pain points in interactive narrative authoring caused by authors' lack of knowledge of underlying computational models [31]. However, the existing research has not yet examined the unique challenges of authoring for systems like Ensemble, wherein content is authored solely as first-order predicate logic rules rather than narrative fragments.

The authoring process may differ greatly depending on the goals of the authors. For example, in early applications of the CiF and Ensemble engines, content authors generally took an informal approach; for example, the authors of the game *Prom Week*–consisting primarily of computer scientists–strove to approximate the sociological and psychological situations portrayed by films in the "teen movies" genre [28], using examples from films of the genre for reference [19]. Subsequent projects like *VESPACE* and *Vox Populi: The Ustradian Games*, however, have required more stringent authoring processes. Both of these projects, being multidisciplinary collaborations between researchers in artificial intelligence, the humanities, and social sciences, required the training of researchers from outside the field of computer science in social physics authoring. In this paper, we will introduce these two projects and outline the various difficulties in author training which they have revealed, as well as the numerous methods which we will employ in our tutorial game in order to address and circumvent them.

Based on experience and feedback from *VESPACE* and *Vox Populi*, several pedagogical issues appear to occur with some regularity in collaborative social physics authoring efforts, and our hope is that documenting these challenges will aid future teachers and authors in their authoring endeavors. In order to address these difficulties head on, the training hurdles enumerated in our analysis have inspired our current tutorial game project, which seeks to guide users in effective social physics authoring by leveraging the unique pedagogical opportunities afforded by open-ended gameplay; much of our tutorial game design has come directly from written responses that *VESPACE* workshop participants took part in and which we will draw from in this paper.

To address the challenges identified in our analysis, we have designed and prototyped a tutorial game to train users by reinforcing learning through exploration, so that learners can immediately experience the expressiveness of the

Ensemble engine through real-time feedback, all while being guided by various challenges and motivational goals. In the game, players will guide a household of pets through social interactions, exploring the narrative and social effects of authorial choices as they complete challenges and unlock new authoring capabilities. The term *"SimCity* effect" has been used to describe video games possessing this ability to develop player understanding of internal structures and mechanisms through gameplay [21,34,35]. We have sought to design our tutorial game with the SimCity effect in mind, utilizing open-ended gameplay and exploration, along with motivating techniques such as skill trees, in order to instill a familiarity with the functionality and potentiality of the Ensemble engine.

## 2   Authoring Projects

In this paper, we focus on the authoring challenges of two major collaborative efforts, the *VESPACE* and *Vox Populi: The Ustradian Games* projects; we chose these two projects based on their complexity and the fact that both projects were interdisciplinary in nature, consisting of collaboration between computer science and artificial intelligence researchers on one hand and humanities and social science scholars on the other. In contrast with other social physics-based interactive narrative games, the authoring for these projects was largely performed by participants with no previous training in social physics or computer science. The *VESPACE* project included an authoring collaboration with French literary historians, which was conducted through numerous authoring workshops that ran in parallel with the development of a collaborative web-based authoring tool. The *Vox Populi: The Ustradian Games* project saw collaboration with education and assessment specialists in order to develop a game which challenges users to think critically as they explore an unfamiliar culture.

### 2.1   Authoring *VESPACE*

The *VESPACE* project, a multidisciplinary collaboration between various universities in the United States and France, has sought to create a virtual reality experience reconstructing the physical and social spaces of eighteenth-century Parisian theatre [7]. The first phase of the project involved the virtual construction of the physical interior of the Saint-Germain Fair theatre based on visual depictions and historical data, leading to the production of a VR experience allowing participants to explore this reconstructed space. Subsequently, the project has focused on the construction of an interactive social game taking place within the virtual environment. Over the course of a year and through a series of workshops, we endeavored to train participating literary historians in the authoring of social physics content, with the ultimate goal of these researchers mining historical texts for social rules capable of producing social experiences which are faithful to period sources. The final game will provide players with an immersive learning environment, allowing users to explore not only the class and gender dynamics of the social mores of eighteenth-century France but also the complexities of historical interpretation [24].

Authoring for the *VESPACE* project has required the construction of a large corpus of rules and a schema tailored to the social norms of 18th century France; importantly, this content must be written by literary historians, with citations supporting each authoring decision. Before the authoring process could begin, we needed to conduct significant training workshops for prospective authors, as well as to develop a new authoring tool facilitating collaborative authoring. We first conducted a series of short workshops as we iterated through the development sprints of the tool, ultimately working up to the deployment of the tool and its use in a week-long remote workshop [6]. The first round of *VESPACE* author training included four half-day workshops, attended by a group of six and guided by three of the participants. Two of the three workshop leaders were computer science researchers, while the other leader was a professor of literary history who had undergone some one-on-one training in social physics concepts and terminologies. The other three participants were graduate students in literary history. These short workshops held a three-fold value: as training sessions for authors, as a means of identifying significant pedagogical challenges in the use of Ensemble, and as beta-testing scenarios for the authoring tool.

The second round of *VESPACE* author training consisted of one week of day-long workshops and was attended by eight participants, including the previous trio of leaders and five graduate and PhD students from various humanities disciplines. The end result of this workshop was a fully-realized schema for *VESPACE* consisting of 10 categories and a total of 113 types, as well as a rich rule set of 230 rules. Following this week-long workshop, we tasked all eight participants with composing an 8–12 page formal reflection outlining their experience, asking them to describe any difficulties they faced. We then conducted an informal analysis of these reflections, maintaining a list of challenges described by the authors. Following the informal analysis, we performed a more thorough analysis, keeping track of the frequency with which each challenge was mentioned, combining closely related challenges into categories, looking for keywords indicating a particular challenge's severity, and collecting illustrative quotes for the paper. The results of this analysis are an important source of experiential data concerning the authorial challenges which we will codify and analyze in this paper.

## 2.2 Authoring *Vox Populi: The Ustradian Games*

*Vox Populi: The Ustradian Games* is a game-based assessment of cross-cultural competency and meta-cognition, created in collaboration with education and assessment specialists, that integrates complex social simulation technologies with gameplay. In the game, players seek to achieve objectives through having conversations with the people of an unknown artificial culture. The player's dialogue options and the non-player character responses are determined by a modified version of Ensemble called the Social Practice Engine [33]. The game roughly conforms to the "Visual Novel" game genre, but rather than simply navigating pre-scripted dialogue trees, the responses are dynamically selected based on the social state and history of player choices. Because the results of conversations are based on a rich model of the non-player character's culture, to successfully play the game, players must focus on gaining an understanding of the culture, rather than memorizing socially appropriate sequences of actions, or simply enumerating all paths through dialogue trees.

The *Vox Populi* project followed a more informal collaborative approach, conducted in the form of meetings and emails, but the conclusions reached were the same as those of *VESPACE*, illustrating how social physics can be used fruitfully for the production of interactive experiences in other cross-disciplinary projects. Creating the artificial unknown culture required the authoring of many social rules and was largely done by a team of education and assessment researchers. Having these non-artificial intelligence researchers create this content required that they be trained in how Ensemble works. This training was done via several day-long workshops, as well as through emails and many remote meetings over the course of two years.

## 3    Challenges in Social Physics Authoring

The collaborative experiences of developing social physics content for *VES-PACE* and *Vox Populi* have revealed numerous difficulties in training social physics authors. In this section, we will enumerate and analyze the most important of those challenges, and later in the paper we will outline our pedagogical approaches for resolving these challenges through the development of a tutorial game.

Authored content for Ensemble can be subdivided into several different data structures and whose relationships can be seen in Fig. 1, including *schema, rules, actions*, and *state*. Of these four, we will discuss significant difficulties in the authorship of the first three, as they have presented the most noteworthy challenges to new authors. By comparison, the authoring of state and the related authoring of characters have posed fewer challenges in workshop, and while we may indirectly address them as they relate to the authoring of schema, rules, and actions, we have refrained from a direct analysis of authoring those structures.

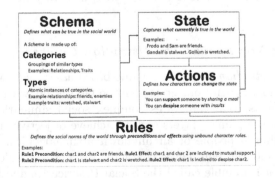

**Fig. 1.** Data structures in ensemble authoring

## 3.1  Schema Authoring Challenges

The realm of possible states and truths in the Ensemble engine are defined in the authoring of a *schema*. Whereas the earlier social physics engine CiF included a predefined schema containing social, psychological, or sociological categories such as character traits, temporary emotional statuses, and relationships, authors using the Ensemble engine must build a schema from scratch, consisting of abstract *categories* which are themselves populated by specific *types*. For example, a category of "relationship" might have types such as "friends" and "enemies." However, this authorial flexibility comes with additional complexity. Schema authoring can be challenging due to its open-ended nature, leading authors to develop schemata which are overdeveloped, underdeveloped, or difficult to use. Experienced Ensemble authors rely on various informal heuristics during schema authoring, but new authors may either feel bewildered or will develop ineffective schemata. The rule authoring process relies on the development of a robust, well-planned schema, but schema authoring is difficult for authors without previous knowledge of social physics or computer science concepts. These authors must first learn these concepts before they can begin the schema authoring process, resulting in a steep learning curve for many authors-to-be.

**Unfamiliar Computer Science Concepts.** Authoring for the Ensemble engine can prove challenging for any author, but it is perhaps most difficult for users who are less familiar with computer science concepts and modalities. At a basic level, many authors will have a tendency to envision rules in terms of individual states, for example "Fido is mean," whereas computer science leverages variables in the form of rule binding, such that "Fido" is replaced by a variable which can potentially bind with any character. In addition, Ensemble leverages even more complex computer science concepts, including networks and graphs, network directionality (and bidirectionality), weighted edges, first-order predicate logic, enums, Boolean and scalar values, and time steps. For example, the abstract schema categories that define the realm of possible states in an Ensemble schema must be declared as either undirected, directed, or reciprocal. For example, if an author were to define a reciprocal category in order to reflect relationships between characters, predicates in that category could be formally represented as a fully-connected network, where all character relationships of a given type could be illustrated in the form of a graph.

The use of computer science terms and concepts has remained a persistent hurdle for new authors of CiF and Ensemble content, and in general, researchers have attempted to strike a balance between minimizing computer science terminology and training authors in the necessary technical concepts. For example, despite the design of the Ensemble system being based on social phenomena and terminology, previous iterations of CiF and Ensemble authoring tools have shielded users from unnecessary terminology. Nevertheless, in some cases, this is unavoidable. For example, during our *VESPACE* training sessions, we found that participants unfamiliar with computer science terminologies found it more difficult in particular to get started in creating schemata, which is reasonable, since schemata are the most abstract data structures in Ensemble and heavily leverage predicate logic and network theory. In order to overcome this, we ultimately designed the schema authoring portion of our authoring tool to function as a questionnaire, in which we asked users a series of questions while providing them with examples. Based on their responses, we empowered users to construct new categories or add new types to existing categories, minimizing as much as possible the use of computer science terms.

**Generalizing Abstractions from Source Material.** For many researchers, such as the literary historians working on the *VESPACE* project, the research process involves a close analysis of source texts for specific examples or citations. Through aggregation of numerous examples, a researcher might extrapolate to develop an abstract grouping or concept, but beginning from observations or individual details helps to prevent the researcher from imposing an abstract concept onto the source material. Therefore, requiring authors to begin with a category and then populate it with types went against the typical research workflow. One *VESPACE* workshop participant described this challenge, stating, "First-time rule authors often try to code the exact scene from the source they are using, but rules authorship is above all an interpretive gesture, in which the literary instance serves as the basis for an abstraction that can be applied across different specific situations." In order to accommodate working from the specific to the general, we designed the schema authoring component of the Ensemble authoring tool such that users first create types and then either add these types to an existing category or build an enclosing category up from the new type.

**Managing Schema Size.** According to our analysis, authors working to design a schema from a large corpus of source texts or from general knowledge have an authorial tendency to create schemata that are too big. This can be a problem, as there is a "non-linear" relationship between schema types and the number of social rules that need to be authored. Ideally, authors should strike a balance between generality and expressivity, but determining the ideal schema size is not immediately intuitive and rather depends on an understanding of the relationship between schema and rules and between rules and actions. For example, if authors create different types for "joyful" and "happy", they will need to create rules pertaining to both, as well as actions for characters to express both states, while the authors may not be particularly attached to the differentiation. There is no right answer as to how many types and classes there should be, but to alleviate the authorial burden introduced by excessive combinations and complexity [1, 4, 25], authors should be conservative when adding to the schema.

Adding to this difficulty is the fact that Ensemble requires the presence of a schema before rules can be authored, meaning authors must start from the most abstract, atomic elements of the world space, which can be quite challenging; authors may define schemata which are too large or too specific, due to an authorial tendency of starting from the specific and moving to the general and abstract. Some *VESPACE* authors found this particularly challenging, with one workshop participant writing that "Complex and less concrete elements in the schema were much more difficult to agree upon and incorporating them revealed both the constraints and the possibilities of thinking within the Ensemble authoring system. For example, my group was very concerned with the issue of theater etiquette, but baffled by the question of how the intricate rules of eighteenth-century public conduct could be summed up by the kind of one-word terms that comprised the schema."

## 3.2   Rule Authoring Challenges

In Ensemble, rules can be thought of as the character tendencies or social norms that the system will use to determine what actions a character might take. This places rules at the core of the Ensemble authoring process, and is where authors must expend the most time and effort. For example, a schema could have between six to ten categories, with perhaps ten to fifteen types each, whereas a given interactive narrative will likely require hundreds or even thousands of rules. Though rule authoring itself is less challenging conceptually than schema authoring, it requires a knowledgeable approach in order to produce a successful experience. For example, the kinds of rules authored–and by extension the number of those kinds–will effect the realm of possible social interactions, and the weights of individual rules can drastically affect the ramifications of player choices. Accounting for these challenges requires the use of several authoring heuristics, which we will endeavor to instill in authors through our tutorial game.

**Achieving Social Rule Coverage.** Developing an effective rule corpus requires achieving sufficient "social rule coverage," which means crafting enough of those rules which define the most generic social norms or behaviors of a particular society or group. Some participants in the *VESPACE* authoring workshops found it difficult to construct rules which would correlate to corresponding actionable behaviors by characters; one participant reflected that "it was challenging to read the texts we chose and then transpose elements from them to write rules governing what the characters in the game would want to do and could actually do, given the particular qualities assigned to them." Related to this, in our experience, authors tend to focus more frequently on highly specific scenarios, but they often do not remember to take into account the "base" effect of single predicate rules. For example, an author might construct a more specific rule defining the concept "the enemy of my enemy is my friend" yet may forget to define the underlying effect of that rule, that "people are less likely to want to be friends with their enemy."

**Determining Authored Rule Space.** Through its relationship with the schema–which defines the realm of all possible states within a given Ensemble social world–the set of rules will occupy some percentage of the total possible "potential rule space." However, the Ensemble authoring tool does not currently provide a means of determining how much of that potential rule space has been covered by authored content. We have developed a general heuristic for approaching this problem in the form of a set authoring order; during the authoring process, we first consider all relationships, then networks, then statuses, and so on. However, this heuristic approach should ultimately be replaced by more exact methods, for example author assistance visualization techniques [8] informing authors on the current authored rule space, which could be filtered by category or type.

### 3.3 Action Authoring Challenges

Actions in Ensemble define the range of all possible decisions that a player or NPC can make in a game. Because actions have preconditions and effects (how the action changes the social state), authors must make deliberate choices when composing both rules and actions, so that rules will have a real effect on the range of possible and probable actions, making for rich social experiences.

**Understanding Action Selection.** One frequent challenge in social physics action authoring concerns the inherent tension between the tendency towards authorial control in traditional authoring and the player freedom and agency offered by emergent systems [3,22], as well as the related balancing act between player agency and character agency [5]. For example, the very concept of dynamic "action selection" (the purpose of Ensemble) caused a lot of confusion with the extended team for *Vox Populi: The Ustradian Games*, with authors developing workarounds to assert more authorial control. Rather than seeing a character's action selection as the emergent result of many rules being true over a semantically meaningful social state that represented the inner feelings of agents, they created actions with effects that merely flagged that specific events had occurred, and then created heavily weighted rules to guarantee that specific characters would choose specific actions subsequently. Authoring in this way eliminated the need to use Ensemble at all, and made the interactive experience a simple branching narrative. Similarly, authors can feel stifled by the uncertain frequency with which characters will choose actions, such as when *VESPACE* authors translating source materials felt anxious about being too general or too specific for effective action selection. One workshop participant noted "if there are too many preconditions for a volition rule, no characters will (likely) meet all the conditions, and the rule will never come into play. Similarly, if there are too few predicates, and the rule is very general and could apply to many or all of the characters... it might become overused in the game."

### 3.4 Time to Feedback

Due to the open-ended nature of social physics experiences, the approach employed in social physics authoring may not be immediately intuitive to authors-in-training; one way to overcome this challenge is to allow authors to learn by doing, which means diminishing the time to feedback or feedback loop becomes an important pedagogical tool. If authors can visualize, experience, and play with the effects of their authorial choices, they can begin to develop an intuitive sense of how authoring decisions relate to the creation of social worlds.

Previous research has identified *expressive range* as a measure of generative space, whereby a set of quantitative metrics and models can be defined for graphing and analyzing an expressive range with an ultimate goal of qualitative interpretation and analysis [16,29,30]. Others have discussed methods for expanding expressive range [15,32], but there may also be uses for decreasing or modulating expressive range depending on the context. Our tutorial game seeks to intentionally constrain the expressive range of the system as players begin, making the range manageable for learning, then gradually releasing that expressive range as players accomplish in-game goals in order to guide them naturally through the learning experience.

## 4 Gameplay as a Pedagogical Answer to Authoring Challenges

Our analysis of the pedagogical challenges in training Ensemble authors, which we have formally codified in this paper, has led naturally to the development of a tutorial game for training aspiring Ensemble authors. Previous social physics-based games have used pre-authored schemata and rules, while our tutorial game will allow players to gradually author their own schemata and rules through gameplay. It will therefore leverage the open-ended exploration and experimentation of social physics-based games in order to deeply integrate learning outcomes and Ensemble familiarity with the mechanics of the game, so that players directly experience the effects of the decisions they make as content authors.

The tutorial game centers around the lives of pets in a household, with the initial cast of characters consisting of three dogs, three cats, and one human. The initial schema will be only minimally predefined, containing four categories–relationships, traits, statuses, and directed statuses; furthermore, players will start the game with an even more simplified active subset of the initial schema, with the option of unlocking categories and types as they complete goals and quests. As players unlock more characters and more social state, each of the characters will have a minimal set of predefined predicates determining the social history of that character. For example, the character Mr. Woof is defined as being a dog (trait), playmates with another dog character named Chaplin (relationship), and hungry (status). Another character named Kitty is defined as being a cat (trait), playful towards Chaplin as well as another cat character named Madame Meow (directed statuses), and social (trait).

Starting from a predetermined schema, cast, social history, and list of actions, players will have the freedom to explore and experiment by adding characters, changing state, and modifying the schema, all while being guided by a system of incentives and quests through which players can level up their skill tree, unlocking new ways to add to or modify the Ensemble authored content. Players will see the effects of their choices gradually play out in the social world, experiencing immediate feedback in the form of character actions and responses that will illustrate the expressive range of the Ensemble engine.

## 4.1   Teaching Schema Authoring Through Gameplay

Recall that an Ensemble schema defines what can be true in the social world. Starting players off with a small, manageable schema will be very important, because as we have found in our analysis of pedagogical challenges, schema authoring tends to be the most daunting authorial process. The four initial categories–trait, relationship, status, and directed status–will be described in detail using colloquial language, leveraging the correlations between Ensemble data structures and natural human sociological states and behaviors. As players level up their schema skill tree, they will first be given the option to add new types to a category, with the possible new types initially determined by the game; beginning with types aligns with our analysis that starting with category authoring is unnatural for many authors, especially researchers who value specificity, evidence, and citation. Furthermore, guiding players through a gradual expansion of the schema will aid authors in gaining an intuitive feel for the effect that schema manipulation and schema size have on the range of possible gameplay scenarios, starting with types and gradually extending to new categories.

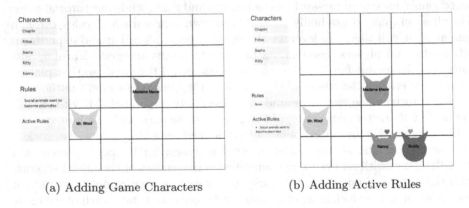

(a) Adding Game Characters          (b) Adding Active Rules

**Fig. 2.** Tutorial game screens

## 4.2   Teaching Rule Authoring Through Gameplay

Rules are the core of the Ensemble authoring process as well as–according to our analysis–one of the more intuitive aspects of authoring. However, while rule authoring itself may be less challenging, the *effects* of rule authoring are less intuitive, especially the relationships between rule authoring and rule coverage, space, and tuning. Therefore, early quests in our tutorial game will challenge users to expand social rule coverage in order to make certain behaviors and responses possible, with the anticipation that experiencing these effects in real time will give authors a more intuitive sense of the correlation between rule authoring and the range of possible social behaviors. We will begin by allowing players to only activate rules from a predetermined set, requiring them to select rules wisely in order to achieve some social responses in the game. As illustrated in Fig. 2(a), not every rule is initially active; only volition rules managed by the player will be leveraged by the game. As a core aspect of gameplay, players can activate rules and experience immediate feedback as they change the range of narrative potential. Figure 2(b) shows that once a player has activated the rule "Social animals want to become playmates" and brought new characters into the game world having the "social" trait, those characters can now be affected by the rule, leading them to potentially become playmates. This is a pedagogically valuable interaction whereby players learn the effects of authoring by experiencing them directly. Gradually, players can unlock the capacity to modify existing rules and to forge new rules, but only after they have witnessed the narrative effects of changes in rule space.

Eventually, as players level up their rule authoring skills, they will gain the option of creating entirely new rules in order to accomplish some goal. As players modify the list of active rules, we will provide visualizations of social rule coverage and existing rule space, in order to illustrate the effects of rule authoring in a more theoretical sense. Due to the importance of weight balancing in the Ensemble authoring process, yet another branch of rule authoring on the skill tree will involve weight tuning, wherein players will gain the ability to modify rule weights so that the impacts of particular rules will change, with quests challenging the player to modify rule weights in order to achieve some goal.

## 5    Conclusions/Future Work

One of the strengths of social physics is its ability to foster collaboration and creative problem solving across disciplines; due to its underlying reliance on first-order logic predicates as opposed to statistical models, researchers and creators of various backgrounds can leverage this authoring paradigm to develop immersive, rich interactive experiences. However, there is a learning curve to the authoring process, which means it will be important to produce effective authoring tools and learning materials that can address the particular difficulties involved in social physics authoring. In this paper, we have compiled data from previous authoring collaborations in order to codify and analyze the most persistent and troublesome challenges in social physics authoring pedagogy. We have also introduced our tutorial game design, which will minimize the feedback loop and gradually introduce player-authors to Ensemble paradigms in intuitive ways, directly addressing the challenges laid out in the paper through the design choices enumerated. With our analysis of pedagogical challenges complete and the tutorial game designed and prototyped, our next step will be to complete development of the game and submit it to user testing and user studies, adjusting game elements as necessary based on user feedback and success studies.

# References

1. Antoun, C., Antoun, M., Ryan, J.O., Samuel, B., Swanson, R., Walker, M.A.: Generating natural language retellings from prom week play traces. In: Proceedings of the PCG in Games (2015)
2. Aylett, R.: Emergent narrative, social immersion and "storification". In: Proceedings of the 1st International Workshop on Narrative and Interactive Learning Environments, pp. 35–44 (2000)
3. Carmichael, G., Mould, D.: A framework for coherent emergent stories. In: FDG (2014)
4. Chen, S., Nelson, M., Mateas, M.: Evaluating the authorial leverage of drama management. In: Proceedings of the AAAI Conference on Artificial Intelligence and Interactive Digital Entertainment, vol. 4 (2009)
5. Cole, A.: Connecting player and character agency in videogames. Text Special (49) (2018)
6. DeKerlegand, D., Samuel, B., Leichman, J.: Encoding socio-historical exegesis as social physics predicates. In: International Conference on the Foundations of Digital Games, pp. 1–9 (2020)
7. François, P., Laroche, F., Leichman, J., Rubellin, F.: Mettre en place les fondations d'un outil de restitution à large audience: Vespace (2018)
8. Garbe, J., Reed, A.A., Dickinson, M., Wardrip-Fruin, N., Mateas, M.: Author assistance visualizations for ice-bound, a combinatorial narrative. In: FDG (2014)
9. Green, D., Hargood, C., Charles, F.: Contemporary issues in interactive storytelling authoring systems. In: Rouse, R., Koenitz, H., Haahr, M. (eds.) ICIDS 2018. LNCS, vol. 11318, pp. 501–513. Springer, Cham (2018). https://doi.org/10.1007/978-3-030-04028-4_59
10. Guimaraes, M., Santos, P., Jhala, A.: CiF-CK: an architecture for social NPCs in commercial games. In: 2017 IEEE Conference on Computational Intelligence and Games (CIG), pp. 126–133. IEEE (2017)
11. Guimarães, M., Santos, P., Jhala, A.: Prom week meets skyrim (2017)
12. Jenkins, H.: Game design as narrative architecture. Computer **44**(53), 118–130 (2004)
13. Koenitz, H.: Narrative in video games (2019)
14. Koenitz, H., Eladhari, M.P.: Challenges of IDN research and teaching. In: Cardona-Rivera, R.E., Sullivan, A., Young, R.M. (eds.) ICIDS 2019. LNCS, vol. 11869, pp. 26–39. Springer, Cham (2019). https://doi.org/10.1007/978-3-030-33894-7_4
15. Thue, D., Schiffel, S., Guðmundsson, T.Þ., Kristjánsson, G.F., Eiríksson, K., Björnsson, M.V.: Open world story generation for increased expressive range. In: Nunes, N., Oakley, I., Nisi, V. (eds.) ICIDS 2017. LNCS, vol. 10690, pp. 313–316. Springer, Cham (2017). https://doi.org/10.1007/978-3-319-71027-3_33
16. Kybartas, B., Verbrugge, C., Lessard, J.: Expressive range analysis of a possible worlds driven emergent narrative system. In: Rouse, R., Koenitz, H., Haahr, M. (eds.) ICIDS 2018. LNCS, vol. 11318, pp. 473–477. Springer, Cham (2018). https://doi.org/10.1007/978-3-030-04028-4_54
17. McCoy, J., Treanor, M., Samuel, B., Mateas, M., Wardrip-Fruin, N.: Prom week: social physics as gameplay. In: Proceedings of the 6th International Conference on Foundations of Digital Games, pp. 319–321 (2011)
18. McCoy, J., Treanor, M., Samuel, B., Reed, A.A., Wardrip-Fruin, N., Mateas, M.: Prom week. In: Proceedings of the International Conference on the Foundations of Digital Games, pp. 235–237 (2012)

19. McCoy, J., Treanor, M., Samuel, B., Tearse, B., Mateas, M., Wardrip-Fruin, N.: Authoring game-based interactive narrative using social games and Comme il Faut. In: Proceedings of the 4th International Conference & Festival of the Electronic Literature Organization: Archive & Innovate, vol. 50. Citeseer (2010)

20. McCoy, J., Treanor, M., Samuel, B., Reed, A.A., Mateas, M., Wardrip-Fruin, N.: Social story worlds with Comme il Faut. IEEE Trans. Comput. Intell. AI Games **6**(2), 97–112 (2014)

21. Mitchell, A.: Reflective rereading and the SimCity effect in interactive stories. In: Schoenau-Fog, H., Bruni, L.E., Louchart, S., Baceviciute, S. (eds.) ICIDS 2015. LNCS, vol. 9445, pp. 27–39. Springer, Cham (2015). https://doi.org/10.1007/978-3-319-27036-4_3

22. Moallem, J.D., Raffe, W.L.: A review of agency architectures in interactive drama systems. In: 2020 IEEE Conference on Games (CoG), pp. 305–311. IEEE (2020)

23. Morais, L., Dias, J., Santos, P.A.: From caveman to gentleman: a CiF-based social interaction model applied to Conan exiles. In: Proceedings of the 14th International Conference on the Foundations of Digital Games, pp. 1–11 (2019)

24. Rubellin, F., François, P.: Le théâtre du xviiie siècle, plus vivant que jamais (2018)

25. Ryan, J., Walker, M.A., Wardrip-Fruin, N.: Toward recombinant dialogue in interactive narrative. In: Seventh Intelligent Narrative Technologies Workshop (2014)

26. Samuel, B., et al.: Playing the worlds of prom week. In: Narrative Theory, Literature, and New Media, pp. 87–105. Routledge (2015)

27. Samuel, B., Reed, A.A., Maddaloni, P., Mateas, M., Wardrip-Fruin, N.: The ensemble engine: next-generation social physics. In: Proceedings of the Tenth International Conference on the Foundations of Digital Games (FDG 2015), pp. 22–25 (2015)

28. Samuel, B.: Crafting stories through play. Ph.D. thesis, UC Santa Cruz (2016)

29. Smith, G., Whitehead, J., Mateas, M.: Tanagra: a mixed-initiative level design tool. In: Proceedings of the Fifth International Conference on the Foundations of Digital Games, pp. 209–216 (2010)

30. Smith, G., Whitehead, J., Mateas, M.: Tanagra: reactive planning and constraint solving for mixed-initiative level design. IEEE Trans. Comput. Intell. AI Games **3**(3), 201–215 (2011)

31. Spierling, U., Szilas, N.: Authoring issues beyond tools. In: Iurgel, I.A., Zagalo, N., Petta, P. (eds.) ICIDS 2009. LNCS, vol. 5915, pp. 50–61. Springer, Heidelberg (2009). https://doi.org/10.1007/978-3-642-10643-9_9

32. Summerville, A.: Expanding expressive range: evaluation methodologies for procedural content generation. In: Fourteenth Artificial Intelligence and Interactive Digital Entertainment Conference (2018)

33. Treanor, M., McCoy, J., Sullivan, A.: A framework for playable social dialogue. In: Proceedings of the AI and Interactive Digital Entertainment Conference (AIIDE 2016) (2016)

34. Wardrip-Fruin, N.: Three play effects-eliza, tale-spin, and sim city. Digital Humanities, pp. 1–2 (2007)

35. Wardrip-Fruin, N.: Expressive Processing: Digital Fictions, Computer Games, and Software Studies. MIT Press, Cambridge (2009)

# An Approach to Multiplayer Interactive Fiction

Mariana Farias[✉] and Carlos Martinho

INESC-ID and Instituto Superior Técnico, University of Lisbon, Lisbon, Portugal
{mariana.farias,carlos.martinho}@tecnico.ulisboa.pt

**Abstract.** In this work, we created an interactive fiction experience designed for two players. We designed it so that players would feel that they were at the same time the protagonists of the story yet different characters. We incorporated mechanics that explore some of the classic features of tabletop role-playing games as the existence of public and character-specific private information and the sharing of a space outside of the instance where players can discuss and make decisions together out of character. Our project promotes cooperation between players and their engagement with the multiple information spaces while keeping the experience fun and interesting. Our evaluation revealed players were very much interested in the prospect of a multiplayer interactive fiction experience and overall appreciated it. However, it quickly came forward that players were having difficulty keeping track of all the different provided dimensions of information. As a result, our model includes mechanics that guide the players' attention, improving their enjoyment of the experience and helping them to follow and understand the story. This work demonstrates it is possible to create a multiplayer interactive fiction experience using our public/private information paradigm. By categorizing the information while crafting the story, we can incorporate mechanics that help guide the players' attention while being especially careful that players do not feel forced to take specific actions as their character.

**Keywords:** Multiplayer · Interactive-fiction · Interactive-storytelling

## 1 Introduction

For a long time, people have been using storytelling as a way of entertainment. In recent years, Tabletop Role-playing Games (TTRPG)[1] have felt a resurgence in popularity [5,6]. It is not far-fetched to assume that, under the right orientation, TTRPG players would also enjoy partaking in Interactive Fiction (IF)[2]. Some TTRPG feature the possibility of separating private information and public information, i.e., a player has access to certain information based on their

---

[1] **Tabletop Role-playing Games:** a form of role-playing game in which the participants describe their characters' actions through speech.

[2] **Interactive Fiction:** a software simulating environments in which players use text commands to control characters and influence the environment.

© Springer Nature Switzerland AG 2021
A. Mitchell and M. Vosmeer (Eds.): ICIDS 2021, LNCS 13138, pp. 48–60, 2021.
https://doi.org/10.1007/978-3-030-92300-6_5

character and the information that makes sense their character to know while keeping it private from other player characters. This happens while simultaneously having the players share the same table and talk with each other, both in character and out of character, giving them the chance to share their private information. TTRPG also have a very strong social component. Being able to play with your friends enhances the experience in a very significant way. Being able to play these kinds of games with a heavy focus on story creation where the player takes an active part but is at the same time interacting with other players as they wish to is something not many digital games have been able to emulate. This act of communication and companionship helps build new relationships and create greater investment in the characters and story. For these reasons, we propose the creation of a new interaction paradigm that fulfills these requirements and offers a fully fleshed-out two-player experience in the form of interactive fiction.

## 2 Multiplayer Interactive Fiction

In most story-driven digital games, players interact with their environment at their own pace. In multiplayer games, players that are sharing a scene are usually prompted to interact with the game at the same time (for example, after a cut scene in the game *A Way Out*[3]). In text-based interactive fiction, this becomes harder to implement because reading a passage of text does not take the same amount of time for everyone. Games like *Monster Prom*[4] deal with this issue by having players play in turns. Another issue with multiplayer interactive fiction is that stories that are designed for multiple players are harder to write. Conventional stories have one single protagonist and the story revolves around them and their decisions. Storylines branch out with one single character making choices. With the inclusion of more than one character acting independently, many new iterations of the story are necessary that the author must account for, increasing writing difficulty. The problem becomes how to design a good experience that uses this new information paradigm and is engaging for multiple players playing experiencing the same story line while in control of distinct characters.

## 3 Interaction Paradigm

Our main objective is to develop a short narrative experience based on the following private vs public information paradigm (see diagram in Fig. 1). We will use a 'couch co-op' approach, where players have access to a shared computer screen and an individual phone screen that also acts as a controller. We will focus on the interaction between two players, each controlling a different character. There is a **public space** that is public to both characters and players. It consists of a shared screen. Whatever is displayed on the screen is known by both

---

[3] A Way Out, https://www.ea.com/games/a-way-out. Last accessed May 19, 2021.

[4] Monster Prom, http://monsterprom.pizza. Last accessed May 19, 2021.

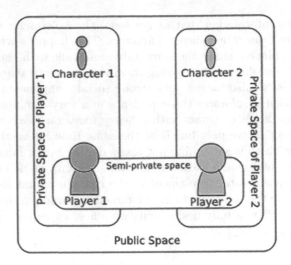

**Fig. 1.** Interaction model.

characters and can be read by both players. There is a **semi-private space** that is public for the players, but private to the characters. It consists of the physical space the players share (e.g. sharing a room or communicating via a voice call). Players use this space to discuss strategies or the story as it progresses, and influence their character's behavior, but this is private information to their characters. Finally, there is a **private space** that is private to the players and characters. This is represented by each phone screen. Whatever is displayed on the phone is private information that the respective player and character know but is private to the rest of the players and their characters.

## 4    Related Work

### 4.1    Shared Screen Multiplayer Games

We started by analyzing common practices in multiplayer digital games that have a strong focus on the story while running on a single screen. We studied a selection of games, e.g. *A Way Out*, *Eon Altar*[5] and *Monster Prom*. From this analysis, we extracted some preliminary guidelines: using a divided screen where players focus on their own character but are aware of what the other player is doing because it is always visible on the screen; more dramatic scenes can be highlighted by being given a greater area on the screen and occasionally players can join in a single frame when their characters are close and participating together in a scene; using a single screen shared by all players with the addition of an extra screen per player as a way to convey private information; a single shared screen that is used, in turns, by all players where they can always see

---

[5] Eon Altar https://eonaltar.fandom.com, Last accessed May 19, 2021.

the actions taken by the currently playing character, without the possibility of interference.

## 4.2    A Framework for Multiplayer IS Interactions

In [8,9], Spawford and Millard analyze multiplayer experiences in a narrative context and define an explicit framework with which we can describe these interactions. They divide the set of characteristics into **general**, **recipient** and **initiator** characteristics. The first category identifies interaction and the other two are specific to the players. A player is said to be a recipient if he is affected by the action of another player and an initiator if it is their own action that triggers the interaction. For general characteristics, they specify likelihood, type, and synchronicity. For recipient characteristics, they specify explicit awareness, deductive awareness, and initiator identifiability. For initiator characteristics, they specify explicit feedback, deductive feedback, and recipient identifiability. We will use this framework to characterize the players' interactions in our game.

## 4.3    Multiplayer Interactive Fiction Experiences

In this section, we review a few examples of experiences in IS especially designed for multiplayer play.

*Card Shark* [1] is a sculptural hypertext[6] tool that resembles a card game. Players have a set of nodes, where each node is represented by a card with a text summary. At first, all cards are connected. The structured story is built by removing unwanted or impossible connections between cards. *Social Shark* [1] is an extension of this concept, taking the same basic ruleset but adding a new player. In Social Shark, two players are dealt seven cards each at the beginning of the game and take turns playing a card. Cards have some points for player one and some other points for player two, so players must play their cards to try and get the most points. The game continues as long as players have playable cards.

*StoryMINE* [7] models a system capable of developing Interactive Fiction based on *MINE*(Multiplayer Interactive Narrative Experiences) and sculptural hypertext. All nodes begin connected but have conditions that eliminate these connections when they are not possible. The system allows the players to have inter-player agency and multiplayer differentiability by having the players participate in the same story, share a reading state and have their actions affect the story nodes available to other players. The system specifies roles to determine what part of the story each player character is experiencing. They identified two problems developers should watch out for. **Starvation** occurs when two players are participating in the story and one player finishes reading their section before

---

[6] **Hypertext** is text displayed on a display with references (hyperlinks) to other text that the reader can immediately access. **Sculptural hypertext** is proposed as an alternative domain for hypertext writing, proceeding by the removal of links rather than by adding links to an initially unlinked text.

the second: the second player will be starved of agency over the story. A way to prevent starvation is to employ **gating**, i.e. the system stays on hold until both players have finished their sections and choose to progress. However, the employment of gating creates **deadlocks**: when one player finishes reading their section before the other player, then the first player will experience a deadlock, i.e. they won't be able to proceed until the second player finishes reading their own section, leaving them stuck without anything else to do.

## 5   Approach

We decided to create an interactive fiction experience that runs for approximately 40 min where two players play simultaneously, each having a different character. We constructed a short story that follows three housemates that do not take each other too seriously. Players control two of these friends while trying to coordinate a surprise birthday party for the third friend, choosing the perfect gift for the occasion. The story is divided into three parts: a shared section where players meet and discuss together the upcoming party, a split section where each character goes to a different store to buy a birthday present and possibly a birthday cake, moving separately, and a final scene where the players are back together with their friend for the party and gift exchange.

The story encourages players to cooperate. We separated public from private information: the players are presented with information privately that directly results from their interactions with the virtual world of the story - this can come from dialogue with Non-Player Characters (NPC), character's emotions, thoughts, etc. They can choose to share this information with the other player either in its entirety, partially or not at all. This, of course, will influence the possible choices the players have in future interactions based on their knowledge. The story progresses and depending on the choices and coordination of the players, different endings are possible. If the players play as intended, coordinating their efforts for the birthday party, they might unlock an ending where they throw the best birthday party of all time. If the players fail this cooperation or one player tries to misguide their partner, they might end up picking a bad gift or there might not be a birthday cake at the party.

The players both share a screen but all their inputs are collected through an application that runs on the player's phone and collects the player's choices in the story. When they are sharing a scene, the public outputs can be displayed simultaneously for both of them but their decisions are kept private by the system. This allows for verbal communication so that the players can strategize their choices or turn the experience into a competition.

## 6   Prototype

### 6.1   Story

The story follows a typical branch-out format applying the foldback strategy [2]. Players can diverge through the story and meet up in key moments. There are

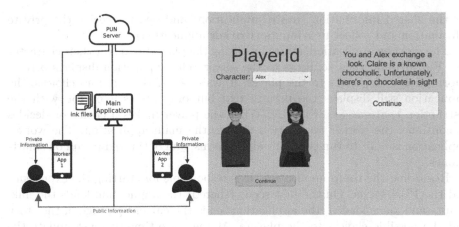

**Fig. 2.** A (left) - architecture. B (middle) - character selection on private interface. C (right) - communicating private information during the game.

shared scenes, equivalent to foldback nodes, and separated scenes, equivalent to divergent nodes. We include the following interactions in accordance with the framework by Spawford and Millard [8,9]. Regarding **general** characteristics, we have *possible likelihood* for interactions that happen between players in different scenes, interactions will be both *mechanical, informational* and *synchronous*. For **recipient** characteristics, recipients will have *possible explicit awareness*, *always possible deductive awareness*, and the initiator will be *always identifiable*. Regarding the **initiator** characteristics, we have *possible explicit feedback*, *always have deductive feedback* and the recipient is *always identifiable*. We also include interactions between the two-player characters, between the players' characters and another non-player character at the same time, and interaction between each playable character and an NPC, without the other character being present.

We opted to use *Ink*[7] to create our story scripts. We created two different types of 'ink' files to separate private from public information. These files share the same number of lines so they can progress simultaneously. Players progress line by line, giving explicit feedback for the file to continue to avoid deadlocks.

## 6.2    Application

We developed our application using *Unity*[8] (see Fig. 2A). To set up a server and establish connections between the user controllers and the application running the experience, we set up a *Photon Unity Networking (PUN)* application with the *Photon Engine*[9]. Then, we launch two instances of the application - one

---

[7] Ink, https://www.inklestudios.com/ink/, Last accessed May 19, 2021.

[8] Unity, https://unity.com/, Last accessed May 19, 2021.

[9] Photon engine, https://www.photonengine.com/en-US/Photon, Last accessed on May 19, 2021.

for the shared information (**main** application) and one to receive the private information and collect user inputs (**worker** application).

The **worker** application, starts by asking the players to select their character (see Fig. 2B) and then connects to the server. The application displays private information and choices to the player, if available. If there are no choices, the application still displays the private text but only shows a button with the instruction *continue* (see Fig. 2C). When the player makes a choice or decides to continue, the worker application notifies the main application. The worker application is built to run on Android platforms, and optimized to run on smartphones.

Regarding the **main** application, it is responsible for starting the experience and the PUN server. On the first scene (shared) the application loads the 'ink' scripts and, once loaded, the application sends the current passage of the story and the possible choices to the players. At the same time, it must update the shared interface to display the sprites of the characters as well as the current text on the public script. Afterward, it awaits feedback from the players. An example of the shared interface for a shared scene can be viewed in Fig. 3A.

This is followed by a split scene, where the characters are separated in the story space. The structure of this scene is somewhat similar to a shared scene, the difference being the presence of two distinct public information sources. Since the characters are separated, the application only has to wait for the answer of a player to update the story state of that player. Once a player finishes their story, the main application must make that player wait until the other player finishes their story. Once both players are done, the application must ensure the loading of the next scene. An example of the split interface can be viewed in Fig. 3B.

The final scene is identical to the first, a shared scene with the exception that previous choices carry over to it. Everything else executes exactly like the first scene. Once the 'Ink' scripts are finished, the story ends.

## 7   Evaluation

### 7.1   Experimental Procedure

Our prototype was designed to be tested in a 'couch co-op' setting, however, due to the pandemic situation that coincided with the period of development of our work, we adapted the procedure. We set up the experiment to be played during a peer-to-peer call (over Skype, Discord, or equivalent). The main application is running on the test supervisor environment and its screen is shared with the players. Each player has the worker application running on their phone. Communication between players is possible at all times - just like it would be if players were in the 'couch co-op' condition.

Before starting the test, the participants fill the demographics section of the questionnaire: gender, age, reading habits and opinions, and experiences with interactive fiction in digital games. Players are then given a brief description of the experience and instructed on how to start. During the experience, the supervisor listens and takes note of the following metrics: the interactions between players - if players were communicative with each other or not and how this

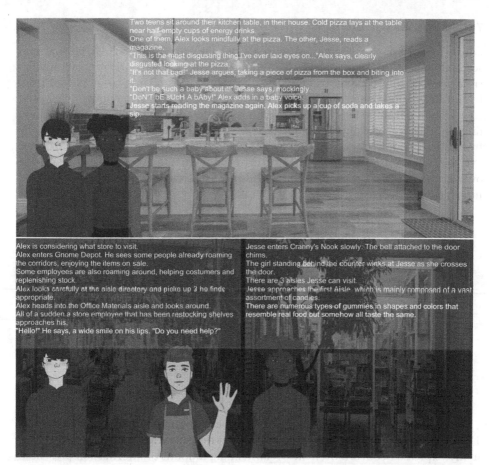

**Fig. 3.** A (top) - shared scene on the public interface. B (bottom) - split scene on the public interface.

varied with the different scenes, as well as the questions asked to the supervisor regarding the application. Other metrics are being automatically recorded by the application, namely the average and maximum time a player waits for the other player's response for the story to progress. After the experience is complete, the players are asked to complete the second part of the questionnaire. This section includes the modules *sensory and imaginative immersion*, *negative affect* and *positive affect* from the *core* module of the Game Experience Questionnaire [4]. We also included the entirety of the *social presence* module to assess how the players felt about the joint experience. This module of the questionnaire encompasses *psychological involvement*, both *empathy* and *negative feelings* as well as *behavioural engagement*. We also included some simple questions to determine how well the paradigm was perceived by the players. After the questionnaire is complete, we conducted a short semi-structured interview with the participant.

## 7.2  First Experiment

During our first experiment, we had 12 participants in pairs. All players had some degree of familiarity with their counterparts to help motivate communication between players. On average, the experience took 45 min to be played from beginning to end. Since our sample size is not comprehensive enough, we opted to use non-parametric statistics over our results. Table 1 depicts the median, minimum, and maximum results from the Questionnaire. These results range from 0 to 4 points and the player's score on each category is determined by their average score on all items of that category [4]. We achieved positive results in overall categories as expected. Players also considered they understood the dual interface architecture.

**Table 1.** Results from the first group of participants.

|  | Median | Min | Max |
|---|---|---|---|
| Positive Affect | 3.10 | 2.40 | 3.80 |
| Negative Affect | 0.50 | 0.00 | 2.00 |
| Sensory and I. Immersion | 2.75 | 1.50 | 3.67 |
| Empathy | 2.29 | 0.86 | 3.29 |
| Negative Feelings | 1.17 | 0.00 | 2.67 |
| Behavioural Engagement | 2.06 | 1.50 | 3.25 |

The majority of players appreciated the metaphor and praised the concept: 11 out of the 12 players complimented the novelty of the experience. However, many expressed concern over the overwhelming amount of information presented to them, especially during the separated scenes. We asked them if they tried to follow along with the other player. The majority of players said they did not. Out of the 6 groups, only one tried to choose adequate gifts with each other. In situations where one player finished the scene before the other, they started reading the other's scene. We asked if it was hard to keep track of both interfaces at the same time. Players uniformly agreed that it needed a lot of effort and even then it was not clear where they should be looking. Many players gave suggestions such as adding a sound effect or vibration effect that would help guide the players' attention or some visual indication to both players when feedback is expected. Aligned with the answers to the previous questions, players had no idea of the actions taken by the other player's character in the separated scene. Apart from that, players considered they had a good understanding of the other player's character's actions.

While playing the story, we had a varying range of interaction behaviors. Some participants spent the entire experience talking about the story while other groups said nothing at all. Even among the groups that communicated, not all tried to achieve a good outcome by discussing their choices. We asked the players what interfered with this communication and what could have been done differently to promote communication. Some players answered they did not feel it was necessary to communicate, they enjoyed playing the interactive fiction as it was. We postulate that, since we are exploring a new concept of interactive fiction that most players had not tried before, these groups that did not display much interaction were focused on how their in-story interactions influenced the story's outcome and for that reason tended to ignore the possibility of verbal interactions. These results, although positive, prompted some changes on our approach.

### 7.3    Prototype Improvements

A common complaint users had at first was about the difficulty they felt when shifting their attention between interfaces while playing through the story. To make the new information more noticeable on the shared screen, we implemented a flashing effect when new lines of text appear. The new lines are also presented in a different color (yellow) from the older lines. To notify the player of new information on the phone, we implemented vibration. This feature is present in both the shared scenes as well as the split scenes since it is private to each player, i.e. only the player holding the phone is notified by its vibration. We also implemented a feature that consisted of visual thought bubbles in the shared scenes: whenever a user receives private information on their private interface, a thought bubble pops up above the corresponding character and it stays there until the player gives feedback. This way, the players have an idea of where to look and know why the story isn't progressing in the case that one of the characters is "still thinking". This does not apply to the split scene. We also included a new passage in each script during the split scene to encourage players to verbally communicate with each other. At a certain point, characters will think something along the lines of *"I wonder what the other character is buying..."*. All playable characters will have this thought at one point or another.

### 7.4    Second Experiment

We tested our new version with 6 new pairs of participants. The duration of the experiment was aligned with the values from the first experiment. Results for the GEQ were again positive and we registered a noticeable increase in *empathy*, which was supported by a Mann-Whitney U-Test ($U = 38.00$, $p = 0.049$) (Table 2). This suggests the new features we implemented in our prototype could help promote empathy between players. Players grasped the concept behind the dual interface, however, some participants felt the private interface was actively trying to push towards certain choices - quoting one participant, when trying to explain what was being presented to him on his phone interface: *"The information on my phone was directed more for my character and to influence my choices."*. A possible explanation is that because we are now guiding where the players should look for novel information, this might have lead players to feel being manipulated in some capacity.

Table 2. Results from the second group of participants.

|  | Median | Min | Max |
|---|---|---|---|
| Positive Affect | 3.50 | 2.80 | 4.00 |
| Negative Affect | 0.63 | 0.00 | 1.25 |
| Sensory and I. Immersion | 3.17 | 1.33 | 4.00 |
| Empathy | 2.71 | 2.00 | 3.86 |
| Negative Feelings | 1.33 | 0.33 | 2.83 |
| Behavioural Engagement | 2.50 | 1.75 | 3.75 |

We asked players what interface they paid more attention to. Responses were mixed. Some players paid more attention to their own private interface while others paid attention to the shared interface. In this second experiment, we got 8 out of the 12 players answering that they paid attention to both interfaces in equal parts – which supports the adequacy of vibration and thought bubbles - although they admit it is still a bit tiring looking from one interface to the other. Many players confessed it was hard to keep track of both interfaces since the shared information moved so fast and a bit taxing looking from one screen to the other. Other players said the fast movement of information was not that disruptive since the screen still kept the info for some time. Players pointed out that, at some points, the experience showed prompts simultaneously on both screens and they considered this behavior to be confusing.

Many more groups confessed to being attentive to the other player's behavior during this round of testing. Players that answered they paid attention to both characters and recalled specific details about these scenes were also the players that reported paying attention to both interfaces at the same time. Players that weren't paying attention to the other admitted that it is taxing trying to pay attention to both shared screens, especially when their counterpart is not doing the same. When asked if they understood all actions taken by the other player's character, answers followed the same pattern from the first experiment. People understood the actions taken by the other character, but were apprehensive about the origin of other player's actions.

We also inquired players about how they felt regarding their verbal inter-actions and what could be done to improve these interactions. Many players expressed that they did not know they were allowed to talk outside of their char-acters. Players felt like communication was not necessary to play the story. Other players still had this communication happen, as before, which helps support our thesis that players can still communicate and this factor is more dependent on the player's personality.

We asked if they felt the vibration and thought bubbles were useful in guid-ing the players' attention. Regarding the vibration, the players' reactions were mixed. Many found it too disruptive to the experience since the vibration was a little bit stronger in some devices than we intended it to be. Other play-ers thought it was helpful to notify them of new information available on the phone. To what concerns the thought bubbles, we instructed players to disable them during the story at least once, even if they decided to enable them again later, so they would experience both iterations. Most players (4 out of the 6 groups) enabled the thought bubbles again after having them disabled. Players thought the thought bubbles helped provide feedback on why the players might be waiting. This helps us support the proposition that this feature was way more informative than distracting.

## 8  Closing Guidelines

In this paper, we explored a new paradigm for multiplayer interactive fiction. We developed a prototype to test our hypothesis and conducted two rounds of tests with players, implementing mechanisms to help guide the players' attention. We concluded that these changes harbored improvements in the overall experience. As a final conclusion of our work, we defined some simple guidelines a project similar to the one we tried to develop should follow to be successful, according to our experience:

- Separate public and private information;
- On split scenes, public information should be described as if it was being seen from a 'faraway' perspective;
- Create a story in a foldback strategy - players should meet on the same shared scene from time to time;
- Pay attention to starvation and deadlocks, while trying to minimize the input needed from the player - our passages prompted the player to spam the "continue" button without much regard to what was written on one of the two interfaces; personalize feedback instructions - players got tired of pressing "continue" over and over.
- Keep short story segments grouped by space, i.e., public or private, in longer story segments - i.e., when instructions are showing up on one screen, the other should not be getting new instructions simultaneously. Do not show new information on both screens at the same time, players will not know where to look.
- Try to keep the story segments the same size for both players, i.e. each passage takes roughly the same time to read. This will help bridge the impact of starvation and deadlocks. Make sure the size of the story segments is not dependent on the players' choices during split scenes, otherwise, players may get very different story lengths, creating long waiting times for one of the players.
- When displaying information on a different screen from the previous screen information was displayed on, warn the player. In our work, we used vibration and thought bubbles to help guide this attention. These changes greatly improved our players' comprehension of the story.

For more implementation and evaluation details, please refer to [3].

**Acknowledgment.** This work was supported by national funds through Fundação para a Ciência e a Tecnologia (FCT) with reference UIDB/50021/2020.

# References

1. Bernstein, M.: Card shark and thespis: exotic tools for hypertext narrative. In: Proceedings of the 12th ACM Conference on Hypertext and Hypermedia, HYPERTEXT '01, pp. 41–50. Association for Computing Machinery, New York (2001). https://doi.org/10.1145/504216.504233
2. Crawford, C.: Chris Crawford on Interactive Storytelling (New Riders Games), p. 366. New Riders Games (2004)
3. Farias, M.: An approach to multiplayer interactive storytelling. Master's thesis, Instituto Superior Técnico, University of Lisbon (2021)
4. IJsselsteijn, W., de Kort, Y., Poels, K.: The game experience questionnaire. Technische Universiteit Eindhoven (2013)
5. Kosa, M., Spronck, P.: Towards a tabletop gaming motivations inventory (TGMI). In: Zagalo, N., Veloso, A.I., Costa, L., Mealha, Ó. (eds.) VJ 2019. CCIS, vol. 1164, pp. 59–71. Springer, Cham (2019). https://doi.org/10.1007/978-3-030-37983-4_5
6. Sousa, M., Bernardo, E.: Back in the game. In: Zagalo, N., Veloso, A.I., Costa, L., Mealha, Ó. (eds.) VJ 2019. CCIS, vol. 1164, pp. 72–85. Springer, Cham (2019). https://doi.org/10.1007/978-3-030-37983-4_6
7. Spawforth, C., Gibbins, N., Millard, D.E.: StoryMINE: a system for multiplayer interactive narrative experiences. In: Rouse, R., Koenitz, H., Haahr, M. (eds.) ICIDS 2018. LNCS, vol. 11318, pp. 534–543. Springer, Cham (2018). https://doi.org/10.1007/978-3-030-04028-4_62
8. Spawforth, C., Millard, D.: Multiplayer games as a template for multiplayer narratives: a case study with dark souls. In: HT (2017)
9. Spawforth, C., Millard, D.E.: A framework for multi-participant narratives based on multiplayer game interactions. In: Nunes, N., Oakley, I., Nisi, V. (eds.) ICIDS 2017. LNCS, vol. 10690, pp. 150–162. Springer, Cham (2017). https://doi.org/10.1007/978-3-319-71027-3_13

# Highlight the Path Not Taken to Add Replay Value to Digital Storytelling Games

Susana Gamito[✉] and Carlos Martinho

INESC-ID and Instituto Superior Técnico, University of Lisbon, Lisbon, Portugal
{susana.gamito,carlos.martinho}@tecnico.ulisboa.pt

**Abstract.** Branching narratives are interactive storytelling formats that present players with moments of decisions that create ramifications within the narrative. However, it is after delivering the consequences that they get a chance to reflect upon them. Through 'actions' and 'inactions', feelings of regret are created within the player, which makes them want to replay the game. Based on the Psychology of regret, this study tests the possibility of conveying more replay value to an interactive storytelling game by providing feedback to those irreversible 'inactions'. To evaluate our approach, we asked 64 participants to play one of two game versions (with the feedback system or without) and report their experience. Results show the feedback of inaction had a positive impact on the players' affective reaction, encouraging players who would not usually do so to replay the game at the expense of players finding it less challenging. Overall, highlighting the path not taken improved the game experience without provoking remorse by hinting at what could have happened and increased the replay value.

**Keywords:** Regret · Inaction · Replayability

## 1 Introduction

Storytelling is key to make a game memorable. It gives purpose to the players from the start and motivates them to play to the end. The decisions taken along this path help reinforce a sense of agency while limiting the experience to a single of multiple available paths. While on that path, players are not always aware of what they 'missed' and could have led to a different experience. We believe providing hints to these alternatives paths during a game helps create a richer experience by giving context to the choices made in a specific playthrough and encouraging replay. We hypothesize that *showing the consequences and leaving subtle hints regarding actions not taken ('inactions') will suggest to the player that a different path could have been taken and promote replay value.* To evaluate this approach, we developed a short story-oriented game and measured the impact of having a toggle that would activate feedback for actions the players

© Springer Nature Switzerland AG 2021
A. Mitchell and M. Vosmeer (Eds.): ICIDS 2021, LNCS 13138, pp. 61–70, 2021.
https://doi.org/10.1007/978-3-030-92300-6_6

did not take to create more desire to replay the game again and explore different outcomes. The feedback was composed of storytelling elements to generate feelings of regret in the players towards the actions they did not take.

## 2    Action, Inaction and Regret

In Psychology, there is a difference between the decision to act (action) and the decision not to act (inaction). One might not consider inaction as a deliberate conscious decision, but it has in fact impact on the world and consequences and can be seen as even more intentional than action [1, 3, 7]. For example, 'inactions' could be deliberate conscious decisions to do nothing through exerting self-control to inhibit emotional reactions and automatic responses, whereas action decisions could reflect impulsiveness, adherence, or primed action, rather than a deliberate conscious self-directed action [12]. Action-inaction is commonly referenced to blame or negative emotions such as regret. These have been shown to be important in many aspects of life, including but not limited to decision-making [5, 10, 15], self-regulation, well-being, and health [4, 16, 18].

The **action effect** [11] is the phenomenon that people tend to feel greater regret over negative outcomes if they are a result of action compared to inaction. These findings are also consistent with the notion that people find it easier to monitor action rather than to monitor inaction. Research on morality has similarly shown that, when the possibility of a negative outcome exists, people prefer harm by omission over harm by command, this is, they rather withhold the truth rather than lie [2, 17]. Although actions produce more regret than 'inactions', other researchers [19] concluded that the action effect was based on decisions made in isolation and ignored that decisions are often made in response to earlier outcomes and the information about a prior outcome was manipulated. Being that, they defended that when prior outcomes were positive or absent, people attributed more regret to action than to inaction. However, as predicted and counter to previous research, following negative prior outcomes, more regret was attributed to inaction, a finding that the authors in [19] labelled the **inaction effect**.

According to **regret theory**, regret is a counterfactual emotion. However, not every "might have been" is supposed to produce regret. Regret is assumed to originate from comparisons between a factual outcome and an outcome that might have been, had one chosen another action [6, 13]. Because one could have prevented the occurrence of the negative outcome by choosing something different, regret is related to a sense of responsibility for the outcome [19]. Regret has been described as a "comparison-based emotion of self-blame, experienced when people realize or imagine that their present situation would have been better had they decided differently in the past" [15]. Alternatively, the attribution of a given bad outcome can be due to external circumstances and misfortune. To that externalization of blame is associated with the emotion of disappointment.

There is an instrument for assessing regret and disappointment in decision-making research: the **Regret and Disappointment Scale** (RDS) [14]. The

RDS assesses these two dimensions of a negative emotional experience by measuring the intensity of the affective reaction and then categorizing the type of emotion experienced based on the cognitive antecedents of regret and disappointment.

Contrary to mere disappointment, which is experienced when a negative outcome happens independently of our own decision, regret is an emotion strongly associated with a feeling of responsibility. This emotion is an important factor in the players' experience especially when the players have moments of decision through action and inaction. Ultimately, it leads the players to want to go back on some of their choices during the playthrough and replay the game in a way they feel better about the outcome. The question is, when will they feel more likely to do so, and how does it influence gameplay?

## 3   "The Ballad of the Wizard and Sacrifice"

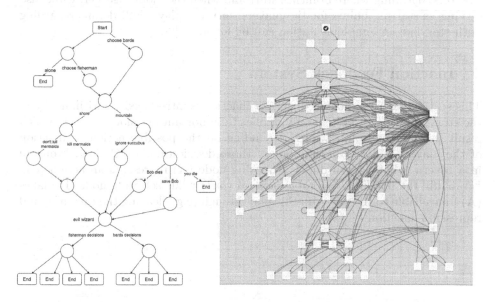

**Fig. 1.** (left) Abstract branching diagram; (right) Twine story graph.

To test our hypothesis, we developed two different versions of "The Ballad of the Wizard and Sacrifice", an original piece of interactive fiction using *Twine*[1]: one version provided standard feedback for actions; while the second provided additional feedback for 'inactions' to appeal to the emotion of regret of the players. This was achieved by manipulating storytelling elements to subtly hint at

---

[1] *Twine* Homepage, https://twinery.org/.

things that could have happened but are no longer available for story advancement (e.g. having the maid bump into a table and break a bottle filled with venom that could have been used to poison a particular character in the story). The idea is to bring to the attention of the players that things have changed and are no longer available (e.g. they could have picked up the bottle earlier in the scene but did not, now it is too late). Additionally, through initial playtesting, we insured that regret was used to make players wonder about their decisions but not feel bad about the overall play experience, in a manner that would make them leave the game annoyed or frustrated. Players would play one or the other version of the game and fill a questionnaire that, in conjunction with logged information from the game, would help us put our assumptions to the test.

Implementation-wise, the system follows a graph architecture where each node represents a decision moment in the storyline leading to new decisions and nodes in the graph (see Fig. 1). We used a world state approach, i.e. by updating variables based on choice and outputting different text based on the value of these variables, we kept the number of nodes manageable. The game is structured in chapters, outlining where branches start and when they join together, while also serving as starting points for the players' future replays. Full details regarding both storyline and implementation can be found in [8].

## 4   Inaction Feedback System

This section describes how feedback for inaction is introduced algorithmically in the story graph. This system only applies to important decision moments which result in different ramifications, depending on the possible action or inaction of the players. Figure 2 depicts one of those decision nodes (C) (e.g. "you are in a tavern, what do you do?"). Choosing node (A) represents an action (e.g. "grabbing the bottle on the table next to you") while selecting node (I) makes (A) unavailable to the player in this playthrough (e.g. "leaving the tavern"), and represents 'inaction'.

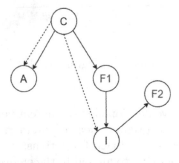

**Fig. 2.** Adding inaction feedback to decision nodes: the dashed line demonstrates the traditional approach and the solid line demonstrates the feedback system approach.

When (A) is chosen, the consequences of the action are directly described to the player and the story moves forward (e.g. "you grab the bottle and quickly hide it from sight before anyone notices."). However, if node (A) is not chosen, and the system realizes (through graph traversal and appropriate tagging) that node (A) is no longer available to be chosen by the player during this playthrough, then, before moving to node (I), an extra node (F1) is triggered that provides feedback regarding the inaction (e.g. "while leaving the tavern, you see the maid bump unto the table next to you, the bottle that seconds ago was standing on the table just breaks into tiny pieces, leaving a poisonous odor in the air"). The intent is to show the player that something important (in terms of story flow) was (voluntarily or involuntarily) missed by the player, and that node (A) is now off-limits. Additionally, a node (F2) is created that reinforces the fact that this option is no longer available to the player (e.g. a new option available to the player in node (I) is to "examine the broken bottle" that would lead to (F2) "the bottle is now broken and its foul content lost forever, who would have left such a bottle unattended?"). Overall, it should be clear by then that another option was available to be chosen.

After all, (F1) and (F2) nodes are created in the story graph, the story designer must fill them with adequate content so the system can provide appropriate inaction feedback when required. This feedback needs to appeal to the player's senses, such as visual cues, sounds, smells, and vibrations.

## 5    Evaluation

We invited a set of participants to play one of two versions of "The Ballad of the Wizard and Sacrifice" and answer a few questions. The inaction feedback was activated in one version and disabled in the other. First, the participants would answer a set of demographic questions and report their familiarity with interactive storytelling. Then, they would play one of the two versions of the game, as much as they wanted, while the game would be logging their choices and progression. Finally, they would fill a second questionnaire in which they would rate their experience with the game and report on emotions related to regret. We measured the game experience with the Game Experience Questionnaire [9] and five complementary items of Choice Perception, Narrative Perception, Agency, Action, and Inaction. The evaluation of the emotions of regret and disappointment was accomplished using the RDS [14]. Finally, we added questions directly related to the game story understanding for control. The participants were not made aware of the manipulation until the end of the experiment. Due to the constraints related to the worldwide pandemic at the time of the experiment, this process was conducted remotely. A link was given to each participant, that would direct them to a website that would guide them, step by step, through the experimental procedure. The average playing time was 20 min but varied based on the number of playthroughs.

## 5.1    Preliminary Evaluation

A pilot was conducted with 4 participants playing the version with inaction feedback. This preliminary evaluation assessed the overall experience of going through the narrative with the inaction feedback and gathered feedback regarding both the game and the evaluation procedure.

Participants expressed a positive feeling while going through the game. The regret index had a much higher score than the disappointment index, which means they attributed the consequences of bad outcomes to their own actions. The experience was overall enjoyable, all participants played the game multiple times and explored different choices when going through the same decision point.

A potential issue was, however, identified in the procedure. All participants reported a positive emotion after playing (regarding the overall experience). Because a participant could have felt regret during a playthrough but being able to cope with this feeling by addressing the issue in the following playthrough (maybe motivated to replay because of this same feeling of regret), asking the question at the end of the experience would have prevented us to detect this effect. To ensure this was not the case, we decided to ask participants to fill the RDS items right after the first playthrough and capture the (eventually induced) emotion of regret after going through the game once.

## 5.2    Final Evaluation

The final evaluation was conducted with a total of 64 participants, equally distributed between the two versions: **V1** implemented the "standard" approach and only provided feedback to the actions of the player; **V2** provided all that V1 provided with the addition of inaction feedback based on our model.

Regarding the results from the **RDS questionnaire**, we found a significant difference[2] in *affective reaction* between V1 and V2 ($t(62) = 2.361$, $p = 0.021$, $\bar{x}(V1) = 1.840$, $\bar{x}(V2) = 0.910$). Participants felt more positive emotions towards V2 and more negative emotions (e.g. sadness, sorrow) towards V1. This could be a result of the players in V1 having less feedback that would provide them with an explanation for the outcome of their actions and 'inactions'. Such feedback would provide them with immediate hints to courses of actions that could change or prevent that outcome. In opposition, the feedback provided in V2 helped players better understand their choice, and could have provided them with a stronger feeling of closure. We found moderate similar feelings of both regret ($\bar{x}(V1) = 1.953$, $\bar{x}(V2) = 1.750$) and disappointment ($\bar{x}(V1) = 1.844$, $\bar{x}(V2) = 1.734$) in both versions.

Results gathered from the **game logs** (see Fig. 3) showed more participants replayed the game in V2 but fewer endings were reached. In opposition, in V1, a greater diversity of endings was explored, but with fewer participants achieving

---

[2] Independent t-tests were used when comparing distributions that both passed the Shapiro-Wilk normality test and a Mann-Whitney U test were used when one of the distribution did not. The test were performed with IBM SPSS 26.

them. On one hand, individual preferences of the participants manifested them-selves, e.g. some participants were completionists and wanted to achieve all that is to achieve in the game, no matter what. On the other hand, hinting at what could have been done, to pique the curiosity of the players, appears to have motivated them to replay the game multiple times. When providing inaction feedback, an important guideline is to maintain uncertainty about the outcome of that alternative path, so that players want to replay the game to discover the unknown parts of the now revealed alternative path.

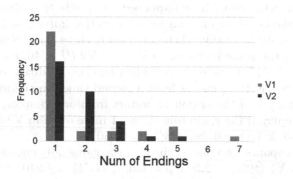

**Fig. 3.** Distribution of the number of endings reached.

In terms of **game experience**, there was no significant difference between the two versions of the game on the dimensions measured by the GEQ. Overall, the experience was rated as moderately positive.

## 6 Discussion

In this section, we discuss some results related to the participants' familiarity with interactive fiction and their inherent preferences regarding this medium.

Players who enjoy and are familiar with branching narratives in video games and replay them multiple times to get different stories, felt more *challenged* when playing V1 than V2 ($U = 91$, $p = 0.022$, $\bar{x}(V1) = 1.750$, $\bar{x}(V2) = 0.950$). This might be a result of the richer feedback provided by V2 when compared to V1. In V1, it is harder to understand the branches the story could take.

Players who do not enjoy interactive fiction or are not familiar with it, reported feeling more *tired* in V1 than V2 ($U = 44$, $p = 0.009$, $\bar{x}(V1) = 0.920$, $\bar{x}(V2) = 0.290$). The feedback given in V2 provided with a more enjoyable ride for these participants, who are not fully aware of what characterises the genre.

Players who reported replaying this type of games more than once, got to play at least *thrice* and felt V2 better conveyed the *consequences* of their actions than V1 ($t(33) = 2.371$, $p = 0.024$, $x(V1) = 2.160$, $\bar{x}(V2) = 2.940$). However, they also reported feeling more *irritated* toward V2 than V1 ($U = 61$, $p = 0.029$, $\bar{x}(V1) = 0.330$, $\bar{x}(V2) = 0.790$). This could be the consequence of V2 regularly pointing that something could have been done differently and they would have to go through the game once more to experience it, which moves the 100% completion goal post further away at each game iteration. This feeling could have been amplified by the repetitive nature of the text-based interface of the game although players were not forced to go through the game from the start, and could resume at the start of any previously visited chapter.

Players who do not feel the need to replay these games after a first playthrough reported a lesser sense of *agency* in V2 than V1 ($t(27) = 2.705$, $p = 0.014$, $\bar{x}(V1) = 3.038$, $\bar{x}(V2) = 2.094$). This could be related to the fact that pointing out what could have happened differently to a player that has no intentions of replaying the game can have a negative impact on this dimension of the experience. Additionally, when considering these same players, we found that more played the game just *once* in V1 than V2 ($U = 46$, $p = 0.007$, $\bar{x}(V1) = 0.670$, $\bar{x}(V2) = 0.170$). As such, providing inaction feedback could motivate such players to replay the game at least a second time. Furthermore, we found that, although they had the option to restart from any chapter, these participants actually replayed the game from Chap. 1 more often in V2 than in V1 ($U = 184$, $p = 0.050$, $\bar{x}(V1) = 0.280$, $\bar{x}(V2) = 0.050$).

Finally, participants who played through the game only once found V2 more *impressive* than V1 ($t(22) = 2.305$, $p = 0.031$, $\bar{x}(V1) = 1.210$, $\bar{x}(V2) = 2.140$). As such, inaction feedback may help with first impressions.

## 7    Conclusions and Future Work

This research assessed the possibility of motivating players to replay a story-oriented digital game by bringing attention to both the actions as well as the 'inactions' of the player. To that end, two versions of a piece of interactive fiction were developed and compared to measure the impact of highlighting the path not taken on replay value. The narrative was written in such a way that feedback would always be provided each time a decision of the player would make a branch in the story graph inaccessible to that player.

Results from a study with 64 participants suggest the approach improves the affective reactions of the players. Even if highlighting the path not taken was not always able to promote actual replay, the use of this regret-based approach was able to improve the game experience without creating remorse in the players. Players became more aware of the impact of their in-game behaviour which added replay value, whether the player actually decided to go through the game once more or not. We additionally found evidence supporting this approach could lead players that usually do not replay such games to actually traverse them multiple times, as the approach makes the experience less tiresome and more impressive.

Further research is still needed to better understand (1) how specific forms of feedback could be used more effectively based on player typology, as not all types of feedback work equally on players with different preferences regarding this genre of games; (2) how we could model those forms of feedback as reusable patterns (e.g. "an important object which has been broken and cannot be used anymore" could be a pattern) in order to be used by narrative designer in their own story/game or by an artificial intelligence to automatically enhance a story graph, and, ultimately, (3), check if this general principle could be transferred, in some way, to other genres and domains.

**Acknowledgment.** This work was supported by national funds through Fundação para a Ciência e a Tecnologia (FCT) with reference UIDB/50021/2020.

# References

1. Albarracin, D., Hepler, J., Tannenbaum, M.: General action and inaction goals. Curr. Direct. Psychol. Sci. **20**, 119–123 (2011). https://doi.org/10.1177/0963721411402666
2. Baron, J., Ritov, I.: Omission bias, individual differences, and normality. Organ. Behav. Human Decis. Process. **94**, 74–85 (2004). https://doi.org/10.1016/j.obhdp.2004.03.003
3. Bohner, G., Dickel, N.: Attitudes and attitude change. Ann. Rev. Psychol. **62**, 391–417 (2011). https://doi.org/10.1146/annurev.psych.121208.131609
4. Connolly, T., Reb, J.: Regret in health-related decisions. Health Psychol.: Off. J. Divis. Health Psychol. Am. Psychol. Assoc. **24**, S29–S34 (2005). https://doi.org/10.1037/0278-6133.24.4.S29
5. Connolly, T., Zeelenberg, M.: Regret in decision making. Curr. Dir. Psychol. Sci. **11**(6), 212–216 (2002). https://doi.org/10.1111/1467-8721.00203
6. David, B.: Regret in decision making under uncertainty. Oper. Res. **30**, 961–981 (1982). https://doi.org/10.1287/opre.30.5.961
7. Diefendorff, J., Hall, R., Lord, R., Strean, M.: Action-state orientation: construct validity of a revised measure and its relationship to work-related variables. J. Appl. Psychol. **85**, 250–63 (2000). https://doi.org/10.1037/0021-9010.85.2.250
8. Gamito, S.: Highlight the path not taken to add replay value to a storytelling video game. Master's thesis, Instituto Superior Técnico, University of Lisbon (2021)
9. IJsselsteijn, W., de Kort, Y., Poels, K.: The game experience questionnaire. Technische Universiteit Eindhoven (2013)
10. Inman, J., Dyer, J., Jia, J.: A generalized utility model of disappointment and regret effects on post-choice valuation. Mark. Sci. **16**, 97–111 (2000). https://doi.org/10.1287/mksc.16.2.97
11. Kahneman, D., Tversky, A.: The psychology of preferences. Sci. Am. **246**, 160–173 (1982). https://doi.org/10.1038/scientificamerican0182-160
12. Kutscher, L., Feldman, G.: The impact of past behavior normality on regret: replication and extension of three experiments of the exceptionality effect. Cogn. Emot. **33**, 901–914 (2019). https://doi.org/10.1080/02699931.2018.1504747
13. Loomes, G., Sugden, R.: Regret theory: an alternative theory of rational choice under uncertainty. Econ. J. **92**, 805–824 (1982). https://doi.org/10.1287/opre.30.5.961
14. Marcatto, F., Ferrante, D.: The regret/disappointment scale: an instrument for assessing regret and disappointment in decision making. Judgm. Decis. Mak. **3**, 87–99 (2008)
15. Pieters, R., Zeelenberg, M.: A theory of regret regulation 1.1. J. Consum. Psychol. **17**, 29–35 (2007). https://doi.org/10.1207/s15327663jcp1701_6

16. Roese, N.J.: Counterfactual thinking. Psychol. Bull. **121**, 133–148 (1997). https://doi.org/10.1037/0033-2909.121.1.133

17. Spranca, M., Minsk, E., Baron, J.: Omission and commission in judgment and choice. J. Exp. Soc. Psychol. **27**, 76–105 (1991). https://doi.org/10.1016/0022-1031(91)90011-T

18. Zeelenberg, M.: Anticipated regret, expected feedback and behavioral decision-making. Other publications tisem, Tilburg University, School of Economics and Management (1999). https://EconPapers.repec.org/RePEc:tiu:tiutis:38371d1b-31fd-45b0-860f-b83a4e416fbf

19. Zeelenberg, M., van den Bos, K., Dijk, E., Pieters, R.: The inaction effect in the psychology of regret. J. Pers. Soc. Psychol. **82**, 314 (2002). https://doi.org/10.1037/0022-3514.82.3.314

# Narrative Text Generation from Abductive Interpretations Using Axiom-Specific Templates

Andrew S. Gordon[(✉)] and Timothy S. Wang

University of Southern California, Los Angeles, CA, USA
gordon@ict.usc.edu, wangtimo@usc.edu

**Abstract.** Structured story graphs have proven to be useful for representing content in pipelines for automated interpretation and narration. Recent progress on interpretation using logical abduction has made it possible to construct these representations automatically, and several methods for converting these structures into narrative text have been proposed. In this paper, we describe a technical approach to narrative text generation from structured story graphs that prioritizes simplicity and ease-of-use, employing full-sentence templates associated with the specific axioms used to construct graphs during the interpretation process. We evaluate our approach using the TriangleCOPA benchmark for narrative interpretation and text generation, comparing our results to human-authored narratives and to the results of previous work.

**Keywords:** Automated interpretation · Text generation · Logical abduction

## 1 Introduction

A popular approach in research on narrative text generation is to first represent story content formally as symbolic structures, which are then converted into natural language text using a variety of approaches. Elson [2] proposed the *Story Intention Graph* as a formalism for encoding the interpretation of stories as symbolic causal structures, reminiscent of the *Causal Network Model* of psychologists Trabasso and van den Broek [18]. Using a software tool for hand-authoring these representations [3], different research teams have succeeded in authoring sizable corpora of story representations, and devising novel algorithms for converting these representations into fluent natural-language texts [2,12]. Although these text-generation systems are typically quite sophisticated in their use of numerous grammatical subsystems and lexical resources, the overall lesson from

The project or effort depicted was or is sponsored by the U.S. Army Research Laboratory (ARL) under contract number W911NF-14-D-0005, and that the content of the information does not necessarily reflect the position or the policy of the Government, and no official endorsement should be inferred.

this line of research is that fluent narratives can be automatically generated if a rich structured representation of the story can be provided by some upstream interpretation process.

Current systems that attempt to automate the interpretation process have their roots in the work of Hobbs et al. [10], who proposed that language interpretation could be cast as a problem of logical abduction. In logic-based reasoning systems, abduction is viewed as a search for the optimal set of assumptions that, if true, would logically entail a set of observations, given a knowledge base of axioms. Hobbs et al. [10] proposed a cost-based method for finding and ranking solutions, where the initial costs assigned into input observations are transferred to antecedents by back-chaining on definite clauses in the knowledge base, i.e., *weighted abduction*. Gordon [4] devised a probabilistic alternative to weighted abduction, *etc.etera abduction*, where the conditional probability of the consequent in a definite clause, given the antecedent, is reified as *etc.etera literals* [9] included in the antecedents of every knowledge base axiom. Back-chaining from observations, solutions consisting entirely of etc.etera literals can be ranked by their joint probability. Although finding an optimal solution via logical abduction requires an intractable combinatorial search process, Gordon [5] devised an incremental algorithm for etc.etera abduction capable of handling large interpretation problems.

While the idea of interpretation as logical abduction grew out of computational linguistics, its applicability to narrative interpretation, more broadly, has been demonstrated in several previous efforts. Gordon [4] applied etc.etera abduction to answer commonsense interpretation problems in the TriangleCOPA benchmark [13], consisting of 100 micro-narratives involving three characters. Gordon [5] applied incremental etc.etera abduction to observable events in the interpretation of the Heider-Simmel film [7], a narrative that is ubiquitously used as a stimulus in social science research. Gordon and Spierling [6] demonstrated how etc.etera abduction could be used for creative narrative interpretation, in the context of a storytelling party game. In each of these efforts, etc.etera abduction produces structured story graphs than can serve as input to downstream narrative text generation systems.

In systems that convert structured representations into natural language text, much of the linguistic complexity arises when composing sentences from multiple nodes in the story graph. For any single node in the graph, a trivial template system is sufficient to produce a fluent sentence or clause. When composing sentences from content across connected nodes, however, the text generation system must be sensitive to a myriad of linguistic concerns, from lexical choice in subordinate clauses, unambiguous use of pronouns, and conjoining noun phrases that share a semantic role in the output sentence. Ahn et al. [1] showed previously how these complexities could be mitigated using the approach of over-generating and ranking. In their method, many possible grammatical rules for combining clauses from connected nodes are exhaustively applied to generate candidate sentences, which are then ranked for fluency using a probabilistic syntactic parser.

In this paper, we explore an alternative approach to this problem that avoids the grammatical complexity of combining phrases altogether, by associating textual templates directly with the axioms used to assemble the story graph in the first place. Using axiom-specific templates, we show that a trivial template system with simple manipulations for noun phrases is sufficient to generate text from formal story graphs that is as fluent as those produced by previous approaches.

## 2 Axiom-Specific Templates

The basic idea in our narrative text generation approach is to utilize sentence-length templates that are specific to individual knowledge base axioms, rather than trying to assemble grammatical sentences from groups of connected nodes in the structured interpretation graph. The rationale is that the knowledge base axioms used to construct the interpretation graph already identify a coherent set of interrelated nodes (logical literals) during the search process. When an axiom participates in building the interpretation, its constituent literals (and their variable bindings) provide all the necessary information to express the inference as a fluent natural-language sentence.

To illustrate this idea, consider the following knowledge base axiom, used by Gordon [4] to correctly answer question 83 of the TriangleCOPA benchmark.

```
(if (and (attack' ?e1 ?y ?z)
         (like' ?e2 ?x ?z)
         (etc3_angryAt 0.9 ?e1 ?e2 ?e ?x ?y ?z))
    (angryAt' ?e ?x ?y))
```

This axiom captures the commonsense idea that if somebody attacks someone that you like, then you are likely to be angry at the attacker. During the interpretation process, this axiom would be used to replace an assumption that unifies with the consequent with the three assumptions in the antecedent, along with the necessary variable substitutions. In a subsequent narration process, a text template can be used to express this inference as a single sentence.

```
Due to a fondness for ?z, ?x was angry at ?y for the attack.
```

In order to correctly substitute the variables in an arbitrary template during narration, the interpretation system must record variable bindings for all uses of each axiom in a given interpretation. Conveniently, etc.etera abduction encodes these substitutions in a unique etc.etera literal that appears in an axiom's antecedent, e.g., the literal with the predicate etc.3_angryAt in the example above. Given the etc.etera literals that constitute a solution to an interpretation problem, the narration system can select templates and make the necessary variable substitutions by matching the antecedents in a knowledge base of textual templates, such as this one:

```
(if (etc3_angryAt 0.9 ?e1 ?e2 ?e ?x ?y ?z)
    (text "Due to a fondness for" ?z ","
          ?x "was angry at" ?y "for the attack."))
```

If an etcetera literal in the interpretation matches the antecedent of this template with substitutions {?x/BOB, ?y/CARL, ?z/DAVID}, the instantiated consequence of the text template is inferred:

```
(text "Due to a fondness for" DAVID "," BOB "was angry at"
      CARL "for the attack.")
```

The particular characteristics of etc.etera abduction, where solutions uniquely identify all axioms that participated in the selected interpretation, afford a simple method for instantiating templates via logical inference. However, the approach is equally applicable to other abductive reasoning methods [11,14], which may require additional bookkeeping to identify the knowledge base axioms that participated in the construction of the selected interpretation. In each case, the basic idea is that the knowledge base axioms are a convenient target for sentence-level templates that express the important interrelationships between nodes in the structured interpretation.

## 3  Proper Nouns, Common Nouns, and Pronouns

After the substitution of bound variables, a text template in our approach will consist of a list of constants. String constants are the linguistic expressions included by the author of the template, e.g., "was angry at". Symbolic constants identify entities that were either identified as arguments in the original observations provided to the interpretation engine, or introduced in the consequence of a knowledge base axiom, e.g., CARL. Skolem constants identify entities whose existence is assumed as a result of the interpretation process, introduced when an existentially quantified variable only appears in the antecedent of a knowledge base axiom, e.g. $4.

Our narrative text generation implementation provides a simple mechanism for replacing symbolic constants with strings for either the proper noun or a common noun of the entity, if they are known. Nouns of these types are provided as logical literals alongside the template axioms, as follows:

```
(proper_noun CARL "Carl")
(common_noun CB1 "city bus")
(common_noun GROUP7 "management team")
```

When converting the text literal into an output string, our implementation will swap symbolic constants for any string constants that have been provided, favoring proper nouns over common nouns.

For common nouns, our system precedes the reference with an indefinite article for its first use in a narrative ("a" or "an") and a definite article on subsequent uses ("the"). When a given common noun has previously been used to reference a different entity in the narrative, an additive determine is used ("another"). A default common noun of "unknown entity" is used for all Skolem constants.

To enable the use of English pronouns, the pronoun class of any entity can be provided as additional information.

```
(pronouns CARL Masculine)
(pronouns CB1 Neuter)
(pronouns GROUP7 Plural)
```

When the pronoun class of an entity has been provided, our implementation will favor referencing it using a pronoun rather than a proper or common noun, guided by specific directives provided by the template author. Our system supports pronoun substitution for subjects (he), objects (her), dependent possessives (their), independent possessives (hers), and reflexive pronouns (herself), as in the following example:

```
(if (etc3_angryAt 0.9 ?e1 ?e2 ?e ?x ?y ?z)
    (text "Due to" DependentPossessive ?x
        "fondness for" Object ?z ","
        Subject ?x "was angry at" Object ?y
        "for" DependentPossessive ?y "attack."))
```

Our implementation attempts to avoid the introduction of ambiguous pronouns into a narrative, guided by the heuristic pronoun resolution approach of Hobbs [8]. Specifically, we inhibit the introduction of subject and object pronouns when the entity has not yet been mentioned in the current or previous sentence, when its pronoun class is the same as another entity in the current or previous sentence, or when its pronoun class has not yet been revealed to the reader of the narrative via a possessive or reflexive pronoun substitution.

We provide an open-source C# implementation of our text generation approach alongside one of the existing distributions of the etc.etera abduction algorithm[1].

## 4    Evaluation

We evaluate our approach by directly comparing it to the previous work of Ahn et al. [1], where over-generating and ranking is used to assemble content from connected nodes in the story graph into fluent sentences. As in their previous work, we apply our approach to 100 formal interpretations of problems in the TriangleCOPA benchmark.

Modelled after the *Choice of Plausible Alternatives* (COPA) benchmark [17] that is widely used in computational linguistics research, TriangleCOPA was conceived as an end-to-end evaluation for systems that jointly perform the tasks perception, interpretation, and narration. Each of its 100 questions consist of a sentence describing a situation involving three characters and a common setting, a question about the commonsense interpretation of the situation, and two plausible answers, where one was uniformly preferred by human raters. Unlike the original COPA evaluation, each TriangleCOPA question includes an animated video clip of the situation to support computer vision research on action recognition, a formal representation of the question and each alternative to support

---

[1] https://github.com/asgordon/EtcAbductionCS.

| a. | Q 5. | *Insults and yelling flew back and forth as the circle and triangle argued loudly in the house. Finally, the triangle had had enough and walked out, slamming the door behind it. As angry as the circle was at the triangle, it was very sad and knew that this may be the end of their relationship.* |
| | Q 83. | *The circle is trying to get away from the cops and pushes the small triangle to get out of its way. The big triangle feels attacked that the circle pushed its friend and chases after the circle too.* |
| b. | Q 5. | *Big Triangle was inside. Circle was inside. Big Triangle argued with Circle because Big Triangle was angry at Circle. Big Triangle exited. He closed a door. Circle moved to the corner because Circle was feeling sad.* |
| | Q 83. | *Circle approached Little Triangle in order to attack Little Triangle. Circle pushed on Little Triangle to attack Little Triangle. Big Triangle chased Circle because Big Triangle was angry at Circle.* |
| c. | Q 5. | *The big triangle argues with the circle. He is inside the box because he is asleep. She is inside it because she is asleep. He exits it and closes the door. She goes to the corner because he argues with her.* |
| | Q 83. | *The circle approaches the little triangle and pushes him in order to attack him. The big triangle chases her because the big triangle likes the little triangle and she attacks the little triangle.* |

**Fig. 1.** Examples of textual narratives for TriangleCOPA questions, (a) authored by Maslan et al. [13], (b) generated by our system, and (c) generated by Ahn et al. [1]

research on automated interpretation, and a human-authored textual narrative of the depicted situation to support research on narrative text generation.

We are aware of no end-to-end system that is capable of answering TriangleCOPA questions given only the video clip as input, but Gordon [4] applied etc.etera abduction to correctly answer 91 of the 100 questions using a knowledge base of 279 commonsense axioms. These 91 automatically-generated interpretations were used by Ahn et al. [1] as input story graphs for their narrative text generation method, yielding a short narrative for each correctly-answered question.

To use our narrative text generation system for this benchmark, we first generated the most probable interpretations for each TriangleCOPA question using Gordon's original knowledge base of 279 commonsense axioms. Then, we hand-authored text templates for each of the 279 axioms, which required approximately 1.5 person-workdays of effort. Finally, we generated textual narratives for each interpretation using our approach, and compared the results to the human-authored narratives in the TriangleCOPA benchmark and to those generated in the work of Ahn et al.

Example human-authored and system-authored narratives for TriangleCOPA questions 5 and 83 are shown in Fig. 1.

We concede that the human-authored narratives for TriangleCOPA would be preferred by human readers for most task contexts, as they exhibit creativity in their interpretation and a fluency that is unmatched by either of the two systems. As well, we see only minor differences in the quality of text generated by either of the automated approaches.

In an effort to quantify the relative performance of each system on this benchmark, we explored the use of language model perplexity as a metric of fluency. Typically, perplexity is used in computational linguistics research to quantify the accuracy of a given language model, where lower scores indicate that the model finds the input language less perplexing. Here we use a single high-quality language model to see which system generates text that is closer in perplexity to that of the human-authored narratives. Specifically, we utilize the transformer-based GPT-2 language model [16] to compute the perplexity of a given text, as $e^{loss}$ given the *loss* of the output tensor. Perplexity scores for narratives were computed using a PyTorch script employing pre-trained models provided in the HuggingFace transformers package.

For each TriangleCOPA question, we computed the perplexity of narratives generated by each of the two systems, and compared them to the perplexity of the corresponding human-authored narrative. To assess whether observed differences were significant, we computed statistical p-values using stratified shuffling, a compute-intensive significance test that is popular in computational linguistics research when comparing different systems on the same test set [19]. In this context, p-values answer the question, What is the likelihood that we would see a difference in mean scores this large if there was actually no difference between the systems that generated these results?

Table 1 shows the results of this comparison of perplexity. The language model finds the narratives produced by our approach to be slightly more perplexing than human-authored texts, and those produced by Ahn et al. to be somewhat less perplexing. These differences are statistically significant only for the Ahn et al. results.

There are many pitfalls in this use of automatic evaluation metrics such as perplexity in research on natural language generation, as they are often shown to have poor correlation with human judgements of language quality [15]. Although we are encouraged that our approach to narrative text generation produces text that more closely matches the perplexity of human-authored narratives, we view these results with caution. To our eyes, the human-authored narratives in this study are superior in quality to the system-generated texts in all cases. We

**Table 1.** Mean perplexity of narratives of TriangleCOPA questions

| Version | $p(version)$ | $|p(gold) - p(version)|$ | p-value |
|---|---|---|---|
| Maslan et al. [13] (gold) | 4.686 | 0 | n/a |
| Our system | 4.790 | 0.104 | 0.444 |
| Ahn et al. [1] | 4.041 | 0.652 | <0.001 |

see several improvements that could be made to our approach, which may not be easily assessed using only the metric of perplexity. Instead, we are most encouraged by the finding that our approach generates text that is at least as good as Ahn et al., using a much simpler method.

## 5   Conclusions

The use of structured graphs to represent story content has aided progress in automated interpretation and narration by allowing researchers to focus their efforts on either of the two different parts of the problem, namely graph construction and natural language generation. However, a downside of this separation is that certain opportunities to exploit synergies across these two processes are not immediately evident. The problem addressed in this paper is one such example, where the assembly of sentences from connected nodes in the graph is greatly simplified by attaching templates directly to the axioms used to make these connections during the interpretation process. Here we exploit a particular feature of interpretations constructed using etc.etera abduction, namely that the etc.etera literals present in a solution indicate exactly which axioms were used in its construction, along with the variable bindings for each universally quantified variable. Using text templates and straightforward methods for including proper nouns, common nouns, and pronouns, the difficult grammatical problems of sentence construction can be largely avoided. While the resulting narrative text is similar in quality to that of more sophisticated approaches, our hope is that the simplicity of our method encourages researchers to shift their development efforts toward more interesting aspects of the narrative text generation problem, such as content selection and discourse planning.

## References

1. Ahn, E., Morbini, F., Gordon, A.S.: Improving fluency in narrative text generation with grammatical transformations and probabilistic parsing. In: Proceedings of the 9th International Natural Language Generation Conference, pp. 70–73. Association for Computational Linguistics, Stroudsburg (2016)
2. Elson, D.K.: Modeling narrative discourse. Columbia University (2012)
3. Elson, D.K., McKeown, K.R.: A platform for symbolically encoding human narratives. In: AAAI Fall Symposium: Intelligent Narrative Technologies, pp. 29–36 (2007)
4. Gordon, A.S.: Commonsense interpretation of triangle behavior. In: Thirtieth AAAI Conference on Artificial Intelligence, pp. 3719–3725. AAAI Press, Palo Alto (2016)
5. Gordon, A.S., USC EDU: Interpretation of the Heider-Simmel film using incremental etcetera abduction. Adv. Cogn. Syst. **6**, 1–16 (2018)
6. Gordon, A.S., Spierling, U.: Playing story creation games with logical abduction. In: Rouse, R., Koenitz, H., Haahr, M. (eds.) ICIDS 2018. LNCS, vol. 11318, pp. 478–482. Springer, Cham (2018). https://doi.org/10.1007/978-3-030-04028-4_55

7. Heider, F., Simmel, M.: An experimental study of apparent behavior. Am. J. Psychol. **57**(2), 243–259 (1944)
8. Hobbs, J.R.: Resolving pronoun references. Lingua **44**(4), 311–338 (1978)
9. Hobbs, J.R.: Ontological promiscuity. In: Proceedings of the 23rd Annual Meeting on Association for Computational Linguistics, pp. 60–69. Association for Computational Linguistics (1985)
10. Hobbs, J.R., Stickel, M.E., Appelt, D.E., Martin, P.: Interpretation as abduction. Artif. Intell. **63**(1–2), 69–142 (1993)
11. Inoue, N., Inui, K.: ILP-based inference for cost-based abduction on first-order predicate logic. J. Nat. Lang. Process. **20**(5), 629–656 (2013)
12. Lukin, S.M., Walker, M.A.: Narrative variations in a virtual storyteller. In: Brinkman, W.-P., Broekens, J., Heylen, D. (eds.) IVA 2015. LNCS (LNAI), vol. 9238, pp. 320–331. Springer, Cham (2015). https://doi.org/10.1007/978-3-319-21996-7_34
13. Maslan, N., Roemmele, M., Gordon, A.S.: One hundred challenge problems for logical formalizations of commonsense psychology. In: Proceedings of the Twelfth International Symposium on Logical Formalizations of Commonsense Reasoning, pp. 107–113. AAAI Press, Palo Alto (2015)
14. Meadows, B.L., Langley, P., Emery, M.J.: Seeing beyond shadows: incremental abductive reasoning for plan understanding. In: Plan, Activity. and Intent Recognition: Papers from the AAAI 2013 Workshop, pp. 24–31. AAAI Press, Palo Alto (2013)
15. Mir, R., Felbo, B., Obradovich, N., Rahwan, I.: Evaluating style transfer for text. In: Proceedings of the 2019 Conference of the North American Chapter of the Association for Computational Linguistics: Human Language Technologies, vol. 1 (Long and Short Papers), pp. 495–504. Association for Computational Linguistics, Minneapolis (2019)
16. Radford, A., Wu, J., Child, R., Luan, D., Amodei, D., Sutskever, I.: Language models are unsupervised multitask learners (2019)
17. Roemmele, M., Bejan, C., Gordon, A.: Choice of plausible alternatives: an evaluation of commonsense causal reasoning. In: Proceedings of the AAAI Spring Symposium on Logical Formalizations of Commonsense Reasoning, Stanford University (2011)
18. Trabasso, T., Van Den Broek, P.: Causal thinking and the representation of narrative events. J. Mem. Lang. **24**(5), 612–630 (1985)
19. Yeh, A.: More accurate tests for the statistical significance of result differences. In: COLING 2000 Volume 2: The 18th International Conference on Computational Linguistics (2000)

# Using Wearable Devices to Participate in 3D Interactive Storytelling

Tsai-Yen Li[✉] ⬥ and Wen-Hsuan Wang

National Chengchi University, Taipei 116, Taiwan
li@nccu.edu.tw

**Abstract.** There exist various ways for a user to participate in a story through interactive narratives. Most previous work uses traditional user interfaces for interactions with limited modifications to story elements. It is a challenge to allow a user to participate in an interactive story through the first-person view in a 3D virtual environment. In this work, we propose to use wearable motion capture (mocap) devices to enable a user to play as a character in a 3D virtual scene and interact with the environment and other virtual characters in real time. The interactions will affect how the story develops as well as the result. In such an interactive storytelling system, we have designed methods to interpret user actions as well as to generate parameterizable animations according to the interactions. We have conducted a user study to evaluate our system by comparing a traditional controller with a wearable device. The experimental results reveal that the interaction methods we have designed are more intuitive and easier to use, compared to the controller. In addition, the users are willing to try to play with the system multiple times, which confirms the replay value of our interactive storytelling system.

**Keywords:** Interactive storytelling · Wearable device · 3D virtual environment · Motion capture · Character animation

## 1 Introduction

As computer technologies advance, there exist more and more opportunities for the audience to change their roles as observers and actively participate in a story in a 3D virtual environment. Through interactions with the virtual environment as well as other characters in a story, one can change the plot of the story or the contents of story elements on the fly. The audience will be able to break the fourth wall of narratives in various ways. In a typical 3D digital interactive storytelling setting, one can use traditional user interface devices such as a keyboard and a mouse to interact with the narrative system by selecting a story branch from a menu or navigating to a Non-Character Player (NPC) to retrieve information and make a conversation. The interaction may not be intuitive and the responses from the system may also be limited. On the other hand, the development of new sensing and VR technologies is opening up new directions for novel applications. For example, somatosensory devices such as Leap Motion, Kinect, and other wearable motion capture devices are becoming more affordable, people are starting to use these devices to develop novel applications for interactive storytelling.

© Springer Nature Switzerland AG 2021
A. Mitchell and M. Vosmeer (Eds.): ICIDS 2021, LNCS 13138, pp. 80–93, 2021.
https://doi.org/10.1007/978-3-030-92300-6_8

As the technologies develop, motion capture (mocap) has become a popular and affordable way to generate character animations in 3D applications. If we use the mocap devices to control the motions of a 3D avatar for the user, how to interpret these motions and generate responsive interactions becomes an important research issue. Besides, captured motions are mostly used as canned motions for NPCs when certain events are triggered or certain conditions for the story or game are satisfied. If the behaviors of NPCs cannot adapt to user interactions, the plausibility of the virtual scene, as well as the replay value of the application, will be greatly reduced. Thus, in this work, we aim to design a 3D interactive storytelling system allowing intuitive 3D avatar control and generation of responsive and appropriate NPC behaviors. We will describe how the system is designed and report the experimental results from a user study.

In the following sections, we will first describe the related work about our research. In Sect. 3, we will describe how we have designed and implemented the interactive storytelling system. Then, we will report the result of the experiment that we have designed to evaluate the system. Lastly, we conclude the paper with some remarks and future research directions.

## 2  Related Work

Interactive storytelling is a form of entertainment allowing the authors and audience to co-create a unique experience of the story through user interactions. 3D interactive narrative is a special form emphasizing using a 3D virtual environment to deliver a story. To realize such an application, many techniques are involved such as drama generation, authoring tools, character animation generation, scripting languages, user interface design, etc. The Oz project [1] is one of the earliest interactive storytelling systems utilizing the concept of agents to provide impromptu interactions with users. Spierling et al. [13] introduced the concept of Narrative Formalism into interactive storytelling and use a layered model to create interactive stories and contents.

Unlike text-based interactive drama creation, the challenges for 3D interactive storytelling are more on the dynamic generation of multimedia contents and the design of multi-modal user interfaces. Kistler et al. [7] and Yang and Li [15] all have proposed to use gestures to interact with the objects in the virtual environment or to select a branch in a story graph. Cavazza et al. [3] have designed a multimodal user interface to allow a user to use voice input to influence the behaviors of virtual characters as well as the plot in an immersive 3D scene. In [4], a gesture recognition module also has been implemented for interactive storytelling. Brown et al. [2] reported a study attempting to find the features of iconic gestures for retelling a story. Piplica et al. [10] presented a system for combining improvisational acting with full-body motions detected through Kinect to support the co-creation of interactive narratives. Mousas et al. [8] proposed to detect user gestures with Kinect to trigger actions of virtual characters. Rhodin et al. [11] proposed to use Kinect and Leap Motion and predefined settings of gestures and velocities to present the corresponding animation of virtual characters. Eubanks et al. [5] recently presented two studies about the investigation of how body tracking fidelity is related to avatar embodiment.

There has been much research on the automatic generation or editing of character animations. For example, Tonneau et al. [14] proposed a technique to edit existing motion clips to respond to large environmental changes on the ground. Shoulson et al. [12] proposed an animation testbed allowing a user to leverage a character's animation and navigation capabilities when authoring both individual decision-making and complex interactions. In [6], the authors used precomputed semantic information about the environment to choose appropriate animation clips for the character to reach a given goal. Mousas et al. [9] also have proposed a system called CHASE allowing a novice user to design scripts with parameters to produce the desired animation. Besides, Yang and Li [15] also proposed to use a scripting language in XML to generate the animations for different story nodes in 3D interactive storytelling.

## 3   System Design and Implementation

To realize our VR system, we have adopted the Unity3D game engine as our experimental platform. In terms of hardware, we have used a relatively low-cost wearable motion capture device, called Perception Neuron, to capture the motion of a player. We have also chosen the HTC VIVE Head-Mounted Display (HMD) and controller as the devices for 3D rendering, audio outputs, and control input. The architecture of our system, as shown in Fig. 1, consists of three main modules: motion interpretation, animation management, and story management. The inputs, except for the ones from the user controller, also include data from external files such as story script, interaction script, and motion database. The authors of the story are in charge of creating the story script and interaction script while the player uses body gestures and the controller to interact with the environment or the NPCs. We will describe the main modules in the following subsections.

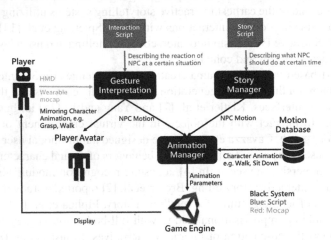

**Fig. 1.** System architecture.

### 3.1   Motion Interpretation Module

The motion interpretation module is in charge of interpreting player motions into regular gestures or specific commands for further processing. The motions are captured through a wearable device mentioned above and inputted into the system in a streaming format (BVH). Since the capture motions have many degrees of freedom, to reduce the control and computation complexity, we have only used a few parts of the body, such as hands and legs, for interpretation. Motion interpretation is needed because some of the player motions are designed to trigger certain events with interaction with the environment or NPCs. In addition, some motions, such as sitting down on a chair, cannot happen in the physical space as in the virtual space. Therefore, we have divided the inputs into two modes: direct input and command input.

**Direct Input Mode.** In this mode, the motions captured for the player are mirrored directly into the motions of the avatar. Therefore, the player can move his body as if he was the avatar. When certain conditions described in interaction scripts are satisfied, corresponding actions from the environment or the NPC will be triggered to respond to the player's intention for interaction. For example, in Table 1, we have listed the types of motions that will be recognized as meaningful actions and trigger events with corresponding motions by the affected objects or the NPC. For example, when the hand of a user avatar approaches an object, such as a glass or a hand of an NPC, and a grasp motion is performed, the object will be snapped into and moves with the hand (Fig. 2). Similarly, an object is released when the player ungrasps. The push motion is similar and can be used to push objects, such as doors, before entering or exiting a room. The motion of a short walk reflects a short-distance walk or position adjustment when the player moves around in the physical space.

**Table 1.** The types of motions recognized in the direct input mode

| Motion types | Procedure to trigger an action |
| --- | --- |
| Grasp | Approach an object and grasp it when it turns red |
| Push | Touch the object and move forward. The object will move along |
| Wave | Raise the hand over the shoulder and wave |
| Short walk | Move the body, and the avatar follows |

**Fig. 2.** The graspable object is highlighted (right) when the hand is close enough

**Command Input Mode.** Unlike the direct input mode where all motions are mapped to the avatar, there could be actions that the player would like to perform in the virtual world but is not physically feasible in the real world. For example, the physical space could be limited and does not allow the player to freely walk for a long distance as one may expect in the virtual world. Similarly, certain motions are not feasible simply because there are no corresponding objects in the real world. For example, when one would like to sit down on a chair in the virtual world, he/she cannot do so because there may not be a chair ready for this in the real world. As a result, we have to design special motions allowing a player to specify his intention for doing this type of motion, which we call the Command Input Mode. In the current implementation, we have designed three motions for command inputs as shown in Table 2. For the long-distance walk, since the player is not transporting his body, the avatar will move along his facing direction. To perform the sit-down motion, the player has to touch a chair first and then bend his knees to tell the system his intention for sitting down. Once the action is triggered, the player can stand up and allow the avatar to display the sit-down animation. Similarly, when the avatar is in a sit-down situation, the player can bend his knees to specify the intention for the avatar to stand up.

**Table 2.** The types of motions recognized in the command input mode

| Motion types | Procedure to trigger an action | Corresponding animations |
|---|---|---|
| Walk | March on the spot by lifting legs alternatively | Avatar moves forward along the facing direction |
| Sit down | Touch a chair and bend the knees | Play the sit-down animation when activated. Walk to the chair if necessary |
| Stand up | Bend the knees when sitting | Play the stand-up animation |

**Animation Enforcing Mode.** There are also some situations where we would like to enforce the display of certain animations to ensure the progress of a story or to simplify the interaction with the environment or NPC. In this mode, the player is still allowed to move his head to watch the display of enforced animations. In our demonstrative example, two situations may trigger this mode. The first case occurs when the story develops to a point where the player is shot by the suspect. Then a lying-down animation will be enforced even though the player does not perform this action. The second case is when the player (playing as a policeman) takes the suspect to the police car after arresting him, both need to enter the car. We choose to enforce the animations for both characters to avoid complex interactions and motion coordination which are not crucial for experiencing the story.

### 3.2 Interaction and Story Scripting

As depicted in Fig. 1, in our system, there are two types of scripts used to describe the interactive story and the interactions with the environment or NPCs: interaction script and story script. The interaction script is used to define how the environment or the NPCs should react to user interaction while the story script defines the story graph with branches for the interaction narratives.

**Interaction Script.** We have designed an interaction scripting language allowing an author to specify the reactions of an NPC when certain conditions are satisfied through the interpretation of player motions in two input modes as described above. The scripting language is an XML-based markup language, and an example is shown in Fig. 3. In the script, we define the conditions for triggering a reaction from an NPC and what kinds of responses (animation) should be taken for the interaction. Currently, there are six attributes defined for the `<InteractMovement>` tag that are used to specify the conditions and responses. For example, in Fig. 3, the interaction scripts for three actors (Suspect, Bartender, and Waiter) are described. In line 5, when the player, playing as a passerby, sits down in a good mood, the interaction movement of "give" for the suspect will be sent to the animation manager for offering a drink for 20 s. In the current system, event types of `RespondMovement` have been implemented.

```
 1  <Interaction>
 2      <Character tag="Suspect">
 3          <InteractMovement PlayerIdentity="Police" PlayerMovement="all" SelfMood="all"
            RespondMovement="shoot" Duration="20"/>
 4
 5          <InteractMovement PlayerIdentity="Passerby" PlayerMovement="sit" SelfMood="good"
            RespondMovement="give" Duration="20"/>
 6
 7          <InteractMovement PlayerIdentity="Passerby" PlayerMovement="grab" SelfMood="good"
            RespondMovement="beCatched" Duration="20" GrabTarget="SuspectStrongHand"/>
 8
 9          <InteractMovement PlayerIdentity="Passerby" PlayerMovement="walk" SelfMood="bad"
            RespondMovement="walk" Duration="20"/>
10
11          <InteractMovement PlayerIdentity="Passerby" PlayerMovement="grab" SelfMood="Great"
            RespondMovement="follow" Duration="100" GrabTarget="SuspectStrongHand"/>
12          <InteractMovement PlayerIdentity="Passerby" PlayerMovement="grab" SelfMood="Great"
            RespondMovement="follow" Duration="100" GrabTarget="SuspectOtherHand"/>
13      </Character>
14      <Character tag="Bartender">
15          <InteractMovement PlayerIdentity="Passerby" PlayerMovement="sit" SelfMood="good"
            RespondMovement="lookat" Duration="20"/>
16      </Character>
17      <Character tag="Waiter">
18          <InteractMovement PlayerIdentity="Police" PlayerMovement="waveHands" SelfMood="good"
            RespondMovement="waveHands" Duration="5"/>
19      </Character>
20  </Interaction>
```

**Fig. 3.** An example of interaction scripts

**Story Script.** Unlike an interaction script which describes the responses of the environment or NPCs, the story script is used to describe the story graph consisting of story nodes connected with branches. It also includes nodes that are time-triggered, which means that some animations may start voluntarily without interactions. Thus, the storyteller can take an initiative to drive the story instead of waiting for the player to interact and trigger events. For example, the script in Fig. 4 describes that the suspect will start to move to a chair by walking for 15 s at an absolute or relative time.

```
<AnimCharacterMove StartTime="0" Duration="15"
ActorTag="Suspect" Movement="walk" destinationTag="Chair" />
```

**Fig. 4.** An example of story scripts

### 3.3 Animation Management Module

The animation management module is in charge of generating natural and responsive animations for the NPCs. In our interactive storytelling system, the animations of the NPCs could be triggered by the story management module because of the need for story development or by the motion interpretation module when the player interacts with the NPC. Since the motion interpretation module deals with real-time interactions with the player, the needs for responsive actions are usually higher. As a result, in the animation management module, we need to have a way to schedule the animations according to their priorities. In addition, the animation management module may also voluntarily insert a necessary transition motion to make the target motion feasible. For example, if the objective is for the NPC to sit down on a chair but the NPC is too far from the chair, the animation manager will issue a walk-to-chair animation for the NPC to reach the chair first.

In Fig. 5, we show an example scenario where the NPC receives animation requests from different modules, and the animation management module needs to arrange these requests according to their priorities. For example, at time t1, the suspect NPC received a request for a sit-down action from the story manager. But the animation manager realized that the suspect was too far from the chair and therefore inserted a walk action ahead of sit-down to reach the chair. At time t3, the player (policeman) walked in and was spotted by the suspect. As a result, the motion interpreter issued a shooting action, which takes the highest priority. Once the shooting is over, the suspect will resume walking to the chair and finally sit down at t6.

| Suspect (t0) | Suspect (t1) | Suspect (t2) | Suspect (t3) | Suspect (t4) | Suspect (t5) | Suspect (t6) |
|---|---|---|---|---|---|---|
| | SM: sit | AM: walk | MI: shoot | AM: walk | SM: sit | |
| | | SM: sit | AM: walk | SM: sit | | |
| | | | SM: sit | | | |

SM: Story Manager, AM: Animation Manager, MI: Motion Interpreter

**Fig. 5.** Animation scheduling in the Animation Manager

In addition to determining the priorities of the animations, the diversity and quality of the animations will also affect a player's immersion experience. By the diversity of animations, we mean that the responses that the player gets from NPC should vary according to the development of the story or the emotion of the NPC. According to the history of interactions with the player, we maintain three emotional states: bad, good, and great for the NPC. When a responsive action needs to be taken by the NPC, the animation manager will select an appropriate animation according to the emotional state of the NPC. Therefore, the responses a player sees may vary at different times of play.

The quality of the animation for an NPC can be considered from several aspects including the factors of cost and complexity. Since most of the animations for the NPCs are prepared and stored in the motion database, the diversity of animations will affect the cost of preparing such an interactive storytelling system. In our animation management system, we have attempted to minimize the need for creating a large animation database by reusing existing motions as much as possible. For example, many motions only focus on a certain part of the body. As such, one can decompose a motion into different parts that can be recomposed to form new animations. For example, as shown in Fig. 6, the hand gesture of the NPC does not depend on the lower body state. Thus, we can decompose the animation for the upper-body gesture and use it when the NPC is sitting on the chair.

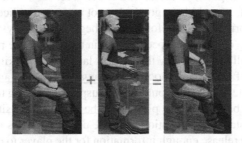

**Fig. 6.** Example of decomposing animation for reuse

In addition to selecting different animation clips for different NPC emotions, the location of the user avatar, as controlled by the player, cannot be determined in advance. Thus, the animation management module may need to make a minor adjustment on the facing direction of the NPC toward the player to conduct a conversation. This kind of minor adjustment also happens when the player needs to have physical interactions with the NPC such as in the situation of arresting the suspect by grasping his hand. As shown in Fig. 7, the configuration of the hand being grasped is adjusted with inverse kinematics according to the player's hand location. We have used the built-in IK controller module in Unity3D for the implementation of this function.

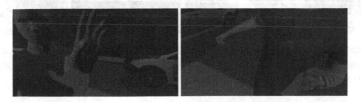

**Fig. 7.** Example of computing hand configurations with inverse kinematics

## 4   Experimental Design and Results

To evaluate the system that we have designed, we have created a demonstrative scenario about an interactive story with multiple branches and endings. We have also designed an experiment with this scene and invite participants to experience the story and provide feedback through questionnaires.

### 4.1   Demonstrative Scenario

The demonstrative scenario is about a story in which a policeman (played by the participant) is asked to find a dangerous suspect of a crime who is reported to be present in the area around a bar. Snapshots of the scene are shown in Fig. 8. The policeman is supposed to find the suspect and arrest him if possible. However, since the suspect is dangerous and armed, it could be a good idea not to wear a police uniform and try to do the investigation privately. Therefore, in the beginning, the system will prompt the player about changing clothes in a special room in the area. If the player decides not to change clothes, he will be spotted by the suspect later when walking to the bar and got shot by the suspect. If the player chooses to change his clothes and enters the bar, he will find that one of the guests that could be the suspect is walking to the bar and will be sitting in front of the bartender. The player will be instructed to sit beside the suspect, and the suspect will start a conversation with the player and tries to offer him a drink. The conversation will release enough information for the player to confirm that the man sitting aside is the suspect. Then, he can decide to arrest the suspect by quickly grasping his hand and take him to the police car outside. If the grasping action is not fast enough, the suspect may find out and run away. In other words, depending on the history of the interactions, the story may develop into multiple endings.

**Fig. 8.** Snapshots of story development during the interactive storytelling (a) mission setup, (b) clothes changing, (c) suspect in a bar, (d) inviting for a drink, (e) releasing crime information, (f) arresting the suspect, (g) taking him to the car, and (h) putting him in prison.

### 4.2   Experimental Settings

We have invited eight subjects to participate in the evaluation. The ages of these subjects range from 22 to 28 with 4 males and 4 females, and half of them are experienced users of VR games while the other half has relatively few experiences.

The procedure for the experiment was a within-subject design and worked as follows. Each subject would experience the story twice with the VIVE controller and the wearable device, respectively. The order of the two experiences was random such that the learning effect could be canceled. Before the formal session started, we first explained to the subjects how the system worked and allowed the subjects to practice how to interact with the objects in a tutorial session through the wearable device and the VIVE controller, respectively. For the VIVE controller, we have adopted the most common ways of interacting with objects. For example, we use a touchpad to trigger teleport, a hair-trigger to grasp, and a grip to switch between sit-down and stand-up. At the end of each formal session, the subjects were asked to fill in a questionnaire about the operations, story, system functions, and immersion of their experiences.

## 4.3  Experimental Results

After each formal session, the subjects were asked to fill in three questionnaires for the evaluation of our system. The questions in the survey are answered on a 5-point Likert scale with 1 to 5 meanings strongly disagree to strongly agree. Three questionnaires are about the assessments on user interface operations, system and story, and immersion experience, respectively. The results (means and standard deviation) for both formal runs (controller and wearable device) are shown in Tables 3, 4 and 5. A paired two-tailed t-test has also been conducted for each question.

**Table 3.**  Assessment of user interface operations

| Questions | Controller | | Wearable | | |
|---|---|---|---|---|---|
| | M | STD | M | STD | t-test |
| 1. The operation of movement is intuitive. | 4.1 | 0.83 | 4.6 | 0.52 | 0.227 |
| 2. The operation of movement is smooth. | 4.1 | 0.99 | 4.3 | 0.71 | 0.785 |
| 3. The operation of movement is interesting. | 4.1 | 0.99 | 4.4 | 0.92 | 0.516 |
| 4. The operation of grasping is intuitive. | 4.0 | 0.93 | 4.8 | 0.46 | *0.048 |
| 5. The operation of grasping is smooth. | 4.1 | 0.99 | 4.1 | 0.99 | 1.000 |
| 6. The operation of grasping is interesting. | 4.1 | 0.64 | 4.6 | 0.52 | 0.104 |
| 7. The operations of sit-down and stand-up are intuitive. | 3.1 | 1.25 | 4.1 | 0.64 | *0.033 |
| 8. The operations of sit-down and stand-up are smooth. | 3.8 | 1.39 | 4.4 | 0.52 | 0.217 |
| 9. The operations of sit-down and stand-up are interesting. | 4.4 | 0.74 | 4.8 | 0.71 | 0.285 |
| 10. I can move my body freely. | 3.8 | 1.39 | 4.5 | 0.76 | 0.303 |

$^*p<0.05$

From the results in Table 3, we can find that the average scores for the wearable device are all higher than the controller. The variation for the wearable device is also lower than the controller. However, only the questions of intuitiveness on the grasping and sit-down and stand-up operations have achieved significant differences between the two types of interfaces. In the interview after the experiment, we also found that the scores for the controller quite depend on the prior experience of the subjects while all subjects consider the wearable devices are more intuitive to use.

**Table 4.** Assessment of story and system functions

| Questions | Controller | | Wearable | | |
|---|---|---|---|---|---|
| | M | STD | M | STD | t-test |
| 11. I can understand the story. | 4.9 | 0.35 | 4.8 | 0.46 | 0.351 |
| 12. I think the story is interesting. | 4.6 | 0.52 | 4.4 | 0.74 | 0.451 |
| 13. I think the progress of the story is smooth. | 4.6 | 0.74 | 4.6 | 0.52 | 1.000 |
| 14. I want to experience different story plots. | 4.6 | 0.52 | 4.9 | 0.35 | 0.170 |
| 15. The audial and textual prompts help me interact properly in the story. | 4.9 | 0.35 | 4.8 | 0.46 | 0.351 |
| 16. I feel that the NPC is interacting with me. | 4.4 | 0.52 | 4.3 | 0.46 | 0.598 |
| 17. I think I have influenced the development of the story. | 4.5 | 0.53 | 4.5 | 0.53 | 1.000 |

*$p<0.05$

The results in Table 4 reveal that the user feedback about the story and system functions are all very positive for either interaction interface but no significant difference has been found. The subjects have found that being able to interact with the NPC and influence the development of the story is interesting.

Table 5 shows the result of assessing the immersion of the player. The subjects are more immersed in the environment with the wearable device but all enjoy playing in the scene with both input devices. The variation of the scores is higher for the controller session probably because their familiarity with the controller varies. On the other hand, from questions 28 and 30, we can find significant differences between the two interfaces, and the wearable mocap device provides a more intuitive interface allowing a player to immerse into the virtual environment more easily.

**Table 5.** Assessment of immersion

| Questions | Controller | | Wearable | | |
|---|---|---|---|---|---|
| | M | STD | M | STD | t-test |
| 18. My mood was up and down as the story develops. | 3.9 | 1.13 | 4.0 | 1.20 | 0.598 |
| 19. I wanted to know how the story developed. | 4.3 | 1.04 | 4.8 | 0.46 | 0.227 |
| 20. I am worried about if I can accomplish the mission. | 4.0 | 0.93 | 4.1 | 1.13 | 0.598 |
| 21. I found myself in the story and would like to dialog with the virtual characters. | 4.1 | 0.83 | 4.5 | 0.53 | 0.285 |
| 22. I enjoy the scene in the game. | 4.3 | 0.71 | 4.4 | 0.52 | 0.351 |
| 23. I enjoy playing the game. | 4.6 | 0.52 | 4.4 | 0.52 | 0.351 |
| 24. I think the operations in the game were easy to learn. | 4.3 | 0.71 | 4.5 | 0.53 | 0.516 |
| 25. I am not aware of using any controller. | 2.4 | 1.30 | 4.5 | 0.76 | **0.001 |
| 26. I can move according to my will. | 4.3 | 0.89 | 4.4 | 0.74 | 0.802 |
| 27. I can interact with the virtual world like in the real world. | 3.3 | 1.16 | 4.1 | 0.64 | 0.087 |
| 28. I was not aware of what was happening in the real world during the play. | 3.4 | 1.06 | 4.3 | 1.16 | *0.021 |
| 29. I felt that the game was my only concern. | 3.9 | 0.83 | 4.1 | 0.64 | 0.351 |
| 30. I would not stop playing the game to see what happened around me. | 3.8 | 0.71 | 4.4 | 0.52 | *0.049 |
| 31. I felt the time flies when I played. | 4.4 | 0.74 | 4.6 | 0.52 | 0.170 |

*$p<0.05$, **$p<0.01$,

## 5 Conclusions and Future Work

There has been much research on interactive storytelling and different ways to design and experience a 3D interactive story. In this paper, we have attempted to design a 3D interactive narrative system allowing a player to wear a mocap device to participate in an interactive story. To realize such a system, in addition to using the wearable device, we also have developed a way to receive user inputs by recognizing the motion and intention of the player under system guidance and to provide plausible responses from the NPC through realistic animations. We have also conducted a study to evaluate the system from several aspects. The experimental result reveals that the interactive storytelling system has achieved the goal of allowing the players to participate in the story through interactions with both the controller and the wearable devices, respectively. The wearable mocap device provides a more intuitive way to interact with the environment or NPCs and is also easier to learn for novice users. Besides, the subjects are better engaged with the story and immersed into the environment with the wearable device and thus have a better story experience in general.

In the current system, the dialogs between the player and the NPC are all pre-determined and pre-recorded. Therefore, although the story has multiple plotlines and endings, the system still cannot change the story on the fly with customized contents or dynamic dialogs. To allow this to happen, more research on dynamic drama creation and scene generation will be necessary. Besides, although the cost for wearable mocap devices is becoming affordable, the quality for stability may be compromised. We will be looking forward to the development of this type of input device for it to become more affordable and precise.

**Acknowledgment.** The authors would like to thank the sponsor of this research: Ministry of Science and Technology in Taiwan under contract MOST108-2221-E-004–007-MY3.

# References

1. Bates, J.: Virtual reality, art, and entertainment. Presence: J. Teleoper. Virtual Environ. **1**(1), 133–138 (1992)
2. Brown, S.A., et al.: Towards a gesture-based story authoring system: design implications from feature analysis of iconic gestures during storytelling. In: Cardona-Rivera, R., Sullivan, A., Young, R. (eds.) ICIDS 2019. LNCS, vol. 11869, pp. 364–373. Springer, Cham (2019). https://doi.org/10.1007/978-3-030-33894-7_38
3. Cavazza, M., Lugrin, J.L., Pizzi, D., Charles, F.: Madame bovary on the HolodeckL immersive interactive storytelling. In: Proceedings of the 15th ACM International Conference on Multimedia, pp. 651–660 (2007)
4. Cavazza, M., Charles, F., Mead, S.J., Martin, O., Marichal, X., Nandi, A.: Multimodal acting in mixed reality interactive storytelling. IEEE Multimed. **11**(3), 30–39 (2004)
5. Eubanks, J.C., Moore, A.G., Fishwick, P.A., McMahan, R.P.: The effects of body tracking fidelity on embodiment of an inverse-kinematic avatar for male participants. In: Proceedings of 2020 IEEE International Symposium on Mixed and Augmented Reality (2020)
6. Kapadia, M., et al.: PRECISION: precomputing environment semantics for contact-rich character animation. In Proceedings of the 20th ACM SIGGRAPH Symposium on Interactive 3D Graphics and Games, pp. 29–37 (2016)
7. Kistler, F., Sollfrank, D., Bee, N., André, E.: Full body gestures enhancing a game book for interactive story telling. In: Si, M., Thue, D., André, E., Lester, J.C., Tanenbaum, T.J., Zammitto, V. (eds) ICIDS 2011. LNCS, vol. 7069, pp. 207–218. Springer, Heidelberg (2011). https://doi.org/10.1007/978-3-642-25289-1_23
8. Mousas, C.: Towards developing an easy-to-use scripting environment for animating virtual characters. arXiv preprint arXiv:1702.03246 (2017)
9. Mousas, C., Anagnostopoulos, C.-N.: Performance-driven hybrid full-body character control for navigation and interaction in virtual environments. 3D Res. **8**(2), Article No. 124 (2017)
10. Piplica, A., DeLeon, C., Magerko, B.: Full-body gesture interaction with improvisational narrative agents. In: Nakano, Y., Neff, M., Paiva, A., Walker, M. (eds.) IVA 2012. LNCS, vol. 7502, pp. 514–516. Springer, Heidelberg (2012). https://doi.org/10.1007/978-3-642-33197-8_63
11. Rhodin, H., et al.: Generalizing wave gestures from sparse examples for real-time character control. In: Proceedings of ACM SIGGRAPH Asia 2015, vol. 34, no. 6, Article No. 181 (2015)
12. Shoulson, A., Marshak, N., Kapadia, M., Badler, N.I.: ADAPT: the agent development and prototyping testbed. IEEE Trans. Vis. Comput. Graph. **20**(7), 1035–1047 (2014)

13. Spierling, U., Grasbon, D., Braun, N., Iurgel, I.: Setting the scene: playing digital director in interactive storytelling and creation. Comput. Graph. **26**(1), 31–44 (2002)
14. Tonneau, S., Al-Ashqar, R.A., Pettré, J., Komura, T., Mansard, N.: Character contact repositioning under large environment deformation. In: Proceedings of the 37th Annual Conference of the European Association for Computer Graphics, pp. 127–138 (2016)
15. Yang, C.C., Li, T.-Y.: Participating in narratives with motion-sensing technologies in a 3D interactive storytelling system. In: Proceedings of Computer Graphics Workshop, Taipei (2015)

# Inbox Games: Poetics and Authoring Support

Chris Martens[1(✉)] and Robert J. Simmons[2]

[1] North Carolina State University, Raleigh, USA
martens@csc.ncsu.edu
[2] Brilliant.org, San Francisco, USA

**Abstract.** This paper defines *inbox games as* a class of interactive storytelling projects in which the story is told through an email inbox-like interface. We contribute a definition and an authoring tool for this category of games.

**Keywords:** Interactive fiction · Epistolary narrative · Authoring tools

## 1  Introduction

Interactive narratives tell stories with some form of reader interaction, but those interactions can take many forms and serve a number of diegetic and thematic purposes. For instance, the player-as-protagonist model (arguably the default) gives the player the point of view of a specific character and asks them to make in-story decisions for that character. Alternatively, a player-as-coauthor model asks the player to draft and/or edit parts of the story (e.g.: *18 Cadence* [23]); a player-as-detective model asks players to examine and iteratively discover fragmented pieces of a story's aftermath to determine a past event sequence (e.g.: *Her Story* [4]); a player-as-director model asks them to manipulate aspects of characters' environment or the actions of multiple characters from an omniscient point of view (e.g.: *Prom Week* [21]). Each of these diegetic framings serves a different type of storytelling.

In this paper, our diegetic framing of interest is what we call the *inbox game*: a work that employs an overlapping set of formal techniques to deliver a narrative by asking the player to send and receive asynchronous messages with non-player characters. We take an expansive view of this idea by including not only games that look like literal email inboxes, but also those that model player interaction on other forms of text-based messaging, such as traditional letter-writing, SMS text-messaging, and social media posting. We are interested in this class of games because we think they can evoke a compelling set of narrative themes, including the conference themes of *disconnection* and *reconnection*. The paradoxical feelings of simultaneous connection and disconnection created by online communication are natural to explore within an interface mimicking one players already use to keep in touch with friends and family online.

© Springer Nature Switzerland AG 2021
A. Mitchell and M. Vosmeer (Eds.): ICIDS 2021, LNCS 13138, pp. 94–106, 2021.
https://doi.org/10.1007/978-3-030-92300-6_9

Our interest in this form has led us to develop an authoring language and game engine designed specifically for this mode of storytelling. We describe this language and its implementation status in Sect. 4.

This paper's contribution is twofold, paralleling the two disciplinary approaches to research methodology. First, we present a theoretical description of the poetic affordances of inbox games, through definition, example, and description of the relationships between formal properties and narrative effects. Second, we present a technical design effort in the form of our software tool for authoring inbox games.

## 2   Related Work

Mawhorter et al.'s work on choice poetics [20] provides a model for this paper by integrating the theoretical foundation of poetics (relations between form and content) [7] with theories of game design and interactive media, such as procedural rhetoric [5] and link pragmatics in hypertext games [29]. As in the choice poetics paper, one of our goals is to provide a preliminary vocabulary for discussing the relationship between formal elements (interface mimesis and epistolary storytelling) and their aesthetic and narrative effects on players. Previous work surveying the *email novel* as a literary form performs similar poetic analysis of a related genre [24, 25], though email novels are not interactive.

Kreminski and Wardrip-Fruin's work defining "storylets" as a model of interactive narrative authorship is structurally similar to ours in that they also catalogue several existing narrative works and outline a design space based on salient common features [15]. The idea of storylets itself is also relevant to this work in that an individual message (e.g. email) could be codified as a storylet, and an engine for inbox games could be adapted to interoperate with storylets as a data structure.

*Grayscale* is an inbox game implemented on top of the *Chimeria* project [10], an engine for modeling group affinities for virtual characters in stories. *Chimeria:Grayscale* represents a central example of the form we are attempting to define and support. Further examples are discussed in the next section.

## 3   Defining Inbox Games

We begin by identifying several examples of games that inform our understanding of the design space. Then we identify an overlapping feature set among these examples that forms our working definition of inbox games.

### 3.1   Examples

Inbox games allow the player to send and receive messages to and from non-player characters, but within those constraints, they vary heavily. We first present a collection of examples that we consider within or adjacent to the space

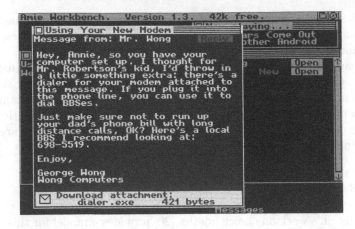

**Fig. 1.** A screenshot of the BBS interface in *Digital: A Love Story*

**Fig. 2.** A screenshot of the email interface in *Chimeria:Grayscale*.

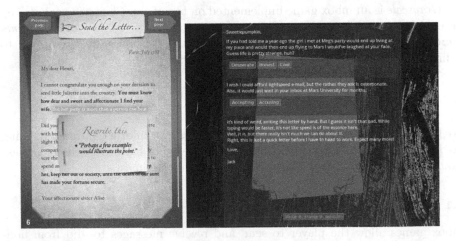

**Fig. 3.** Screenshots of the drafting interfaces in *First Draft of the Revolution* and *13 min of Light*.

of inbox games and identify some of their key characteristics. Table 1 summarizes the games and characteristics discussed.

There are two existing games we are aware of that do this with an interface that simulates an email inbox: *Digital: A Love Story* [16] and *Grayscale* [10]. Screenshots of their interfaces can be seen in Figs. 1 and 2. In both cases, an opening frame story transitions quickly to the interface of an email client, in which the player progresses by reading emails and sending replies. In *Digital*, a reply is sent by clicking on the "reply" button, but the contents of the player's message are left implicit. In *Grayscale*, the player usually has several choices for how to respond, and the choice affects the outcome of the game. It is implied that the text in the choice links for the player is the literal text of the email that is sent.

There are a few other examples of games that emphasize the "epistolary" nature of inbox games—sending and receipt of messages—without emphasis on digital interface mimesis, including *First Draft of the Revolution* [27] and *13 min of Light* [14], which simulate writing handwritten letters (Fig. 3). (Notably, *13 min of Light* also has a portion of gameplay that mimics Reddit's forum interface.) These games also allow the player to *edit* the message before sending it, which adds an element of coauthorship to the player's role, rather than simply selecting pre-authored responses.

There are several other games that emphasize digital interface mimesis but deviate from the strictly asynchronous epistolary nature of email. *We Should Talk* [30], Lifeline [1], and A Normal Lost Phone [2] all imitate text messaging interfaces for in-game dialogue. Don't Take it Personally, Babe [17] (by the same author as Digital: A Love Story) mimics the social network dynamics of Facebook walls, and HoloVista [3] specifically evokes Instagram, including posting photos with filters and receiving likes and comments.

### 3.2   Inbox Game Characteristics

The above examples form a Wittgensteinian family resemblance [22] in that they share a meaningful set of overlapping formal features with an empty intersection. These formal features include:

- **Response Choice:** Players can (sometimes or always) select among multiple choices for how to respond to a received message.
- **Response Drafting:** Once a general response scheme is selected, players can edit, draft, or otherwise fine-tune specific components of the response independently.
- **Multithreading:** There are active conversations with multiple parties simultaneously that can be engaged with in an order decided by the player.
- **Interface Mimesis:** There is a diegetic interface in the game designed to evoke a particular real-world counterpart.

We summarize selected examples in terms of these characteristics in Table 1 and discuss them in more detail presently.

**Table 1.** Summary of inbox games and characteristics. Key: RC = response choice; RD = response drafting; M = multithreading; IM = interface mimesis (see Sect. 3.2).

| Game | RC | RD | M | IM |
|---|---|---|---|---|
| Digital: A Love Story | | | ✓ | BBS/Email |
| Grayscale | ✓ | | ✓ | Email |
| Holovista | | | | Instagram |
| A Normal Lost Phone | | | ✓ | Email and text messages |
| First Draft of the Revolution | ✓ | ✓ | | Handwritten letters |
| 13 min of Light | ✓ | ✓ | | Handwritten letters/Reddit |
| Don't Take it Personally, Babe | | | ✓ | Facebook |
| Lifeline | ✓ | | | Text messaging |
| We Should Talk | ✓ | ✓ | | Text messaging |

**Response Choice.** Epistolary fiction centrally involves communication between two or more characters as a mode of storytelling. In this way, it has some things in common with dialogue—*how* something is said matters as much as what is said, and choices of action primarily affect the mental states of characters rather than the physical state of the world. In inbox games that are modeled more on text messaging or direct-messaging than email, this correlation is especially evident.

For that reason, games with an interest in character AI and modeling the mental states of virtual characters may offer interfaces that allow varying degrees of choice in response. *Grayscale:Chimeria*, for example, was written primarily to showcase the Chimeria engine's "flexible, and dynamic model of how humans categorize members of various groups" [9], and the choices one can make in how to respond hook into this engine to determine non-player character responses and eventual outcomes.

Not all inbox games offer a choice of how to reply, and some don't even show the player the "text" of their message. For instance, in *Digital: A Love Story*, clicking the "Reply" button closes the window and (potentially) results in another message showing up in your inbox sometime in the future, responding to an implied message sent by your character that is never shown. This choice parallels a common video game design decision to make the player character silent in dialogue, often with the justification that this makes them easier for the player to project themself onto.

**Response Drafting.** A common difference between dialogue messages and epistolary messages is that the latter tend to be longer, potentially multiple paragraphs. In this case, it makes sense to simulate the process of drafting and editing. Mechanics for drafting and editing are central to games like *First Draft of the Revolution* and *13 min of Light*. Even games where messages are shorter and more dialogue-like sometimes allow for this fine-tuning, as in *We Should*

*Talk's* text messaging interface where individual words and subphrases of a single message can be selected and modified independently. This mechanic extends the metaphor of the inbox beyond reply selection and into reply *composition*, which is why Emily Short classifies them as "games of coauthorship" [26].

**Multithreading.** By contrast with synchronous dialogue, traditional epistolary fiction based on handwritten letters carries the implication of a much longer passage of time between messages received and sent, during which an unknown amount of real-world time may pass. This diegetic assumption affords some interesting storytelling techniques. First, the text of the story can allude to *implied* actions that take place "off-screen," leading the reader to infer what happens between the messages. Second, narrative state is implicitly saved within threads, but not shared across them (unless the recipients overlap). This means that stories can advance alongside each other, potentially calling back to or juxtaposing with one another, or evolve independently. Finally, even when there is no diegetic relationship between threads, in an interactive context, they can *mechanically* gate each other: the player may need to reach a certain point in one thread in order to unlock progress in another.

**Interface Mimesis.** The technique of so-called diegetic interfaces has been employed in the games industry to make routine, logistical interactions with gameworlds more natural and cohesive for the player [11]. Inbox games, insofar as they take place entirely within a digital space, have a ready advantage in this arena since they can easily repurpose existing computer interfaces.

Several of them do this: the mixed-reality mobile game *Holovista* [3] alternates interaction modes where the player is photographing a physical environment and then posting photos and captions to an Instagram-like social media platform. The familiar elements of a news feed, comments, and likes are present. *Tentacles Growing Everywhere* [28]—arguably not an inbox game because it lacks direct replies from non-player characters—replicates the affordances of LiveJournal. *A Normal Lost Phone* simulates a number of functions of a smartphone, including text messaging. The hit mobile "texting adventure" *Lifeline* [1] adopts the pretense that the player is on Earth, texting with an astronaut on an unfamiliar planet, and (by default) includes long delays between replies.

We refer to the adoption of diagetic interfaces in digital message-sending games as *interface mimesis*. Interface mimesis relies on the player's assumptions about how familiar interfaces work, supplied by their cultural context and digital literacy within that context, to get away with teaching fewer mechanics and interface conventions. For example, a player familiar with text messaging will immediately understand that a repeated animation of three dots in a text messaging window indicates that the other party is in the process of composing a message.

When Google Mail (GMail) adopted the "reply suggestion" feature that allows the user to click on various options that generate example responses to emails, it exposed a huge number of computer-users to the idea of choice-based

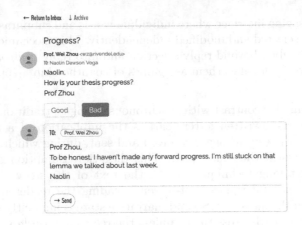

**Fig. 4.** An inbox game can build a response choice mechanic on top of an interface for selecting suggestions that Google has already taught to a large population of users.

interfaces. Grayscale had to invent its own choice interface for email replies, but in the system we describe in Sect. 4, we can simply reappropriate Google's interface to provide the user with a choice-based interface they are likely to have already encountered (Fig. 4).

### 3.3 Narrative Themes

> "I've learned that real-world human-to-human tactile contact will kill you, and that all human interaction, whether it be social, political, spiritual, sexual, or interpersonal should be contained in the much more safe, much more real interior digital space. That the outside world, the non-digital world, is merely a theatrical space in which one stages and records content for the much more real, much more vital digital space.
> One should only engage with the outside world as one engages with a coal mine. Suit up, gather what is needed, and return to the surface."
>
> — Bo Burnham, *Inside* [6]

Narrative themes supported by inbox games include both the good and bad of mediated communication: a sense of being separated from physical intimacy and connection, but also learning new languages of intimacy that can be expressed in unfamiliar ways. Many LGBTQ+ millennials and zoomers grew up with the internet as the main space that felt safe to express and explore their identity during adolescence [18], and this experience is reflected in games like *Digital: A Love Story* and *A Normal Lost Phone*.

At the same time, especially during the COVID-19 pandemic, lots of people experienced feelings of dissociation and being "trapped" behind digital interfaces, struggling to express intimacy and nuance through them. danah boyd

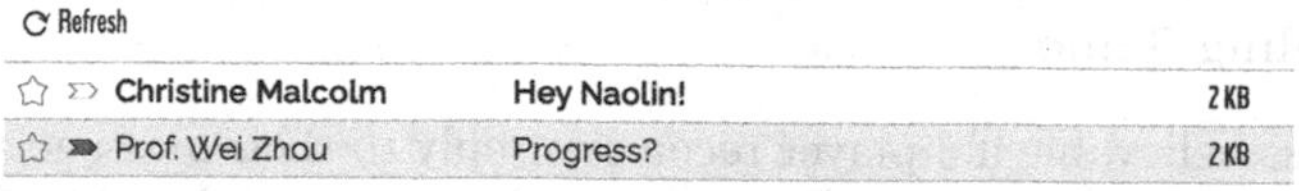

↻ Refresh

| ☆ ≫ **Christine Malcolm** | **Hey Naolin!** | 2 KB |
| ☆ ➤ Prof. Wei Zhou | Progress? | 2 KB |

**Fig. 5.** The multithreading presentation created by *Inbox*.

coined the term "context collapse" [8,19] to explain one facet of this phenomenon: internet spaces like email inboxes often collide social worlds from the workplace, family, and extracurricular spaces. *Grayscale* emphasizes that challenging emotional and political labor can take place in the email inbox [9], despite the medium's apparent lack of conversational nuances associated with embodied communication (e.g.: sexual harassment can take place via the strictly verbal medium of email, not only via physical touch). *HoloVista* traps its protagonist in a space generated by their own internal turmoil, employing themes of cognitive distance from reality and difficulty distinguishing one's internet presence from one's reality.

## 4   Authoring Support

Inspired by this emerging genre, we designed an authoring tool called *Inbox*, consisting of a custom markup language and a rendering engine, to allow an author to create an inbox game. We take inspiration from Twine [13] and Ink [12] in terms of language minimality and prioritizing the writing of legible narrative text over control flow code. Our design of *Inbox* served as an investigation into the minimal set of authoring affordances that could support multithreading and response choice.

### 4.1   Email Engine

Modern email inboxes are threaded: rather than an inbox consisting of a chronological sequence of individual messages, an inbox consists of a sequence of *threads*, each of which is a chronological sequence of messages with the same subject. This design is reflected in the design of *Inbox*: a story is authored as a group of threads, and the story evolves when the engine or the player manipulates a thread. The engine can add new threads, append new emails to existing threads, and modify the actions available to the player. The player, in turn, interacts with the story by taking any of the actions available on any thread. Figure 5 shows an example of what the "top level" player inbox might look like in a game rendered by *Inbox*.

The primary player action is selecting one of a fixed number of available email responses and then choosing to send that response (see Fig. 4). This appends their response to the thread and returns the player to the inbox view.

By default, our engine ends the game when player reaches "Inbox 0" (no messages left in the inbox), which can be achieved by archiving all messages. To make this concept work as a game mechanic, messages are not archiveable by default, e.g. if there is still a response the player can send on that thread that could prompt a reply.

## 4.2    Modeling Time

It will feel less believable if a player receives a reply to their message *immediately* after sending it. There are a few different possible ways to solve this: for example, *Grayscale* simply adds a timed delay between sending an email and receiving new emails. Our design choice for *Inbox* is to modify the inbox *only* when an email is sent, returning the player to an inbox that has already changed rather than ever showing an email's arrival. To model the "time" it would take for a recipient to respond to their sent messages, we essentially add a one-step delay: the effects of a player's action won't happen until they take a subsequent action. In other words, the player can take an action on a thread, but any responses to that action won't appear until immediately after the player takes an action on a different thread.

This interaction style won't be the only one that authors want, but it is one that promotes an experience of *context collapse* (as described in Sect. 3.3): taking an action on a given thread instantaneously redirects the player's attention back to an unrelated thread. This model also allows us to greatly simplify the engine due to fact that the most recently received email can be thought of as the "current scene," which entirely defines the set of available actions. On the other hand, it limits the expressive affordances for authoring. There is no way, for example, to permit a player to send multiple emails on a thread in a row: sending an email is an action, and no other action will be available until the engine adds a new scene to the thread, which won't happen until the player takes action on a different thread. Additionally, since it is more straightforward to implement responses that always react to the last email received, *Inbox* does not naturally facilitate authoring a conversation where the set of available responses shifts as the conversation evolves.

## 4.3    The *Inbox* Authoring Language

The *Inbox* authoring language gives authors three main expressive affordances, *threads*, *scenes* and (player) *actions*. A *thread* is a list of scenes associated with an email subject. A *scene* corresponds to a single email received by the player. In addition to the usual data and metadata associated with an email (text, attachments, a list of senders and recipients), a scene defines a set of *actions*, which include response choices and their effects.

In Fig. 6, a complete *Inbox* script is provided, written in a markup language called Camperdown designed for flexible interactive authoring.[1] (Both Fig. 4 and Fig. 5 are taken from this script.) The threads are marked by lines starting with single  #   marks (lines 11 and 20), and additional scenes in the second thread are marked by lines starting with a pair of  #   marks (lines 49 and 56, which are additional scenes in the thread that starts on line 20).

The most common player action is responding to the thread by sending an email. The author lists the player's available responses in the script by specifying

---

[1] https://package.elm-lang.org/packages/brilliantorg/backpacker-below/latest/.

```
1    ! contact Me "naolin@rivendel.edu"
2       |> full "Naolin Dawson Vega"
3
4    ! contact Prof "wz@rivendel.edu"
5       |> full "Prof. Wei Zhou"
6       |> short "Wei"
7
8    ! contact Recruiter "christine@upprcut.com"
9       |> full "Christine Malcolm"
10
11   # Hey Naolin!
12   ! email |> from Recruiter |> to Me
13   My company is hiring research engineers! You should
14   apply!
15
16   Love, Cece
17
18   ! archive
19
20   # Progress?
21   ! email |> from Prof |> to Me
22   Naolin,
23
24   How is your thesis progress?
25
26   Prof Zhou
27
28   ! respond [Good]
29      |> to Prof
30      |> triggers "good_progress" >>
31   Prof Zhou,
32
33   It's going well actually! I proved that lemma I
34   was stuck on last week.
35
36   Naolin
37
38   ! respond [Bad]
39      |> to Prof
40      |> triggers "bad_progress" >>
41   Prof Zhou,
42
43   To be honest, I haven't made any forward
44   progress. I'm still stuck on that lemma we talked
45   about last week.
46
47   Naolin
48
49   ## good_progress
50   ! email |> from Prof |> to Me
51   Great! Let's meet about it tomorrow.
52
53   WZ (sent from my iPhone)
54   ! archive
55
56   ## bad_progress
57   ! email |> from Prof |> to Me
58   Ok. Let's discuss tomorrow.
59
60   WZ (sent from my iPhone)
61   ! archive
```

```
1    INBOX GAME
2    -> inbox
3    VAR msgs = 2
4    VAR thesis_progress = "unknown"
5
6    === inbox ===
7    Your inbox contains {msgs} messages.
8    <- friend_email
9    <- advisor_email
10   + [delete all] -> END
11
12   === friend_email ===
13   + [From: Cecelia Burns] -> email1
14   = email1
15      Hey Naolin!
16      My company is hiring research engineers! You
17         should apply!
18      Love, Cece
19      + [Back] -> inbox
20
21   === advisor_email ===
22   + {thesis_progress == "unknown"}
23      [From: Prof. Wei Zhou] -> email1
24   + {thesis_progress == "good"}
25      [From: Prof. Wei Zhou] -> good_reply
26   + {thesis_progress == "bad"}
27      [From: Prof Wei Zhou] -> bad_reply
28   = email1
29      Naolin,
30      How's your thesis progress?
31      Prof Zhou
32      + [Good] -> good_progress
33      + [Bad] -> bad_progress
34      + [Back to inbox] -> inbox
35   = good_progress
36      Prof Zhou,
37      It's going well actually! I proved that lemma
38         I was stuck on last week.
39      Naolin
40      + [Send] Message sent.
41         ~thesis_progress = "good"
42         -> inbox
43      + [Reconsider] -> email1
44   = bad_progress
45      Prof. Zhou,
46      To be honest, I haven't made any forward
47         progress. I'm still stuck on that lemma we
48         talked about last week.
49      Naolin
50      + [Send] Message sent.
51         ~thesis_progress = "bad"
52         -> inbox
53      + [Reconsider] -> email1
54   = good_reply
55      Great! Let's meet about it tomorrow.
56      WZ (sent from my iPhone)
57      + [Back] -> inbox
58   = bad_reply
59      Ok. Let's discuss tomorrow
60      WZ (sent from my iPhone)
61      + [Back] -> inbox
```

**Fig. 6.** The same inbox story written in *Inbox* (left) and in Ink (right).

contents of each response, allowing for response choice (but not response drafting). The structure of the !respond command detailing a potential response is shown in Fig. 7.

Because the *archive* action is disabled by default, the author must explicitly indicate where the player may archive the thread. In Fig. 6, the !archive command appears on lines 18, 54, and 61.

## 4.4   Assessment: Comparison with Ink

The right-hand side of Fig. 6 represents an attempt to capture the multithreading and response-choice aspects of the *Inbox* script on the left-hand side of that figure. The Ink implementation lacks certain details that the *Inbox* script includes

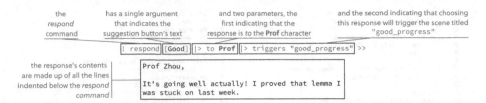

**Fig. 7.** Authoring an email response in the markup language used for *Inbox*.

for interface mimesis—lines 1–9 of the *Inbox* script, for example, serve only to connect characters with the identifying information that an email client would normally expose.

An inbox game in Ink seems to require at least one bit of state per thread to track the current "scene position" of that thread—though because the first thread has no scenes, this particular script only requires the variable on line 4 to track the state of the second thread.

The most notable difference between the two presentations, though, is not state but circularity. An inbox game fundamentally proceeds forward as new messages received and sent. The possible evolutions of an inbox game form a directed graph, and the *Inbox* script is a straightforward linearization of this directed graph. An Ink representation of an inbox game, on the other hand, has little choice but to loop back on itself in order to implement response choice and multithreading. Every [Reconsider] action must point back to its parent email, and every sent email must return to the inbox. For an inbox game, this is inessential complexity, as the simpler structure of the *Inbox* script demonstrates.

## 5    Future Work

### 5.1    Planned Language Extensions

The current implementation of *Inbox* was intended to include the minimum set of functionality needed to tell stories with a threaded inbox. We avoided adding a relatively important feature to our first prototype: at present, scene selection is the only way of influencing the story's state. Text, actions, and scenes cannot depend on choices the player made more than one choice in the past, and message threads cannot influence one another. An earlier prototype included such state-manipulation primitives, and we removed them in the interest of creating a "minimum viable product" in which a context collapse experience was emergently generated by multithreaded conversation. However, we came to the conclusion that this restriction is probably too limiting in the long run.

A natural extension of our language and implementation is to allow choices to be enabled or disabled, and allow message delivery to be blocked, based on whether users have received or viewed certain scenes. This simple mechanism adds an enormous amount of expressive power, as demonstrated by Ink's similar functionality of automatically supporting conditional tests on whether the player has seen any named piece of content. For example, this feature would grant enough expressive power to gate scenes on the user having reached a certain point in multiple conversations across multiple threads. It would not be difficult to support arbitrarily complex state tracking, giving threads and scenes the same expressive affordances as storylets, but our current approach is to grow the language conservatively, driven by authorial need.

In addition, the consequences of any particular action are always delayed by exactly one player action, as described in Sect. 4.2. We plan to implement a more general set of message delay controls, including delaying for any number of player actions, delaying until some condition is set in the global state, and delaying for specified wall-clock time (as in *Grayscale*'s approach).

## 5.2 Tool Evaluation

In the future, we plan to more formally evaluate *Inbox*'s expressiveness by authoring additional case study examples in *Inbox* and using quantitative code complexity measures to compare equivalent implementations in tools like Twine and Ink. Further, we plan to conduct a human subjects evaluation through a game jam and subsequent developer survey.

## 6   Conclusion

In this paper, we defined a class of games called inbox games, citing several examples and identifying poetic relations between form and function in these games. We describe an implementation of a novel authoring language for inbox games and demonstrate how it supports key formal elements of the genre.

Our analytical process identifies that the epistolary diagetic framing and use of familiar digital interfaces lend themselves particularly well to ICIDS 2021's conference theme of [Re|Dis]Connection. Specifically, these games explore narrative themes of digitally mediated intimacy, isolation, surveillance, and context collapse. We posit that these narrative themes are especially relevant today in a world of global (though inequitably distributed) internet connectivity and global pandemic, and our work contributes an effort to support technical forms that assist storytellers with adopting these themes more effectively.

## References

1. 3 Minute Games: Lifeline (2015). https://www.3minute.games/
2. Accidental Queens: A normal lost phone (2017). https://anormallostphone.com/
3. Aconite Studios: HoloVista (2020). http://www.aconite.co/holovista/
4. Barlow, S.: Her story (2015). http://www.herstorygame.com/
5. Bogost, I.: Persuasive Games: The Expressive Power of Videogames. MIT Press, Cambridge (2010)
6. Burnham, B.: Inside (2021)
7. Butcher, S.H., et al.: The Poetics of Aristotle. Macmillan, London (1907)
8. Davis, J.L., Jurgenson, N.: Context collapse: theorizing context collusions and collisions. Inf. Commun. Soc. **17**(4), 476–485 (2014)

9. Hardesty, L.: 3Q: D. Fox Harrell on his video game for the #MeToo era. MIT News (2018). https://news.mit.edu/2018/3q-d-fox-harrell-video-game-metoo-sexual-misconduct-0119
10. Harrell, D.F., Ortiz, P., Downs, P., Wagoner, M., Carré, E., Wang, A.: Chimeria: Grayscale: an interactive narrative for provoking critical reflection on gender discrimination. MATLIT: Materialidades da Literatura 6(2), 217–221 (2018)
11. Iacovides, I., Cox, A., Kennedy, R., Cairns, P., Jennett, C.: Removing the HUD: the impact of non-diegetic game elements and expertise on player involvement. In: Proceedings of the 2015 Annual Symposium on Computer-Human Interaction in Play, pp. 13–22 (2015)
12. The ink narrative scripting language. Inkle Studios (2021). https://www.inklestudios.com/ink/, version 1.0.0
13. Jane, F.: Untangling Twine: a platform study. In: DiGRA 3913 - Proceedings of the 2013 DiGRA International Conference: DeFragging Game Studies, August 2014
14. Jod: 13 minutes of light (2016). https://jod.itch.io/13-minutes-of-light
15. Kreminski, M., Wardrip-Fruin, N.: Sketching a map of the storylets design space. In: Rouse, R., Koenitz, H., Haahr, M. (eds.) ICIDS 2018. LNCS, vol. 11318, pp. 160–164. Springer, Cham (2018). https://doi.org/10.1007/978-3-030-04028-4_14
16. Love, C.: Digital: A love story. Love Conquers All Games (2010). https://scoutshonour.com/digital/
17. Love, C.: don't take it personally, babe, it just ain't your story. Love Conquers All Games (2011). https://scoutshonour.com/donttakeitpersonallybabeitjustaintyourstory/
18. Lucero, L.: Safe spaces in online places: social media and LGBTQ youth. Multicult. Educ. Rev. 9(2), 117–128 (2017)
19. Marwick, A.E., Boyd, D.: I tweet honestly, i tweet passionately: Twitter users, context collapse, and the imagined audience. New Media Soc. 13(1), 114–133 (2011)
20. Mawhorter, P., Mateas, M., Wardrip-Fruin, N., Jhala, A.: Towards a theory of choice poetics. In: Proceedings of the 9th International Conference on Foundations of Digital Games (2014)
21. McCoy, J., Treanor, M., Samuel, B., Mateas, M., Wardrip-Fruin, N.: Prom week: social physics as gameplay. In: Proceedings of the 6th International Conference on Foundations of Digital Games, pp. 319–321 (2011)
22. Medin, D.L., Wattenmaker, W.D., Hampson, S.E.: Family resemblance, conceptual cohesiveness, and category construction. Cogn. Psychol. 19(2), 242–279 (1987)
23. Reed, A.: 18 Cadence (2014). http://aaronareed.net/18-cadence/
24. Rettberg, J.W.: Email novel. The Johns Hopkins Guide to Digital Media, pp. 178–79 (2014)
25. Rotunno, L.: User IDs: email novels and the search for identity. A/B: Auto/Biogr. Stud. 21(1), 70–82 (2006)
26. Short, E.: Games of coauthorship. Emily Short's blog (online) (2015). https://emshort.blog/2015/01/14/games-of-co-authorship/
27. Short, E., Daly, L.: First draft of the revolution (2012). https://www.inklestudios.com/firstdraft/
28. Squinkifer, D.: Tentacles growing everywhere (2015). https://squinky.itch.io/tentacles
29. Tosca, S.P.: A pragmatics of links. In: Proceedings of the eleventh ACM on Hypertext and hypermedia, pp. 77–84 (2000)
30. Whitethorn Games: We should talk. Whitethorn (2020). https://whitethorndigital.com/we-should-talk

# A Plan-Based Formal Model of Character Regret

Martin Martinelli and Justus Robertson(✉)

College of Computing and Software Engineering, Kennesaw State University,
Kennesaw, USA
mmart248@students.kennesaw.edu, justus.robertson@kennesaw.edu

**Abstract.** Regret is an important emotion in narrative. It is often built into backstories, influences character arcs, and motivates action. Regret is also an important emotion for interactive stories. While linear narratives allow audiences to empathize with and understand characters through their feelings of regret, an interactive context allows participants to feel regret about their own actions and influence on events. A formal model of regret will allow automated interactive storytellers to identify and generate situations where characters, including the participant, feel regret about an action or outcome. To this end, we introduce a formal narrative planning-based model of regret based on character goals and choice. Using our model, we show how character regret is identified in the context of an example dilemma. Finally, we enumerate and discuss types of regret the model has not yet formalized.

**Keywords:** AI planning · Formal models of narrative · Regret

## 1 Introduction

The feeling of regret is central to many different types of stories. For example, remorse and regret of past choices or mistakes provides the background and motivation to change for many characters in redemptive arcs, like Darth Vader in the *Star Wars* [15] saga. Regret can also prompt non-redemptive character growth, like Kevin McCallister in *Home Alone* [7] who comes to appreciate his family after regretting a wish that they would disappear. Sometimes characters feel a sense of loss and regret about an outcome even when they are happy with and confident about their past choices, like Mia and Sebastian in *La La Land* [5]. In addition to empathizing with characters in linear stories, regret is amplified in interactive narrative contexts where participants can regret their own actions and influence on story events and outcomes [17]. A formal model of regret would allow linear and interactive narrative systems to identify, reason about, and generate situations that produce regret for narrative characters and human participants. In this paper, we present a formal model of *commissive* character regret in the context of *explicit, discrete* choices in plan-based narratives.

© Springer Nature Switzerland AG 2021
A. Mitchell and M. Vosmeer (Eds.): ICIDS 2021, LNCS 13138, pp. 107–117, 2021.
https://doi.org/10.1007/978-3-030-92300-6_10

Our model is based on narrative AI planning and identifies regret using character goals and choice actions. The plan-based choices our model uses have *explicit* framings and outcomes. They also have a *discrete* number of choice options. Psychological work has identified regret can arise through either action or inaction that results in an unfavorable outcome [10]. Regret caused by an action is called *commissive* and regret caused by inaction is called *omissive*. Our model focuses on commissive regret, which is caused by the character's past actions. Regret arises from a counterfactual reasoning process that compares the current situation to an alternate possible world where the reasoner took a different past action and received a more favorable outcome. For example, a commonly reported regret is not finishing college or graduate school [10]. To identify this regret, the person reflects on the time in their life they stopped pursuing education and imagines their life if they had instead continued. They imagine the fulfillment or opportunities they would have and feel regret about their decision to stop. Similarly, our model works by identifying when character actions make a goal they have in the story world unachievable along with an alternate possible world where the goal is achieved or still possible.

We begin by discussing related work in narrative planning, choice poetics, and the study of regret. We then introduce our formalism and model mechanics. We give an example of the mechanics using a dilemma based on the film *La La Land*. Finally, we discuss situations in which characters may feel regret that are not currently supported by our formalization.

## 2    Related Work

This section provides background on narrative planning, choice poetics, and non-computational approaches to studying regret. We begin with narrative planning, which is the computational paradigm our model is built in.

### 2.1    Narrative Planning

AI planning is a popular approach to computationally modeling and generating linear and interactive narratives [39]. AI planners generate narratives by solving a planning problem, which requires sequencing character actions from an initial world representation to a conclusion provided by the problem author. However, off-the-shelf planners have no ability to reason about narrative-specific structures [38] and can produce simplistic or counter-intuitive stories. Over the years, work has focused on increasing the richness of plan-based narrative representations as well as making narrative planning systems more robust and efficient.

Much of the representation work has focused on allowing characters to act believably and enriching how the generated narratives are told. Many plan-based narrative systems focus on generating plot, which are the abstract events of the story, or discourse, which is how the plot is communicated to an audience. Representational advancements include modeling character plot-level goals and intentions [22], modeling and generating plot and discourse-level suspense [1,9],

sequencing discourse-level camera shots to convey plot [13], modelling conflicting characters goals [34], personality [2], and character beliefs [6]. Work has also
been done to make narrative planning more efficient, moving from partial order
planning to off-the-shelf compilations [12], multi-agent planning [33], and heuristic planning methods [36]. In this paper, we show how an intentional narrative
planning model can be further extended to identify commissive character regret.

In addition to linear narratives, our model could be applied to identifying
regret in real-world data sets and real-time participant regret in interactive narrative systems. Symbolic narrative structures have been used to tell stories in
real-world domains [3, 14, 26]. Narrative planning and plan structures have also
been used for generating interactive stories [20, 21, 23, 25, 27, 28, 31, 35] in a number of mediums [24, 29, 30, 37]. Our plan-based model of regret could not only
help to create better narratives in these domains, but also serve as an aspect of
player modeling. Regret has been posed as an important aspect of user experience in interactive narrative domains as part of the study of narrative choices,
*choice poetics*.

## 2.2   Choice Poetics

Choice and action are how we come to understand characters in narratives. It
is especially important in interactive narratives where human participants help
shape the progress of events. A common type of choice is one that is *explicit* and
*discrete*, meaning the choice is clearly presented to a character with very specific
possible actions and outcomes. These choices can be defined as containing a
*framing*, *options*, and an *outcome*. A frame is the context or situation in which
the choice is made, the options are the possible actions the character can choose
between, and the outcome is the situation that results from the chosen action.
This choice structure is the basis for *choice poetics* [17,18], a formalization of
ways in which choices can have meaning for a player in an interactive story.
Choice poetics identifies regret as a dimension of player experience important
to players in a branching narrative. In this paper, we build a plan-based model
of character regret for explicit and discrete choices that could be applied to
system and human-controlled narrative characters. Additionally, choice poetics
has led to a number of empirical evaluations that test how choice structures
and outcomes impact player psychology [4,8,16]. Regret has also been studied
empirically by psychologists and a robust model of regret in narrative contexts
could be evaluated with human subject tests.

## 2.3   Regret

In psychology literature, regret is viewed as a "counterfactual emotion". This
means regret arises from a comparison between a real-world outcome and a
counterfactual possible world where a more favorable outcome was reached [32].
Additionally, regret can be felt over the short or long-term and stems from acts
of *omission* or *commission* [11]. Omissive regret stems from actions never taken,
like never learning to speak a second language. Commissive regret from a taken

action, like ordering a bad dish at a restaurant. In this paper, we establish a plan-based model of commissive narrative character regret. Our model establishes regret over a narrative interval by identifying a choice action, outcome, character goal, and counterfactual outcome that produce commissive regret. We give a *La La Land* example to show this process in the context of a particular type of choice called a dilemma. A dilemma is a type of choice structure where each choice option leads to an undesirable outcome for the character [16]. In the next section, we introduce our plan-based model of regret.

# 3    Plan-Based Regret Model

In this section, we give a technical description of intentional narrative planning and present our regret model. We begin by introducing planning, which serves as our narrative world and action model. We give formal and detailed descriptions of narrative planning mechanics as a base to build our regret model.

## 3.1    Intentional Planning

Intentional narrative planning [22] is similar to off-the-shelf AI planning, but includes modifications that allow the planner to reason about character intentions. As a result, intentional planners never add actions to the story unless they are motivated by a character goal. Intentional planners use a first-order logic language, similar to the Planning Domain Definition Language [19] (PDDL). PDDL is a first-order logic language with constant symbols called *objects*, relation symbols called *predicates*, and variable symbols. An intentional planning problem is represented with the tuple $\Pi = \langle S_0, G_a, G_c, \mathcal{O} \rangle$ where $S_0$ is a set of ground atoms called the *initial state*, $G_a$ is a closed formula called the *author goal*, $G_c$ is a set of ground atoms associated with story characters that represent *character goals*, and $\mathcal{O}$ is a set of *action operators*. The initial state and operators form a state machine of world configurations connected by possible character actions.

**Definition 1.** *Initial State* - A *state* is a snapshot of the story world at a particular time. The *initial state*, $S_0$, is a snapshot of the story world at the start of the story. It is represented by a set of logical statements, called atoms, that describe how the story world is configured.

Plans are a series of actions that transform the initial state into a goal state. The goal allows a human author to specify how the generated narrative will end.

**Definition 2.** *Author Goal* - $G_a$ describes a set of state configurations where the author wants the story to end. The planning problem is solved if a story state is reached that satisfies the author's goal specification.

In addition to the author goal, intentional planning allows individual story characters to have, set, and work towards their own individual goals. These character goals do not have to be achieved in order for an author goal to be reached and the story to end.

**Definition 3.** *Character Goals* - $G_c$ is a set of state literals indexed to story characters that describe aspects of the story world state that different characters want to be true or false.

Finally, characters can act in the story world and change the state by taking actions described by operators. Each operator $o = \langle l_o, p_o, e_o, c_o \rangle \in \mathcal{O}$ consists of a unique name or label $l$, a conjunctive set of first-order literal *preconditions* $p$, a conjunctive set of first-order literal *effects* $e$, and a set of characters that must consent to the action being taken. The set of free variables that occur in an operator's preconditions and effects are called the operator's *parameters*.

**Definition 4.** *Action Operators* - $\mathcal{O}$ is a set of templates used by characters to take action and change the story world. If an action's preconditions $p_o$ are true in a state, the action can be taken by a character. When an action is taken, a new state is created by making the action's effects $e_o$ true.

In order for actions to be performed by story characters, operators with parameters must first be *grounded* by substituting concrete objects, which represent story world characters, things, and locations, for operator parameters. A series of grounded actions is a trajectory through the narrative world state machine that is called a *world history*.

**Definition 5.** *World History* - $h_n$ is a series of story character actions and resulting states that leads from the initial state $S_0$ to the current state $s_n$. This represents everything done in the story world from the start of the story to a particular state. The *length*, $n$, of the history corresponds to how many actions it contains. A world history leads to a current state, $s_n$, which is the $n$th and final state in the trajectory.

Next, we define aspects of the model needed to identify commission-based character regret in the context of intentional narrative plans using counterfactual reasoning and character goals.

## 3.2   Regret Model

Character goals allow intentional planners to restrict narrative plans to only contain actions that are motivated by something the character wants to happen in the world. They are useful for ruling out possible stories where characters act against their own interests. However, not all character goals have to be achieved in order for an author goal to be satisfied and the narrative planning problem to be solved. This aspect of intentional planning, along with counterfactual possible worlds reasoning, is used to plan for narrative conflict between characters [36]. Here, we use character goals and counterfactual reasoning to identify situations where characters will feel commissive regret. It begins by identifying when a character action leads to a portion of the narrative state space where one of their goals becomes *inaccessible*.

**Definition 6.** *Accessibility* - A literal is accessible from a given state $s$ if a sequence of character actions exists that can make the literal true. Conversely, a literal is *inaccessible* from state $s$ if no possible sequence of character actions can make the literal true.

A character $c$ will feel commission-based regret with regard to one of their character goals $g$ if a choice they make leads to $g$ becoming inaccessible when it otherwise would remain accessible or be fulfilled. For this to happen, there must be an *inciting action* and an *alternate action* that leads to an *alternate possible world* where $g$ is still accessible or true.

**Definition 7.** *Inciting Action* - An inciting action $a$ for character $c$ to feel commission regret about character goal $g$ is one such that $g$ is accessible from every state before $a$ in the world history but inaccessible from every state after $a$.

An inciting action is the decision made that directly makes a desired outcome inaccessible in the future. For this action to be part of a choice, there must also be an alternate action where the goal remains accessible.

**Definition 8.** *Alternate Action* - Given an inciting action $a$ performed in state $s$ by character $c$ that produces commission regret about character goal $g$, there must be an alternate action $a^*$ that is also enabled for $c$ in $s$. To be an alternate action, $a^*$ must produce an alternate possible world where $g$ remains accessible.

This alternate action produces an alternate possible world where the character's goal can still be achieved or is true.

**Definition 9.** *Alternate Possible World* - Given a world history $h_n$ that leads to a state $s_n$, an alternate possible world $s_n^*$ is a state reached by a world history $h_n^*$ of the same length as $h_n$, starting from the same initial state $S_0$, and using actions from the same operator set $\mathcal{O}$.

This alternate possible world provides the counterfactual evidence needed to produce the feeling of regret. Together, we can now identify a class of explicit, discrete choices that produce commission-based regret with respect to a particular character goal due to the character's choice making the goal irrevocably unachievable.

**Definition 10.** *Commission-Based Regret Choice* - A choice produces commissive regret for character $c$ with respect to a character goal $g$ in any state following $s_i$ in a world history $h_n$ if there exists an inciting action $a_i \in h_n$ performed by $c$ where $g$ is accessible in every state before $s_i$ but is inaccessible in every state after $s_i$. Additionally, there must exist an alternate action $a_i^*$ that $c$ could have taken in $s_i$ to produce alternate possible history $h_n^*$ such that $g$ is accessible or achieved in every state $s \in h_n^*$.

This type of choice will create commission-based regret for character $c$ with respect to their goal $g$ in every state after $s_i$, because their goal will never become true as a result of the action $a_i$. Additionally, there is at least one alternative action $c$ could have taken in state $s_i$ to keep their goal $g$ accessible in the future. In the next section we illustrate these mechanics with an example dilemma based on the film *La La Land*.

## 4  Example

To illustrate our model we use an example dilemma from the film *La La Land* [5]. The film is in Los Angeles and is about an unlikely relationship between an aspiring actress, Mia, and jazz pianist, Sebastian. At the start of the film, Mia is struggling to begin her career while Sebastian dreams of owning his own jazz club. Near the end of the story, Mia is offered a breakout acting role in Paris. Sebastian encourages her to follow her dream while he works to build his jazz club. The two pursue and ultimately attain their dream careers, but lose touch with one another in the process. For our purposes, we will treat this situation as an explicit dilemma for Mia, with a choice between pursuing a career on her own or staying with Sebastian. A dilemma is a type of choice structure where each option leads to an undesirable outcome for the character [16]. No matter what Mia chooses, she has one positive and one negative outcome. Pursuing her career has the explicit outcome of not ending up with Sebastian and staying together has the outcome of not attaining her dream career. Either Mia finishes the story with her relationship with Sebastian or her career, but not both.

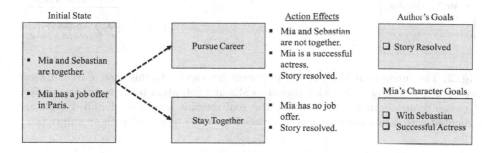

**Fig. 1.** A formalization of Mia's dilemma.

## 4.1  Setup

We use a simple planning problem to characterize the example dilemma. The problem begins with an initial state where Mia and Sebastian are together in Los Angeles and Mia has a job offer in Paris. A lone choice exists from the initial state. Mia chooses to either stay together or pursue her career. As a result of staying in the relationship, Mia will be with Sebastian but will not become a successful actress. As a result of pursuing her career, Mia will be a successful actress but will not be with Sebastian. Figure 1 illustrates the dilemma setup. It shows the initial state, the two possible actions and their effects, the author's goal, and Mia's two character goals.

## 4.2   Result

No matter what Mia decides, our model predicts she will experience regret with respect to one of her character goals. If Mia chooses to stay in the relationship she will not be a successful actress, so staying in the relationship is an inciting action. Additionally, there is an alternate action where she pursues her career which produces an alternate possible world where she becomes a successful actress. Our model identifies that Mia will regret not becoming a successful actress with respect to her decision to stay in the relationship. Conversely, if Mia chooses to pursue her career she will not be with Sebastian, so pursuing her career is an inciting action. Additionally, there is an alternate action where she stays in the relationship which produces the outcome the she and Sebastian are still together. Our model identifies that Mia will regret not being with Sebastian with respect to her decision to pursue her career. This outcome is illustrated in Fig. 2.

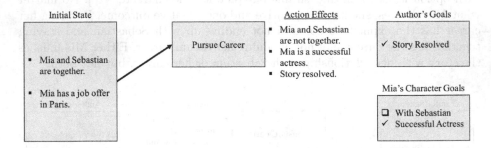

**Fig. 2.** The outcome of Mia's choice to pursue her career. In this case, *Pursue Career* becomes the inciting action with regard to Mia and Sebastian being together and *Stay Together* is an alternate action where the goal remains accessible. Fulfilled goals are indicated with a check-mark while unsatisfied goals are indicated with an empty box.

## 5   Conclusion

In this paper, we present a plan-based model of regret. This model identifies commission-based narrative structures that produce feelings of regret in the context of discrete, explicit choice structures. Regret is an important aspect of the human condition and factors into many narratives, especially as a motivator for character arcs and change, so the ability to systematically identify when characters feel regret about their decisions and narrative outcomes is an important step towards a larger, more complete formal model of narrative.

# References

1. Bae, B.-C., Young, R.M.: A use of flashback and foreshadowing for surprise arousal in narrative using a plan-based approach. In: Spierling, U., Szilas, N. (eds.) ICIDS 2008. LNCS, vol. 5334, pp. 156–167. Springer, Heidelberg (2008). https://doi.org/10.1007/978-3-540-89454-4_22
2. Bahamón, J.C., Barot, C., Young, R.M.: A goal-based model of personality for planning-based narrative generation. In: Twenty-Ninth AAAI Conference on Artificial Intelligence (2015)
3. Barot, C., et al.: Bardic: generating multimedia narrative reports for game logs. In: Proceedings of the 10th Workshop on Intelligent Narrative Technologies at the 13th AAAI Conference on Artificial Intelligence and Interactive Digital Entertainment (2017)
4. Cardona-Rivera, R.E., Robertson, J., Ware, S.G., Harrison, B., Roberts, D.L., Young, R.M.: Foreseeing meaningful choices. In: AAAI Conference on Artificial Intelligence and Interactive Digital Entertainment, vol. 10, pp. 9–15 (2014)
5. Chazelle, D.: La La Land (2016)
6. Christensen, M., Nelson, J., Cardona-Rivera, R.: Using domain compilation to add belief to narrative planners. In: AAAI Conference on Artificial Intelligence and Interactive Digital Entertainment, vol. 16, pp. 38–44 (2020)
7. Columbus, C.: Home alone (1990)
8. Fendt, M.W., Harrison, B., Ware, S.G., Cardona-Rivera, R.E., Roberts, D.L.: Achieving the illusion of agency. In: Oyarzun, D., Peinado, F., Young, R.M., Elizalde, A., Méndez, G. (eds.) ICIDS 2012. LNCS, vol. 7648, pp. 114–125. Springer, Heidelberg (2012). https://doi.org/10.1007/978-3-642-34851-8_11
9. Fendt, M.W., Young, R.M.: Leveraging intention revision in narrative planning to create suspenseful stories. IEEE Trans. Comput. Intell. AI Games 9(4), 381–392 (2016)
10. Gilovich, T., Medvec, V.H.: The experience of regret: what, when, and why. Psychol. Rev. 102(2), 379 (1995)
11. Gilovich, T., Medvec, V.H., Kahneman, D.: Varieties of regret: a debate and partial resolution. Psychol. Rev. 105(3), 602 (1998)
12. Haslum, P.: Narrative panning: compilations to classical planning. J. Artif. Intell. Res. 44, 383–395 (2012)
13. Jhala, A., Young, R.M.: Cinematic cisual discourse: representation, generation, and evaluation. IEEE Trans. Comput. Intell. AI Games 2(2), 69–81 (2010)
14. Kokkinakis, A.V., et al.: DAX: data-driven audience experiences in esports. In: ACM International Conference on Interactive Media Experiences, IMX 2020, pp. 94–105. Association for Computing Machinery, New York (2020)
15. Lucas, G.: Star Wars: Episode IV - A New Hope (1977)
16. Mawhorter, P., Mateas, M., Wardrip-Fruin, N.: Generating relaxed, obvious, and dilemma choices with Dunyazad. In: AAAI Conference on Artificial Intelligence and Interactive Digital Entertainment, pp. 58–64 (2015)
17. Mawhorter, P., Mateas, M., Wardrip-Fruin, N., Jhala, A.: Towards a theory of choice poetics. In: International Conference on the Foundations of Digital Games. ACM (2014)
18. Mawhorter, P., Zegura, C., Gray, A., Jhala, A., Mateas, M., Wardrip-Fruin, N.: Choice poetics by example. In: Arts, vol. 7, p. 47. Multidisciplinary Digital Publishing Institute (2018)

19. McDermott, D., et al.: PDDL - the planning domain definition language. Technical report CVC TR98003/DCSTR1165, Yale Center for Computational Vision and Control (1998)
20. Miller, C., Dighe, M., Martens, C., Jhala, A.: Crafting interactive narrative games with adversarial planning agents from simulations. In: Bosser, A.-G., Millard, D.E., Hargood, C. (eds.) ICIDS 2020. LNCS, vol. 12497, pp. 44–57. Springer, Cham (2020). https://doi.org/10.1007/978-3-030-62516-0_4
21. Ramirez, A., Bulitko, V.: Automated planning and player modeling for interactive storytelling. IEEE Trans. Comput. Intell. AI Games **7**(4), 375–386 (2014)
22. Riedl, M.O., Young, R.M.: Narrative planning: balancing plot and character. J. Artif. Intell. Res. **39**, 217–268 (2010)
23. Riedl, M.O., Bulitko, V.: Interactive narrative: an intelligent systems approach. AI Mag. **34**(1), 67 (2013)
24. Robertson, J., Cardona-Rivera, R.E., Young, R.M.: Invisible dynamic mechanic adjustment in virtual reality games. In: IEEE International Conference on Artificial Intelligence and Virtual Reality, pp. 282–289. IEEE (2020)
25. Robertson, J., Jhala, A., Young, R.M.: Efficient choice enumeration for narrative world design. In: International Conference on the Foundations of Digital Games, pp. 1–10 (2019)
26. Robertson, J., et al.: Wait, but why?: assessing behavior explanation strategies for real-time strategy games. In: 26th International Conference on Intelligent User Interfaces, IUI 2021, pp. 32–42. Association for Computing Machinery, New York (2021)
27. Robertson, J., Young, R.M.: Finding Schrödinger's gun. In: Proceedings of the AAAI Conference on Artificial Intelligence and Interactive Digital Entertainment, pp. 153–159 (2014)
28. Robertson, J., Young, R.M.: Gameplay as on-line mediation search. In: Proceedings of the AAAI Artificial Intelligence and Interactive Digital Entertainment Conference, pp. 42–48 (2014)
29. Robertson, J., Young, R.M.: Automated gameplay generation from declarative world representations. In: Proceedings of the AAAI Artificial Intelligence and Interactive Digital Entertainment Conference, pp. 72–78 (2015)
30. Robertson, J., Young, R.M.: Interactive narrative intervention alibis through domain revision. In: Intelligent Narrative Technologies Workshop at the AAAI Artificial Intelligence and Interactive Digital Entertainment Conference, pp. 49–52 (2015)
31. Robertson, J., Young, R.M.: Perceptual experience management. IEEE Trans. Games **11**(1), 15–24 (2019)
32. Roese, N.J., Morrison, M.: The psychology of counterfactual thinking. Hist. Soc. Res./Historische Sozialforschung 16–26 (2009)
33. Teutenberg, J., Porteous, J.: Efficient intent-based narrative generation using multiple planning agents. In: International Conference on Autonomous Agents and Multi-Agent Systems, pp. 603–610 (2013)
34. Ware, S., Young, R.M.: CPOCL: a narrative planner supporting conflict. In: Proceedings of the AAAI Conference on Artificial Intelligence and Interactive Digital Entertainment (2011)
35. Ware, S.G., Garcia, E.T., Shirvani, A., Farrell, R.: Multi-agent narrative experience management as story graph pruning. In: AAAI Conference on Artificial Intelligence and Interactive Digital Entertainment, vol. 15, pp. 87–93 (2019)

36. Ware, S.G., Young, R.M.: Glaive: a state-space narrative planner supporting intentionality and conflict. In: Proceedings of the 10th AAAI international conference on Artificial Intelligence and Interactive Digital Entertainment, pp. 80–86 (2014). (Awarded Best Student Paper)

37. Ware, S.G., Young, R.M.: Intentionality and conflict in the best laid plans interactive narrative virtual environment. IEEE Trans. Comput. Intell. AI Games **8**(4), 402–411 (2015)

38. Young, R.M.: Notes on the use of plan structures in the creation of interactive plot. In: AAAI Fall Symposium on Narrative Intelligence, pp. 164–167 (1999)

39. Young, R.M., Ware, S.G., Cassell, B.A., Robertson, J.: Plans and planning in narrative generation: a review of plan-based approaches to the generation of story, discourse and interactivity in narratives. Sprache Datenverarbeitung Spec. Issue Formal Comput. Models Narrative **37**(1–2), 41–64 (2013)

# Narraport: Narrative-Based Interactions and Report Generation with Large Datasets

Colin M. Potts$^{(\boxtimes)}$ ⓘ and Arnav Jhala ⓘ

North Carolina State University, Raleigh, NC, USA
{cmpotts,ahjhala}@ncsu.edu

**Abstract.** There is an increasing demand for rapid content filtering in relation to topics like digital forensics for legal cases, cybersecurity, and social media conduct monitoring. While there have been significant advances in algorithms and frameworks for media processing, this task requires an ensemble of tools and algorithms that are not well-understood by human analysts, thereby reducing their trustworthiness. In this paper, we present a novel perspective on this problem through the development of an intelligent system that generates reports from large email datasets in the form of short stories. The stories generated by the system are based on identifiable plot structures in popular media. These structures are used as semantic sensemaking templates to organize data for further filtering and triage. The end-to-end system, accessible through an interactive dashboard, incorporates unsupervised annotation modules (such as speech acts and sentiment), topic discovery, communication network analysis, character personality profiles, and automated text and visualization generators. This emerging application prototype is developed and internally deployed in collaboration with analysts and researchers actively working in this area.

## 1 Introduction

Large amounts of data are currently being produced and stored relating to all aspects of our daily lives. By some estimates, we generate around 2.5 quintillion bytes of data daily spread over social media platforms. This wealth of data is often of great interest to analysts and researchers working on digital forensics in cases where there is data associated with legal cases. The size and scope of data analysis makes this a challenging tasks for analysts working within our legal system. This challenge is intensified further due to the variety of tools that need to be incorporated into the analysis process and their outputs need to be presented in interpretable and verifiable reports for non-experts. For this task analysts need to effectively filter and triage data in order to ensure that retrieve relevant data and are able to succinctly present their analysis results.

In legal cases pertaining to corporate malfeasance, public attorneys and investigators need to work with analysts to triage through large numbers of communications such as email, chat messages, and social media messages to look for evidence. For this task, analysts and researchers develop workflows that incorporate available computational tools to effectively sort through this data. Further, they need to then document and create summary reports for further discussion, integration of segments assigned to multiple analysts, and generation of reports for final outcomes of the investigation [17].

ⓒ Springer Nature Switzerland AG 2021
A. Mitchell and M. Vosmeer (Eds.): ICIDS 2021, LNCS 13138, pp. 118–127, 2021.
https://doi.org/10.1007/978-3-030-92300-6_11

As part of evaluating and building this system we worked extensively with a team comprised of two analysts and two scientists specializing in research supporting analysts. We worked with them for over a year in an iterative development process. Analysis of large datasets where there is not a clear target is an iterative process [22]. This is usually characterized by transitions between high-level exploration followed by a deeper look into elements of interest. This process iteratively leads to more specific filters along different dimensions. For instance, an analyst may want to look at the frequency of emails about a particular topic over time as a temporal chart. Then they identify peaks or valleys in the chart and focus on patterns of email within the month in the neighborhood of these features. Even after this step, they end up with several hundred emails to analyze. From here they could filter by emails that only include senders or receivers at the upper-management level or based on other meta-data such as emails that include attachments. Eventually, the process leads to one or a chain of emails of interest that leads them through the process of discovery of relevant content to their investigation. Finally, they generate a multi-modal (text+charts) report that summarizes their exploration and presents items or patterns of interest with justifications for them.

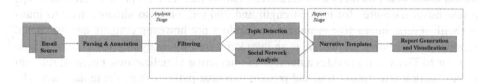

**Fig. 1.** A pipeline for the storytelling with data paradigm from emails sources.

This paper describes two contributions with respect to AI support for analysts. First, we describe the integration of a pipeline (see Fig. 1) of established AI tools and algorithms in the workflow for analysts. Second, we present a novel idea for automatically filtering data and generating reports that are constructed with narrative frames that are instantiated based on constraints satisfied by trends and relationships in the underlying data. These narrative frames encode a number of recognizable data patterns that can be presented as stories from the dataset.

We tested our system on both the Enron [12] dataset (about $500K$ emails) and the Avocado Research Email Collection (closer to $1M$ emails) [16]. The Enron scandal [18] was a well-known corporate collapse with corresponding investigation. Avocado was an information technology software and services firm developing products for the mobile internet market, operating from the late 1990s to the middle of the first decade of the 21st century. We used this collection extensively in our work with analysts but the license prohibits most sharing of information about the dataset.

Our system uses an assortment of existing NLP and social network analysis techniques to analyze our email datasets. The key dynamic we are seeking to capture is the relationship between users over time. This will allow us to identify patterns of change that correspond to narrative patterns that we can exploit later. We parse the dataset and store as a directed hyper-graph where nodes are email addresses and edges are messages. There are other representations that afford better performance depending on the desired metric [7], but in terms of application to narrative patterns we leave this to further research. There are many topics of discussion in a large organization. An important filter for emails in this dataset is based on relevance of messages and message threads by topics. For topic modeling we use Latent Dirichlet Analysis (LDA) [4]. We further extend the LDA model used in this paper, following the work of TIARA [13], to compute topic strength over time. This allows analysts to filter emails based on topic across different time frames through an interactive interface. For social network analysis, we use graph based measures over the graph of all email address units in the dataset. These include in/out degree and proximity prestige, where these different measures offer different views of the social network [21].

## 2 Related Work

This work builds on a basis of natural language processing and social network analysis algorithms. These are rich areas of research. We present a system for using currently popular techniques and algorithms to generate automated reports. The field of automated email analysis includes interactive systems like TIARA [13]. TIARA develops a few novel measures for topic strength and ranking, but also allows a user to interact with several interactive visualizations. It does not however, contain any automated reporting capabilities. Bardic [2] is an interactive tool for analyzing video game relays. Similar to TIARA, it provides a number of interactive visualizations, but most relevant to this work it attempts to find and present narrative patterns from the replay data. The approach is similar in that it uses a decomposition planner to match and apply narrative templates. Unlike Bardic, we externally solve for story patterns then use the planner to exclusively solve the corresponding presentation plan. Sultan *et al.* [11] use a hierarchical deep-learning approach to automatically generate narrative captions for images. Battad and Si [3] also do co-generate of visual plots and narrative captions. Our work is more expansive than either because we do co-generation of complete narrative reports with multiple visual artefacts (as see in Fig. 3).

Vesanto and Hollmén [19] consider the processes of data mining in general, and present an automated system for the generation of preliminary reports. This phase is meant to be followed by interactive analysis. It takes a similar approach in that it begins by generating a number of standard measures over a target data source and presents that information alongside visualizations. The intent of this report is to enable a data miner to further explore and thus is about getting a general understanding of the data source.

Erete *et al.* [8] examine the use of storytelling by non-profit organizations. NPOs use narratives to help engage stakeholders promote causes. McKenna *et al.* [14] did a user study on popular data-driven narratives on the web to determine the effect of different visual encodings. Traditional timelines used for data may not fit ideally with storytelling approaches. Brehmer *et al.* [6] consider this question and explore the additional dimensions that can be explore in narrative. We find this relevant to our work because we present a timeline in our narrative templates based upon detected inflections points in data that we use an story inflection points. An interesting contemporary system is DataShot [20]. Given a tabular data source, the system automatically generates a fact sheet using a number of visual techniques. While we use email data, both systems attempt to create engaging visual artefacts. DataShot does not attempt to create reports however, or use storytelling techniques.

## 3  Identifying Story Elements for Narrative Frames

We provide a representation of narrative patterns in this work with templates that include variables bound through constrained queries to the annotated dataset. First we discuss how to identify these patterns (content selection) and then how to present it (content presentation). Here each narrative pattern has both a recognizable visual pattern in data and a rhetorical strategy for presentation. The key elements in a story are the setting, characters, plot, and resolution state or outcome. We can define the setting in this work as a temporal interval of interest given by the analyst. We define characters as email accounts along with their personalities (features such as verbosity, sentiment, influence, etc.). Finally we have a representation of basic plot patterns in Table 1.

We want to identify people who have influence over topics, groups of people, events, email volume, and others. We can compute these measures by combining topics and social graphs. We also want to compute relationships, this is primarily achieved by looking at email volume between small sets (e.g., pairs, triples, clusters). We use an annotation scheme similar to Battad *et al.* [3] to represent numeric measures. This involves identifying minima/maxima of a given measure over time. This corresponds to the visual features of a measure when plotted [10] and we show how these correlated to narrative patterns. These local minima/maxima are annotated with local intervals. Patterns then are describe as constraints over these descriptors. To communicate these patterns using stories, we then look at how they evolve over time. Note that even if the measures do not change, we can still potentially match against common tropes. Patterns can also be applied at varying scales. For instance, to introduce a person into a report we could use the *rags to riches* pattern (more details below). Alternatively, we could use the same pattern over the entire report to focus on a particular persons gain in influence over the entire time period in question.

Each pattern in this work focuses on an individual or set of people as the "main characters" of the story. The patterns also include aspects related to typical story progression. These include the following (in order) which should correspond to inflection points in the data, namely, Anticipation, Dream, Frustration, Nightmare, and Resolution [5]. These patterns were developed in conjunction with our analyst partners and can be applied not only automatically by the system, but can also be directed by the user interactively. For instance, if while doing a deep-dive a user decides they want more information about a particular entity, they can explicitly search for applicable patterns.

### 3.1  A Selection of Patterns

Now we present a selection of hybrid narrative/data patterns for use in our report generation. These are not meant to be exhaustive but ones that are easily identifiable and relevant to the patterns in our dataset. The representation of stories is in terms of templates with rules that are based on statistical properties of the underlying data. These templates can be nested. Our representation is inspired from early storytelling systems such as James Meehan's Tale-Spin [15] that incorporated a set of heuristic rules over a knowledge base of predicates about the world to create sequences of actions for characters based on logical inference over STRIPS-style operators [9].

For instance, the *rags to riches* pattern discussed later can be used to frame a entire report as one person gaining influence, or to introduce a communicative partner. The system reasons over these templates to ensure that all parties discussed are properly introduced. The sample patterns are named for their narrative counterparts. Five of the patters are described below with the corresponding rules presented in Table 1.

**Table 1.** Details of narrative templates. Here "Person" refers to any email addresses with email volume above a given threshold. A "relative set" is one or more other email addresses above the same threshold. A measure $f$ is either message volume (total or by topic) or an influence proxy. "Introduce", "Visualize", "Highlight", and "Contrast" correspond to presentation plans. The constraints correspond directly to visuals that will be inserted into the final reports and the presentation plans are partial plans to be solved by the discourse planner.

| Pattern name | Parameters | Constraints | Presentation Plan |
|---|---|---|---|
| Rags to riches | Person $p$<br>Measure $f$<br>Relative Set $r$<br>Intervals $t_0, t_{max}$,<br>$t_{min}, t_e$ | $t_0 < t_{max} < t_{min} < t_e$<br>$f_p < avg(f_r)$ over $t_0$<br>$t_{max}$ contains a local maxima<br>$t_{min}$ contains a local minima<br>$f_p > avg(f_r)$ over $t_e$ | Introduce $p, r, f$<br>Visualize $f_p$ with $avg(f_r)$<br>Highlight $f_p < avg(f_r)$ over $t_0$<br>Foreshadow $f_p > avg(f_r)$ over $t_e$<br>Highlight local maxima $t_{max}$<br>Highlight local minima $t_{max}$<br>Highlight $f_p > avg(f_r)$ over $t_e$ |
| Fall from grace | Person $p$<br>Measure $f$<br>Relative Set $r$<br>Intervals $t_0, t_{min}$,<br>$t_{max}, t_e$ | $t_0 < t_{min} < t_{max} < t_e$<br>$f_p > avg(f_r)$ over $t_0$<br>$t_{min}$ contains a local minima<br>$t_{max}$ contains a local maxima<br>$f_p < avg(f_r)$ over $t_e$ | Introduce $p, f$<br>Visualize $f_p$ with $avg(f_r)$<br>Highlight $f_p > avg(f_r)$ over $t_0$<br>Foreshadow $f_p < avg(f_r)$ over $t_e$<br>Highlight local minima $t_{min}$<br>Highlight local maxima $t_{max}$<br>Highlight $f_p < avg(f_r)$ over $t_e$ |
| Best buddies | Person $a$<br>Person $b$<br>Measure $f$<br>Intervals $t_0, t_{max}$,<br>$t_{min}, t_e$ | $t_0 < t_{max} < t_{min} < t_e$<br>$f_{a,b} < avg(f_{a,b})$ over $t_0$<br>$t_{max}$ contains a local maxima<br>$t_{min}$ contains a local minima<br>$f_{a,b} > avg(f_{a,b})$ over $t_e$ | Introduce $a, b, f$<br>Visualize $f_{a,b}$ with $avg(f_{a,b})$<br>Highlight $f_{a,b} < avg(f_{a,b})$ over $t_0$<br>Foreshadow $f_p > avg(f)$ over $t_e$<br>Highlight local maxima $t_{max}$<br>Highlight local minima $t_{min}$<br>Highlight $f_{a,b} > avg(fa, b)$ over $t_e$ |
| Falling out | Person $a$<br>Person $b$<br>Measure $f$<br>Intervals $t_0, t_{min}$,<br>$t_{max}, t_e$ | $t_0 < t_{min} < t_{max} < t_e$<br>$f_{a,b} > avg(f_{a,b})$ over $t_0$<br>$t_{min}$ contains a local minima<br>$t_{max}$ contains a local maxima<br>$f_{a,b} < avg(f_{a,b})$ over $t_e$ | Introduce $a, b, f$<br>Visualize $f_{a,b}$ with $avg(f_{a,b})$<br>Highlight $f_{a,b} > avg(f_{a,b})$ over $t_0$<br>Foreshadow $f_p < avg(f)$ over $t_e$<br>Highlight local minima $t_{min}$<br>Highlight local maxima $t_{max}$<br>Highlight $f_{a,b} < avg(fa, b)$ over $t_e$ |
| Juxtaposition | Person $a$<br>Person $b$<br>Relative Set $r$<br>Measure $f$<br>Intervals<br>$t_{a,0}, t_{a,max}$,<br>$t_{a,min}, t_{a,e}$<br>$t_{b,0}, t_{b,min}$,<br>$t_{b,max}, t_{b,e}$ | $a, r, f, t_{a,0}, t_{a,max}, t_{a,min}, t_{a,e}$<br>satisfy *rags to riches*<br>$b, r, f, t_{b,0}, t_{b,min}, t_{b,max}, t_{b,e}$<br>satisfy *fall from grace* | Introduce $a, b, r, f$<br>Visualize $f_a$ & $f_b$ with $avg(f_r)$<br>Highlight $f_a < avg(f_r)$ over $t_{a,0}$<br>– Contrast $f_b > avg(f_r)$ over $tb, 0$<br>Foreshadow $f_a > avg(f_r)$ over $t_{a,e}$<br>Foreshadow $f_b < avg(f_r)$ over $t_{b,e}$<br>Highlight local maxima $t_{a,max}$<br>– Contrast local minima $t_{b,minx}$<br>Highlight local minima $t_{a,min}$<br>– Contrast local maxima $t_{b,max}$<br>Highlight $f_a > avg(f_r)$ over $t_{a,e}$<br>– Contrast $f_p > avg(f_r)$ over $t_{a,e}$ |

**Rags to Riches.** We identify a user who along any of several metrics (topic influence, email volume, etc.) shows a dramatic increase. This corresponds to the difference between the user's least and most active periods. We also need to identify at least one inflection point where their influence reaches a relative maximum, followed by a relative minimum, followed by another increase. Next we foreshadow their eventual success in text, followed by a visual representation showing increase from their initial low point. Finally we show their final state making sure to contrast both with the original comparison but also with their initial state. Visually the report keeps the overall graph, showing the entire trajectory, in view. Through use of text templates, the reader is guided to focus on interesting parts of the visual.

**Fall from Grace.** This is the reverse of *rags to riches* and involves the same data conditions in reverse. The presentation largely follows the same pattern both in visual representation in terms of choice of graphs and in textual template descriptions.

**Pairs: Best Buddies.** Here we look for two people in our graph that develop a closer relationship over time. This could also be between an individual and a group. Characterized on mutual email volume both in terms of sent and received emails. We look for patterns where the interaction begins with low volume then builds. Several interesting visualizations are generated to provide details of the relationship such as distribution of topic terms over time, length, frequency, sentiment of emails.

**Pairs: Falling Out.** Opposite of *best buddies* where the relationship appears to diminish over time. This one is a little more challenging to characterize because someone leaving a company often shows this pattern where their emails abruptly stop. As such the presentation accounts for the uncertain nature of the decrease.

**Juxtaposition of Rise and Fall.** This is another common narrative trope where there is a juxtaposition of rise and fall of influence or relationships. This is a meta pattern in that we either recognize a *best buddies* and a *falling out* or a *rags to riches* and a *fall from grace*. This meta pattern then realizes the overall report by correlating the trajectory of both sub-patterns. A single combined visual for both patterns is used as the primary focal point. This includes both data trajectories visual coded to contrast, enabling the reader to draw their inference about the significance of the correlation. This pattern is also visible during internal personnel changes in significant roles.

## 4  Narrative Report Generation

We use narrative planning to implement the patterns described in Table 1. Specifically we use an evolution of the DPOCL [23] algorithm used in the Bardic system [2]. Instead of using a story encoding and letting the planner solve for applicable discourse patterns, we instead pre-identify story patterns then use the planner to solve the partial narrative patterns described. This allows flexibility in the report generation to handle different cases and reason about required introductory text among other concerns.

To illustrate the output of the system we will walk through a specific generated report (Fig. 3) including visualizations and supporting text. Consider the first sub-figure of that report. This shows sent email volume by topic for gerald.nemec@enron.com over time. This visual matches the *rag to riches* pattern. The system might select this from the set of matching *rags to riches* candidates (which also includes elizabeth.sager@enron.com and vince.kaminski@enron.com). The second sub-figure of the report shows sara.shackleton@enron.com fitting the *fall from grace* pattern, which is a common fit for the Enron dataset and includes others such as tana.jones@enron.com and kay.mann@enron.com. An important thing to note, is the the ending time period selected in all these cases correspond exactly with the downfall of Enron (as reported by the New York Times [18] and others). This helps support the idea that points of narrative interest correlate with ones that were selected by human analysts from the dataset.

Since gerald.nemec matches *rags to riches* and sara.shackleton matches *fall from grace*, and both matches use the same measure (sent email volume), together they match the *rise/fall juxtaposition* pattern. Moreover, the sub-intervals also match, simplifying the application of the template. The report begins by introducing each person. This includes presenting summary statistics and any external information (such as job title) and that they both work at Enron. Following their introductions, the report presents a comparison of colleagues with similar communication patterns. Next the report includes a the sub-figures discussed about showing the visual aspect of the selected story patterns. This is followed by expository text mentioning their high and low respective volumes at the beginning, paired with a highlight of the corresponding region in the graphic. The report then foreshadows the rise and fall to come in text highlights changes in the next interval. Finally visualize and describe narrative tension by highlighting how each regresses to their starting point (Fig. 2).

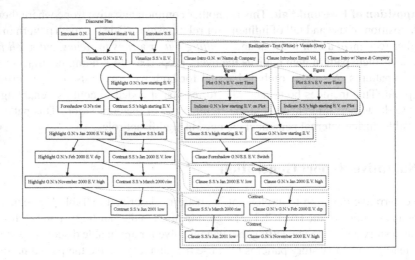

**Fig. 2.** Partial discourse and realization plan for Fig. 3. The story-layer is omitted because we use a modified version of the tripartite model from Barot *et al.* [1,2] where we select a pattern externally from the planner.

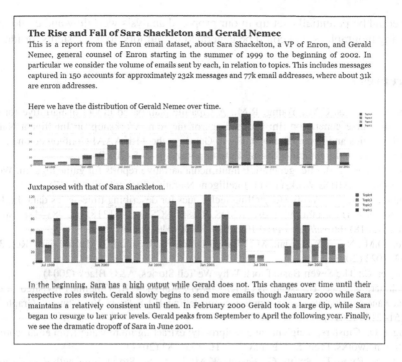

**Fig. 3.** Narrative report generated based on matching story pattern.

## 5   Conclusions and Future Work

We have presented a practical application and workflow with the integration of several AI algorithms to generate narrative reports on large structured datasets. This project has been developed by a team of analysts and researchers to improve the triage and reporting aspects of their tradecraft. For this paper, we focus on the report generation aspect which is challenging as human-analysts are tasked with both sifting through data, collaboration, reporting, and integration of their analysis outcomes. We focused on a rule-based system to map underlying data patterns to narratives about people using an illustrative set of recognizable templates. Narrative presentation, as with any methodology, has the potential to introduce bias and thus should be studied carefully to understand the effects on the conclusions inferred by analysts before deployment. While the representation of these frames is in the form of fixed scripts, the overall approach shows promise based on feedback from analysts. We are exploring future work in terms of rigorous formal representations of narratives as discourse plans with specific communicative goals that would seamlessly integrate narrative, visuals, and linguistic descriptions in the generation process. Several narrative representations are of interest to us including plot units, plot graphs, and classical plan-based ones. While we have shown the use case of legal investigative analysis through the Enron corpus, other applications such as reports based on analysis of research paper topics over time within an area in terms of citation networks could be potentially set up in our proposed analysis workflow and could lead to interesting biographies that could be generated for authors, tools, systems, or ideas.

# References

1. Barot, C., Potts, C.M., Young, R.M.: A tripartite plan-based model of narrative for narrative discourse generation. In: Proceedings of the Joint Workshop on Intelligent Narrative Technologies and Social Believability in Games at the 11th AAAI Conference on Artificial Intelligence and Interactive Digital Entertainment, pp. 2–8 (2015)
2. Barot, C., et al.: Bardic: generating multimedia narrative reports for game logs. In: Working Notes of the AIIDE Workshop on Intelligent Narrative Technologies (2017)
3. Battad, Z., Si, M.: Apply storytelling techniques for describing time-series data. In: Rouse, R., Koenitz, H., Haahr, M. (eds.) ICIDS 2018. LNCS, vol. 11318, pp. 483–488. Springer, Cham (2018). https://doi.org/10.1007/978-3-030-04028-4_56
4. Blei, D.M., Ng, A.Y., Jordan, M.I.: Latent Dirichlet allocation. J. Mach. Learn. Res. 3(Jan), 993–1022 (2003)
5. Booker, C.: The Seven Basic Plots: Why We Tell Stories. A&C Black (2004)
6. Brehmer, M., Lee, B., Bach, B., Riche, N.H., Munzner, T.: Timelines revisited: a design space and considerations for expressive storytelling. IEEE Trans. Vis. Comput. Graph. 23(9), 2151–2164 (2017)
7. Engel, O.: Clusters, recipients and reciprocity: extracting more value from email communication networks. Proc. Soc. Behav. Sci. 10, 172–182 (2011)
8. Erete, S., Ryou, E., Smith, G., Fassett, K.M., Duda, S.: Storytelling with data: examining the use of data by non-profit organizations. In: Proceedings of the 19th ACM Conference on Computer-Supported Cooperative Work & Social Computing, CSCW 2016, pp. 1273–1283. Association for Computing Machinery, New York (2016)
9. Fikes, R.E., Nilsson, N.J.: STRIPS: a new approach to the application of theorem proving to problem solving. Artif. Intell. 2(3–4), 189–208 (1971)
10. Freeman, H.: Shape description via the use of critical points. Pattern Recogn. 10(3), 159–166 (1978). https://doi.org/10.1016/0031-3203(78)90024-9. https://www.sciencedirect.com/science/article/pii/0031320378900249. The Proceedings of the IEEE Computer Society Conference
11. Nahian, M.S.A., Tasrin, T., Gandhi, S., Gaines, R., Harrison, B.: A hierarchical approach for visual storytelling using image description. In: Cardona-Rivera, R.E., Sullivan, A., Young, R.M. (eds.) ICIDS 2019. LNCS, vol. 11869, pp. 304–317. Springer, Cham (2019). https://doi.org/10.1007/978-3-030-33894-7_30
12. Klimt, B., Yang, Y.: The Enron corpus: a new dataset for email classification research. In: Boulicaut, J.-F., Esposito, F., Giannotti, F., Pedreschi, D. (eds.) ECML 2004. LNCS (LNAI), vol. 3201, pp. 217–226. Springer, Heidelberg (2004). https://doi.org/10.1007/978-3-540-30115-8_22
13. Liu, S., Zhou, M.X., Pan, S., Song, Y., Qian, W., Cai, W., Lian, X.: TIARA: interactive, topic-based visual text summarization and analysis. ACM Trans. Intell. Syst. Technol. (TIST) 3(2), 1–28 (2012)
14. McKenna, S., Henry Riche, N., Lee, B., Boy, J., Meyer, M.: Visual narrative flow: exploring factors shaping data visualization story reading experiences. Comput. Graph. Forum 36(3), 377–387 (2017)
15. Meehan, J.R.: TALE-SPIN, an interactive program that writes stories. In: IJCAI, vol. 77, pp. 91–98 (1977)

16. Oard, D., Webber, W., Kirsch, D.A., Golitsynskiy, S.: Avocado research email collection LDC2015T03. Linguistic Data Consortium, Philadelphia (2015). https://doi.org/10.35111/wqt6-jg60
17. Robertson, J., Harrison, B., Jhala, A.: Interactive summarization for data filtering and triage. In: The Thirty-Third International Flairs Conference (2020)
18. Staff, E.: Timeline: a chronology of Enron corp. New York Times (2006). https://www.nytimes.com/2006/01/18/business/worldbusiness/timeline-a-chronology-of-enron-corp.html
19. Vesanto, J., Hollmén, J.: An automated report generation tool for the data understanding phase. In: Abraham, A., Jain, L., van der Zwaag, B.J. (eds.) Innovations in Intelligent Systems. Studies in Fuzziness and Soft Computing, vol. 140, pp. 203–219. Springer, Heidelberg (2004). https://doi.org/10.1007/978-3-540-39615-4_8
20. Wang, Y., Sun, Z., Zhang, H., Cui, W., Xu, K., Ma, X., Zhang, D.: DataShot: automatic generation of fact sheets from tabular data. IEEE Trans. Vis. Comput. Graph. **26**(1), 895–905 (2020)
21. Wilson, G., Banzhaf, W.: Discovery of email communication networks from the Enron corpus with a genetic algorithm using social network analysis. In: 2009 IEEE Congress on Evolutionary Computation, pp. 3256–3263 (2009)
22. Wongsuphasawat, K., et al.: Voyager 2: augmenting visual analysis with partial view specifications. In: Proceedings of the 2017 CHI Conference on Human Factors in Computing Systems, pp. 2648–2659 (2017)
23. Young, R.M., Pollack, M.E., Moore, J.D.: Decomposition and causality in partial-order planning. In: AIPS, pp. 188–194 (1994)

# Lean-Back Machina: Attention-Based Skippable Segments in Interactive Cinema

Niels Erik Raursø$^{(\boxtimes)}$ , Malte Elkær Rasmussen , Mikkel Kappel Persson ,
Tor Arnth Petersen , Kristinn Bragi Garðarsson ,
and Henrik Schoenau-Fog

Department of Architecture, Design and Media Technology, Aalborg University,
Copenhagen, Denmark
{nraurs18,marasm18,kgarda18}@student.aau.dk,
contact@mikkelkappelpersson.com, toap@itu.dk, hsf@create.aau.dk

**Abstract.** Interactive cinema appears as an enticing blend of cinema and games. However, active control has been argued to disrupt the appeal of the cinematic experience, and so-called lean-back interactions have been proposed. Such experiences seek to increase narrative immersion without posing demands to the user, or them necessarily being conscious of the control. This paper seeks to investigate how such mechanism can be designed by leveraging attention-measuring Brain-Computer Interface to cater to individuals' interests and increase narrative engagement for interactive films. This is done by skipping seamlessly ahead to the next exciting plot point when detecting drops in viewer's attention, thereby tailoring parts of the film while keeping the overarching story. A short prototype film was produced with virtual production techniques and evaluated in a between group experimental design (n = 24). Participants in the experimental condition watched an interactive version of the film, which contained skippable segments based on viewers' level of attention, while those in the control condition watched a non-interactive version with an edit matching one from the experimental group. The results showed no significant difference in narrative engagement; however, the experimental group showed a significantly higher overall attention than the control group. This suggests that attention-based skippable segments could have some impact on viewer engagement, and it may be beneficial for creating personalized edits for viewers, although further investigations are needed.

**Keywords:** Brain-controlled film · Neurocinema · Lean-back vs Lean-forward interaction · Interactive cinema · Narrative engagement · Attention

## 1 Introduction

The fruition of interactive cinema provides new opportunities for telling stories within large entertainment industries. Interactive cinema offers both new venues

A. Mitchell and M. Vosmeer (Eds.): ICIDS 2021, LNCS 13138, pp. 128–141, 2021.
https://doi.org/10.1007/978-3-030-92300-6_12

for artists to explore and new types of experiences for the audience. Because the opportunities appear so vast, understanding how to design the experiences that maintain cinema's appeal is essential.

The term lean-back serves as a metaphor that describes traditional media experiences such as cinema [16,26] – We lean back, and behold the spectacle unfolding unlike lean-forward mediums such as games [11]. For the narrative absorption, it has been argued that active choice becomes a disruption [5,27] - including even just the mediation of choice through an interface [25].

Passive Brain-Computer Interfaces [33] (BCIs) have therefore become of interest in recent projects of brain-controlled film [23,27] as a mean to tap into the mind of the viewer, and to apply passive control for changes in a film for a more personalized experience. Previous studies have sought to artistically augment and personalize the film experience, such as using BCI measurements of attention and eyelid blinks to control sound, shots, and timelines [22]. It appears however that conscious control, though passive, can still disrupt the narrative immersion [22,26]. Proposed lean-back interactions seek to increase narrative immersion without posing demands to the user, or them necessarily being conscious of the control [26].

This project seeks to leverage lean-back interactions in a practical manner for the viewer. Cinema as a product for the masses arguably suffers, as smaller tangents of a plot or embellishments of its story world are discarded to provide a lean product with mass appeal—sometimes seen with director's cut opposed to the studio's cinematic version. Here, interactive cinema can earn a functional quality as a way to indulge both the creator's and viewers' interests at a more individual and subjective level.

Therefore, this project investigates how individual interests can be catered to with the use of a framework for skipping past segments of a film found boring by the viewer, while maintaining a coherent narrative with authorial control. Our own short film, which was an adaptation of scenes from the movie *Ex Machina* (2014)[1], included 4 zones with content that could be skipped based on the viewer's attention. With a between-subject research design, we aimed to find a difference in narrative engagement. Though no significant difference was found between the two versions of the experiences in self-reported narrative engagement, there is still knowledge to inform future endeavors with brain-controlled film.

This paper will first review related work, then present the background for brain-controlled cinema and areas researched for the presented framework. Then we will describe the experiment and the evaluation methods, followed by a discussion of the main findings of the study, and a conclusion.

## 2 Related Work

Interactive cinema has been experimented with for many decades [27], though the first to apply passive control by measuring physiological responses was Tikka's

---

[1] https://www.imdb.com/title/tt0470752/.

installation 'The Obsession' [31]. Since then, the term of 'neurocinematics' has been coined by Hasson et al. [13] who investigated films' effect on our brains, and now, in turn, how this can affect the film itself, with the field of brain-controlled films. This section will look into some examples of these.

In a study by Pike et al. [22] with the film called *The Disadvantages of Time Travel* [2], the occurrence of viewers' eyelid blinks, as well as attention and meditation levels, are used to control the view of the narrative as well as blending between video layers. In continuation of this research, Ramchurn et al. [26] conducted a study of the brain-controlled film *The MOMENT* [3]. The film blends narrative threads and soundtracks using an attention-based algorithm with data from the previous scene to determine the combination. The algorithm was designed to maintain continuity while also allowing for variation and subconscious control. A drop in attention triggers a cut between threads, the thread continues if attention is maintained or increased. Pike et al. reflected on their work with brain-controlled films [24], and proposed themes for research questions yet to be answered, among them, how individuals' subjectivity can be catered to and whether viewers should be conscious of control.

Kierkels and Pun [17] investigated if the viewer's interest in movie scenes could be discerned using various physiological measures, not including EEG. They found no correlations between interest and movie genre, arousal and valence, but that changes in interest level across a scene and between viewers were detectable. Kirke et al. [19] used physiological measurements, among them EEG, evaluated at specific points in order to determine which ending of the film a viewer would find most exciting. They found that their system was possibly able to succeed in this task, but that it was inconclusive to what degree the system did so by appropriate selection of measurements.

This study attempts to explore how consumer-grade BCIs can be leveraged further in designing experiences with practical benefits for the audience and does not require the creators to completely rethink their art in the creation of interactive films.

## 3    Background

As this study aims at exploring the research area of catering to individuals' interests, this section will firstly look into some of the arguments and assumptions of these previous projects before presenting the theoretical basis for this project's suggested solution.

With the term 'interactive cinema', it is naturally implied that some interaction has to take place. Over the years, there have been many different takes on interactive cinema, ranging from more traditional active decision making, as for example in Netflix's title: *Black Mirror: Bandersnatch (2018)* [1], and for more passive or sometimes even non-conscious interactions bending conventional understanding of interaction.

The ambiguous space of control has been considered in previous projects [22,27], and has been further reflected upon with Benford et al.'s conceptual framework of contested control [6], where control is considered along the dimensions of surrender of control (voluntary/involuntary), self-awareness of control, and looseness of control (how predictable the relationship between measurements and system output is).

The previous studies on brain-controlled films featured control that shifted across these dimensions as users consciously tried exerting control, or forgot they had it. While notions as subconscious control might appear contradictory, it relates to the state of Csíkszentmihályi's flow [10], the mental state of full immersion in ones activity, as has been previously argued [6,22]. Flow relies on a balance between boredom and anxiety; in context of interaction, this requires the controls to take background and allow the activity itself, or narrative, to take foreground for it to stay engaging [25]. This has been acknowledged to be the challenging predisposition of lean-back interactions [26]. Attention offers an interesting control as it too shifts, and is an inherent part of the viewer's engagement with the narrative. If interactive systems are able to rightfully adjust to viewers' attention, they could offer less friction in the interaction.

Attention is a profusely complex phenomena to study, as Siler puts it *"studying attention is like peering into an ocean of data that covers and connects the entire human sensorium, and interpreting the flow of data, currents and all the other changing details"* [29] (p. 191). The 'attention' measurement of consumer-grade BCIs, such as products by Neurosky[2], produces this metric using proprietary non-open source algorithms, therefore introducing some validity concerns. This means that it is not clear how 'attention' is derived, though studies have found that it does correlate with the cognitive process of attention [7,18,20]. Films however offer a very controlled environment for studying attention. Smith investigated how attention is guided across cuts with his Attentional Theory of Cinematic Continuity [30]. In this study the bottom-up and top-down processes that drive our attention are described. Bottom-up processes are involuntary, as our eyes follow movement, look at the bright parts of the image, or gravitate towards faces. Top-down driven processes are driven by our cognition as we formulate and ascribe meaning and connections to our observations. This type of processing is more cognitively effortful, as they require the viewer to actively connect the dots.

Vorderer et al.'s model of the media experience [32] presents the viewer's interests as one prerequisite for enjoyment. This intangible subjective interest of the user as a prerequisite to engage just for the sake of doing so. For this project, it is the top-down processes between viewers we would like to differentiate, to investigate if viewers' interests and engagement with content can be derived from the measurement of 'attention'. The following sections investigate what motivates our attention to seek more, and how this could be considered structurally to both engage and reengage the audience.

---

[2] http://neurosky.com.

## 3.1  Curiosity and Factors that Drive It

Gottlieb et al. [12] investigated the factors that drive curiosity from a neural and computational perspective, not only in humans, but as underlying mechanism of the brain that motivates exploratory behavior. Curiosity is the desire to obtain more information, an intrinsic motivation, as the goal is to know more, simply for the sake of knowing it. Unlike the rewards of extrinsic motivation, e.g., money or food, the rewards of intrinsic motivation are more challenging to quantify. They investigate the mechanism of this complex and subjective experience and provide the factors of surprise, novelty, reward, and uncertainty that describe its structure.

**Surprise** is the subversion of expectations, and is therefore context-specific on the situation and beliefs of the observer. **Novelty** on the other hand, is dependent on the amount of the observer's prior exposure to the observation. Gottlieb et al. cite a model of novelty from a computational point of view as the dissimilarity between a stimulus and the representation of similar stimuli in the observer's brain [4]. Novelty and surprise elicit attention from the observer without necessarily being part of a goal-directed task, i.e., as part of obtaining knowledge to satiate curiosity. The factors of **reward** and **uncertainty** are more top-down driven, as the viewer selectively directs their attention to items of perceived importance; items that either close information gaps, or items that simply arouse a feeling of pleasure due to prior experiences.

## 3.2  Structural-Affect Theory

Brewer and Lichtenstein's Structural-Affect Theory describes how entertainment stories organize and present events [8]. **Suspense event structures** present critical information which outcome is first revealed later on. Due to the uncertain consequences of the critical event, this structure builds suspense to the point when the outcome is revealed. A **surprise event structure** also contains critical event information early in the discourse, yet this information is not shown, and the viewer is unaware that the information is being omitted. Surprise will be evoked when the omitted information is revealed. Similar to the surprise event structure, in a **curiosity event structure** an initiating critical event is omitted from the viewer, but here the viewer knows that the information is missing, making the viewer become curious about the withheld information. The curiosity is later resolved by gradually providing enough of the missing information for the viewer to reconstruct the omitted event.

The inclusion and awareness of these structural elements of surprise, suspense, and curiosity will be useful for this project to build a narrative that keeps the audience engaged in the story.

# 4  Design of the Short Film

This section will first provide overview of the proposed framework, then how the short film was produced, and how the framework was implemented for the short film.

We propose using drops in the viewer's attention level, as indication that the current segment of the film is of no particular interest for the viewer and should therefore be 'skippable'. Skippable is to be understood in the sense that the viewer unknowingly skips ahead in the story in a seamless manner, past the segment of little interest – while maintaining story continuity. If a specific segment of a film particularly arouses the interest of a viewer, we assume that more attention will be allocated to it, as they engage with the content on a deeper, and hopefully, measurable level. To provide structure to the segments, the notion of an attention zone is proposed as illustrated in Fig. 1.

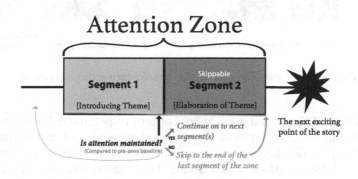

**Fig. 1.** The conceptual framework for Attention Zones and its segments.

A zone contains at least two segments, as first, the viewer needs to be introduced to the content before it can be determined whether there is an interest in the topic. The first segment serves as a hook, to assess if the succeeding segments are of interest. Therefore, only succeeding segments are skippable. Attention is compared to a pre-zone baseline, with no major plot points that could spike attention. If there is more than two segments, then baseline for the third segment is the second segment. If a particular segment is not of interest to the viewer and the segment is thereby skipped, we also need to consider what comes after the segment. After all, if the viewer was disinterested in a particular aspect or part of the story, continuing with something boring would risk losing the interest altogether. So, we want to re-engage them with a new beat of the story - here, elements of suspense, surprise and curiosity should be considered as a way to amend lowered interest.

To apply this framework, an interactive film needed to be produced. Due to resources and scope of the project, it was decided to base our short film production on an existing movie. The movie *Ex Machina* (See footnote 1) is about the programmer Caleb who performs a Turing test on tech mogul Nathan's newest creation, the humanoid AI Ava. It was chosen as it covers different topics that could be elaborated upon or condensed and featured several plot points that could be used in a short film of its own right.

The short film created that applies this framework contains four zones with content that can be skipped if the viewer's attention drops. The content of the zones was considered for how they elaborate on topics of the film, topics that might be of different interest to viewers. Zone 1, as illustrated in Fig. 2, features entirely new content in the film, while the remaining zones and film are adapted from several scenes of the original *Ex Machina* script.

[Caleb shows interest in Ava's drawings, and brings up Fibonacci Sequence ]    Ava: Do you want to be my friend?

**Fig. 2.** Overview of zone 1 of the film featuring three segments.

The themes of the remaining 3 zones concern respectively; Caleb's work and his personal life, the philosophical *Knowledge Argument*, and Ava testing Caleb. The exciting plot developments for each of these zones are respectively; Ava asking if Caleb likes Nathan, Caleb asking Ava if she knows he is brought there to test her, and Ava asking what will happen if she fails his test.

The short film used in the experimental setup can be seen here[3], and lasts 13 min, 3 min of which are skippable. The link features annotations for when the different zones and segments starts. Our short film production was made using virtual production techniques, more specifically with the use of live LED wall in-camera virtual production. This is a state of the art technique where output from the real-time game engine Unity to a live LED video wall. to a live LED wall is used together with real-time DMX lighting and camera tracking to create final-pixel imagery in camera, and has been employed in the recent and popular series *The Mandalorian*[4] [14, 15].

## 5   Methods

To evaluate if the presented framework can be used to increase narrative engagement, a lean-back interactive short film was produced as described in the previous section.

With a between-subject experimental design, two independent groups were tested; The experimental group viewed an interactive version, and the control group viewed a non-interactive version. Sampling of participants was done by convenience sampling. To ensure equal distribution of skips in both groups, participants in the non-interactive group watched a previous participant's version from the experimental group. The setup featured a projector to give a cinema-like

---

[3] https://youtu.be/9qROrN4eVkU.
[4] https://www.imdb.com/title/tt8111088/.

experience. Both groups wore a NeuroSky MindWave Mobile 2 EEG headset[5], and were not told about the experiment's purpose and controls. The measurements of 'attention' was used to determine whether a skip should occur. If attention dropped more than 10% compared to a baseline, a skip occurred. This was evaluated few frames before a segment ended. For the first segment, the baseline was the viewers average attention leading up to the beginning of the zone. These pre-zone baselines were of different lengths, as to ensure that no peak in attention could be caused by any larger plot points. For remaining segments, the baseline was the average value from the preceding segment.

While a participant was watching the film, an observer took note of their behavior and reactions. Following the film, feedback from participants' self-reported narrative engagement was gathered. First, according to Busselle and Bilandzic's Likert scale for measurement of narrative engagement [9], which has sub-scales that could highlight different aspects of the solution. Then, according to Schoenau-Fog et al.'s Continuation Desire assessment method [28] participants responded to the single statement: *"When the film ended, I wanted the film to continue."* Along with basic demographic data, participants were also asked whether they had seen the original movie or not. After answering the questionnaire, a short semi-structured interview was conducted with questions related to the film's tempo, and whether they felt bored or 'zoned out'. The participants were also asked for each of the zones how interesting or exciting a zone's theme was to them, and were asked to give each zone a rating on a 10-point scale.

The ratings were used to assess the performance of the skipping algorithm which was evaluated. A confusion matrix was developed to assess the correlation between the participants' non-conscious control of the film and their interests in the topics of the four zones. The confusion matrix was developed by classifying a zone with low interest (below 5), and thereby an *expected skip*, as positive, and the opposite as negative. Likewise, a *determined skip* by the skipping algorithm was classified as positive, where no skip was classified as negative. These classifications were done for all participants. For the control group, however, calculations were made for each participant's attention data, to find out where skips would have occurred if they had seen the interactive version of the film. Various derivations were then made from the confusion matrix to assess the performance of the algorithm.

The algorithm was assessed according to gender differences, and whether participants had seen the original movie. Having seen the original movie could prove a large confounding variable, as viewers could compare the versions, removing elements of surprise and novelty. However, due to low availability of participants, it was chosen not to be a disqualifying factor. Gender differences was investigated as differences in attention between male and female has been found in a previous study [21].

---

[5] https://store.neurosky.com/pages/mindwave.

# 6    Results

The experiment was conducted on 24 students, 9 females and 15 males in age range of 20–27 years old. Two participants had only seen some of the original movie, 11 had seen it, and 11 had not. In the control group six participants had not seen the original movie, two had seen some if it. In the experimental group, five had not seen it. The following sections will first present findings between the experimental and control conditions, then qualitative data gathered from interviews and observations, and finally results of assessment of the skipping algorithm.

## 6.1    Experiment

A normal distribution was observed in the data with Shapiro-Wilk test ($p > .05$) homogeneity of variance with Levene's test ($p > .05$). A two-tailed independent t-test was used to detect significance in the result data. No significant difference was found in the total self-reported narrative engagement scores between the group viewing the interactive version ($M = 41.08$, $SE = 6.39$) and the group viewing the non-interactive version ($M = 41.92$, $SE = 6.53$), $t(22) = -.32$, $p = .76$, $r = .07$.

Upon deeper inspection of the data, the narrative engagement sub-scales showed no indication of difference, nor did the continuation desire: Both conditions had almost the same scores, with the control condition having a slightly higher but non-significant score in both scales. However, the attention levels between the groups (see Fig. 3 (A)) differed, as the group viewing the interactive version ($M = 46.77$, $SE = 5.14$) had higher attention levels than the group viewing the non-interactive version ($M = 43.11$, $SE = 4.44$), $t(22) = 1.87$, $p = .04$, $r = .39$.

## 6.2    Interviews and Observations

In order to compare the algorithm's identification of attention with viewers' own interests, we compared these as well. The self-reported interest scores from participants in relation to each zone can be seen in Fig. 3 (C).

Regarding pacing or tempo, four participants explicitly noted that the film was *too* slow. All of them were in the control group. Looking at the attention data of those four, two would have skipped 2 segments, one would have skipped 3 segments and one would have skipped 5 segments, and half of these skips corresponded with their self-reported interests.

Concerning the topic of 'zoning out', 5 participants stated that they did not zone out. Other participants noted that they reflected on the story and the characters, but nothing unrelated to the film. For comments relating to boredom or zoning out, 9 were possible to pinpoint to specific zones, and 10 only to a lesser degree. Of the zone-specific, six of them were in respect to zone 1, two to zone 2, and one to zone 4.

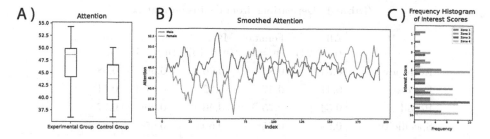

**Fig. 3. A)** Box-plots depicting the measured attention between experimental and control group. **B)** Depicts the attention levels across the film with smoothed by a rolling average. **C)** Depicts the self-reported interest scores for each of the zones.

One participant in the control group vocalized a large amount of mind-wandering. Thoughts revolved around intricate implications of the story, the film's production, and the experiment itself. Had this participant taken part in the experimental group, the film would have skipped three times, though it should not have in respect to his self-reported interests.

One participant noted a great deal of confusion in zone 3 in relation to its content, and its meaning to the story. No skips were identified, though it should have based on her self-reported interest score.

Multiple of the participants who had watched the original movie brought it up in some form during the interviews. One participant who had recently watched the original movie, mentioned doing comparisons between the two versions in relation to actors, mise-en-scène, and changes to the story. Other participants mentioned being able to remember or recognize close to nothing. Some suddenly recalled aspects of the film they had forgotten.

### 6.3   Assessment of the Skipping Algorithm

The confusion matrix, which was developed to assess the performance of the skipping algorithm compared to expected skips based on participants' interest ratings, showed the following results: true positive (correctly identified skip) = 12, true negative (correctly identified no skip) = 49, false positive (incorrectly identified skip) = 25, false negative (incorrectly identified no skip) = 10. Derivations from the confusion matrix are presented in Table 1.

## 7   Discussion

The experiment described above showed no difference in narrative engagement between the experimental and control group, but it did indicate that the experimental group had significantly higher attention. Together with the fact that all participants who thought the film was *too slow* were in the control group, this indicates that the interactive skippable segments could have some sort of effect.

**Table 1.** Derivations from confusion matrix.

|  | All (n = 24) | Female (n = 9) | Male (n = 15) | Seen (n = 11) | Not Seen (n = 11) |
|---|---|---|---|---|---|
| Accuracy | 0.64 | 0.84 | 0.60 | 0.59 | 0.68 |
| F-score | 0.41 | 0.57 | 0.32 | 0.61 | 0.51 |
| Recall | 0.54 | 0.75 | 0.46 | 0.29 | 0.77 |
| Specificity | 0.66 | 0.75 | 0.60 | 0.65 | 0.65 |
| Precision | 0.32 | 0.46 | 0.24 | 0.13 | 0.48 |
| Cohen's Kappa | 0.17 | 0.42 | −0.05 | −0.04 | 0.35 |

The short film was well-received according to the measurements of narrative engagement, despite containing parts some viewers did not find particularly interesting. This is likely a result of the skippable content being too short to make a measurable impact, and the content zones were too generally enjoyable, as only the zone 1 appeared controversial in relation to the viewers self-reported interest scores. Another factor relating to the lack of difference in narrative engagements relates to the design of the film. While some viewers rated some zones rather low, it did not affect their overall experience. This could be due to the design amending transient lowered interest by re-engaging them with an exciting plot point. Future studies could feature longer additional and more controversial content to more clearly assess the effect of skipping certain content.

The assessment of the skipping algorithm showed that it did not correlate with participants' interest scores in any high degree, as it only performed slightly better than random. Inspecting Cohen's Kappa for the sub-groups indicate that the algorithm performed poorer than chance for males and viewers of the original movie, while it did appear to more correctly evaluate skips for females and those who had not seen the original movie. A previous study on gender differences in 'attention' showed that males' are higher, but declines, while females' are more stable [21]. In this experiment, a similar tendency is indicated, with the addition that females' attention increased across the short film. Although further experiments with more participants are needed to make any generalizations, if such gender differences are existent they could be needed taken into account. In relation to having seen the original movie, it is somewhat obvious that this likely affected the experiment. With novelty and surprise reduced, it is likely that this would have a diminishing effect on attention levels. How it could have affected the design or evaluation is however not entirely accounted for with this experiment - The participants in this sub-group was however somewhat equally distributed between the experimental and control conditions. Future experiments with adaptions of existing content could be more inquisitive in this aspect, as it indicates it could have an effect on the viewers perceptions and attention.

In this experiment, participants were not informed of the control they had. Future experiments could investigate how knowledge of control in a design like this would work. Ramchurn et al. [26] found that while their lean-back mechanism was ambiguous and covert it its working, some users still attempted to exert control. In our design, could viewers be able exert control over their attention to elicit skips by disengaging with the content? How this would work at a conscious or subconscious level, and how this relates to the viewing experience, and if it is even desirable, require further research to be answered.

## 8   Conclusion

In recent years, the usage of passive control in interactive cinema has opened unexplored territory with the field of brain-controlled cinema. Previous projects had used a 'loose' mapping in assigning functionality to the metric of 'attention' from consumer-grade Brain-controlled Interfaces.

With this project it has been explored how individual film viewers' subjective interests can be catered to, by attempting to use the attention measurement as an indication of interest in specific parts of a film. A short prototype film adaptation of scenes from the movie *Ex Machina* was made, that contained 4 zones with content that could be skipped according to the viewer's level of attention.

The results from the between-subject test showed no significant difference in narrative engagement between the experimental and control group. There was however an indication of a significant difference found in their measured attention-levels, with the experimental group having a higher average attention than the control group. Furthermore, there appeared to be indications that gender differences in attention-levels affected the performance of the skipping algorithm, as well as whether participants had seen the original film. Additionally, it was found that skips often did not seem to correlate with participants' self-reported interests in the presented topics to any reliable degree. Uncertainties about how the attention data can be interpreted and how affected it was by external factors make it difficult to form any definitive conclusions. However, due to the average attention being significantly higher for the experimental group, it suggests that the interactive film with skippable segments did have some impact that remains to be fully accounted for.

**Acknowledgments.** Thanks to Copenhagen-based film director Oliver Pilemand (http://www.oliverpilemand.com/) and actors Jonas Bau Ellertsson and Lina Csillag for elevating the professionalism of the short film for this project.

## References

1. Imdb - black mirror: Bandersnatch. https://www.imdb.com/title/tt9495224/. Accessed 15 Oct 2021
2. Imdb - the disadvantages of time travel. https://www.imdb.com/title/tt8072006/. Accessed 15 Oct 2021
3. Imdb - the moment. https://www.imdb.com/title/tt7853742/. Accessed 15 Oct 2021
4. Barto, A., Mirolli, M., Baldassarre, G.: Novelty or surprise? Front. Psychol. **4**, 907 (2013)

5. Ben-Shaul, N.: Can narrative films go interactive? New Cinem.: J. Contemp. Film **2**(3), 149–162 (2004)
6. Benford, S., et al.: Contesting control: journeys through surrender, self-awareness and looseness of control in embodied interaction. Human-Comput. Interact. **36**, 1–29 (2020)
7. Bitner, R., Le, N.-T., Pinkwart, N.: A concurrent validity approach for EEG-based feature classification algorithms in learning analytics. In: Nguyen, N.T., Hoang, B.H., Huynh, C.P., Hwang, D., Trawiński, B., Vossen, G. (eds.) ICCCI 2020. LNCS (LNAI), vol. 12496, pp. 568–580. Springer, Cham (2020). https://doi.org/10.1007/978-3-030-63007-2_44
8. Brewer, W.F., Lichtenstein, E.H.: Stories are to entertain: a structural-affect theory of stories. J. Pragmat. **6**(5–6), 473–486 (1982)
9. Busselle, R., Bilandzic, H.: Measuring narrative engagement. Media Psychol. **12**(4), 321–347 (2009)
10. Csikszentmihalyi, M.: Flow: The Psychology of Optimal Experience. Harper Perennial (1991)
11. Dewdney, A., Ride, P.: The New Media Handbook. Routledge, London (2006)
12. Gottlieb, J., Lopes, M., Oudeyer, P.Y.: Motivated cognition: neural and computational mechanisms of curiosity, attention, and intrinsic motivation. In: Recent Developments in Neuroscience Research on Human Motivation. Emerald Group Publishing Limited (2016)
13. Hasson, U., Landesman, O., Knappmeyer, B., Vallines, I., Rubin, N., Heeger, D.J.: Neurocinematics: the neuroscience of film. Projections **2**(1), 1–26 (2008)
14. Kadner, N.: The Virtual Production Field Guide volume 1, vol. 1. Epic Games (2019)
15. Kadner, N.: The Virtual Production Field Guide Volume 2, vol. 2. Epic Games (2021)
16. Katz, H.E.: The media handbook : a complete guide to advertising media selection, planning, research, and buying/Helen Katz. LEA's Communication Series, 3rd edn. L. Erlbaum Associates, Mahwah (2006)
17. Kierkels, J.J.M., Pun, T.: Towards detection of interest during movie scenes. In: First International Workshop on Multimodal Interactions Analysis of Users in a Controlled Environment (MIAUCE2008) (2008)
18. Kim, Y., Moon, J., Lee, H.J., Bae, C.S., Sohn, S.: Integration of electroencephalography based services into consumer electronics. In: 2012 IEEE 16th international symposium on consumer electronics, pp. 1–2. IEEE (2012)
19. Kirke, A., et al.: Unconsciously interactive films in a cinema environment-a demonstrative case study. Digit. Creat. **29**(2–3), 165–181 (2018)
20. Lim, C.G., et al.: A brain-computer interface based attention training program for treating attention deficit hyperactivity disorder. PLoS ONE **7**(10), e46692 (2012)
21. Pari-Larico, S., Llerena-Urday, B., del Carpio, Á.F., Rosas-Paredes, K., Esquicha-Tejada, J.: Evaluation of brain attention levels using Arduino and Neurosky Mindwave EEG according to age and sex (2020)
22. Pike, M., Ramchurn, R., Benford, S., Wilson, M.L.: # scanners: exploring the control of adaptive films using brain-computer interaction. In: Proceedings of the 2016 CHI Conference on Human Factors in Computing Systems, pp. 5385–5396 (2016)
23. Pike, M., Ramchurn, R., Wilson, M.L.: # scanners: integrating physiology into cinematic experiences. In: Proceedings of the 2015 ACM SIGCHI Conference on Creativity and Cognition, pp. 151–152 (2015)

24. Pike, M., Ramchurn, R., Wilson, M.L.: Two-way affect loops in multimedia experiences. In: Proceedings of the 2015 British HCI Conference, pp. 117–118 (2015)
25. Polaine, A.: The flow principle in interactivity. In: Proceedings of the Second Australasian coNference on Interactive Entertainment, pp. 151–158 (2005)
26. Ramchurn, R., Martindale, S., Wilson, M.L., Benford, S.: From director's cut to user's cut: to watch a brain-controlled film is to edit it. In: Proceedings of the 2019 CHI Conference on Human Factors in Computing Systems, pp. 1–14 (2019)
27. Ramchurn, R., Martindale, S., Wilson, M.L., Benford, S., Chamberlain, A.: Brain-controlled cinema. In: Nijholt, A. (ed.) Brain Art, pp. 377–408. Springer, Cham (2019). https://doi.org/10.1007/978-3-030-14323-7_14
28. Schoenau-Fog, H., Louchart, S., Lim, T., Soto-Sanfiel, M.: Narrative engagement in games - a continuation desire perspective. In: Proceedings of the 8th International Conference on the Foundations of Digital Games (FDG 2013). Foundations of Digital Games Conference Proceedings, vol. 8, pp. 384–387. Society for the Advancement of the Science of Digital Games (2013). sNO/CNO: 156495 Foundations of Digital Games Conference Proceedings; Foundations of Digital Games: The 8th International Conference on the Foundations of Digital Games, FDG 2013; Conference date: 14-05-2013 Through 17-05-2013
29. Siler, T.L.: Neurotranslations: interpreting the human brain's attention system. AIMS Med. Sci. 3(2), 179–202 (2016)
30. Smith, T.J.: The attentional theory of cinematic continuity. Projections 6(1), 1–27 (2012)
31. Tikka, P., Vuori, R., Kaipainen, M.: Narrative logic of enactive cinema: obsession. Digit. Creat. 17(4), 205–212 (2006)
32. Vorderer, P., Klimmt, C., Ritterfeld, U.: Enjoyment: at the heart of media entertainment. Commun. Theory 14(4), 388–408 (2006). https://doi.org/10.1111/j.1468-2885.2004.tb00321.x
33. Zander, T.O., Kothe, C.: Towards passive brain-computer interfaces: applying brain-computer interface technology to human-machine systems in general. J. Neural Eng. 8(2), 025005 (2011)

# A Quantified Analysis of *Bad News* for Story Sifting Interfaces

Ben Samuel[1]([✉]), Adam Summerville[2], James Ryan[3], and Liz England[1,2,3]

[1] University of New Orleans, New Orleans, USA
bsamuel@cs.uno.edu
[2] Cal Poly Pomona, Pomona, USA
asummerville@cpp.edu
[3] Carleton College, Northfield, USA
jryan@carleton.edu

**Abstract.** *Bad News* is an award winning game, simulation, and performance art piece which depends on story sifting and live acting performed simultaneously and in real time by two human performers taking on two roles: a *Wizard* and an *Actor*. This paper offers a quantified analysis of eighty-one playthroughs of *Bad News*, identifying common patterns that were frequently used by the story sifting *Wizard* to unearth narratively salient content buried in the simulation to reveal to the player. This analysis informs the design of an in-development *WizActor* interface; a tool intended to reduce the cognitive overhead of story sifting such that future pieces of computationally assisted performance might only depend on one person to fulfill both roles.

**Keywords:** Bad news · Computationally assisted performance · Story sifting · Kismet · Social simulation · WizActor

## 1 Introduction

Social simulation has demonstrated itself to be a powerful tool for creating works of interactive digital storytelling [18,20,22]. Social relationships and dynamics are often a core part of resonant stories, and therefore finding ways to computationally represent them remains an important area of research for the interactive narrative community. Thus far, many narratives driven by social simulation have relied on the properties of emergent narrative [32], in which no formal representation of narrative structure (e.g., an Aristotelian dramatic arc [2]) is encoded, and instead narrative patterns naturally emerge through the actions of the simulated agents. These patterns are then surfaced to readers/players through mechanisms appropriate to the experience in question, in a process that has come to be known as story sifting [15,29]: somehow searching the simulated space to find narratively salient gold amidst the dross of other simulated output.

Story sifting technology is still nascent, however, with ample room for exploration. A notable example of this can be seen in the award-winning

© Springer Nature Switzerland AG 2021
A. Mitchell and M. Vosmeer (Eds.): ICIDS 2021, LNCS 13138, pp. 142–156, 2021.
https://doi.org/10.1007/978-3-030-92300-6_13

game/theatrical performance piece *Bad News* [34]. Powered by the social simulation system *Talk of the Town* [30], *Bad News* asks players to explore a unique procedurally generated small American town with one hundred and forty years of simulated history. The player is tasked with three objectives: discovering the identity of a resident that has recently passed away, searching for the deceased's next of kin, and delivering the eponymous bad news of their passing. Interaction in this piece is real-time spoken communication between the player and a live human performing as the game's *Actor*, who may be asked to assume the role of any of the hundreds of the town's residents. Behind the scenes, another human deemed the *Wizard* (so termed from Wizard-of-Oz interaction techniques [31]) is performing the role of story sifter; scouring the simulated history for material that is narratively salient. In truth, the *Wizard* bears the responsibility of both story sifter and drama manager [23], as the material they find must not only be narratively salient, but also in service of the ultimate quality of the player's experience, whose needs are dynamically changing based on a number of factors. A simple example of one such factor is the experience duration; the designers of *Bad News* determined that the ideal length for a playthrogh is between forty-five and sixty minutes. Thus, the *Wizard* had the task of searching the simulated history for interesting narrative patterns (e.g., starcrossed lovers, rival businesses, disgruntled family dynamics, and other stressors of smalltown life), but revealing them in such a way as to not make the game too easy or too hard (e.g., laying breadcrumbs that would bring the player to the next of kin immediately upon the start of play—even if narratively salient—would likely produce a short and ultimately narratively unsatisfying experience). This is all made more complex by virtue of the fact that the Wizard does not present their findings directly, but rather conveys this information to the *Actor*, who bears ultimately responsibility over how and when any of this information is revealed to the player. Moreover, the simulated history has no GUI interface; it can only be explored via Python code. This led to the *Bad News* experience resulting in the *Wizard* livecoding in Python, the *Actor* performing with the player, and the *Wizard* and *Actor* simultaneously communicating with each other via text messages while performing their respective roles.

Though perhaps the spectacle of this is unique to *Bad News*—and indeed likely contributed to its positive reception—it renders the game frustratingly difficult to distribute. The work presented in this paper is an attempt to enable all of the above in a manner which consolidates the responsibilities of *Wizard* and *Actor* into a single role. At present, the cognitive load of simultaneously role playing and story sifting are too much for a single person to perform. Thus, we present the initial development of an interface intended to enable the consolidation of the *Actor* and *Wizard* roles, tentatively titled the **WizActor** interface. Its design draws directly from quantitative and qualitative data drawn from dozens of *Bad News* playthroughs. However, though *Bad News* informs the design of this interface, it is intended to be generalizable enough to be applicable in any situation in which an interactive narrative driven by social simulation and storysifting leverages a human storyteller. This has a wide range of application areas, from entertainment based experiences such as tabletop role-playing games to simulated role-playing exercises for training and education.

The contributions of this paper are the following: We present for the first time a quantitative analysis of logs of previous *Bad News* playthroughs. These logs are complete records of every Python command typed by the *Wizard*, but do not include any communication between the *Wizard* and *Actor*, nor do they include any input from the Player. Though the complete theatrical experience can't be recreated from a log alone, each log still offers an invaluable lens into the overall flow of the experience. Exploring them provides a concrete look at the types of stories and relationships that were most prevalent in *Bad News*, and serves as the first quantified evaluation of this award winning game. Additionally, this paper will present an in-development prototype of a computational story-sifting assistant: the aforementioned *WizActor* interface, whose design is informed by this analysis of *Bad News*. The data used in this preliminary presentation of the *WizActor* interface was generated via the small social simulation system *Kismet* [38], a system designed to enable authors to create simulation-rich *Bad News*-like playable theatrical experiences of their own. The *Kismet* simulation itself depicts a regency-era ball, authored by a professional developer with a specialty in world simulation and procedurally generated content.

## 2  Related Work

This work finds itself at a cross section of many different branches of research and practice (akin to other cross-disciplinary techniques such as Research Creation [33]). One such branch is the theatre, both traditional and experimental. *Bad News* is a piece of interactive theatre such as *Coffee! A Misunderstanding*, *Sleep No More*, and the performances of Improbotics [13,19,41]. Of these three it is most closely aligned with Improbotics, as they are both fully improvised. However, *Bad News* dialogue is informed by the simulation but is generated by the human *Actor*, whereas improbotics uses natural language generation techniques to produce dialogue for both human and robotic performers. *Bad News* is also a piece of procedural content generation. Though there are many approaches to procedural content generation [39,40], *Bad News* takes much inspiration from the world generation and simulation techniques of *Dwarf Fortress* [1]. It is also a piece of table top role-playing akin to *Dungeons and Dragons* [9], a domain which has seen its own share of of PCG research ranging from the generated music of *Bardo* [25], the characters and relationships of *Fiascomatic* [11], and the settings and story beats of *Dear Leader* [12].

Gamalyzer [24] analyzed playthroughs of *Prom Week* in a quantitative manner, but was concerned with similarity/dissimilarity between playthroughs as opposed to any specific patterns found in the playthroughs. Rameshkumar and Bailey [27] performed high-level textual analysis of role playing sessions from the *Critical Role* series, but as with Gamalyzer, there was no assessment of patterns in the playthroughs. Leece and Jhala [16] used sequence mining similar to our approach to find patterns of actions in *StarCraft*, but to our knowledge no one has investigated logs of actions of simulation sifting/role playing before.

*Kismet* is a tool for social simulation. While other social simulation approaches, such as *PsychSim* and *Comme il Faut*, are large systems that attempt to operationalize specific theories from the psychology literature [17, 21], *Kismet* is intentionally designed to be smaller and more accessible. Authoring for *Kismet* is intended to not depend on the use of a specialized authoring tool [35] like other social simulation systems [6]. Its design was informed by the easy-to-use philosophy of Casual Creators [5], akin to other creativity enabling tools such as *Tracery* [4] and *Imaginarium* [10].

The *WizActor* interface is intended to be a computational assistant for performing many of the roles currently borne by the *Wizard*. These roles include story-sifting through generated content to find salient emergent narrative as backstory [14, 15], as well as performing drama management [28] to find relevant dramatic moves to further the ongoing narrative, and even aspects of player modeling [36] to shape content around the player's predilections. Though intended to be used as a computational assistant during live play, the *WizActor* interface can also be used as a lens into the expressive range [37] of any *Kismet*-powered system, assisting authors in their design of the simulation [8].

## 3   Quantitative Analysis of *Bad News* Wizard Logs

As mentioned above, *Bad News* is a "game about death, death notification, and everyday life, combining deep social simulation and live performance." [34] The two most critical non-player roles are those of the *Wizard* – the one who interprets commands from the player and interfaces with the simulation – and the *Actor* – the one who takes on the role of characters in the simulation. One of the key interactions between *Wizard* and *Actor* is where the *Wizard* queries the simulation and then communicates the salient information to the *Actor*. In looking to support the fusion of *Wizard* and *Actor*, we analyzed records of the commands used by the *Wizard* during playthroughs of *Bad News*. The end goal being an understanding of what types of information the *Wizard* found salient and useful, so as to streamline the information gathering process for the *WizActor*.

In total, we analyzed the logs from 81 playthroughs. The *Wizard* interface for a *Bad News* playthrough is an interactive Python terminal that allows the *Wizard* to execute arbitrary code – in this analysis we wanted to find commonalities between these commands, especially in how they relate to querying, saving, and storing information from the simulation. As such, there were two major forms of command:

- **Print** command – A command that took the form of
  `print(SUBJECT.INFORMATION)` or `print(INFORMATION)`, where the `SUBJECT` is one of the default named entities found in *Bad News* (e.g., pc = 'Player Character', d = 'Deceased', etc.) or a previously assigned entity from an **Assignment** command, and `INFORMATION` is the specific piece of information that is being requested (e.g., current location, family structure, residence address, etc.).

- **Assignment** command – A command that took the form of LABEL = VALUE, where LABEL is the *Wizard* assigned label for the queried information (e.g., mom, dad, bar, susan) , and VALUE is the specific piece of information or entity being assigned to that label.

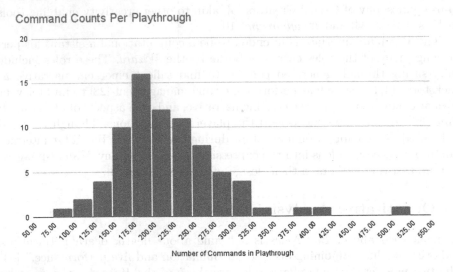

**Fig. 1.** A histogram of the number of commands per playthrough across 81 runs of *Bad News*.

The 81 playthroughs comprise 12,084 commands, with median length of 209 commands in a playthrough (see Fig. 1 for a histogram of number of commands per playthrough). Of these 12,084 commands 16,866 (71.6%) were either a **Print** or **Assignment** command.

Looking to the **Print** commands, we found that the single most common subject (the deceased) showed up on 28.4% of all print commands (3,199 commands in total), while subjects that showed up only once only accounted for 3.8% of print commands (432 commands) – the 5 most common subjects were (1) deceased at 3,199 commands, (2) player at 1,392, (3) mom at⌊542, (4) dad at 463, and (5) next-of-kin at 293. Figure 2a shows the full Cumulative Distribution Function (CDF) of **Print** command subject counts. The most common information was in fact, no information – which in Python would display the entire object – occurring 33.4% of the time (3,757 commands), and again the information that was requested only once occurred 6.2% of the time (694 commands) – the 5 most common pieces of information were (1) ∅ at 3,757 commands, (2) location at 404, (3) occupation at 404, (4) occupations at 387, and (5) home at 311. Figure 2b shows the full Cumulative Distribution Function (CDF) of **Print** command information counts.

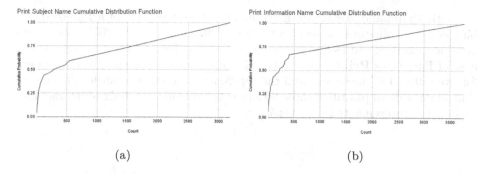

Fig. 2. Cumulative distributions for print related commands (2a for Subject, 2b for Information)

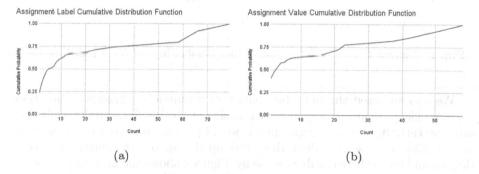

Fig. 3. Cumulative distributions for assignment related commands (3a for Label, 3b for Value)

Turning to the **Assignment** commands, we first note that they were much less common than the **Print** commands – 1,048 **Assignment** vs 11,260 **Print** commands. Another note is that the **Assignment** commands are not as extreme as **Print** commands – the most common label ('bars') only accounts for 7.5% and the most common value (d.mother, d.father) only accounts for 6.8% of the **Assignment** commands respectively. We note that the discrepency in that the most common label does not match the most common information – this comes from the fact that 'bars' was often assigned to multiple times in the face of missing information (e.g., First g.city.businesses_of_type('Bar'), then g.city.businesses_of_type('Hotel'), and finally g.city.former_businesses_of_type('Bar')). The five most common labels were (1) bars at 79 commands, (2 & 3) mom & dad at 66, (4) 'sibs' (siblings) at 58, and (5) hotel at 32. Figure 3a shows the CDF for assignment labels. The five most common values were (1) d.mother, d.father at 66 commands, (2) d.siblings at 58 , (3) g.city.businesses_of_type('Bar') at 44, (4) d.love_interest at 37, and (5) nok[0] at 24. Figure 3b shows the CDF for assignment information.

Both **Print** and **Assignment** commands take the form of a Pareto distribution [26] – sometimes known as the 80–20 distribution (i.e., 80% of outcomes are due to 20% of causes and 20% of outcomes are due to 80% of causes). In the case of Bad News **Print** commands – the top 5 most common subjects account for over 50% of all use-cases, and the top 20 account for two-thirds. This means that being able to prioritize those 20 subjects will cover the bulk of interactions, easing the requirements for a *WizActor*.

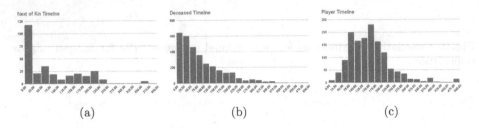

(a)                     (b)                     (c)

**Fig. 4.** Command usage as a function of turn number in *Bad News* playthroughs.

We also analyzed the time distribution of commands – knowing when they are more likely occur can help orient the design of the *WizActor* interface. If they show up early in a playthrough, then it would perhaps be best to include them in an initialization step, while if they show up throughout the playthrough then they should be easily accessible on the fly. Figure 4 shows the histogram of when a subject appears in the course of the playthroughs. We see that there are a range of patterns that appear in *Bad News*. The next of kin is mostly referenced at the beginning, and would be well suited to mostly being handled in an initialization step. The deceased is referenced most at the beginning, but is also referenced throughout the playthrough. Finally, the player character is not referenced much at the beginning, but is referenced throughout the playthrough, mostly for the sake of being moved around the world. The differences in these usage patterns speaks to the need to design different ways of accessing and manipulating the simulation depending on the type of entity.

Finally, we wanted to assess the kinds of patterns found in the commands. If certain patterns of commands show up commonly together, then it stands to reason that the creation of *macros* to handle those patterns might be useful in easing the burden of the *WizActor*. To assess this, we used Byte Pair Encoding (BPE) [7] – a technique where the most common pair of tokens is replaced with a new token, a process that is repeated until a vocabulary of token sequences is filled up to a certain size. In this case, we first anonymized the variable names – e.g. if there was a command sequence of:

```
dad.occupations[-1]
dad.occupations[-1].terminus.date
```

We would want it to be considered the same as:

```
patricia.occupations[-1]
patricia.occupations[-1].terminus.date
```

I.e., we only care about the macro pattern of "Find the last job this person had, and its end date". So we turn those into:

```
ENTITY.occupations[-1]
ENTITY.occupations[-1].terminus.date
```

After running a character level BPE to fill up a vocabulary of size 5,000, we sort the vocabulary by size, to find long, common sequences. We found some interesting patterns emerge:

"Get general info and job information of the person you are speaking to."

```
print ENTITY.all_interlocutors[INT]
print ENTITY.all_interlocutors[INT]
print ENTITY.all_interlocutors[INT].occupations
print ENTITY.all_interlocutors[INT].occupations[INT]
print ENTITY.all_interlocutors[INT].occupations[INT]
```

"Get the family tree of a person"
```
print ENTITY.father
print ENTITY.father.father
print ENTITY.mother
print ENTITY.mother.father
print ENTITY.mother.father.father
print ENTITY.mother.father.father.father
print ENTITY.mother.father.father.occupations
```

"Get the personality traits of a person"
```
print ENTITY.personality.e
print ENTITY.personality.a
print ENTITY.personality.o
print ENTITY.personality.c
print ENTITY.personality.n
```

All of these are sequences of commands that could be turned into macros that get all of the information at once. Furthermore, the different types of information could (and should) be presented to the *WizActor* in different ways. A family tree is different than a history is different than the presentation of 5 numbers – each should be presented in ways to assist the *WizActor* in understanding the most salient details quickly and easily.

## 4    The *WizActor* Interface

The *WizActor* tool is currently a prototype and in active development. As discussed above, its primary purpose is to provide an interface that makes exploring the underlying simulation for dramatic backstory elements and inspiring future moves simple and accessible. Though ultimately intended for use in many simulation-driven performance experiences, in the parlance of *Bad News*, it is intended to facilitate the *Wizard*'s most common needs (outlined in Sect. 3), such that the roles of *Actor* and *Wizard* could conceivably be collapsed and performed by a single individual with minimal cognitive overhead.

The prototype is being developed as a web application using *Data Driven Documents* (the *D3.js* library) [3]. Figure 7 depicts an early version of the tool, demonstrating its initial functionality. Though the inspiration for the design of this tool comes in part from the aforementioned analysis of *Bad News* playthroughs, it is intended to be usable for a variety of domains and game experiences that depend on human performers (e.g., the Bad News "actor", a Tabletop Role Playing Game "game master", etc.) parsing through, discovering, and delivering simulation-generated content. To showcase a different narrative domain, the underlying data used in the following examples was generated via a *Kismet* simulation that represents a collection of thirty regency era socialites attending a ball. Each character in the simulation is composed of individual character traits (such as "snoopy", "extrovert", and "drunkard"), statuses (such as "sad", "drunk", and "embarrassed") and is depicted as a node in a *D3* force directed graph. The edges of the graph are directed and represent the source character's affinity towards the target; unbounded integers that could be negative (indicating disdain) or positive (indicating affection). In the following figures the solid green edges represent positive affinities and the dashed red edges represent negative ones.

Figure 5 presents a view of the entire interface. The top portion depicts the complete cast of characters, who can be added or removed from the graph individually via checkboxes. Beneath that there is a slider that adjusts the "relationship threshold" value which impacts how many edges between nodes are drawn. Beneath that is trait and status information about a selected character (here Penelope Leosfel), and to the right of that are buttons that highlight narratively salient patterns (such as "Find a Rival" or "Find all Friends"). Beneath all that is, finally, the graph itself.

Being able to add characters to the graph individually is helpful; in *Bad News*, for example, players were often most concerned with learning more information about characters they had already met. This allows for the *WizActor* to gradually add characters as the player encounters them, focusing the information offered by the *WizActor* interface to be most pertinent to the current game. However, as discussed in Sect. 3, the *Wizard* also commonly needs to query the simulation for information regarding characters that the player has yet to encounter – either at the start or in media res. However, these queries nearly always were in relationship to characters the player had already encountered or learned about – e.g., finding the family tree of an encountered character. The *Kismet* world used for this didn't have familial relations, but finding friends, love interests, and rivals are spiritually similar tasks. There are a set of buttons (e.g., *Find a Friend* and *Find a Rival*) that adds a new character to the graph who fulfills the desired pattern when pressed. This automated search for patterns is

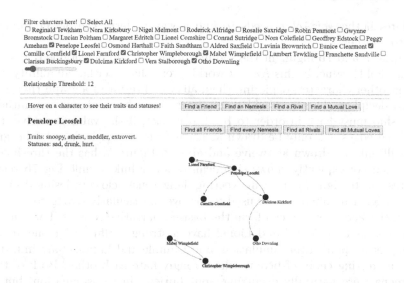

Filter charcters here!  ☐ Select All
☐ Reginald Tewkham ☐ Nora Kirksbury ☐ Nigel Melmont ☐ Roderick Alfridge ☐ Rosalie Saxridge ☐ Robin Penmont ☐ Gwynne Bromstock ☐ Lucian Poltham ☐ Margaret Edritch ☐ Lionel Comshire ☐ Conrad Sutridge ☐ Nora Colefield ☐ Geoffrey Edstock ☐ Peggy Ameham ☑ Penelope Leosfel ☐ Osmond Harthall ☐ Faith Sandtham ☐ Aldred Saxfield ☐ Lavinia Brownritch ☐ Eunice Clearmont ☑ Camille Comfield ☑ Lionel Farnford ☑ Christopher Wimpleborough ☑ Mabel Wimplefield ☐ Lambert Tewkling ☐ Franchette Sandville ☐ Clarissa Buckingsbury ☑ Dulcima Kirkford ☐ Vera Stalborough ☑ Otho Downling

Relationship Threshold: 12

Hover on a character to see their traits and statuses!

**Penelope Leosfel**

Traits: snoopy, atheist, meddler, extrovert.
Statuses: sad, drunk, hurt.

**Fig. 5.** An early prototype of the *WizActor* interface using generated *Kismet* data simulating a regency era ball. Solid green lines signify positive affinities, dashed red lines represent signify negative affinities. (Color figure online)

a simple form of story-sifting, and enables the *WizActor* to quickly discover new characters to weave into the story. The patterns presented here ("friend", "rival", etc.) were authoring decisions specific to this particular simulated world. *Kismet* permits authors to create their own patterns of arbitrary complexity, and the *WizActor* interface dynamically populates its search functionality based on the current world.

Though its primary intended use case is to facilitate live story-sifting while in-game, the *WizActor* interface is also a helpful mechanism for better understanding the generative space of a *Kismet* simulation, and can serve as a tool to verify that generated content is desirable. Figures 6, 7a, and 7b highlight some of this sanity checking.

Figure 6 depicts the results of clicking the "Find all Friends" button; it introduces into the graph every character who appears in the "Friends" pattern. Note how the resulting graph is clearly partitioned; the simulation has naturally created a group of people who all love each other (through the mutually connected solid green lines towards the top of the graph) and another group that all despise each other (connected through the dashed red lines towards the bottom). This is an interesting phenomenon in and of itself—it enables the author of the simulation to reflect on whether this result is desirable and to modify the *Kismet* file accordingly—but it also reveals potentially interesting characters for narrative moves. Here, there are a few characters, such as Peggy Ameham, Geoffrey Edstock, and Dulcima Kirkford who are generally liked but who also have connections to the "angry" group. Those characters serve as narratively interesting candidates if the *WizActor* needs to find a way to ferry the player from one group to another.

Figures 7a and 7b highlight the significance of the aforementioned "relationship threshold" value. In this *Kismet* world, every character has an affinity value for every other character; depicting them all would result in a graph that is difficult to decipher. The threshold value determines the minimum magnitude a relationship must have in order to be drawn (e.g., if the value is twelve, then dashed red edges will only be drawn at negative twelve or less, and solid green edges will only be drawn at twelve and above). Figure 7a has the threshold at twenty, and consequently shows significantly fewer links, while Fig. 7b relaxes the threshold to eight (and begins veering dangerously close to losing decipherability). Higher numbers can be used to discover particularly strong connections between characters, which can form the basis of narrative content. For example, Fig. 7a tells us that Alfred and Lionel have a stronger affinity for one another than any other pair in the simulation, and Camille and Lambert are linked via a very interesting chain of people who strongly hate each other. Both of these phenomena were naturally occurring—but buried—in the simulation, but the *WizActor* tool unearthed them easily, offering potential narrative fuel to in turn to be surfaced to the player. Similarly, lowering the threshold consequently shows more links, further confirming the two 'factions' here and revealing additional characters that could be considered "on the border" between the two groups.

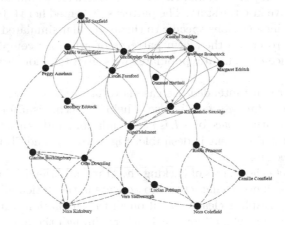

**Fig. 6.** A depiction of the interface after the "Find all Friends" button is pressed

## 5    Conclusion and Future Work

This paper presents initial findings from a quantified analysis of *Wizard* logs from the game *Bad News*. These findings revealed the commands most often entered by the *Wizard* while playing *Bad News*, which in turn speaks to the simulated information and emergent narrative most crucial to be surfaced for

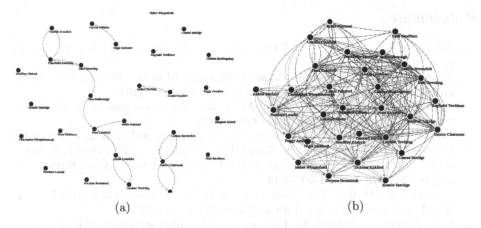

(a) (b)

**Fig. 7.** Two *WizActor* graphs depicting character affinities. Figure 7a includes all thirty characters with the "relationship threshold" value set to twenty. 7b is the same but with the value at eight.

a successful play-through. These findings have informed the development of a *WizActor* interface, intended to be used in any piece of computationally assisted table-top role-playing powered by the social simulation system *Kismet*. Though the interface is still in its early stages, it shows promise as both a mechanism for story-sifting, as well as for visualizing the generative space of *Kismet* simulations. Additionally, the authors hope this work highlights why these types of evaluations are important, as the insights garnered from them have the potential to enable entirely new sets of work. We encourage other researchers and developers to analyze their own playthrough data (or make it publicly available) to enable these valuable lines of research.

There is ample future work remaining on this project. Further analysis of *Bad News*, taking player actions and *Wizard-Actor* communication into account, remains to be performed. There is still additional wisdom learned from the existing *Bad News* analysis to integrate into the *WizActor* interface. As this work continues, the authors hope to leverage *Kismet* and the *WizActor* interface to develop a new "*Bad News*-like" game to serve simultaneously as evaluation of these systems, and a standalone piece of creative work. Once completed, the ultimate plan is to provide these tools to all, to nurture a blossoming genre of computationally assisted performance games. Additionally, a professional developer has been working with *Kismet* and the *WizActor* interface, offering their insight and feedback on using these tools. Codifying this feedback could be valuable future work of interest to interactive storytelling researchers that aspire to produce narrative content and tools that are relevant in both academic and industry circles.

# References

1. Adams, T., Adams, Z.: Dwarf fortress. Game [Windows, Mac, Linux], Bay 12 (2006)
2. Aristotle: Poetics (Penguin Classics). Penguin Classics (1997). http://www.amazon.com/Poetics-Penguin-Classics-Aristotle/dp/0140446362
3. Bostock, M., Ogievetsky, V., Heer, J.: $D^3$ data-driven documents. IEEE Trans. Vis. Comput. Graph. **17**(12), 2301–2309 (2011)
4. Compton, K., Kybartas, B., Mateas, M.: Tracery: an author-focused generative text tool. In: Schoenau-Fog, H., Bruni, L.E., Louchart, S., Baceviciute, S. (eds.) ICIDS 2015. LNCS, vol. 9445, pp. 154–161. Springer, Cham (2015). https://doi.org/10.1007/978-3-319-27036-4_14
5. Compton, K., Mateas, M.: Casual creators. In: Proceedings of the Sixth International Conference on Computational Creativity, p. 228 (2015)
6. DeKerlegand, D., Samuel, B., Leichman, J.: Encoding socio-historical exegesis as social physics predicates. In: International Conference on the Foundations of Digital Games, pp. 1–9 (2020)
7. Gage, P.: A new algorithm for data compression. C Users J. **12**(2), 23–38 (1994)
8. Garbe, J., Reed, A.A., Dickinson, M., Wardrip-Fruin, N., Mateas, M.: Author assistance visualizations for ice-bound, a combinatorial narrative. In: FDG (2014)
9. Gygax, G., Cook, D.: The Dungeon Master Guide, No. 2100, 2nd edn. (Advanced Dungeons and Dragons). TSR, Inc., Lake Geneva (1989)
10. Horswill, I.: Imaginarium: a tool for casual constraint-based PCG. In: Proceedings of the AIIDE Workshop on Experimental AI and Games (EXAG) (2019)
11. Horswill, I.D.: Fiascomatic: a framework for automated fiasco playsets. In: Eleventh Artificial Intelligence and Interactive Digital Entertainment Conference (2015)
12. Horswill, I.: Dear leader's happy story time: a party game based on automated story generation. In: WS-16-21. pp. 39–45. AAAI Workshop - Technical Report, AI Access Foundation, 12th AAAI Conference on Artificial Intelligence and Interactive Digital Entertainment, AIIDE 2016; Conference date: 08–10-2016 Through 09–10-2016 (January 2016)
13. Kiai, D.: Coffee! a misunderstanding (2014)
14. Kreminski, M., Dickinson, M., Mateas, M.: Winnow: a domain-specific language for incremental story sifting. In: Proceedings of the AAAI Conference on Artificial Intelligence and Interactive Digital Entertainment, vol. 17, pp. 156–163 (2021)
15. Kreminski, M., Dickinson, M., Wardrip-Fruin, N.: Felt: a simple story sifter. In: Cardona-Rivera, R.E., Sullivan, A., Young, R.M. (eds.) ICIDS 2019. LNCS, vol. 11869, pp. 267–281. Springer, Cham (2019). https://doi.org/10.1007/978-3-030-33894-7_27
16. Leece, M.A., Jhala, A.: Sequential pattern mining in starcraft: brood war for short and long-term goals. In: Tenth Artificial Intelligence and Interactive Digital Entertainment Conference (2014)
17. Marsella, S.C., Pynadath, D.V., Read, S.J.: Psychsim: agent-based modeling of social interactions and influence. In: Proceedings of the International Conference on Cognitive Modeling, vol. 36, pp. 243–248 (2004)
18. Mateas, M., Stern, A.: Façade: an experiment in building a fully-realized interactive drama. In: Game Developers Conference, vol. 2, pp. 4–8 (2003)
19. Mathewson, K.W.: Humour-in-the-loop: improvised theatre with interactive machine learning systems (2019)

20. McCoy, J., Treanor, M., Samuel, B., Reed, A.A., Wardrip-Fruin, N., Mateas, M.: Prom week. In: Proceedings of the International Conference on the Foundations of Digital Games, pp. 235–237 (2012)

21. McCoy, J., Treanor, M., Samuel, B., Reed, A.A., Mateas, M., Wardrip-Fruin, N.: Social story worlds with comme il faut. IEEE Trans. Comput. Intell. AI Games 6(2), 97–112 (2014)

22. Meehan, J.R.: Tale-spin, an interactive program that writes stories. In: Proceedings of the 5th International Joint Conference on Articial Intelligence, Aug. 1977. vol. 1, pp. 91–98 (1977)

23. Nelson, M.J., Mateas, M., Roberts, D.L., Isbell, C.L., Jr.: Declarative optimization-based drama management (dodm) in the interactive fiction anchorhead. Comput. Graph. Appl. 26(3), 32–41 (2006)

24. Osborn, J.C., Samuel, B., McCoy, J.A., Mateas, M.: Evaluating play trace (dis) similarity metrics. In: Tenth Artificial Intelligence and Interactive Digital Entertainment Conference (2014)

25. Padovani, R.R., Ferreira, L.N., Lelis, L.H.: Bardo: emotion-based music recommendation for tabletop role-playing games. In: Thirteenth Artificial Intelligence and Interactive Digital Entertainment Conference (2017)

26. Pareto, V.: Cours d'économie politique: professé à l'Université de Lausanne, vol. 1. F. Rouge (1896)

27. Rameshkumar, R., Bailey, P.: Storytelling with dialogue: a critical role dungeons and dragons dataset. In: Proceedings of the 58th Annual Meeting of the Association for Computational Linguistics, pp. 5121–5134 (2020)

28. Roberts, D.L., Isbell, C.L.: A survey and qualitative analysis of recent advances in drama management. Int. Trans. Syst. Sci. Appl. Spec. Issue Agent Based Syst. Hum. Learn. 4(2), 61–75 (2008)

29. Ryan, J.: Curating simulated storyworlds. Ph.D. thesis, UC Santa Cruz (2018)

30. Ryan, J.O., Summerville, A., Mateas, M., Wardrip-Fruin, N.: Toward characters who observe, tell, misremember, and lie. In: Eleventh Artificial Intelligence and Interactive Digital Entertainment Conference (2015)

31. Ryan, J.O., Summerville, A.J., Samuel, B.: Bad news: a game of death and communication. In: Proceedings of the 2016 CHI Conference Extended Abstracts on Human Factors in Computing Systems, pp. 160–163 (2016)

32. Ryan, M.L.: From narrative games to playable stories: toward a poetics of interactive narrative. Storyworlds A J. Narrative Stud. 1, 43–59 (2009)

33. Sadati, S.H., Mitchell, C.: Serious game design as research-creation to address sexual and gender-based violence. Int J Qual Methods 20, 16094069211046130 (2021)

34. Samuel, B., Ryan, J., Summerville, A.J., Mateas, M., Wardrip-Fruin, N.: Bad news: an experiment in computationally assisted performance. In: Nack, F., Gordon, A.S. (eds.) ICIDS 2016. LNCS, vol. 10045, pp. 108–120. Springer, Cham (2016). https://doi.org/10.1007/978-3-319-48279-8_10

35. Shibolet, Y., Knoller, N., Koenitz, H.: A framework for classifying and describing authoring tools for interactive digital narrative. In: Rouse, R., Koenitz, H., Haahr, M. (eds.) ICIDS 2018. LNCS, vol. 11318, pp. 523–533. Springer, Cham (2018). https://doi.org/10.1007/978-3-030-04028-4_61

36. Smith, A.M., Lewis, C., Hullett, K., Smith, G., Sullivan, A.: An inclusive taxonomy of player modeling. University of California, Santa Cruz, Technical report. UCSC-SOE-11-13 (2011)

37. Smith, G., Whitehead, J.: Analyzing the expressive range of a level generator. In: Proceedings of the 2010 Workshop on Procedural Content Generation in Games, pp. 1–7 (2010)
38. Summerville, A., Samuel, B.: Kismet: a small social simulation language. In: Summerville, A., Samuel, B. (2020, September). Kismet: a Small Social Simulation Language. In: 2020 International Conference on Computational Creativity (ICCC). (Casual Creator Workshop). ACC (2020)
39. Summerville, A., et al.: Procedural content generation via machine learning (pcgml). IEEE Trans. Games **10**(3), 257–270 (2018)
40. Togelius, J., Yannakakis, G.N., Stanley, K.O., Browne, C.: Search-based procedural content generation: a taxonomy and survey. IEEE Trans. Comput. Intell. AI Games **3**(3), 172–186 (2011)
41. Worthen, W.B.: The written troubles of the brain: sleep no more and the space of character. Theatre J. 79–97 (2012)

# Digital Storytelling and Social Interaction in Cultural Heritage - An Approach for Sites with Reduced Connectivity

Ektor Vrettakis[1,2], Akrivi Katifori[1,2(✉)], and Yannis Ioannidis[1,2]

[1] ATHENA Research Center, Artemidos 6 & Epidavrou, 15125 Maroussi, Greece
{ekvre,vivi,yannis}@di.uoa.gr

[2] Department of Informatics and Telecommunications, National and Kapodistrian University of Athens, Panepistimioupolis, Ilissia, Greece

**Abstract.** As mobile devices gradually became more pervasive, there has been an evolution in their use in the museum and cultural heritage context. Traditionally, audio guides and mobile mediated narratives in general, have been a single user experience. However, as a museum visit is, in most cases, social in nature, different experimental applications attempt to implement sociality in a variety of experience designs. In this work, we seek to support digitally-mediated social interaction for collocated users experiencing digital storytelling in a cultural heritage context, addressing the issue of decentralized communication across devices that are collocated, without a single point of coordination. This requirement stems from the fact that most cultural sites lack the reliable infrastructure to support network connectivity of any kind. To support social interaction, we extend an IDN authoring framework with support for collaborative experiences and evaluate it through a study with twelve participants.

**Keywords:** Interactive digital storytelling · Authoring tool · Social interaction · Cultural heritage

## 1 Introduction

Audio guides have played a significant role in museums and heritage sites [33]. As mobile devices gradually became more pervasive, there has been an evolution in the use of this technology, yet its full potential still has not been fully realized. The technology is there, however the issue has shifted to that of an effective experience design that would convey successfully the objective to promote visitor engagement. Digital storytelling is one of the recognized and widely used approaches to that effect [21, 27] and an increasing number of cultural institutions employ narratives of different forms to enhance the visitor experience, "overextending" in some cases the use of the term "digital storytelling" to even include purely informational content [13].

Traditionally, mobile mediated narratives in this context have been a single user experience [34, 36, 37]. Visitors are given a device or asked to download an app, and are left to wander alone, isolated by the other visitors by the use of headphones. However, a

© Springer Nature Switzerland AG 2021
A. Mitchell and M. Vosmeer (Eds.): ICIDS 2021, LNCS 13138, pp. 157–171, 2021.
https://doi.org/10.1007/978-3-030-92300-6_14

museum visit is in most cases social in nature [3, 7, 18, 19] as people rarely come alone [2]. Cultural sites have been characterized as "social places where people in groups gather to collectively share their experiences and collectively make meaning" [6]. And mobile devices have indeed been accused of isolating the visitor from their surroundings and each other [30]. Past research has confirmed that the use of personal mobile devices by collocated users often isolates the group's members, absorbing their attention on their device – creating thus an isolating bubble or "cocoon" [10, 25]. Recent work has been attempting to reconcile sociality in heritage sites with mobile digital experiences and to reverse this effect, turning the mobile phones into the incentive or focus for meaningful communication and interaction between the visitors [1, 12, 14, 20].

In this work we focus on digitally-mediated social interaction for collocated users experiencing mobile-mediated digital storytelling in a cultural heritage context. In this experience type, the users are allowed to proceed in parts of the experience at their own pace. At specific points, they are asked by the system to interact with each other, either by engaging in conversation in relation to the narrative themes or in another type of shared activity. We build upon previous work, that focused on the conceptual aspects of this approach [14], to explore an implementation of system-based synchronization of the collocated devices, beyond user-initiated coordination. To that end, we propose an implementation framework, building upon the Story Maker tool authoring tool for interactive digital narratives [28, 29]. Our objective is (a) to explore the effect of this type of system-driven synchronization on the visitor experience and (b) to address the authoring aspects of the approach, taking into account that the content creators in this context are not experienced programmers but rather digital heritage practitioners. As an additional challenge, we address the issue of decentralized communication across devices that are collocated, without a single point to orchestrate the synchronization.

In Sect. 2 we present in more detail the background research that has been the motivation for this work, while in Sect. 3 we identify specific requirements for our implementation, offer a brief description of the Story Maker framework and present our implementation approach which extends this framework. Section 4 focuses on the user evaluation, followed by the Conclusions in Sect. 5.

## 2  Background and Motivation

Social interaction has been examined in a cultural context as an aspect of the visit e.g. [5, 22, 35] and from the perspective of the study of group behavioral patterns [4, 24]. Existing research has sought to promote specific forms of social interaction between groups, including situations where visitors are not in close proximity [16, 17]. Different applications implement sociality in a variety of experience designs. Gamified approaches are typically based on a treasure hunting theme [2, 15], whereas other approaches employ individual user trajectories that combine isolated exploration and reflection with shared activities and may include collocated interactions [8, 20]. An example of this latter type combines mobile drama with coordinated narrative variations to induce conversations in small groups [1, 9].

Our work focuses on the use of digital storytelling in a cultural heritage context as an individual mobile user experience, combined with points where the users are guided, by the device, to interact with each other, usually to engage in some type of common exploration activity or, most often, dialogue. One example is the facilitated dialogue experience for a group of 6–8 users for the York Minster Cathedral described in [11]. In this case one of the users assumes an enhanced role, to facilitate the dialogue that is prescribed as a social activity in between the storytelling parts of the experience.

The work in [14, 23] describes a mobile-based digital storytelling experience for two users, "The story of Building 52", developed for the archaeological site of Çatalhöyük, near Konya in Turkey. The experience follows a story-centric, drama-based digital storytelling approach where two fictional characters, Abla, a Neolithic inhabitant and Archie, an archeologist, narrate events from their past on the site. The evaluation of the experience has established with statistical significance the positive outcomes of designing explicit social interaction points between the users into digital storytelling. Conversation between group members has positive effects on visitors' engagement with the overall experience and significantly fosters historical empathy and learning. The same study also confirmed that integrating social interaction points in a digital storytelling, experienced individually by each user, does not break the user's engagement with the story flow.

In this case a technologically minimalistic approach was adopted. The interaction points were implemented as individual prompts to each user to initiate the interaction. There was no underlying synchronization mechanism to ensure that the digital storytelling experiences proceeded in parallel. In other words, there was no means to control whether users reached the same interaction point at the same time, so as to start the activity together. The users themselves controlled their own experience pace, coordinating (or not) their actions. The study observed a variety of approaches by the users, concluding that "the decision not to enforce or even technically support synchronization did not seem to hamper the experience for users. Participants were able to drift apart if they wanted to, and pairs who decided to align their experiences were able to socially coordinate their digital stories, while at the same time maintaining individual control of their personal device" [14], finding this result consistent with the work of [8].

An important point, however, was that the ease with which the participants' self-coordinated is most likely due also to other factors and cannot be considered a generalizable argument against the use of system-supported synchronization, at least not without more targeted experiments to explore participant self-coordination. The authors consider the specific story design, including "structure, branching factor and depth over the script level, temporal placement and frequency of interaction points, etc." [14] as important factors to that effect, becoming even more crucial if significant differences are introduced between the narrative variations offered to the participants.

Furthermore, the fact that the experience type is an interactive narrative, even if it is designed for the users to proceed in a roughly parallel trajectory, the fact that users are "able to proceed at their own pace, exploring in-depth some parts of the story, or moving along quickly, or even skipping other parts", does "not guarantee that they will arrive at any given [social] interaction point at the same time" [14].

In this sense, as the authors also conclude, although Suh et al. point out that social negotiation is more or less a prerequisite for shared experiences [26], it cannot technically support synchronization. To this end, in this work we propose and assess an approach to system-driven synchronization, attempting to address specific requirements, inspired by [11] and [14].

A horizontal design decision we made was to implement for reduced, unstable or no connectivity, which is the case for both the aforementioned use cases. The Çatalhöyük Neolithic site is located in a rural area of Turkey, at a relatively great distance from cities or towns. For different reasons, including the lack of security personnel during the winter, it is not practical to install on site the equipment needed to guarantee stable Wi-Fi coverage. On the other hand, mobile network coverage is unstable, rendering it unreliable to guarantee a seamless user experience with a high demand of network communication. The case of the York Minster Cathedral is similar, as the building offers no Wi-Fi coverage while it features basements where there is no 4G coverage. For this reason, in both cases, any digital experience implementation requiring network connectivity most certainly does not guarantee a smooth and uninterrupted user experience.

Although it may be hard to believe, the aforementioned use cases are fairly common in cultural heritage sites and not the exception, when it comes to network connectivity. Especially in the case of the more remote sites, which in reality would benefit more from a mobile-based approach as they usually lack curated supplementary informational content on-site, this need is even more prominent.

## 3 System Overview

In this section we present our approach, starting from the definition of requirements.

### 3.1 System-Driven Synchronization Requirements

The storytelling approach we seek to support foresees individual exploration that is interleaved with social interaction points. The users proceed within the experience at their own pace. At specific interaction points they cannot proceed further and they have to wait for the other participant(s) in their group. Once they all reach this specific point, they can join the specific group activity. Different activities can be described for these social interaction points, including:

**Content Variations.** The users are simultaneously shown content, which is different for every user, and then prompted to discuss with their companion(s) about it. This activity aims to support the information gap technique where users are presented each with different information and asked to exchange their perspectives on the topic. As an example, the user following the character of Abla in the story example of the Çatalhöyük "Building 52" will be presented with a representation of the Neolithic home whereas Archie, with a view of the home as it was while excavated.

**Prompted Exploration or Reflection on the Same Content.** This activity presents the same content to all users. In contrast to the previous requirement, the aim is to give the participants a common point for prompted reflection and conversation.

**"Gift Giving" Activity.** One user may offer a virtual object to another user. The object may appear on the other user's screen. This object is selected from a collection, motivating users to explore more deeply this collection so as to decide which is more appropriate. An example in the context of the Çatalhöyük digital storytelling experience could be "Select the most appropriate funerary object for your companion. Explain to them the reasons for this choice."

**Facilitator Control.** One of the participants can be assigned the role of facilitator. This role has advanced rights in comparison with the others, allowing the user to control the pace of the experience and make decisions for the whole group in branching points.

**Polling Branching Point.** Participants are asked to select an option in a menu, representing a branching point of the story. Then, the system evaluates their choices to make an informed decision for the path of the story they will all, collectively follow. The author can choose between different activity variations, in which users can see the polling results and, optionally, a pie-chart with the vote distribution. This activity aims to engage users in a decision-making process based on the current state of the experience. In case of a tie, the final decision can be either facilitator-driven or system-driven.

Lastly, our implementation aims to address the issue of reduced connectivity by exploring solutions for decentralized communication across devices that are collocated, without a single point to orchestrate the synchronization.

In the remainder of this section we focus on our implementation approach for these requirements, aiming for the right balance between promoting visitor engagement through social interaction and an authoring approach appropriate for non-experts.

### 3.2  The Story Maker Framework

For this work we build upon the Story Maker [28] authoring tool. The Story Maker offers a framework for creating IDN experiences, from start to end. It consists of a) the Story Design Editor (SDE) used to define the structure and concept of the branching narrative, and b) the Storyboard Editor (SBE) [29] used to transform the author's concept into an interactive experience.

SDE's objective is to support the design of the story concept (i.e. the story plot) and structure through the use of a WYSIWYG editor, extended with additional features for branching narrative creation. The narrative text can be organized in Parts, defined as coherent parts of the narrative and Branches that interconnect them. Parts are defined as abstract building blocks that can be used to define the different pieces of the narrative. They can be freely linked together using Branches, leading from one Part to another. Branches help define the possible paths of the experience. For the authors to control the availability of a path at any given point of the experience, we introduced the use of Conditions and Tags. Tags can be associated with Parts or Branches, and be used in a Branch condition to show or hide the specific Branch, giving the authors additional control over the flow of the experience, depending on the paths selected by the users. The conditions are determined by enforcing boolean constraints on the tags a user has encountered, defining whether a tag has been met during an experience, or not.

The Story Maker Storyboard Editor (SBE) covers the production of the final IDN experience. Parts of the script can be implemented in multimedia format through sets of Screens and Branches through Menus or Jumps. Jumps are implicit transitions, selected automatically according to conditions that are set while the user proceeds.

When complete, the produced experience can be made available through a web-based player as well as a native mobile application for Android devices. In this work, we extend the latter by adding support for collaborative and facilitated features, as described in the following section.

### 3.3 Implementation

To address the need for the framework to be effective in a context of reduced connectivity, we opted to use Google's Nearby Connections [31] for the P2P functionality. Google's Nearby Connections is a P2P networking framework that enables an application to discover, connect to, and exchange data with other nearby devices, regardless of network connectivity status. It leverages a variety of wireless interfaces available on modern mobile devices (i.e. Wi-Fi, Bluetooth and BLE) to offer high-bandwidth, low-latency, encrypted P2P networking. Nearby Connections aims to eliminate the vagaries posed by different android versions and wireless interface hardware vendors.

Our framework provides three types of requests: a) Base Requests, b) Screen Requests and c) Menu Requests.

**Base Requests:** The Base Requests class contains requests related to framework-specific actions such as handling the player component's status, moving between screens, bookkeeping, exception handling, etc.

All requests not directly handled by the Story Player (i.e. Base Requests) are delegated to the respective Screen's MVC to handle them. Programming hooks (i.e. handleRequest) are exposed to enable developers to easily extend any Screen type (and their subtypes) with collaborative features.

**Screen Requests:** Screen requests are specializations of Base Requests, extending them with an ID attribute. The ID corresponds to the ID of the Screen the request refers to; if the request ID attribute matches the ID of the Screen currently shown, the handler associated with the request gets called. An example would be toggling between the text and image views of a Screen.

**Menu Requests:** Menu requests are a specialization of Screen Requests, extending them with the Branch attribute selected (if any) by the user.

**Types of Menu Requests.** We have implemented three types of Menu Requests: a) Role Requests, b) Poll Requests and c) Remote Choice Requests.

**Role Requests:** Role requests are tightly coupled with role assigning menus. A role can be used to restrict the user's navigation to certain paths of the story, thus introducing role-specific subpaths that serve alternative content between users of the same experience. Currently, the cardinality of the relationship between users and roles is 1–1 but one could consider a future extension to also handle role-groups. A collaborative experience can have at most one instance of this type of menu. This limitation is imposed by the way we chose to implement the dynamic nature of roles. The role essentially acts as a prefix for Tags collected while traversing the experience graph. Using the example of the "Building 52" experience, the two variations of the story, implementing the perspective of Abla and Archie can be realized by the corresponding two roles. By making a choice on a Role Menu, the user acquires a role Tag, that can also be used for conditionals. So in the story we may denote that the user with the role Abla, while viewing the Screen about Bucrania (the decorative use of bull's horns), "collects" the tag "PerspectiveBucrania" with the expression Abla:PerspectiveBucrania).

**Poll Requests:** Poll requests are tightly coupled with voting menus. These menus give the ability for a group of users to collectively choose which path of the story they want to follow. Users can change their votes as many times as they want while the voting procedure is still open. The voting procedure stops when all users have successfully voted at least once. The result is either the Branch that gathered the majority of votes or a random selection between the finalist Branches in case of a tie.

**Remote Choice Requests:** Remote choice requests enable a user to change the course of the plot for another user. Conceptually, this functionality can be thought of as the ability of a user to remotely make a Branch selection for the other. This request type may support the implementation of the gift giving activity, described in Sect. 4.

Currently, the Story Maker tool framework provides four distinct templates for menus (i.e. Simple, QR-Code, Interactive Image and NFC). Every Screen or Menu can be easily converted to its collaborative counterpart; i.e. we can add polling capabilities to any menu type just by implementing the related API hooks. These new collaborative capabilities, effectively provide us with twelve new types of menus.

**Identifying Terminal Storytelling Engine States.** A Storytelling Engine State consists of a) the index of the last Screen the user viewed in a Part, b) the ID of that Part c) a set containing the Tags the user encountered so far (i.e. Part or Branch Tags). Transitioning to a new Part is equivalent to creating a new State and pushing the old down the stack. Undoing user actions becomes as simple as replacing the current State with the stack's top. To define terminal states, we have to describe the inner workings of the Storytelling Engine's principle of operation.

Parts are defined as discrete pieces of the plot, however, they effectively act as Screen containers. The majority of Screen subtypes Story Maker provides, materialize content views with one prominent exception, Jumps. Jumps are special types of non-user-visible Screens, acting as direct transitions to other Parts if their conditional expression evaluates to True.

For a user to transition to another Part, she has to follow a Branch either explicitly (i.e. through a Menu) or implicitly (i.e. through a Jump). Formally speaking, a Branch is considered eligible (i.e. qualified for selection by the user) if and only if the state of the Storytelling Engine satisfies all the conditions posed by the Branch.

To prevent the user from following paths where there's no visible content (e.g. a user may follow a Branch leading to a Part that consists only of an unsatisfied Branch), we had to enforce some rules. Specifically, we require all state transitions to leave the

Storytelling Engine in a valid state (i.e. there has to be at least one user-visible Screen or an eligible Branch that leads to a user-visible Screen). Thus, to identify terminal states, it is enough to explore all of the outgoing Branches of a Part; if there is no transition leading to a Part bearing some user-visible content, then the state is considered terminal. To identify whether the user can reach a valid state, the Storytelling Engine traverses the story graph in a Depth-First Search manner until an eligible path gets discovered.

**Authoring User Synchronization Points.** Let us consider the following scenario: A user has to wait for others to reach a Synchronization Point before moving forward.

Synchronization points exploit the underlying condition evaluation mechanism by allowing the author to express requirements such as "specific roles to have acquired specific tags. For an example of three story variations according to the Roles of Abla, Archie and Felix, the tags "Abla", "Archie:House", "Felix:Horns" translate to the following conditions a) the user's Role is "Abla", b) the users with the roles "Archie" and "Felix" to have acquired the Tags "House" and "Horns" respectively for the branch in question to be eligible. Role names must be unique and have no conflicts with other Tags. This extension also allows us to have role-specific Branches.

It is easy to identify users that have to wait for others due to unfulfilled condition constraints. This does not apply to the last user who meets all the criteria to immediately move forward. Thus, we have to devise a mechanism to artificially hold up the last user, for all the users to collectively move forward. Our solution requires having all user devices, upon receiving state updates, determine if the latest state updates lead to paths that were previously non-accessible. If the previous holds, the user has to be held up. The system provides haptic (i.e. vibration) and visual feedback if an event broadcasted by another user's device affects the eligibility of an underlying option. There is also an optional delay between the haptic and the visual cue to re-engage the user with the activity. Lastly, we provide a configurable timer (defaulted to 3 s) to delay the user from moving forward, which triggers when all required roles have synced.

**Evaluating the Global Experience State.** Tags are essentially equivalent to globally scoped Boolean variables; the existence of a tag corresponds to logical True while the absence of it, to a logical False. Tags can be combined to represent Boolean conditions except for OR. This poses some limitations on the conditionals that an author can express. The user acquires tags by visiting parts or following Branches. Tags can also be set as prerequisites for certain graph paths; if the user's tag inventory matches the criteria imposed for following a certain path, then the user can follow that path.

We have extended the Branch condition evaluation mechanism to support tags in the form Abla:House. The previous expression states that the user with the role Abla needs to acquire the tag House to follow a specific Branch. Having a global view of each user's state, lets us express and evaluate conditionals that range beyond the scope of a single device. This way tags can be used to implement synchronization primitives. We can distinguish several patterns of usage for this mechanism, some of which are:

The author may want to establish explicit synchronization points in which all the users wait for the "slowest" user to reach them (i.e. barriers). To this end, they need to follow these steps:

- Create a branch $l_i$ for transitioning $r_i$ to $p_t$, $r_i \in$ Roles. Let $p_i$ be the part $l_i$ is in. The $l_i$'s may belong to different parts.
- Let also $p_i$ assign the tag $t_i$ when visited.
- Add the condition $r_i$ on each $l_i$.
- Add the condition $r_j{:}t_j$ on each $l_i$, $\forall\, r_j \in$ Roles $\setminus \{\, r_i \,\}$.

For example, suppose we have three users, bearing the roles of Abla, Archie and Felix that are currently in parts $p_{Abla}$, $p_{Archie}$ and $p_{Felix}$ respectively. We also have the branches $l_{Abla}$, $l_{Archie}$, $l_{Felix}$ that are in $p_{Abla}$, $p_{Archie}$ and $p_{Felix}$ respectively and point to $p_{target}$. Lastly, $p_{Abla}$, $p_{Archie}$ and $p_{Felix}$ assign the tags $t_{Abla}$, $t_{Archie}$ and $t_{Felix}$ respectively when visited. Then the conditional expressions for the respective branches will be:

Abla AND Archie: $t_{Archie}$ AND Felix: $t_{Felix}$ for $l_{Abla}$
Archie AND Abla: $t_{Abla}$ AND Felix: $t_{Felix}$ for $l_{Archie}$
Felix AND Abla: $t_{Abla}$ AND Archie: $t_{Archie}$ for $l_{Felix}$

If the Storytelling Engine, taking into account the global story state, evaluates the conditions of $l_i$ to True, then $l_i$ can be selected by the user with the role $r_i$, $r_i \in \{$Abla, Archie, Felix$\}$. Following the same strategy, the author can impose synchronization points on a subset of users, just by including only the roles in question.

**Authoring Synchronization Points.** In this section we present the definitions of unilateral and bilateral synchronization points. These can be mixed, thus creating complex synchronization primitives between users.

*Unilateral Synchronization Points:* There exists p, p $\in$ Parts such that the users with $r_1$, $r_2 \in$ Roles paths cross on p. Let's suppose that we want $r_2$ to transition to p before $r_1$; in other words, we want to block $r_1$ from reaching p as long as $r_2$ has not. To achieve this behavior, we have to do the following steps:

- Create two Branches, $l_1$ and $l_2$, dedicated for transitioning $r_1$ and $r_2$ to p; $l_1$, $l_2$ may belong to different parts.
- Add the condition $r_2$ to $l_2$ and let $l_2$ assign the tag t when followed.
- Add the conditions $r_1$ and $r_2{:}t$ to $l_1$.

The condition $r_1$ ensures that the branch will be followed only by the user bearing the role $r_1$ and $r_2{:}t$ renders $l_1$ unavailable while $r_2$ hasn't acquired t.

*Bilateral Synchronization Points.* There exists p, p $\in$ Parts such that the users with $r_1$, $r_2 \in$ Roles paths cross on p. Let's suppose that we want $r_1$ and $r_2$ to be able to transition to p together. To achieve this behavior, we have to do the following steps:

- Create two Branches, $l_1$ and $l_2$, dedicated for transitioning $r_1$ and $r_2$ to p; $l_1$, $l_2$ may belong to different parts.
- Add the conditions $r_1$ and $r_2{:}t_2$ to $l_1$. The condition $r_1$ ensures that the branch will be followed only by the user holding role $r_1$ and $r_2{:}t_2$ renders $l_1$ unavailable while $r_2$ hasn't acquired $t_2$. Let also the part containing $l_1$ assign the tag $t_1$ to $r_1$.

- Add the conditions $r_2$ and $r_1$:$t_1$ to $l_2$. The condition $r_2$ ensures that the branch will be followed only by the user holding role $r_2$ and $r_1$: $t_1$ renders $l_2$ unavailable while $r_1$ hasn't acquired $t_1$. Let also the part containing $l_2$ assign the tag $t_2$ to $r_2$.

For example, suppose we want the user with the role Archie to have viewed the Screen "Bucrania" thus having collected the tag "PerspectiveBucrania", as well as the user with the role Abla to have collected the tag House to let them both move forward.

**Fig. 1.** Example of a synchronization point implementing a content variation social activity

In Fig. 1, on the left device, the user gets informed that they should wait for their partner, while in the middle, we can see that the next button is no longer available and therefore the user is forced to wait for their partner. Once the user of the device on the right reaches the synchronization point (right), the next-screen button becomes available again on both devices, allowing the users to proceed.

# 4  Evaluation

To assess the users' outlook on the enforced synchronization points, we have organized and conducted six trial sessions with twelve participants in six groups of two members each. Our objective was to examine general user experience aspects of the approach as well as how the users negotiated synchronization with user control over the experience.

After a brief introduction to the research objectives and the signing of consent forms, the users were handed one mobile device each. For the purposes of the evaluation we used the digital storytelling experience "The story of building 52" [14, 23]. The users experienced the story off-site, in a room dedicated to the evaluation and after a brief video presentation about the site. They were instructed to proceed within the experience as they saw fit, even to end it if they wished to. While engaged in the experience, an evaluator was discreetly observing and took notes. At the end of the session, the users filled in a brief questionnaire. Each session took approximately 45 min to complete.

The participants' age ranged between 19 and 45 years old (3 were in the range 19–25, 5 in 26–35 and 4 in 36–45). 75% identified themselves as "female" while the rest 25% as "male". Most participants stated moderate to high interest in History (91.6%) and Archaeology (83.3%). The participants were selected so as to be familiar with each other (group-wise), either as friends or colleagues. This was a study design decision since in real conditions people that visit a cultural site together know each other.

The questionnaire to be completed by all users at the end of the evaluation [32] was based on the one in [14] and included visitor demographic characteristics, quality of experience, social presence and questions related to the user agency and sense of control. This last part focused on how the users perceive the interaction points in terms of their effect on their sense of control over the experience. The questionnaire combined statements, rated by the respondents on a five-point Likert scale, from "Strongly disagree" to "Strongly agree", with open-ended questions designed to record qualitative feedback. The original questionnaire was presented in Google Forms format.

## 4.1 Results

Our study showed that most participants were positive about sharing an IDN experience with another person ($\mu = 4.58$, $\sigma = 0.51$). The participants enjoyed the time spent on conversation activities stimulated by the narrative ($\mu = 4.67$, $\sigma = 0.49$). However, further research is needed to validate this finding (e.g. would a group of non-acquainted participants also share a positive view on shared experiences?). The majority of the participants ($\mu = 4.58$, $\sigma = 0.51$) found the mobile experiencing app easy to understand and use.

All participants were in favor of synchronized experiences, also arguing that the kind of experience we delivered would not be possible without it. The majority (75%) mentioned that the interactive nature of the experience helped them keep their focus on the plot while also creating a sense of responsibility towards their partners. Several of the participants (66.6%) stated that the topics raised by the experience for discussion motivated them to work in tandem, provoked interesting discussions and information sharing, something they would otherwise be reluctant to do. Moreover, we observed that most pairs of participants had a, give-or-take, steady pace relative to their partner's. We believe that this is due to the careful design of the experience and the appropriate placement of the synchronization points. All participants stated that at some point they had to wait for their companion. The majority used the waiting time as an opportunity to review the information offered (either on the screen they were in or by moving to previous screens) and to reflect in order to prepare for the discussion with their companions regarding the questions posed by the narrative. We also noticed that some of the users indulged in looking over their companions' screens.

The most prominent negative aspect was that some participants felt insecure while waiting for their companions. This feeling of insecurity stemmed from not knowing in what state their companion was in (i.e. has she made a selection or is she waiting for me?). Lastly, two participants stated they would prefer to receive additional status updates for the actions performed by their partners (i.e. which role they chose, etc.).

## 5   Conclusions and Future Steps

In this work we extend the Story Maker framework to support social interaction in digital storytelling for cultural heritage. This meant that we had to adapt the principles of a framework initially designed for single user interactive, to work in a multi-user setting. To this end, we had to enforce guidelines for authoring the story structure and implement synchronization principles. An additional aim was to implement the collaborative experience in a decentralized fashion, to address the fact that most cultural sites lack the reliable infrastructure to support stable network connectivity.

The evaluation results provided useful insights regarding the usability and effectiveness of our approach as most of our users were quite positive about sharing an IDN experience with another and argued in favor of system based synchronization, feeling that it would not be possible without it. Taking into account that the implementation of synchronization and the social interaction points is based on the use of tags and conditions and does not require programming skills, we are confident that with brief training authors would be able to use the tool to create group digital storytelling activities. However, further evaluation is needed to validate this approach with story creators.

Additionally, our design, by exposing programming hooks, enables developers to easily extend Screens (and any subtype of it) with collaborative features and is also open to further extensions. As an example, taking advantage of the byte stream payload type provided by the Nearby Connections API to support features such as streaming audio or video between devices (i.e. a tour guide acting as a facilitator, could use her device to show every participant a specific exhibit through live video feed). File-sharing can also be used to share in-app recorded streams and commemorative photos.

Furthermore, we aim to introduce physical user collaboration aspects. For example, many devices come with an integrated NFC tag reader/writer; one could think of an extension that will utilize the underlying hardware by exploiting Android BEAM API. This could introduce playfulness to some activities by requiring the users, for example, to touch their devices together for a specific interaction to happen (e.g. "Put your devices together to unite the house's floor plan and explore all its objects"). Android's BEAM can also be used to provide functionality similar to Remote Choice Requests.

The development of such collaborative functionality in the Story Maker tool implies enhancements for the authoring tool itself. Specifically, conditional branches are a topic of Story Maker tool that is not thoroughly tested and its API may completely change in the future (i.e. there are thoughts about developing a simple domain-specific language that will add support for actual variables, a full set of Boolean algebra operators, and more). Moreover, the tool could be extended to provide semi-automated functionality aiding the author in specifying roles of the user and other similar functionalities. Finally, the authoring tool could identify problems of the plot (for example unreachable paths) at authoring time and not at runtime.

**Acknowledgements.** This research has been co-financed by the European Regional Development Fund of the European Union and Greek national funds through the Operational Program Competitiveness, Entrepreneurship and Innovation, under the call RESEARCH –CREATE –INNOVATE (project "ARIA - Augmenting the Reception of music through Innovative solutions and Archives", code:T2EDK-02084)".

# References

1. Callaway, C.B., Stock, O., Dekoven, E.: Experiments with mobile drama in an instrumented museum for inducing conversation in small groups. ACM Trans. Interact. Intell. Syst. **4**(1), 1–39 (2014)
2. Cabrera, J.S., et al.: Mystery in the museum: collaborative learning activities using handheld devices. In: Proceedings of the 7th International Conference on Human Computer Interaction with Mobile Devices and Services (MobileHCI 2005). Association for Computing Machinery, New York, NY, USA, pp. 315–318 (2005)
3. Dierking, L.D., Falk, J.H.: Family behavior and learning in informal science settings: a review of the research. Sci. Educ. **78**, 57–72 (1994)
4. Dim, E., Kuflik, T.: Group situational awareness: being together. In: Workshop on Personalization in Mobile and Pervasive Computing, in Conjunction with UMAP 2009. Trento, Italy (2009)
5. Emmanouilidis, C., Koutsiamanis, R.A., Tasidou, A.: Mobile guides: taxonomy of architectures, context awareness, technologies and applications. J. Netw. Comput. Appl. **36**(1), 103–125 (2012)
6. Falk, J.H., Dierking, L.D.: Learning from Museums, 2nd edn. Rowman & Littlefield, Lanham, Maryland (2018)
7. Falk, J.H.: Identity and the Museum Visitor Experience. Left Coast Press, Walnut Creek, CA (2009)
8. Fosh, L., Benford, S., Reeves, S., Koleva, B., Brundell, P.: See me, feel me, touch me, hear me: trajectories and interpretation in a sculpture garden. In: Proceedings of the SIGCHI Conference on Human Factors in Computing Systems. ACM, New York, pp. 149–158 (2013)
9. Huws, S., John, A., Kid, J.: Evaluating the affective dimensions of Traces-Olion: a subtle mob at St Fagans National Museum of History, Wales. In: IEEE Proceedings of the 3rd International Congress and Expo of Digital Heritage, San Francisco, USA, pp. 26–30, October 2018. IEEE, San Francisco (2018). (in press)
10. Jarusriboonchai, P., et al.: Personal or social? designing mobile interactions for co-located interaction. In: Proceedings of the 8th Nordic Conference on Human-Computer Interaction: Fun, Fast, Foundational (NordiCHI 2014). Association for Computing Machinery, New York, NY, USA, pp. 829–832 (2014)
11. Gargett, K.: Re-thinking the Guided Tour: a Critical Exploration of the use of Co-creation, Dialogue and Facilitation Practices for Democratic Social Engagement at York Minster. MA in Cultural Heritage Management, Department of Archaeology. University of York, UK (2018)
12. Katifori, A., Kourtis, V., Perry, S., Pujol, L., Vayanou, M., Chrysanthi, A.: Cultivating mobile-mediated social interaction in the museum: towards group-based digital storytelling experiences. In: MW2016: Museums and the Web 2016. Published 15 January 2016. Consulted 24 July 2019. https://mw2016.museumsandtheweb.com/paper/cultivating-mobile-mediated-social-interaction-in-the-museum-towards-group-based-digital-storytelling-experiences/
13. Katifori, A., Karvounis, M., Kourtis, V., Perry, S., Roussou, M., Ioanidis, Y.: Applying interactive storytelling in cultural heritage: opportunities, challenges and lessons learned. In: Rouse, R., Koenitz, H., Haahr, M. (eds.) ICIDS 2018. LNCS, vol. 11318, pp. 603–612. Springer, Cham (2018). https://doi.org/10.1007/978-3-030-04028-4_70
14. Katifori, A., et al.: Let them talk!": exploring guided group interaction in digital storytelling experiences. ACM J. Comput. Cult. Heritage (2020). https://doi.org/10.1145/3382773
15. Klopfer, E., Perry, J., Squire, K., Jan, M.F., Steinkuehler, C.: Mystery at the museum: a collaborative game for museum education. In: Proceedings of the 2005 Conference on Computer Support for Collaborative Learning: Learning 2005: The Next 10 Years! (CSCL 2005). International Society of the Learning Sciences, pp. 316–320 (2005)

16. Kuflik, T., Sheidin, J., Jbara, S., Goren-Bar, D., Soffer, P., Stock, O., Zancanaro, M.: Supporting small groups in the museum by context-aware communication services. In: Proceedings of the 12th International Conference on Intelligent User Interfaces (IUI 2007). ACM, New York, pp. 305–308 (2007)

17. Kuflik, T., Stock, O., Zancanaro, M., Gorfinkel, A., Jbara, S., Kats, S., Sheidin, J., Kashtan, N.: A visitor's guide in an active museum: Presentations, communications, and reflection. J. Comput. Cult. Heritage (JOCCH), 3–11 (2011)

18. Leinhardt, G., Knutson, K.: Listening in on Museum Conversations. Altamira Press, Walnut Creek, CA, USA (2004)

19. McManus, P.M.: Good companions: more on the social determination of learning-related behaviour in a science museum. Int. J. Mus. Manage. Curatorship 7, 37–44 (1988)

20. Perry, S., Roussou, M., Mirashrafi, S., Katifori, A., McKinney, S.: Collaborative, shared digital experiences supporting sites, meaning-making at heritage sites. In: Lewi, H., Smith, W., Cooke, S., vom Lehn, D. (Eds.) The Routledge International Handbook of New Digital Practices in Galleries, Libraries, Archives, Museums and Heritage Sites. Routledge International Handbook, Routledge (2019)

21. Pujol, L., Roussou, M., Poulou, S., Balet, O., Vayanou, M., Ioannidis, Y.: Personalizing interactive digital storytelling in archaeological museums: the CHESS project. In: Earl, G., Sly, T., Chrysanthi, A., Murrieta-Flores, P., Papadopoulos, C., Ro-manowska, I., Wheatley, D. (Eds.) Archaeology in the Digital Era. Papers from the 40th Annual Conference of Computer Applications and Quantitative Methods in Archaeology (CAA) (2013). Southampton, UK, pp. 26–29, March 2012. Amsterdam University Press (2012). https://arno.uva.nl/cgi/arno/show.cgi?fid=545855

22. Raptis, D., Tselios, N., Avouris, N.: Context-based design of mobile applications for museums: a survey of existing practices. In: Proceedings of the 7th Conference on Human-Computer Interaction with Mobile Devices and Services, Mobile HCI, Salzburg, Austria, pp. 153–160 (2005)

23. Roussou, M., Pujol, L., Katifori, A., Chrysanthi, A., Perry, S., Vayanou, M.: The museum as digital storyteller: collaborative participatory creation of interactive digital experiences. In: MW2015: Museums and the Web 2015. Published 31 January 2015. Consulted 28 September 2015. http://mw2015.museumsandtheweb.com/paper/the-museum-as-digital-storyteller-collaborative-participatory-creation-of-interactive-digital-experiences/

24. Tolmie, P., Benford, S., Greenhalgh, C., Rodden, T., Reeves, S.: Supporting group interactions in museum visiting. In: Proceedings of the ACM Conference on Computer Supported Cooperative Work (CSCW 2014), pp. 1049–1059 (2014)

25. Turkle, S.: Alone Together: Why We Expect More from Technology and Less from Each Other. Basic Books, New York (2011)

26. Suh, Y., Shin, C., Woo, W., Dow, S., MacIntyre, B.: Enhancing and evaluating users' social experience with a mobile phone guide applied to cultural heritage. Pers. Ubiquit. Comput. 15(6), 649–665 (2011). https://doi.org/10.1007/s00779-010-0344-2

27. Twiss-Garrity, B., Fisher, M., Sastre, A.: The art of storytelling: enriching art museum exhibits and education through visitor narratives. In: Trant, J., Bearman, D. (Eds.) Museums and the Web 2008. Montreal, Quebec, Canada: Archives & Museum Informatics (2008)

28. Vrettakis, E., Kourtis, V., Katifori, A., Karvounis, M., Lougiakis, C., Ioannidis, Y.: Narralive – creating and experiencing mobile digital storytelling in cultural heritage. Digit. Appl. Archaeol. Cult. Heritage 15, e00114 (2019)

29. Vrettakis, E., et al.: The story maker - an authoring tool for multimedia-rich interactive narratives. In: Bosser, A.-G., Millard, D.E., Hargood, C. (eds.) ICIDS 2020. LNCS, vol. 12497, pp. 349–352. Springer, Cham (2020). https://doi.org/10.1007/978-3-030-62516-0_33

30. Wessel, D., Mayr, E.: Potentials and challenges of mobile media in museums. Int. J. Interact. Mobile Technol. 1(1), 32–39 (2007)

31. com.google.android.gms.nearby.connection. https://developers.google.com/android/refere nce/com/google/android/gms/nearby/connection/package-summary. Accessed 28 July 2021
32. Storytelling evaluation questionnaire. https://osf.io/x2rkh
33. Tallon, L.: Introduction: mobile, digital and personal. In: Tallon, L., Walker, K. (eds.) Digital Technologies and the Museum Experience: Handheld Guides and Other Media. Altamira Press (2008)
34. Roussou, M., Katifori, A.: Flow, staging, wayfinding, personalization: evaluating user experience with mobile museum narratives. Multimodal Technol. Interact. **2**, 32 (2018)
35. Cesário, V., Petrelli, D., Nisi, V.: Teenage visitor experience: classification of behavioral dynamics in museums. In: Proceedings of the 2020 CHI Conference on Human Factors in Computing Systems (CHI 2020). Association for Computing Machinery, New York, NY, USA, pp. 1–13 (2020). https://doi.org/10.1145/3313831.337633
36. Lombardo, V., Damiano, R.: Storytelling on mobile devices for cultural heritage. New Rev. Hypermedia Multimedia **18**(1–2), 11–35 (2012). https://doi.org/10.1080/13614568.2012. 617846
37. Pau, S.: Audio that moves you: experiments with location-aware storytelling in the SFMOMA app. In: MW17: Museums and the Web 2017. Published 31 January 2017. Consulted 24 July 2019

# Beats and Units Framework: A Story-Game Integration Framework for the Ideation Stage of Narrative Design of Serious Games

Nelson Zagalo(✉) ⓘ, Ana Patrícia Oliveira ⓘ, and Pedro Cardoso ⓘ

DigiMedia, Department of Communication and Art, University of Aveiro, Aveiro, Portugal
{nzagalo,apoliveira,pedroccardoso}@ua.pt

**Abstract.** There are no recipes or rules to develop games, any more than there are to develop stories. Our aim was to develop a serious game with the goal of promoting discussion and awareness among children around nutrition: FlavourGame. For this purpose, we needed not only to design game mechanics, but also to create a narrative that provided meaning to the game experience, in order to ensure substrate to the context of nutrition. In this paper, we present a framework that serves as a narrative design tool used in the development of this game and which can be employed in the creation of serious story-based games.

**Keywords:** Narrative design · Serious games · Storytelling · Play · Creativity process · User experience design

## 1   Introduction

Narrative design has emerged in the world of game design only in the last decade [1, 2], as a way of uniting story writing and game design [3–5]. The complexity of this union arises from the fact that they are both central systems for generating human experience, and as such, when united they collide by the force with which they draw to themselves the control of experiences [6]. Therefore, we are facing a process still fluid in ways of doing [7].

In this paper, we present the *beats&units story-game integration framework*, which consists of a layered information management system that supports the ideation stage of narrative design of serious games. It is organized in two levels: 1) the *operational level*, composed by a single layer materialized into a set of cards that can be used to build de narrative with the game; and 2) the *informational level*, constituted the several base layers with the information useful to operate the operational level.

## 2   The Beats and Units Framework

The *beats&units framework* (Fig. 1) is an instrument for the ideation of narrative design in serious games. It features the *operational level*, that builds and integrates the narrative

© Springer Nature Switzerland AG 2021
A. Mitchell and M. Vosmeer (Eds.): ICIDS 2021, LNCS 13138, pp. 172–176, 2021.
https://doi.org/10.1007/978-3-030-92300-6_15

with the game, and the *informational level,* in which features the information about the story and the game. These are organized in four groups: the *conceptual layers,* in which layer 1 is focused on framing of possibilities of meaning, layer 2 on the mechanics, and layer 3 on narrative structure; the *design layers,* in which layer 4 inspects the gameplay, and layer 5 the game plot; the *units layer,* which expands the units of narrative; and the *surface layer,* which is the tool that results from all the other layers.

| | | |
|---|---|---|
| Operational level | Surface layer | Layer 7 – Beats |
| Informational level | Units layer | Layer 6 – Units |
| | Design layers | Layer 5 – Game plot |
| | | Layer 4 – Gameplay |
| | Conceptual layers | Layer 3 – Story (Fable) |
| | | Layer 2 – Mechanics |
| | | Layer 1 – Intent (Nexus) |

**Fig. 1.** The *beats&units framework.*

## 2.1 The Conceptual Layers

*Conceptual layer 1* is based on Aristotle's elements of circumstance [8] — the know scheme: *Who, What, When, Where, Why* and *How.* According to the project's intent, these serve as the framing of possibilities of meaning, delimiting the scope of the game and story.

*Conceptual layer 2* follows Schell's work [9], restricting mechanics to: *space, objects, actions, rules, skills,* and *uncertainty.* Uncertainty is perhaps the most relevant mechanic here as it defines the great goal of the game and what is at stake for the characters and the plot of the narrative.

*Conceptual layer 3* invokes Todorov's structure [10], which defines narrative structures: *equilibrium, disruption, recognition, repair,* and *new equilibrium.* It allows us to start from the natural state of the world to then propose different disruptions in it, until we find one that matches the game's intent.

## 2.2 The Design Layers

To connect story and game, *layer* 4 resorts to the *Forest Paths* method by Alexander Swords [11], modeling the relationship between the character's story, and player's actions. It establishes the player as a starting point and the goal as the finishing line, whereas in the middle is where the game process is developed that guarantees the player's involvement with the storyworld.

Up until layer 4, we have the story that we want people to retain in their heads, a fable, but that is different from the artifact that stimulates the fable itself. In this sense, *layer 5* takes Todorov's [10] structure and adapts it to Freytag's [12], abandoning the chronology of the story, and following the plot as an organization of information capable of generating interest and surprise.

## 2.3  The Units Layer

The *units layer* follows previous theoretical work [13] indicating the *setting*, *characters*, and *events* as the core units of narrative design, to which we now add *player* and *narration* as core units of player participation.

## 2.4  The Surface Layer

The *surface layer* operationalizes everything by taking the shape of a set of cards in which each features a form that includes *Scenes*, *Beats*, and *Units* (Fig. 2). These three elements are used in the domain of scriptwriting [14] and serve the scriptwriter in designing the information management of the experience. *Scenes* are sections that frame concrete moments in which something happens, the so-called conflicts or incidents that produce perfectly delineable and autonomous spaces of information. *Beats* are actions that break scenes into smaller structural units. McKee defines *Beats* as "an exchange of behavior in action/reaction" [14]. These may concern what the characters (narrative) or players (game) do. *Units* subdivide a Scene and a Beat into 5 elements that consist of a generalization of the game-story in a mode of abstraction, clashing with the fundamental needs of the game and the stories. Regarding the Units: *Narration* is about the scene's information in each beat; *Setting* refers to the place in the game, the place in the story; *Characters* relates to who is in the portrayed moment, including dialogues and voice overs; *Events* describe the actions of each element in the Scene/Beat; *Player* is aimed at what can or should the player do.

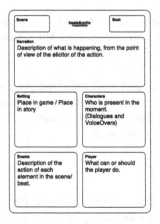

**Fig. 2.**  Layer 7 – A Beat (card).

Each card represents a Beat (Fig. 3) in a specific Scene. The cards are building blocks of the relationship between narrative and gameplay, able to be combined into linear or multilinear sequences of events with no fixed numbers of Scenes or Beats per Scene.

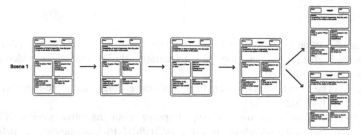

**Fig. 3.** Each card represents a Beat. By interconnecting Beats, one can work on flow, pacing and balancing in linear and non-linear sequences of events.

## 3 Conclusions and Next Steps

The current version of the *beats&units framework* allowed us to speed up the understanding of the game and story experience, making the information visual and hierarchical in time. By resorting to it we were able to understand what the player knows and does not know about the game and the story, at each moment. It thus becomes possible to measure the evolution of each character, in the eyes of the player, to evaluate the narrative progression, to understand its moments of tension and breathing, and to adjust the game progress with the narrative progress.

In a first moment, we used the tool to define the fundamental information to offer just before the game starts, as well as the information to introduce in the dialogues. The goal of any game lays in its interaction, so we cannot continuously stop the game to tell the story in non-interactive modes, we need to work on the different modes of exposition, from the dialogues to the scene objects – e.g. character presentation, space, setting, etc. – in order to introduce the information that allows the evolution of the characters and the progression of the narrative. So, the tool was very useful in determining these elements, because as the information is introduced in the game, and appears in the *beats&units framework*, we can better understand the flow of the experience, and understand if we need to speed up the exposure or slow it down.

We consider that the tool has delivered as expected, in terms of supporting the creation and management of narrative design. Naturally, for larger projects, it might be necessary to take the structure and apply it in a programmable environment, which could offer us links between cells, transportation of variables, as well as incorporating dialogues and actions directly into the final implementation of the game.

The next steps are to finalize the implementation of the game, and to perform sets of tests with users, namely working pre-tests and post-tests, to understand how much the game experience may or may not contribute to future behavioral changes, and consequently find about the level of truth infused in the game intent.

**Acknowledgments.** The authors would like to acknowledge POCI-FEDER and FCT for funding this Project, under the Grant Agreement No. POCI-01–0145-FEDER-031024.

# References

1. Brunette, L.: What's a Narrative Designer? https://web.archive.org/web/20171110210044/ http://www.bigfishgames.com/blog/guide-to-narrative-design-and-writing-video-game-sto ries/. Accessed 15 July 2021
2. Jubert, T.: The Narrative Designer. http://litshowcase.org/content/the-narrative-designer/. Accessed 15 July 2021
3. Batchelor, J.: Four questions to help improve your narrative design [Chris Bate-men]. https://www.gamesindustry.biz/articles/2019-07-16-four-questions-to-help-improve-your-narrative-design. Accessed 15 July 2021
4. Heussner, T., Finley, T.K., Hepler, J.B., Lemay, A.: The Game Narrative Toolbox. Routledge, Burlington (2015). https://doi.org/10.4324/9781315766836
5. McRae, E.: Narrative Design for Indies: Getting Started. Fiction Engine Limited (2017)
6. Zagalo, N.: Engagement Design: Designing for Interaction Motivations. Springer, Cham (2020). https://doi.org/10.1007/978-3-030-37085-5
7. Heussner, T.: The Advanced Game Narrative Toolbox (2019).https://doi.org/10.1201/978135 1014397
8. Sloan, M.C.: Aristotle's nicomachean ethics as the original locus for the septem circumstan-tiae. Class. Philol. **105**, 236–251 (2010). https://doi.org/10.1086/656196
9. Schell, J.: The Art of Game Design: A Book of Lenses. Morgan Kaufmann (2008)
10. Todorov, T., Weinstein, A.: Structural analysis of Narrative. Nov. A Forum Fict. (1969). https://doi.org/10.2307/1345003
11. Swords, A.: Forest Paths Method For Narrative Design. Alexander Swords, Melbourne (2020).
12. Freytag, G.: Technique of the Drama: An Exposition of Dramatic Composition and Art. University Press of the Pacific, Forest Grove (1864)
13. Zagalo, N.: Design de Narrativa, Desenho de significado na experiência interativa. Convoc. - Rev. Ciências Da Arte. **7**, 57–76 (2019)
14. McKee, R.: Story: Substance, Structure, Style and the Principles of Screen Writing. Harper Collins, New York (1997)

# Interactive Narrative Theory

# Monster Power. Rebel Heart. Gay Sword.

## Queer Structures and Narrative Possibility in PbtA Tabletop Roleplaying Games

PS Berge(✉) (iD)

University of Central Florida, Orlando, FL 32816, USA
hello@psberge.com

**Abstract.** Much of the scholarship on tabletop roleplaying games (TRPGs) has focused on representation of queer characters and 'cues' that signal to queer audiences [1]. Yet recent independent TRPGs have moved beyond cues that queer play is merely tolerated and instead integrate ludonarrative structures that actively encourage queer interactions. Drawing from queer game scholarship and discussions by queer game designers, this article uses the idea of the 'playground' of game design [2, 3] to identify queer structures in three Powered by the Apocalypse (PbtA) TRPGs: *Voidheart Symphony* (2020), *Thirsty Sword Lesbians* (2021), and *Apocalypse Keys* (forthcoming). In this case study, I show how these games frame key elements (safety tools, Conditions, personal doom, Bonds, and media inspirations) as structures [4] that actively support queer narrative possibility. I argue that these structures engender shared outcomes, namely: encouraging emotions, showcasing messy characters, clarifying the power of fiction, recognizing tension between community and self, reframing violence, and building inter-player support.

**Keywords:** Queer games · Tabletop roleplaying games · Powered by the Apocalypse

# 1 Introduction

## 1.1 Queer TRPGs: A Troubled Legacy

The history of tabletop roleplaying games (TRPGs, often stylized TTRPGs) and queerness is contentious. On the one hand, mainstream TRPGs (like *Dungeons and Dragons*) have been constricted by the conservative roots of the medium. As Stenros & Sihvonen note in their history of queer representation in TRPG sourcebooks, "queer sexualities started to figure in the role-playing game books towards the end of the 1980s. However, in these early depictions, male homosexuality is presented as especially villainous, traitorous, and deceitful" [5]. Early TRPGs featured limitations on character gender [6] and even labeled queer identities as "sexual disorders" [5, 7]. Broadly speaking, the evolution of queerness in TRPGs, like queer video games, has followed a two-pronged path: 1) industry-supported games have made limited effort towards basic representation while 2) independent TRPGs push the boundaries of queer game possibilities.

© Springer Nature Switzerland AG 2021
A. Mitchell and M. Vosmeer (Eds.): ICIDS 2021, LNCS 13138, pp. 179–192, 2021.
https://doi.org/10.1007/978-3-030-92300-6_16

In TRPG spaces, like other game spaces, queerness can be understood in two modes: 1) representing the experiences and identities of queer folks and 2) "as a way of being, doing, and desiring *differently*" [8]. As queer game scholar Bo Ruberg notes [8], this latter model builds on decades of queer theory [9–11] that examines queerness as a force that disrupts hegemonic structures. Queer game scholarship that addresses TRPGs has focused predominantly on queer representation, usually by examining sourcebooks and social dynamics. Stenros & Sihvonen argue for increased queer representation when they write "even the most fleeting mention, a veiled remark, would signal that the game world does indeed feature queer people" [5]. They call such signals 'cues' for queer players—noting that "cues for queer play remain a controversial issue… The publisher and designer, the creators of the urtext, signal if queer play is tolerated, encouraged, or expected" [1]. While signals for queer representation in TRPGs are important, overfocusing on cues neglects possibilities for queer play that goes "beyond representation into the mechanics, aesthetics, interfaces, and development practices of games" [3]. While games like *D&D* have recently added invitations for queer players and characters [6], mainstream TRPGs have struggled to develop meaningful queer *structures*.

While game scholars have begun exploring independent video games and the "Queer Avant-Garde" [3], less notice has been paid to indie TRPGs built around queer structures. Designer Naomi Clark noted in an interview with Ruberg that she didn't want her roleplaying card game, *Consentacle*, to be "about queerness at the level of characters or narrative. Instead, the queerness comes out in the interactions between people" [12]. Likewise, Avery Alder said that "games are made queer when they have structural queerness. Structural queerness is fundamentally about challenging the frameworks of how stories get told. It's about subverting systems through queer mechanics and creating new ways of seeing desire" [4]. This idea of 'structural queerness' is fundamental to TRPG design that reshapes the narrative possibilities of play through queer interactions. This study examines such structures across three Powered by the Apocalypse TRPGs—*Voidheart Symphony* (*VS*) by Minerva McJanda, *Thirsty Sword Lesbians* (*TSL*) by April Kit Walsh, and *Apocalypse Keys* (*AK*) by Jamila R. Nedjadi—to explicate a toolkit for storygame design that opens possibilities for queer play.

## 1.2 Dragons on the Playground: Queer Cues vs. Queer Structures

Before we define and observe "queer structures" [4], and how can they be differentiated from shallower instances of representation, it is important to delineate how structures in TRPGs differ from other mechanical game systems. Ruberg writes that queer game designers have "demonstrate[d] how queerness can operate in video games beyond representation, and how game-making can function as a playground in its own right for exploring queer messes" [3]. This idea of an explorative 'playground' mirrors a framework in TRPG design, as Jay Dragon notes in a lyrical article titled "A Dozen Fragments on Playground Theory" [2]. Dragon describes a growing frustration with the characterization of TRPGs as rigid rule systems that players engage with in fixed ways. Instead, Dragon—like Ruberg—offers the metaphor of a playground, drawing an analogy to physical structures: slides, monkey bars, etc. While playground features might have an intended use, the *actual* use of such structures is interpreted by children (the players). As Dragon writes: "I have added a slide, because it is fun to slide down, and because sometimes that is all that is needed. There are metal bolts exposed on the side of the slide, and the kids have invented their own game with those bolts..." [2]. TRPG mechanics intended to work one way by the designer(s) can be ignored or reinterpreted by players. At the same time, play might take place in what Dragon calls the "wide open field" where "structure is unneeded" [2]. The playground, as a metaphorical lens, is useful for examining TRPG systems not as singular, fixed mechanics (defined rules with concrete outcomes), but as structures (acted upon by players) within a flexible system of inter-pretation. Unlike most videogame narratives, where players only engage the surface of the system through "abstracted interface" [13, 14] players interact with the struc-tures of TRPGs directly [4]. In the same way that the physical structures of a playspace anticipate, shape, and encourage the possibilities of play—so too the structures of a role-playing game shape emergent narrative *possibility*. In this sense, my analysis of these games focuses on 1) how their mechanics comprise larger structures of play, and 2) how those structures support queer narratives.

In looking at queer TRPG structures, we must note how such structures are distinct from more superficial elements. Llaura McGee describes a problem in video games that interpret queerness through an oversimplified "shallow coating," and notes "the metaphor is in the mechanics, but the mechanics are so simplified that the metaphor is meaningless" [15]. Likewise, Alder criticizes games that approach queerness through characters and narrative but neglect queer mechanics—noting that 'desire' mechanics in her game *Monsterhearts* stemmed out of a need to "make those mechanics queer" [4]. To this end, I'm defining game elements that provide superficial signals and representational flavor (what Anna Anthropy has called a "gay button" [16]) as queer *cues* [1], separate from queer *structures* that shape and anticipate narrative play.

To help distinguish these, here's an example: many TRPGs provide a space for pronouns on character sheets. This is a mechanical cue to players that knowing and respecting the pronouns of other players and characters is important, that they should not be assumed, and is a "signal that the game world does indeed feature queer people" [5]. Compare this, however, to Jay Dragon's game *Sleepaway*, which gives the following prompt, "For each camper, choose 2 genders (1 from each column):

- **Column 1:** "Masculine, Feminine, Full, Empty, Open, Closed, Ajar, Adjacent, Crossing Past, Above, Below Inbetween, Overflowing, Vacant"
- **Column 2:** "Cicada, Fox, Eagle, Pillbug, Worm, Faux Wolf, Dragon, Robin, Coyote, Lion, Moth, Butterfly, Tree" [17].

*Sleepaway*'s mechanics for describing characters' gender(s) go far beyond being a cue that queerness is "tolerated, encouraged, or expected" [1]. By prompting players to 1) choose two genders, 2) consider the multiplicity of gender, and 3) think about whether they are more of an "Empty Faux Wolf" or an "Overflowing Worm," *Sleepaway* structurally reshapes the game narrative with queer possibility [17]. While both takes on pronouns are important, one mechanic *leaves space* for queerness while the other *actively encourages queer interactions*. As Jack Halberstam has said, "rather than just hunting for LGBT characters in the worlds of gaming, we want to seek out queer forms, queer beings, and queer modes of play" [18]. In this way, I focus on how each game in this study reshapes play with queer and 'disorienting' [11] narrative possibility. While any analysis of TRPG mechanics based on sourcebooks alone is likely to be reductive, analyzing how queer game structures are framed across multiple titles provides a more comprehensive glimpse of queer possibility in TRPGs.

### 1.3 A Brief History of the *Apocalypse*

Vincent and Meguey Baker's *Apocalypse World* (*AW*, 2010) marked the beginning of a critical era in 'fiction-first' TRPG design. As Aaron Reed notes, *Apocalypse World*, as a collaborative storygaming system, "prioritizes Generation of ideas over simulationist Administration, flipping the dynamic present in traditional rules-heavy games" [19]. A violent, dystopian, wasteland-punk game, *AW* itself is less important to the legacy of independent TRPGs than the Bakers' invitation to other designers: "If you've created a game inspired by *Apocalypse World*, and would like to publish it, please do" [20]. The *AW* website lists 89 games that designers have since self-designated with the genealogical marker "Powered by the Apocalypse" (PbtA) as of this writing. What designates a game as PbtA is complicated. As Vincent Baker writes, the label "isn't the name of a kind of game, set of game elements, or even the core design thrust of a coherent movement. (Ha! This last, the least so.)" [20]. Instead, the label is an unpoliced 'homage'—designers may choose to signal a relationship between their game and *AW* using the label and a logo. In other words, "PbtA" is not a branding or a mechanical linkage to *AW*'s system, but a mark of ludic etymology.

The three games in this study are all part of this distributed legacy of PbtA games and all share several mechanical influences from *AW* itself:

- Each game relies on "playbooks" that designate the different roles the characters take in the game (i.e. "The Beast" [*TSL*], "The Watcher" [*VS*], "The Fallen" [*AK*]).
- Gameplay is oriented around "moves." Moves pause and shape the action of the fiction and generally involve dice-rolls and/or choices. Moves are activated by a narrative 'trigger' that happens during collective storytelling (i.e. in *AK*, if a character confides in another, they will trigger the 'Reveal Your Heart' move).
- Play and the fiction are structured as a 'conversation' between one MC ("Keeper of the Doors" in *AK*, "Gaymaster" in *TSL*, and "Architect" in *VS*) and the players: sharing what their characters (or NPCs and the world) are doing, saying, and thinking.

These games also draw from two influential PbtA titles: *Masks: A New Generation* by Brendan Conway and *Monsterhearts* (*MH*) by Avery Alder (who was part of development for both *TSL* and *AK*). *Masks* is a superhero game focused on teen drama and cartoon-violence—with a robust system for relationships and emotional defeat. Both *VS* and *TSL* note *Masks* as an inspiration, and Nedjadi has talked about his experiences running *Masks* as motivation for designing *AK*. Similarly, numerous scholars and designers point to Alder's work (*MH* and *MH 2* in particular) as a turning point in the legacy of both PbtA games and queer TRPGs [1, 7, 19, 21, 22]. *MH*, a messy drama about monsters in high school, brought the queer potential of PbtA games to the fore. In this sense, *VS*, *TSL*, and *AK* are products of a complex ecology within the independent TRPG scene. While this study accounts for only a sample of PbtA games, I hope it illuminates some of the ways that independent TRPG designers have developed a shared toolkit for supporting queer narrative play.

## 1.4   The Table is Everywhere: The Games in Context

The TRPG scenes of today extend beyond physical tabletops—remote play, online distribution, and digital affordances are now commonplace parts of the medium. Virtual tabletops (VTTs) such as Roll20, Fantasy Grounds, rollwithme.xyz, Foundry VTT, and Tabletop Simulator provide means of playing mainstream and independent TRPGs online, often augmented through voice/video chat software such as Zoom or Discord. The material components of TRPGs (character sheets and playbooks, dice, cards, handouts, sourcebooks) have likewise adapted to iterations across apps, online generators and dice rollers, PDFs, and digital assets. During the COVID-19 pandemic, the ubiquity of online play has exploded: sites like Roll20—which allow players to advertise online games— were used by libraries, game stores, and friend groups to move game night online. The distribution of independent TRPGs likewise relies on digital platforms: games are funded and circulated through Kickstarter and Backerkit, itchfunding, and other pledge-based programs. Digital game marketplaces like itch.io and DriveThruRPG are central hubs for selling indie content. The games analyzed here are, as modern TRPGs, enmeshed in this complex digital ecology [23]. The networked backdrop of independent TRPGs is not only an important reality, but key context for queer play—where the conversative legacy of TRPGs has often excluded marginalized players, digital tabletops have changed the game for queer community. Not everyone has access to, or is comfortable, joining public tables at the local game store, but queer TRPG communities are thriving online. The table is everywhere—the games examined here operate between their analog roots and the new affordances of digitality.

*Thirsty Sword Lesbians*, written by April Kit Walsh (she/her, gay/ghem), was published by Evil Hat and supported by a Kickstarter campaign that raised just shy of $300k USD (15 times the game's funding goal). *TSL* is the most genre-flexible game in this study, as the opening paragraph states: characters "may be fantasy heroes, or may inhabit a galaxy of laser swords and starships. Anywhere that swords cross and hearts race, thirsty sword lesbians are there" [24]. Rather than focus on a singular game genre (stealth-action, mystery, etc.) *TSL* pulls its 'genre' inspiration from queer-coded lesbian media (direct examples are discussed in Sect. 2.6 as media inspirations). Characters fight and flirt with villains, and playbooks use sword-lesbian archetypes such as The Nature Witch ("Oblivious Horse Girl," "Plant Geek Babygay") and The Infamous ("Former Villain," "Escaped Henchperson"). As of this study, *TSL* is the most commercially known—with an established publisher (Evil Hat), its own third-party license ("Powered By Lesbians"), and official assets and modules for Roll20's online marketplace.

Written by Minerva McJanda (she/her) and published through UFO Press, *Voidheart Symphony* was also funded via Kickstarter and distributed through itch.io with physical books and card decks shipped to backers. *VS* builds on McJanda's previous work with PbtA design (*Legacy: Life Among the Ruins* [25], among others). *VS* is heavily inspired by the videogame *Persona 5* and imitates its core gameplay loop. In *VS*, characters are rebels: mundane people in a modern city with the power to enter demonic, otherworldly labyrinths called Castles. Castles contain the reflections of a Vassal—powerful, evil figures—and by infiltrating them and defeating their Vassals, the rebels change the state of the real world. Rebels must also manage a host of relationships (called Covenants) represented by tarot cards. Rebel playbooks (The Authority, The Icon, The Heretic) note characters' civilian strengths and otherworldly powers.

Currently in development by Jamila R. Nedjadi (they/he), *Apocalypse Keys* was originally distributed through itch.io during its beta releases, but is now being produced by Evil Hat (also the publisher of *TSL*). This study used official playtest materials for the game; content quoted here is subject to change. In *AK,* players are monstrous agents working for a secretive, occult government branch called the DIVISION. Inspired by storyworlds such as *Hellboy*, the players are monsters investigating monsters: stopping Harbingers of the apocalypse from opening Doom's Door. Yet each monstrous agent's playbook (The Last, The Surge, etc.) foretells a doomed future: as characters embrace their Powers of Darkness, they risk becoming harbingers themselves.

## 2 Finding Queer Structures

### 2.1 Overview

Despite their disparate genres (lesbians, heist-action, mystery), the three sourcebooks adopt shared structures that encourage queer narrative possibility: 1) safety tools 2) Conditions 3) personal doom 4) Bonds and 5) drawing from extant media. These structures, though uniquely framed, all anticipate queer play and interactions. Notably, these structures are not *exclusively* queer, but support both queer narrative possibility and marginalized play across identities. Below, I characterize these structures and examine how they are presented across each title:

### 2.2 Safety Tools: Beginning with Boundaries

All these games foreground the importance of safety tools—used to manage boundaries, scope, and tone for play. Each game either links to or references tools from the TTRPG Safety Toolkit (curated and maintained by Kienna Shaw and Lauren Bryant-Monk), which is prevalent in independent TRPGs [26]. These include the use of:

- *The X-Card* (by John Stavropoulos), which gives players a card (digital or material) that signals a need to pause the game in response to player discomfort or trauma.
- *Script Change Tools* (by Beau Jágr Sheldon) that allow players to signal (via cards, gesture, or chat) a request to rewind, fast-forward, or pause the narrative.
- *The CATS sheet* (by Tomer Gurantz, adapted from Patrick O'Leary) that helps the MC describe the Concept, Aim, Tone, and Subject Matter of the game.
- A system for sharing *Lines* (topics players don't want to exist in the story) and *Veils* (things they don't want to see 'onscreen'), developed by Ron Edwards.

In addition, these games provide discussions of consent-based gaming and storytelling. *VS* encourages players to preemptively discuss how they feel about antagonism between characters and what kinds of enemies they are comfortable going up against

[27]. *TSL* includes re-flavored versions of many of these tools (a check-in card, lines and veils, and the X-card) and also a discussion about "The Palette" of the game, where players share what story elements they wish to focus on [24]. *AK* refers players to the toolkit, includes a digital CATS sheet, and a Greed/Red/Yellow system for describing content players want to see and avoid (an adaptation of Lines and Veils) [28]. In every case, these safety tools are frontloaded as the first and most crucial part of setup.

As community game designer Elizabeth Sampat wrote about her game *Deadbolt*, "If *Deadbolt* is queer, it's because it's a safe space to be queer" [29]. Safety tools allow players to establish boundaries for play and fiction—defining the narrative playground through shared, consent-based rulebuilding. As Ashwell notes, these mechanics are not framed as an attempt to limit content, rather "the stress is… that it makes a greater range of content *possible*" [22]. Notably, safety tools also serve as a queer cue in that they clarify audience and signal to marginalized players that safety is valued. *TSL* even includes a clear statement "No Fascists or Bigots Allowed" (a strategy developed by *iHunt* designer Olivia Hill [30]) along with a detailed list of the game's expectations for players' social awareness and political values. Clark has noted the importance of designing space for consent in tabletop games [12]. While the power dynamics of TRPGs can fall into toxic tropes (relying on, say, antagonism between the facilitator and players), these safety tools are rooted in trust. Rather than asking players to agree to 'terms' or relying on implied consent, these tools are based around shared boundary-setting (through the "palette," lines, and veils), active consent (revoked at any time via the X-card or "Pause" tools), and shared satisfaction.

## 2.3 Conditions: Pain and Possibility

Conway's *Masks* developed a system called 'Conditions,' which reimagined the mechanics for harm and physical violence used in *AW*. *Masks*, a game about adolescent superheroes, notes "how much physical harm can an invulnerable space alien take before they go out?… *Masks* isn't about that—in *Masks*, [characters'] responses to getting punched are far more important." [31]. *Masks'* Conditions system tracks the emotional fallout of conflict as characters become emotionally embroiled ("The alien gets Angry"). Each game in this study adapts the Conditions system to emphasize emotional consequences over physical harm. As players amass Conditions, they are expected to roleplay the responses of their thwarted characters.

*VS* uses variations of the same Conditions as *Masks*: characters might become Angry, Callous, Cowed, Overwhelmed, or Scared—each leading to a mechanical penalty for certain rolls. If characters accrue too many Conditions, they are removed from the scene and receive a complication in the mundane world. This is a motivation for players to use emotional support moves and to manage the mental health of characters. *VS* links this back to player safety: on the page delineating Conditions, there's a highlighted note that only *characters*, not players, should be dealing with unwanted feelings. *TSL* likewise uses five conditions: Angry, Frightened, Guilty, Hopeless, and Insecure. If all are marked, characters are Defeated, and the player momentarily loses narrative control of the character. Like *VS*, players can clear Conditions through support moves, but also by taking destructive actions such as lashing out (Angry), running away (Frightened), or confronting an object of jealousy (Insecure) [24]. *AK* takes a different approach:

each Playbook has its own four Conditions, and players can earn Darkness Tokens (a crucial resource spent on moves) by roleplaying a Condition that affects them. Because Conditions are unique to each Playbook, they build on that Playbook's theme: The Last (a grief-stricken survivor) might become Distant, Merciless, or Despairing. The proud Fallen, on the other hand, turns Lustful, Raging, Forlorn, or Obsessed.

By choosing not to focus on physical harm, the Conditions system lingers on the emotional aftermath of conflict. Unlike physical wounds, where characters might sleep or drink a healing potion to 'reset' bodily harm, Conditions can't be cleared by time. Instead, they haunt the characters, and can only be resolved through care and support by companions (at best) or by lashing out (at worst). Rather than framing Conditions as a *consequence* (emphasizing the infliction as punishment), the focus is on *the character's response*—an opening of possibility for hurt and healing in the fiction.

Conditions are a queer reimagining of damage and pain. Importantly, these systems do not *demand* that players or characters be messy or vulnerable, but instead encourage experimentation with what Ruberg has called for in video games: a "rich array of emotions… that can in fact shape a game's message as much as (if not more than) its content and mechanics" [32]. Characters get vicious and fearful—rejecting an expectation of happiness, victory, and heroism. Conditions drive players to consider context: a character who reacts to something by becoming Lustful ($AK$) must now think about how that desire might shape the fiction. By confronting context through consensual pain [33], these games invite players to "feel what we aren't supposed to feel" [32] and engage with emotional volatility and messy possibility.

## 2.4 Personal Doom: Power and Ruin

Given that the Conditions system doesn't allow characters to be killed, the stakes of these games are defined elsewhere: in characters' personal transformations. Rather than focusing on whether a character will survive physically, these games focus on what personal values characters will compromise to continue surviving. They structurally highlight personal doom, as players make hard choices about where their characters will draw their power from. For example, in $AK$, players accrue points of Ruin whenever they are tempted by their dark future or choose to push their Powers of Darkness. When players reach five Ruin, they take a Ruin Advance, which unlocks new, devastating moves (e.g. the ability to instantly kill a vulnerable NPC or a pathway to godhood). But there is a catch: once characters take their ninth Ruin Advance, the player 'retires' the character, makes a new one, and the original character emerges as the antagonist of the next investigation. In this way, players (and characters) are tempted by the power of Ruin—but because these abilities often require players to mark additional Ruin whenever they are used, characters who over-rely on Ruin moves will find themselves in a rapid descent into doom. This is reflected in the move, Torn Between, where a character must decide to "Let [their] monstrous nature show" or "Describe how [they] diminish [their] power to conform to what society demands." While the player's characters can't 'die,' there is a threat of personal failure that is put in conflict with the characters' values. Rather than "will my character survive?" the question becomes: "Will my character resort to their ruinous powers? How will this change them?".

In *TSL*, the structure for balancing personal doom is unique to each playbook. For example, The Beast playbook has a "Feral" meter and a warning: "You may walk in civilized circles, but sooner or later your feral truth will come to the fore" [24]. Depending on the action The Beast takes in the fiction, they will increase or decrease their Feral score: if their meter reaches zero, they lose access to all their Beast playbook moves. If their meter reaches four, they Transform into their monstrous self and gain powerful moves but expose themselves and allies to danger. Other playbooks in the game feature a similar balancing act. The Chosen has a 'Destiny' that they must embrace or reject, while The Trickster must balance their 'Feelings' meter. Each of *TSL*'s Playbooks feature self-conflict and a precarious balance between the characters' want for power/freedom and cultural expectation. This also emerges in a special move, "Call on a Toxic Power" which triggers when characters parlay with an evil entity: "You can approach them and you may even find them helpful at times, but only those with strong Spirit can engage with them and emerge unscathed" [24].

*VS* takes a similar approach through its use of the modified tarot. As characters make choices, they build attunement with two cards: The World ("World is 'you matter,' a hand reaching down to pull others back up to their feet.") and The Void ("Void is 'I matter,' fists raised up in defiance against a hostile universe.") [27]. Like the other games, characters balance these two sources of power hand-in-hand: community obligations, relationships, and the everyday vs. an internal, isolating, devastating power and "taking your enemy's strengths for yourself" [27]. When characters go too far and reach three ranks in either attunement, they trigger one of two moves:

- **Overwhelmed by the World:** One of the character's Covenants charges recklessly into danger, the character becomes unable to help an ally and loses their commitment, or the character gives up life as a rebel and can only help in mundane ways.
- **Overwhelmed by the Void:** The character loses a Covenant ("they just don't mean anything to you anymore"), the character's own darkness manifests new demons, or the character becomes a monster themselves in the Castle otherworld [27].

This structure reshapes narrative with possibilities for queer—and especially trans-gender—tension: between helping your community and protecting yourself, between hiding from and standing up to the world. As game designer Kara Stone has said, "hardness goes with softness… the decision between whether you are going to heal or destroy. Sometimes it's not the right answer to put your healing energy towards something that doesn't love you back" [34]. As tensions escalate, players must make choices about whether their characters are willing to grow closer to ruin, transform into beasts, or channel dark powers from the Void to survive.

### 2.5  Bonds: Featuring Relationships

These games use systems for relationships based on Bonds (developed in *Masks* and *MH*). *AK* uses the most direct adaptation of this system: when players create characters, they mark Bonds with other agents, NPCs, and with "What the Darkness Demands of You." During play, players can spend Bonds to change the outcomes of rolls by narrating a short flashback or detail about how that character has shaped the outcome.

Bonds can also be nurtured when characters trigger the "Reveal Your Heart" move and can be destroyed by activating some Ruin abilities. Bonds represent opportunities to put mechanical teamwork into the fiction, but *AK* clarifies that Bonds aren't always positive: rivalries and tense relationships can also grow as Bonds. While Bonds suggests a two-way relationship, *TSL*'s Strings (as in 'heartstrings') allow players to "Influence With a String" and tempt a character or alter a roll. Strings give characters subtle (but incomplete) power over one another, allowing players to boost their own experience and grow closer in a short scene. In *TSL,* players also share Strings when a character becomes Smitten with someone, foregrounding romantic possibility. Finally, *VS* adopts this structure through its use of Minor Covenants and Major Covenants. Covenants are defined by their role in the tarot deck and a brief description that states how a Covenant will help a character and what help they require themselves. Characters may struggle to protect and nurture their Covenants, or even betray them—making *VS*'s social system a complex cycle of managing character's needs and the needs of their Covenants.

These games continue the project that Alder has described with *MH*—which famously includes a move to 'turn on' other monsters [35], prompting players "to contend with what that desire means for their characters" [4]. Like structures for personal doom, these mechanics support a queer world of social bonds filled with mutual empowerment, grief, needs, and desire [36]. Bonds reshape characters' influences over one another—opening possibility for queer play amidst rivalry, love, and friendship.

### 2.6  (Re)drawing from Queer Media

These games draw from established media and in doing so, reimagine the queer potential of extant genres—building on a long legacy of queer readings and queer remixing of media [8, 10, 37, 38]. For example, *VS* pulls extensively from the *Persona* franchise— a videogame series about adolescents who can transform from ordinary civilians into powerful, costumed heroes who wield inner-demons. Yet, as Jordan Youngblood has pointed out, this franchise is riddled with homophobic and transphobic messaging and reinforces heteronormative values [39]. *VS* rebuilds *Persona*'s ludic premise (and queer potential), opening narrative possibility for trans-empowerment narratives of transformation and queer stories about navigating identities under crisis. Similarly, while the *Hellboy* franchise (an inspiration for *AK*) rarely explores queerness directly, the potential of the themes of 'dual-monstrosity' [4] demands queer remix: as *AK* characters encounter alienation, transformation, and reject self-narratives. *TSL* is overtly queer in its messaging, and its sample adventures reference established queer media (like "Monster Queers of Castle Gayskull," which parodies *She-Ra and the Princesses of Power*). Yet *TSL* also references media with queer baggage. One adventure, "Sword Lesbians of the Three Houses," reimagines Nintendo's *Fire Emblem: Three Houses*—a game popular in queer shipper fandoms but which included queerbaiting [40]. By opening space for reinterpretations of established media, these games prompt queer remix and subversive play against normative genres.

# 3  Queer Narrative Possibility

## 3.1  Shared Outcomes

In imagining the playground, play is not determined by rules but by player interaction. These structures can be revised, ignored, and even misused. Independent TRPG designers have pointed out that safety tools (such as the X card) can be abused by bad actors to manipulate other players [41]. Likewise, game structures themselves do not necessarily create, demand, or imply queer play. The structures explored here are queer because they *open possibilities* for players to safely "bring-your-own-queerness" to the table [12]. When put in conjunction with one another, we can see what interactions these structures anticipate and the shared outcomes they proliferate in game narratives:

*Encouraging emotions:* Giving players agency over the content of the game through safety tools opens possibilities for emotional narrative. *TSL* encourages players to "Feel Deeply and Often," which it links to safety and consent, noting that groups should aim to "foster an environment where your fellow players feel safe exploring intense feelings and potentially difficult topics." [24]. Likewise, *AK* encourages players to embrace entanglements, and "fight, fall in love, succumb to your emotions, be vulnerable" [28]. As Ruberg writes: "Let us play anger. Let us play what hurts. Let us play in ways that are just as different and just as queer as we are as players" [32]. By redefining the narrative playground, these games support a counter-normative range of feelings.

*Showcasing messy characters:* These games draw from media that highlights nuanced characters, from disaster lesbians to monster agents. As *TSL* states: "even friends can hurt each other's feelings, and no one is perfect, particularly not the complex, conflicted PCs in [*TSL*]" [24]. These structures grant permission to player characters and enemies to embrace messiness. Rather than 'soldiering on' and ignoring the Conditions that affect their characters, players are mechanically rewarded for embodying Conditions. *AK* grants crucial Darkness Tokens for roleplaying doom in the fiction, and *TSL* lets players clear Conditions by lashing out in destructive ways. These allow players to explore both the messiness of identity [3] and emotions beyond 'fun' and 'victory' [32].

*Clarifying the power (and danger) of fiction:* By noting the need for boundaries, these sourcebooks affirm the affective power of shared storytelling. *VS* clarifies that the story "can easily go very dark, and it's important to respect the comfort of the actual people in your group over the desires of fictional characters" [27]. *VS* includes an invocation to players: "if we want a better world we'll need group solidarity, community accountability, individual empowerment, and a dream of a better way, just like this game's rebels" [27]. These messages not only welcome marginalized players and validate players' lived experiences, but invite (rather than ignore) real political context.

*Recognizing tension between community and self:* Each of these games structurally present queer tension between a destructive, powerful force rooted in the self and a healing, yet demanding force located in community. Characters must narratively balance their need to "let your monstrous nature show" and "conform to what society demands" [28]. In *AK*, marking Ruin means that an agent can accrue new devastating powers, but that they also slowly descend into their "darkest" self as a harbinger. Yet *AK* does not frame this descent as a bad thing, only a new direction of the fiction. Likewise, *TSL* foregrounds characters' dual-needs to remain secretive and find power in transformation.

This is loudest in *VS*: turning to the self (Void) gives characters destructive power that can only be calmed with community support (World). At the same time, characters who overcommit to the needs of their Covenants struggle to maintain their edge against the Vassal. These are struggles of queer energy: between supporting the community around you and fighting against larger, external systems of oppression.

*Reframing violence:* Conditions shape how these games frame physical violence. In combat-focused TRPGs, a character's ability to physically destroy and dominate an enemy is paramount. Yet Conditions open possibilities for modes of conflict and recognize that being *defeated* is different from being *killed*. In these games, violence is only one avenue to defeating a potential enemy; players are prompted to rethink the impact of their actions on an opponent. *TSL* especially drives this point: "Bear in mind that inflicting Conditions is emotionally violent, and sometimes physically violent… that said, some things are worth fighting for and conflict is often necessary before oppression and toxic behavior can be halted" [24]. This is reinforced by the way these games approach power: characters who take the 'strongest' moves are also prone to experience Ruin (*AK*), struggle against the Void (*VS*), or expose themselves to danger (*TSL*). In this way, they resist optimization and elevate character story over domination.

*Building support between players:* These games meaningfully underscore support with other characters and the need to blow off steam. *VS*'s "Check In" move, *AK*'s "Reveal Your Heart" move, and *TSL*'s "Emotional Support" move are triggered when characters open up to others, clearing Conditions and gaining Bonds. These games encourage scenes where characters support one another—driving roleplay that focuses on teamwork and tension, healing and community, relationships and reciprocity.

## 3.2 Conclusion: Beyond Cues

The games in this study mark a transition from TRPGs that include cues that "queer play is tolerated, encouraged, or expected" [1]. Notably, these games do include such cues—*AK* features gender diversity in the characters of its mysteries and many of the example Vassals in *VS* are described as posing a danger to queer communities. *TSL* has so many overtly queer references that it actually includes a cue to *non-queer* players, in its section "What If… Not Lesbians?" [24]. But while cues are important because they welcome queer audiences—queer audiences are already here. Thanks to the new hybrid ecology of TRPGs, queer players and designers are now a permanent force in the tabletop roleplaying scene. Queer folks are playing, making (podcasts, actual plays, hacks, fan art, games), and telling new, subversive stories through roleplaying games.

The examples presented here represent a distillation of the tools being used by independent TRPG designers of PbtA games—but they are not the whole picture. Queer TRPG designers are working in every subgenre, from old-school dungeon crawlers to lyric games [21]. It's my hope that this case study can not only draw greater attention to the important work of queer, independent TRPGs, but provide a chance for game scholars and designers to learn from these structures and imagine new modes of play, new playgrounds, and new possibilities for queer interactive storytelling.

# References

1. Sihvonen, T., Stenros, J.: Cues for queer play: carving a possibility space for LGBTQ role-play. In: Harper, T., Adams, M.B., Taylor, N. (eds.) Queerness in Play. PGC, pp. 167–184. Springer, Cham (2018). https://doi.org/10.1007/978-3-319-90542-6_10
2. Dragon, J.: A dozen fragments on playground theory. Medium, 24 May 2021
3. Ruberg, B.: The Queer Games Avant-Garde: How LGBTQ Game Makers Are Reimagining the Medium of Video Games. Duke University Press, Durham (2020)
4. Avery, A., Ruberg, B.: Avery alder: queer storytelling and the mechanics of desire. In: The Queer Games Avant-Garde: How LGBTQ Game Makers Are Reimagining the Medium of Video Games, pp. 183–191. Duke University Press (2020)
5. Stenros, J., Sihvonen, T.: Out of the dungeons: representations of queer sexuality in RPG Source books. In: Evan, T. (eds.) Analog Game Studies. vol. 2, pp. 71–92. Carnegie Mellon University (2017). https://doi.org/10.1184/R1/6686720.v1
6. Stokes, M.: Access to the page: queer and disabled characters in Dungeons and Dragons. In: Aaron Trammell, Evan Torner, Emma Leigh Waldron, and Shelly Jones Analog Game Studies, Volume 4, ed., 105–123. Carnegie Mellon University (2020). https://doi.org/10.1184/R1/11929782.v1
7. Brown, A.M.L., Stenros, J.: Sexuality and the erotic in role-play. Routledge, In Role-Playing Game Studies (2018)
8. Ruberg, B.: Video Games Have Always Been Queer. NYU Press, New York (2019)
9. Butler, J.: Undoing Gender. Routledge, New York, London (2004)
10. Sedgwick, E.K.: Novel Gazing: Queer Readings in Fiction. Duke University Press, Durham (1997)
11. Ahmed, S.: Queer Phenomenology: Orientations, Objects. Duke University Press, Others (2006)
12. Clark, N., Ruberg, B.: Naomi clark: disrupting norms and critiquing systems through "Good, Nice Sex with a Tentacle Monster." In: The Queer Games Avant-Garde: How LGBTQ Game Makers Are Reimagining the Medium of Video Games, pp. 102–112. Duke University Press (2020)
13. Tan, K., Mitchell, A.: Dramatic narrative logics: integrating drama into storygames with operational logics. In: Bosser, A.-G., Millard, D.E., Hargood, C. (eds.) ICIDS 2020. LNCS, vol. 12497, pp. 190–202. Springer, Cham (2020). https://doi.org/10.1007/978-3-030-62516-0_17
14. Wardrip-Fruin, N.: Expressive Processing: Digital Fictions, Computer Games, and Software Studies. MIT Press, Cambridge (2009)
15. McGee, L., Ruberg, B.: Llaura McGee: leaving space for messiness, complexity, and chance. In: The Queer Games Avant-Garde: How LGBTQ Game Makers Are Reimagining the Medium of Video Games (2020)
16. Anthropy, A.: Rise of the Videogame Zinesters: How Freaks, Normals, Amateurs, Artists, Dreamers, Drop-outs, Queers, Housewives, and People Like You Are Taking Back an Art Form. Seven Stories Press, New York (2012)
17. Dragon, J.: Sleepaway. Possum Creek Games (2020)
18. Halberstam, J.: Queer gaming: gaming, hacking, and going turbo. In: Ruberg, B., Shaw, A. (eds.) Queer Game Studies. University of Minnesota Press, Minnesota (2017)
19. Reed, A.A.: Changeful Tales: Design-Driven Approaches Toward More Expressive Storygames. University of California, Santa Cruz (2017)
20. Powered by the Apocalypse (2021). http://apocalypse-world.com/pbta/policy. Accessed 8 June 2021

21. Torner, E.: Lyric games: geneaology of an online "Physical Games" Scene. DiGRA 2020 – Proceedings of the 2020 DiGRA International Conference: Play Everywhere: 4 (2020)
22. Ashwell, S.K.: What Is A Storygame? These Heterogenous Tasks (2016)
23. Trammell, A.: Analog Games and the Digital Economy. Analog Game Studies (2019)
24. Walsh, A.K.: Gay Spaceship Games. Thirsty Sword Lesbians. Evil Hat Productions (2021)
25. McJanda, M., Mota, D.S.: Legacy Life Among the Ruins, 2nd edn. Modiphius Entertainment Limited, UFO Press, Postapocalyptic RPG Hardback (2019)
26. Shaw, K., Lauren, B.-M.: TTRPG Safety Toolkit Guide v2.4 (2021)
27. McJanda, M.: Voidheart Symphony. 1.0. UFO Press (2021)
28. Jamila, N.: Sword Queen Games. Apocalypse Keys. Playtest Edition. Evil Hat Productions (2021)
29. Sampat, E., Ruberg, B.: Elizabeth Sampat: safe spaces for queerness and games against suffering. In: The Queer Games Avant-Garde: How LGBTQ Game Makers Are Reimagining the Medium of Video Games (2020)
30. No fascists. RPG Museum (2021). https://rpgmuseum.fandom.com/wiki/No_fascists. Accessed 17 June 2021
31. Conway, B.: Masks: A New Generation. Magpie Games (2016)
32. Ruberg, B.: No fun: the queer potential of video games that annoy, anger, disappoint, sadden, and hurt. QED: J. GLBTQ Worldmaking 2, 108–124 (2015). https://doi.org/10.14321/qed.2.2.0108. (Michigan State University Press)
33. Brice, M., Ruberg, B.: Mattie brice: radical play through vulnerability. In: The Queer Games Avant-Garde: How LGBTQ Game Makers Are Reimagining the Medium of Video Games The Queer Games Avant-Garde: How LGBTQ Game Makers Are Reimagining the Medium of Video Games, Bo Ruberg. Duke University Press (2020)
34. Stone, K., Ruberg, B.: Softness, strength, and danger in games about mental health and healing. In: The Queer Games Avant-Garde: How LGBTQ Game Makers Are Reimagining the Medium of Video Games (2020)
35. Alder, A.: Monsterhearts 2. HT Publisher (2019)
36. Shaw, A.: The trouble with communities. In: Studies, I.Q.G. (ed.) Adrienne Shaw and Bo Ruberg, pp. 153–162. University of Minnesota Press (2017)
37. Pow, W.: A trans historiography of glitches and errors. Feminist Media Histories 7, 197–230 (2021). https://doi.org/10.1525/fmh.2021.7.1.197. (University of California Press)
38. Macklin, C.: Finding the queerness in games. In: Studies, I.Q.G. (ed.) Bo Ruberg and Adrienne Shaw, pp. 249–258. University of Minnesota Press (2017)
39. Youngblood, Jordan. "C'mon! Make me a man!": Persona 4, Digital Bodies, and Queer Potentiality. Ada: A Journal of Gender, New Media, and Technology (2013). https://doi.org/10.7264/N3QC01D2
40. Berge, P.S., Britt, R.K.: Dance With Me, Claude: Creators, Catalyzers, and Canonizers in the Fire Emblem: Three Houses Slash-Ship Fandom. Game Studies (Forthcoming, December 2021)
41. cavegirl. And like, you can't design safety tools to account for this sort of thing. You just can't. Any tools you present will be weaponised by bad actors. (4/6). Tweet. @DyingStylishly (2021)

# Emergent Gameplay, Emergent Essaying

Kirsty Dunlop(✉) ⓘ

University of Glasgow, Glasgow G12 8QQ, UK
k.dunlop.4@research.gla.ac.uk

**Abstract.** Within our current post-internet landscape of Web 2.0, in which we exist as intermedial beings increasingly engaging with cross-media forms, I propose Emergent Essaying as a connective term, merging the milieu of game design with hybrid creative writing approaches. Emergent Gameplay is 'a game design term that refers to video game mechanics that change according to the player's actions'. Emergent Essaying utilizes gameplay techniques within an active digital-born form of essaying, to invite more open, playful, collaborative and changeable modes of thinking, encouraging ambivalence, multiplicity, and fluidity over fixed, finished thinking. Expanding upon creative theorists Lisa Robertson and Anne Carson's approach to the verb 'essaying' as an act of trying, in this digital, hybrid writing context I conceive of Emergent Essaying as an act of playful reimagining from both writer/designer and reader/player, in which the essay is more narrative based, enacting a conversation between ideas rather than focusing on argument. I combine game design techniques with the approaches to hybrid/digital work adopted by indie writers to inform my own practice as a cross-form, cross-genre writer, as reflected both in this paper, and via a link to a digital-born, creative iteration of this work which enacts Emergent Essaying. In a world increasingly controlled by Big Tech and optimization, through Emergent Essaying I advocate for more empathetic digital modes of connection and understanding, valuing the concepts of 'glitch' and 'glitching', reader/player control and intervention, and the opportunities for nuanced expression afforded by the intertwining of digital environment and language.

**Keywords:** Emergent Gameplay · Emergent Essaying · Glitching · Hybridity

## 1 In Motion

In our post-internet[1] landscape of Web 2.0, we have become used to the continual motion of language and thought performed by us and before us on screen, enacted in the constant updating of pages and the ability to repeatedly edit posts on social media with the expectation of instant feedback. We are now intermedial beings, consumers and readers, with the virtual and the actual no longer easily distinguishable. As Russell

---

[1] 'The postinternet is kind of to say, we don't even log on anymore; this is just being. [...] The postinternet is kind of to say, what would still constitute an online experience of the sublime? Is there a resistant potential in pursuing this, or staying with the sheer sense of the internet's dailiness?' SPAM zine & Press, '>What is post-internet?' [1].

© Springer Nature Switzerland AG 2021
A. Mitchell and M. Vosmeer (Eds.): ICIDS 2021, LNCS 13138, pp. 193–202, 2021.
https://doi.org/10.1007/978-3-030-92300-6_17

argues in *Glitch Feminism* [2], it is now more accurate to state you are AFK (away-from-keyboard), rather than existing IRL (in-real-life) (p. 5). Paralleling this blurring of the environment, the framework of game design is beginning to spill over into creative and experimental writing fields. The combination of Emergent Gameplay and experimental essaying is a hybrid mergence, particularly apt and arguably vital to the rapidly shifting rhythms of our everyday digital lives in the contemporary moment.

Emergence invokes the shifting motion of an ongoing creative process; there is a tension and multiplicity in the word emergence, between quick action and slow unravelling, of what is sudden and urgent (an "emergency"[2]) and what is unfurling. Whilst this undercurrent is felt in the process of writing page-based forms, we are assured that the writing is complete through our interaction with a finite physical manuscript. A digital-born work, on the other hand, carries emergence, at the forefront of its thinking and creation as well as its interaction with the reader, with both text and reader performatively enacting a sense of ongoing-ness. Here, we must embrace the difficulties and pacing of the continual evolution emanating from the screen, whether we feel able to explore a digital environment freely or are entrapped in a narrative.

Emergent Gameplay is a recognized aspect of game design where interactivity and narrative come together: generally understood as 'a game design term that refers to video game mechanics that change according to the player's actions [...] Emergent gameplay can also be created by adding multiple players to the same game environment and having their individual actions impact the overall game narrative.' (Techopedia) [4]. Horowitz and Loony [5] add to this definition that 'the term refers to complex outcomes that can result from the interaction of simple rules [...] There are two types of emergence commonly referred to by scholars, intentional and unintentional' (p. 11). The combination of simple actions and complex outcomes, intentionality and unintentionality, emphasizes the nuance and openness of Emergent Gameplay's narrative potential for communicating complex affective responses and plot tension, as well as blurring the boundaries between creator and player.

In writing an interactive work or game, the writer(s) must be hyper-aware of the effects of this Emergent Gameplay, both on the over-arching structure and with regard to the key micro moments. The writer must shift between experiencing the game as player and creator, in order to understand how decision-making will impact the experience of playing the game, thinking beyond a single frame of text or play. Emergent Gameplay is rich with possibilities. The uncertainty this multiplicity and reactiveness embeds becomes intricately connected to the notion of the glitch and the verb glitching (considered further below). Its complexity and potential is also related to notions of essaying, hybridity, and experimentation on the page, and adds a specific kind of interactive quality and effect, which shall be seen within the hybrid framework of Emergent Essaying.

---

[2] 'And the state of emergency is also always a state of *emergence*.' writes Bhabha in *The Location of Culture* (p. 59) [3].

## 2   From Wandering to Glitching

In her hybrid essay *A Field Guide to Getting Lost*, Solnit [6] writes: '[…] to be lost is to be fully present and to be fully present is to be capable of being in uncertainty and mystery. And one does not get lost but loses oneself, with the implication that it is a conscious choice, a chosen surrender […]' (p. 13). Solnit's statement connects to the idea of wandering, in both the thinking required for the creative process and in the interaction that can be experienced in a digital-born work. The physical act of wandering brings unintentional discovery, ideas emerge into sharp focus from the chaos of disordered thoughts. Wandering implies a slowing down, which can be uncomfortable in the Big Tech[3] post-internet capitalist environment, which heavily promotes optimization. There is a desire to provide a better, faster, cleaner mode of engagement, which can, ironically, hold us in a singular space for longer. Wandering is about expanding a field, encouraging a slowed down opening up of complexity; it is anti-optimization. The act of getting lost connects to wider thinking about failure and error; if we choose to go down a lesser known path, not linear or with a concrete goal, in many ways we are allowing ourselves to become more vulnerable to error; it is within this space of potential that I see a movement from wandering to the role of the glitch and the act of glitching within Emergent Essaying.

   'Glitch' is a mode of error, yet it holds more exuberance and potential than the word 'failure'. In practice, glitch becomes intrinsically linked to openings, portals into the unexpected, inviting an affective response of hope and possibility, alongside chaos, confusion, and anxiety. Glitch is an emergent term in its shifting definitions: it appears both specific to a technological landscape yet holds within this specificity a number of hybrid movements. We might consider glitch in its dictionary definition: 'a minor malfunction [in a computer system] […] may have derived from the Yiddish *glitsh*, meaning "slippery place"' (Merriam-Webster) [8], but we might also look at it through a wider lens, as its associations expand into further contexts: Glitch Music, Glitch Art, the act of glitching in video game communities, and increasingly its use as a theoretical framework (a recent example being Russell's *Glitch Feminism* [2]). Glitch artist Rosa Menkman has revealed new possibilities of the mode as an aesthetic practice, and this framework is what is commonly at the forefront of academic, theoretical, and practice-based discussions. In *The Glitch Moment(um)*, Menkman [9] writes 'Glitch, an unexpected occurrence, unintended result, or break or disruption in a system, cannot be singularly codified, which is precisely its conceptual strength and dynamic contribution to media theory.' (p. 26). Menkman posits the glitch in her theoretical unpickings alongside her Glitch Art, with its deliberate subversion of resolution, as a dynamic site of potential. Writer/coder myers [10] has crafted her own approach to the glitch as aesthetic radical renewal through the creation of 'glitcherature', the title of a Python script she created to apply glitch aesthetics to the texture of text, immediately glitching any writing the user inserts. Through these overt acts, we become aware that a glitch has to begin in a site of familiarity, that it can be both intentional and unintentional (and yet still be surprising and open in both

---

[3] 'Big Tech' refers to the hegemony major technical companies have over society. For more on the links between this control and the attention economy in our era, see Tanner in *The Circle of the Snake: Nostalgia and Utopia in the Age of Big Tech* [7].

versions), and that it is this departure from the familiar that can act as a catalyst for joy, potential, and unease, to engender a myriad of complex affects that revel in surprise. I look towards Stewart's [11] theoretical work *Ordinary Affects* to conceptualize these responses: 'Ordinary affects are the varied, surging capacities to affect and be affected that give everyday life the quality of a continual motion of relations, scenes, contingencies, and emergence.' (p. 2).

How then does this subversion and consequent generation of affective responses relate to Emergent Essaying, connecting back to ideas of wandering and losing one's way? Glitch must first be understood as it stands within these many fields and contexts, as an active digital-born mode that creates entries into new beginnings or alternative continuations. The verb 'glitching' here also brings another mode into play: game scholars, such as Meades and Consalvo, theorize glitching as a collective act of players unlocking faults within a game to carve their own playing experience. Meades [12] promotes the ideas of thinking through glitching as more complex than a negative interference whilst Consalvo [13] connects glitching more overtly to acts of cheating, promoting the idea that it is not a wholly negative intervention, but rather an important collaboration between player, game, and writer, offered up by the specific emergent techniques enabled by the technologies of the form. Glitching functions as an interventional act of emergence, handing over control of the narrative structure to the reader and the potentialities of the text itself. Page-based text can be open to varied interpretations and viewpoints, but in the digital environment this occurs performatively, with the text and game never wholly stable. The underwiring of the code is revealed, reflecting the fragility of binary (closed) thought as further collaborative choices are opened within the context of the work.

Additional tensions also exist within the effects and purposes of glitching. After a recent talk, I was asked whether the act of speed-running in a video game can be considered a radical emergent glitching within the framework I am proposing. Speed-running as framed by Scully-Blaker [14] is indeed an Emergent Gameplay practice: 'the process of completing a game as quickly as possible without the use of cheats or cheat devices'. Whilst this act of racing through a game is a radical intervention by the player, it does not fall into the expansive wandering that I am positing with Emergent Essaying. If speed-running exists as 'post(human) performance art' as posited by Hay [15], in which speculation, competitiveness, and instant gratification are at the forefront, then slow meandering through choice, and a re-framing of glitching with essaying as a means to travel in different directions, inserts the human mind with all its errors and capabilities of discovery back into the digital sphere.

The mode of glitching I envision within Emergent Essaying is subverting the optimization rhythms of quick movement and success, so often geared towards solutionism rather than the chaotic and difficult slower presence of our thoughts, which are capable of curiosity, change, and alternative directions. This builds upon the definition of experimental essaying posited by Lopate, 'The essay is a notoriously flexible and adaptable form. It possesses the freedom to move anywhere, in all directions.' (p. xxxvii) [16]. This takes on new relevance in Emergent Essaying, where digital writing tools such as Twine turn readers into players, literally wandering between ideas. By embracing performative glitches along with the potential for genuine errors, we can enact a playful spatiality to wander and become lost in language. This thinking is in line with Robertson's [17] words from 'Time in the Codex': 'It is the most commodious sensation I can imagine, this being lost.' (p. 13). Commodious implies a comfortable space in which to roam freely and explore. What roominess might gameplay offer us?

With that question in mind, there have been an increasing number of commercial games that have reveled in a slower, more observant explorational narrative movement. One example is the action-adventure game *Subnautica* [18], an open world survival game that encourages the slow exploration of the ocean of an alien planet.

Alternative commodious modes of play can interact with the commodious sensation of thinking in relation to reading, writing, and time, which is the experience and feeling Robertson is describing. A rejection of the flattened idea of quick success and point scoring as the primary mode of glitching makes room for more of the wonder that can be found in the space of non-linear thinking and variables, discussed further below. Here, in this liminality of the hybrid, is the possibility for a more exuberant "slippery space".

## 3 To Try, To Play

Think of essay as a verb, as a becoming. To essay is to try within an experimental, creative context. I parallel this with Carson's statement [19]: 'Consider incompleteness as a verb' (p. 29), from the hybrid collection *Plainwater: Essays and Poetry*. Emergent Essaying seeks to expand this notion of ongoing-ness into the sphere of digital-born play. What does it mean to play into an idea, to write into the glitch?

Hybridizing essaying with gameplay feels ever more important in our increasingly digitalized world, where concepts of digital play can easily slide into a framework of optimization. Instead, we can re-conceptualize play in line with emergence as a more nuanced unravelling of thought and creation: a nexus of multiple ideas and genres. Play invokes desire. Experimental essayist Blau DuPlessis writes: 'The essay is restless [...] always a little too thirsty.' (p. 38) [20]; the merging of gameplay and playfulness in language can enhance this sensation of continuous reaching, with the addition of obstacles supplanting neat, conclusive arguments.

Emergent Essaying intertwines the acts of trying and playing. Here, the thinking is innately interdisciplinary, combining elements of interactive fiction, gameplay techniques, and hybrid essaying. Academic digital theory has traditionally focused on hypertext—the joining of fragmented pieces of text, through links, a form which Coover [21] argues 'offers the patient reader [...] just such an experience of losing oneself to a text'. However, digital writers and researchers, such as Montfort [22] have been increasingly promoting the in-depth study and value of interactive fiction. Emergent Essaying exists at the intersection of literary hypertext, the gameplay of interactive fiction, and hybrid essaying, with the multi-potential layering of these seemingly disparate forms and techniques.

A multi-media writer whose work embraces an essayistic approach, is Carpenter, whose electronic writing/art often concerns the collision of historical documents with the contemporary digital framework. In *The Pleasure of the Coast* [23], the user accesses the work through a non-linear format, scrolling horizontally rather than vertically, to enact an exploration of landscape. The work recalls the aesthetics of chapbooks, albeit with the sense of space afforded by the digital realm. Pencil line drawings are joined with kinetic text, playfully layering historical found text and fictional narration.

Carpenter uses the layering of aesthetics and user experience, forming a palimpsest of image and text alongside the scrolling mechanic, to create an alternative mapping effect that is imperfect and in motion, encouraging the user/reader to slow down and examine how they engage with the work. The simplicity of the infinite coast, and the performative glitch effect of forever scrolling sideways, asserts a lack of closure.

Carpenter also encourages a mode of error-making in writing, stating that 'imperfections are deliberate', including errors of translation. Here, the digital techniques and artistic practice inform one another, leading to new slants in seeing and comprehending, in the real-time pace of the on-screen reading experience.

When examining Carpenter's expansion of essaying, apt connections can be found in the Web 1.0 hypertext works of Jackson, whose landmark text *Patchwork Girl* [24], brings together Mary Shelley's *Frankenstein* [25], with contemporary understandings of the post-human as posited in Haraway's *A Manifesto for Cyborgs* [26], resulting in a sprawling, monstrous conception of the female body through the rhizomatic form of the hypertext reading structure. The movement of following a hyperlink to another page of text induces an awareness of multi-layering: what is not accessed immediately is still knowingly an integral part of the narrative.

Modes of critique and essaying which borrow from hypertextual rhythms are cropping up in page-based creative-critical writing such as 'hypercriticism', highlighted by Manifold Press as 'an exploitation of hypertextual possibilities' [27]. Emergent Essaying adds layers of performance and interactivity, with the reader/player existing as a vital part of the writing, performing this more 'blissful' mode of reading, that is 'writerly,' as posited by Barthes [28]. Emergent Essaying engages with gameplay techniques, such as non-linearity, variables (collecting objects or scores that affect later parts of the narrative), external data, randomization (diverging points emerging through chance for different players), and intentional glitches alongside the potential for genuine malfunctions, to influence how readers/players understand and engage with the thinking and poetic effects of the work. The tension created by Ludonarrative Dissonance (described by Hocking as 'a powerful dissonance between what it is about as a game, and what it is about as a story', in relation to the game Bioshock [29]) must be kept in mind during the writing and playing of Emergent Essaying. Techniques should not simply be implemented because they are available in the digital realm but because they create new experiences of understanding through play that are linked to the themes and connections the writer is exploring. This ethos must be embraced when working with game writing tools such as Twine, in which the author must also inhabit the role of player, creating an environment in which gameplay influences essaying and vice versa.

Game designer Sampat subverts the idea that games are simply a mode of eliciting empathy, instead arguing that they can function as empathetic machines, if empathy is directly built into their structure by the designer(s) [30]. Here, not only content but also structural systematic understanding can be subverted, demonstrated in *Am I Part of the Problem?* [31], in which the player must address their own biases and approaches, offering direct critical insight, tailored to the individual, as they answer questions in order to understand their role in a conflict situation. The game recognizes that it holds no definitive solutions. Instead, through play, it offers a look into the self that does not feel prescriptive or reductive in its assumptions about the player. In combining elements from the examples above, Emergent Essaying opens up a new cross-form conversation, reconfiguring and expanding the expectations of the essay in a multimedia landscape by inviting the term 'essay' to co-mingle performatively with 'play'.

Within this context, play must be understood in its many facets, beyond gameplay; Huizinga [32] regards the function of play as just as important as work in society, a "free" mode; the motivation of play being the experience it offers rather than the concrete goal. We can connect this to Halberstam's [33] conceptualization of low theory, as a mode of play and child-like pleasure in process, crafted through error. The digital gameplay of Emergent Essaying promotes a more playful approach to understanding, with language play intertwining with digital interactive gameplay, each informing and driving the other to capture new ways of seeing, doing, asking, and inviting. This layering of play encourages us to think more receptively, questioning our knowledge and opening us up to new experiences and information. Through play, we move beyond the individual to a collective and collaborative space of thought. Thinking merges with play, emerges from within it, sometimes consciously, often unconsciously.

## 4 Emergent Essaying: Time and Practice

Time and pacing are integral to both writing and experiencing Emergent Essaying. Key questions must be considered during the planning and writing, such as: how long will the player remain in the text, and will its duration impact the player's emotional connection to the work? Will the player feel trapped, will this give a feeling of stasis, will slow thinking or fast thinking be created through links and choices? Pacing takes on an important role in this process, as the writer and text impact the experiences of the player/reader, not only through length at a syntactic level, but also on a wider scale via choice, repetition, and looping. The distinct conceptualization of temporality in game-time has been expanded by Jayemanne [34], who has crafted a methodology called "chronotypology" as an approach to 'facilitate literary approaches to video game temporality' using terms such as "synchrony" to demonstrate the layers of temporality built up through the gameplay, as distinct from other literary modes.

In considering the importance of time in the game environment, I am drawn to Zoe Quinn's *Depression Quest* [35], which labels itself as an interactive (non)-fiction about the everyday realities of living with depression. The game has hundreds of different options and would take the average player around half an hour to navigate. Throughout the piece, choices become limited by the player's previous decisions, resulting in different narrative outcomes. The text is accompanied by ambient music, altering in response to player choices, with sound, play, and narrative tone informing one other. Alternative choices can often be seen but are scored out, letting you know that, based on the current state of you/the character's emotions, certain options are no longer available (reflecting the lack of bodily and mental control experienced during deep bouts of depression). Here it is clear that timing has been carefully considered; although there are large chunks of text to be read in each fragment, the intimacy and momentum created by the narrative response to player choices encourages users to complete the game in a single sitting. The use of second person here enhances the sense of immediacy; that we are a vital part of the text's inner workings, capable of creating pathways that may diverge from others' experiences of the work.

If our sense of time is thwarted by the short attention spans and immediate responses of Web 2.0, Emergent Essaying has the capability to expand how we experience and consider time in this virtual world. Writers of these experimental digital forms can continually re-frame their own considerations of narrative time, through the reflective, slow thinking required to create complex linkages and gameplay techniques. Returning to this idea of wandering, digital-born works have the capability to deliberately slow down a player/reader's mind through Emergent techniques, as well as providing them with a sense of freedom to individually navigate the text.

The 'glitch' is an integral aspect of time in the practice of writing and experiencing Emergent Essaying, as it exists as a moment of stasis and potential. I often think of the glitch in relation to Derrida's notion of 'hauntology' [36], a reminder of the work's past state and flux, its ghostly underpinnings, the mark the writer has left on the machine and that the reader has yet to leave. There is also the sense of temporality and fragility, in the awareness that the essay can 'break' or be meddled with by the reader, which opens a more ambivalent mode of thinking.

The term Emergent Essaying creates immediate connections between what are often thought of as disparate fields: bringing together elements of game design and experimental essaying. It challenges the ideas around what a game entails and an essay involves, centering itself more around narrative exploration of ideas than the concrete pursuit of goals of the former or the neat conclusive arguments of the latter. If essaying is a mode of trying, Emergent Essaying inserts a more playful practice, understanding and enacting of questioning and intervention, through a continually shifting dynamic between player, writer, and game.

**In order to demonstrate the practice of Emergent Essaying, and give the reader an experience of one iteration it might take, a digital-born, alternative and experimental version of this paper, written in Twine, can be accessed here:** http://kirsty dunlop.com/EmergentGameplayEmergentEssaying/digital.

## References

1. SPAM zine & Press, ">What is post-internet?" https://www.spamzine.co.uk/what-is-post-int ernet. Accessed 09 July 2021
2. Russell, L.: Glitch Feminism: A Manifesto. Verso Books, London (2020)
3. Bhabha, H.K.: The Location of Culture. Routledge, London (1994)
4. Techopedia def. Emergent Gameplay. https://www.techopedia.com/definition/27043/eme rgent-gameplay. Accessed 09 July 2021
5. Horowitz, S., Looney, S.: The Essential Guide to Game Audio: The Theory and Practice of Sound for Games. Focal Press, Burlington (2014)
6. Solnit, R.: A Field Guide to Getting Lost. Viking Penguin, New York (2005)
7. Tanner, G.: The Circle of the Snake: Nostalgia and Utopia in the Age of Big Tech. Zero Books, London (2020)
8. Merriam-Webster def. Glitch. https://www.merriam-webster.com/word-of-the-day/glitch-2019-05-15. Accessed 09 July 2021
9. Menkman, R.: The Glitch Moment(um). Institute of Network Cultures, Amsterdam (2011). https://networkcultures.org/_uploads/NN%234_RosaMenkman.pdf. Accessed 09 July 2021
10. Myers, R.: glitcherature (2014). https://robmyers.org/glitcherature/. Accessed 09 July 2021

11. Stewart, K.: Ordinary Affects. Duke University Press, Durham & London (2007)
12. Meades, A.: Why we glitch: process, meaning and pleasure in the discovery and documentation, sharing and use of videogame exploits. In: Well Played: a Journal on Video Games, Value and Meaning, pp. 79–98, Carnegie Mellon University: ETC Press, Pittsburgh, PA (2013)
13. Consalvo, M.: Cheating: Gaining Advantage in Video Games. MIT Press, Cambridge (2009)
14. Scully-Blaker, R.: A practiced practice: speedrunning through space with de certeau and virilio. Game Stud. Int. J. Comput. Game Res. **14**(1) (2014). ISSN: 1604–7982. http://gam estudies.org/1401/articles/scullyblaker. Accessed 09 July 2021
15. Hay, J.: Fully optimized: the (Post) human art of speedrunning. J. Posthuman Stud. **4**(1), 5–24. The Pennsylvania State University, University Park, PA (2020). https://www.jstor.org/stable/10.5325/jpoststud.4.1.0005
16. Lopate, P.: The Art of the Personal Essay. First Anchor Books, USA (1995)
17. Robertson, L.: Time in the Codex. In: Nilling: Prose Essays on Noise, Pornography, The Codex, Melancholy, Lucretius, Folds, Cities and Related Aporias, pp. 9–18, 2nd edn. Book*hug Press, Toronto (2012)
18. Cleveland, C.: Subnautica, 16 December 2014. https://store.steampowered.com/app/264710/Subnautica/. Accessed 09 July 2021
19. Carson, A.: Plainwater: Essays and Poetry, Reprint Vintage Books, New York (2000)
20. DuPlessis, R.B.: Blue Studios. The University of Alabama Press, Alabama (2006)
21. Coover, R.: Praise for Patchwork Girl by Shelley Jackson (Eastgate) (1995). https://www.eas tgate.com/catalog/PatchworkGirl.html. Accessed 7 July 2021
22. Montfort, N.: Twisty Little Passages: An Approach to Interactive Fiction. MIT Press, Cambridge (2005)
23. Carpenter, J.R..: The Pleasure of the Coast (2019). http://luckysoap.com/pleasurecoast/en/index.html. Accessed 09 July 2021
24. Jackson, S.: Patchwork Girl. Eastgate, Watertown, MA (1995). CD-ROM
25. Shelley, M.: Frankenstein, New Alma Classics, London (2014)
26. Haraway, D.J..: A Manifesto for Cyborgs: Science, Technology and Socialist Feminism in the 1980s (1985). https://monoskop.org/images/4/4c/Haraway_Donna_1985_A_Manifesto_for_Cyborgs_Science_Technology_and_Socialist_Feminism_in_the_1980s.pdf. Accessed 09 July 2021
27. Manifold Press Submissions. https://www.manifoldcriticism.com/submissions. Accessed 09 July 2021
28. Barthes, R.: The Pleasure of the Text. Trans. Richard Miller. Reissue edn. Farrar, Straus & Giroux Inc, New York (1975)
29. Hocking, C.: Ludonarrative dissonance in Bioshock. In: Click Nothing: Design from a Long Time Ago, 07 October 2007. https://clicknothing.typepad.com/click_nothing/2007/10/ludona rrative-d.html. Accessed 09 July 2021
30. Sampat, E.: Empathy Engines: Design Games that are Personal. Political and Profound. CreateSpace Independent Publishing Platform, Scotts Valley, California (2017)
31. Sampat, E.: Am I Part of the Problem? (2017). https://elizabethsampat.itch.io/am-i-part-of-the-problem. Accessed 09 July 2021
32. Huizinga, J.: Homo Ludens: A Study of the Play-Element in Culture. Maurice Temple Smith Ltd, London (1970)
33. Halberstam, J.: The Queer Art of Failure. Duke University Press, Durham, North Carolina (2011)
34. Jayemanne, D.: Chronotypology: a comparative method for analysing game time. In: Games and Culture, **15**(7) (2019, 2020). https://journals.sagepub.com/doi/10.1177/155541201984 5593. Accessed 09 July 2021

35. Quinn, Z., Patrick, L., Isaac, S.: Depression Quest, 14 February 2013. http://www.depressio nquest.com/. Accessed 09 July 2021
36. Derrida, J.: Specters of Marx: the State of the Debt, the Work of Mourning and the New International. Routledge, New York (1994)

# Tale: Defamiliarizing Ludonarrative Puzzles

Antonino Frazzitta and Charlie Hargood[✉]

Bournemouth University, Poole, UK
{s5117080,chargood}@bournemouth.ac.uk

**Abstract.** Tale is a puzzle platformer game which explores a changing relationship between two characters through challenges in communication and experimentation, to loneliness and the anxiety it brings, and finally to reunification, collaboration, and growth. The game does not make use of traditional storytelling techniques such as text or dialogue, but rather employs ludonarrative design through mechanics as metaphor and defamiliarization. In this demo paper we present our design and approach to using these concepts to tell the story of our characters principally through movement and puzzles.

**Keywords:** Interactive narrative · Ludonarrative · Mechanics as metaphor · Puzzles · Game design

## 1 Introduction

Tale[1] is a 2.5D puzzle-platformer that seeks to explore and demonstrate ludonarrative design through an approach based on Mechanics as Metaphor and defamiliarization. Developed in Unity 3D Tale follows the relationship between two nameless protagonists through a ruined fantasy world across 3 levels and 9 puzzles. The puzzles include a variety of platformer mechanics designed to explore the emotional state of the protagonists and the nature of their relationship. There is no text or dialogue, the play alone delivers a tale of communication and experimentation, loneliness and anxiety, and collaboration and growth.

Ludonarrative narrative design seeks a blend of play and storytelling [1] where by the mechanics of the game themselves may reinforce, and even tell, the story through play. A common approach to this is the notion of mechanics as metaphor where by the form and interaction of a gameplay mechanic becomes a metaphor within the narrative. The earliest mention of this concept was likely Jason Rohrer in a personal essay on his work on Passage [6] where the progression from left to right and changing visuals are a metaphor for the passage of life, though numerous other designers and scholars have discussed the concept. This can be effectively paired with defamiliarization within design, a notion with its origins in formalism [8] but more recently explored within ludonarrative [5]. A design may be defamiliarized by subverting player expectations, breaking the games

---

[1] Tale can be played here: https://ninofrazzitta.itch.io/tale as of 08/10/2021.

© Springer Nature Switzerland AG 2021
A. Mitchell and M. Vosmeer (Eds.): ICIDS 2021, LNCS 13138, pp. 203–207, 2021.
https://doi.org/10.1007/978-3-030-92300-6_18

own established rules, or surprising the player with new rules and systems. This draws the players attention and can serve to highlight an element of ludonarrative design, a mechanical metaphor, or even serve as a metaphor itself. While ludonarrative is a well established concept in our field, particularly in analysis, in this demonstration we provide an example of its use in practical design and our own approach to its use in movement, puzzles, and defamiliarization.

## 2   Tale

Tale narrates a small adventure of a young boy entering a mysterious world where he finds and frees a young girl belonging to an ancient civilization. The story revolves around the theme of companionship, and the player will explore three fundamental stages of this relationship as they progress with the game.

Firstly the player starts with the discovery of this new relationship focusing on the sense of communication and experimenting with new things. The second part has the two characters separated by an uncontrollable force, exploring loneliness and oppressive anxiety. And finally, the characters are reunited and we explore developing collaboration and growth. Through the duration of the game the player as "the boy" will work with "the girl" as they take their journey through the ancient ruins. The interactions between the two underline that they need each other in order to progress on their journey. This is achieved by having the boy pushing boxes and interacting with leavers, etc. while the girl uses magic powers such as teleporting to progress.

The two characters come from different worlds and have different languages so they cannot communicate properly with each other. The story explores their struggles communicating and how they grow as time passes, showing how their bond becomes stronger. While superficially the story may at first seem to have a "save the princess" premise, this is quickly dispelled with a shift in focus to the collaboration of the two characters. The story finishes the girl completing her journey and taking her place at the ruins summit.

### 2.1   Game Design

Our design makes use of Jesse Schell's lenses of unification [7] helping the design to bring together a cohesive experience that supports a dominant emotion of collaboration. There are three levels in the game, the forest, the underground dungeon, and the sky temple forming a three-act arc in the game, each is designed to support the core emotional themes (communication and experimentation, followed by loneliness and anxiety, followed by collaboration and growth). The level design of those areas is meant to build the right context mirroring the character state of mind - following Zammitto's colour principles [9] that associate colours to certain emotions, and Bura's principles of emotion engineering [2] modifying gameplay using framing devices such as music and visuals to build the appropriate context allowing us to elicit the right emotions in time. In addition to that, we have designed the player's elevation based on the Lopez blockbuster intensity graph [4] allowing us to further regulate the game emotional intensity (Fig. 1).

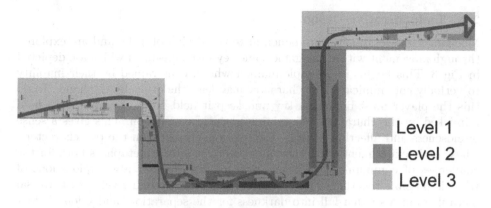

Fig. 1. The structure of Tale's 3 levels

The game presents classic platformer movements and interactions. The player controls "the boy" with standard controls while "the girl" moves either in response to leading and teleportation mechanics, or later moves in response to puzzle context. The game is divided into small areas that contain environmental puzzles. To complete a puzzle both characters must reach the end (which most of the time is signified by a stone portal). For the basic mechanics, the game has "classic" interactions such as pushing boxes, climbing ladders, pulling levers, navigating lifts and moving platforms, and collecting keys. The core mechanic used is the teleportation of "the girl" who can be positioned on platforms or switches to complete the puzzle using initially static teleportation stones, and later moveable teleporter orbs (as depicted in Fig. 2. Puzzles are solved through careful positioning of both characters in order to collect keys and reach the exit, While the player has fine control over the position of one character movement of the other is more challenging and limited by teleportation and leading mechanics, but becomes more flexible as the game progresses.

Fig. 2. Movement is key to Tale and teleportation stones and orbs are part of that

## 2.2  Ludonarrative Design

Mechanics as Metaphor is fundamental to the design of Tale, and are explored through movement within the game some key mechanisms of which are depicted in Fig. 3. This begins in a simple manner where, constrained by their inability to verbally communicate, one character may lead the other by the hand. To do this the player must depress a key and keep it held down, maintaining a hold mimicked by the character maintaining physical connection. This gives a sense of closeness and affection defining the relationship between the two characters. These early experiments with movement serve as strong metaphors both for the challenges of communication in an early relationship but also explorations of what is possible together. The design bookends the second level with traversal metaphors in a sudden fall into darkness for the separation, and a long ladder ascent into the reunification of the third level. Our reflective descent and ascent not only evokes Campbell [3] but also serves as a metaphorical movement towards and away from the darker anxiety of this level. The portal mechanic continues to build on the movement metaphor in that the portals require both characters to be together to enter and, as they are reunited on the 3rd level, the portal itself must be put back together by pushing its component parts.

**Fig. 3.** Movement mechanics: leading, climbing, and bringing the portal together.

We pair this use of mechanical metaphor with defamiliarization. Having completed the first level and explored what is possible between the two characters with teleportation and movement this is then defamiliarized in the second level when the characters are separated, the player is left alone with "the boy" and must solve puzzles, that would be trivial with the teleportation of "the girl", without her. The sudden separation draws the players attention to the absence of a useful mechanic and frequent reminders of the loss in deactivated teleportation stones build the anxiety of the 2nd level. Similarly in the final level as the characters are reunited, while "the girl" and teleportation returns it is now not through static stones that the character will only stand at, but through a moveable and throwable orb that "the girl" will move from on her own accord to trigger interactions in a helpful manner. By subverting the established expectations of teleportation we defamiliarize the mechanic again, drawing the players attention both to the reunification but also that the relationship has grown and the characters are more effective in their collaboration.

# References

1. Aarseth, E.: A narrative theory of games. In: Proceedings of the International Conference on the Foundations of Digital Games, FDG 2012, pp. 129–133. Association for Computing Machinery, New York (2012). https://doi.org/10.1145/2282338. 2282365
2. Bura, S.: Emotion engineering in videogames: toward a scientific approach to understanding the appeal of videogames (2008). http://www.stephanebura.com/emotion/
3. Campbell, J.: The Hero with a Thousand Faces, vol. 17. New World Library (2008)
4. Lopez, M.: Gameplay fundamentals revisited: harnessed pacing & intensity. Gamasutra **12**, 2008 (2008)
5. Mitchell, A., Kway, L., Neo, T., Sim, Y.T.: A preliminary categorization of techniques for creating poetic gameplay. Game stud. **20**(2) (2020)
6. Rohrer, J.: What i was trying to do with passage. Jason Rohrer's webpage, November 2007. http://hcsoftware.sourceforge.net/passage/statement.html. Accessed 20 July 2021
7. Schell, J.: The Art of Game Design: A Book of Lenses. CRC Press, Boca Raton (2008)
8. Shklovsky, V.: Art as Technique. University of Nebraska Press, Lincoln (1965)
9. Zammitto, V.L.: The expressions of colours. In: DiGRA Proceedings of the 2005 DiGRA International Conference: Changing Views: Worlds in Play (2005)

# Emergent Narrative and Reparative Play

Jason Grinblat[1], Cat Manning[2], and Max Kreminski[3(✉)]

[1] Freehold Games, Walkerton, USA
jason@freeholdgames.com
[2] Santa Cruz, USA
[3] University of California, Santa Cruz, USA
mkremins@ucsc.edu

**Abstract.** Eve Sedgwick's theory of reparative reading offers a mode for interpreting text that is "additive and accretive" and "wants to assemble and confer plenitude on an object". It was developed in response to what Sedgwick calls "paranoid reading", which embodies the desire to locate a stable, canonical meaning and is therefore hostile to the notions of multiplicity and surprise. We argue that interactive digital narrative can be productively understood through the paranoid/reparative framing, and that in particular, narrative sandbox games—games that lean heavily on emergence to produce a narrative effect—invite a kind of reparative play. Narrative sandbox systems function by producing deliberately incomplete artifacts that facilitate a diversity of reparative meaning-making processes by the player; they invite repair by arriving in disrepair.

**Keywords:** Emergent narrative · Ludonarrative hermeneutics · IDN theory

## 1 Introduction

Recent work on *ludonarrative hermeneutics* [10,12] has attempted to address the question of how players make sense of narrative meaning in interactive digital narrative (IDN) systems, including narrative games. To date, this work has largely focused on the analysis of games in which a strong *protostory* is deliberately embedded by the designers: in other words, games that attempt to communicate certain preauthored narrative events to the player on every playthrough, regardless of variations that might arise from one playthrough to the next. In attempting to apply a hermeneutic approach to the analysis of narrative sandbox games such as *The Sims*, where no particular narrative events are fixed in place by the game's creators, we are left with an open question: how do players go about interpreting narrative meaning when the units of narrativity embedded in a game by its designers are much smaller, much more abstract, and much more freely recombined than in the archetypal cases of heavily protostory-laden narrative games? To address this question, we propose that the narrative

C. Manning—Independent.

A. Mitchell and M. Vosmeer (Eds.): ICIDS 2021, LNCS 13138, pp. 208–216, 2021.
https://doi.org/10.1007/978-3-030-92300-6_19

meaning-making process in narrative sandbox games can be understood through the lens of *reparative reading*, as articulated by Eve Sedgwick [15].

Reparative reading was coined by Sedgwick in *Touching Feeling*, as an alternative for what she considered the "paranoid" turn in critical studies as exemplified by New Historicism (among others). Instead of looking to create a strict framework that anticipates outcomes, reparative reading offers a "weak" network: that is to say, flexible, mutable, and capable of being rearranged. Sedgwick's work here is grounded in psychoanalytic and queer theory, but the very mutability of reparative reading as an approach makes it adaptable across multiple different fields and frameworks [5, 8, 9].

Others have already moved to bring reparative reading practices into games. In particular, scholars operating in the queer games studies tradition have used techniques of reparative reading to reinterpret a wide variety of games from a queer perspective [13]. Kara Stone has also proposed the practice of *reparative game design*, in which the creator's process serves to repair overdetermined spaces in the medium [17]. However, our notion of reparative play differs from existing work in how it calls attention to the way that games themselves can orient players toward particular modes of interpretation—in the case of narrative sandbox games, a reparative mode.

The reparative process is active; the reader turns to the "part-objects" of a text and assembles them to engender a kind of personal meaning. Sedgwick notes that "the desire of a reparative impulse [...] is additive and accretive. Its fear, a realistic one, is that the culture surrounding it is inadequate or inimical to its nurture; it wants to assemble and confer plenitude on an object that will then have resources to offer to an inchoate self." Repair involves reassembly into, as Sedgwick says, "something like a whole—though, I would emphasize, not necessarily like any preexisting whole" [15, p. 128]. Because narrative sandbox games contain no pre-assembled narrative, only fragmented pre-narrative bits of structure for the player to manipulate and interpret, they invite the practice of repair, first in the interpretative act of making sense of the raw, real-time experience of the interaction loop, and then in the effective act of guiding the further development of the emerging narrative.

Sedgwick suggests that reparative practices can teach us about "the many ways selves and communities succeed in extracting sustenance from the objects of a culture" [15, p. 150]. In this sense, reparative practices offer a new context for understanding how meaning is made out of play experiences, most legibly in narrative sandbox games, but also across the breadth of interactive digital storytelling as a medium. Furthermore, in arguing that narrative sandbox games orient their players toward reparative reading and play, we open investigation into how the mechanics of any given work of interactive digital narrative might be orienting its users toward particular modes of reading and play.

## 2   Background

Key to the argument of how narrative sandbox games invite reparative reading, and from there reparative play, is the idea that a work of interactive digital narrative, or a class of such works, can invite a particular reading practice at all. To get there, it's useful to examine how the theory of interpretation has penetrated the field of interactive digital storytelling. Roth, van Nuenen, and Koenitz [12] have put forth their own "ludonarrative hermeneutics" as an extension to Koenitz's *System, Process, Product* model of IDN [6]. Their extension, the "hermeneutic strip", imports Heidegger's hermeneutic circle and adds a second circle; the part-whole interpretation loop of an unfolding narrative coincides with and mutually reinforces the player-system interactions that are causing the unfolding. Narrative meaning making occurs as iteration through the resulting *double circle*.

Another conceptual tool in the wider territory of ludonarrative hermeneutics is the *story volume*, a mapping in narrative space of all the possible stories a work of IDN can produce. Story volumes "enclose a family of emergent stories" that "explore similar themes or invoke a similar mood" [4]. The idea is analogous to the SPP model's *protostory*, which "describes the concrete content of an IDN system as a space of potential narratives" [6]. The story volume framing differs from the protostory in its emphasis on the shape of the Product stories and de-emphasis on any narrative cohesion prescribed by the System; as we'll see in our look at narrative sandbox games, story volumes can be spun out of works that have very little concept of a protostory.

If we accept that hermeneutics are now operative in IDN, we might next investigate how one particular hermeneutic or class of hermeneutics differs in operation from another. Insofar as the double circle model makes room in the meaning making process for the intervention of game systems and their affordances (inside the upper circle), how might the particularities of a system's design give texture to the interpretative loop? Games are ergodic objects that require "nontrivial effort" in the production of their narratives [1, p. 1]. We might consider how the arrangement of components in System pushes or pulls us into an orientation congruent with one or another particular mode of interpretation. This is the perfect entry point for Sedgwick, who positions reparative reading in an ecosystem of reading practices: a hermeneutic among hermeneutics.

In particular, Sedgwick defines reparative reading against what she sees as the dominant form of critical interpretation—what is "perhaps by now nearly synonymous with criticism itself"—*paranoid reading* [15, p. 124]. Paranoid reading, as Sedgwick explains, is sourced in what Paul Ricoeur calls the "hermeneutics of suspicion" [15, p. 124]. It is *anticipatory* and "places its faith in exposure" [15, p. 130], or the teasing out of "true" meaning from a text. Here Sedgwick quotes Ricoeur on Marx, Nietzsche, and Freud, the three intellectual progenitors whose ensuing traditions Ricoeur invented the category to describe.

> For Marx, Nietzsche, and Freud, the fundamental category of consciousness is the relation hidden-shown or, if you prefer, simulated-manifested.... Thus the distinguishing characteristic of Marx, Freud, and Nietzsche is the general hypothesis concerning both the process of false consciousness and the method of deciphering. The two go together, since the man of suspicion carries out in reverse the work of falsification of the man of guile [15, p. 125]

Consider narrative discovery games, which position the player as investigator ferreting out a narrative truth, "carrying out in reverse the work of falsification" perpetrated by the game object and its designers, using an interactive toolkit supplied by those same perpetrators. These games ask specific questions and give you the tools to dig up their specific answers; in *Outer Wilds*—what happened to the Nomai; in *Return of the Obra Dinn*—where is everyone on the ship's manifest; in *Her Story*—did she really do it? All the narrative energy is tied up in answering these questions; all the ergodic friction comes from grinding against the systems that makes answering them a challenge. These games, then, invite paranoid readings. We might say they have *strong* protostories; that is, the narratives that emerge in the Product, that get read out through the iteration of the hermeneutic strip, are tightly tethered to the prefigurations in System. Discovering pieces of the narrative in different orders changes the texture of the protostory but in relatively undramatic ways. Conversely, we might say their story volumes are *closed*. The volumes are hard-boundaried; they purport to fully and cleanly encapsulate their inner spaces. For an extreme reading of this kind of constrained multiplicity, we can look at an ancestor to IDN theory in Umberto Eco's *The Open Work* and his analysis of a particular hermeneutic of allegory from the Middle Ages that "posited the possibility of reading the Scriptures (and eventually poetry, figurative arts) not just in the literal sense but also in three other senses: the moral, the allegorical, and the anagogical." Of this he writes, "What in fact is made available is a range of rigidly pre-established and ordained interpretative solutions, and these never allow the reader to move outside the strict control of the author." [2, Ch. 1, p. 6]

Sitting in contrast to narrative discovery games are narrative sandbox games, typified by genre exemplars *Dwarf Fortress* and *The Sims*. For these games, there are no prefigured narratives to discover; their protostories are weak. Narrative coheres *only* via iteration through the hermeneutic strip as the player interacts with System via Process and makes sense of the output in Product. Of Melanie Klein's "depressive" position that is a precondition for the reparative orientation, Sedgwick writes, "this is the position from which it is possible [in turn] to use one's own resources to assemble or 'repair' the murderous part-objects into something like a whole—though, I would emphasize, *not necessarily like any preexisting whole*" [15, p. 128; Sedgwick's emphasis]. The narrative project of the *Sims* player is to take the pre-narrative part-objects of the game and assemble them into "something like a whole". This cannot look like any preexisting whole because there is none. The narrative must be repaired, because it arrives in disrepair.

How does this repair happen, and what, in this mapping, are "one's own resources"? They are, oddly, the narrative connections that sit outside the game's systems. This is a move vital to the work of the ludonarrative interpreter who's to make sense of a narrative sandbox experience with no referent; they must fill in the lacunae—unavoidably present in a weak prototype—by "confer[ing] plentitude on an object" that isn't up to the task of doing so itself. This conference of plentitude is the pulling in of threads from an outside context to mend the narrative that's spun out of the upper circle. Of course the object will contain ludonarrative devices that assist this process and anticipate aspects of the emerging narratives (things like mechanics, tone-setting art styles and sound design, etc.). In this way we might say narrative sandbox games' story volumes are *open*; they sketch their boundaries to suggest shape but are less concerned with strict in/out delineation. Sedgwick positions reparative as a *weak* theory in contrast to the *strong*, totalizing impulse of the paranoid. (This is not disparaging; Sedgwick points to reparative reading's acceptance of its limitations as a strength of the theory.) Here we see the weakness in action; because the emerging narrative does not benefit from an author's prefiguration, because it may wander into a thorny corner of its open story volume, the scope of its coherence may be local instead of global, but it has the potential to be nourishing nonetheless.

It's tempting to think of the narratives in narrative discovery games as also arriving in disrepair. But the tools of repair, in the Sedgwickian formulation, are furnished from "one's own resources" and cannot be shipped with the game object as part of its suite of mechanics. It's more accurate to say these narratives arrive intact but buried (think of the digging metaphor we used earlier) and that you're given tools of revelation: a compass to find the relevant sites and a hammer and chisel to excavate them. How intact these buried narratives are can vary, and this gives a bit of reparative flex to these broadly paranoid systems. *Her Story* famously doesn't communicate when you've satisfactorily unearthed what it has hidden [16]. *Return of the Obra Dinn*, on the other hand, explicitly reifies the revelation of its truths; it's difficult (but humorous) to imagine the *Obra Dinn* player who correctly matches three crewmates to their fates and triggers the validation sequence but who persists in their doubt of the results.

We've formulated reparative *reading* in the context of IDN, but the reparative practice is coextensive with the move from the hermeneutic circle to the hermeneutic strip. The reparative work of interpretation happening in the lower circle flows back to the upper; the repairer moves from interpreting events that are occurring to reifying their interpretation as game actions that trigger the next iteration of events. Reparative *reading* becomes reparative *play*; interpretation begets actions, and the cycle is repeated. Here the repairer acts as co-author to the narrative object, using game affordances[1] to mine narrative material [14] and sculpting this material into a narrative work.

## 3    Reparative Play: A *Sims* Case Study

Consider the iconic narrative sandbox franchise *The Sims*. Its story volume is open, a sketch of a sanitized version of 21st century suburbia. Within that story volume, the game does not dictate to players what they ought to be doing or what their sims' narratives will be; the furthest it goes is to suggest potential actions players can take based on their sims' needs. If a romance sim has a fear of getting married, the marriage option is still available to the player; the sim

---

[1] Beyond the affordances of the game itself, modding offers another domain of reparative play possibilities, but those practices are outside this paper's scope.

may go into aspiration failure, but that failure then becomes another part-object to be assembled.

Because *The Sims* doesn't prefigure its narratives, narrative must cohere as the player moves through the hermeneutic strip, taking actions, witnessing their effects, and interpreting the results. The player must interpret *why* a specific action is happening at any given moment. A spontaneous flirt might be interpreted as a result of a sim's promotion putting them in a good mood and boosting their self-esteem, or it might be seen as a sign of true love. The chosen reading then offers shape to the player's next choices: if the autonomous flirt is interpreted as a sign of the sim's interest, then the player may choose to send their sim on a date with the NPC of interest. The game actions taken as a result of this interpretation then engender their own consequences that are in turn subject to interpretation, and the cycle continues. These narrativizations are influenced by a player's "own resources", the stories they're most interested in telling through this sort of imaginative play. The process by which this happens is one of *extrapolative narrativization* [7]: in making narrative sense of *Sims* play, players do not simply transcribe the series of game events as it unfolds. Instead, they confer additional layers of interpretation on these events, adding extra details to the narrative-as-perceived—which then influences what actions the player is inclined to take next.

Sims' speech bubbles are a common intervention point for this extrapolative narrativization. Player-authors of *Sims* retellings [3] often attempt to attribute a meaning to the game's abstract dialogue icons in order to shore up an interpretation. In roBurky's *Alice and Kev* [11]—a notable *Sims 3* retelling centered on a homeless father and daughter—the author looks at Alice's first real adult conversation with an NPC as a site of potential meaning, suggesting that a lake might represent her sleeping rough in parks and a Yeti figure might be her ogre of a father. Because Alice's life in the story has been so shaped by roBurky's roleplaying of her as homeless, the author confers meaning on this conversation by attributing referents to the otherwise ambiguous dialogue icons that would cast the interaction as a meaningful opening-up. Another conversation between two different sims involving a lake and a Yeti might suggest an entirely different reading, such as a camping trip gone wrong. The same speech bubbles interpreted differently might lead players to take two very separate sets of actions; in roBurky's reading, a player might be moved to deepen the relationship with the NPC, where in the camping trip scenario, a player might decide to send their sim on another, hopefully more successful camping trip. Extrapolative narrativization is the key by which players become co-authors, as their interpretive frameworks overlay the game's mechanics, guide them to actions that fulfill the narratives suggested by their frameworks, and ultimately allow them to assemble a cohesive, satisfying narrative through reparative play.

Even *The Sims*'s pre-structured scenarios, which could be considered pre-assembled narrative pieces for discovery, are malleable to players' intentions. *The Sims 2* shipped with several scripted events in its base neighborhoods; events were set to trigger, but players could ignore those scenarios and instead focus on playing their own created characters. If the households with queued narrative were opened after players had already changed the world state, the designer-prefigured events would sometimes not be able to trigger, or their conditions would cause them to play out differently as a result of the player's previous decisions elsewhere in the neighborhood. Players who wanted Cassandra Goth's wedding to Don Lothario to succeed rather than fail, as it was scripted to do under default conditions, could go to his house and invite her over, raising his relationship with her past the threshold at which he would not leave her at the altar. That completed, they could reopen the Goth household to the wedding scenario, still set up exactly as scripted, and complete the wedding as they desired it to go. Mary-Sue Pleasant was scripted to always fail the chance card that came up when her household was loaded, regardless of the action the player took, causing her to come home and potentially catch her husband cheating on her with their maid. Players discovered that ignoring the chance card entirely avoided the trap; others simply had her husband send the maid home after she was finished cleaning. When a player had decided how they wanted the scripted event to play out, regardless of the game's structure, their next actions could subvert the game's suggestions and instead offer a reparative reading in which the player's own preferred meaning would take precedence over the story suggested by the game.

This sort of reassembly could not happen without the part-objects that Sedgwick discusses and which characterize narrative sandbox games. All *Sims* narratives arrive in disrepair, made up of small actions with specific game verbs that have specific effects on the world state. These are most often very limited in scope, affecting one sim or one household at a time; it is only through the assemblage of many of these actions that major changes, like marriages and promotions, occur. Game verbs like "study a skill" are part-objects in the larger narrative of "Cassandra Goth got promoted"; without them, the latter cannot occur mechanically, but also cannot be meaningful narratively. Any verb can be a part-object, depending on what is meaningful to the player; that is what makes *The Sims* such a clear instance of an open story volume. Reparative play, and the hermeneutic strip, enable one to cut through a dizzying plethora of possible meanings. As the player reifies an ever-evolving interpretation of events and takes further actions that stem from that emerging interpretation, a disparate mass of narrative parts, player-provided resources, and player-conferred meanings coalesce into a satisfying narrative: "something like a whole".

## 4    Conclusion

Altogether, we hold that a Sedgwick-inspired theory of reparative play represents a powerful new lens for understanding narrative meaning-making in narrative sandbox games and in interactive digital storytelling at large. Sedgwick's figuring of "part-objects" is a useful framework for thinking about how units of narrative get assembled into cohesive stories. The player's reparative instinct to confer meaning that the system does not already provide maps cleanly to the idea of extrapolative narrativization, through which the player brings their own resources to bear on what the game offers. By interpreting game events, which then spur further actions and interpretations, players engage in the hermeneutic strip of meaning-making—but rather than narrowing in on a canonical, designer-intended narrative meaning, the player instead constructs an assemblage of narrative part-objects whose meaning is derived partly from the resources that this player in particular has brought to bear. As a counterpart to a ludonarrative hermeneutics of suspicion, Sedgwick's framework thus points the way to a parallel ludonarrative hermeneutics of repair, and from there, toward an investigation into broader paradigms of interpretive orientation.

# References

1. Aarseth, E.J.: Cybertext: Perspectives on Ergodic Literature. Johns Hopkins University Press, Baltimore (1997)
2. Eco, U.: The Open Work. Harvard University Press, Cambridge (1989)
3. Eladhari, M.P.: Re-tellings: the fourth layer of narrative as an instrument for critique. In: Rouse, R., Koenitz, H., Haahr, M. (eds.) ICIDS 2018. LNCS, vol. 11318, pp. 65–78. Springer, Cham (2018). https://doi.org/10.1007/978-3-030-04028-4_5
4. Grinblat, J.: Emergent narratives and story volumes. In: Short, T., Adams, T. (eds.) Procedural Generation in Game Design. CRC Press (2017)
5. Hawthorne, S.M.: Reparative reading as queer pedagogy. J. Fem. Stud. Relig. **34**(1), 155–160 (2018)
6. Koenitz, H.: Towards a specific theory of interactive digital narrative. In: Koenitz, H., Ferri, G., Haahr, M., Sezen, D., Sezen, T.I. (eds.) Interactive Digital Narrative: History, Theory and Practice, pp. 91–105. Routledge (2015)
7. Kreminski, M., Samuel, B., Melcer, E., Wardrip-Fruin, N.: Evaluating AI-based games through retellings. In: Proceedings of the AAAI Conference on Artificial Intelligence and Interactive Digital Entertainment, vol. 15, pp. 45–51 (2019)
8. Love, H.: Truth and consequences: on paranoid reading and reparative reading. Criticism **52**(2), 235–241 (2010)
9. Ohito, E.O.: Refusing curriculum as a space of death for Black female subjects: a black feminist reparative reading of Jamaica Kincaid's girl. Curric. Inq. **46**(5), 436–454 (2016)
10. Rezk, A.M., Haahr, M.: The case for invisibility: understanding and improving agency in black mirror's Bandersnatch and other interactive digital narrative works. In: Bosser, A.-G., Millard, D.E., Hargood, C. (eds.) ICIDS 2020. LNCS, vol. 12497, pp. 178–189. Springer, Cham (2020). https://doi.org/10.1007/978-3-030-62516-0_16
11. roBurky: Alice and Kev (2009). https://aliceandkev.wordpress.com/
12. Roth, C., van Nuenen, T., Koenitz, H.: Ludonarrative hermeneutics: a way out and the narrative paradox. In: Rouse, R., Koenitz, H., Haahr, M. (eds.) ICIDS 2018. LNCS, vol. 11318, pp. 93–106. Springer, Cham (2018). https://doi.org/10.1007/978-3-030-04028-4_7
13. Ruberg, B., Shaw, A.: Queer Game Studies. U of Minnesota Press, Minneapolis (2017)
14. Ryan, J.: Curating Simulated Storyworlds. Ph.D. thesis, University of California, Santa Cruz (2018)

15. Sedgwick, E.K.: Paranoid reading and reparative reading, or, you're so paranoid, you probably think this essay is about you. In: Touching Feeling, pp. 123–152. Duke University Press, Durham (2003)
16. Steam forum users: What to do? : Her Story General Discussions (2015). https://steamcommunity.com/app/368370/discussions/0/530645446308194754/
17. Stone, K.: Time and reparative game design: queerness, disability, and affect. Game Stud. **18**(3) (2018)

# Text, Retelling, and the Digital: Reimagining the Mahabharata Through Interactive Games

Ritwik Kar[✉], Garvita Jain, Muskan Aggarwal, and Payel C. Mukherjee

Indraprastha Institute of Information Technology, Delhi, New Delhi 110020, India
ritwik18306@iiitd.ac.in

**Abstract.** Mahabharata, is a multi-faceted and multi-dimensional epic layered with complex narratives and discursive interpretations. Being an ancient Sanskrit text, it houses several perceptions towards marginal characters like Hidimba, a Rakshasi or demoness, who marries a royal prince, Bheema. The case of Hidimba is complex, and is at the crux of our exploration through the essay. The transformation in her portrayal from Ved Vyasa's traditional Mahabharata to a 15th century retelling by Sarala Das, an Odia poet, is fascinating as it subverts the notions of marginality by incorporating voices from the fringes and targeting to audiences who are not expected to indulge in elite Sanskrit literature. We are in the process of creating a game that allows the player to exercise the power of decision making from a subaltern perspective through inclusion of the narratives of marginalised characters. As an extension to the first iteration of the game, we study how people percieve "Rakshasas" and why. The motivation of building an interactive storytelling format for the ancient texts and retellings of the Mahabharata stems from the need to bring the lesser known stories into the mainstream media.

**Keywords:** Epics · Mahabharata · Marginalisation · Retelling · Interactive storytelling · Interactive games

## 1  Introduction

Mahabharata, one of the great Indian epics, unravels the complexities of human thought and condition. This paper focuses on the stories of marginalized characters which remain unnoticed in the reader's pursuit to uncover the popularly known stories. With a contemporary lens of caste hierarchy and patriarchal marginalization, "Hidimba"[1] stands out as one of the characters who has the strength to influence the plot but lacks the power to exercise her agency. As we

---

[1] Hidimba is also called "Hidimba", "Hidimbi" and "Hidimbaki" at different places. We refer to her as Hidimba in this paper. Hidimba is referred to as "Asuri" and "Rakshasi" (which roughly translates to a demoness). For the sake of this paper, we call her a Rakshasi.

© Springer Nature Switzerland AG 2021
A. Mitchell and M. Vosmeer (Eds.): ICIDS 2021, LNCS 13138, pp. 217–221, 2021.
https://doi.org/10.1007/978-3-030-92300-6_20

focus on the Odia retelling by Sarala Das, a 15th century Shudra[2] poet, we bring to light one such episode from the epic which depicts the strength of Hidimba' character [2,7]. The narration of this story as a digital game aims to sensitize the users about the existing biases and prejudices prevalent in our society and to familiarise them with the ideas of agency, identity and perception. The game unfolds differently for each user based on their choices at every juncture in the episode, thus shifting the control of the story from the narrator to the user [5].

## 2    Decoding Hidimba: Marginality and Agency

Hidimba - the queen of the Rakshasa clan was the first wife of Bheema, one of the five Pandava brothers[3]. A noble and liberated character, yet at times she submitted to the patriarchal and classist societal norms. Her strength is never given an independent spotlight in the Vyasa Mahabharata. The instances involving Hidimba provide only an illusion of power drawn from the fact that she is a Rakshasi. Many instances in Sarala Das' version are absent elsewhere and point towards Sarala's goal of making the epic more relatable for his audience [6]. Sarala Das gives her character the mobility to the main landscape and strength to make her own decisions.

The episode we chose for our pilot study has primarily three characters; Hidimba, her son Ghatotkacha and Draupadi, where Hidimba confronts Draupadi, the Pandava queen, for cursing Ghatotkacha. Although her representation has strength, it is never accessible to the readers in either of the two versions. However in Sarala Das' version, she stands up for herself and her son against the upper-caste society and their oppression. It also talks about Hidimba as a "good" wife and her sacrifices; which provokes the thought as to why, despite her stature and abilities, Hidimba is left to lurk in the shadows [1]. Exploring the change in her portrayal, we come across complex attributions - the authors of each version and their societal status[4], the times they were written in, and their target audiences. All these attributes have led to a shift in the portrayal of Hidimba's agency between the Vyasa and Sarala Mahabharata.

## 3    Into the Digital Portrayal

Our gamified approach to present the epic attempts to create a contemporary social lens. The users' power of decision making in the game allows them to engage with the complexity of the plot and critically analyze the decisions made

---

[2] Link to a diagram of the Prevalent Caste System in the 15th century referred from Ambedkar, D.B.R.: Who Were the Shudras? Ssoft Group, INDIA (Jul 2014),google -Books-ID: JGI0BQAAQBAJ.

[3] King Pandu had 5 sons, namely Yudhishtira, Bheema, Arjuna, Nakula and Sahadev. They were collectively known as the "Pandavas". Link to the Genealogy of the Pandavas.

[4] Ved Vyasa was an upper caste Brahmin while Sarala Das belonged to the Shudra caste.Link to Indian Caste System.

by the characters given their situation. In this manner, it becomes easier and more fulfilling for the user to experience and practice empathy [3].

The pilot edition of the game[5] was conducted through a Google Form. In this pilot study, we narrate the confrontation between Hidimba and Draupadi drawn from an episode in the Sarala Mahabharata. At the moment, the game allows the user to make decisions on behalf of Hidimba. At every decision point, the player gets to choose between two options[6]. The story moves ahead on the basis of these choices and consequently has multiple endings. One of the branches leads to the original end whereas all others are created from the researchers' poetic liberty. We attempted to create alternatives that would agree with the characters' personality yet spin the story in a different direction. The players are also required to give reasoning for their choice of action. The set of choices are unique to each user and indirectly represent their personality traits.

## 4   Perceptions for the Virtual

The pilot study was conducted with 39 participant- 20 females and 19 males. Majority of our respondents belonged to the age group of 18–25 and 36–50 years. It was observed that Hidimba, the protagonist of our pilot study, was one of the most recognised marginal characters from the epic. The feedback suggested that the dialogues which served as the background for each decision point needed more clarity to encourage better decision making. We observed that when provided with options which do not affect a person in their real life, they always tend to choose the more righteous option. It was difficult for the respondents to realise the actual limitations of the situation and were inclined to choose the ideal action. However, on further reflection and on being provided a similar dilemma drawn from their personal experiences, they became more critical of their choices and the rationale behind choosing them. The most prominent limitation of the first iteration of this game was its textual character introductions which romanticised Hidimba. It did not allow the users to form an impartial opinion of the characters as one of our respondents said, "the introductions themselves seemed to idolize certain characters".

New media and technology have gathered a vast audience to share a wide spectrum of content, including mythological stories. These stories have come a long way from language specific literature to more experiential formats. The visual representation plays a key role in driving the viewer's imagination and thought process. A "malicious" demon will be represented with features that viewers attribute as scary and harmful. While a docile character would probably be given softer features. It is observed that viewers are often shown what is more desirable and conventionally acceptable, which often builds upon the pre-existing biases even at the cost of straying away from authenticity [4].

---

[5] Link to Pilot Study on Mahabharata.
[6] Link to Flow of the Game.

We conducted a survey to find out the general understanding of rakshasas in terms of perception and visualisation[7]. We touched upon various physical aspects, including body size, expressions, environment and clothing. The collection of words used to associate expressions of Rakshasas were mainly negative - aggression, vengeance, hatred, anger and terror. Many participants thought that their devilish nature was situation-driven. Approximately 37.7% of the participants were convinced that rakshasas are evil. While 61.3% couldn't put rakshasas in fixed brackets of good or evil, and reasoned that it depends on situations, characters and inferences.

**Fig. 1.** Character illustrations and introductory poems

The introduction of the characters of the episode are, now, in the form of short poems[8]. Poems are a great form of abstraction and allow user interpretation to a large extent. The same lines can be interpreted by a reader in their own subjective way based upon their life experiences, mindset and thought process thus reducing any bias introduced by the creators of the game. The characters as shown in Fig. 1 have been designed keeping in mind the perception of viewers in combination with the literature. For example, Draupadi is represented as a lean built fair woman in mainstream media, which aligns with the socially accepted beauty standards in the modern world. This is different from how she is described in the texts where she has a darker complexion. Similarly, Hidimba, in mainstream media, is portrayed as a vicious rakshasi with "dehumanising" features, like fangs, bone ornaments, deformities. The motivation behind redesigning these characters is to challenge and try to eliminate social biases and stereotypes based on physical appearances.

Using this interactive game as a tool, we break down Hidimba and all other characters into entities everyone can relate to. We challenge the public idea of a Rakshasi, and question the basis of their perception. When forced to think about why the stories they read or the plays they've watched as children have a particular representation of the character- both physical and behavioral - people begin to realise the flexibility of these characters. They don't necessarily fit into a given mold. The game gives the users a chance to create their own opinion about the marginalized characters from the Mahabharata, while experiencing empathy and compassion for them in stories which deserve to be heard.

---

[7] Link to the study of Visual Perception.
[8] Link to the poetic character introductions.

# References

1. Patnaik, B.N.: Sarala Mahabharat: when Hidimbaki and Draupadi met...,
   May 2008. https://saralamahabharat.blogspot.com/2008/05/when-hidimbaki-and-
   draupadi-met.html
2. Dash, K.C.: Discourse of literary tradition and its socio-historical perspective. Lokaratna **4** (2011). http://citeseerx.ist.psu.edu/viewdoc/download?doi=10.
   1.1.737.4099&rep=rep1&type=pdf
3. Flottemesch, K.: Learning through narratives: the impact of digital storytelling on intergenerational relationships. Acad. Educ. Leadersh. J. **17**(3), 53–60
   (2013). https://www.proquest.com/openview/3f3d0c08463329dd46d6f8fd4e9ce761/
   1?pq-origsite=gscholar&cbl=38741
4. Goldschmidt, G., Smolkov, M.: Variances in the impact of visual stimuli on design
   problem solving performance. Design Stud. **27**(5), 549–569 (2006). https://doi.
   org/10.1016/j.destud.2006.01.002. https://www.sciencedirect.com/science/article/
   pii/S0142694X06000172
5. Robin, B.: The educational uses of digital storytelling, pp. 709–716. Association for
   the Advancement of Computing in Education (AACE), March 2006. https://www.
   learntechlib.org/primary/p/22129/
6. Sahu, D.U.N.: The great Indian epic: Mahabharat in Orissa, Assam and Ben-
   gal, pp. 48–50, November 2008. http://magazines.odisha.gov.in/Orissareview/2008/
   November-2008/engpdf/48-50.pdf
7. Satpathy, S., Nayak, J.K.: Sarala Mahabharata: introduction. Indian Lit. **58**(3
   (281)), 7–14 (2014). https://www.jstor.org/stable/44753707. Publisher: Sahitya
   Akademi

# A Coauthorship-Centric History
# of Interactive Emergent Narrative

Max Kreminski[✉] and Michael Mateas

University of California, Santa Cruz, Santa Cruz, CA 95060, USA
{mkremins,mmateas}@ucsc.edu

**Abstract.** We trace the history of emergent narrative as both a term and a concept, with a particular focus on *interactive emergent narrative* (IEN): the use of emergent narrative as an approach or solution to the problems presented by the combination of interactivity and narrativity. We argue that discussion of IEN—both historical and modern—often fails to distinguish between two contrasting uses of IEN: to enable player *participation* as a character in an authored storyworld, and to enable player *authorship* of new stories. We additionally advocate for a clearer distinction between these perspectives, so that IEN systems which aspire to enable player authorship can be developed, studied and evaluated on their own terms.

**Keywords:** Emergent narrative · History of IDN · IDN theory

## 1 Introduction

Interactive emergent narrative (IEN) is an approach to the construction of interactive digital narrative experiences that aims to create computational systems from which narrative naturally emerges, bottom-up, through simulation and user interaction. Since the 1995 introduction [7] and 1999 popularization [2] of the term "emergent narrative", IEN has predominantly been framed as a solution to the problem of creating narrative play experiences in which the player may meaningfully *participate* as a character in an authored storyworld. For almost as long, however, there has also existed an alternative perspective on the purpose of IEN. This alternative perspective frames IEN as an approach to the creation of play experiences in which the player takes on the role of the *author* of the "emergent" narrative, rather than a participant. From this perspective, the goal of IEN can be viewed as the provision of the user with *creativity support* [32]: IEN games and systems must give the user the tools and materials they need to construct a story of their own, even in the presence of barriers to player creativity that might obstruct or inhibit the construction of a successful story [14].

These two contrasting perspectives on IEN, despite the substantial differences between them, have remained rhetorically entangled due to the lack of a clear distinction between the play-pleasures of authorship and the play-pleasures of participation. Additionally, when IEN is discussed in a modern context, it is

A. Mitchell and M. Vosmeer (Eds.): ICIDS 2021, LNCS 13138, pp. 222–235, 2021.
https://doi.org/10.1007/978-3-030-92300-6_21

often taken to stand specifically for the form of IEN that targets participatory user experiences.

We believe that several recent developments in the study of interactive digital narrative justify a reexamination of the player-authorship perspective on IEN. The study of *retellings* [6], or the stories that players tell about their play experiences (often in IEN games like *The Sims* and *Dwarf Fortress*), has called attention to the cultural significance of these stories—and to the extensive work that players do in constructing them, for instance by embellishing or extrapolating beyond the bare events of play to craft a better story [13, 22] and constructing stories that ironically comment on or critique the IEN systems with which they were produced [33]. James Ryan [26] has drawn a clear distinction between the raw material of simulation and a particular telling or narrativization of this material, proposing a new *curationist* perspective on emergent narrative that highlights the work done by the human interactor in crafting a coherent story from the disorderly and overwhelming outputs of a simulation engine. In tabletop roleplaying games, recent years have seen the emergence of a clearer distinction between games that focus on enabling player participation in a story (like the traditional *Dungeons and Dragons* style of tabletop roleplaying) and games that intend to enable player coauthorship of a story (like the "GM-less" games *Microscope* and *The Quiet Year*) [8]. And several recent efforts have been made to construct digital IEN games in which the intended player experience is one of coauthorship, rather than one of participation [10–12, 30].

In this paper, we attempt to trace the history of emergent narrative (EN) as both a term and a concept, with a particular focus on *interactive emergent narrative* (IEN): the use of emergent narrative as an approach or solution to the problems presented by the combination of interactivity and narrativity. Walsh [34], Ryan [26] and Larsen et al. [16] have all made significant attempts to disentangle the history of emergent narrative, and we draw extensively on their efforts here. These existing histories, however, stop short of drawing a clear distinction between two frequently conflated uses of IEN: the use of IEN to enable participation play and the use of IEN to enable authorship play. We therefore focus especially on drawing out and clarifying this distinction, with an eye to how this distinction can inform the design of IEN systems intended to facilitate each kind of play.

We argue that one central play-pleasure of IEN lies in the use of IEN systems by players to actively compose narratives. In this context, the computer functions as a storytelling partner that supports the player's storytelling practice, often by keeping track of complicated storyworld state; elaborating on the player's actions in unexpected ways, or otherwise suggesting new directions in which the narrative could be taken; and providing *curatorial affordances* [26] that assist the player in extracting particularly resonant details of the play experience into narrative form.

This use of IEN to enable player *authorship* of narrative is distinct from the use of IEN to support the player's *participation* in a storyworld through the embodiment of a particular character. Although these uses are sometimes compatible within a single IEN play experience, they are also frequently at odds with one another. Artificially limiting the player's viewpoint and agency to align with that of a single character, for instance, may help to strengthen player identification with the character in question (and thus the player's sense of participation in the world), but may simultaneously inhibit the player's ability to tell stories about storyworld events to which their point-of-view character did not directly bear witness, or to "nudge" the storyworld in certain desirable ways in order to promote the development of a particular narrative direction or theme. Therefore, it is useful to consider the play-pleasures of participation and the play-pleasures of authorship as related but distinct phenomena, and to maintain a consistent awareness of which play-pleasures you intend to prioritize during IEN design.

One reason for confusion around the concept of emergent narrative is that people have discussed the concept without using the term, and have also used the term to talk about several different related concepts. In this paper, we will first discuss early usage of the concept of emergent narrative prior to the appearance of the term. Then we will discuss the birth, popularization, and development of the term itself, including two distinct strands of thought that view emergent narrative primarily through the lens of player participation and player authorship respectively, as well as an additional expansive perspective that attempts to situate both interactive and non-interactive EN systems within a common framework.

For the purposes of this paper, we adopt a definition of "authorship" that follows earlier scholarship on emergent narrative—particularly the definition given by Louchart and Aylett (2004) [18], which holds that an author is someone who "seeks control over the direction of a narrative in order to give it a satisfying structure". Though we recognize that this definition sidesteps the debate over the boundary between reader and author that has taken place in hypertext communities (e.g., in Landow's work [15]), not to mention the extensive debate over the broader concept of authorship that has unfolded in modern and postmodern literary theory, we hope that this definition can nevertheless serve as a useful jumping-off point from which to survey existing literature in the interactive digital narrative tradition. Reconciliation of how authorship is discussed in an IDN context with how it has been conceived of in literary theory more broadly remains a potentially fruitful direction for future research.

## 2    Pre-interactive EN

James Ryan [26] argues that emergent narrative as a computational approach to storytelling originated several decades before the term "emergent narrative" was coined. In particular, he identifies the early story generators *Saga II* (1960), Sheldon Klein's murder mystery generator (1967-73), and Meehan's *Tale-Spin* (1975-77) [21] as some of the earliest works of computational emergent narrative. In all of these systems, narrative is treated as the emergent product of bottom-up interactions between a variety of simulated agents or characters, rather than something that is scripted into being from the top down.

**Table 1.** A timeline of key moments in the evolution of "emergent narrative" as a term with respect to Louchart and Aylett's three proposed user roles (spectator, participant, and author) [18] over time. Rows are publications; the S/P/A columns are marked if a publication's definition of emergent narrative includes spectatorship, participation, or authorship modes of user involvement respectively.

| Publication | S | P | A | Notes |
|---|---|---|---|---|
| Early worldsim story generators, e.g. *Tale-Spin* (1975) [21] | ✓ | | | Predate coinage of EN as a term, but retroactively included by Ryan (2018) |
| Galyean (1995) [7] | | ✓ | | First academic use of EN as a term |
| Aarseth (1997) [1] | | ✓ | ✓ | Discusses EN without using term directly; treats MUD players mostly as participants but sometimes uses coauthorship language |
| Murray (1997) [23] | | ✓ | | Discusses EN without using term directly |
| Aylett (1999, 2004) [2,18] | | ✓ | | Introduces definition of EN that remains most widely used today |
| Mateas (2002) [20] | | | ✓ | Cites Aylett but interprets EN differently, without comment |
| Jenkins (2004) [9] | | | ✓ | Cites and disagrees with Murray; doesn't cite Galyean/Aylett/Mateas |
| Ryan, Marie-Laure (2006) [29] | ✓ | ✓ | ✓ | First occurrence of expansive definition |
| Walsh (2011) [34] | | | ✓ | Cites and disagrees with Ryan (2006) |
| Ryan, James (2015) [27] | | ✓ | | Closely follows Aylett's definition |
| Ryan, James (2018) [26] | ✓ | ✓ | ✓ | Pivots from Ryan (2015) to an expansive definition |

Dehn [4] critiqued *Tale-Spin* for its limitations—particularly its need to begin a simulation run with all eventually-necessary characters, props, locations, and so on already invented in advance—and instead proposed an alternative approach to story generation, founded not in *Tale-Spin*'s *world simulation* (simulation of agents with various needs, desires, and so on) but in *author simulation*: the simulation of the process by which a human author assembles a story. In Dehn's view, human authors take a variety of actions beyond placing characters in a storyworld and allowing them to produce a story through their interactions. For instance, authors may invent characters, props, and locations on the fly as needed; plan out desired plot beats far in advance; deliberately develop characters and plotlines to engage with or comment on specific themes; or rearrange the order in which events are presented to achieve a desired effect on the reader. Dehn's approach represented a break from emergent narrative, and helped to found an alternative tradition of story generation founded on author simulation, which is continued in part today by the robust field of planner-based story generation [24,36]. The analog story generation framework *Plotto* (1928) [3], which was later operationalized as a digital story generator [5], can also be viewed as an early manifestation of story generation via author simulation.

In the early context of story generation, then, the emergent narrative approach can largely be identified with bottom-up world simulation as opposed to top-down author simulation. However, neither the early world simulation-driven story generators nor their author simulation-driven counterparts present themselves as live interlocutors that can take input from a user midway through the story generation process and adapt the story in response. Instead, these systems aim to produce fully formed static narratives without a human in the loop. Due to our focus on interactive emergent narrative specifically, we thus consider these story generators to be largely outside the scope of our interest here.

## 3   The Participatory View of IEN

This brings us to the origins of the term "emergent narrative", which appears to have been coined in parallel by several different scholars and practitioners in the 1990s. Ryan traces the earliest academic use of the term to Tinsley Galyean's dissertation in 1995 [7]. Galyean makes only brief use of the term, discussing emergent narrative primarily as a contrast to the approach he intended to introduce: "narrative guidance of interactivity", which involves the use of interactivity to tell the specific story the author of the game wants to tell [7, p. 27]:

> In the narrative guidance model the presentation is manipulated to assure that the user will be told the story regardless of their interaction. In other words, the story remains the same at a high level while the presentation of the story varies.

Critically, however, it is at this stage in the history of emergent narrative that interactivity becomes key to its definition. Emergent narrative for Galyean specifically represents a potential solution to a challenge that would later come to be known as the *narrative paradox*: the difficulty of conveying a coherent story in the presence of an unpredictable human interactor [18]. Galyean's main intent was not to provide an extended characterization of EN, but to present narrative guidance of interactivity as a potential alternative solution to the narrative paradox—in opposition to emergent narrative, which for Galyean had already proven itself viable as the approach taken by a number of successful interactive experiences, such as flight simulators, *DOOM*, and *Myst*. Nevertheless, it is a Galyean-esque understanding of emergent narrative as a prospective solution to the narrative paradox that Ruth Aylett appears to have been responding to in her own work, which substantially developed and popularized emergent narrative as both a term and an approach.

Aylett (1999) [2], the first of Aylett's papers to lay claim to "emergent narrative" as a term, frames itself around the central question "What structures are needed to produce narrative often enough and with enough complexity to satisfy the user?". This framing makes clear the fact that the locus of interest for Aylett is on the system's production of narrative, not on the player's.

Louchart and Aylett (2004) [18] develop this distinction and make it more explicit. Here, Louchart and Aylett present three contrasting perspectives on the role of the user in interactive storytelling (user-as-spectator, user-as-participant, and user-as-author), and frame emergent narrative as an attempt to solve the problems associated with the user-as-participant perspective specifically:

> The role of the user is a key issue in interactive storytelling, with whether the user is considered as an author or a participant within the story having a major impact on theoretical approaches. The contradiction between authorship and participation is an important element of the narrative paradox previously mentioned. On the one hand an author seeks control over the direction of a narrative in order to give it a satisfying structure. On the other hand a participating user demands the autonomy to act and react without explicit authorial constraints. Casting the user either as a spectator, with no ability to act, or as the author him or herself avoids this problem, however it does not offer a solution for a participating user in real-time interaction within a narrative display. It also limits the storyline to a single entity. We argue that a serious consideration of the user as participant can actually present a solution to the narrative paradox, in the sense that it would encourage the emergence of several storylines while still leaving the user with the responsibility of conducting real-time meaningful actions within the unfolding narrative.

This distinction between user roles in IEN is particularly useful for understanding how different authors understand the scope of emergent narrative as a term or concept. In the remainder of this paper, we will make frequent reference to Aylett's proposed user roles in order to contextualize the design goals of different EN systems and approaches to EN system design.

Aylett's conceptualization of emergent narrative as fundamentally based in participation play is further supported (if only implicitly) by two early key works of interactive narrative scholarship: Espen Aarseth's *Cybertext* [1] and the first edition of Janet Murray's *Hamlet on the Holodeck* [23]. Both texts were published in 1997, shortly after the first appearance of the term "emergent narrative", but prior to Aylett's arrival on the scene in 1999. At the time, the term "emergent narrative" was not yet in wide use, but both texts engage with emergence and its relationship to interactive narrative. Moreover, although neither text explicitly draws a clear distinction between participant and author as user roles, both deal primarily with play experiences in which the user directly controls a particular embodied character in the storyworld, and both tend to come down on the side of narrative as either "merely" emergent from interaction or primarily produced by the system rather than by the participating human user.

Aarseth's interest in narrative emergence centers largely on the phenomenon of collaborative improvisatory storytelling in multi-user dungeons, or MUDs. He describes this collaborative storytelling as analogous to a "jazz jam session" [1, p. 158] and frames players in MUDs as "literary cyborgs" [1, p. 160], collaborating both with one another and with autonomous bots to construct textual or literary "happenings" that may lack the "grand structural schemes" of "prose narrative", but that are worthy of treatment as texts. This characterization seems to position MUD players somewhere between participants and authors from a narrative perspective, while largely avoiding the question of narrativity one way or the other. Simultaneously, for Aarseth, "to be an 'author' means to have configurative power over not merely content but also over a work's genre and form" [1, p. 164]. Through this lens, authorship may or may not be available to players of MUDs and other highly malleable IEN systems (that allow users, for instance, to define new commands or interaction mechanics), and remains clearly out of reach for users of more closed IEN systems (such as *The Sims*, *Dwarf Fortress*, and other IEN games that are widely known today).

The tension between Aarseth's desire to characterize MUD play as a form of collaborative storytelling and his hesitance to assign users of computational systems the status of "author" may be attributable to Aarseth's view of early IEN systems (like the MUD) as texts in and of themselves, rather than as tools for producing texts. This conflation—the same one that Ryan [26] argues against, with his admonition that the simulated storyworld is not itself an emergent story—leads Aarseth to treat the unedited transcripts of MUD play sessions as the artifacts of narrative interest. Without the distinction between narrative material and retelling advanced in more recent work [6,13,14,16,22,26,33], Aarseth's view on the role of the user in IEN ends up suspended ambiguously between the user-as-participant and user-as-author perspectives.

Murray's position, meanwhile, is less ambiguous in its strong association of narrativity with participation. Her discussion of MUDs positions the MUD as a "collective creation" and a "digital narrative environment" in which stories can take place [23, p. 103], but does not treat the MUD itself as a narrative per se. MUDs for Murray are essentially a form of "participatory theater" [23, p. 152], and the central design issue that they pose is not one of co-creativity but of "discovering the conventions of participation" [23, p. 153] that will preserve the participant's sense of immersion. Similarly, in her discussion of different player attitudes toward *SimCity*, Murray states that "for the wife, [the game] was a narrative" [23, p. 105], but places the wife in the role of receiving the story rather than creating it. This attitude is made more explicit by Murray's assertion that the "narrative quality" of *SimCity* is "expand[ed]" by changes in later versions that "[allow] the player to live inside a more-detailed three-dimensional city rather than only manipulate it from on high" [23, p. 106]—or, essentially, that a simulation game becomes more of a narrative experience the more closely identified a player becomes with a particular character in the storyworld. Ultimately, Murray's goal is not to produce play experiences that center around player authorship, but to extend into computational media the pleasures of experiencing a story that someone else has authored. To Murray, "once we understand simulations as interpretations of the world, the hand behind the multiform plot will feel as firmly present as the hand of the traditional author" [23, p. 347]—and it is this firm sensation of authoredness that she believes interactive narrative systems should ultimately aspire to provide.

Today, the term "emergent narrative" has become strongly associated in many research communities with the work of Aylett and her collaborators (including Sandy Louchart, Mariët Theune, Ivo Swartjes, and others). Moreover, this research program has consistently maintained its strong focus on participatory experiences. For instance, Louchart et al., in a more recent (2015) characterization of the history of IEN [19], still frame the central problem that EN as an approach is intended to solve as one of "reconcil[ing] the demands of a carefully structured story experience with the necessary freedoms (movement, decisions) one would expect to grant an interactive user." This framing carries forward the focus on the interactor-as-participant-in, not the interactor-as-author-of, the emergent narrative, and consequently the close identification of the interactor with a particular player character. Similarly, Weallans, Louchart and Aylett's 2012 work on distributed drama management [35] essentially attempts to reconcile the idea of the "drama manager" from interactive drama research [17,25] with the bottom-up approach taken in emergent narrative design in order to produce a particular kind of narrative experience from the perspective of the player character inhabited by the user. This work takes it as a technical requirement that the user is strongly identified with a particular player character.

As a result, it may appear that IEN research is concerned primarily with systems in which the user's role is that of a participant in a simulated story-world. But in parallel with Aylett's early work in the late 1990s and early 2000s, an alternative conceptualization of emergent narrative was also taking form. This alternative view, which treats "emergent" stories as having been actively coauthored by the users of IEN systems, has significant but often-overlooked implications for how IEN systems should be designed.

## 4   The Player-Authorship View of IEN

Perhaps the first concrete evidence of this alternative view can be found in Mateas's 2002 dissertation [20]. Like Galyean before him, Mateas does not spend much time on emergent narrative, listing it as one of a wide variety of potential alternatives to the interactive drama approach to interactive narrative on which he prefers to focus. But Mateas's definition of emergent narrative is focused on player authorship: for him, "emergent narrative is concerned with providing a rich framework within which individual players can construct their own narratives, or groups of players can engage in the shared social construction of narratives", and emergent narrative can be explicitly contrasted with the traditional view of narrative as "highly structured experiences created by an author for consumption by an audience" [20, p. 20]:

> Rather than viewing narratives as highly structured experiences created by an author for consumption by an audience, emergent narrative is concerned with providing a rich framework within which individual players can construct their own narratives, or groups of players can engage in the shared social construction of narratives. Autonomous characters may be

designed in such a way that interactions among autonomous characters and between characters and the player may give rise to loose narratives or narrative snippets [Stern 2002; Stern 1999; Aylett 1999]. Multi-user online worlds, including textbased Multi-User Dungeons (MUDs), avatar spaces, and massively multiplayer games such as Everquest and Ultima Online, create social spaces in which groups co-construct ongoing narratives. And simulation environments such as *The Sims* may be used by players to construct their own stories. Using the ability to capture screen shots and organize them into photo albums, plus the ability to construct new graphical objects and add them to the game, players of *The Sims* are constructing and posting online thousands of photo album stories.

Although Mateas cites Aylett (1999) for support in his discussion of emergent narrative, his definition in fact conflicts with Aylett's. Aylett frames emergent narrative not in terms of narrative construction by the user, but in terms of getting the user to participate correctly in a narrative that is "emerging" naturally from the bottom-up interactions of virtual agents. Aylett particularly spends time considering how to ensure the user is watching from the right place when interesting emergent events take place. For Mateas, in contrast, it is always the player's role to "construct" narrative from the "narrative snippets" that interaction produces.

Jenkins cites neither Mateas, Aylett, nor Galyean directly, but his 2004 treatment of emergent narrative [9] falls into the same category as Mateas's. He positions emergent narrative alongside three other kinds of game narrative (evoked, enacted, and embedded narratives) and explicitly suggests that one game design goal may be to "[produce] game platforms which support player-generated narratives", framing the player as the ultimate creator of the emergent narrative and cautioning designers against "attempt[ing] to totally predetermine the uses and meanings of the spaces they create". Further, Jenkins specifically asserts that it is the designer's responsibility to provide players with "highly legible" narrative material to aid them in the construction of their own narratives—although he does not quite go so far as suggesting that designers ought to provide players with tools to help them assemble this material into narratives.

And perhaps the strongest existing articulation of the player-authorship perspective on emergent narrative can be found in Walsh (2011) [34]. Walsh argues that narrative is necessarily "a semiotic activity, a sense-making process, rather than a product of other modes of representation or action"—and, therefore, that it cannot merely emerge as an "inherent result of running a simulation or interacting with a simulated environment". Instead, Walsh concerns himself with what he views as the "semiotic use of a simulation" by players: the deliberate use of narrative sense-making facilities to create a story, rather than to "remediate" a narrative that naturally emerges from play. Walsh highlights Marie-Laure Ryan's characterization of the central play-pleasure of *The Sims* as "coaxing a good story out of the system" [29] to underscore his argument, claiming that

> This description implies the semiotic use of a simulation; such an approach
> to a *Sims* session would involve using the representational logic of the

simulation and the directive influence of your own intervention to create a narrative.

For Walsh, then, the central responsibility of the IEN system designer is to design a system that generates "narratively legible" behavior, and thus "[invites] narrative interpretation". But like Jenkins before him, even Walsh—despite his strong characterization of player storytelling behavior as active and deliberate— stops just short of suggesting that IEN systems can essentially be viewed as tools or instruments of narrative authorship.

## 5    The Expansive View of EN

One outlier definition of emergent narrative, which subsumes both the participation-focused and authorship-focused views of IEN under a single label, can be found in the writings of narrative theorist Marie-Laure Ryan. In her 2006 book *Avatars of Story* [29], Ryan distinguishes between a wide variety of narrative "modes", and discusses three modes that she considers especially important for digital narrative: the "emergent", "simulative", and "participatory" modes. For Ryan, the emergent mode includes all works of narrative media in which discourse (how story is presented to the recipient) and "at least some aspects of story" (the events occurring within the storyworld) are "created live through improvisation". Improvisation may occur within a single human storyteller, as in oral storytelling; between a cast of human actors, as in commedia dell'arte; within a computer program, as in what Ryan calls the "simulative" narrative mode; or between a human "recipient-participant" and a larger storytelling system, as in hypertext, tabletop roleplaying games, interactive drama, and computer games.

Ryan views the simulative and participatory modes as subcategories of the emergent mode. Her simulative mode is "specific to digital media" and characterized by its use of simulations, or "productive engines that generate many different courses of events through a combination of fixed and variable parameters", to implement the improvisatory dynamism of emergent narrative. Her participatory mode, meanwhile, contains works of narrative media in which the recipient plays an "active role" in shaping either the events presented by the narrative (story-level participation) or the narrative presentation of those events (discourse-level participation). In hypertext fiction, for instance, the recipient plays an active role in shaping the discourse by traversing the node-link structure in a particular order and thereby determining the sequence in which the events of the narrative are presented, while in Dungeons and Dragons, the recipient "impersonates an active character who influences the evolution of the storyworld", and thereby participates at a story level.

Ryan's definition of emergent narrative is thus the most expansive of the definitions we consider here, and in fact, we can recognize works of narrative media that cast the user in all three of Aylett's user roles (spectator, participant, and author) within Ryan's definition of EN. Spectatorship-oriented story generators based on world simulation, for instance, clearly fall within EN from Ryan's perspective, as do participation-focused non-digital roleplaying games. Authorship play, meanwhile, is represented most clearly in Ryan's work by her characterization of *The Sims*, which she discusses several times in *Avatars of Story* but also unpacks further in her 2005 essay "Narrative and the Split Condition of Digital Textuality" [28]. Here, Ryan discusses the game's "story mode" (in which players "create comic strips by taking snapshot of the screen and adding their own text"—an early example of what James Ryan would later term "curatorial affordances") and points out that some "players have been known to manipulate the game, in order to get the snapshots that will fit into the plot they have in mind". Moreover, she asserts that the game does not afford users "enough control over the plot" to truly serve those users who aspire to authorship, and suggests that the game should provide more tools to give players control over what's going on in the characters' heads. For Ryan, "the most important problem to resolve for emergent systems of the future is to find the right balance between computer-generated and user-controlled events"—and, in some cases, the right balance lies much more on the side of user authorship of narrative than other contemporary theorists of emergent narrative tend to acknowledge.

Marie-Laure Ryan is not alone in adopting an expansive definition of EN. James Ryan, in his early (2015) writing on emergent narrative [27], cited and relied on Aylett's participation-focused definition of EN. However, he later shifted (in his 2018 writing) to an expansive definition [26] that more closely follows the definition given in *Avatars of Story*. This rhetorical shift was likely driven by Ryan's desire to incorporate early world simulation-based story generation systems into his conception of EN, and thereby to subsume both non-interactive and interactive forms of EN under a single model. The resulting curationist model holds that emergent narrative is always the product of a multi-stage process which refines the raw material of narrative potentiality into fully-realized narrative through active curation and narrativization—sometimes by a human user, as in the case of Ryan's own *Bad News* [31], but sometimes by a computer system that implements "story sifting" techniques, as in the case of Ryan's more recent project *Sheldon County* [26]. By exploding the process of emergent narrative creation into a series of steps with a number of distinct roles that either a human or a computational system could perform, Ryan simultaneously endorses the importance of user authorship in contemporary emergent narrative creation and attempts to present a path by which computational systems could engage in the construction of emergent narrative entirely on their own, without a human in the loop.

## 6    Conclusion

Emergent narrative is a historically contested term. For Galyean (perhaps the first to introduce the term to the scholarly literature) and especially Aylett (who initially popularized the term), emergent narrative represented a particular approach to designing interactive narrative systems in which the user takes up the role of a participant in a simulated storyworld. But almost from its introduction, as evidenced by Mateas's early interpretation of the term, "emergent narrative" as a category was also taken to include interactive narrative systems in which the user takes up the role of an author.

This sideways bleed of the term, and the resulting rhetorical confusion, mirrors the confusion present in early discussions of storytelling-oriented tabletop roleplaying games, where design strategies for promoting the "emergence" of stories around player participants were routinely conflated (on a rhetorical level) with mechanics that enabled the players to participate as authors in a process of story construction. The move to distinguish "GM-less" from traditional tabletop roleplaying games helped to resolve some of this rhetorical confusion by defining a new category of play experiences that center the play-pleasures of authorship as distinct from the pleasures of participation. As a result, design patterns for authorship play can now be discussed more clearly, due to the lack of constant compensation for the fundamental but unresolved discrepancy between two kinds of storygames. We hope that a similar turn can advance understanding of the differences between two analogous and oft-conflated types of digital storygames—thereby opening the door to a new category of IEN play experiences and design strategies intended to facilitate authorship play as a distinct mode of player interaction.

# References

1. Aarseth, E.J.: Cybertext: Perspectives on Ergodic Literature. Johns Hopkins University Press, Baltimore (1997)
2. Aylett, R.: Narrative in virtual environments - towards emergent narrative. In: Proceedings of the AAAI Fall Symposium on Narrative Intelligence, pp. 83–86 (1999)
3. Cook, W.W.: Plotto: The Master Book of All Plots. Tin House Books, Portland (2011)
4. Dehn, N.: Story generation after TALE-SPIN. In: International Joint Conference on Artificial Intelligence, pp. 16–18 (1981)
5. Eger, M., Potts, C., Barot, C., Young, R.M.: Plotter: operationalizing the master book of all plots. In: Proceedings of the AAAI Conference on Artificial Intelligence and Interactive Digital Entertainment, vol. 11 (2015)
6. Eladhari, M.P.: Re-tellings: the fourth layer of narrative as an instrument for critique. In: Rouse, R., Koenitz, H., Haahr, M. (eds.) ICIDS 2018. LNCS, vol. 11318, pp. 65 78. Springer, Cham (2018). https://doi.org/10.1007/978-3-030-04028-4 5
7. Galyean, T.A.: Narrative Guidance of Interactivity. Ph.D. thesis, Massachusetts Institute of Technology (1995)
8. Guzdial, M., et al.: Tabletop roleplaying games as procedural content generators. In: International Conference on the Foundations of Digital Games (2020)
9. Jenkins, H.: Game design as narrative architecture. Computer 44(3), 118–130 (2004)
10. Kreminski, M., et al.: Cozy mystery construction kit: prototyping toward an AI-assisted collaborative storytelling mystery game. In: Proceedings of the 14th International Conference on the Foundations of Digital Games (2019)
11. Kreminski, M., Dickinson, M., Mateas, M., Wardrip-Fruin, N.: Why are we like this?: Exploring writing mechanics for an AI-augmented storytelling game. In: Electronic Literature Organization Conference (2020)

12. Kreminski, M., Dickinson, M., Mateas, M., Wardrip-Fruin, N.: Why are we like this?: The AI architecture of a co-creative storytelling game. In: International Conference on the Foundations of Digital Games (2020)
13. Kreminski, M., Samuel, B., Melcer, E., Wardrip-Fruin, N.: Evaluating AI-based games through retellings. In: Proceedings of the AAAI Conference on Artificial Intelligence and Interactive Digital Entertainment, vol. 15, pp. 45–51 (2019)
14. Kreminski, M., Wardrip-Fruin, N.: Generative games as storytelling partners. In: Proceedings of the 14th International Conference on the Foundations of Digital Games (2019)
15. Landow, G.P.: Hypertext: The Convergence of Contemporary Critical Theory and Technology. Johns Hopkins University Press, Baltimore (1991)
16. Larsen, B.A., Bruni, L.E., Schoenau-Fog, H.: The story we cannot see: on how a retelling relates to its afterstory. In: Cardona-Rivera, R.E., Sullivan, A., Young, R.M. (eds.) ICIDS 2019. LNCS, vol. 11869, pp. 190–203. Springer, Cham (2019). https://doi.org/10.1007/978-3-030-33894-7_21
17. Laurel, B.K.: Toward the Design of a Computer-Based Interactive Fantasy System. Ph.D. thesis, The Ohio State University (1986)
18. Louchart, S., Aylett, R.: The emergent narrative theoretical investigation. In: Narrative and Interactive Learning Environments Conference, pp. 21–28 (2004)
19. Louchart, S., Truesdale, J., Suttie, N., Aylett, R.: Emergent narrative: past, present and future of an interactive storytelling approach. In: Interactive Digital Narrative, pp. 185–199. Routledge (2015)
20. Mateas, M.: Interactive Drama, Art and Artificial Intelligence. Ph.D. thesis, Carnegie Mellon University (2002)
21. Meehan, J.R.: TALE-SPIN, an interactive program that writes stories. In: International Joint Conference on Artificial Intelligence (1977)
22. Murnane, E.: Emergent Narrative: Stories of Play, Playing with Stories. Ph.D. thesis, University of Central Florida (2018)
23. Murray, J.H.: Hamlet on the Holodeck: The Future of Narrative in Cyberspace. MIT Press, Cambridge (1997)
24. Porteous, J.: Planning technologies for interactive storytelling. In: Nakatsu, R., Rauterberg, M., Ciancarini, P. (eds.) Handbook of Digital Games and Entertainment Technologies. Springer, Singapore (2016). https://doi.org/10.1007/978-981-4560-52-8_71-1
25. Roberts, D.L., Isbell, C.L.: A survey and qualitative analysis of recent advances in drama management. Int. Trans. Syst. Sci. Appl. Spec. Issue Agent Based Syst. Hum. Learn. 4(2), 61–75 (2008)
26. Ryan, J.: Curating Simulated Storyworlds. Ph.D. thesis, University of California, Santa Cruz (2018)
27. Ryan, J.O., Mateas, M., Wardrip-Fruin, N.: Open design challenges for interactive emergent narrative. In: Schoenau-Fog, H., Bruni, L.E., Louchart, S., Baceviciute, S. (eds.) ICIDS 2015. LNCS, vol. 9445, pp. 14–26. Springer, Cham (2015). https://doi.org/10.1007/978-3-319-27036-4_2
28. Ryan, M.L.: Narrative and the split condition of digital textuality. In: The Aesthetics of Net Literature: Writing, Reading and Playing in Programmable Media, pp. 257–281. Columbia University Press (2005)
29. Ryan, M.L.: Avatars of Story. University of Minnesota Press, Minneapolis (2006)
30. Samuel, B., Mateas, M., Wardrip-Fruin, N.: The design of writing buddy: a mixed-initiative approach towards computational story collaboration. In: Nack, F., Gordon, A.S. (eds.) ICIDS 2016. LNCS, vol. 10045, pp. 388–396. Springer, Cham (2016). https://doi.org/10.1007/978-3-319-48279-8_34

31. Samuel, B., Ryan, J., Summerville, A.J., Mateas, M., Wardrip-Fruin, N.: Bad news: an experiment in computationally assisted performance. In: Nack, F., Gordon, A.S. (eds.) ICIDS 2016. LNCS, vol. 10045, pp. 108–120. Springer, Cham (2016). https://doi.org/10.1007/978-3-319-48279-8_10

32. Shneiderman, B.: Creativity support tools: accelerating discovery and innovation. Commun. ACM **50**(12), 20–32 (2007)

33. Sych, S.: When the fourth layer meets the fourth wall: the case for critical game retellings. In: Bosser, A.-G., Millard, D.E., Hargood, C. (eds.) ICIDS 2020. LNCS, vol. 12497, pp. 203–211. Springer, Cham (2020). https://doi.org/10.1007/978-3-030-62516-0_18

34. Walsh, R.: Emergent narrative in interactive media. Narrative **19**(1), 72–85 (2011)

35. Weallans, A., Louchart, S., Aylett, R.: Distributed drama management: beyond double appraisal in emergent narrative. In: Oyarzun, D., Peinado, F., Young, R.M., Elizalde, A., Méndez, G. (eds.) ICIDS 2012. LNCS, vol. 7648, pp. 132–143. Springer, Heidelberg (2012). https://doi.org/10.1007/978-3-642-34851-8_13

36. Young, R.M., Ware, S.G., Cassell, K.B., Robertson, J.: Plans and planning in narrative generation: a review of plan-based approaches to the generation of story, discourse and interactivity in narratives. Sprache und Datenverarbeitung Spec. Issue Form. Comput. Models Narrative **37**(1–2), 41–64 (2013)

# Wrestling with Destiny: Storytelling in Perennial Games

Bjarke Alexander Larsen[✉] and Elin Carstensdottir

University of California, Santa Cruz, USA
{balarsen,ecarsten}@ucsc.edu

**Abstract.** "Games-as-a-service" games like League of Legends, Destiny, and Fortnite have been overlooked in terms of how their storytelling contributes to the audience's experience. This paper wants to rectify that by defining these games as storytelling experiences, by drawing on long-form inspirations like sports, wrestling and serialized TV. This paper defines and describes the area of "perennial" experiences as live, on-going narrative experiences that are perpetual, temporally continuous, and have a universal chronicle. These experiences are created through on-going interaction between the authors, the audience, and the experience itself. A case study of the game Destiny is presented to understand how these experiences tell stories over long periods of time, how players and authors interact with the game during that time, and how that experience affects the audience. Perennial experiences tell stories very slowly over real-time. This causes strange diegetic behavior where the real world affects the fictional continuously and they create and enforce myths through their own story-making and live events, which the players and audience partake in and share, making them real. Perennial games are some of the most popular games in the 2021 market, and it is therefore important to understand how they tell stories to better understand the player experience of millions of players.

**Keywords:** Perennial games · Live games · Games-as-a-service · Storytelling · Narrative · On-going · MMOs · Destiny · Diegesis · Sports · Wrestling

## 1 Introduction

"Games-as-a-service" [28,88] are the most popular form of games on the current market[1]. Games like Minecraft [67], League of Legends [81], Fortnite [41], and

---

[1] Exact player counts are difficult to ascertain because they are often company secrets unless announced, as e.g. Fortnite did [97], yet there are sources such as the Steam Charts [98] (which only shows Steam games) or the updated Wikipedia entry on most-played video games by player count https://en.wikipedia.org/wiki/List_of_most-played_video_games_by_player_count. Purveying these two lists give a clear overall picture of the popularity of games-as-a-service.

© Springer Nature Switzerland AG 2021
A. Mitchell and M. Vosmeer (Eds.): ICIDS 2021, LNCS 13138, pp. 236–254, 2021.
https://doi.org/10.1007/978-3-030-92300-6_22

Destiny [25] have changed not only how games are made and distributed [39] but also how they are played [111]. They are all "on-going", with consistent updates, patches and refreshments of their content, keeping players interested and wanting to come back for more. It is proving to be a very successful business model, and part of the undescribed success of these games lie in their storytelling, their ability to tell on-going stories for and with the players. We argue that it should be considered an important part of the experience of playing them. Initially, one might assume their persistent, on-going nature renders them unfit for plotted storytelling, as they cannot accomodate individual player actions as meaningful change. In this work we instead focus on describing and analyzing these experiences as storytelling experiences for whole audiences.

MMOs (Massive Multiplayer Online) can be considered a precursor to this format. However, existing research provides few answers on how MMOs function as storytelling experiences. At the height of research into Everquest and World of Warcraft [5,53,75], many described MMOs as unable to tell stories in the "traditional" sense: No three act structure, no plot [6,59]. The authored stories of MMOs have not been in focus, despite plenty of plots one can get from World of Warcraft (Sect. 4.1). Beyond games, there are many precedents for on-going storytelling. Professional wrestling [73,105] has been telling on-going, live stories since the 80s [49], along with sports, reality TV, soap operas, long-running book and comics series, that all share common traits with these on-going games. When viewed as storytelling experiences, there are clear similarities. It can even be associated to how mythological storytelling operates more broadly. League of Legends has consistently added to its narrative world through websites, cinematics, and in-game changes [43,82], and traditional MMOs like World of Warcraft are no different. We argue that these games tell traditionally plotted stories, yet on an entirely diffcrent temporal scale than, say, Mass Effect [8].

We define these experiences as *"perennial experiences"*: Experiences that are perpetual, temporally continuous, and has a universal chronicle. All games which are perennial experiences can be called *"perennial games"*. The word perennial is chosen because it encapsulates the perpetuity and recurrence of these experiences: They repetitiously add new content (a new TV episode is released, a new update to a game, a new sports match is played), but it is never fully repetitious—it is always a new match, always a ncw patch, always a new episode. The second aspect is that it takes *time* for these experiences to develop and change. One update might not drastically change the status quo, but over many, the fabric of their universes slowly becomes something new. Perennial games are not a new genre of video games, in the popular understanding of genre as defined by the primary interactions (such as "Shooter" or "RPG" (role playing game)) [32,110], nor a genre of storytelling as defined in film studies, by stylistic similarities [110]. The perennial nature of a game is not defined by its gameplay, as a perennial experience is not defined by its storytelling content. Rather, it is a form of storytelling many genres and media can perform, and it is in fact often transmedic [50,85] in nature (although it does not have to be).

While perennial games have been discussed in storytelling terms [45,59,80, 94], this is the first time perennial experiences have been defined as a form of storytelling experience across games and not-games. This work aligns these otherwise disparate experiences, and allows new ways to describe them. Using the case study of Destiny [25, 26], we highlight how this manifests in an existing perennial game, how these stories naturally have a muddled diegesis and how they create myths. These qualities have always been present in MMOs, yet it takes significant time (as in real-world waiting time) to see it unfold. Perennial games are among the most watched and played media in the world in 2021, and is therefore of interest to the interactive storytelling community. While clearly effective for storytelling, this aspect has been woefully understudied.

## 2    Definition of Perennial Experience

Perennial experiences follow a specific set of requirements that do not refer to the specific interaction nor assert assumptions on its subject matter. These requirements are a set of functions of the temporality and universality of its narrative content. We consider sports, professional wrestling, reality TV, soap operas, Twitch Plays, long-running book- and tv-series, and comics to all be examples of perennial experiences. We consider the games World of Warcraft, League of Legends, Blaseball [102], Destiny, Magic: The Gathering [112], and Fortnite to all be examples of perennial games[2]. The requirements are as follows:

- **Perpetuity**. These experiences are perpetual. They do not have stated end or explicit final goal: League of Legends has no obvious ending in sight. New content, events, episodes, or updates can always add to the experience, and the audience can always expect more for one reason or another. They *might* end, as City of Heroes did in 2012 [34], but the ending is arbitrary rather than planned from the outset. (This excludes most narratives.)
- **Temporal Continuity**. These experiences are tied to real-world time [113] rather than experiential time [70]. The fictional space persists even when the audience is not actively engaging with it: Wrestling matches occur without you watching them, the "World" of Warcraft is there despite you being in it, Doctor Who episodes aired before you watched them. The story does not retract or repeat, it always appears in sequence and does not go backwards[3]. The fictional time might not flow 1:1 with the real world (though it can, in e.g. Destiny), but it is operating in a similar fashion to the real world in the sense that it does not revolve around a single person's perception—even the author's. It is *always* progressing forward and changing, intermingled with

---

[2] Referencing the earliest release date for these is inherently misleading, as these games have changed from their release state. Therefore, whenever we reference a specific example, we reference relevant version number or date-identifying information, along with supplemental material showing recorded cinematics, dialogue transcripts etc. as there is often no way of experiencing this inside the game experience today.

[3] Spin-offs, flashbacks, reboots, or alterations of the timeline muddle this significantly. The existence of such narrative devices could signify a lack of temporal continuity, but we can still view the audience experience as linear and sequential regardless.

the time of the real world. A common signifier is how these experiences have live, missable moments [83, 109, 114] where you "had to be there" [100]. (This excludes static spaces and stories that only progress when engaged with.)

- There exists a **Universal chronicle**[4] that is shared by all participants. While there might be audience-individual events and narratives, there is a large-scope chronicle of diegetic events that the author and entire audience has access to and can agree upon as true. (This excludes single-person games such as Dwarf Fortress [1] or table-top role playing games (TTRPGs)[5].)

The experiences have further two delineations based on their representation of their fictional worlds. They have either "virtual worlds" as defined by Pearce [75] and Klastrup [53] (as persistent, inhabitable online spaces) or not:

- **Shared Virtual World**. There is one identifiable world (even if it is instanced on servers) that all players exist within, with shared geography they all traverse equally. Within this is experiences like Destiny [25], Second Life [58, 75], EVE Online [31], and World of Warcraft [13].
- **Shared Fiction**. There is a shared fictional space, but it is not a virtual world—it is not traversable or inhabitable. Yet there is still a requirement of a single shared, unified idea of the fiction, that stems from the universal chronicle. Within this is experiences like Blaseball [102], League of Legends [81], sports, and Doctor Who [7].

A few edge-cases will illustrate the margins of this definition.

Sports might not seem fictional, and they are not in the sense that they are "made up". Rather, sports are fictionalised because the audience and the players create and partake in stories about and inside them. The shared fiction should be understood in the sense that there is a shared fabric of events, a common understanding of the players at stake and a shared narrative they are involved in. This is very much the case in sports.

Serialized fiction such as television or book series, like Doctor Who, bends the temporal continuity requirement significantly, as there is less direct correlation between the temporality of the fictional space and the real world. Yet, the waiting time in between episodes affects the story experience, causing continuity-esque effects: The writers may change story beats based on how the audience responds and the audience has to actively wait for the next episode. This is part of the perennial experience.

The universal chronicle requirement can, likewise, be removed for other effects. A game like "Mountain" by David OReilly [74] is an example of a "personal" perennial game. In it, the player "takes care" of a mountain where elements change over time when the player is not looking, similar to a Tamagotchi

---

[4] The word "chronicle" should be understood in the same sense as in Ryan's work on curated stories [84]: A chronicle is not a narrative by itself, but rather a series of events that can lead to a narrative when storified.

[5] Non-game experiences are almost exclusively universal—non-universality seems to be an affordance of simulation.

[2]. Here, each instance is unique to each player, so it is a personal chronicle despite perpetuity and temporal continuity being in full effect. Groups, similarly, can have shared chronicle of, for example, a unique TTRPG campaign.

These examples all function as perennial experiences and many lessons can be learned from them even if they bend or exclude one of the requirements. The definition of this space is only half of the story however, as any experience with perpetuity, temporal continuity, and a universal chronicle is shaped by three interdependent aspects, and this is vital to how these experiences work.

## 3   The Trifecta of Influence

All perennial stories share a trifecta of control between an author, a game/world /system/story/space, and an audience, who all interact in real time *over time*. This is visualised in Fig. 1. Across any kind of representation of the fiction is a shared diegesis that author and audience agree upon as being "part of the world", which is wherein events can shape the universal chronicle, although the specifics of that can be and are up for negotiation at run-time (there is in fact *only* run-time for these experiences as a whole): When something goes wrong in the world of Destiny, it has already happened, and the authors (Bungie employees) have to fix it in real-time.

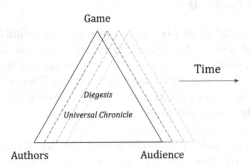

**Fig. 1.** This triangle shows the trifecta of control as shared between the author, the game or system, and the audience, as they negotiate the diegesis and universal chronicle. These then evolve concurrently over time, as shown by the figure's third dimension, which shapes the experience through the control all three exert.

The author, the game, and the audience are all progressing forward through time, during the experience. In a traditional narrative process, the author grows and changes during development, then publishes a fixed story to the audience, who then are influenced by this story moving forward. But in a perennial experience, all three continuously move forward in time, change and mold the experience as they do. Each aspect of the experience is consistently reflected by the other two. Perennial experiences embody the old saying "no one steps into the same river twice", through their very design.

As a natural consequence of this three-part interaction, the storytelling process is an ongoing social negotiation between the three parties. The creation of the universal chronicle, thus, is a social, cultural process that happens over time. Every one of the perennial experiences mentioned in this paper share this quality: They create, facilitate and strengthen communities of play [75]. It is already well known how playing MMOs is a social experience [33,68,75,77], but this sociality extends to the interactions between the audience and the authors as well. Through the audience interacting with the other two aspects and other audience members, the universal chronicle is formed (and enforced).

Note the use of the word "audience", rather than "players". The primary interaction with a perennial experience is moreso that of an audience, than as players. Sports or wrestling are useful examples of audience-bound storytelling. Sports are well known as emergent storytelling phenomenae [3] but the perennial experience of a sport is bound to the audience: They are the people who we'd say have the storytelling experience of the sport. It is not tied to the playing of an individual match, but rather the story arcs that spring forth over a season, over multiple seasons. One match might be pivotal to that story, but it is through the context understood by the audience that the experience comes to life: The players are not who the experience is for. The players actuate the experience; they are, in other words, actors of the game, and thus belong more in the game part of the trifecta.[6]

In video games, many people who play them are both players and audience. This is the commonly understood experience of playing a game: We enter a world and act within it, to see the outcome of our actions. We play for an audience of ourselves, and a single person thus fulfills both roles. But it is important to note that when we are talking about *playing* these experiences, it is a different action than *experiencing them as stories*, even if both can and will occur simultaneously.[7] Examples in Sect. 4 will make this clear.

Being an audience does not mean they are non-interactive. While a player can play for months without story advancement and the story then can suddenly shift drastically without player input (see Sect. 4), these experiences are still fundamentally interactive. Wrestling is a good example of a medium where the audience can have direct influence over the outcomes of matches and storylines [35,63,72,90], through acting as an audience.

## 3.1   The Spectrum of Perennial Experiences

To illustrate the complicated relationship of control between author and audience, perennial experiences can be mapped onto a two-dimensional spectrum of control, which can be seen in Fig. 2. This is an example of how to think about the authorial control in perennial experiences, to try to understand this very storied

---

[6] This doesn't discount players: Play is necessary for the perennial game to function.

[7] This split should not be understood as a person can only engage with one or the other exclusively, but rather as different lenses to understand the experience of interacting with a piece of media.

question [3,15,60], as perpetuity in no way simplifies the matter. The horizontal axis shows the authorial control, with sports (very little authorial control) in one extreme and serialized fiction (much authorial control) on the other. Note here that the aspect of control mentioned is specifically over the outcome of the experience: In football, those who make the rules have little control over the outcome of a match, despite how much control they have on the rules themselves (which might influence future matches). On the other axis is the spectrum of audience control with tells us how much in control the audience has over the outcome of the experience.

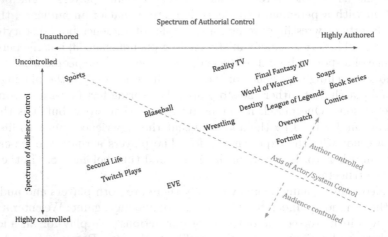

**Fig. 2.** This two-dimensional spectrum shows the various degrees of control the author has (horizontal) and the audience has (vertical). While an inverse correlation that less author control means more audience control exists in many cases, it is not always the case, as highlighted by the diagonal line in the middle, which focuses on experiences where neither have complete control. Note that the specific placements of the experiences are exhibitory and should not be considered exact.

While there are experiences where clear lack of authorial control leads to a high degree of audience control, there are also experiences where neither is in full control; sports and sports-like experiences like Blaseball and wrestling being the most obvious examples. The authors and audience each have a degree of control, yet there is an element with much more to say: The emergence of the system itself. No individual player, coach, audience member or television promoter of a football match is in total control over what happens. The game is decided by many players and systems coalescing into an emergent experience [3] that is in no-one's entire control. In Blaseball, the randomness of the game gives a high degree of uncertainty for both the audience and the creators [61]. Similarly, in wrestling, neither the wrestlers or the writers or the audience are in full control of the experience [35,63]. This is an example of how less authorial control does not necessarily lead to more audience control, and while it is most clear in sports-likes, a degree of it happens in any perennial experience, not the least due to the perpetual, unpredictable nature of time.

## 3.2 Temporal Diegesis

Through the creation of the universal chronicle over time by the three aspects, a sense of diegesis[8] is formed about what is part of the narrative world and what is not. However, that is often a very blurry, shifting line. Wrestling is a great example of this. It is common knowledge that wrestling is a "fake" sport, that is, its matches are prescripted [4,63,91]. However, the real, unscripted outside world frequently impacts the storytelling of wrestling, causing its pre-written narrative to change in real-time to react to real-world events, and each participant will frequently negotiate what is a part of the storyworld and what isn't [63,73]. Simultaneously, as Sect. 4.2 will show, the fact that the audience experiences the world in real-time causes the "virtual" events that happen in perennial stories to become real, because they happen to real people in real situations. The universal chronicle of perennial experiences runs parallel to the real world, and this causes the distinction between what is part of the storyworld and what isn't to blur and weave, at all times. The trifecta of a perennial experience will always be in a negotiation of what is part of its world, and what is not.

The case study of the video game Destiny will help to illustrate these effects in a game context and how the properties of perennial experiences lead to this kind of storytelling experience.

## 4 Case Study: Destiny

Destiny[9] is a widely known game that has been studied with a view on identity [30,48], player profiling and modelling [37,86,92,99], social media [29,38,107] player networks and communication [9,76,77,87,103,106,108], economics [65], competitive multiplayer [78,93], skill development [51,55,96], character creation [64,89], archeology [40,79], and visuals [57,66,101], yet, on its story has only been said it was poorly received at launch [14]. Since then, Destiny has turned into a *quintessential* perennial game. The former Game Director for Destiny, Luke Smith, defined Destiny as an *"Action MMO in a single, evolving world"* [20], and while the genre itself doesn't matter to its perennial status, the notion of a "single, evolving world" is telling. It is perpetual and on-going, and its temporal state is 1:1 with the real world: 1 day in our world is 1 day in the Destiny fiction; events that happened a year ago, happened a year ago in both[10]. To understand

---

[8] Diegesis is here understood in the terms from Kleinman et al. [54].

[9] We discuss Destiny [25] and Destiny 2 [26] as a single franchise and universe. The story is a direct continuation, and they exist in the same narrative world, so there is little reason to distinguish between them, other than distribution.

[10] This is evident through a range of dialogue and interactions [36,47], for example a character referring to the Traveller coming alive *"a year ago"*, in 2018, referencing an event that happened at the end of the Red War, in 2017 [47].

how the universal chronicle in Destiny is formed, we need to understand how the game tells its stories.

Destiny's position in the spectrum of control shows how it is a perennial experience with quite heavy author control. This authorial power is exercised in several ways. Destiny employs well-trodden avenues from narrative video games, like dialogue and cut-scenes and scripted missions—yet often only for yearly expansions and pivotal moments—combined with depictions of the world through "lore cards", item descriptions, and embedded text, which are often accounts of happenings in the world by fictional characters, either current or historical. However, the assembly of these narratives into a sensible chronicle is, for the most part, left to the players, such as when the lorebook "Truth to Power", released to the players over months, yet was slowly revealed to be full of lies [19,26, Patch 2.0.2.1 and onwards]. The players are also given the task of actuating and propulsing many of the story's agendas, such as when, during the "Forsaken" expansion, the area of the "Dreaming City" became cursed through a spell triggered by the players slaying a dragon. This occurred in September 2018, and is now a historical event (the city is, as of this writing, still cursed) [26,46,71, Patch 2.0.2.1 and onwards]. This is the primary way Destiny creates its universal chronicle: Through authored events actuated and enforced by players. However, sometimes players cause events to feed back into the world such as the infamous "Loot Cave" [25,44, Original release], a cave of endlessly spawning enemies players were using to get equipment, which the developers then had to disable. However, the Loot Cave showed up later in Destiny 2 in 2020 as an empty cave full of corpses [26,42, Beyond Light, Patch 3.0.0.1]. This is an example of an unintended behaviour in the game affecting player behaviour, and then feeding back to the authors to support the universal chronicle of Destiny. By reimplementing the cave, the developers are telling the players that the endless shooting into a cave that happened in 2014 was in fact real, echoing how every event expands Destiny's world and moves it forward, regardless who or what caused it.

Seeing a moment of gameplay of Destiny will not reveal any of this. At its gameplay core, a player in Destiny shoots aliens. While some parts of the story-telling is front and center, much of it can be entirely ignored, and is not required to *play* the game successfully. Here, the split player/audience is helpful. A player of Destiny is interacting with the gameplay systems, whereas the audience for the perennial game of Destiny is experiencing the storytelling. For many players, this happens concurrently, as it is part of playing for them to experience the story, read the lore cards and learn about the fictional world. Yet, you could play without paying attention to the story or the *reverse*; read lore cards on a website (like https://www.ishtar-collective.net/) and watch lore recaps by "My Name is Byf" on YouTube [27] to experience the story without participating in it. To what extent this happens in reality is out of the scope of this paper, yet it can still deductively and anecdotally be understood as a possible way to experience these stories. Furthermore, a player joining later and learning about previous events other players did in the space, can be said to have a pure audience-relation to those events, since they did not participate in them.

## 4.1 The Speed of Storytelling

Destiny, for our purposes, is an MMO, despite its shooter trappings. It has a consistent, inhabitable virtual world, rather than a fragmented fiction. MMOs were, by Bartle and others, not seen as games with traditional storytelling potential: *"...virtual worlds do not have, nor ever can they have, narrative in the conventional sense. They're places. Players can act out narratives of their own within them, but the virtual worlds can't impose a three-act structure or anything like it."* [6,52,59]. To contrast, here is a story from the universal chronicle of Destiny. In 2017, early Destiny 2, Mithrax [17] was nothing more than an unnamed NPC of an enemy faction, who was surprisingly not agressive towards us, the players [16], but over the years he has slowly revealed his identity and intentions, turning him from a rogue ally [21], to an insubordinate Fallen helping us overthrow a new tyrant [23], to recently, where he has fully allied with the players, and been given asylum in a part of the human city [24]. We hope this example illustrates how the previous notion is wrong. The story of Mithrax is a quite conventional story of learning to trust an unexpected ally; it just took 3.5 years to unfold. To take another example, we today have the power of seeing all the changes that happened to the "World" of Warcraft in the 17 years since its inception, and it is no small story. Kings (plural) have died [11–13, Legion, Patch 3.3.0]. Entire continents upheaved [10,13, Cataclysm]. Ancient trees burned to the ground [13,62, Patch 8.0.1]. This was not something a player could experience in 2004, when the game released. This highlights a crucial property of perennial storytelling: It is *slow*. Spending mere hours or days with any perennial experience—even "long" hours by traditional game standards—will not reveal its true nature, and it is therefore vital to let them take their time: It is only over *time* their worlds develop, which is how the storytelling happens. This is what viewing games as perennial experiences gives us: We can see that what was previously considered a static world in snapshots has rather obvious parallels with experiences like wrestling, sports, or serialized television, and there are important lessons from these we can draw.

## 4.2 Diegesis and Myth

One of those lessons is in how perennial games work diegetically. The pace and temporal continuity of Destiny causes its world to flow interchangeably in and out of diegesis with the real world, as its events are forever tied to real-world events—just as the real world has changed over the last 3 years, so has the world of Destiny. Yet, it gets much weirder. You could (until recently [26, Beyond Light, Patch 3.0]) go back and re-experience The Red War from 2017, in a motion that simulates re-watching an old wrestling or sports match for nostalgia or historical reverence, as it, fictionally, only occurred once. Likewise, as in most online games, many missions can be repeated ad nauseum for rewards, without explanation for how the enemies reappear (with some rare exceptions, where respawning is actually fictionalised within the world of Destiny [18], making the instances where it is not even stranger). Destiny's temporality also causes its fiction to be impacted by the real world: Its 2020 expansion got delayed by two months because of the Covid-19 pandemic, causing the entire fiction of Destiny to "wait" until it was ready, with no diegetic explanation. Another, recent example is how the official Twitter account of the developer Bungie got "overtaken" by a fictional character from the world of Destiny, and spoke as if she existed in the real world [104]. Note how this is similar to wrestling and other long-form transmedia storytelling: The specific examples of how the diegesis breaks is different but it is still a fundamental aspect that the dual-diegetic elements arise because of the perennial nature—specifically the temporal continuity and universal chronicle—which causes anything that isn't temporally continuous or part of the universal chronicle to be inherently odd. However, the fiction-breaking implications of respawning villains and recurring events are not necessarily any diegetically stranger than the incorporation of real-life movies into the fiction of wrestling [73, Monday Night Raw, November 24, 2008]. And in both, the audience does not seem to care. This is evident purely through the popularity of these experiences: If diegetic breaks like these were enough to make the storytelling experience fall apart, they wouldn't be as consistently popular and well regarded by their fans as they are. This diegetic power is also in part because of the inherent affordances perennial games have to create myths about themselves, through continuity and universality.

The pseudo-historical nature of these games cause a strange effect to happen upon the veracity of their events. They are still undoubtedly fictional, yet there is something true about them. To understand what we mean, here is an example of an event that happened in Destiny: *We shot down the Almighty*[11] [22]. This is true. It did happen. Every player (first author included) who was part of this can attest to the fact that it happened. Therefore, while the world is fictional, as Krzywinska said, *"we nonetheless do "real" things in that world"* [56]. This statement is different from most narrative events as it is not an individual experience: It didn't happen separately to each person—yes, each player had their unique perspective on the event, but the event itself is part of the universal chronicle: Every player who played in the seasonal event helped gather the required resources, and every player who was in Destiny at 10 AM PST on June 6th, 2020 saw the Almighty explode in the sky [22]. And any player who was not can only hear the story of it. This is how perennial games become historical; become mythological: They create events which become myth. The destruction of the Almighty, the fall of the moon "Dalamud" in Final Fantasy XIV [69,95, Pre-patch 2.0 and transition to A Realm Reborn], the black hole in Fortnite [41,109, Oct 13-15, 2019], the opening of the gates of Ahn-Qiraj [13,83,114, Patch 1.9.0] are all examples of the most mythological of these types of events: They were big, earth-shattering (literally) events that changed the fabric of their universes. They are foundational myths upon which their universal chronicles stand. These myths are kept alive through records and retellings and *become* myths through player action.

---

[11] A space station on a collision course with Earth.

Furthermore, to Krzywinska [56], the repetition of quests, traditionally thought as a negative for storytelling, makes perfect sense mythologically, as traditional myths were repeated, battles were fought over and over again, stories were told and retold. Understanding these worlds as mythological, rather than factual or logical, makes their diegetically and temporally strange occurrences perceivable as storyable, too. Note here that the world is not a "myth" in itself, as it exists, but rather it functions mythologically, and is able to present myth.

# 5   Conclusion

This paper has described and defined the "perennial game", and above it, the "perennial experience" as an experience that is perpetual, temporally continuous, and has a universal chronicle, with either a shared fiction or a shared world. Each perennial game exists in relation and negotiation with the authors, the game itself, and the audience, with players directly interacting with the game, whereas the audience (who can and do overlap with the players) experiences it. Perennial games exists within the larger scope of perennial experiences, and the commonalities between them make comparisons useful. A spectrum of experiences was presented, showing how various examples of this form mapped onto authorial and audience control. Understanding all of these experiences as perennial opens the possibility for us to draw teachings from wrestling, sports, Reality TV, etc. into video games, as the storytelling findings they have from their decades of run-time could be useful for these types of games.

A case study of Destiny was presented as an example of how perennial games tell perennial stories over long periods of time. It shows itself through lasting change in the world, and through social player engagement within it. Perennial worlds or fictions become mythological through evocative and detailed histories and mythologically functioning events. The worlds and stories are both real and not-real, as they fluently flux into and out of reality, through their mimicry of (and existence within) reality's time.

Perennial games have truly exploded within the last 10 years, so there is a much broader wealth of experiences to analyse and study than ever before. They span the most popular games on the planet right now, and they show little sign of slowing down. In this paper we outline their definition to create a common ground upon which we can begin to disseminate and discuss the possibilities and pitfalls of these games, by showing how their experiences echo other forms of media. There are still many questions to be explored within this form both in terms of how they are experienced (what is the effect of real-time and constant (re)negotiation of the story space for the audience? How much does time affect the experience?) and how they are made (how to continue to develop new content for an experienced audience, while also remaining accessible to newcomers?).

The popularity of these games have demonstrated the power of perennial storytelling experiences, and are therefore of inherent interest to the interactive storytelling research community. This paper presents a first step in the direction of trying to wrestle with this form of games, to help answer the questions of what they are, how they are experienced, and what we can do with them.

# References

1. Adams, T., Adams, Z.: Dwarf fortress (2006)
2. Akihiro Yokoi (WiZ), A.M.B.: Tamagotchi (1996)
3. Aylett, R.: Narrative in virtual environments-towards emergent narrative. In: Proceedings of the AAAI Fall Symposium on Narrative Intelligence, pp. 83–86 (1999)
4. Barthes, R.: The world of wrestling, chap. 2, pp. 23–33. Duke University Press (1972)
5. Bartle, R.: Hearts, clubs, diamonds, spades: players who suit muds. J. MUD Res. 1(1), 19 (1996). http://www.mud.co.uk/richard/hcds.htm
6. Bartle, R.A.: Designing Virtual Worlds. New Riders, Indianapolis (2004)
7. BBC, Newman, S., Webber, C.E., Wilson, D.: Doctor Who. Television Series on BBC (1963–Now)
8. BioWare: Mass effect (2007)
9. Birk, M.V., et al.: The effects of social exclusion on play experience and hostile cognitions in digital games. In: Proceedings of the 2016 CHI Conference on Human Factors in Computing Systems, CHI 2016, pp. 3007–3019. Association for Computing Machinery, New York (2016). https://doi.org/10.1145/2858036.2858061, https://doi-org.oca.ucsc.edu/10.1145/2858036.2858061
10. Blizzard: World of warcraft patch notes: Patch 4.0.3a: the shattering of azeroth (2010). https://worldofwarcraft.com/en-us/news/1214741/patch-403a-the-shattering-of-azeroth-now-live
11. Blizzard: Fall of the lich king ending (youtube video) (2011). https://www.youtube.com/watch?v=qAIrj_Vqdfc. Accessed 17 Jan 2021
12. Blizzard: Death of Varian Wrynn- world of warcraft: Legion (youtube video) (2016). YouTube "Tom's Hardware": https://www.youtube.com/watch?v=T9Z3eLEpxQ8. Accessed 17 Jan 2021
13. Blizzard Entertainment Ltd.: World of warcraft (2004)
14. Bowey, J.T., Mandryk, R.L.: Those are not the stories you are looking for: using text prototypes to evaluate game narratives early. In: Proceedings of the Annual Symposium on Computer-Human Interaction in Play, CHI PLAY 2017, New York, NY, USA, pp. 265–276. Association for Computing Machinery (2017). https://doi.org/10.1145/3116595.3116636, https://doi-org.oca.ucsc.edu/10.1145/3116595.3116636
15. Bruni, L.E., Baceviciute, S.: Narrative intelligibility and closure in interactive systems. In: Koenitz, H., Sezen, T.I., Ferri, G., Haahr, M., Sezen, D., Ç atak, G. (eds.) ICIDS 2013. LNCS, vol. 8230, pp. 13–24. Springer, Cham (2013). https://doi.org/10.1007/978-3-319-02756-2_2
16. Bungie: "chances and choices: enemy of my enemy". From destiny 2 original release (no longer playable as of beyond light), November 2020. Destiny 2 Story Mission. Enemy Captain does not fight the player (2017). Video and transcript can be found at https://www.ishtar-collective.net/transcripts/quest-chances-and-choices-enemy-of-my-enemy#mithrax by Isthar Collective. Accessed 17 June 2021
17. Bungie: Mithrax (Misraaks). Non-playable character in Destiny 2 (2017–2021). https://www.ishtar-collective.net/categories/mithrax by Isthar Collective for overview. Accessed 17 June 2021

18. Bungie: Dialogue from destiny 2 strike: The hollowed lair (added in the forsaken expansion, 2018). Replayable Strike Mission in Destiny 2 (2018). Dialogue Transcripts available at https://commons.ishtar-collective.net/t/the-hollowed-lair-st rike/2106, by Isthar Commons. Youtube video of relevant dialogue at https://www.youtube.com/watch?v=rShQFTvPeBw&list=PLS2hBTtCDufSzVXI2EJM cP4-BCSACYuy&index=17, posted by Destiny Lore Vault. Both URLs Accessed 16 June 2021
19. Bungie: Truth to power (2018). Lorebook from Destiny 2, hosted on https://www.ishtar-collective.net/categories/book-truth-to-power
20. Bungie: Bungie vidoc - the moon and beyond (2019). https://www.youtube.com/watch?v=mEvVKCKdtfw
21. Bungie: "zero hour". From destiny 2's "season of the drifter", May 2019 (no longer playable as of beyond light (2020). Destiny 2 Repeatable Story mission. Mithrax is passive NPC who starts the mission, and shows up during to help the player (2019). Video and transcript can be found at https://www.ishtar-collective.net/transcripts/quest-fallen-transponder-and-zero-hour-outbreak-perfected by Isthar Collective. Accessed 17 June 2021
22. Bungie: The crash of the almighty. Live event inside Destiny 2, 10 AM PDT, June 6th, 2020. First author can report being present at the event (2020). Second-hand video can be seen at https://www.youtube.com/playlist?list=PLS2 hBTtCDufSxtSjyvzjtXIGOPL5VigE-. Article about the event can be seen at https://www.polygon.com/2020/6/5/21279660/destiny-2-almighty-event-tower-damage-emblem-seraphs-wings-crash-date-time Both URLs Accessed 16 June 2021
23. Bungie: Quest: Evacuation. Story mission in Destiny 2: Beyond Light (2020). Player helps evacuate skiff with refugees to Mithrax's "House of Light" (2020). Transcript and video can be seen at https://www.ishtar-collective.net/transcripts/quest-evacuation-beyond-light by Isthar Collective. Accessed 17 June 2021
24. Bungie: The lost splicer. Opening story mission in Destiny 2: Season of the Splicer (2021). Mithrax is now a fully voiced and singular character (2021). Videos can be seen at https://www.youtube.com/watch?v=ty9nRvTE26A&list=PLS2hBT tCDufQgZAAvRPamiMCkJ-r_Pef3&index=2 and https://www.youtube.com/wa tch?v=ZiteIeg3riY&list=PLS2hBTtCDufQgZAAvRPamiMCkJ-r_Pef3&index=3 by Destiny Lore Vault. Accessed 17 June 2021
25. Bungie and Activision: Destiny (2014)
26. Bungie and Activision: Destiny 2 (2017), as of 2019, Activision is not affiliated with Destiny. https://kotaku.com/bungie-splits-with-activision-1831651740
27. My name is Byf: Youtube channel: "my name is byf" (2014–Now). https://www.youtube.com/c/MynameisByf/videos
28. Cai, W., Chen, M., Leung, V.C.: Toward gaming as a service. IEEE Internet Comput. **18**(3), 12–18 (2014)
29. Canossa, A., Azadvar, A., Harteveld, C., Drachen, A., Deterding, S.: Influencers in multiplayer online shooters: evidence of social contagion in playtime and social play, New York, NY, USA, pp. 1–12. Association for Computing Machinery (2019). https://doi-org.oca.ucsc.edu/10.1145/3290605.3300489
30. Carroll, A.E.: Identity within destiny: virtual selves in virtual worlds. Master's thesis, University of Colorado Denver (2016)
31. CCP Games: Eve Online (2008)
32. Clearwater, D.: What defines video game genre? Thinking about genre study after the great divide. Loading **5**(8), 29–49 (2011)

33. Cole, H., Griffiths, M.D.: Social interactions in massively multiplayer online role-playing gamers. Cyberpsychol. Behav. **10**(4), 575–583 (2007)
34. Cryptic Studios: City of heroes (2004)
35. De Garis, L.: The Logic of Professional Wrestling, chap. 9, pp. 192–213. Duke University Press (2005)
36. dobby_rams: Dreaming city dialogue reddit post (2018). https://www.reddit.com/r/DestinyLore/comments/9z0gtk/dreaming_city_dialogue/. Accessed 19 Jan 2021
37. Drachen, A., et al.: Guns and guardians: comparative cluster analysis and behavioral profiling in destiny. In: 2016 IEEE Conference on Computational Intelligence and Games (CIG), pp. 1–8. IEEE (2016)
38. Drescher, C., Wallner, G., Kriglstein, S., Sifa, R., Drachen, A., Pohl, M.: What moves players? Visual data exploration of twitter and gameplay data. In: Proceedings of the 2018 CHI Conference on Human Factors in Computing Systems, CHI 2018, New York, NY, USA, pp. 1–13. Association for Computing Machinery (2018). https://doi.org/10.1145/3173574.3174134. https://doi-org.oca.ucsc.edu/10.1145/3173574.3174134
39. Dubois, L.E., Weststar, J.: Games-as-a-service: conflicted identities on the new front-line of video game development. New Media Soc. (2021). https://doi.org/10.1177/1461444821995815
40. Emery, K.M., Reinhard, A.: Trading shovels for controllers: a brief exploration of the portrayal of archaeology in video games. Public Archaeol. **14**(2), 137–149 (2015)
41. Epic Games: Fortnite (2017)
42. Gach, E.: They brought back destiny's loot cave, but not the loot (2020). Kotaku article. https://kotaku.com/they-brought-back-the-loot-cave-but-not-the-loot-1845638914. Accessed 30 Apr 2021
43. Gilliam, R.: The history of the league of legends (2018). https://www.riftherald.com/2018/4/13/17231028/history-lol-league-of-legends-institute-of-war-summoners. Accessed 17 Jan 2021
44. Good, O.S.: Here's how to find destiny's 'loot cave' and plunder it for endless riches (2014). Polygon article. https://www.polygon.com/2014/9/21/6760715/destiny-loot-cave-engrams-farming. Accessed 30 Apr 2021
45. Gursoy, A.: "We're excited to chart this unknown territory together": storytelling strategies in patch notes documents. In: Proceedings of DiGRA 2020 (2020)
46. Isthar Collective: Ishtar collective's last wish cinematic transcript. Transcript of in-game cinematic displayed upon the first canonical completion of the "Last Wish" Raid, part of the Forsaken campaign (2019). https://www.ishtar-collective.net/transcripts/last-wish-cinematic?highlight=curse. Accessed 19 Jan 2021
47. Isthar Collective: Ishtar collective's visions of light transcript. Transcript of in-game mission during the original Forsaken campaign. The important quote is "Ghost: The Traveler's been alive for a year. Why has it waited so long to speak to us?" (2019). https://www.ishtar-collective.net/transcripts/visions-of-light. Accessed 19 Jan 2021
48. Jedruszczak, B.: Identity creation and world-building through discourse in video game narratives. Master's thesis, Syracuse University (2016)
49. Jenkins, H.: 'Never Trust a Snake': WWF Wrestling as Masculine Melodrama, chap. 3, pp. 33–67. Duke University Press (2005 (1997))
50. Jenkins, H.: Convergence Culture. New York University Press, New York (2006)

51. Joshi, R., et al.: A team based player versus player recommender systems framework for player improvement. In: Proceedings of the Australasian Computer Science Week Multiconference, ACSW 2019. Association for Computing Machinery, New York, NY, USA (2019). https://doi.org/10.1145/3290688.3290750

52. Karavatos, A.: "What is Your DPS, Hero?": Ludonarrative dissonance and player perception of story and mechanics in MMORPGs. Master's thesis, University of Skövde (2017)

53. Klastrup, L.: A poetics of virtual worlds. In: Digital Arts and Culture. RMIT University (2003)

54. Kleinman, E., Carstensdottir, E., Seif El-Nasr, M.: A model for analyzing diegesis in digital narrative games. In: Cardona-Rivera, R.E., Sullivan, A., Young, R.M. (eds.) ICIDS 2019. LNCS, vol. 11869, pp. 8–21. Springer, Cham (2019). https://doi.org/10.1007/978-3-030-33894-7_2

55. Kokkinakis, A.V., Cowling, P.I., Drachen, A., Wade, A.R.: Exploring the relationship between video game expertise and fluid intelligence. PLoS One 12(11), 1–15 (2017). https://doi.org/10.1371/journal.pone.0186621

56. Krzywinska, T.: Blood scythes, festivals, quests, and backstories: world creation and rhetorics of myth in world of warcraft. Games Cult. 1(4), 383–396 (2006)

57. Lee, Y., Armstrong, T., Spataro, J.: Destiny character-animation system and lessons learned (full text not available). In: ACM SIGGRAPH 2014 Courses, SIGGRAPH 2014, New York, NY, USA. Association for Computing Machinery (2014). https://doi.org/10.1145/2614028.2615458, https://doi-org.oca.ucsc.edu/10.1145/2614028.2615458

58. Linden Lab: Second Life (2003)

59. Lohmann, B.: Storytelling in massively multiplayer online games. Master's thesis, IT University of Copenhagen (2008)

60. Louchart, S., Aylett, R.: Solving the narrative paradox in VEs – lessons from RPGs. In: Rist, T., Aylett, R.S., Ballin, D., Rickel, J. (eds.) IVA 2003. LNCS (LNAI), vol. 2792, pp. 244–248. Springer, Heidelberg (2003). https://doi.org/10.1007/978-3-540-39396-2_41

61. Manning, C., Ashwell, S.K.: The gods play dice: procedural content in blaseball (2021). Medium Article https://medium.com/the-game-bland/the-gods-play-dice-procedural-content-in-blaseball-a9487dec0310. Accessed 16 June 2021

62. Marshall, C.: World of warcraft's latest story campaign has ignited the fanbase (2018). https://www.polygon.com/2018/8/1/17639398/world-of-warcraft-battle-for-azeroth-sylvanas-story-war-thorns-campaign

63. Mazer, S.: 'Real'Wrestling/'Real'Life, chap. 4, pp. 67–88. Duke University Press (2005)

64. McArthur, V., Teather, R.J., Jenson, J.: The avatar affordances framework: mapping affordances and design trends in character creation interfaces. In: Proceedings of the 2015 Annual Symposium on Computer-Human Interaction in Play, CHI PLAY 2015, New York, NY, USA, pp. 231–240. Association for Computing Machinery (2015). https://doi.org/10.1145/2793107.2793121, https://doi-org.oca.ucsc.edu/10.1145/2793107.2793121

65. Miller, W.: The role of spontaneous order and choice in video games: a case study of destiny. Available at SSRN 2953791 (2016)

66. Misztal, S., Carbonell, G., Schild, J.: Visual delegates - enhancing player perception by visually delegating player character sensation. In: Proceedings of the Annual Symposium on Computer-Human Interaction in Play, CHI PLAY 2020, New York, NY, USA, pp. 386–399. Association for Computing Machinery (2020). https://doi.org/10.1145/3410404.3414238, https://doi-org.oca.ucsc.edu/10.1145/3410404.3414238

67. Mojang: Minecraft (2011)

68. Nardi, B., Harris, J.: Strangers and friends: collaborative play in world of warcraft. In: Proceedings of the 2006 20th Anniversary Conference on Computer Supported Cooperative Work, pp. 149–158 (2006)

69. Nelva, G.: The story of how final fantasy XIV players marched together to the battle that ended the game (2019). https://twinfinite.net/2019/08/final-fantasy-xiv-anniversary-march/. Accessed 17 Jan 2021

70. Nitsche, M.: Mapping time in video games. In: DiGRA Conference (2007)

71. O'Connor, A.: Destiny 2's groundhog day curse is a neat touch that's easy to miss. Rock Paper Shotgun (2019). https://www.rockpapershotgun.com/2019/01/31/destiny-2-the-dreaming-city-curse-cycle/. Accessed 19 Jan 2021

72. Oglesby, B.: Daniel Bryan & the negotiation of kayfabe in professional wrestling. Master's thesis, University of South Florida (2017)

73. Oliva, C., Calleja, G.: Fake rules, real fiction: professional wrestling and videogames. DiGRA (2009)

74. OReilly, D.: Mountain (2014)

75. Pearce, C.: Communities of Play: Emergent Cultures in Multiplayer Games and Virtual Worlds. MIT Press, Cambridge (2011)

76. Perry, R., et al.: Online-only friends, real-life friends or strangers? Differential associations with passion and social capital in video game play. Comput. Hum. Behav. **79**, 202–210 (2018)

77. Pirker, J., Rattinger, A., Drachen, A., Sifa, R.: Analyzing player networks in destiny. Entertain. Comput. **25**, 71–83 (2018)

78. Ravari, Y.N., Spronck, P., Sifa, R., Drachen, A.: Predicting victory in a hybrid online competitive game: the case of destiny. In: Proceedings of the AAAI Conference on Artificial Intelligence and Interactive Digital Entertainment, vol. 13 (2017)

79. Reinhard, A.: Archaeogaming: An Introduction to Archaeology in and of Video Games. Berghahn Books, New York (2018)

80. Rimington, E., Blount, T.: Lore v. representation: narrative communication of power with regard to gender in league of legends. In: CEUR Workshop Proceedings, vol. 1628, pp. 1–5 (2016)

81. Riot Games: League of Legends (2009)

82. Riot Games: League of legends universe website (2021). https://universe.leagueoflegends.com/en_US/. Accessed 17 Jan 2021

83. Rousseau, S.: 'world of warcraft' recreates one of its biggest events, including broken servers (2020). https://www.vice.com/en/article/ep4wqj/world-of-warcraft-recreates-one-of-its-biggest-events-including-broken-servers. Accessed 17 Jan 2021

84. Ryan, J.: Curating simulated storyworlds. Ph.D. thesis, UC Santa Cruz (2018)

85. Ryan, M.L.: Transmedia storytelling: industry buzzword or new narrative experience? Storyworlds: J. Narrat. Stud. **7**(2), 1–19 (2015)

86. Schaekermann, M., et al.: Curiously motivated: profiling curiosity with self-reports and behaviour metrics in the game "destiny". In: Proceedings of the Annual Symposium on Computer-Human Interaction in Play. CHI PLAY 2017, pp. 143–156. Association for Computing Machinery, New York (2017).https://doi.org/10.1145/3116595.3116603, https://doi-org.oca.ucsc.edu/10.1145/3116595.3116603

87. Schiller, M.H., et al.: Inside the group: investigating social structures in player groups and their influence on activity. IEEE Trans. Games 11(4), 416–425 (2018)

88. Schreier, J.: Top video game companies won't stop talking about 'games as a service' (2017). https://kotaku.com/top-video-game-companies-wont-stop-talking-about-games-1795663927. Accessed 17 Jan 2021

89. Schwind, V., Wolf, K., Henze, N., Korn, O.: Determining the characteristics of preferred virtual faces using an avatar generator. In: Proceedings of the 2015 Annual Symposium on Computer-Human Interaction in Play. CHI PLAY 2015, pp. 221–230. Association for Computing Machinery, New York (2015). https://doi.org/10.1145/2793107.2793116, https://doi-org.oca.ucsc.edu/10.1145/2793107.2793116

90. Sciarretta, E.: The use of social media as part of a transmedia storytelling strategy in WWE's professional wrestling. In: Meiselwitz, G. (ed.) HCII 2019. LNCS, vol. 11578, pp. 556–570. Springer, Cham (2019). https://doi.org/10.1007/978-3-030-21902-4_39

91. Sehmby, D.S.: Professional wrestling, whooo!: a cultural con, an athletic dramatic narrative, and a haven for rebel heroes. Master's thesis, University of Alberta, Edmonton (2000)

92. Sifa, R., Drachen, A., Bauckhage, C.: Profiling in games: understanding behavior from telemetry. In: Social Interactions in Virtual Worlds: An Interdisciplinary Perspective (2018)

93. Sifa, R., et al.: Controlling the crucible: a novel PvP recommender systems framework for destiny. In: Proceedings of the Australasian Computer Science Week Multiconference, pp. 1–10. ACM (2018)

94. Sown, H.H., Jeon, S.K.: Storytelling characteristics of the MOBA with a comparison to the MMORPG: focused on< league of legends>. Asia Digit. Art Des. 2013(12), 430–433 (2013)

95. Square Enix: Final Fantasy XIV (2013)

96. Stafford, T., Devlin, S., Sifa, R., Drachen, A.: Exploration and skill acquisition in a major online game. In: The 39th Annual Meeting of the Cognitive Science Society (CogSci), York (2017)

97. Statt, N.: Fortnite is now one of the biggest games ever with 350 million players. The Verge (2020). https://www.theverge.com/2020/5/6/21249497/fortnite-350-million-registered-players-hours-played-april. Accessed 21 Jan 2021

98. Steamcharts: Steamcharts' top games by current players (2021). https://steamcharts.com/top. Accessed 17 Jan 2021

99. Tamassia, M., Raffe, W., Sifa, R., Drachen, A., Zambetta, F., Hitchens, M.: Predicting player churn in destiny: a hidden Markov models approach to predicting player departure in a major online game. In: 2016 IEEE Conference on Computational Intelligence and Games (CIG), pp. 1–8. IEEE (2016)

100. Tassi, P.: Destiny 2's 'you had to be there' philosophy is turning off players. Forbes article (2020). https://www.forbes.com/sites/paultassi/2020/01/22/destiny-2s-you-had-to-be-there-philosophy-is-turning-off-players/?sh=6e886c641b3a. Accessed 25 June 2021

101. Tatarchuk, N.: Character creation pipeline and rendering in destiny (full text not available). In: ACM SIGGRAPH 2014 Courses. SIGGRAPH 2014. Association for Computing Machinery, New York (2014). https://doi.org/10.1145/2614028. 2615457, https://doi-org.oca.ucsc.edu/10.1145/2614028.2615457

102. The Game Band: Blaseball (2020). https://www.blaseball.com/

103. Toups, Z.O., Hammer, J., Hamilton, W.A., Jarrah, A., Graves, W., Garretson, O.: A framework for cooperative communication game mechanics from grounded theory. In: Proceedings of the First ACM SIGCHI Annual Symposium on Computer-Human Interaction in Play. CHI PLAY 2014, pp. 257–266. Association for Computing Machinery, New York (2014). https://doi.org/10.1145/2658537.2658681, https://doi-org.oca.ucsc.edu/10.1145/2658537.2658681

104. Valle, C.G.D.: 'destiny 2' Twitter, Facebook taken over by villain caiatl; zavala storyline cutscene leaked [video] (2021). Techtimes article https://www.techtimes. com/articles/257864/20210309/destiny-2-twitter-facebook-taken-over-villain-caiatl-zavala-storyline.htm. Article has images of tweets in question with corresponding avatar icon and name (the acconut has since been rebranded back to "Destiny 2" https://twitter.com/DestinyTheGame. Also see Reddit thread from the time https://www.reddit.com/r/DestinyTheGame/comments/m0kggb/destinythegames_twitter_profile_has_changed_his/ and community conversation about it at https://twitter.com/MyNameIsByf/status/1369991874539311104

105. McMahon, V., World Wrestling Entertainment, Inc.: World wrestling entertainment, Inc (WWE) (1980 (As Titan Sports), 1998 (As WWF), 1999 (as WWE)). https://www.wwe.com/

106. Wallner, G., Kriglstein, S.: Introducing planet: a tool for visualizing player communities. In: Proceedings of the 13th International Conference on the Foundations of Digital Games. FDG 2018, Association for Computing Machinery, New York (2018). https://doi.org/10.1145/3235765.3235808, https://doi-org.oca.ucsc.edu/10.1145/3235765.3235808

107. Wallner, G., Kriglstein, S., Drachen, A.: Tweeting your destiny: profiling users in the twitter landscape around an online game. In: 2019 IEEE Conference on Games (CoG), pp. 1–8. IEEE (2019)

108. Wallner, G., et al.: Beyond the individual: understanding social structures of an online player matchmaking website. Entertain. Comput. **30**, 100284 (2019)

109. Webster, A.: With the apocalyptic black hole event, Fortnite's storytelling has grown increasingly ambitious (2019). https://www.theverge.com/2019/10/14/20913541/fortnite-game-shutdown-black-hole-event-storytelling. Accessed 17 Jan 2021

110. Whalen, Z.: Game/genre: a critique of generic formulas in video games in the context of "the real". Works Days **22**(43/44), 289–303 (2004)

111. Williams, M.: Rise of the lifestyle game: Gaming as your second job (2014). https://www.usgamer.net/articles/rise-of-the-lifestyle-game-gaming-as-your-second-job. Accessed 17 Jan 2021

112. Wizards of the Coast: Magic: The Gathering (1993)

113. Zagal, J.P., Mateas, M.: Time in video games: a survey and analysis. Simul. Gaming **41**(6), 844–868 (2010)

114. Ziebart, A.: WoW archivist: The gates of Ahn'Qiraj (2011). https://www. engadget.com/2011-04-19-wow-archivist-the-gates-of-ahnqiraj.html. Accessed 17 Jan 2021

# Blabbeur - An Accessible Text Generation Authoring System for Unity

Jonathan Lessard[1]([✉])[iD] and Quinn Kybartas[1,2][iD]

[1] Concordia University, Montréal, Québec, Canada
jonathan.lessard@concordia.ca
[2] McGill University, Montréal, Québec, Canada

**Abstract.** We present Blabbeur, a generative, context-aware, text generation system for Unity. It provides a simple, accessible context-free grammar inspired syntax allowing conditional generation and the surfacing of variables. Content requests are easily invoked in Unity scripts with relevant variables passed either as property dictionaries or through class interfaces. A persistent testing environment allows authors to quickly test their grammars against different contexts.

**Keywords:** Text generation · Context-free grammars · Authoring · Unity

## 1 Another Text Generation System?

In this demo paper, we present *Blabbeur*, a generative, context-aware, text generation system for the Unity game engine[1]. Blabbeur was designed for a multi-member game development team making an emergent narrative game in Unity. For the game, it is necessary to generate text communicating greatly varying world states and events to players, the scale of which prevents hand-authoring. As a result, we sought to use a text generation tool, which would meet the following requirements:

1. **Easy to author** – Team members without programming background should be able to quickly learn to create content with it.
2. **Context-aware** – Authors should be able to set conditions qualifying or disqualifying text fragments. They should also be able to surface specific values in the text.
3. **Generative** – The tool should easily allow for variations in the generated text.
4. **Easy to troubleshoot** – Authors should be able to quickly test context scenarios without having to wait for them to be naturally occurring in the system.

---

[1] Blabbeur is available here: https://bitbucket.org/lablablab/blabbeur/.

© Springer Nature Switzerland AG 2021
A. Mitchell and M. Vosmeer (Eds.): ICIDS 2021, LNCS 13138, pp. 255–259, 2021.
https://doi.org/10.1007/978-3-030-92300-6_23

5. **Compatible** – It should be easy to communicate system states to the tool and request text generations.
6. **Supports collaboration** – Multiple authors should be able to contribute simultaneously.

Requirements 1, 2 and 3 are commonly found in research focused text generation systems, namely Expressionist [6], Tracery [3], and STEP [4]. We considered each system as a possibility for our requirements, but each system typically fell short of one or more of requirements. Out of the three, Expressionist was the initial clear choice, being heavily inspired by the existing functionality of Tracery, but also provided the functionality of requirement 2, whereas Tracery does not provide any built in conditional checks, or value surfacing.

The major limitation which was found with Expressionist, is that it is implemented in Python, and would require a code port to Unity's native coding language of C#. This proved non-trivial namely due to Expressionist's use of the EVAL() function to evaluate conditions and effects. EVAL essentially allows the execution of an arbitrary string as though it was a line of Python code, but this function is not available in C# and is non-trivial to implement. STEP, being already implemented in Unity, is an obvious alternative, but the PROLOG-like syntax was found to be overly hard for the non-technical authors to learn. While re-implementing may seem a trivial issue, it nonetheless highlights the different challenges required in the actual use of text generation systems in real world projects. Elements such as cost, differently skilled team members and integration limit the acceptance of research systems in a broader context, e.g. while Tracery is considered a successful system, it only became common use with the development of Twitter [2] and Twine [1] integrations. We therefore, in addition to the contribution of the tool itself, present the specifics of the Blabbeur design, in hope that it can help other researchers or practitioners understand the more practical side of tool development.

## 2   Blabbeur

In this section we present the syntax, system communication and debugging features of Blabbeur. As stated before, the system is not particularly novel for text generation, but rather the focus is on implementation, and the needs of a game development team.

**Syntax.** A Blabbeur grammar is written as a basic text file. This has many advantages, such as not being tied to any particular editor, and being particularly easy to track on source control systems. Syntax was designed to be legible and intuitive, and contains the following components:

*Symbols* – Grammar symbols are defined as labels followed by colons, the first one being the point of entry (in Fig. 1, "Wiki_Accident"). Non-terminal symbols that need to be resolved are expressed within brackets. In Fig. 1, the generation will first resolve [description] and then [damage]. Multiple outputs of a symbol can be

```
// Wiki output for accidents
// Requires: Damage (int), TypeOfAccident (string), victim (human)

Wiki_Accident: [description] [damage];

damage: and I lost <Damage> health points, leaving me with <victim.healthpoints>.;

description:    {TypeOfAccident == ""} [generic_accident];
                {TypeOfAccident == "agriculture"} [agriculture];
                {TypeOfAccident == "fishing"} [fishing];
                {TypeOfAccident == "hunting"} [hunting];

generic_accident:   I had a freak accident;
                    I messed up big time;
                    I was minding my business, when suddenly [misfortune];

agriculture:    I hurt my [bodypart] with a [farmingtool];
                I suffered heatstroke from working all day under the sun;
                I grabbed what I thought was my [farmingtool], but it was a snake. It bit me;
                I sprained my [bodypart] pulling out weeds;
```

**Fig. 1.** Excerpt from a Blabbeur grammar file used to generate accident descriptions.

defined by separating them with semicolons. In this case, the [generic_accident] symbol can randomly resolve either as "I had a freak accident", "I messed up big time", or "I was minding...". Symbols can be nested ad infinitum.

*Conditional Expressions* – Authors can make a symbol conditional by preceding it with an expression in curly braces. Only the symbols whose conditions are met will be considered as possible outputs at the moment of generation. In Fig. 1, for example, the author redirects the resolution of [description] by checking what kind of accident they are dealing with. If the "TypeOfAccident" variable is set to "agriculture", only the second symbol will be considered valid, thus leading to the resolution of [agriculture]. Currently, the following operators are supported: !=, ==, <, >, &&, ||

*Variables* – Variables that have been passed along the generation request can be used within conditional expressions or surfaced directly within the text. This is done by placing a condition within angle brackets. In Fig. 1, <Damage> and <victim.healthpoints> will be replaced with the variables' values. Values can be numerical, strings, enumerators, or conditionals.

*Comments* – Any line preceded with "//" are disregarded as comments.

**System Communication** – The Blabbeur system is implemented as a singleton and is accessible at any point of the project's code. Blabbeur communication is done through requests, passing the name of the top-level symbol of the desired grammar, as well as a custom Blabbeur Object containing an arbitrary set of variables describing the state of the request. The generated text is returned as a string.

*Blabbeur Object* – A Blabbeur object is a <string,value> dictionary which matches a variable string from the grammar to its appropriate value. It is further possible to "nest" blabbeur objects, e.g. the "victim" shown in Fig. 2, is assigned to the actor object, which then contains its own dictionary, e.g. name, age, etc.

```
Blabbeur.Objects.PropertyDictionary blabvars = new Blabbeur.Objects.PropertyDictionary("blabvars");
blabvars.Add("Damage", Damage);
blabvars.Add("TypeOfAccident", TypeOf);
blabvars.Add("victim", actor);
return Blabbeur.TextGen.Request("Wiki_Accident", blabvars);
```

**Fig. 2.** A Blabbeur content request in C#

*Blabbeur Interface* – Blabbeur objects can also be implemented through a C# interface, where a class can be treated as a blabbeur object by implementing the required functions of the interface. In Fig. 2, the actor is a "Human" class which implements the Blabbeur interface and is therefore treated as a nested Blabbeur object (Fig. 3).

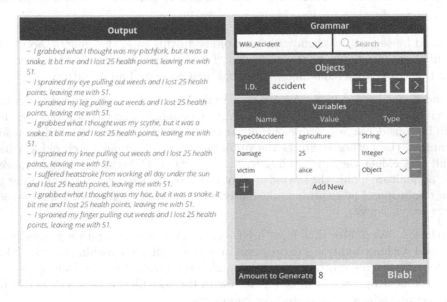

**Fig. 3.** The Blabbeur test environment

**Testing Environment** – As underlined in Lessard et al. [5] productivity with generative text tools depends on the availability of a robust testing environment. We have designed for Blabbeur a Unity interface allowing authors to test their grammars against different states. Testing involves selecting a grammar and creating or modifying custom Blabbeur objects to create a number of possible game scenarios.

## 3  Conclusion

We have been using this system for months now and it has proven easy to use and efficient. With less than an hour of training, authors can immediately begin producing new content. We already have more than 40 grammars in our system and they are a key component in communicating with players. As we stress test Blabbeur, we are also noting requests and comments from authors to increase usability, focusing on elements such as error feedback, and accessing another grammar from within a grammar.

# References

1. Balousek, M.R.F.: Twincery. https://github.com/mrfb/twinecery. Accessed 07 June 2021
2. Buckenham, G.: Cheap bots done quick. Accessed 07 June 2021
3. Compton, K., Kybartas, B., Mateas, M.: Tracery: an author-focused generative text tool. In: Schoenau-Fog, H., Bruni, L.E., Louchart, S., Baceviciute, S. (eds.) ICIDS 2015. LNCS, vol. 9445, pp. 154–161. Springer, Cham (2015). https://doi.org/10.1007/978-3-319-27036-4_14
4. Horswill, I.: Generative text using classical nondeterminism. In: Joint Proceedings of the AIIDE 2020 Workshops, Worcester, MA (2020)
5. Lessard, J., Brunelle-Leclerc, E., Gottschalk, T., Jetté-Léger, M.A., Prouveur, O., Tan, C.: Striving for author-friendly procedural dialogue generation. In: Proceedings of the International Conference on the Foundations of Digital Games - FDG '17. ACM Press (2017). https://doi.org/10.1145/3102071.3116219
6. Ryan, J., Seither, E., Mateas, M., Wardrip-Fruin, N.: Expressionist: an authoring tool for in-game text generation. In: Nack, F., Gordon, A.S. (eds.) ICIDS 2016. LNCS, vol. 10045, pp. 221–233. Springer, Cham (2016). https://doi.org/10.1007/978-3-319-48279-8_20

# Enhancing Interactivity in Propp-Based Narrative Generation

Luis Mienhardt and Marco Volpe[(✉)]

Institute of Cognitive Science, University of Osnabrück, Osnabrück, Germany
{lmienhardt,mvolpe}@uos.de

**Abstract.** In this paper, we recall the main limitations of interactive storytelling (IS) systems based on Propp's *Morphology of the Folktale*, in particular with respect to the degree of interactivity that they offer, and propose an adapted morphology. Namely, we allow the original Propp functions to have a reversed outcome, we study how to combine sub-plots, and we introduce the use of flashbacks. We claim that such modifications enhance the interactivity of Propp-based IS systems.

## 1 Introduction

Since the emergence of computational storytelling, Vladimir Propp's *Morphology of the Folktale* [14] has received great consideration (see, e.g., [4,5,9]) because of its quite formal nature. In particular, in the context of interactive storytelling (IS), the early two thousands saw a number of Propp-based systems [3,11,13,16]. After that, however, a phase of decline occurred; in fact a recent overview paper [8] does not mention any later Propp-based IS system. [18] focuses on the issues that Propp-based systems suffer from and claims that Propp's morphology is inherently unable to provide adequate interactivity. After presenting some background notions (Sect. 2), we recall the main criticisms of [18] and others (Sect. 3) and suggest some adaptations to Propp's morphology aiming at enhancing interactivity of Propp-based IS systems (Sect. 4).

## 2 Propp's Morphology and Interactivity

Propp's morphology formalizes the plot structure of folktales by dividing them into universal components, called *functions* [14], which are independent of the how and by whom of a particular story. Building upon this notion, a *move* is the smallest sequence of functions that can be considered a tale. Propp defines a clear ordering of all the functions in a move. A move starts with its introductory functions, followed by a villainy or a lack function, then a series of functions representing a struggle or test for the hero, resulting in the liquidation of misfortune that resolves the villainy or lack, and finally some kind of reward function.

In this paper, we will refer to *interactivity (with a story)* as a meaningful intervention of a player within the story representation as a work of art [2]. Interactivity can be considered at two different levels: (*i*) at the function-level, the

© Springer Nature Switzerland AG 2021
A. Mitchell and M. Vosmeer (Eds.): ICIDS 2021, LNCS 13138, pp. 260–265, 2021.
https://doi.org/10.1007/978-3-030-92300-6_24

player's input influences the selection of a specific function; (ii) at the plot-level, it affects the ordering of the function sequence. More specifically, a condition for interactivity is that the player's decisions are meaningfully connected to their outcome [15]. We define a *meaningful decision* as an affordance [10] that makes it obvious to the player that the action he takes is a significant intervention on the function-level and/or on the plot-level. This implies that the player can sensibly reason about the decision's consequences both before and after he makes it.

## 3   Issues in Propp-Based Interactive Storytelling

Although only [18] analyzes in detail the difficulties of its IS system with respect to interactivity, other Propp-based approaches [3,11,13,16] seem to suffer from similar problems. In this section we briefly recall some of such issues, while in the next one we propose changes to the morphology aiming at addressing them.

**Missing Influence of Player Decisions.** When applied to IS, Propp's functions seem to only provide decisions that lack a substantial influence over the plot. What prevents them from being meaningful decisions is their fixed outcome: e.g., no matter how the player decides to act, the hero has to somehow defeat the villain, if a subsequent function that is necessarily part of the plot needs the villain to be defeated.

**Lack of Interactivity at the Plot-Level.** According to [18], interactivity on the function-level can be achieved by choosing or skipping certain functions, but plot-level interactivity is not possible because Propp's morphology does neither allow to rearrange the order of functions nor to use a given function multiple times. Clearly this severely limits the player's influence and reduces interactivity.

**Dead-Ends.** In IS the player can, by means of interaction with the system, influence the story in a way that prevents it from evolving towards any interesting or desirable ending. We call such situations dead-ends (see, e.g., [1]). Although not specific of Propp-based systems, dead-ends can also harm interactivity, since the player might not be able to identify which decisions led to them.

## 4   An Adapted Morphology

### 4.1   Negative Reaction Functions

Many of Propp's functions come in an action/reaction pair, such as the victory following a struggle. In Propp's morphology, given one action, only one reaction function is possible, e.g., the hero always wins a fight. A *negative function* is a Propp's function with its outcome reversed. In the running example of Table 1, showing an interaction between a player and an ideal IS system based on our adapted morphology, we introduce, e.g., a defeat function where the hero (Siegfried) loses the fight against the dragon. Propp himself makes sporadic use of negative functions in examples, and [7] adopts only a few negative functions such that the story ends when they occur. We propose to use the negative functions in a systematic way in order to augment the influence of player's decisions. Our proposed set of negative reaction functions appears in Table 2.

**Table 1.** Example of an interaction between a player (P) and an ideal IS system (N).

| Primary move | | | | |
|---|---|---|---|---|
| | | | N: | Siegfried lives in peace in his village. His father tells him not to talk to dragons |
| | | | P: | Siegfried obeys his father |
| | | | N: | A dragon kidnaps Kriemhilde |
| | | | P: | Siegfried decides to rescue Kriemhilde |
| | | | N: | So Siegfried goes on the journey |
| | Replacement move | | N: | But he doesn't know where to look for her |
| | | | P: | He decides to search for information on the dragon's lair |
| | | | N: | A figure with a dragon's lair's map riddles him: "What walks on four legs ...?" |
| | | | P: | "A daydreamer???" |
| | | | N: | Siegfried guesses wrong. The mysterious figure leaves with the map |
| | | | P: | Siegfried fights the mysterious figure |
| | | | N: | Siegfried wins the fight. He takes the map. He knows the location of the lair |
| | | | P: | Siegfried travels to the dragon's lair. He challenges the dragon in a fight |
| | | | N: | He loses and learns that he needs a magical sword. He can't rescue Kriemhild |
| | Complication move | | N: | Siegfried gets imprisoned because he lost the fight |
| | | | P: | He decides to fight the dragon again |
| | | | N: | Second fight with the dragon. Flashback to some days before |
| | | Flashb. | N: | Sigfried is in his village. He learns of Hagen having a sword |
| | | | P: | Sigfried decides to steal the sword from Hagen |
| | | | N: | Siegfried manages to steal it while Hagen is hunting. He has now a sword |
| | | | N: | Return to the fight. Siegfried defeats the dragon with the sword. He is free |
| | | | N: | He can rescue Kriemhild |
| | | | P: | He returns to his village |
| | | | N: | A big feast is hold for the victorious Siegfried |

**Table 2.** Negative reaction functions.

| Initiating functions | Original reaction | Negative reaction |
|---|---|---|
| Interdiction | Violation of interdiction | Compliance with interdiction |
| Reconnaissance | Information delivery | No information delivery |
| Trickery | Complicity of the victim | Resisting the trickery |
| Donor's test | Hero's reaction | Wrong hero reaction |
| Test + reaction | Transfer of magical agent | Magical agent held back |
| Struggle | Victory | Defeat |
| Pursuit | Rescue of the hero | Capture of the hero |
| Difficult task | Solution | Task failure |
| Disguise | Recognition of the hero | Hero is not recognized |
| False hero | Exposure of the false hero | Failed exposure |
| Villainy, ... | Liquidation of misfortune | Failed liquidation |

## 4.2  Combination of Moves

In [14], Propp suggests that moves can be combined; however he does not integrate a method for that in his morphology. We plan to provide a comprehensive formalization of move combinations. The basic idea consists in allowing one move to replace, and thereby expand, one or more functions occurring in another move. This works especially well for action/reaction pairs, where we can create a new move with the desired outcome of the reaction function as a lack function. The liquidation of this lack, if successful, equals a positive outcome of the reaction function and, if not successful, equals the negative outcome. In Table 1, a *replacement move* for a map search substitutes the pair donor's test/hero reaction. By emphasizing an aspect of the story, a replacement makes it obvious to the player that his success or failure will have consequences on the plot development. It also allows the player to have different ways to success, as he is not restricted to pass the donor's test to receive the map, but can attack the donor afterwards.

As a special case, replacing the liquidation of misfortune function can have a slightly different form, to which give the name of *complication move*. It is based on the intensification method mentioned in [12] and [10]. To create such an intensification, we reincorporate [17] the events of a previous move into the next one. I.e., instead of resolving the first move, we replace the liquidation function with a second move that uses a further villainy and intensifies the hero's struggle.

We then release the tension in a climax point when both villainies are resolved. In our example, Siegfried loses the fight with the dragon. This defeat is built upon in the next move and consequently he is imprisoned by the dragon. A causal relation between the two moves is created and transforms the decision to fight the dragon into a meaningful decision.

### 4.3 Flashbacks

In order to avoid imminent dead-ends, we propose to use flashbacks. As [6] points out, a flashback in IS has to be interactive. In our view, this means that the player, when taken back in time, can either find a solution to the dead-end or not. In Table 1, Siegfried faces a dragon, but he misses a magical sword to defeat him. We take Siegfried back to his village before he sets out for the dragon and give him a chance to get a sword. Flashbacks allow us to deal with dead-ends only when they occur and to not restrict player decisions beforehand.

## 5   Conclusion

In this paper we recalled the criticism of [18] and others with respect to the use of Propp's morphology in the context of IS systems. The problems that we consider harmful to interactivity are the lack of influential decisions and the rigidity of the morphology when it comes to plot-level changes. For both problems we provide ideas on how they can be resolved. In particular, we extend the morphology by negative versions of the original functions in order to allow different reactions to player decisions and we give such decisions plot-level relevance by embedding additional moves into the existing story line. We also suggest to use the narrative device of flashbacks to overcome dead-ends that might occur due to player interactions. The approach presented in this paper is still at a preliminary stage. We are currently working on its comprehensive formalization, which we believe could be used as a foundation for future IS system implementations.

## References

1. Barros, L.M., Musse, S.R.: Towards consistency in interactive storytelling: tension arcs and dead-ends. Comput. Entertain. 6(3), 1–17 (2008)
2. Cameron, A.: Dissimulation: Illusions of interactivity. Millenium Film J. 28 (1995). http://mfj-online.org/journalPages/MFJ28/Dissimulations.html
3. Fairclough, C.: Story games and the OPIATE system: using case-based planning for structuring plots with an expert story director agent and enacting them in a socially simulated game world. Ph.D. thesis, University of Dublin, Trinity College (2004)
4. Gervás, P.: Propp's morphology of the folk tale as a grammar for generation. In: Finlayson, M.A., Fisseni, B., Löwe, B., Meister, J.C. (eds.) 2013 Workshop on Computational Models of Narrative, CMN 2013, August 4–6, 2013, Hamburg, Germany, OASICS, vol. 32, pp. 106–122. Schloss Dagstuhl - Leibniz-Zentrum für Informatik (2013)

5. Gervás, P.: Computational drafting of plot structures for Russian folk tales. Cogn. Comput. **8**(2), 187–203 (2016). https://doi.org/10.1007/s12559-015-9338-8
6. Guy, O., Champagnat, R.: Flashback in interactive storytelling. In: Nijholt, A., Romão, T., Reidsma, D. (eds.) ACE 2012. LNCS, vol. 7624, pp. 246–261. Springer, Heidelberg (2012). https://doi.org/10.1007/978-3-642-34292-9_17
7. Hartmann, K., Hartmann, S., Feustel, M.: Motif definition and classification to structure non-linear plots and to control the narrative flow in interactive dramas. In: Subsol, G. (ed.) ICVS 2005. LNCS, vol. 3805, pp. 158–167. Springer, Heidelberg (2005). https://doi.org/10.1007/11590361_18
8. Kybartas, B.A., Bidarra, R.: A survey on story generation techniques for authoring computational narratives. IEEE Trans. Comput. Intell. AI Games **9**, 239–253 (2017)
9. Lakoff, G.P.: Structural complexity in fairy tales. Study Man **1**, 128–150 (1972)
10. Mateas, A.S.M.: The game design reader: a rules of play anthology. In: Interaction and Narrative, pp. 642–669. MIT Press (2006)
11. Machado, I., Prada, R., Paiva, A.: Bringing drama into a virtual stage. In: CVE '00 (2000)
12. Murray, J.: Hamlet on the Holodeck: The Future of Narrative in Cyberspace. MIT Press, Cambridge (1997)
13. Peinado, F., Gervás, P., et al.: Transferring game mastering laws to interactive digital storytelling. In: Göbel, S. (ed.) TIDSE 2004. LNCS, vol. 3105, pp. 48–54. Springer, Heidelberg (2004). https://doi.org/10.1007/978-3-540-27797-2_7
14. Propp, V.: Morphology of the Folktale. University of Texas Press, Austin (1968)
15. Salen, K., Zimmerman, E.: Rules of Play: Game Design Fundamentals. MIT Press, Cambridge (2003)
16. Spierling, U., Grasbon, D., Braun, N., Iurgel, I.: Setting the scene: playing digital director in interactive storytelling and creation. Comput. Graph. **26**, 31–44 (2002)
17. Tomaszewski, Z.: On the use of reincorporation in interactive drama. In: Intelligent Narrative Technologies (2011)
18. Tomaszewski, Z., Binsted, K.: The limitations of a Propp-based approach to interactive drama. In: AAAI Fall Symposium: Intelligent Narrative Technologies (2007)

# The Applicability of Greimassian Semiotics to Meaningful Procedural Quest Generation

Luis F. T. Meza[1]([✉]) [iD] and David Thue[2,3] [iD]

[1] School of Humanities, University of Iceland, Reykjavík, Iceland
lft1@hi.is
[2] School of Information Technology, Carleton University, Ottawa, ON, Canada
david.thue@carleton.ca
[3] Department of Computer Science, Reykjavik University, Reykjavik, Iceland

**Abstract.** We present the semiotics of Algirdas J. Greimas as an analytical method that may be useful to the procedural generation of quest narratives in interactive games. We focus on summarizing the tools introduced by Greimas to describe a narrative's meaning, and we explain them using a sample analysis of Monterroso's microstory "The Dinosaur". Finally, we sketch our vision of how these tools can be used in the context of a generative system that could create stories where a deeper meaning is identifiable by players.

**Keywords:** Semiotics · Procedural quest generation · Story generation

## 1 Introduction

Procedural Content Generation (PCG) has long since been used as a feature of digital games, with varying degrees of success. In her historical analysis of PCG, Smith observed that by delegating the creation of game content to computer systems, "any ability for providing meaning in the generated characters or consideration for player experience was lost" [1]. She added that it is "harder to create *meaningful* content or to understand the qualities of generated content in terms of player experience" [1] and highlighted the detrimental effects that using randomness in the generation of encounters, monsters, and items can have on the players' experience of a game.

We believe that Smith's call for meaning refers to the perceived absence of a *theme* in procedurally generated content. This idea of theme corresponds to what Howard called "meaningful action" [2], or an allegorical set of correspondences where game players find statements about the real world by interacting with a fictional world. Thus, we raise the question: How can a procedural quest generator provide such a meaning to its generated stories? To answer it, we turn to the semiotics proposed by Algirdas J. Greimas [3] as a tool that an algorithm might use to generate quests that mimic Howard's meaningful action.

We propose that Greimas's method of analysis offers a compelling precursor for an envisioned quest generation algorithm that prioritizes meaning. We believe this for the following reasons. First, it formally describes the concept of theme as a "relation

A. Mitchell and M. Vosmeer (Eds.): ICIDS 2021, LNCS 13138, pp. 266–279, 2021.
https://doi.org/10.1007/978-3-030-92300-6_25

of various units of the signified distributed throughout the length of the story" [4] that follows concrete, procedural rules. Second, Greimas's equation has been applied as a method to describe the theme of a complete story and is able to describe and predict thematically relevant events in a story [5]. Third, it presents a model of narrative grammar that focuses on theme [6] as well as a way to establish how actions performed by story actants [7] are related to the story's theme.

## 2 Related Work

Among the most influential works to discuss the idea of "meaning" within interactive narratives are those of Aarseth [8] and Bogost [9]. Aarseth created a conceptual toolset to understand texts using a function-oriented perspective, and studied them as a machine for the production and consumption of signs. Aarseth's work observes elements of texts and the functions that they serve in the process of communication. The study created a compelling basis for an ontology of the text, but it does not discuss the processes of meaning production at an authorial level. In contrast, Bogost's unit analysis seeks to assist critics in finding the "discrete meaning-making in texts of all kinds."

Bogost's approach is aimed at the critical study of interactive texts. He makes the claim that critics and creators work with similar tools. In his view, the similarity of these tools teaches us to read both technology-based works and non-technology-based works "from the single perspective of their shared procedurality" [9]. This view supports our position that a detailed analysis of meaning is a precursor of the procedural generation of meaning.

Eladhari applied the semiotics of Algirdas Greimas and others to the study of meaning production in videogames [10]. Eladhari focused her application of Greimas as a "conceptualization that breaks down the parts of a story into force fields that make it possible for the narrative to come into existence" [10]. These "force fields" refer to the devices of meaning production and the contextualization of actions and events. Eladhari further wrote that the analysis of the dynamic elements (actions) and static (characters and settings) helps us observe the semantic syntax which gives a game its meaning. The view is based on Budaniekiewicz's syntactic study of action [11], which presupposes the *modal*, i.e., motivating factors such as wants, goals and plans, as an antecedent state of the actualization of actions.

In what is perhaps a more relevant study for interactive computing Yu et al. [12] use Greimas's actantial model as a tool in computer-based narrative by studying character interactions to classify them ontologically by their relationship to the story's subject. They conclude that continued tests would further evidence the similarity between human and system identifications of characters as subjects, helpers, or opponents. Nonetheless, we find that these studies, originally conceived as tools of analysis, could contribute to interactive narrative design.

Szilas used elements of structuralism, including Greimas's canonical narrative schemata in his study of the narrative act. He described this act as "a type of meta-action in which the embedded action is one of the core actions of the story" and stated that such acts "constitute the main sequence (or plot) in the story" [13]. His system, IDtension [14, 15], works by organizing concrete actions through generated meta-actions. Szila's contribution to the formalization of what Chatman refers to as the "content/form" of stories is invaluable. However, we argue that a formal process through which Szilas's narrative acts can be filtered to reflect what Chatman calls "the codes of the author's society" which determine the "content/substance" of the story [16].

The focus on the "content/form" that Szilas proposed has been shown to have limitations. For example, Riedl and Young's IPOCL focuses on two attributes of narratives that they considered to be relatively universal: "the logical causal progression of plot and character believability" [17]. The project found that the generator was unable to communicate comedy and tragedy given the inability to produce narrative structures where a character failed to achieve one of its goals.

To address this issue, Shirvani and Ware drew on the Ortony, Clore and Collins model of emotions to constrain possible actions and add variety to possible plots [18] and "ensure that agents only act in ways that they expect to contribute to achieving their goals" [19]. The model works by explaining such actions, enabling a system-user communication of character personality traits, by which they judge the characters to be more relatable [19]. Similarly, the CONAN engine "seeks to produce novel and coherent quests in a videogame context by having NPCs make plans to solve their goals in accordance with their preferences" [20]. CONAN presents each NPC as a planning problem, which computes a quest by imposing a point cost to the possible actions characters can take.

We find that the above-mentioned models do not address the lack of an overarching theme in stories: understandable characters with consistent emotions and motivations do not necessarily make stories with a central thematic message. These are made instead via "correspondence" or allegory, which Howard presents as central for the design of meaningful action [2], and which we believe Greimas has formalized, based on the work of Propp.

The goal of having a theme in computer-authored narrative has led many authors to adopt narratological structures such as the ones described by Propp [21] and Campbell [22] or a combination of both. One such system used Case Based Reasoning to generate stories by following a principle of "story fragment interchangeability" [23]. To exemplify this modularity, we can look at Burstenev's Overall Story Arc, in which "a designer can make sure that a narrative [...] follows the simple rules of the 'Heroes Journey' [sic] and can quickly set a skeleton framework to the game which can then be populated with more clearly defined level design" [24].

However, Propp's generative model has proved more popular. Examples of its use include Minstrel Remixed [23], a reconstruction of the Turner 1993 original [25]; Grabson, Spierling and Braun's GEIST [26], Ogata's plot generator module [27], and Gervás's ProtoPropp system [28]. Despite their successes as technical constructions, using Propp for narrative generation has not been without critique. Sjöstrom points out that game stories that adhere to Propp's structure do not offer players a significant range of choice in what happens in a story and notes that in such cases "the narrative sequence must always be complete and the player may therefore not fail" [29], an issue reminiscent of the shortcomings that Riedl and Young identified in IPOCL [17].

Perhaps more significantly, Gervás later wrote of Propp's morphology that "the brevity in which this generative procedure is described in Propp's book inevitably leaves many things unsaid and a large number of open problems". One of them is an apparent difficulty to identify functions that allow stories to end in a satisfactory manner; another is the difficulty in recognizing dependencies between non-consecutive story events [30].

These approaches attempt to add meaning to stories by arranging a sequence of events following a restrictive formula which only allows permutations at critical points, while the rest is determined with constrained randomness. This allows only for limited variations within the same narrative structure, and do not present particularly meaningful opportunities to engage with a thematic message more than once. To this end, we propose the further study of Greimassian semiotics.

## 3  Greimassian Semiotics and a Sample Analysis

This paper proposes using the model presented in Greimas's "On Meaning" [3] as a narrative morphology to generate quests in which:

1. Events and characters seem connected to a story message or theme.
2. Different ways for players to advance are recognized and responded to accordingly.
3. Story structures are malleable, so the system can alter them to suit player actions.

Greimas's model attempts to explain how the human mind constructs complex cultural objects [5], starting with simple elements and following a constrained trajectory. In this section, we will outline this process with an example analysis to introduce the terms and conceptual tools used by Greimas. This will clarify our discussion section, which explains how these tools might help an algorithm assemble meaningful computer game quests.

Describing Greimassian semiotics is best done with examples. Greimas worked with myths and folktales, whereas Budnikiewicz [11] worked with West's Miss Lonelyhearts (a US literature classic), and Hébert [31] worked with biblical stories, Greek classics, and fairy tales. In our sample analysis, we work with Monterroso's microstory "The Dinosaur"; which we will use as a running example throughout the text. The story, quoted in its entirety is: "Cuando despertó, el dinosaurio seguía allí" [32]. Grossman translated it as: "When he awoke, the dinosaur was still there" [33]. However, we will not use this translation given that it ignores the null-subject quality of the original. Instead, we will work with a more technical (though perhaps less appealing) translation:

**Table 1.** Technical translation of Monterroso's "The Dinosaur".

| Cuando | | despertó, | el dinosaurio | seguía allí |
|--------|----------|-----------|---------------|-------------|
| When | he/she/it | awoke, | the dinosaur | remained there |

According to Greimas, the construction of this "meaningfulness" is a compound process with three structured stages. The first is the *deep structure*, which "accounts for the achronic apprehension of the signification of all stories that could possibly be generated by a given semantic micro universe" [6]. The second structured stage is *surface structure*, which uses the elements described in the deep structure to define the characters, actions, happenings, and settings that are susceptible to manifestation by means of a *semiotic grammar*. The *structure of manifestation* is the third stage of the process. It produces the text that is visible to interactors. This last stage is beyond the scope of this paper, as it would only be observable in a finished game. It is nonetheless useful to be aware of, as we use it as the starting point of the example analyses that follow.

Our translation in Table 1 attempts to reflect word by word the manifest structure that Monterroso published in 1959. As the process of translation shows, the ideas: (1) someone awakes, and (2) they realize a dinosaur remains at a known place; are independent of the manifest structure used (such as the original text, or our translation or Monterroso's original). Greimas describes the surface structure as a stage in which actants (anthropomorphized performers) and their actions follow a syntax to create a meaningful story. By contrast, the deep structure (which he also called *elementary morphology*) describes the thematic significance of story actions or happenings.

### 3.1 The Deep Structure

There are two events in Monterroso's story: the act of awakening and the act of remaining. Because these actions are the only elements of the text that evidence the presence of a meaningful sentiment in the story, we identify them as *elementary concepts* of the story. Elementary concepts are the basic units of meaning from which a story is drawn, and form the basis of Greimas's taxonomic model to study the deep structure.

Greimas proposes that the events carried out by actants are arranged syntactically to communicate meaning, and that they do so by proposing elementary concepts in an oppositional relation. Monterroso's microstory has only two elementary concepts to contrast: (a) awareness, asserted by the awakening of the implied someone or something and (b) presence, implied by the fact that the dinosaur remains. In our analysis, the word "awareness" refers to the active function of perceiving Monterroso's story world, and "presence" refers to the passive function of being there or being perceivable in the story world. Figure 1 shows the elementary concepts in Monterroso's story as part of Greimas' *semiotic square*, which shows ten different ways in which meaningful events, characters and settings can occur or exist in a story world. Each elementary concept corresponds to a corner, edge, or diagonal of the semiotic square.

In any analysis, the choice of (a) and (b) is subjective but relies on the observation of constant values proposed by the main character's actions and the challenges they overcome. (a) and (b) are subset to (e), the complex term, which represents the meaningful message of any story. In the case of "The Dinosaur," we see (e) manifest in any number of subjective meanings that one could assign to Monterroso's contrast between awareness and presence, such as the opinions a reader can have about the meaning of the story, or the ways in which a film maker might re-tell "The Dinosaur." The neutral term, (f), indicates the limitations of the story, which can be understood as the things that the author(s) did not mean to communicate. As stories become more complex, (e) and (f) may not be as evident as they are in our example story. Greimas includes contradictory terms (c) and (d) as neutralizing operators that are subset to (f), so that $a+d = 0$ and $b+c = 0$. In the case of "The Dinosaur" it is simple to find a word that encompasses $d = -a = unawareness$

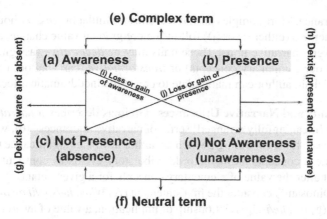

**Fig. 1.** Greimas' semiotic square, used to analyze Monterroso's "The Dinosaur".

but this is not always required; (d) could remain as *non-awareness*. Contrary terms are calculated as follows:

$$d = -a \qquad c = -b \tag{1}$$

(g) and (h) are called *deixes* by Greimas. They refer to a micro-ontology of actants (including characters, settings, and events) determined by their relationship to the elementary concepts of a given story. In "The Dinosaur", we might classify actants as belonging to the set (g) because they cause or bring about awareness or absence. On the other hand, actants organized in (h) will cause or bring to attention the concept either presence or unawareness in opposition to the actants in set (g). Although these are not discussed here at length, deixes (g) and (h) form the basis of Greimas' actantial model, where (g) includes helpers and opponents and (h) includes senders and receivers.

(i) and (j) are the transformative functions. Greimas originally expressed these as oriented syntactic operations, in the forms $f(a) = a \to d$ or $f(d) = d \to a$ and conversely $f(b) = b \to c$ or $f(c) = c \to b$ [6]. These describe the possible actions that actants (g) and (h) can perform to propose either of the elementary concepts at a particular point of story time. We depart from Greimas toward adding more mathematical meaning to the notation. We give (a) a value of 1 when our main character is aware. We can therefore understand a function (i) such as "*he/she/it awoke*", as follows:

$$a_{n+1} = \max(\min(a_n + ut_n, 1), -1) \tag{2}$$

This equation represents (i) in Fig. 1, and describes the process by which our person in (g) awakens, or gains awareness, going from a moment where they are unaware and towards a moment when they are aware. For example, we can say that at the moment of awakening, $a_0$ has a value of -1 and the story segment *he/she/it awoke* adds a contribution value $ut_0 = 2$. The result is $a_1 = 1$, indicating that our character is now aware, changing the state of the meaningful variables of Monterroso's story.

This narrative unit creates a full transformation from ($d = 1$) unawareness to ($a = 1$) awareness. It is therefore a *simple* narrative unit, consisting of one function (i), that is, one narrative utterance. More complex narratives follow a similar process, although the transformative functions (either (i) or (j)) follow a more gradual value change, and therefore consist of several narrative units. These units may be *declarative* (assigning or restating values of our elementary concepts) or *transformative* (carrying out transformative functions which an author can manipulate to create distinct dramatic effects).

**Narrative Units and Narrative Utterances.** Greimas describes a *narrative unit* as a "syntagmatic [meaningfully arranged] series of narrative utterances" [6], while a *narrative utterance* is a function through which an author attributes significance to the actants of a story. These concepts allow us to describe story events as consecutive operative functions that alter the value of elementary concepts for a given actant.

In "The Dinosaur", consider the first statement (A) *When he/she/it awoke.* We assign our actant in (g) *he/she/it*, by relationship of implication, a value of awareness (a) equal to -1. In our analysis, this value indicates that the actant is unaware. In general, the value 1 indicates that an actant (in either (g) or (h)) is defined by an elementary concept (a) or (b). A value of -1 indicates the actant is defined by the contrary concept. We therefore understand the narrative utterance *he/she/it awoke* as an instance of Eq. 2 where the initial awareness (a) of our actant in (g) has an initial value of -1 (it is not aware) and a resulting value of 1 (it is aware).

Because "The Dinosaur" is a very short story, narrative units and narrative utterances are indiscernible in context. The contrast between them can be seen more easily in the context of two adaptations:

(Y) *"He came back from an uneasy slumber. Slowly, he opened his eyes and began to rise as he yawned lazily. He didn't immediately scan the room, but when he did; the dinosaur remained there."*

(Z) *"He came to slowly. He opened his eyes and began to rise tentatively. The wound in his eye made it difficult for him to look around, so he treated it as best he could. When he was done, he saw that the dinosaur remained there."*

In adaptation (Y), the act of waking up takes 5 distinct actions, whereas in (A), it takes only one. The individual actions in (Y) are considered narrative utterances, which comprise the general act (and narrative unit) of awakening. Table 2 compares the three adaptations, showing that the fluctuation of value (a) as difference narrative utterances add a contribution value following Eq. 2. to compute a new value of (a) of our actant in (g), the main character who awakens.

We begin Table 2 by dividing it in three sections, corresponding to our analyzed statements. We then present the narrative unit type describing the act of awakening as a function of our actant in (g) going along axis (i) in the semiotic square (see Fig. 1) by having its current (a) value (-1, indicating the subject is unaware) fluctuate towards our desired (a) value (1, indicating the subject is aware). We represent the fluctuation with the addition of variable $(ut_n)$, to which we attribute a value representing the degree in which a given utterance (with number $n$) contributes to the value of (a). Variable $(ut_n)$ has an arbitrary value that describes the contribution an utterance makes to the value with which we describe an actant. Longer narrative units will contain more functions

**Table 2.** Narrative units contrasted with narrative utterances.

| | Narrative unit type | Utterance number (n) | $(a_n)$ Starting value | $ut_n$ | Computation | $(a_{n+1})$ End value |
|---|---|---|---|---|---|---|
| A | $i_g = d \rightarrow a$ | 1 | $-1$ | 2 | $a_0 = -1 + 2$ | 1 |
| Y | $i_g = d \rightarrow a$ | 1 | $-1$ | 0,4 | $a_1 = -1 + 0,4$ | $-0,6$ |
| | | 2 | $-0,6$ | 0,4 | $a_2 = -0,6 + 0,4$ | $-0,2$ |
| | | 3 | $-0,2$ | 0,4 | $a_3 = -0,2 + 0,4$ | 0,2 |
| | | 4 | 0,2 | 0,4 | $a_4 = 0,2 + 0,4$ | 0,6 |
| | | 5 | 0,6 | 0,4 | $a_5 = -0,6 + 0,4$ | 1 |
| Z | $i_g = d \rightarrow a$ | 1 | $-1$ | 0,4 | $a_1 = -1 + 0,4$ | $-0,6$ |
| | | 2 | $-0,6$ | 0,3 | $a_2 = -0,6 + 0,3$ | $-0,3$ |
| | | 3 | $-0,3$ | 0,3 | $a_3 = -0,3 + 0,3$ | 0 |
| | | 4 | 0 | 0,6 | $a_4 = -0 + 0,6$ | 0,6 |
| | | 5 | 0,6 | $-0,3$ | $a_5 = 0,6 - 0,3$ | 0,3 |
| | | 6 | 0,3 | 0,3 | $a_6 = 0,3 + 0,3$ | 0,6 |
| | | 7 | 0,6 | 0,4 | $a_7 = -0,6 + 0,4$ | 1 |

with lower values of $(ut_n)$. In (A) the act of awakening takes one narrative utterance, and therefore $(ut_1)$ *"when he awoke"* has its maximum value (2) when the new value of (a) is calculated. To contrast this, in (Y), we observe a more gradual awakening, and therefore $(ut_n)$ has lower values that happen in sequence. Note that every utterance in (Y) has a value in the positive axis, and are therefore *conjunctive functions*, that is, they modify the value of (a) so that it fluctuates towards our desired value.

In (Y), the inclusion of narrative utterance 5 *"The wound in his eye made it difficult to look around"* is a *disjunctive function,* where variable $(ut_5)$ has a value in the negative range, causing the value of (a) to fluctuate towards its value at $ut_0$. This potentially describes a story in which the elementary concept (a) has a more interesting development, where characters must overcome obstacles, or encounter opponents or situations that propose (a)'s contrasting value (d).

Figure 2 shows the values of elementary concept (a) in our three versions of "The Dinosaur". The three narrative units are superimposed in the same chart, where the vertical axis reflects the value of (a) awareness, and the horizontal axis represents the number of utterances in each unit.

From this comparison we present the following conclusions. First, narratives can be understood as the sequence of narrative utterances which arise from both stated and

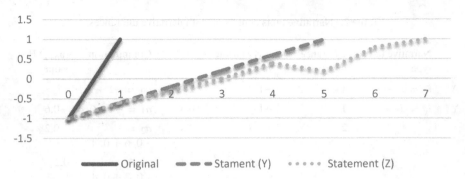

**Fig. 2.** Contrast of the value of (a) awareness in different renditions of "The Dinosaur"

inferred narrative units. Second, narrative units are transformations of the story world, represented by the value fluctuation of elementary concepts to their contrary values (1, -1), and these can be experienced in chains of sequential narrative units that have varying lengths. Furthermore, a narrative unit describes the way in which actants (characters or settings classified in deixies (g) or (h)) perform functions (i) or (j) causing the values of elementary concepts to fluctuate.

### 3.2   The Surface Structure

In our discussion of narrative units and utterances, we have presented how the actions and happenings of a story can be represented as thematic operations. The sequential listing of these operations (expressed in the terms of the deep structure) constitutes a representation of the surface structure. We do this by listing narrative units ($Nu_n$) in sequence, where the integer $n$ indicates their logical progression. We assign the number 0 to the narrative unit in which the reader enters the story (e.g., when he/she/it awakens in "The Dinosaur"). By relationship of implication, some narrative units are inferred to have happened before this moment, and thus count along negative values of $n$.

Table 3 shows the surface structure of "The Dinosaur", where we present the manifest discourse as evidence of our identification of meaning from left to right. We proceed to assign a number to each narrative unit that we identify, starting from the furthest that can be logically inferred towards the last one indicated by the manifest discourse. We continue by providing information on its "type," which describes the thematic operation it performs in terms of the deep structure. Next, we present each unit's function and assign values to variables. We conclude by providing an interpretation using natural language to exemplify the meaning of the abstract operations that we work with.

The reader enters the story during $Nu_0$, when the subject of the story becomes awake, and readers await more information. Manifest statement (A), however, indicates $Nu_{-1}$, a non-manifest moment in which the subject was unaware. By the word "remained" used in (B), we can infer $Nu_{-3}$, a previous moment in time where the subject was aware and the dinosaur was present, as well as a function that occurs during $Nu_{-2}$, where the subject somehow became unaware. Following (B) we understand that the subject somehow becomes aware of the dinosaur during $Nu_2$. But again, the word "remained" indicates that the subject expects in $Nu_1$ that the dinosaur would be absent.

**Table 3.** The surface structure of "The Dinosaur"

| Manifest discourse | Narrative unit | Narrative unit type | Functions & values | Interpretation |
|---|---|---|---|---|
| None, but implied by (B) | $Nu_{-3}$ | $a, b$<br>$c = -b$<br>$d = -a$ | $a = 1$<br>$b = 1$<br>$c = -1$<br>$d = -1$ | Person in (g) is aware of the presence of the dinosaur in (h) |
| (A) When he/she/it awoke | $Nu_{-2}$ | $a \rightarrow d$<br>$ut = -2$ | $a_g = a_g + ut_1$ | Person (g) goes from state: aware to state: unaware |
| | $Nu_{-1}$ | $a, b$<br>$c = -b$<br>$d = -a$ | $a = -1$<br>$b = 1$<br>$c = -1$<br>$d = 1$ | Person (g) is unaware |
| | $Nu_0$ | $d \rightarrow aut = 2$ | $a_g = a_g + ut_1$ | Person (g) goes from state: unaware to state: aware |
| (B) the dinosaur remained there | $Nu_1$ | *ability* :<br>$b \rightarrow c$<br>$ut = -2$ | *ability* :<br>$b_h = b_h + ut_1$ | Person is aware that the state of the dinosaur in (h) can change from present to absent |
| | $Nu_2$ | $a, b$<br>$c = -b$<br>$d = -a$ | $a = 1$<br>$b = 1$<br>$c = -1$<br>$d = -1$ | Person becomes aware of the dinosaur's (h) state: present |

$Nu_1$ is a virtual function. According to Greimas, actants "possess a virtuality of the particular doing that will make them able to accomplish [a value] transfer operation" [6]. Virtuality occurs in four modes that Greimas identifies. The first three are knowledge, ability, and want, which are prerequisites of the fourth mode, performance, the actualization of a function. In "The Dinosaur," all narrative units other than ($Nu_1$), which is a statement of virtuality, are performances.

This analysis of "The Dinosaur" exemplifies three kinds of statements that can be made. The first is *descriptive statements* (see $Nu_{-3}$, $Nu_{-1}$ and $Nu_2$). These are important because they represent a recalculation of the elementary concept's value and present a view of the current world state. The second is *function statements*, which describe state transformations (see $Nu_{-2}$ and $Nu_0$), where actants belonging to (g) or (h) conduct operations by altering the value of elementary concepts (a, b, c and d). The third is *virtual statements*, which can be subjectivized by either the author or the reader to enrich the meaning even further during the telling or re-telling of a story.

### 3.3  The Investment of Meaning

In Table 2, we presented and analyzed the types of narrative units that can occur in a story by enlisting the resources employed by Monterroso to communicate "The Dinosaur." In it we observed we have a single virtual narrative unit, $Nu_1$, which communicates the dinosaur's ability to become absent. It is here that we turn back to the fact that the original story gives readers little manifest evidence to discern its true meaning. Although we instinctively appreciate that the dinosaur can become absent, as most things are, Monterroso does not fully express the virtuality of the value transformation of the variable (b) presence. The following information is missing:

1. Whether the dinosaur wants to become absent.
2. Whether the subject wants the dinosaur to become absent.
3. Whether the dinosaur knows how to leave.
4. Whether the subject knows how to make the dinosaur become absent.
5. Whether the subject has the ability make the dinosaur become absent.

These unknowns represent questions that are answered by readers and interpreters. When they write that the story suggests that "our intellectual slumber prevents us from exacting social change" [34] Ramírez and Toledo identify the dinosaur as an allegorical figure that represents political authority and assumes that the subject (a figure representing society) wishes it to become absent. On the other hand, Aguilar's cinematographic adaptation of "The Dinosaur" [35] manifests all the narrative units presented in Table 2 by creating characters, including a drug dealer called "The Dinosaur", a young man who purchases drugs, and drugs that cause the young man's unawareness.

The pronounced differences between Ramírez and Toledo's and Aguilar's interpretations can be explained by referring to the process that Greimas calls "*investment*" [7]. This process defines characters that propose the elementary concepts of the narrative at the level of the *aesthetic* (with characters and settings), the *virtual* (defining wants, knowledge and abilities) and finally the *moral* (subjective interpretations).

Contrasting these two interpretations shows us that the aesthetic investment and the virtual investment need not remain the same for a deeper message to be communicated. The stories remain recognizable as adaptations of "The Dinosaur" because they follow the same message of contrast. We present this message in Eq. 3.

$$i : changes\,in\,awareness \neq j : changes\,in\,presence \qquad (3)$$

## 4  Proposed Application to Quest Generation

Our application of Greimassian semiotics to interactive narrative design begins with the conception that meaningful stories have messages generated by the contrasting relationship of two elementary concepts as shown in the semiotic square (Fig. 1). We have highlighted four different tools as relevant to interactive story design: (i) A model of the message and the process of investment; (ii) A representation of narrative units that describe actions and states in terms of numerical values attributed to elementary concepts of the semiotic square; (iii) A description of narrative unit types at the author level by their function, including the descriptive, the virtual, and the functional; and (iv) A description of the component parts of narrative units and narrative utterances, including a demonstration of how they can present modular variations without compromising the story's message.

Having studied these conceptual tools, we argue that a generative system might rely on them to direct happenings, present optional events to users, and provide players with quest plots where they may select a role to play and that they can invest with a moral message. We now sketch the operation of a system that follows these principles.

1. Given an elementary concept (such as need), select an appropriate contrasting concept (such as greed) and select a target message. This could be achieved with a library of elementary concepts and common contrasts in other stories or quests.
2. Build the story space by identifying possible functions related to the target message and identify actants (characters, objects, and settings), and assign them as proponents of a particular elementary concept (e.g., a farmer who needs medicine; need, an alchemist that sells medicine at a ridiculous price; greed).
3. Identify logical narrative units for a quest arc (player must identify the needy farmer, get medicine, present medicine), e.g., through narrative planning processes like Shivani & Ware's [19] or Breault, Ouellet and Davies's [20].
4. Identify possible narrative utterances (e.g., ways for the player to acknowledge the need, the greed, and their causes, ways to relieve the need or to participate in the greed, and ways in which actants might respond to such actions) and assign contribution values to each ($ut_n$).
5. Use the identified utterances to generate narrative units, extending those units that might provide interesting developments. For example, the number of narrative utterances in "get medicine" could be extended by introducing an actant with the directive "steal medicine." This expansion requires a library of different narrative units with associated contribution values.
6. As the story unfolds, identify player actions that might allow them to propose elementary concepts. Should the player get the medicine, they might either give it and relieve the need, or sell it to a farmer at a better price than the alchemist.
7. At the conclusion of the story, restate the significance of the player's actions in the story world, presenting or evidencing the contrasting terms of the story by comparing the initial world state and end world state, as well as presenting the system's understanding of the character's role of the generated story.

## 5  Conclusions and Future Work

In this work, we explained how the analytical tools of Algirdas J. Greimas can be used to create and communicate the general meaning of a story through action, and we sketched how a theorical system might use those tools to generate stories.

Greimas's work was conceived primarily to analyze stories – not generate them. Therefore, applying several of the tools that we discussed will require inferring additional precision (toward enabling computation) beyond what Greimas explicitly states.

Furthermore, several of the steps of the system we have sketched will be non-trivial to automate completely, and thus the support of a substantial body of authored and annotated content will be required. Finding a viable balance between authoring and automation remains as future work. In the meantime, we hope that our summary of Greimas's tools can support further work that seeks to produce interactive narratives that convey a message – be they hand-authored, generated, or some combination of the two.

Looking forward, it would be useful to analyze more works of literature, both traditional and interactive, with the goal of describing the dramatic resources that human authors have used to communicate their messages through action. This is because more complex stories will contain more than one message, or the message might not be as simple as it is in Monterroso's "The Dinosaur." We theorize that observing different messages with this methodology will allow our theorical system to produce more complex stories with the use of a library of contrasting elementary concepts.

Another benefit further analysis of stories would be the appreciation of narrative utterance design. This would allow us to better understand the relationship between a narrative unit's emotional effect and the value fluctuation of the $ut_n$ variable we introduced to measure each utterance's contribution to the value of our elementary concepts. We suspect that works within particular story genres (such as comedy, tragedy or suspense) will present similar patterns in how the values of elementary concepts fluctuate across their narrative utterances.

# References

1. Smith, G.: An analog history of procedural content generation. In: FDG (2015)
2. Howard, J.: Quests: Design, Theory and History in Games and Narratives. A K Peters, Ltd., Wellesley, MA (2008)
3. Greimas, A.J.: On Meaning. University of Minesota Press, Minneapolis (1987)
4. Greimas, A.J.: Toward a Semiotics of the Natural world, in On Meaning. University of Minessota Press, Minneapolis, pp. 17–47 (1987)
5. Greimas, A.J.: The Interaction of Semiotic Constraints, in On Meaning. University of Minessota Press, Minneapolis, pp. 48–62 (1987)
6. Greimas, A.J.: Elements of a Narrative Grammar, in On Meaning. University of Minnesota Press, Minneapolis, pp. 48–83 (1987)
7. Greimas, A.J.: Actants, Actors, and Figures, in On Meaning, pp. 106–120. University of Minessota Press, Minneapolis (1987)
8. Aarseth, E.: Cybertext: Perspective on Ergodic Literautre. JHU Press, Baltimore (1997)
9. Bogost, I.: Unit operations: An Approach to Videogame Criticism. MIT press, Cambridge (2008)
10. Eladhari, M.P.: Re-tellings: the fourth layer of narrative as an instrument for critique. In: Rouse, R., Koenitz, H., Haahr, M. (eds.) Interactive Storytelling. ICIDS 2018. LNCS, vol. 11318. Springer, Cham (2018). https://doi.org/10.1007/978-3-030-04028-4_5
11. Budniakiewicz, T.: Fundamentals of Story Logic: Introduction to Greimassian Semiotics. John Benjamins Publishing, Amsterdam/Philadelphia (1992)
12. Yu, H.-Y., Kim, M.-H., Bae, B.-C.: Actantial model-based character role recognition using emotional flow graph among characters in text stories. J. Internet Comput. Serv. 22(1), 51–63 (2021)

13. Szilas, N., et al.: The study of narrative acts with and for digital media. Digit. Scholarsh. Humanit. **35**(4), 904–920 (2020)
14. Szilas, N.: IDtension: a narrative engine for interactive drama. In: Proceedings of the Technologies for Interactive Digital Storytelling and Entertainment (TIDSE), Darmstadt:Fraunhofer (2003)
15. Szlias, N.: A computational model of an intelligent narrator for interactive narratives. Appl. Artif. Intell. **21**(8), 187–203 (2007)
16. Chatman, S.: Story and Discourse. Cornell University Press, Ithaca (2021)
17. Riedl, M.O., Young, R.M.: Narrative planning: balancing plot and character. J. Artif. Intell. Res. **39**, 217–268 (2010)
18. Shirvani, A., Ware, S.G.: A formalization of emotional planning for strong-story systems. In: Proceedings of the Sixteenth AAAI Conference on Artificial Intelligence and Interactive Digital Entertainment (2020)
19. Shirvani, A., Ware, S.G.: A plan-based personality model for story characters. In: Proceedings of the AAAI Conference on Artificial Intelligence and Interactive Digital Entertainment, Atlanta, Georgia (2019)
20. Breault, V., Ouellet, S., Davies, J.: Let CONAN tell you a story: procedural quest generation. Entertain. Comput. **38**, 100422 (2021)
21. Propp, V.: Morphology of the Folktale. University of Texas, Austin (2010)
22. Campbell, J.: The Hero with a Thosand Faces. New World Library, Novato (2008)
23. Tearse, B., Wardrip-Fruin, N., Mateas, M.: Minstrel remixed: procedurally generating stories. In: Proceedings of the Sixth AAAI conference on Artificial Intelligence and Interactive Digital Entertainment, vol. 5, no. 1 (2010)
24. Brusentsev, A., Hitchens, M., Richards, D.: An investigation of Vladimir Propp's 31 functions and 8 broad character types and how they apply to the analysis of video games. In: Proceedings of the 8th Australasian Conference on Interactive Entertainment: Playing the System (2012)
25. Turner, S.R.: Minstrel: A Computer Model of Creativity and Storytelling. Diss. University of California, Los Angeles (1993)
26. Grabson, D., Spierling, U., Braun, N.: Setting the scene: playing digital director in interactive storytelling and creation. Comput. Graph. **26**(1), 31–44 (2002)
27. Ogata, T.: Computational and cognitive approaches to narratology from the perspective of narrative generation. In: Ogata, T., Akimoto, T. (eds.) Computational and Cognitive Approaches to Narratology. IGI Global, Hershey, pp. 1–74 (2016)
28. Gervás, P., Díaz-Agudo, B., Peinado, F., Hervás, R.: Story plot generation based on CBR. In: Macintosh, A., Ellis, R., Allen, T. (eds.) Applications and Innovations in Intelligent Systems XII. SGAI 2004. Springer, London (2005). https://doi.org/10.1007/1-84628-103-2_3
29. Sjöström, J.: Morphology of digital narrative: prototyping digital narratives using the theories of Vladimir Propp. DiVA Archive (2013)
30. Gervás Gómez-Navarro, P.: Reviewing Propp's story generation procedure in the light of computational creativity. In: 40th Annual convention of the Society for the Study of Artificial Intellingence and the Simulation of Behaviour, London, UK (2014)
31. Hébert, L.: Tools for Text and Image Analysis: An Introduction to Applied Semiotics. Routledge, New York (2020)
32. Monterroso, A.: Obras Completas (y otros cuentos). Ediciones Era, Mexico, DF (1990)
33. Complete Works and Other Stories. University of Texas Press, Austin, Texas (1996)
34. Ramírez, J., Toledo, J.: El Dinosaurio de Monterroso: La exégesis Política más Breve del Mundo, Perro Negro, 1 October 2015. http://revistaperronegro.com/el-dinosaurio-de-monterroso-la-exegesis-politica-mas-breve-del-mundo/. Accessed 19 July 2020
35. Aguilar, S.: Youtube, 8 December 2016. https://www.youtube.com/watch?v=37EPAHbur50. Accessed 27 July 2021

# Interactive Narrative Impact and Applications

# Interviews Towards Designing Support Tools for TTRPG Game Masters

Devi Acharya(✉)⬤, Michael Mateas⬤, and Noah Wardrip-Fruin⬤

University of California, Santa Cruz, USA
dacharya@ucsc.edu, {michaelm,nwf}@soe.ucsc.edu

**Abstract.** In running tabletop roleplaying games (TTRPGs), game masters (GMs) are tasked with helping create and facilitate the building of a shared story between players based on player choices. In this paper, we look at how we can inform the design of computational tools for GMs through the use of qualitative interviews. We present GMs with a prototype of a computational tool built based on a beginner TTRPG module that has some of the features we believe would be useful in a GMing assistant, such as consolidating information for easier reference and helping GMs keep track of what has happened in the game world. From these interviews, we found which features GMs liked and what could be improved with our digital prototype.

**Keywords:** Role-playing games · Game masters · Requirements analysis

## 1 Introduction

In running tabletop roleplaying games, game masters (GMs) lead the game and take on a variety of roles, including providing challenges to players and improvising new content based on the player's character backstories, choices, and actions in the game world. In order to do this, GMs must be able to adapt the game on the fly, improvising from both prepared materials and the GM's imagination to build new elements of the game world. This can be a difficult task, and one that is especially daunting to new GMs. In this paper, we use qualitative interviews with GMs in order to assess a digital prototype for helping GMs. This requirements analysis helps us understand how computational tools can help to support GMs and inform next directions for the design of such tools.

## 2 Related Work

Currently there exist many different digital commercial and research tools for helping run TTRPGs. While there are many tools to help GMs facilitate their games such as virtual tabletop platforms or rulebook references for lookup, we

ⓒ Springer Nature Switzerland AG 2021
A. Mitchell and M. Vosmeer (Eds.): ICIDS 2021, LNCS 13138, pp. 283–287, 2021.
https://doi.org/10.1007/978-3-030-92300-6_26

focus here on the most relevant work related to facilitating GMing. One example is *Undercurrents*, a tool that helps to facilitate hidden information communication within tabletop roleplaying games by helping the game master share information with only a single or a few players [3]. This helps maintain hidden information in what is traditionally an open space of information, and provides a way of keeping track of what has happened in the game so far. Another example is *Imaginarium*, which uses procedural text generation to provide descriptions that are constrained by the author but still have variations to them, using an authoring language similar to natural language [6]. Horswill poses this as a casual authoring tool for game masters to develop semi-randomized content on the fly, for instance descriptions of monsters.

There has also been previous work theorizing how one might build digital tools based on these techniques. Bergström uses interviews with TTRPG players and their own experience with TTRPGs to create categories of "frames" of storytelling, such as diegetic and non-diegetic communication, using this to inform the design of digital tools for TTRPG communication [3]. Peinado discusses how GMing techniques could be applied in a digital domain, such as for modeling improvisation in a text adventure game. Our work builds on these and other studies on TTRPGs and using qualitative interviews, such as [8] and [11].

Finally, we use techniques informed by requirements analysis, in which interview insights can help to inform the design and iterative development of digital tools. Nelson & Mateas [7] provide game design assistive tools to several groups of game designers with various needs, perform interviews with them about their needs and how they can use the tools provided to help with those needs, and iterate on the tool's design based on the results of these interviews. Grow's [4] approach to evaluating AI architecture authoring tools is similar, using three different case studies to evaluate three different architectures, and looking at how different architectures require different methods of authoring. Gustafsson, Holme, and Mackay analyze the play experiences and players' stories of important objects from their play using interviews and questionnaires, using these to inform the design of new game architectures that provide a greater support for player narratives [5].

## 3    Methods

In order to give GMs a baseline from which we could discuss the design and functionality of a TTRPG digital assistant, we created a digital prototype of a tool for GMs that had some of the features that we were interested in assessing. We based this prototype on beginner *Dungeons & Dragons* 5th edition module *Lost Mine of Phandelver*, because it is a scenario meant for new GMs using a popular TTRPG system, and thus could be the introduction to GMing for many new GMs. For modeling out the scenario, we focused on Chapters 2 and 3 of *Lost Mine* because these offered some interesting variance in play style (social, hub-based quests and combat) and player options. The static version of the visualization laid out story and character information and connections between them in a flowchart-style interface, providing information on the various paths that the players could take through the story and a list of characters. The interactive version was the same flowchart representation in which nodes and the connections between them could be edited, added, or removed by the user.

We used similar methods to our previous study [2], interviewing six of the GMs interviewed for that study as well as two more contacted based on convenience sampling [9] from a pool of students and faculty members in the area. Before the interview, we asked GMs to review the module *Lost Mine of Phandelver*. We then conducted hour-long interviews with each GM individually to get insights into their GMing process and how a digital assistant could help with this. We both asked questions related to how the GM would run the module and questions related to the digital prototype–the information being displayed, how it might be helpful, and what the GMs would want to see changed about it. For the interview, GMs were given a PDF version of the *Lost Mine of Phandever* module, as well as links to both the static and interactive versions of the digital prototype. As with our previous study [2], we then performed qualitative coding as informed by [10] on the interview notes and video interviews in order to pull out both general categories and specific examples that arose throughout the interviews.

## 4  Requirements Analysis

Overall, GMs commented that they liked the tool and were interested in the potential for computational tools to help with GMing. Many of the GMs liked that the tool condenses the many pages of information found in the module into a more accessible form that can be referenced in either planning for a next session or during play. GMs also talked about how the tool could be used to keep track of information, such as information the players know, or things that they have done, which could be used to help map out the rest of the story and determine effects from previous player actions.

That said, GMs had many recommendations for improvements and features that they would like to see. One area that GMs wanted to see improved was in information visualization. The current prototype has some limited information on NPCs–names, occupations, and a few relationship indicators such as whether characters are family members–but GMs discussed more features that they would like to see, and different desired functions, such as being able to sort, filter, and tag information (1, 2, 5). GMs also wanted more visualizations of information for storytelling, such as showing relationships between characters or factions (5). GM #2 added that they would also like to keep track of faction goals–what members of the factions want, and the next steps that they will take to accomplish this. This helps to drive the story based around the characters and their motivations.

GMs also talked about other uses for computation in supporting GMing. One of the main areas that GMs wanted support for was in being able to swap around existing content or add their own content, which was partially supported by the current prototype. Some of this was based on tailoring content to players. For example, GMs #2, 4, and 6 talked about cutting down on the content that was provided in the module and swapping elements to help create player investment such as providing encounters with monsters that the player characters dislike (2), or using encounters to convey different narrative themes (4). Swapping content can also be helpful changing content around if needed to help advance the story. GM #6 gives an example of this from *Lost Mine*–if Hamun the necromancer has information that you want the players to know but they decide they don't want to pursue that route, you can provide that information on another NPC, for example having the players find this information after defeating Iarno, the leader of the Redbrands (6). It would be interesting to further explore how computational tools could facilitate this content swapping, either manually or automatically through an AI suggesting changes to tailor scenarios to the players' backstory, theme, or interests. As GM #1 points out, swapping things around arbitrarily could lead to more complications down the line as the GM changes information or key characters for story progression. This could also be a potential area for computational intervention.

Another area in which GM #1 talked about creating new content for the game was in helping realize character and faction beliefs in the game. For example, if the general of a faction has the belief that the best defense is a good offense, how is this behavior contextualized and seen during play? GM #1 discusses how it might be nice to have some provided framing questions in order to help them better establish the kinds of actions that groups would take in the world to convey their beliefs. They offer the example of having the tool prompt the GM with questions–for example, how the given faction might take a fort (by force, by coercion, by stealth, etc.) or if the town was taken over by a tyrannical leader, how a member of the faction might deal with that.

Finally, GMs (5, 6) also talk about having improvisational prompts for things that can happen next. GM #6 discussed how this would be good for beginners, especially for modules that are large, expansive worlds (the GM gives the example of *Storm King's Thunder* [1]). In such games, there is a lot of content, but at any one time players (and the GM) might be at a loss for what to do next, and there may be large distances (either physically or narratively) between each chapter of the story, with player potentially missing the plot hooks connecting them (6). Potentially, a computational system with some knowledge of what has already happened and story threads could provide prompts for potential events that could happen next, or stepping stones to help guide players to the next part of the story.

## 5   Conclusions and Future Work

While there are some limitations to the data collected here, such as the number of participants interviewed, we believe that this is a strong starting point for understanding how we can better design computational assistive tools for GMs. Next steps for this work likely include building out some of these speculative designs as actual functioning tools that GMs can use, and evaluating these tools through user studies, particularly with a target demographic such as novice GMs.

# References

1. Wizards of the Coast, Inc., Perkins, C.: Storm King's Thunder. Wizards of the Coast, Renton (2016)
2. Acharya, D., Mateas, M., Wardrip-Fruin, N.: Story improvisation in tabletop role-playing games: Towards a computational assistant for game masters. In: Conference on Games (2021)
3. Bergström, K.: Framing storytelling with games. In: Si, M., Thue, D., André, E., Lester, J.C., Tanenbaum, T.J., Zammitto, V. (eds.) ICIDS 2011. LNCS, vol. 7069, pp. 170–181. Springer, Heidelberg (2011). https://doi.org/10.1007/978-3-642-25289-1_19
4. Grow, A., Gaudl, S., Gomes, P., Mateas, M., Wardrip-Fruin, N.: A methodology for requirements analysis of AI architecture authoring tools. In: Proceedings of the 9th International Conference on the Foundations of Digital Games (2014). https://games.soe.ucsc.edu/methodology-requirements-analysis-ai-architecture-authoring-tools
5. Gustafsson, V., Holme, B., Mackay, W.E.: Narrative substrates: reifying and managing emergent narratives in persistent game worlds. In: International Conference on the Foundations of Digital Games, pp. 1–12 (2020)
6. Horswill, I.: Imaginarium: a tool for casual constraint-based PCG (2019)
7. Nelson, M.J., Mateas, M.: A requirements analysis for videogame design support tools. In: Proceedings of the 4th International Conference on Foundations of Digital Games - FDG 2009. ACM Press, New York (2009)
8. Reyes, M.C.: Measuring user experience on interactive fiction in cinematic virtual reality. In: Rouse, R., Koenitz, H., Haahr, M. (eds.) ICIDS 2018. LNCS, vol. 11318, pp. 295–307. Springer, Cham (2018). https://doi.org/10.1007/978-3-030-04028-4_33
9. Robinson, O.C.: Sampling in interview-based qualitative research: a theoretical and practical guide. Qual. Res. Psychol. 11(1), 25–41 (2014)
10. Saldaña, J.: The Coding Manual for Qualitative Researchers. Sage, Thousand Oaks (2015)
11. Strugnell, J., Berry, M., Zambetta, F., Greuter, S.: Narrative improvisation: simulating game master choices. In: Rouse, R., Koenitz, H., Haahr, M. (eds.) ICIDS 2018. LNCS, vol. 11318, pp. 428–441. Springer, Cham (2018). https://doi.org/10.1007/978-3-030-04028-4_50

# The Ethics of Virtual Reality Interactive Digital Narratives in Cultural Heritage

Jonathan Barbara[1](✉) , Hartmut Koenitz[2] , and Ágnes Karolina Bakk[3]

[1] St. Martin's Institute of Higher Education, Hamrun, Malta
jbarbara@stmartins.edu
[2] Södertörn University, Huddinge, Sweden
hartmut.koenitz@sh.se
[3] Moholy-Nagy University of Art and Design Budapest, Budapest, Hungary
bakk@mome.hu

**Abstract.** As IDNs are used to represent complex phenomena, we are bound to assess the ethical dimension of these representations in order to help IDN mature as a practice and a discipline. In this paper, we consider ethical aspects arising from applications of IDN in VR for Cultural Heritage experiences. Using a discussion of ethical aspects of cultural heritage and virtual reality as a foundation, and considering a range of IDN VR cultural heritage experiences, we derive a set of ethical questions for IDN design in general and for cultural heritage specifically as the basis for the development of standard ethics guidelines and help start a conversation on the topic in the community.

**Keywords:** Interactive digital narratives · Ethics · Ethics guidelines · Virtual reality · Cultural heritage

## 1 Introduction

The question of the effects of mediated products on their audiences has been studied for a considerable time [1–3]. As the field of Interactive Digital Narratives (IDNs) matures [4], questions arise that have been asked of other disciplines [5], and starting to address these questions helps the field develop further. One such question is the issue of ethics: what are the ethical considerations of IDNs? The approach taken by this paper is to focus on ethical questions pertaining to a specific platform and application for IDNs, Virtual Reality (VR) and cultural heritage. Concretely, we start with a catalogue of general concerns and then take a bottom-up approach in considering IDNs developed as VR experiences in cultural heritage. The connection to cultural heritage enables us to take in insights developed in this more established field, and consider ethical aspects of VR technology which has been used in the preservation of cultural heritage sites and artefacts over the past two decades. Bringing together these lessons and our initial catalogue, we identify specific concerns for VR in cultural heritage applications.

A crucial prerequisite to discussions of ethical questions in IDN design is an understanding of its specific qualities in contrast to fixed narratives forms. IDN as a dynamic,

A. Mitchell and M. Vosmeer (Eds.): ICIDS 2021, LNCS 13138, pp. 288–292, 2021.
https://doi.org/10.1007/978-3-030-92300-6_27

systemic form is principally open to unexpected consequences and unintended uses and this central aspect shifts a part of the responsibility to the audience as interactors. On this basis, we can identify questions for ethical implications of IDN productions in general and VR products for cultural heritage specifically. The following catalogue of questions is intended as a starting point for a framework of ethical IDN production as part of the further development of the field.

- How can multi-perspective experiences be created in a way that each perspective gets a fair treatment?
- How can an IDN scaffold an experience for the interactor in a complex situation so that they arrive at an understanding of how their actions have resulted in the outcome?
- How can undue simplification and trivialization of a complex situation in an IDN be prevented?
- How can an IDN design accommodate interactors with different levels of experience with interactive artifacts?
- How can an IDN design accommodate interactors with different levels of prior knowledge in regards to the topic of the artefact?

## 2  Ethics of VR IDNs in Cultural Heritage

The ability of IDNs to contain multiple perspectives and offer choices make it an attractive medium through which cultural heritage can be represented. Before we consider the above ethical concerns, we need to also consider the ethical considerations introduced by the technological platform of choice. Built to visually and aurally immerse the wearer into a virtual world, VR technology has been the platform of choice for over two decades in digital heritage experiences [6]. Examples of such IDN cultural heritage applications are *The Last Goodbye* [7], *Nefertari: Journey to Eternity* [8], *Chauvet: The Dawn of Art* [9] and *The Book of Distance* [10].

In 2016, Michael Madary and Thomas K. Metzinger proposed a possible code of conduct for VR [11]. The authors emphasize that the main motivation behind their investigation is VR's ability to enable the illusion of embodiment and argue that this can have a manipulative effect, especially if "illusions of embodiment are misused" [11]. Madary and Metzinger point out the importance of informing the interactors about potentially lasting psychological effects of VR and "the possibility of using results of VR research for malicious purposes" [11]. Furthermore, the authors discuss a potential danger of excessive use of VR, which can lead to a condition where VR users could "experience the real world and their real bodies as unreal, effectively shifting their sense of reality exclusively to the virtual environment" [11].

Importantly, IDNs are not just the 'interactivisation' of traditional media [12]. In this regard, Rebecca Rouse reminds of the active role of the audience, created by these experiences, which traditionally "has been reserved for the curator and exhibit designer" [13]. The interactivity in IDNs differs considerably from earlier fixed forms of narration and thus require a novel starting point, such as Koenitz' SPP model [14]. For the same reason, we have to reframe the ethical considerations explored above within the framing of IDN work including VR.

The use of a head-mounted device in VR brings the interactor in the immediate vicinity of the projected world which heightens the 'authenticity-of-feelings' [15] but also introduces ethical questions. Conversely, IDNs in general facilitate experiences as part of the possibility space of the protostory [14] and its intended understanding.

In IDN, there is an implicit contract between interactor and designer, an act of "active creation of belief" [16] that is also the responsibility of the audience. From the ethical perspective this creates the question at what point does a possible failure to reach the intended understanding stop belonging to the interactor and start being attributed to the IDN designer?

## 2.1 Ethical Issues in Example Application

Since spatiality is an essential characteristic of the digital medium [16], navigation is a critical component, but this is tackled superficially in the first three examples of VR experiences in 3D space. In *The Last Goodbye*, a drone-avatar diminishes the player's presence while in *Nefertari* and *Chauvet: Dawn of Art* unnatural teleportation systems are used. Similarly, IDNs attempt to model some complex aspect of life (real or fictional) and provide means for the interactor to 'navigate' through it. The level of realism implemented in the IDN system, the fidelity of the system to the complex phenomenon all contributes to the interactor's feeling of being 'inside it'.

The fourth example, *The Book of Distance*, is different from the other three because the interaction is not based on navigation, but on agency within the story. Effectively serving the progress of the narrative, the interactions allow the player to contribute to the story, serving as a side-kick to whoever is currently leading the narrative. There is an emphasis here on plausibility over realistic place illusion as the player's interaction with the space around them helps the interactor to actively create the illusion themselves that the depicted scenario is actually occurring. Moreover, as the player's actions visibly affect the state of the space around them, there is self-location, agency, body ownership, indeed embodiment [17]: the player feels that their real life actions of hitting and dropping are actually helping build a fence, sowing seeds etc. The player not only learns how to do these actions but gets visual feedback. A lesson for IDNs here is that mimetic performance is to be preferred over narrative diegesis in order to teach the interactor the meaning of their actions. Having players perform actions just for the sake of doing something, of interaction without agency, without conveying the results and possible underlying meaning of that action is unethical IDN design in the context of the represented intangible cultural heritage.

Where the *Book of Distance* does not deliver, is on the level of emotional connection, elements of which have been found to be positively affected by spatial presence, especially in VR interactive narratives whose main purpose is not entertainment [18]. However, due to the design choice of not giving a fixed role to the VR player [10], there is no emotional attachment to any of the three main characters in the experience as the player's actions help each of these in different stages of the experience. There is even no rational empathy because interactors are not presented with any moral choices: each action that is presented has to be done, otherwise the narrative does not progress.

Taking the issue of emotional connection a step further, we can ask whether it is ethical to expect empathy from a VR player who is taught to re-enact some form of intangible cultural heritage without having the cultural insider's knowledge necessary for a full understanding. The vision of VR as the 'ultimate empathy machine' [19] is problematic for several reasons (also see [20]), one of which we can see in *The Book of Distance*. What the IDN designer should aim for is instead 'radical compassion': 'an ethical stance that embraces an openness to understanding and refuses to assimilation others' experience into one's own self' [21].

## 3 Specific Concerns of VR IDNs in Cultural Heritage

Drawing from the initial questions and the above examples, the following ethical questions should be considered in future VR cultural heritage projects:

- How can the role of the interactor be defined, such that no prior knowledge of a specific cultural tradition is required, and yet enables an understanding of it?
- How can interactors with different knowledge levels about a specific cultural heritage tradition be accommodated?
- How can an experience be respectful to a given tradition, but does not submerge contemporary values to it (e.g. oppression due to gender, origin, religion etc.)?
- How can newly discovered knowledge (e.g. new archeological finds, novel historical insights) be integrated into an IDN artifact?
- How can undue trivializing of the depicted original behavior be avoided?
- How can the responsibility of the interactor in a cultural heritage experience be clearly communicated?

## 4 Conclusion

In this paper, we have provided a starting point for a framework of ethical IDN production by analyzing ethical considerations arising from applications of IDN in VR for Cultural Heritage experiences. Building upon ethical aspects of cultural heritage and virtual reality separately, we have developed a set of ethical questions for IDN design in general and specifically for the application of IDN in VR representing cultural heritage. From these questions, initial guidelines can be developed by the community, with the aim to define a standard applicable to on an international level in the future.

**Acknowledgments.** The authors acknowledge the support of the EU COST Association in the form of the COST Action 18230 INDCOR (Interactive Narrative Design for COmplexity Representations). https://indcor.eu.

## References

1. Benjamin, W.: Das Kunstwerk im Zeitalter seiner technischen Reproduzierbarkeit. Frankfurt am Main, Suhrkamp (1969)
2. Horkheimer, M., Adorno, T.: The culture industry: enlightenment as mass deception. In: Durham, M.G., Kellner, D.M. (eds.) Media and Cultural Studies: KeyWorks (2006)

3. Habermas, J.J.: The Structural Transformation of the Public Sphere: An Inquiry into a Category of Bourgeois Society. (T. Burger, Trans. & F. Lawrence, Trans.) (1989)
4. Koenitz, H.: Thoughts on a discipline for the study of interactive digital narratives. In: Rouse, R., Koenitz, H., Haahr, M. (eds.) Interactive Storytelling. ICIDS 2018. LNCS, vol. 11318, pp. 36–49. Springer, Cham (2018). https://doi.org/10.1007/978-3-030-04028-4_3
5. Koenitz, H., Eladhari, M.P.: Challenges of IDN research and teaching. In: Cardona-Rivera, R., Sullivan, A., Young, R. (eds.) Interactive Storytelling. ICIDS 2019. LNCS, vol. 11869, pp. 26–39. Springer, Cham (2019). https://doi.org/10.1007/978-3-030-33894-7_4
6. Ch'ng, E., Cai, Y., Thwaites, H.: Special issue on VR for culture and heritage: the experience of cultural heritage with virtual reality: guest editors' introduction. PRESENCE Teleoperators Virtual Environ. 26, iii–vi (2018). https://doi.org/10.1162/pres_e_00302
7. Zalewska, M.: The Last Goodbye (2017): Virtualizing Witness Testimonies of the Holocaust. 8 (2017)
8. Experius VR, Curiosity Stream: Nefertari: Journey to Eternity (2018). https://store.steampowered.com/app/861400/Nefertari_Journey_to_Eternity/
9. Tanant, J.: Google Arts & Culture, Atlas V: Chauvet: The Dawn of Art (2020). https://experiments.withgoogle.com/chauvet
10. Oppenheim, D., Okita, R.L.: The book of distance: personal storytelling in VR. In: ACM SIGGRAPH 2020 Immersive Pavilion, pp. 1–2. ACM, Virtual Event USA (2020). https://doi.org/10.1145/3388536.3407896
11. Madary, M., Metzinger, T.K.: Real virtuality: a code of ethical conduct. Recommendations for good scientific practice and the consumers of VR-technology. In: Frontiers in Robotics and AI, vol. 3 (2016)
12. Koenitz, H.: Reframing interactive digital narrative: toward an inclusive open-ended iterative process for research and practice (2010). https://smartech.gatech.edu/bitstream/handle/1853/34791/koenitz_hartmut_a_201008_phd.pdf
13. Rouse, R.: Someone else's story: an ethical approach to interactive narrative design for cultural heritage. In: Cardona-Rivera, R.E., Sullivan, A., Young, R.M. (eds.) ICIDS 2019. LNCS, vol. 11869, pp. 47–60. Springer, Cham (2019). https://doi.org/10.1007/978-3-030-33894-7_6
14. Koenitz, H.: Towards a specific theory of interactive digital narrative. In: Interactive Digital Narrative, pp. 91–105 (2015)
15. Mochocki, M.: Heritage sites and video games: questions of authenticity and immersion. Games Cult. 155541202110053 (2021). https://doi.org/10.1177/15554120211005369
16. Murray, J.H.: Hamlet on the Holodeck: The Future of Narrative in Cyberspace. Simon and Schuster, New York (1997)
17. Kilteni, K., Groten, R., Slater, M.: The sense of embodiment in virtual reality. Presence Teleoperators Virtual Environ. 21, 373–387 (2012)
18. Barreda-Ángeles, M., Aleix-Guillaume, S., Pereda-Baños, A.: An empathy machine or a just-for-the-fun-of-it machine? Effects of immersion in nonfiction 360-video stories on empathy and enjoyment. Cyberpsychol. Behav. Soc. Netw. 23, 683–688 (2020)
19. Milk, C.: How virtual reality can create the ultimate empathy machine (2015)
20. Fisher, J.A.: Empathic actualities: toward a taxonomy of empathy in virtual reality. In: Nunes, N., Oakley, I., Nisi, V. (eds.) Interactive Storytelling. ICIDS 2017. Lecture Notes in Computer Science, vol. 10690, pp. 233–244. Springer, Cham (2017). https://doi.org/10.1007/978-3-319-71027-3_19
21. Bollmer, G.: Empathy machines. Media Int. Aust. 165, 63–76 (2017)

# Exploring Multiple Perspectives in Citizenship Education with a Serious Game

Erik Blokland, Caroline Cullinan, Doreen Mulder[✉], Willie Overman,
Marin Visscher, Amir Zaidi, Mijael R. Bueno Pérez, and Rafael Bidarra

Delft University of Technology, Delft, The Netherlands
d.mulder@student.tudelft.nl, R.Bidarra@tudelft.nl

**Abstract.** Within citizenship education, a new focus is being laid upon what is expected of citizens within a diverse and lightning-fast society: more emphasis is placed on teaching students how to understand and respect other people's opinions, regardless of how they may contrast with one's own. However, learning to be tolerant with others' viewpoints comes with hurdles, as currently it is quite easy to become stuck within one's own worldview. We developed *Diermocratie*, an in-classroom game aimed at encouraging a more open conversation, which breaks through these hurdles and addresses key competencies such as empathy and argumentation. By role-playing metaphors that parallel real-world events, students explore their own predispositions, are made aware of the perspectives of others, and are enabled to discuss issues objectively. From a preliminary evaluation, most students could identify the parallelism between the in-game metaphor and real-world situations. They also indicated that the game motivates them to further talk to each other, approaching sensitive topics among them.

**Keywords:** Multiple perspectives · Citizenship education · Diversity · Serious games

## 1 Introduction

Traditionally, citizenship education has laid the focus on teaching students to become 'well-behaved' citizens. However, over the last decade or so, this paradigm has been shifting. In addition to highlighting which morals are expected from citizens, a new focus is being placed on shaping citizens who think critically and participate actively in society. This change in paradigm can be attributed, in part, to the fact that society has become more fast-paced than ever. It has never been easier to acquire information or connect with like-minded individuals that share common thoughts and opinions. While such advancements have brought our standard of living to a new high, there are some significant downsides to these developments as well. Polarization, the phenomenon where

A. Mitchell and M. Vosmeer (Eds.): ICIDS 2021, LNCS 13138, pp. 293–306, 2021.
https://doi.org/10.1007/978-3-030-92300-6_28

opposing attitudes become increasingly divergent making it difficult for different groups of people to communicate effectively, has increased significantly over the last decades [27]. Through emphasizing the importance of critical thinking skills and opinion acceptance within citizenship education, new education efforts attempt to address early on issues such as polarization. With such an approach, students of varying levels can realize the value of different opinions, as well as learn to think critically about where their own opinions originate from. It is expected that this approach should lead to more open and participating citizens.

However, actually applying this strategy in the classroom has proven to be quite challenging [21,22]. Topics that are both relevant to the students and useful in this context are often sensitive to discuss in class. In Dutch vocational college, for example, where classrooms are most diverse in terms of demographic background, vastly different opinions limit an open discussion. In such settings, teachers may not have the necessary skills and comfort to lead such complex discussion. Moreover, leading complex discussions becomes even more challenging as teachers recognize that their own point of view could also influence the debate.

In this paper we explore how some of these hurdles can be overcome through the use of serious gaming. By encouraging a fictional discussion in a multiplayer environment we investigate whether vocational college students are more open to discussion and self-reflection when faced with a metaphorical parallel of a real-life debate. The research question we try to answer with this paper is:

*How could a serious game provide a metaphorical analogy of a real-life scenario, which promotes open conversations about complex and sensitive topics among students in vocational education?*

Through this research, we contribute insights to the debate around polarization, and we demonstrate how the effects of clashing worldviews may be mitigated through the use of metaphorical gameplay. In acknowledging related work, we build upon existing research in the domain of education and critical discussion, and we explore the role of serious gaming in facilitating open discussion in an education context. We then introduce our game design, its prototype implementation, and its evaluation in serving as a tool for educators to encourage a multi-perspective approach to conversation in the classroom. Finally, we conclude with a summary of our findings and the implication that this research has for serious games in educational settings.

## 2    Related Work

Among the most notorious barriers to open conversation in the classroom are sensitive topics, groupthink, and clashing worldviews. We briefly survey existing research on these specific barriers of open conversation, as well as on how they can relate to citizenship education and serious games.

## 2.1   Barriers to Classroom Conversation

There is extensive research regarding the discussion of sensitive topics in the classroom. A good example is a 2016 paper by Kello [17], which notes that multiple factors ranging from fear of a backlash from their students to feeling restrained by their own belief, prevent teachers from leading classroom discussion about these sensitive topics. A disconnect between instructor and student culture can also lead to instructors feeling as if they do not possess the cultural literacy to approach sensitive social issues which affect students very differently. Because of this, instructors can often feel uncomfortable facilitating and leading conversation about sensitive topics. If classroom instructors lack the experience, skills, and confidence to facilitate open conversation about socially sensitive topics with students, then it is likely very difficult not only to ensure any deep conversation at all, but also to facilitate critical self-reflection and exploration of multiple perspectives.

The second barrier is groupthink, or the phenomenon of a group of people shifting towards a complacent decision that often disregards individual perspectives [15]. This is something that strongly applies to classroom dynamics. As indicated by Johnson & Weaver [16], "students rarely enter into lengthy conversations regarding course material with other students or teachers outside the classroom context. When such conversations do take place, it seems more common to hear a recitation of things heard in class rather than a disparaging or challenging of class statements or positions." In order to avoid social exclusion or in an attempt not to offend others, groups of students might not accurately represent their range of opinions due to groupthink.

A person's worldview is the way in which a person gives meaning to their surroundings through their own values and expectations. However, when different worldviews clash, this may form a barrier in the classroom. In a recent article by Brandt & Crawford [8], a clear overview is given on how through the protection of their own worldview, people are likely to reject conflicting worldviews. This study found that prejudice through worldview conflict is present in almost all worldviews, regardless of, for example, openness or cognitive ability. Since there are many different worldviews colliding within the multicultural classrooms of vocational college education, it may very well be that certain prejudices are expressed, or even formed, within this setting. This would greatly impact open conversation and truly understanding other people's opinions.

## 2.2   Dutch Citizenship Education

In the Netherlands, a citizenship curriculum has been developed to cope with the challenges that students may encounter in current society. This curriculum is broken down into three themes: democracy, diversity, and globalization. Particularly, the theme of diversity is relevant to this research. The curricular theme of diversity is focused on a set of competencies that are to be developed by the students. Competencies like self-awareness, context, empathy, argumentation, and complexity of relations are critical for diversity education. These competencies give us an understanding of what is expected of students in diversity education curricula. In the following subsection we will dive into how we can best achieve these goals through gameplay.

*Self-awareness*, or critically evaluating one's own actions and thoughts, is key to an open discussion. Benbassat & Baumal [7] discuss six teaching methods for enhancing self-awareness in medical students. Of these, two techniques appear to be applicable to our scenario: *classroom discussions* of emotionally challenging situations, and *small-group discussions* in which personal experiences are shared. In particular, the latter has been used to address prejudices in medicine, by asking questions to determine whether individual students have themselves felt prejudice against particular patients.

Understanding the *social context* of a certain discussion and its stakeholders, is also crucial for it to be open. Luckily, through peer-to-peer communication, people are able to develop implicit social inferences which serve as context [29]. This context encourages conversation, thus promoting social interaction [1]. Thus, in developing context through peer-to-peer interaction, students can learn to engage in conversation with one another, no matter the diversity and differences in their backgrounds.

*Empathy*, or the capacity to recognize the feelings of other people, needs to be present as well. Through group learning experiences, such as cooperative learning, vocational college students can develop empathy [4]. They can then use their developed empathy to inform knowledge and skills obtained in the classroom for conscious action [13].

*Argumentation* is a key competency in citizenship as well. Structuring arguments leads to a better understanding of your own rationale. A common argumentation framework is the Toulmin method, presenting a model in which arguments are broken down into six parts: claim, grounds, warrant, qualifier, rebuttal, and backing [18]. This method has been used in classroom exercises to build argumentation skills [10], and may be applicable to a serious game, should that game want to confront students with arguments that they need to analyze.

Finally, it must be understood by students that relations within a debate are inherently *complex*, especially those within a diverse educational setting. Disproportionate representation within a classroom, in combination with cultural misunderstandings, can strain relationships in multicultural education settings. Dynamic and engaging cooperative learning can encourage vocational college students to interact with one another and forge meaningful relations with each other, regardless of the complexity associated with diversity [14].

## 2.3   Serious Gaming in Social and Educational Contexts

Serious games have long been successfully designed and deployed to change, or at least influence, the mindset of players regarding very disparate and complex topics, from dealing with prejudices around home retrofitting [11] to raising understanding for the complexities of large infrastructure systems [3]. In educational contexts, there has also been increasing research into designing serious games that help students overcome known personal and social hurdles in their student life, including overcoming obstacles to their personal productivity [24], providing early ice-breaking within newly-formed teams [26], and stimulating psychological safety among project colleagues [2].

Starks [28] provides a comprehensive overview of important elements of serious game design. One finding that stands out from her research is that students learn best when the information is presented in a real-world setting and when the information incorporated is of the students' interest. According to Starks, self-awareness seems to be promoted when the player experiences empathy during gameplay.

*Darfur is Dying* [25], a game world situated in Darfur, western Sudan, is an example of an empathy-provoking serious game. In this game, the player plays a refugee who has to find water for their village while not being captured by soldiers. The game attempts to let the player experience life as a Darfuri refugee and, as a result, to bring attention to the war situation by increasing empathy in the player.

Such empathy-provoking methods for game immersion can also ensure player engagement. As James Paul Gee puts it: "Games can show us how to get people to invest in new identities or roles, which can, in turn, become powerful motivators for new and deep learning in classrooms and workplaces" [12]. In addition, Starks [28] also describes two additional ways to create immersion: realistic graphics, and a first-person perspective where players can identify with the character they are playing. Aging simulations may also increase empathy with people who are older than the player [9].

Some studies suggest that video games designed to increase empathy do have positive effects on adolescent players [20]. While there was no evidence of group difference in behavioral change, participants who engaged more with the emotional aspects of gameplay in the empathy training game *Crystals of Kaydor* showed an increase in empathic accuracy. The authors note that this research is still in its early stages; however, they do mention that their results provide evidence that empathy-related brain functions can be improved in adolescents by using game mechanics that rely on empathy, such as perspective taking and emotional regulation. Additional research is needed to determine whether this kind of empathy training could lead to improvements in empathic behavior.

Belman & Flanagan [6] formulated four design principles for designing games to foster empathy. The first principle describes how players usually only empathize when they make an effort to do so at the beginning of the game - otherwise, people play "unempathically". The second principle recommends giving players recommendations about how their actions affect the issues in the game. The third principle describes how short bursts of emotional empathy work well if the desired outcome of playing the game does not require major shifts in the player's beliefs. Lastly, the fourth principle states that it is beneficial to put emphasis on points of similarity between the player and the people who the player is supposed to empathise with.

Serious games have also been used within a citizenship curriculum. The serious game *TimeMesh* [5], for example, is a collaborative multiplayer game designed to teach students about significant events in Portuguese history. The game has a non-linear storyline, where players time travel to different periods in history to influence historic events and change the 'present reality'. Lorenzini et al. created *LawVille* [23], a serious game designed to teach citizenship topics, primarily the Italian constitution and lawmaking process, to secondary school students. Like *TimeMesh*, *LawVille* contains collaborative aspects in which players may communicate with each other while playing the game, although there is no interaction within the game world itself.

## 3   Game Design

The goal of promoting open conversation around sensitive topics guided the design of *Diermocratie*. In order to achieve this goal, many game choices that were taken are directed towards avoiding groupthink and mitigating the influence of players' predispositions.

### 3.1   Game Synopsis

In an authoritarian farm regime, students play as different kinds of livestock that are presented with a dilemma imposed by the ruling farmers. The players get a small briefing about the dilemma and their species' role in that dilemma. Subsequently, they may get to know the other species' perspectives, by communicating with other players. Eventually, they will have to democratically decide on a solution to resolve the issue. In these scenarios, players have to role-play with an assigned opinion, which otherwise might not normally be theirs. Through player-to-player communication, a player's opinion has the possibility of changing. After the final democratic vote, a debriefing session revisits the process and relates the events during the game to a real-world scenario.

This synopsis fits into the SPP framework for interactive digital narratives defined by Koenitz [19], which divides digital narratives into three parts: System, Process and Product. The *system* contains a collection of potential narratives, also known as proto-stories. In our case, one of such narratives is chosen by the teacher to match the topic of the current lecture. The *process* involves the players interacting with the system, in this case, the students participating in the anonymous debate on the dilemma that affects the farm and its population. During the process, the player will need to consider which strategies to use while interacting with the other animals on the farm, as their ability to persuade others will help determine the outcome of the story. According to Koenitz, this players' need to consider their actions and the level of control they have on the narrative is a crucial component to an interactive digital narrative. Finally, the *product* is the instantiated narrative: which solution to the dilemma will the students pick? After the final decision has been made, the debriefing session aims to explore the process and product further, analyzing why the narrative has played out the way it did, giving the students a means to reflect on the actions of themselves and their peers.

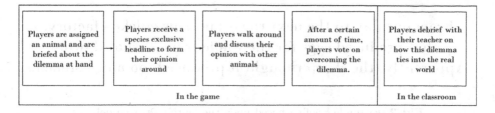

**Fig. 1.** Illustration of the main game loop.

## 3.2  Game Mechanics

The above synopsis, together with the game loop of Fig. 1, reveal the more tangible ways in which the game is perceived by the players. However, below the surface there are some overarching mechanics that help this game reach its intended goals. In the following section we go into the metaphorical, motivational, and concluding aspects of our game. As a visual aid, we also provide a trailer[1] of *Diermocratie* sample gameplay (in Dutch).

**The Metaphor.** The key element in *Diermocratie* is the metaphor. Through the use of a metaphor, players are able to look at, and discuss, a given dilemma without any predispositions holding them back. The metaphor must still be relatable, though, as this will help the players get into character. The metaphor manifests itself in the game in multiple different ways: the setting, the character assignment, the briefing, and the headlines.

The game takes place in a farm setting, with the playable characters being farm animals. This environment was chosen because it is easy to relate to for almost anyone, as it creates an amenable role-playing atmosphere. This role-playing is necessary to stimulate empathy among the students, which is one of the citizenship competencies. A farm setting is also easier to translate dilemmas into, as most people are already familiar with anthropomorphizing animals. Furthermore, in assigning players to different animal groups, a 'tribe mentality' is induced, as players connect to their animal and its specific group, thus fueling the notion that multiple and diverse perspectives exist within a society.

The briefing is the most prominent manifestation of the metaphor. Mainly, the briefing sets the scene with game rules and potential game outcomes, and it also provides players with a short description of their assigned animal and its viewpoints. The briefing translates an existing societal dilemma or debate into a farm and animal context. With such a briefing, player immersion can be more easily and quickly facilitated. It also enables the player to understand the true context of the dilemma, which links to the key competencies of citizenship as well. Through the briefing, the translated societal concern should be unrecognizable as the specific dilemma on its own, however it should still be recognizable during the classroom debriefing session through guided discussion. An example

---

[1] https://surfdrive.surf.nl/files/index.php/s/imRlGKFsRfLilSZ.

> From one day to the next the brand new chicken factory,
> that produced eggs for the whole farm, is shut down.
> Apparently, the sheep thought it produced too much stench.

**Fig. 2.** Example briefing based upon the Dutch nitrogen debate.

briefing can be seen in Fig. 2. The briefing wording itself is not recognizable as the Dutch nitrogen debate, however the link to farmers being the chickens and environmentalists being the sheep can easily be made.

An important implementation aspect of our use of the metaphor is the anonymity afforded by a digital game. While many of the gameplay elements described could translate to a physical tabletop game, role-playing would become more difficult as there would be a clear relation between actual players and roles. Since *Diermocratie* is intended to be played among classmates, anonymizing players by giving them a virtual avatar both minimizes the effect of pre-existing relationships and enhances players' immersion into the game, improving the role-playing quality.

**Motivational Mechanics.** Next to creating an environment in which role-playing is encouraged, the players must also be motivated to actually play the game as intended. To do this, several motivational mechanics have been implemented, including: headlines, communication, time, and voting.

Each animal group receives a potentially biased headline from their local news source with species-exclusive coverage about the posed dilemma, as shown in Fig. 3. The headlines motivate the players to form a specific opinion based on their assigned species and on the news they have been provided. The headlines will often imply consequences for said species, and they encourage the players to move around the game world, and to communicate with players of other species, using a chat function, in order to spread their viewpoints and influence the final

| **Chicken News** | **Sheepy Times** |
| --- | --- |
| Sensitive sheep cause our factory to close. Huge layoffs imminent. | Factory closed! We can finally graze outside again without stuffing our noses with wool. |

**Fig. 3.** Example species exclusive headlines that are paired with the briefing from Fig. 2.

vote. The headlines and the consequent communication around them, facilitate multiple diverse perspectives and conversation surrounding a polarizing topic. It also connects to the *argumentation* competency of citizenship. After a set time for gameplay, the final vote is held, requiring the players to act immediately as time is a limited resource. With the final vote and the subsequent outcome announcement, the players are informed of the results of their discussion. The actual tally is not that important, as the game revolves mostly about getting an understanding of the democratic process as a whole. The results can, however, be used as input to the final debriefing between teacher and students.

**Debriefing the Students.** Following gameplay, students engage in an instructor-lead debriefing session where they have the opportunity to exchange their thoughts and experiences about the game session. Through this debriefing, students are particularly encouraged to translate game scenarios into real-world situations. In exploring the parallels between the metaphorical game scenarios and real life, discussion is encouraged about the students' experiences with polarizing topics and the diverse opinions of others. In this debriefing, self-awareness amongst students should be fostered, and the complexity of relations explored.

### 3.3 Implementation Aspects

In implementing this game, a communicative multi-player approach has been chosen. It deploys a server for handling all players in a session, and transparently manages all chat functionality for player-to-player communication, easily ensuring that players' diverse perspectives can be exchanged and explored. As more players participate in the game, more conversation can emerge. Additionally, because all chat content is made visible to everybody in the game world, every player is able to see the opinions, questions and objections stated by all others. As a result, pursuing further conversation is strongly stimulated.

## 4  Game Evaluation

### 4.1  Method

In order to evaluate the extent to which the game was effective in its purpose to promote an open conversation about difficult topics, multiple play sessions were held with vocational college classes of approximately 20 students each. Due to current societal constraints, play sessions varied between taking place fully online, entirely on location or in a half-and-half setting. During each session, students were given a short presentation to get familiar with the functionality of the game. After this brief introduction, the students were asked to play the game.

In order to give students an opportunity to debrief and voice their experiences and concerns, after each playing round they were divided into smaller focus groups of approximately five students, in which their views could be further discussed with their instructor. Because of the subjective nature of the topic, conversation was initially centered around evaluative topics of game concept, engagement, goal achievement and how comfortable they felt in expressing their opinions. Eventually, debriefing conversation was directed towards exploring parallel real-world dilemmas, as students were encouraged to discuss how elements of the game dilemma transpire in society. In exploring parallels between the game world and the real world, students were led by instructors in discussion about other sensitive and societal relevant topics.

Finally, to assess the impact of this prototype game and subsequent debriefing on the perceptions of the students, they were asked to fill out a survey.

### 4.2    Results and Discussion

It was noticeable that students were more involved in the in-person sessions than when they played online. Debriefing sessions were also more actively attended, allowing for better discussion on societal issues to match the game purpose. The survey was filled in by a total of 60 students.

Regarding the communication among players (see Fig. 4), about half of the players report they were motivated to talk to other players, as can be seen in Fig. 4a. That said, Fig. 4b indicates that 45% of the players talked to less than 2 people, which is a clear concern. During the debriefing sessions it came forward that excessive spamming was one of the major reasons players were less motivated to talk to each other. Because of this, especially dyslexic people were having a hard time to keep up with the conversation. Measures should be taken to prevent spamming and improve the UI so the chat is more organized, for example by displaying the chat in a sidebar. With these improvements in

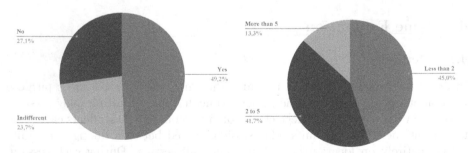

(a) Were you motivated to talk to other players?    (b) How many players have you talked to?

**Fig. 4.** Survey results regarding player communication (N = 60)

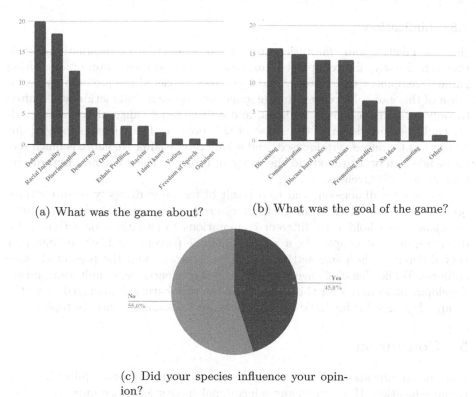

(a) What was the game about?       (b) What was the goal of the game?

(c) Did your species influence your opinion?

**Fig. 5.** Survey results regarding game mechanics, topic and purpose (N = 60)

mind, we believe it is perfectly achievable to have each player talk to at least two people.

Although not every student took the game seriously, the topic and purpose of the game seem to have been clear for the large majority (see Fig. 5). Questions like "What was the game about?", Fig. 5a, were mostly answered with mentions to debates (20), racial inequality (18), and discrimination (12). Likewise, students' perception of the goal of the game was to practice discussions (16), improving communication between people (15), facilitate talking about harder topics (14), and talking about and listening to others' opinions (14) (see Fig. 5b). These are quite promising results, since they show that the purpose of the game is clearly conveyed, even when gameplay was not optimally experienced.

Finally, 45% of the participants reported that their own species had an effect on their opinion, indicating that a considerable amount of people were influenced by the role-playing aspect of the game, as shown in Fig. 5c.

## 4.3  Limitations

Here we identify some limitations present in conducting the evaluation of this research. Firstly, limited playtesting sessions and student interaction during game development undoubtedly and inevitably impacted the preliminary evaluation of this game. Moreover, during game development, interaction was limited to only a few educational facilities, and only a small range of course materials could be considered in the scope of this project. The current scope of this research is therefore very focused, and a long term evaluative effort is much recommended, in order to extend the range of topics in the game and improve its impact and effectiveness.

On another dimension, and as a result of the large diversity of subcultures present, we realized that the metaphors used in the game, including *animal metaphors*, can hold very different connotations to situations or activities for diverse groups of people. As a result, different players are likely to interpret very differently the game setting, specific characters, and the presented game scenario. While this challenge was currently experienced as a limitation, future development scenarios for this game could use this feature, if managed correctly, as an advantage for fueling diversity of perspectives about sensitive topics.

## 5  Conclusion

Citizenship education is increasingly regarded as an important pillar in vocational education. However, many educational institutions face important challenges to adapt to modern demands in this domain.

We designed and developed *Diermocratie*, an in-classroom game aimed at promoting open conversations within diverse classes among vocational college students. The game empowers students to grow in diversity-related competences, including self-awareness, empathy and argumentation. By means of role-playing metaphors, players successfully explore their predispositions, becoming aware of each other's perspectives. This progress is further supported by a debriefing session, led by an instructor. As a result of a preliminary evaluation, we have concluded that the game motivated students to discuss with their colleagues different perspectives on a complex scenario.

Compared to other serious games around citizenship topics, as e.g. *TimeMesh* [5] and *LawVille* [23], *Diermocratie* stands out in both the flexibility for potential discussion topics and the crucial role of player interaction in achieving the game goals. *Diermocratie* was not designed to teach a fact-based curriculum, but rather to promote open conversations around sensitive topics. Conversations between players, therefore, take a much more central role, and shape the outcome of the story rather than being simply a tool for players to progress through a story.

We believe that *Diermocratie* provides a valuable and effective assistance to vocational college instructors in challenging citizenship education topics. We therefore expect the game to continue being further developed, extended with carefully designed scenarios for more specific topics, and rolled out in more educational institutions.

**Acknowledgments.** We thank Anouck Wolf and her team at Critical Mass for the inspiring discussions and feedback throughout this project.

# References

1. Abowd, G.D., Dey, A.K., Brown, P.J., Davies, N., Smith, M., Steggles, P.: Towards a better understanding of context and context-awareness. In: Gellersen, H.-W. (ed.) HUC 1999. LNCS, vol. 1707, pp. 304–307. Springer, Heidelberg (1999). https://doi.org/10.1007/3-540-48157-5_29
2. Alaka, S., Cunha, M.L., Vermeer, J., Salamon, N.Z., Balint, J.T., Bidarra, R.: Stimulating ideation in new teams with the mobile game Grapplenauts. Int. J. Serious Games **6**(4), 87–101 (2019)
3. Alderliesten, D., Valečkaitė, K., Salamon, N.Z., Timothy Balint, J., Bidarra, R.: MainTrain: a serious game on the complexities of rail maintenance. In: Gentile, M., Allegra, M., Söbke, H. (eds.) GALA 2018. LNCS, vol. 11385, pp. 82–89. Springer, Cham (2019). https://doi.org/10.1007/978-3-030-11548-7_8
4. Aronson, E.: Building empathy, compassion, and achievement in the jigsaw classroom. In: Improving Academic Achievement, pp. 209–225. Elsevier (2002)
5. Baptista, R., Carvalho, C.V.d.: TimeMesh - a serious game for European citizenship. EAI Endorsed Trans. Game-Based Learn. **1**(1), e2 (2013). https://doi.org/10.4108/trans.gbl.01-06.2013.e2
6. Belman, J., Flanagan, M.: Designing games to foster empathy. Int. J. Cogn. Technol. **15**(1), 11 (2010)
7. Benbassat, J., Baumal, R.: Enhancing self-awareness in medical students: an overview of teaching approaches. Acad. Med. **80**(2), 156–161 (2005)
8. Brandt, M.J., Crawford, J.T.: Worldview conflict and prejudice. In: Advances in Experimental Social Psychology, vol. 61, pp. 1–66. Elsevier (2020)
9. Chen, A.M., Kiersma, M.E., Yehle, K.S., Plake, K.S.: Impact of the geriatric medication game® on nursing students' empathy and attitudes toward older adults. Nurse Educ. Today **35**(1), 38–43 (2015)
10. Dawson, V.M., Venville, G.: Teaching strategies for developing students' argumentation skills about socioscientific issues in high school genetics. Res. Sci. Educ. **40**(2), 133–148 (2010). https://doi.org/10.1007/s11165-008-9104-y
11. Dikken, O., et al.: A serious game for changing mindsets about loans for home retrofitting. In: Marfisi-Schottman, I., Bellotti, F., Hamon, L., Klemke, R. (eds.) GALA 2020. LNCS, vol. 12517, pp. 347–361. Springer, Cham (2020). https://doi.org/10.1007/978-3-030-63464-3_33
12. Gee, J.P.: What video games have to teach us about learning and literacy. Comput. Entertain. (CIE) **1**(1), 20–20 (2003)
13. Gerdes, K.E., Segal, E.A., Jackson, K.F., Mullins, J.L.: Teaching empathy: a framework rooted in social cognitive neuroscience and social justice. J. Soc. Work Educ. **47**(1), 109–131 (2011)
14. Irvine, J.J.: Complex relationships between multicultural education and special education: an African American perspective. J. Teach. Educ. **63**(4), 268–274 (2012)
15. Janis, I.L.: Groupthink. IEEE Eng. Manag. Rev. **36**(1), 36 (2008)
16. Johnson, S.D., Weaver, R.L., II., et al.: Groupthink and the classroom: changing familiar patterns to encourage critical thought. J. Instr. Psychol. **19**(2), 99 (1992)
17. Kello, K.: Sensitive and controversial issues in the classroom: teaching history in a divided society. Teach. Teach. **22**(1), 35–53 (2016)

18. Kneupper, C.W.: Teaching argument: an introduction to the toulmin model. Coll. Compos. Commun. **29**(3), 237–241 (1978)

19. Koenitz, H.: Towards a theoretical framework for interactive digital narrative. In: Aylett, R., Lim, M.Y., Louchart, S., Petta, P., Riedl, M. (eds.) ICIDS 2010. LNCS, vol. 6432, pp. 176–185. Springer, Heidelberg (2010). https://doi.org/10.1007/978-3-642-16638-9_22

20. Kral, T.R., et al.: Neural correlates of video game empathy training in adolescents: a randomized trial. npj Sci. Learn. **3**(1), 1–10 (2018)

21. Leeman, Y., Nieveen, N., de Beer, F., Van der Steen, J.: Teachers as curriculum-makers: the case of citizenship education in Dutch schools. Curric. J. **31**(3), 495–516 (2020)

22. Leeman, Y., Pels, T.: Citizenship education in the Dutch multiethnic context. Eur. Educ. **38**(2), 64–75 (2006)

23. Lorenzini, C., Brondi, R., Carrozzino, M., Nistico, M., Evangelista, C., Tecchia, F.: LawVille: a collaborative serious game for citizenship education. In: 2014 6th International Conference on Games and Virtual Worlds for Serious Applications (VS-GAMES). IEEE, September 2014. https://doi.org/10.1109/VS-Games.2014.7012163

24. Raateland, W., et al.: A serious game for students to acquire productivity habits. In: Marfisi-Schottman, I., Bellotti, F., Hamon, L., Klemke, R. (eds.) GALA 2020. LNCS, vol. 12517, pp. 335–346. Springer, Cham (2020). https://doi.org/10.1007/978-3-030-63464-3_32

25. Ruiz, S.: Take action games: Darfur is dying. https://susanaruiz.org/takeactiongames-darfurisdying

26. Sjölund, A., et al.: Misusing mobile phones to break the ice: the tabletop game Maze Maestro. In: Proceedings of FDG 2020 - International Conference on the Foundations of Digital Games (2020)

27. Spohr, D.: Fake news and ideological polarization: filter bubbles and selective exposure on social media. Bus. Inf. Rev. **34**(3), 150–160 (2017)

28. Starks, K.: Cognitive behavioral game design: a unified model for designing serious games. Front. Psychol. **5**, 28 (2014)

29. Uleman, J.S., Adil Saribay, S., Gonzalez, C.M.: Spontaneous inferences, implicit impressions, and implicit theories. Annu. Rev. Psychol. **59**, 329–360 (2008)

# Digital Narrative and Temporality

Serge Bouchardon[1](✉) and Erika Fülöp[2]

[1] Université de Technologie de Compiègne, Compiègne, France
serge.bouchardon@utc.fr
[2] Lancaster University, Lancaster, UK
e.fulop@lancaster.ac.uk

According to Paul Ricoeur (1984), "Time becomes human to the extent that it is articulated through a narrative mode, and narrative attains its full meaning when it becomes a condition of temporal existence". From this perspective, narrative is our principal tool for situating ourselves in time—and for experiencing time within ourselves. The digital, on the other hand, may be characterized as "a tool for the phenomenal deconstruction of temporality" (Bachimont 2014). This is reflected in its two main tendencies: that of real time calculation, conveying the impression of immediacy, and that of universality of access, conveying the impression of availability. The digital could thus lead to constant present, without any impression of the passage of time. What happens then when we exploit the particularities of digital technology to tell a story? What kind of temporal experiences are constructed by new forms of digital narrative, and how are they constructed? Reciprocally, what new narrative forms, or even new concepts of narrative, do these new temporal experiences provided by digital technology offer to us? Through the example of three types of digital stories, including a smartfiction based on notifications, a web narrative based on real-time data flow, and the widely used social media feature of *stories*, this paper raises the question of the diverging potentialities of the relationship between the digital, temporality, and narrative.

## 1 Narrative Games for the Smartphone Built Around Notifications

Narrative can help to (re)construct in a coherent manner the incoherence of the information flow, particularly manifest through smartphone notifications. Our first example looks at how certain digital narratives stage this flow of what is happening in order to render it coherent. On mobile application distribution platforms (Google Play and App Store), one can find more and more interactive narratives for smartphones, also called *smartfictions* (Picard 2021). These fictions rely on ordinary daily practices on a smartphone, realtime chats, for instance, but also notifications. *Bury me, my Love* (*Enterre-moi, mon* amour 2017, http://enterremoimonamour.arte.tv/) is a narrative game in which the reader incarnates the character of Majd, the husband of Nour, a Syrian woman attempting to reach Europe. The reader exchanges messages with Nour via an instant messaging platform. The communications take place in pseudo real time: if Nour must accomplish an action which is supposed to take her several hours, the reader will not be able to contact her during this time lapse. When she returns, a notification will inform the reader that she is available again. The piece plays with temporality through the intrusion of the reader's real time, which is also the fictional character's.

© Springer Nature Switzerland AG 2021
A. Mitchell and M. Vosmeer (Eds.): ICIDS 2021, LNCS 13138, pp. 307–311, 2021.
https://doi.org/10.1007/978-3-030-92300-6_29

Through the notifications, smartfictions thus create the impression of a co-presence. As readers of, or actors in a smartfiction, when we make a choice, our actions in a way render a fictional character present in our own reality. Moreover, this notion of presence is further reinforced when we respond to a character's solicitation via a notification. In this way we invite the other's temporality (as well as that of the fiction) to interact with our own. The temporality of the fictional character (and of events) coincides with the reader's temporality via the notifications, so that the reader interiorizes the duration of the story. This interplay relies on the fact that the smartphone is the device which we now use for an increasing portion of our communications. If this characteristic lends a reality effect to a fictional narrative, we also realize, due to the fiction's notifications that have a blurring effect on our own reality, that the smartphone is itself in some ways a derealization medium: it builds a fictional layer which is external to the *real* world (Bouchardon 2019). Thanks to such fictional works, we come to understand that the smartphone has already become a medium for fiction (and for narration), bringing a new relationship with temporality as well as with fiction and narrative.

## 2   Narratives Built Around Real Time Data Flows

If the digital manifests itself through an increasing overflow of data, it produces this data flow through a calculatory logic, whereby time is no longer present as a horizon of expectation and anticipation, as we are dealing with results based on the world understood as input data, rather than occurrences. Is it possible to re-establish a temporal experience, notably the power of expectation, based on these calculated results? Our second example is a narrative based on real time data flow. The strongest limit imposed on a narrative by real time data flow is that the causality of events is replaced by the sequentiality of real events (Chambefort 2020). Yet according to consensual definitions (Schmid 2005; Revaz 2009), the causal link between events is a *sine qua non* condition for narrativity, and may even be considered as its constitutive feature. A simple sequence of events or data cannot therefore become a narrative without the intervention of a consciousness and ensuing representation creating a link between them. At the same time, the technical specificity embodied by reliance on a real time data flow injects life's contingencies into the narrative (Chambefort 2020).

Françoise Chambefort's *Lucette, gare de Clichy* (2017 http://fchambef.fr/lucette/int ro.php) is a web narrative connected to real time through data from the Paris region rail network. The interface is like a triptych. On the left, train times are displayed (trains may be late, or cancelled), in the middle is a succession of photographs of Lucette, the fictional character, and on the right, we can access her stream of thoughts. The viewer's attention oscillates between the real and fictional poles. If they feel empathy for the character, they will live an exceptional temporal experience and the vulnerability of an old person who has little control over her life (Chambefort 2020). The train schedule's calculated time becomes existential time, a waiting period that becomes full of meaning. The fact that this creation is not interactive reinforces the temporal experience. The author emphasizes the non-interactivity of her creation, as if to offer greater incitation to the user to pay more attention to old people suffering from loneliness in the physical world. Although *Lucette, gare de Clichy* is of course built around the calculated time of a real time data flow, it is at the same time a "pure experience of time", based on the temporal experience of the fictional character (Chambefort 2020). Chambefort refers to this work as a "narrative". If we can speak of a narrative, it is mainly thanks to the words attributed to Lucette and the unifying force of her perspective. Yet *Lucette* is no doubt situated at the frontier of what constitutes a narrative, just like *Bury me, my love*. The latter can indeed be categorized as a "narrative game". *Lucette* raises the question as to how far we can stretch digital narratives before they cease to be narratives, and whether database narratives may be able to help us deal with the digital data flows we are constantly exposed to, or even to foster a different relationship with them and better situate them in time.

## 3 From Storytelling to Storyshowing: The *Stories* on Social Networks

Our third case study concerns the *story*[1] feature, in particular on *Facebook* and *Instagram*. This feature allows users to display a sequence of one or more 15 s *stories* available for 24 h[2], which we could refer to as the viewer's "storyline". It is possible to create sequences of photos, videos, texts, etc., but they will always be displayed as a collection of fragments rather than a unique continuous video sequence. Each *story* must not only adhere to strong temporal (and therefore formal) constraints, but also conform to inclusion in a chain of *stories* created by algorithms. Facebook presents *stories* as "a visual medium which is ideal for sharing authentic *moments*"[3], explicitly and deliberately destined to remain fragments. The *story* thus creates a continuous succession of fragmented sequences, which, once activated, displays a non-stop chain of *stories* until the user interrupts it – unlike the newsfeed, which requires the user to repeat an interactive swiping gesture. At the same time, the integration of these fragments in the chain of *stories* of a network of friends contributes to building an artificial continuity between the *stories* of various people without any causal link among them. Rather than individuals' "narrative identity,"[4] it is the digital identity *of a network* that emerges.

Rather than inviting to tell actual stories, Facebook's official recommendations insist on combining visual attractiveness with speed to capture the viewer's attention. According to classical and cognitive narratological theories[5], narratives induce emotions and activate other cognitive functions by presenting human experiences. This capacity of the narrative is directly linked to the fact that it establishes temporal and causal links.

---

[1] We will be using the italics here to distinguish the social media feature from the traditional meaning of "story".

[2] The programmed disappearance can be avoided on Instagram by highlighting a story, while Facebook conserves archives which are accessible only to the publication's author.

[3] See the guidelines for companies: https://www.facebook.com/business/help/304846896685 564?id=2331035843782460

[4] Mayer and Bouchardon (2020) put forward the hypothesis of a "poetic identity" built around a collection of snapshots, moments and fugacious impressions which, reinforced by social media, would coexist alongside Ricoeur's "narrative identity".

[5] See Ricoeur's theory, already quoted here, as well as the works of Monika Fludernik (2009), David Herman (2013), Nancy Easterlin (2012) and Lisa Zunshine (2006), among others.

Here we witness a very different logic, appealing to the senses to provoke simple and immediate emotional response. Not only does the *story* fail to impose any criteria for narrativity, narrativity even seems to be an obstacle to the *stories'* immediate efficacy.

## 4 Further Questions

Our first two examples show that interactivity and dataflows raise questions around temporality, intertwined with the question of fictionality[6]. If the classical narrative aims for and encourages *immersion* through movement from real space-time towards fictional space-time, the new narrative forms allow the *emergence* of fictional space-time in real space-time, via a movement that not only crosses, but also deconstructs frontiers.

Our third example invites us to rethink our conception of narrative as it is defined by classical and post-classical narratology, adopting the term and using it to designate entirely different phenomena and practices. This radical otherness also expresses itself through the relation to time: the temporality imposed by the feature, that of the content it proposes, and that of the users. The function of these *stories* is no longer to establish temporal or causal links between events, but simply to include them in what could be referred to as "the life of the network(s)". In 1984, Ricoeur observed that "new narrative forms, which we do not yet know how to name, are already being born, which will bear witness to the fact that the narrative function can still be metamorphosed, but not so as to die". The question today is how far this metamorphosis can go, and how far we can push the limits of narrative without it losing its traditional use. To what extent do our consciousness and thinking depend on narratives, and how prepared are we to consider alternative modes of functioning?[7] We may not be facing a total and definitive disappearance of narratives, of course, but perhaps a relativisation of their place in our culture, history and theoretical constructions, and a multiplication of modes of representing and performing time.

## References

Bachimont, B.: Availability and the transformation of objects into heritage: digital technology and the passing of time. In: Dufrêne, B. (ed.) Heritage and Digital Humanities: How Should Training Practices Evolve?, pp. 49–70. LIT, Berlin (2014)

Bouchardon, S.: Mind the gap! 10 gaps for digital literature?", Electronic Book Review (2019). http://electronicbookreview.com/essay/mind-the-gap-10-gaps-for-digital-literature/

Chambefort, F.: Lucette, gare de Clichy (2017). http://fchambef.fr/lucette/

Chambefort, F.: Sortir de l'écran : Lucette, Gare de Clichy. In: Gervais, B., Marcotte, S. (eds.) Attention à la marche ! Penser la littérature électronique en culture numérique. Montréal: Les Presses de l'Écureuil - ALN/NT2, pp. 327–338 (2020). ISBN 979-10-384-0004-7

Easterlin, N.: A Biocultural Approach to Literary Theory and Interpretation. Johns Hopkins UP, Baltimore (2012)

Fludernik, M.: An Introduction to Narratology. Routledge, Londres (2009)

---

[6] On this subject see Fülöp (2021).

[7] Galen Strawson, in a well-known article (2008), already suggests that "There are deeply non-Narrative people and there are good ways to live that are deeply non-Narrative".

Fülöp, E.: Virtual mirrors: reflexivity in digital literature. In: Fülöp, E. (ed.) In collaboration with Priest, G. and Saint-Gelais, R., Fictionality, Factuality, and Reflexivity across Discourses and Media, pp. 229–254. De Gruyter, Berlin (2021)

Herman, D.: Storytelling and the Sciences of Mind. MIT, Cambridge (2013)

Mayer, A., Bouchardon, S.: The digital subject: from narrative identity to poetic identity? Electronic Book Review, May 2020. https://electronicbookreview.com/essay/the-digital-subject-from-narrative-identity-to-poetic-identity/

Picard, M.: La smartfiction, quand l'environnement numérique fictionnel s'hybride à l'environnement numérique personnel. XXIIème congrès de la SFSIC (2021). https://sfsic2020.sciencesconf.org/333005

Revaz, F.: Introduction à la narratologie. Action et narration. De Boeck, Brussels (2009)

Ricœur, P.: Time and Narrative, vol. 1. University of Chicago Press, Chicago (1984)

Schmid, W.: Elemente der Narratologie. de Gruyter, Berlin (2005)

Strawson, G.: Against narrativity. In: Real Materialism and Other Essays. Clarendon Press, Oxford (2008)

The Pixel Hunt, Figs, Arte France (2017). Enterre-moi, mon amour. http://enterremoimonamour.arte.tv/

Zunshine, L.: Why We Read Fiction? Ohio UP, Columbus (2006)

# "You Write Your Own Story": Design Implications for an Interactive Narrative Authoring Tool to Support Reflection for Mental Health in College Students

Sarah Anne Brown[1,2](✉) ⓘ and Sharon Lynn Chu[1,2] ⓘ

[1] University of Florida, Gainesville, FL 32611, USA
sarah.brown@ufl.edu
[2] Embodied Learning and Experience (ELX) Lab, Gainesville, USA
https://elxlab.cise.ufl.edu/

**Abstract.** Mental health therapy often involves the reflection and reconstruction of one's life narrative. However, few, if any existing digital interventions support a narrative-oriented therapeutic reflective process. College students may benefit from a digital support for mental health therapy, as they often need accessible, self-help ways for mental health support and are at a stage of life when their narratives are in flux. We propose the use of interactive story authoring to facilitate the process of reflection in college students to support their mental health, as it could guide them in independently externalizing and restructuring their life narratives, which are inherently non-linear. We conducted an interview study with college students and college counselors, and extracted themes detailing their experiences in order to extract aims and implications for the design of a life narrative authoring tool for mental health.

**Keywords:** Interactive story authoring · Authoring tools · Life reflection · Therapy · Mental health · College students

## 1 Introduction

The use of narrative and storytelling in mental health therapeutic practice has been widely documented [1,10–12,15,19,20,22,23,29]. Across techniques used in mental health therapy, the restructuring or forming of new narratives with a patient over time is a common theme. One way we engage or restructure our personal narratives both on our own and in the context of therapy is through self-reflection, a term we use here to describe any process in which an individual reviews their life. However, digital self-help tools for mental health therapy often lack the guidance of a therapist found in a formal therapeutic setting.

For populations such as college students, digital self-help tools for mental health therapy can be enormously useful since they often face high levels of anxiety and depression, demand for mental health services continues to outpace

A. Mitchell and M. Vosmeer (Eds.): ICIDS 2021, LNCS 13138, pp. 312–321, 2021.
https://doi.org/10.1007/978-3-030-92300-6_30

supply, and they are also familiar with technology [16–18]. The challenge we perceive thus is: how do we provide a digital intervention for college students which facilitates the narrative process found in mental health therapy through a guided reflection they can perform on their own?

Our proposed approach is the design of an interactive story authoring tool made explicitly to support the reflective process with the support and guidance found in mental health therapy. The primary aim of interactive story authoring tools is to provide authors the ability to construct and revise non-linear narratives. This is also necessary in the narrative processes of therapy and reflection, given that our life narratives are non-linear in the way they branch out into different future possibilities. This is particularly applicable to college students who are at a stage of their lives where their personal narratives are in a natural state of flux, due to a number of stressful life changes [14, 28].

Many authoring tools for interactive narratives exist, but they naturally tend to focus on the final creative output. None are designed to support the process of reflection on one's life narrative for mental health support. To design such authoring tools for college students, we must first understand the nature of how students engage with their life narratives, and how counselors work with students to guide their narratives with the goal of improving mental health. This paper presents findings from a series of interviews that we conducted to fulfill that purpose. From these findings, we derived design implications for an interactive story authoring tool for reflection for mental health. Thus, the goals of our study were as follows: (i) to understand how college students guide their own personal narratives through reflection and maintain their mental health over time; (ii) to understand how counselors who treat college students form narratives with their patients to maintain their care between sessions, and how they guide those narratives over time; and (iii) to derive design aims for an interactive story authoring tool to facilitate reflection on college students' narratives to support their mental health. We first summarize relevant background and related work, followed by a description of our chosen methodology, a summary of the interview study we conducted, and our subsequent analysis. The findings we present focus on design aims and implications extracted from our analysis.

## 2  Background and Related Work

In the use of storytelling or narrative in therapy, there seems to be two broad camps of methodology: practices which involve an interaction with the patient's story [1, 10, 19], and practices which involve stories that are told *to* the patient, often children [10, 12, 15, 22, 23, 29]. We focus on the former, an approach which relies heavily on theories such as Bruner's, who proposes that we understand, communicate with each other, and experience the world through the lens of narrative, and indeed construct our reality via narrative [3, 4]. Of the existing therapeutic techniques which involve the patient's personal narrative, narrative therapy is perhaps the most relevant. Butler et al. [5] provide a clear overview of the general steps undertaken in narrative therapy, most notably including the process of restorying. In restorying, the patient assigns meaning to unique outcomes discovered in therapy, which are "any thought, behavior, feeling, or event that contradicts or is at odds with the dominant story" [5]. With methods like this, narrative therapy serves to re-author a personal narrative that is in conflict with the patient's lived experience [6]. Similarly, in narrative medicine, physicians guide their patients' narratives surrounding their illness or condition into ones of healing [25].

Interactive story authoring tools scaffold the process of authoring complex, non-linear narratives through a specially designed interface. We identified a few examples of digital story authoring for mental health in the literature, though these systems do not necessarily qualify as interactive (i.e. non-linear) authoring tools. My Mobile Story is an application which allows patients to author their experiences or bring digital artifacts to therapy sessions on their phone [21]. The authors acknowledge the restructuring of personal narrative and identity found in narrative therapy and psychotherapy, however their intervention serves as a means of communication between the therapist and their patient. Another example is the 3MR_2 system [27], which allows patients to reconstruct memories across multiple modalities, including a timeline overview. This intervention features a virtual agent which assists in exposure to traumatic events through a system of questions which facilitate memory recollection. Lastly, Chittaro and Sioni use the term *existential video games* to describe games that encourage reflection on the topics of death, freedom, isolation, or meaninglessness [9]. Their work does not seek to facilitate reflection, but rather incites it through thoughtful design of the environment, interactions, and the dialogue of a virtual agent.

We found one example of an interactive story authoring tool used to support mental health, although not explicitly designed for it. Twine has been explored as a means to cathartic story authoring through a series of case studies [26]. The authors note the non-linear nature of stories in writing therapy, and their description of the benefits of non-linear authoring resembles the process of narrative reconstruction found in therapy and reflection. While interactive story authoring was studied here in a therapeutic context, it was explored by examining authors who experienced catharsis and benefits to their mental health by using Twine outside of a formal therapy setting. The authors explain the potential to explore existing non-linear authoring platforms such as Twine as tools in existing writing therapy practice, rather than as a standalone technology designed explicitly to support therapeutic narrative restructuring and reflection. However, their work gives our proposed approach promise, and we aim to further explore this area by investigating how we may design an authoring tool that actively facilitates the process of life reflection, with a target population of college students.

## 3   Methodology

Our goals were to understand how college students and counselors interact with student personal narratives and work to improve their mental health, in order to derive aims for the design of an authoring tool to facilitate therapeutic reflection in college students. We seek to better understand college students in this context, as such a tool should align closely with their experiences, to allow for ease of adapting said tool into their routine, as well account for unique struggles of this population. Wielding the grounded theory method, we conducted analysis between rounds of data collection to build an understanding of student experiences, and to assess the need to revise interview questions or collect additional data. Open-ended interviews with college students were our primary data source, and we conducted analysis after every 2 to 3 participants. Supplemental interviews were also conducted with college counselors, in order to understand from a professional standpoint how care is provided to this population and how counselors interact with students' personal narratives. The themes and questions for both sets of interviews were derived from the first two goals of our study.

## 4 Study Details

The study consisted of open-ended interviews with college students and college counselors, lasting a maximum of one hour. We conducted and recorded these interviews remotely over Zoom, and transcribed them for analysis. Students were recruited via word of mouth and through our department's SONA recruitment system, which allowed students to participate in our study for extra credit. Fourteen students in total participated in our study: 10 male, 4 female. Ages ranged from 17 to 44 years, with an average age of 21.43 years. The ethnicities of the student participants were distributed as follows: 2 identified as Asian, 3 as Hispanic or Latino, 8 as White/Caucasian, and 1 as Two or More Races. Participants' majors were primarily in a STEM field, with 11 in Computer Science or Engineering, 1 in Aerospace Engineering, 1 in Physics, and 1 in a double-major. College counselors were recruited via a digital flyer distributed to university counseling centers and groups. 2 female counselors participated in our study, aged 51 and 53 years, and both identified as Hispanic or Latino.

## 5 Analysis

Our coding process for the interviews followed recommendations made by Charmaz [7]. First, we performed an *Initial Coding* of the data, by combing through interview transcripts for responses relevant to the goals of our analysis, and creating codes which directly captured what the participant said. Next came *Focused Coding*. Initial codes were compared for common themes to create focused codes. Interpretation of the data began at this stage. Lastly, we performed *Theoretical Coding*. Our process for creating theoretical codes was to qualitatively create relationships between the focused codes. For the student interviews, coding was jointly performed by 2 researchers for the first few rounds, with 1 researcher performing the remainder of the analysis. We concluded the study upon establishing that we had sufficient data to derive significant implications for design. Upon completion of the interview analysis, theoretical and focused codes were examined and grouped for common themes to determine general aims for design. Design aims were constructed with a combination of student and counselor codes, in order to capture both an individual and professional perspective.

# 6 Study Findings

Our first two research goals were to understand how college students and college counselors guide students' personal narratives and maintain their mental health over time. Two mappings of themes were extracted from our interviews through our analysis. The maps consist of our theoretical codes, which draw connections and establish relationships between these themes, and are supplemented with further detail by the focused codes that are encapsulated by them. The map of the college student interviews consists of 30 theoretical codes and 64 focused codes. The map of the college counselor interviews contains 10 theoretical codes and 27 focused codes. For brevity, we do not present these mappings, and instead reference the most relevant codes in the following section.

## 6.1 Design Aims and Implications

Our third research goal was to derive design aims for an interactive story authoring tool to facilitate the process of reflection on college students' personal narratives. Seven aims were extracted from the theoretical and focused codes of our analysis. As we describe the implications for design associated with each of the design aims below, we will differentiate **theoretical codes** and *focused codes* by using boldface and italics. We will only include the most relevant codes in our discussion of the design aims for the sake of brevity and clarity. The presented implications for design are comparable to sensitizing concepts, and aim to share relevant observations from our interviews with college students and counselors. [24]. Thus, their value is less in their prescriptive nature, and more in their ability to generate novel designs in future work.

**Aim 1: The tool should allow the author to externalize and manipulate individual experiences in a manner that allows for easy reflection.** The codes *Reflecting results in a step-back perspective* and *Reflecting by comparing past experiences to the present* indicate the need to overview the narrative in a way that allows for easy comparison and isolation of relevant experiences. Additionally, while an autobiographical retelling of a person's story lends itself well to a temporal structure, reflection can involve the comparing of experiences in causal terms. Causal relationships between events are common in interactive narratives, however in reflection, there exists a potential for the same memories to be re-structured depending on the context of a given reflection. The author should be able to create multiple configurations of life experiences, connected differently based on the context of reflection, and visually manipulate the boundary between past/present experiences to future ones. We propose the term *reflection context* to describe a specific configuration of externalized experiences for the purpose of reflection. Lastly, in the context of existing authoring tool paradigms (as identified by Green et al. [13]), we suggest that a graph-based format could best support the process of reflection. This paradigm is perfectly situated to scaffold the author's process of extracting specific experiences and restructuring the narrative, by merit of an interactive visualization of the narrative structure.

**Aim 2: The tool should support the process of narrative reflection in a therapeutic way.** Through this aim, we identify key aspects of the reflection process undertaken by college students that the tool should aim to support. Our codes indicate the existence of an assessment phase (as shown by codes such as *The session begins with uncovering/recap before work begins*, and *Counselors help the patient determine what they want/need*), where the student reviews their experiences and the goals of reflection. Given that students' personal narratives exist both within and outside of the tool, the tool must be frequently updated with relevant experiences. We propose that the tool accomplishes this during the assessment phase, through prompts and questions which guide the author in recording past and present experiences into the tool.

This is followed by a second phase, where the bulk of reflection exists and the narrative branches into future possibilities through asking what options there are (indicated by codes such as *They ask themselves questions about different options they have*). In the second phase, it is important to challenge the student's perspectives or assumptions (informed by codes such as *Counselors use probing questions to make patients reconsider ideas*). Through the use of probing questions, we can expect narrative restructuring to occur, as the author is asked to question their initial telling of the narrative. Thus, the second phase should also allow for the easy revisiting of already authored experiences, to review and compare them, as well as update them with new perspectives and ideas.

**Aim 3: The tool should lower barriers to and promote motivation.** Codes such as *Motivation to journal comes from need*, *Low motivation for tracking/journaling*, *Low commitment to therapy is a barrier to care*, and *Patients don't do homework*, portray a clear need to promote motivation and lower barriers in engaging college students in mental health interventions. For the proposed tool, this can be done by addressing the medium of the narrative, such as by allow students to author and read back their narratives via both text and speech, as not all enjoy writing. In order for the tool to be ready-at-hand for when the user is prompted to reflect, the best platform may be a mobile or cross-platform application. Lastly, gamification, or the use of game-like mechanisms outside of games, has been explored in mental health technologies to increase adherence to and engagement with a given intervention [2,8], and could also be used to reward students for engaging in regular reflection. While traditional authoring tools only need concern themselves with a singular input, output, and platform, and have no issue of author motivation, thoughtful design in these regards could go far in the adoption of an authoring tool that promotes regular reflection.

**Aim 4: The tool should adapt to different reflection contexts.** We determined two common contexts for reflection: daily reflection, and reflection in response to a personal crisis. Daily reflection was informed by the codes *They work on their mental well-being daily* and *Daily reflection is important*, implying the need to accommodate reflection sessions which consist of regular maintenance of the student's narrative. Reflection in response to a crisis emerged from the codes *They work on their mental well-being when things are bad*, *Negative events prompt reflection*, and *Focusing on crises is a barrier to care*. Although the counselor interviews suggested that focusing on crises distracted from the overarching goals of therapy, this does not mean the tool should ignore such a scenario. Crisis support may come in the form of streamlining the author into the appropriate reflection context to address the crisis upon an initial assessment, or by redirecting them to additional resources depending on the situation's severity.

**Aim 5: The tool should capture and be informed by the author's identity.** The codes under **Foci** (which contained various foci or priorities in students' narratives), and the counselor codes *Counselors help patients determine what they want/need* and *Need to account for patient identity* suggest that for our proposed authoring tool, the author's identity as they undergo the authoring process is uniquely important, not just the end creative product. This is natural, given that the story in question is composed of the author's own life experiences. The system should thus capture relevant aspects of the author, both in promoting motivation (i.e. Aim 3) and providing guidance. For the latter, there may be benefits in the system identifying an author's narrative or behavioral patterns and bringing attention to them, as a counselor might during a session. This may require some form of artificial intelligence or natural language processing, as the system would need to analyze the author's content and draw appropriate conclusions from it. Further research is needed to determine precisely what aspects of the author should be captured, and how it should be utilized in the system.

**Aim 6: The tool should allow the author to share their story.** This goal was informed by codes such as *Sharing the story outside of therapy helps maintain care*, which indicated that additional support can stem from the student sharing their personal narrative outside of an individual or therapy context. Thus, the narrative product created by the student should be shareable with others, such as their peers and family. However, care should be taken in giving the author control over what aspects of their life narrative is shared.

**Aim 7: The tool should be safe and positive in design.** Not everyone enters reflection in a positive state, as shown by codes such as *They struggle with exaggerating things negatively during reflection* and *Reflection can involve thinking about bad times*. In therapy, counselors form an important connection with their patient (E.g. *Connecting with their counselor allows students to open up*), and often have to react to serious situations and traumas in the context of care (E.g. *Counselors need to account for patient traumas*). Thus, the tool's user experience, from visuals to system dialogue, should aim to promote positive affect and provide a safe space for the author. However, the tool should not pretend to be as capable as qualified professionals, and include some form of disclaimer and easily accessible links to appropriate resources.

# 7  Discussion

Our implications for design describe requirements for an interactive story authoring tool primed to support college students through the process of therapeutic reflection. Unlike prior digital story authoring tools for reflection, we identify the need for a holistic approach to fully facilitate the process in a standalone, self-help tool. This includes features such as an assessment phase to identify the general context of reflection and initiate the externalization of life experiences; a phase which fosters narrative restructuring; and the accounting for the author's identity within the tool itself. We also provide design implications which seek to accommodate struggles our target population of college students has in reflection and maintaining their mental health, namely the need for features which promote motivation or lower barriers to engaging in the process of reflection.

Such features augment recommendations from prior work on interactive storytelling for mental health, and are necessary in the context of a self-help tool, where a user lacks the support of a counselor to both guide and motivate them. For instance, while Mobile Story [21] and the 3MR_2 system [27] allowed for experiences and memories to be externalized, they do not necessarily facilitate the process of reflection from start to end, and require the intervention of a therapist. On the other hand, existential video games as defined by Chittaro and Sioni may incite reflection, but do not provide guidance through the reflection process [9]. Our design aims instead detail how a system could be designed to fully cover an ongoing process of narrative reflection in the lives of college students, without the need for a therapist present. Our findings also expose questions that future research could address. For instance, *What would these narratives look like? What form would the prose take, and how would they be connected into a non-linear narrative by student authors?* Another question that comes to mind is *How would the various prompts and specifics of the reflection interactions be designed?* We acknowledge that our study was limited by the few counselors who took participated, due to limited access to this specific population. Lastly, our student participants were primarily white, male, and enrolled in a STEM major - future research would benefit from a more diverse participant pool.

## 8   Conclusion

We contribute aims and implications for the design of an interactive story authoring tool that facilitates the process of how college students reflect on their lives as a narrative, to support their mental well-being. We conducted and analyzed interviews with college students and college counselors, which resulted in two maps of codes detailing their experiences in interacting with student narratives and their mental health. These were examined to form aims for design, which we use to propose implications for the design. We then discuss how our findings relate to the existing literature, and identify future avenues for research. Our work situates itself within existing technologies for mental health as a uniquely interactive narrative approach, addressing the non-linear nature of the narratives we construct through life reflection.

**Acknowledgements.** We thank Tristan Funicelli for his assistance in designing the interviews, running the initial studies, and conducting the initial analysis.

# References

1. Becvar, D.S., Becvar, R.J.: Storytelling and family therapy. Am. J. Fam. Ther. **21**(2), 145–160 (1993)
2. Brown, M., O'Neill, N., van Woerden, H., Eslambolchilar, P., Jones, M., John, A.: Gamification and adherence to web-based mental health interventions: a systematic review. JMIR Mental Health **3**(3), e39 (2016)
3. Bruner, J.: The narrative construction of reality. Crit. Inq. **18**(1), 1–21 (1991)
4. Bruner, J.: Narrative, culture, and mind. Telling stories: language, narrative, and social life, pp. 45–49 (2010)
5. Butler, S., Guterman, J.T., Rudes, J.: Using puppets with children in narrative therapy to externalize the problem. J. Mental Health Couns. **31**(3) (2009)
6. Carr, A.: Michael white's narrative therapy. Contemp. Fam. Ther. **20**(4), 485–503 (1998)
7. Charmaz, K.: Constructing Grounded Theory. Sage (2014)
8. Cheng, V.W.S., Davenport, T., Johnson, D., Vella, K., Hickie, I.B.: Gamification in apps and technologies for improving mental health and well-being: systematic review. JMIR Mental Health **6**(6), e13717 (2019)
9. Chittaro, L., Sioni, R.: Existential video games: proposal and evaluation of an interactive reflection about death. Entertainment Comput. **26**, 59–77 (2018)
10. Divinyi, J.: Storytelling: an enjoyable and effective therapeutic tool. Contemp. Fam. Ther. **17**(1), 27–37 (1995)
11. Friedberg, R.D.: Storytelling and cognitive therapy with children. J. Cogn. Psychother. **8**(3), 209–217 (1994)
12. Giuliani, F., Couchepin Marchetti, B., El Korh, P.: Is storytelling therapy useful for children with autism spectrum disorders and severe mental retardation? Adv. Tech. Biol. Med. **4**(1) (2016)
13. Green, D., Hargood, C., Charles, F.: Contemporary issues in interactive storytelling authoring systems. In: Rouse, R., Koenitz, H., Haahr, M. (eds.) ICIDS 2018. LNCS, vol. 11318, pp. 501–513. Springer, Cham (2018). https://doi.org/10.1007/978-3-030-04028-4_59
14. Holmbeck, G.N., Wandrei, M.L.: Individual and relational predictors of adjustment in first-year college students. J. Couns. Psychol. **40**(1), 73 (1993)
15. Kagan, R.M.: Storytelling and game therapy for children in placement. Child Care Q. **11**(4), 280–290 (1982)
16. Kraft, D.P.: One hundred years of college mental health. J. Am. Coll. Health **59**(6), 477–481 (2011)
17. Lattie, E., Cohen, K.A., Winquist, N., Mohr, D.C.: Examining an app-based mental health self-care program, intellicare for college students: single-arm pilot study. JMIR Mental Health **7**(10), e21075 (2020)
18. Lattie, E.G., Lipson, S.K., Eisenberg, D.: Technology and college student mental health: challenges and opportunities. Front. Psych. **10**, 246 (2019)
19. Launer, J.: A narrative approach to mental health in general practice. BMJ **318**(7176), 117–119 (1999)
20. Lawlis, G.F.: Storytelling as therapy: implications for medicine. Altern. Ther. Health Med. **1**(2), 40–45 (1995)
21. Matthews, M., Doherty, G.: My mobile story: therapeutic storytelling for children. In: CHI 2011 Extended Abstracts on Human Factors in Computing Systems, pp. 2059–2064 (2011)

22. Parker, T.S., Wampler, K.S.: Changing emotion: the use of therapeutic storytelling. J. Marital Fam. Ther. **32**(2), 155–166 (2006)
23. Reichert, E.: Individual counseling for sexually abused children: a role for animals and storytelling. Child Adolesc. Soc. Work J. **15**(3), 177–185 (1998)
24. Sas, C., Whittaker, S., Dow, S., Forlizzi, J., Zimmerman, J.: Generating implications for design through design research. In: Proceedings of the SIGCHI Conference on Human Factors in Computing Systems, pp. 1971–1980 (2014)
25. Shapiro, J.: The use of narrative in the doctor-patient encounter. Family Syst. Med. **11**(1), 47 (1993)
26. Starks, K., Barker, D., Cole, A.: Using twine as a therapeutic writing tool for creating serious games. In: Marsh, T., Ma, M., Oliveira, M.F., Baalsrud Hauge, J., Göbel, S. (eds.) JCSG 2016. LNCS, vol. 9894, pp. 89–103. Springer, Cham (2016). https://doi.org/10.1007/978-3-319-45841-0_8
27. Tielman, M.L., Neerincx, M.A., Bidarra, R., Kybartas, B., Brinkman, W.P.: A therapy system for post-traumatic stress disorder using a virtual agent and virtual storytelling to reconstruct traumatic memories. J. Med. Syst. **41**(8), 1–10 (2017)
28. Towbes, L.C., Cohen, L.H.: Chronic stress in the lives of college students: scale development and prospective prediction of distress. J. Youth Adolesc. **25**(2), 199–217 (1996)
29. Wynne, E.: Storytelling in therapy and counseling. Child. Today **16**(2), 11–15 (1987)

# Applying Animated Parables to Gamification in Daily Context: An Expert Evaluation Study

Kenny K. N. Chow(⌧)

School of Design, The Hong Kong Polytechnic University, Kowloon, Hong Kong
sdknchow@polyu.edu.hk

**Abstract.** Latest studies regarding gamification for behavior change have suggested using meaningful stories for long-term effects. Drawing on psychological studies related to narrative transportation and mental simulation, this paper extends the idea of animated parables and argues that selecting stories to frame gamified systems should consider perceived causality between the real-life action and the simulated diegetic effect. This study employs expert evaluation on a collection of parables regarding perceived usefulness, novelty, and perceived causality. Results show that parables consensually rated by experts as both useful and novel are also prominent in perceived causality, which supports the argument that perceived causality underpins perceived persuasiveness of parables.

**Keywords:** Gamification · Behavior change · Interactive narratives · Animated parables · Blended causality · Consensual assessment technique

## 1 Introduction

Latest studies regarding gamification have shown that basic game elements (e.g., points, levels, and leaderboards) can be effective in short-term interventions; for long-term effects, they have suggested using meaningful stories to frame users' goals [1–4]. Fictional narratives have proved to be effective in changing beliefs via mental transportation [5, 6]. Yet, experimental psychology and neuroscience research results seem to cast doubt on transportation regarding interactive fictions [7]. Interactivity in gamification narratives need to be more implicit. With ubiquitous sensing and visualization technologies, a gamified system of today can track users' actions in life routines and present simulated outcomes blended in relevant contexts. One simply feels that the real-life action causes the simulated effect in the narrative world.

Chow [8] introduces the idea of animated parables, which refers to a kind of data-driven interactive visual narrative wherein outcomes depend on real-life actions in daily context. Animated parables can be applied in gamified systems that support self-management or habit formation. With proposed design guidelines and evaluation metrics, Chow reports the analyses of a collection of about 50 parables generated from a series of design workshops, arguing that similarities in embodied experiences between the real-life activity and the narrative likely render the action-outcome links easy to interpret. This paper reports a study that extends to compare the parables in terms of

A. Mitchell and M. Vosmeer (Eds.): ICIDS 2021, LNCS 13138, pp. 322–332, 2021.
https://doi.org/10.1007/978-3-030-92300-6_31

perceived causality, novelty, and usefulness. The study invites domain experts to rate the parables, which are illustrated using the same blending diagram template. Comparison of the scores shows that parables consensually rated as both useful and novel are also prominent in perceived causality. Discussion about the results is given.

## 2 Theoretical Framework

### 2.1 Narrative Transportation and Mental Imagery

Transportation refers to a reader's mental journey to the fictional world of a narrative [5]. When one is "absorbed" into a story, one can picture the events, imagine being in them, feel with the characters in the narrative, want to know how it ends and even "what if." Studies show that transportation is positively correlated with story-consistent beliefs, even though one knows the story is fictional [6]. Transportation entails mental imagery, which is powerful in persuasion. Imagining a hypothetical event and being the main character in it has proved to increase perceived likelihood of the event [9] and affect corresponding intention [10]. The increased likelihood estimates and intention may also lead to behavior [11]. Hence, reading (or listening to) narratives (e.g., a hypothetical situation) and constructing corresponding mental images have become an approach, so-called "mental simulation," to behavioral interventions [12–17].

### 2.2 Computer Simulations for Interactive Narratives

Narrative transportation and mental imagery are found positively correlated with perceived realism (individuals' subjective evaluations of the plausibility of stories) even to those without relevant prior experience [18]. Yet, some people may lack concrete sensory images in the "mental library" for constructing particular "unseen world" [19]. Using interactive visualization technologies can provide artificial sensory images that facilitate one's imagination. For example, Chow and colleagues [20] demonstrate that through showing an animated character on the mobile screen that becomes tired with increasing screen time, participants' reported imagination of mistreating the character is positively correlated with reduction in daily screen time. Immersing individuals in virtual environments that simulate hypothetical scenarios (e.g., showering in coal, seeing the old self) have been found effective in changing attitudes [21–23] and motivating behaviors [24]. Hence, computer-generated simulations (2D images on screens or panoramic images on head-mounted displays) can be applied to create images of interactive narratives that facilitate transportation.

### 2.3 Animated Parables for Gamification

Gamified systems with goals framed in stories can simulate outcomes in artificial sensory images (virtual rewards or penalties) according to one's real-life actions. Yet, many story-based gamified apps supporting self-management (e.g., Fortune City [25], Habitica [26], Forest [27]) rely on users' self-input of activity logs. Self-input is "cumbersome" to keep in a daily fashion [28]. With ubiquitous sensing and visualization technologies of today, a gamified system can track users' actions in life routines (e.g., flights of stairs climbed) and present simulated effects (e.g., pictures taken when hiking) in relevant context (e.g., on a picture frame in office). The purpose is to let one act in real life and perceive the simulated diegetic outcomes seemingly blended in the real world.

To maintain narrative transportation, diegetic outcomes should be relevant to real-life actions based on the user's knowledge. When one prepares to act, the brain tests the reality of the action and its outcome. Failing the reality-test disrupts "suspension of disbelief" and transportation [7]. For instance, walking in real life causing a virtual fish to grow (e.g., Fish 'n' Steps [29]) is easily judged as unreal, because their relation cannot be easily explained. Yet, if walking in real life rewards a new pair of virtual shoes (e.g., Fitbit badges [30]), one could interpret that the old pair retired after long journeys. Interpretable causal links can be "temporarily" treated as true (pass reality-test) and easily imagined, which make one more confident in the truth of the causality [31]. Chow names it "blended causality" [30] which links real-life actions to diegetic outcomes. This blending of the non-diegetic into the diegetic, rather than breaking the "fourth wall," actually relocates it and echoes what Conway calls "expansion of the magic circle" (the fictional game world) which arguably enhances immersion [32].

For interpretable and imaginable action-outcome links in gamification, Chow [8] proposes blending the real-life activity with an imaginary cause-effect narrative wherein they have similar causal actions. Chow introduces the idea of animated parables, which refers to a kind of data-driven interactive visual narrative that presents positive or negative outcomes metaphorically mapped with real-life actions. Chow reports the generation of parables from a series of design workshops according to proposed design guidelines, followed by evaluation based on proposed conceptual metrics. Drawing on embodied cognition [33], Chow argues with analyses that similarities in embodied experiences (embodied mapping) between the real-life activity and the simulated narrative render better parables in terms of the metrics.

## 2.4 Novelty and Usefulness

Each animated parable in Chow [8] is generated through blending a real-life activity and a cause-effect narrative. The two inputs share similarities in terms of sensorimotor (visual, auditory, kinesthetic, etc.) and spatiotemporal (spatial relations like container or proximity) experiences. Meanwhile, differences between the activity and the narrative are also crucial for novelty. When the differing parts of the narrative are simulated and blended into daily context (e.g., a mountain top photo displayed after climbing stairs to office), the user can interpret the parable through the similarities (e.g., climbing) meanwhile appreciating the nuances (e.g., different views between mountains and urban cities), which render the gamified system more intriguing and appealing. Thus, novel parables benefit system adoption and adherence.

Usefulness not only means that a system effectively meets the user's needs, but also that it is easy or convenient to use. Usefulness can be assessed via user evaluation on minimum viable prototypes. In earlier stages of design processes, perceived usefulness [34] can be assessed via expert evaluation on proof-of-concept prototypes (e.g., visualized use-case scenarios), which provides health check before proceeding to more costly implementation stages. In assessing animated parables for gamification, perceived usefulness informs perceived persuasiveness.

Indeed, novelty and usefulness are regarded as major criteria of creativity [35–37], whose assessment relies on a "suitably knowledgeable social group" as informed by the sociocultural definition of creativity [35]. The most widely used evaluation method is the Consensual Assessment Technique (CAT) wherein each product in a specific set is rated against the whole set by two or more domain experts independently, and the average rating is a measure of the product's creativity [38, 39]. Studies have shown that the ratings of experts highly correlate in general [35].

## 3 Expert Evaluation (Consensual Assessment)

This study conducts expert evaluation on the set of animated parables from Chow [8] regarding appropriateness, perceived usefulness, novelty, and perceived causality. Each parable is visualized using the author-modified conceptual blending diagram template and presented in random order to each expert participant, who rates each of the above attributes on a Likert scale. Following the CAT, a small number of expert participants are often able to produce coherent results. Those parables acquired good and coherent results (i.e., high means and low standard deviations) across measures are juxtaposed and compared. The objective is to uncover correlations among the attributes.

### 3.1 Participants

Seven expert participants have been recruited. Four of them are design practitioners with relevant work experiences ranging from five to thirty years. Two are researchers in Design and Technology respectively, with sixteen and fifteen years of relevant experience. One is educator in Linguistics with fifteen-year experience. Their self-ratings on knowledge regarding creativity and metaphor fall between three and four on a five-point scale (five is highest).

### 3.2 Materials: Parables in Blending Diagrams

There are totally 51 parables in this study, wherein the first parable alludes to the classical imaginative play "Trashcan Basketball" for comparisons with other parables from Chow [8]. Each parable is visualized using the author-modified conceptual blending diagram template. It starts with two horizontally aligned circles respectively representing a real-life activity (B) and a hypothetical event (C). They are blended into a circle below them representing the parable (P), which is elaborated into positive and negative action-outcome paths underneath. Figure 1 is an example parable "Staircase Hiking" that blends climbing stairs with hiking. It rewards the user with a beautiful mountain view whenever one walks up the stairs or shows a doddery image in case of using the elevator.

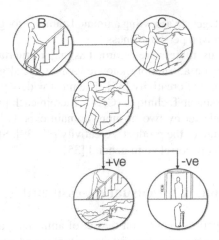

**Fig. 1.** The presented blending diagram of the parable "Staircase Hiking"

### 3.3 Measures

Each parable is first presented with the visualizations of (B) and (C), followed by a statement saying "a product that rewards you with" a positive outcome in the parable (e.g., a beautiful mountain view) whenever "you" perform a positive action (e.g., walk up the stairs).

**Appropriateness and Usefulness.** One side of criteria in the sociocultural definition of creativity typically refers to comparable attributes including appropriateness and usefulness of an idea [35]. In this survey, expert participants were asked to respond to the question: "How appropriate do you judge this product?" on a seven-point scale ranging from "not appropriate at all" to "extremely appropriate". The next closely related question is "How useful do you think the above product to target audience?" and the options are on a seven-point scale ranging from "not useful at all" to "extremely useful".

**Novelty.** The other major criterion in the sociocultural definition of creativity is novelty [35]. In this survey, expert participants were asked to respond to the question: "How novel do you judge this idea?" on a seven-point scale ranging from "not novel at all" to "extremely novel".

**Perceived Causality.** The survey then presents visualizations of the positive and negative action-outcome paths of the parable. Expert participants were then asked to indicate the level of agreement to the two statements, one about the positive outcome (e.g., "I feel like walking up the stairs causes a lively body image on the mountain view to appear") and the other about the negative outcomes ("I feel like taking the elevator causes only a doddery image to appear"). Five options were given: not at all, not much, moderately, quite much, and absolutely. They corresponded to a five-point scale ranging from 1 to 5.

# 4  Results

Responses from the seven expert participants to the survey were collected and aggregated. To detect consensus among our expert participants, parables with high mean scores and low standard deviations over each measure were selected. On the seven-point scale, the selection criterion is mean score minus one standard deviation staying above four. On the five-point scale, the selection criterion is mean score minus one standard deviation staying above three. Table 1 shows all selected parables with their descriptions as presented in the survey. Table 2 shows their mean scores and standard deviations over the corresponding measures.

**Table 1.** Parables that championed in the expert evaluation and their descriptions.

| Parable | Product/System description |
| --- | --- |
| 1. Trashcan Basketball | A smart bin that rewards you with successful basketball shot every time you accurately throw paper in the trashcan |
| 2. Viobrush | A smart toothbrush that rewards you with good music every time you brush teeth completely and adequately |
| 3. Hatcher | A smart cushion that rewards you with a virtual hatched chick (on your phone) after you sit on a cushion before too long |
| 10. Pond & Pipe | A smart tap that rewards you with a pond full of fish (on mirror) every time you conserve water in the sink |
| 12. Ice Breaker Scale | A smart scale that shows you (on its surface) with unbroken ice whenever you maintain a good weight |
| 14. Smoked House | A smart ashtray connected with a digital picture frame that rewards you with an unclouded, clean picture when you avoid smoking |
| 21. Bathroom Singer | A smart showerhead that rewards you with a lush forest with animals whenever you regulate water consumption when showering |
| 22. Staircase Hiking | A system that rewards you with a beautiful mountain view (projected on the wall) whenever you walk up the stairs instead of the elevator |
| 26. Sleeping Charging | A system that that rewards you a fully charged phone after you sleep well |
| 29. Tetridge | A smart fridge that shows you (on its door) a cleared tetris board whenever you consume food before its expiry |
| 32. A Cup of Care | A tabletop installation that rewards you and your friends with opened cups whenever you talk and listen to each other |
| 34. Daily Eye Usage | A smart lamp that generates more brightness and even flashes whenever you blink your eyes too frequently |
| 41. Bean | A smart mirror that rewards you with a smile (emoticon) whenever you smile at it |
| 46. TV Exercise | A smart TV that rewards you with bullseye darts whenever you stretch you arms while watching TV |
| 48. I Got Your Back | A shape-changing cushion that rewards you with a well-shaped clay seat every time you maintain proper sitting posture |

The juxtaposition across the measures shows that a few parables excel at two or more attributes. Four parables, namely 12. Ice Breaker Scale, 14. Smoked House, 22.

**Table 2.** Selected parables with high mean scores and low standard deviations in each measure. Perceived causality includes positive (+) or negative (−) outcome measures.

| Appropriateness (Criterion: M-SD > 4) | Usefulness (Criterion: M-SD > 4) | Novelty (Criterion: M-SD > 4) | Perceived Causality (Criterion: M-SD > 3) |
|---|---|---|---|
| 1. Trashcan Basketball (M = 5.625, SD = 1.408) | 1. Trashcan Basketball (M = 5.375, SD = 1.188) | | 1. Trashcan Basketball +(M = 4.125, SD = 0.835) |
| 2. Viobrush (M = 5.25, SD = 1.165) | | | 2. Viobrush +(M = 3.875, SD = 0.835) |
| 3. Hatcher (M = 4.875, SD = 0.835) | | 3. Hatcher (M = 5.375, SD = 1.061) | |
| 10. Pond & Pipe (M = 5.375, SD = 0.916) | 10. Pond & Pipe (M = 4.875, SD = 0.641) | | |
| 12. Ice Breaker Scale (M = 5.625, SD = 0.916) | 12. Ice Breaker Scale (M = 5.625, SD = 1.061) | 12. Ice Breaker Scale (M = 5.625, SD = 1.302) | 12. Ice Breaker Scale −(M = 4.375, SD = 0.916) |
| 14. Smoked House (M = 5.500, SD = 0.756) | 14. Smoked House (M = 5.375, SD = 0.744) | 14. Smoked House (M = 5.500, SD = 0.926) | 14. Smoked House +(M = 4.000, SD = 0.535) −(M = 4.000, SD = 0.535) |
| | | 21. Bathroom Singer (M = 5.625, SD = 1.188) | |
| 22. Staircase Hiking (M = 6.375, SD = 0.518) | 22. Staircase Hiking (M = 6.125, SD = 0.354) | 22. Staircase Hiking (M = 5.750, SD = 1.282) | 22. Staircase Hiking +(M = 4.750, SD = 0.463) |
| 26. Sleeping Charging (M = 6.125, SD = 0.641) | 26. Sleeping Charging (M = 6.250, SD = 0.886) | | 26. Sleeping Charging +(M = 4.625, SD = 0.518) −(M = 4.500, SD = 0.535) |
| 29. Tetridge (M = 5.500, SD = 0.926) | 29. Tetridge (M = 5.375, SD = 1.061) | 29. Tetridge (M = 5.625, SD = 0.916) | 29. Tetridge +(M = 4.000, SD = 0.535) |

(*continued*)

**Table 2.** (*continued*)

| Appropriateness (Criterion: M-SD > 4) | Usefulness (Criterion: M-SD > 4) | Novelty (Criterion: M-SD > 4) | Perceived Causality (Criterion: M-SD > 3) |
|---|---|---|---|
| | | | 32. A Cup of Care +(M = 3.625, SD = 0.518) |
| | | 34. Daily Eye Usage (M = 5.375, SD = 1.302) | |
| 41. Bean (M = 5.500, SD = 0.756) | 41. Bean (M = 5.125, SD = 5.125) | | |
| | | 46. TV Exercise (M = 5.250, SD = 1.165) | |
| | | | 48. I Got Your Back +(M = 3.625, SD = 0.518) |

Staircase Hiking, and 29. Tetridge, have high rating in both usefulness (appropriateness as well) and novelty. Meanwhile, our expert participants are consensually able to feel the causal links in these four creative parables.

## 5  Discussion

The list under appropriateness largely overlaps with that under usefulness. The socio-cultural definition of creativity informs that a creative product should be judged to be "novel" on one hand, and "appropriate, useful, and valuable" on the other [35]. Appropriateness sounds like the basic requirement, followed by usefulness and then value. In our survey, expert participants were asked to judge the appropriateness of an imagined product that embodies the parable idea, whereas usefulness was assessed in relation to target users. With the target users in their minds, expert participants could be more critical in assessing usefulness.

The four creative parables that are rated highly novel and useful (appropriate as well) also score high in perceived causality. This aligns with the embodied mapping analyses by Chow [8]. These four parables consist of structural similarities (i.e., image schemas [40] e.g., path, containment, proximity, support) directly relating the causal actions (e.g., walk up from a low to a high level, fill or empty a confined space, move near to a surface, step on a plane) to the simulated diegetic outcomes (e.g., a view from a mountain top, the filled fridge, dust on the picture, cracks on the ice). They also show surface similarities (by design) (e.g., mountains, tetrominos, dust/dirt, cracks) that prompt the corresponding narrative frame (e.g., hike, tetris, air pollution, ice cracking) in participants. The nuances, including structural similarities and surface similarities by design, seemingly increase novelty.

Four parables consensually rated as novel but not useful include 3. Hatcher, 21. Bathroom Singer, 34. Daily Eye Usage, and 46. TV Exercise. They feature surface similarities by design (e.g., shaking of hatched chicks, forest animals, flashing light, bullseye darts), which contribute to novelty. But they are all rated as low perceived causality. This suggests that perceived causality may be a necessary condition for perceived usefulness when assessing a gamified system framed by a parable.

Four parables are listed as useful but not novel. They are 1. Trashcan Basketball, 10. Pond & Pipe, 26. Sleeping Charging, and 41. Bean. Trashcan Basketball is familiar imaginative play, which expectedly decreases its novelty. Pond & Pipe combines the act of opening a water tap in a sink and that of opening a valve draining water from a pond. It seems like surface similarities in the bodily actions by nature, not by design (e.g., turning something clockwise by hand) may affect novelty.

## 6  Conclusion and Future Work

Results of this study show that parables consensually rated as both useful and novel are also prominent in perceived causality, which supports that perceived causality underpins perceived persuasiveness. Discussion suggests that structural similarity can facilitate perceived causality, and surface similarity by design increases novelty. In this study, the standard deviations of some measures are high. Future work includes revising the visualizations of those parables with low perceived causality and examining the profiles of those participants with scores deviating from the means in hope of identifying key expertise that might lead to better consensus in assessments.

**Acknowledgements.** This research benefits from projects supported by The Hong Kong Polytechnic University.

## References

1. Laschke, M., Hassenzahl, M.: Mayor or patron? The difference between a badge and a meaningful story. In: CHI 2011. ACM (2011)
2. Zuckerman, O., Gal-Oz, A.: Deconstructing gamification: evaluating the effectiveness of continuous measurement, virtual rewards, and social comparison for promoting physical activity. Pers. Ubiquit. Comput. **18**(7), 1705–1719 (2014). https://doi.org/10.1007/s00779-014-0783-2
3. Mekler, E.D., Brühlmann, F., Tuch, A.N., Opwis, K.: Towards understanding the effects of individual gamification elements on intrinsic motivation and performance. Comput. Hum. Behav. **71**, 525–534 (2017)
4. Rapp, A.: Drawing Inspiration from world of warcraft: gamification design elements for behavior change technologies. Interact. Comput. **29**, 648–678 (2017)
5. Gerrig, R.J.: Experiencing Narrative Worlds: On the Psychological Activities of Reading. Yale University Press, New Haven (1993)
6. Green, M.C., Brock, T.C.: The role of transportation in the persuasiveness of public narratives. J. Pers. Soc. Psychol. **79**, 701–721 (2000)

7. Holland, N.N.: Spider-Man? Sure! The neuroscience of suspending dislief. Interdisc. Sci. Rev. **33**, 312–320 (2008)
8. Chow, K.K.N.: Crafting animated parables: an embodied approach to representing lifestyle behaviors for reflection. Digit. Creat. **32**, 1–21 (2021)
9. Sherman, S.J., Cialdini, R.B., Schwartzman, D.F., Reynolds, K.D.: Imagining can heighten or lower the perceived likelihood of contracting a disease: the mediating effect of ease of imagery. Pers. Soc. Psychol. Bull. **11**, 118–127 (1985)
10. Anderson, C.A.: Imagination and expectation: the effect of imagining behavioral scripts on personal intentions. J. Pers. Soc. Psychol. **45**, 293–305 (1983)
11. Gregory, W.L., Cialdini, R.B., Carpenter, K.M.: Self-relevant scenarios as mediators of likelihood estimates and compliance: does imagining make it so? J. Pers. Soc. Psychol. **43**, 89–99 (1982)
12. Pham, L.B., Taylor, S.E.: From thought to action: effects of process- versus outcome-based mental simulations on performance. Pers. Soc. Psychol. Bull. **25**, 250–260 (1999)
13. Wynd, C.A.: Guided health imagery for smoking cessation and long-term abstinence. J. Nurs. Scholarsh. **37**, 245–250 (2005)
14. Armitage, C.J., Reidy, J.G.: Use of mental simulations to change theory of planned behaviour variables. Br. J. Health. Psychol. **13**, 513–524 (2008)
15. Knäuper, B., McCollam, A., Rosen-Brown, A., Lacaille, J., Kelso, E., Roseman, M.: Fruitful plans: adding targeted mental imagery to implementation intentions increases fruit consumption. Psychol. Health **26**, 601–617 (2011)
16. Chan, C.K.Y., Cameron, L.D.: Promoting physical activity with goal-oriented mental imagery: a randomized controlled trial. J. Behav. Med. **35**(3), 347–363 (2012). https://doi.org/10.1007/s10865-011-9360-6
17. Conroy, D., Sparks, P., Visser, R.D.: Efficacy of a non-drinking mental simulation intervention for reducing student alcohol consumption. Br. J. Health Psychol. **20**, 688–707 (2015)
18. Green, M.C.: Transportation into narrative worlds: the role of prior knowledge and perceived realism. Discourse Process. **38**, 247–266 (2004)
19. Bailenson, J.: Experience on Demand: What Virtual Reality Is, How It Works, and What It Can Do. W. W. Norton & Company (2018)
20. Chow, K.K.N., Leong, B.D., Lee, B.Y.H.: Imagining consequences of excessive smartphone use via a character-based mobile application. Int. J. Ment. Heal. Addict. **16**(6), 1420–1434 (2018). https://doi.org/10.1007/s11469-018-9984-7
21. Ahn, S.J.G., Bailenson, J.N., Park, D.: Short- and long-term effects of embodied experiences in immersive virtual environments on environmental locus of control and behavior. Comput. Hum. Behav. **39**, 235–245 (2014)
22. Bailey, J.O., Bailenson, J.N., Flora, J., Armel, K.C., Voelker, D., Reeves, B.: The impact of vivid messages on reducing energy consumption related to hot water use. Environ. Behav. **47**, 570–592 (2015)
23. Ahn, S.J.G., Bostick, J., Ogle, E., Nowak, K.L., McGillicuddy, K.T., Bailenson, J.N.: Experiencing nature: embodying animals in immersive virtual environments increases inclusion of nature in self and involvement with nature. J. Comput.-Mediat. Commun. **21**, 399–419 (2016)
24. Hershfield, H.E., et al.: Increasing saving behavior through age-progressed renderings of the future self. J. Mark. Res. **48**, S23–S37 (2011)
25. https://fortunecityapp.com/en/
26. https://habitica.com/static/home
27. https://www.forestapp.cc/
28. Rapp, A., Cena, F.: Personal informatics for everyday life: how users without prior self-tracking experience engage with personal data. Int. J. Hum Comput Stud. **94**, 1–17 (2016)

29. Lin, J.J., Mamykina, L., Lindtner, S., Delajoux, G., Strub, H.B.: Fish'n'Steps: encouraging physical activity with an interactive computer game. In: Dourish, P., Friday, A. (eds.) UbiComp 2006. LNCS, vol. 4206, pp. 261–278. Springer, Heidelberg (2006). https://doi.org/10.1007/11853565_16

30. Chow, K.K.N.: Toward a language of blended causality for transforming behavioral data into reflective user experiences. In: The ACM Conference on Creativity and Cognition. ACM Press (2019)

31. Koehler, D.J.: Explanation, imagination, and confidence in judgment. Psychol. Bull. **110**, 499–519 (1991)

32. Conway, S.: A circular wall? Reformulating the fourth wall for videogames. J. Gaming Virtual Worlds **2**, 145–155 (2010)

33. Lakoff, G.: Explaining embodied cognition results. Top. Cogn. Sci. **4**, 773–785 (2012)

34. Davis, F.D.: Perceived usefulness, perceived ease of use, and user acceptance of information technology. MIS Q. **13**, 319–340 (1999)

35. Sawyer, R.K.: Explaining Creativity: The Science of Human Innovation. Oxford University Press, New York (2012)

36. Boden, M.A.: The Creative Mind: Myths and Mechanisms. Routledge, London (2004)

37. Boden, M.A.: Computer models of creativity. AI Magazine, vol. Fall 2009 (2009)

38. Amabile, T.M.: Social psychology of creativity: a consensual assessment technique. J. Pers. Soc. Psychol. **43**, 997–1013 (1982)

39. Getzels, J.W., Csikszentmihalyi, M.: Problem finding and creativity. In: The Creative Vision: A Longitudinal Study of Problem Finding in Art, pp. 236–251. Wiley, New York (1976)

40. Lakoff, G., Johnson, M.: Philosophy in the Flesh: the Embodied Mind and its Challenge to Western Thought. Basic Books, New York (1999)

# Creativity and Collaboration During COVID-19: Creating an Alternate Reality Game in the Face of a Pandemic

Diego L. Faverio(✉) ⓘ, Iulia V. Popescu ⓘ, and Matthew Mosher

University of Central Florida, Orlando, FL 32816, USA
{diegofaverio,iulpop}@knights.ucf.edu, matthew.mosher@ucf.edu

**Abstract.** This paper describes the design, development, and implementation of an alternate reality game (ARG) created by a small team of graduate students in the Digital Media program at the University of Central Florida. The paper specifically focuses on how social distancing as a result of the COVID-19 pandemic hindered traditionally collaborative college campus environments and what techniques the team took to overcome those limitations in order to create a fun and engaging experience for players. The solution for overcoming those limitations included designing an ARG that promoted a sense of involvement by framing the game as a student-run organization for those interested to join. Through the utilization of engaging puzzle games, fictional narratives, and online platforms, the ARG known as the *Fairy Investigation Club* was a unique medium for collaboration and involvement in the face of a global pandemic.

**Keywords:** Alternate reality games · Social distancing · Interactive games · Coronavirus pandemic · Human-computer interaction

## 1 Introduction

In-person collaborative environments have been drastically altered during the COVID-19 pandemic. In hopes of preserving the spirits of undergraduate students who may be experiencing university life for the first time amidst a pandemic, the team set out to inspire collaboration among University of Central Florida (UCF) students in a creative way. The alternate reality game (ARG) the team designed blurred the lines between the real world and fantasy by inviting undergraduate students to become members of the *Fairy Investigation Club* (FIC), an unofficial club at the university. Alternate reality games began growing in popularity during the early 2000s [7]. These games deliberately blurred the lines between the in-game and out-of-game experience for players, which is what the team hoped to mimic with the creation of the fictional club. *In Rethinking the Library Game: Creating an Alternate Reality with Social Media*, the Puppet Masters, or the ones who typically release the puzzles in response to real-time gameplay, demonstrated that leveraging social media in ARGs can be beneficial in gaining an audience and creating a more realistic feel to the game [2]. Likewise, the UCF team took advantage of popular platforms such as Instagram and Discord to advertise the game and enhance gameplay.

© Springer Nature Switzerland AG 2021
A. Mitchell and M. Vosmeer (Eds.): ICIDS 2021, LNCS 13138, pp. 333–337, 2021.
https://doi.org/10.1007/978-3-030-92300-6_32

Similar to the study outlined in *Participation, Collaboration, and Spectatorship in an Alternate Reality Game* surrounding the ARG *MeiGeist*, the team's use of daily blog posts, online discussion forums, and social media activity aided in building a powerful sense of ethos around the *Fairy Investigation Club* [6]. The following video describes the creation and context of FIC: https://drive.google.com/file/d/1z4Llru_CD6wW2I29n yaNmletOmZda1lb/view.

## 2  Design and Development

The design and development process for this alternate reality game presented a unique challenge due to the limitations brought on by the COVID-19 pandemic. Not only was the team designing a game for students to enjoy while social distancing, but the designers themselves were social distancing while collaborating on the development of the project. The design process consisted of allocating responsibilities via departments (narrative, art, puzzle creation, and web development) to effectively complete tasks. Weekly updates were conducted using various online video conferencing platforms.

### 2.1  The Design

The team took on the task of solving the question: "how could we design an alternate reality game for undergraduate students that affords them an interactive and entertaining experience in the face of a pandemic?" To do this, each department focused on what the ARG would look like, how it would function on a technical level, and how to structure the puzzles and narrative in a way that challenged players to think creatively about solutions. It was through an iterative design process that the team refined the story, the aesthetics, and the overall gameplay experience that players would have [3]. After seven weeks of ideaphoria, the final game took an additional seven weeks to complete. That time was spent creating graphical assets, modifying the complexity of the puzzle games, and integrating everything into an interactive web-based experience. By designing and branding the game as a "club," it allowed players to feel a sense of belonging from the start by fictitiously joining this club during a time where joining a real club on campus was impossible [4].

To avoid large social gatherings, the team hosted a pre-release scavenger hunt where 3D-printed gnomes were placed in discrete locations on campus with links of the website on them. Hints to locate the gnomes were left via cryptic captions on Instagram. This advertising tool was a deliberate design feature that the team included which allowed players to explore campus in a creative way that did not require face-to-face interactions. The gnomes were all taken, leaving the team satisfied that whoever discovered them was exposed to information about the FIC whether they simply stumbled upon them or located them through Instagram.

Informal user testing was utilized to gain insight into the effectiveness of each game aspect. Playtests were conducted over the course of a week where members of the team met virtually with a total of 10 play testers to observe them play through the game in real-time. Time on task, error rates, and perceived enjoyment of the game were all recorded during these sessions. The playtest included a 7-point Likert scale pre-survey and an open-ended post-survey to gather information on the participant's experiences as well as general design heuristics. These informal observations helped the team refine the design of the FIC website, visual aesthetics, and narrative structure in order to create an interactive and entertaining experience.

## 2.2 A Technical Overview

The ARG consists of a series of blog posts constructed using Wix.com, a cloud-based web development service. Each blog post serves to advance the narrative of the FIC and challenge the players to complete puzzles to unlock new information. The team utilized Google Forms as a platform for players to verify their solutions and continue to the next set of blog posts. The game was deployed episodically over the course of five days, where each day 2–3 blog posts and puzzles were published for the players to complete (Fig. 1). The team was able to control the pace of the game through this method. To further promote collaboration and interconnectedness, the team created and advertised a community Discord server where players could interact with each other. The final blog post was hosted on a password-protected page on the site, using the answer of the penultimate puzzle as the password, to ensure that players did not skip to the ending without solving key puzzles and reading crucial narrative blogs. Audio files, video files, original photographs, and QR codes were implemented in the puzzles to create a multimedia experience.

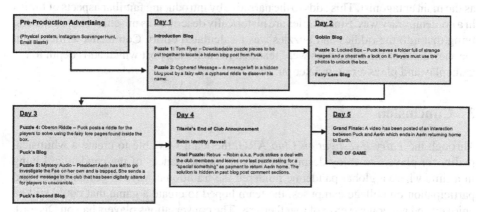

**Fig. 1.** Flow chart diagram of the narrative blog posts and puzzles in order of which they were released.

## 2.3 Gameplay

The FIC took a whimsical design approach while still maintaining the common themes of mystery and investigation typically found in ARGs [1, 5, 8]. Through the club website, players were able to familiarize themselves with characters, such as the Club President, and others who each had a unique personality and role in the FIC. At the start of the game, it appears as though players are simply members of a group aiming to observe the many mystical fairy sightings on the university's campus until circumstances grow increasingly more peculiar as Aerin, the Club President, vanishes and club members must solve puzzles to bring her home (Fig. 2). The online modality of the ARG contributed to allowing players to participate in the game whenever and wherever they were located during this time.

**Fig. 2.** Screenshots from the FIC blog website depicting two of the puzzles.

The final game consisted of a series of ten tasks, communicated through puzzles and blog posts that were released over the course of five days, commencing after the university's Spring Break in mid-April of 2021. The ARG features a well-known Fae character, Puck, or Robin Goodfellow, from Shakespeare's *A Midsummer Night's Dream* as the main antagonist. This adds to the narrative by introducing familiar aspects of fairies in a contemporary way. Since fairies are historically described as mischievous pranksters, tying that into the riddles and puzzles was a calculated effort. Comments written from the viewpoint of the characters were featured in each blog post which adds depth to the gameplay and plays a role in later puzzles.

## 3 Conclusion

Through the *Fairy Investigation Club* ARG, the team was able to create a whimsical reality for players to enjoy despite the current circumstances of the pandemic. Living in a time where a global pandemic hindered the traditional ways of collaboration and participation on college campuses, the team hoped to create a game that could still be enjoyed and generate a sense of togetherness. The conversations players had on Discord, such as sharing stories of their fairy encounters, demonstrated to the team a sense of group interaction. It would be helpful in future games to potentially take a poll of what site to message on once the game begins to ensure that a majority of people are able to participate in this aspect of the gameplay more easily. The entire team hopes that despite the tribulations encountered during the game's design process, this experience may challenge other digital media professionals to seek alternate methods of collaborating with their peers and to think more deeply about how they might create meaningful experiences for their users.

# References

1. Alice & Smith: The Black Watchmen. Game [PC]. Alice & Smith, Montreal, Quebec, Canada, 25 June 2015 (2015)
2. Battles, J., Battles, J., Glenn, V., Shedd, L.: Rethinking the library game: creating an alternate reality with social media. J. Web Librariansh. **5**(2), 114–131 (2011). https://doi.org/10.1080/19322909.2011.569922
3. Bonsignore, E., Hansen, D., Kraus, K., Visconti, A., Fraistat, A.: Roles people play: key roles designed to promote participation and learning in alternate reality games. In: Proceedings of the 2016 Annual Symposium on Computer-Human Interaction in Play (2016). https://doi.org/10.1145/2967934.2968108
4. Evans, E., Christopherson, L., Strum, B., King, E., Haefele, C.: Alternate reality games: a realistic approach to gaming on campus. In: Proceedings of the 38th Annual Fall Conference on SIGUCCS - SIGUCCS 2010 (2010). https://doi.org/10.1145/1878335.1878376
5. Mihell & Lycos: Forever has Fallen. Game [Web]. Mihell & Lycos, Adelaide, Australia, 5 September 2020 (2020)
6. O'Hara, K., Grain, H., Williams, J.: Participation, collaboration, and spectatorship in an alternate reality game. In: Proceedings of the 20th Australasian Conference on Computer-Human Interaction Designing for Habitus and Habitat - OZCHI 2008 (2008). https://doi.org/10.1145/1517744.1517787
7. Piatt, K.: Using alternate reality games to support first year induction with ELGG. Campus-Wide Inf. Syst. **26**(4), 313–322 (2009). https://doi.org/10.1108/10650740910984646
8. O'Connell, W.: Subtext. Game [Mobile]. William O'Connell, Alexandria, Virginia (2018)

# Interacting with Climate Change: A Survey of HCI and Design Projects and Their Use of Transmedia Storytelling

Marta Ferreira[1]($\boxtimes$) (iD), Nuno Nunes[2] (iD), and Valentina Nisi[2] (iD)

[1] ITI/LARSyS, FCT, U. Nova Lisboa, Lisbon, Portugal
hello@amartaferreira.com
[2] ITI/LARSyS, IST, U. Lisboa, Lisbon, Portugal

**Abstract.** Climate change is arguably one of the most debated issues today. The scale and global reach of this crisis doesn't afford a universal solution and requires widespread global mobilization. Public engagement is essential for the success of any initiative on this topic. However, sometimes communicating the facts is not enough. Interactive storytelling and transmedia narratives have an important part to play in communicating climate change, especially in shifting from a mere transmission of data to a narrative that is more engaging, positive and action focused, that considers diverse audiences and active participation. Following this premise, we conducted a survey on climate change applied research projects addressing the general public to understand how the fields of interactive media, HCI and Design are using transmedia narratives. The intention of this study is to gather what has been done regarding these topics and the strategies used, to further the debate among the community and inform future research.

**Keywords:** Communication · Climate change · Transmedia · Storytelling · Design · Interaction

## 1 Introduction: Climate Change – A Communication Challenge

Climate change is possibly the most pressing crisis of our time [1, 2]. All fields of knowledge can contribute to help mitigate the consequences of the Anthropocene and solutions to complex global problems require a multidisciplinary perspective. ICIDS theme for 2021 is "Interconnectedness and Social Impact" and it perfectly encompasses this need to connect diverse stakeholders and audiences to address the need for climate action in all areas of society – from individual action to systemic political and social shifts. Effective communication is a crucial part of this process [3, 4], and *how* this crisis-related information is imparted is of paramount importance to the success of the exchange. In this survey, we will map what has been done in applied research regarding transmedia storytelling as a way to foster engagement with the climate crisis.

Because of its pressing nature, the discourse around climate change has been mainly one of urgency, alerts, and, in many cases, "end-of-the-world" rhetoric. This way of communicating climate change has been effective in highlighting the scale and urgency

A. Mitchell and M. Vosmeer (Eds.): ICIDS 2021, LNCS 13138, pp. 338–348, 2021.
https://doi.org/10.1007/978-3-030-92300-6_33

of the issue [5, 6], but also in associating the topic with the frames of fear, anxiety and even hopelessness [7, 8]. Climate change is now a much debated and mediated issue, but arguably what we need now are effective ways of engaging the general public with positive, action-focused exchanges that will lead to action [9–11]. We argue that communication techniques such as storytelling and transmedia can play a crucial part in shifting the dialogue from the negative, defeatist tone into a more positive, entertaining, engaging, and inclusive one. Therefore, understanding what has been done to date will help position future work in these areas.

Interactive digital narratives (IDN) is a rapidly evolving area of research [12, 13] and transmedia narratives can contribute to the development of the field, especially when dealing with applied research. Previous work [14] has analysed how the HCI research community has been addressing climate change to the general public, especially their interaction, storytelling and media choices. In this study, we take this analysis further by doing a survey on interactive media, HCI and Design applied research focused on climate change interactions and looking specifically into their media strategies, with a special focus on transmedia. This analysis used the Grounded Theory Literature Review method [15]. By looking into the databases of ICIDS, SIGCHI, Interact, DRS, TDJ, JDR, DS, and She Ji it returned 680 results for the keywords "climate change", climate crisis" and "global warming" for Jan. 2010 to Dec. 2020. From these results, we gathered N = 40 interaction projects that used storytelling. A keyword analysis points to a limited focus in narrative-related topics. Further inquiry on their media strategies concluded that n = 33 use *mono-media*, n = 2 use *multimedia*, and n = 5 use *transmedia*. We focused on the five transmedia projects to gather their narrative choices based on current proposals for effective climate change communication.

## 2 Interactive Storytelling, Transmedia and Climate Change

### 2.1 The Message: Using Interactive Storytelling

In this analysis, we consider the definition of storytelling as a form of discourse shaped by an imaginative process of meaning-making, which organizes knowledge and experience according to a narrative form [16]. Therefore, we investigated how the projects transmitted their message and if there was an effort to transform the information, the raw data, into a form of structured discourse that would guide the audience in their process of interpretation.

When creating interactive experiences related to climate change, simply presenting data most likely will not engage the majority of people without a scientific background. Climate literacy is an important step in this communication path, but knowledge by itself isn't likely to be enough for people to change their behaviours, promoting collective or systemic change. Other issues like incentives, barriers to action or social norms need to be addressed as well [17]. By using interactive storytelling in crafting messages, communicators can leverage the use of emotion as it is a central part of people's decision making and ethical judgments about climate change [18], with messages adapted to their perceptions and values [19]. *Games for change*, for example, encourage game creators and social innovators to incentivize real-world change through games and immersive media [20]. Environmental topics, including climate change, are already being prolifically explored through this interactive venue.

The complexity of the issue and the diversity of people being engaged means that no single story will trigger widespread attention [21]. Likewise, physical vulnerability in general does not impact people's risk perceptions, but political or ideological affiliation and connection to local impacts of climate change does [22]. These results suggest that crafting a narrative linking climate change to local impacts is more effective than generalised information.

When discussing the importance of a more positive and action-focused story associated with climate change, highlighting paths for action are an important step in the interaction. If the information is not accompanied by specific recommendations on how to actually respond, the audience might just accept the fatalism of the situation and won't be prompted for action [23]. Furthermore, overdramatization can easily be exploited by skeptics to discredit the importance of the issue [24]. Pratten [9] advocates for this action and solution focused approach in a call for *transmedia for change* (T4C) stating that storytellers should engage the audience with positive messages that inspire and motivate, and that they should provide solutions to guide the audience in their path towards change.

Going forth, climate change storytelling is increasingly focusing on this need for change and action, and the best methods to achieve these goals. The present analysis of applied interaction experiences about climate change intends to understand how researchers have been developing these narratives, including if the message focuses on generalized or local issues, if it presents actionable steps, and if the storytelling/narrative process is a focus of the research.

## 2.2 The Media: Using Transmedia Strategies

Definitions and transmedia structures have been extensively debated in the academic community. We decided to focus on the definition of transmedia as "any story that is told through more than one medium" [25]. Transmedia storytelling allows for an exploration of the information through multiple media outlets, from more analogue to more digital, from more direct to more immersive. The challenge with crafting a transmedia story is taking into account the overall narrative so the different channels all work as a larger storytelling system [26]. Unlike multimedia strategies that convey the same content through different media (e.g., the same game that is available through a website or an app), transmedia supports the expansion of content in each channel. Another important aspect in transmedia is encouraging audience's participation [27].

Robert Pratten [28] has divided transmedia storytelling into three types: franchise, portmanteau, and complex. In transmedia franchise, we have multiple stories through multiple media. These stories are part of the same overall narrative but are somewhat independent, so they can be enjoyed together or as standalones, and allow for different entry points to the narrative. In transmedia portmanteau, one story consists of multiple media that are somewhat dependent on each other for a good enjoyment of the experience. Complex transmedia is a combination of the previous two. We will use this classification in the transmedia project analysis.

Concerning climate change communication, if we consider the enormous scale of potential audiences to address, a transmedia project could potentially reach a wider range of people with different social backgrounds, interests, and even political affiliations. Each part of the story is a possible entry point to the discussion. Henry Jenkins calls transmedia storytelling "entertainment for the age of media convergence" [27], an age when computing, communication and content are brought together as a consequence of the digitization of media content and the ubiquitousness of the Internet. This media convergence transformed the established media landscape and allowed for the emergence of entirely new forms of content and storytelling. Furthermore, he presents this type of transmedia experience as entertainment for the age of collective intelligence – a shared or group intelligence that comes from collaboration and collective efforts from many individuals. This prescient notion has taken a deeper meaning recently, with many scholars arguing for more inclusive, plural, socially aware perspectives in sustainability and climate change research that account for participation, co-production and collective action [29–36], and for community and social interaction [37, 38]. The need for systemic change highlights the importance of these strategies [39–46]. Besides, digital media practitioners now need to work on services, experiences and networks that take into consideration these complex socio-technical systems [47].

In any transmedia strategy, the media literacy of the audience in question needs to be carefully considered. In a world of participatory culture, for example, true engagement comes only from active participation. If the person addressed does not possess the tools to actively take part in the exchange, then communication fails. However, if the medium is adequate for the public it addresses, the possibilities are endless. Users find transmedia stories engaging and versatile, evoking creativity and collaboration [48]. Participatory mechanisms allow for constant feedback and participation from the audience. Especially for social causes, this willingness for participation can be harnessed to help solve problems [49]. The potential offered by interactive media allows for storytelling to explore more deeply the intersection between personal experience and community action, and for a complex topic like climate change, this is a crucial factor to explore.

Nowadays, communicators deal with a complex media landscape where multiple media channels, shared authorship, social networks, sharing and interaction, are an everyday reality. Interactivity and entertainment should be leveraged to increase public engagement and allow for diverse pathways for different audiences to enter the conversation. With this in mind, we set out to understand if and how researchers are using transmedia in climate change related interactions.

## 3 Survey: Interactive Media and Transmedia for Change

### 3.1 Interaction Projects on Climate Change: Analysis Criteria

For this survey, we conducted an analysis of interaction projects focused on climate change that made use of storytelling. We adopted the Grounded Theory Literature Review method [15] for a systematic and rigorous analysis from which we could derive themes and opportunities for future work. The analysis focuses on applied interaction narratives, so we looked at interactive media, human-computer interaction (HCI) and design. Therefore, the following databases were reviewed: ICIDS proceedings, ACM SIGCHI proceedings, IFIP-13 Interact proceedings, the Design Research Society proceedings, The Design Journal, the Journal of Design Research, Design Studies journal, and She Ji: The Journal of Design, Economics, and Innovation. These libraries allow for a multidisciplinary, comprehensive scope with an international representation.

The data selection criteria were: (1) climate change as the main topic of the project; (2) target audience: a general public outside academia; (3) projects that have an interaction component; (4) projects that use storytelling to convey a message.

The analysis was restricted to the past decade – from Jan. 2010 to Dec. 2020 – for timewise relevant results, and to the search terms "climate change", "climate crisis" or "global warming" to focus on climate change related narratives.

The initial search returned 680 results, divided as follows: ICIDS: 7; SIGCHI: 395; Interact: 38; DRS: 102; TDJ: 58; JDR: 17; DS: 16; She Ji: 47. Each result was scrutinized through its title and abstract. If it mentioned an interaction or communication project, it was added to the list. This list was then refined by checking if the projects corresponded to the first three points of the selection criteria, resulting in a final list of 77 projects: ICIDS: 3; SIGCHI: 43; Interact: 9; DRS: 12; TDJ: 6; JDR: 1; DS: 2; She Ji: 1. Lastly, we analyzed if the projects used storytelling to convey a message – criteria four – and ended up with a final data set of 40 projects: ICIDS: 3; SIGCHI: 26; Interact: 2; DRS: 4; TDJ: 4; JDR: 1; DS: 0; She Ji: 0. Therefore, from the initial list of 680 results of papers and articles that mentioned climate change, 40 (5,9%) mentioned applied projects for the general public that use storytelling strategies to communicate a message. In the following section, we present further questions asked of this final dataset with the purpose of better understanding the storytelling strategies used.

### 3.2 Keyword Analysis

In a first stage, we surveyed the keywords of each of the 40 papers, to gather if narrative, storytelling, or media choices were a key concern of the projects. Related with these issues, we found the following keywords: *visual rhetoric* (n = 1); *visualization* related keywords (n = 4); *design fiction* (n = 2); *interactive narrative design* (n = 2); *media narratives* (n = 1); *storytelling* (n = 1); *tangible narrative* (n = 1). No project mentioned *transmedia* in their keywords, and one instance of *interactive narrative design* and *media narratives* are from the same article. There is some interest in the exploration of the visualization of data and a limited mention to narrative-related topics.

The fact that our dataset consists of 40 projects that explore a storytelling component points to the importance of using these strategies. However, the lack of specific keywords about storytelling, media use or media strategies, suggest that these areas of research are not one of the focuses of the evaluations of these works. The applied projects organically use storytelling as part of the message creation, but its development and potential is generally not one of the objects of study.

### 3.3 Analysis of Media Strategy

Since our dataset is already a selection of applied research that uses some form of storytelling to convey information, we intended to better understand the strategies connected to the use of interactive media. Therefore, we asked of our data set if the projects used one of the following media strategies: a) *mono-media* – one media output, either digital or analogue; b) *multimedia* – the same content presented in different media platforms; c) *transmedia* – different parts of the story conveyed across different media.

The analysis resulted in: a) *mono-media* n = 33; b) *multimedia* n = 2; c) *transmedia* n = 5. Results highlight a minority of project adopting multimedia or transmedia strategies to communicate climate change and clear preference for the use of mono-media.

## 3.4 Analysis of Transmedia Application

In this section we look in more detail at the five projects that employed transmedia, including: a) summary of the project and its story/message; b) transmedia strategy employed (based on Pratten's classification [28]); c) if the message focuses on local or generalized topics; d) what is the audience's participation component.

1. *London Phenological Clock* [50]: a) Uses analogue clocks and a data visualization website to represent the annual timing of life cycle events for species in urban ecosystems. b) Transmedia franchise strategy. c) Local impacts: local plants and animal's characteristics and habits. d) Participation component: the data is gathered by citizen scientists or volunteers from their neighborhood.
2. *Vox Populi* [51]: a) Uses a card game, software package support, and theatre performance to build an interactive narrative about the importance of media for elections, fake news, and the refugee crisis. This project is part of the ongoing transmedia storyworld "Shatterland". b) Transmedia portmanteau strategy. c) Generalized topics (even though based in two European cities for an European context). d) Participation component: players have an active role inside the interactive story.
3. *Spilltime* [52]: a) Formed of three objects, each focusing on a different form of showcasing and experiencing one's carbon footprint – a water tank, a wearable, and a mirror, also with the support of a coach. b) Transmedia franchise strategy. c) Generalized topics. d) Participation component: data based on user action.
4. *Angstfabriek* [53]: a) An interactive installation that uses different media to tell a story about people's fears, including climate change – VR, corporate-like videos, QR code scans, analogue elements in lockers, etc., as part of the same interactive narrative. b) Transmedia portmanteau strategy. c) Generalized topics. d) Participation component: audience is part of the live experience and plays a part in the story.
5. *Econundrum* [54]: a) A sculpture and an app to input data and allow for user participation. The physical data sculpture represents the small community's food habits and the consequent carbon emissions. b) Transmedia portmanteau strategy c) Local impacts: individual's choices and their impact. d) Participation component: data inputted by the participants.

The five projects are quite balanced in terms of transmedia strategy used with n = 3 for Transmedia portmanteau, and n = 2 for Transmedia franchise. Likewise for the focus on local or generalized topics, with n = 3 for generalized and n = 2 for local. In terms of audiences, *Spilltime* considers the advantages of having different objects with different characteristics for different users – one possibly appealing more to an 80-year-old person while another to a seven-year-old child. The *London Phenological Clock*, being a physical installation and a data visualization website, allows for interaction with different types of users in different contexts. The *Vox Populi* interactive narrative, the *Angstfabriek* installation, and the *Econundrum* sculpture are experiences where the different media work for the same users. Nevertheless, having different outputs with varying levels of complexity and participation can help in considering users with varying media literacies even within the same experience.

### 3.5   Analysis of Suggestions for Action as Part of the Message

As discussed in Sect. 2.1, Pratten advocates that projects should provide solutions as a "pathway to success", and we also pointed to the importance of associating new, more positive narratives with climate change. Therefore, we asked of the projects if they showcase solutions or actionable steps as part of the exchange. The results were: a) *No* (n = 27); b) *Yes* (n = 13).

If we look specifically at the five projects that used a transmedia strategy, the results are: a) *No* (n = 4); b) *Yes* (n = 1). The sample is very limited, but these results point to the need of developing more action-focused narratives within this subset of storytelling.

## 4   Discussion and Future Work

Discussions around *transmedia for good*, *transmedia for change* and *transmedia activism* have been around for years. This survey returned five transmedia projects linked to climate change topics to an audience of non-experts. This result points to a relative lack of actual applied research of these concepts. Nevertheless, 2020 was the year with the highest number of projects found in general, and all five transmedia projects are from 2017 and onwards, with two from 2019 and one from 2020. The growing interest in the topic and consequent increase in applied research is encouraging.

As Pratten states: "If future projects are to create greater impact, they need to connect to people where the people are – they're mobile, they're in the real world and of course they're across platforms" [9]. As highlighted in Sect. 2.2, using a transmedia strategy to communicate climate change topics has the potential of engaging multiple audiences with different characteristics and media literacies and engage them with a complex topic in a way that connects with them. However, deeper analysis on the impact and efficacy of these strategies when compared to others still needs to be further developed. Especially with a topic like climate change with long-term consequences and applications, testing of these strategies is challenging and new methods to analyze communication effectiveness need to be considered.

The need to shift climate change communication towards more positive stories is especially pressing since our survey only returned one transmedia project that communicated explicit suggestions for action. Pratten's call for positive communication echoes other scholars' [10, 11, 55, 56]. One way to support positive climate action is focusing more on systemic change and not only on individual behavior [36–38, 43, 46, 57]. Informing and empowering action related to social, political, and community issues, and system changes, can help avoid a defeatist narrative.

Other sources of inspiration for future work in applied climate change communication are the more inclusive and diverse perspectives being debated around sustainability and biodiversity. Many researchers are pressing for a deeper consideration of non-human agents and cohabitation [58–61], more-than-human perspectives and decentering humans in design [50, 62], more-than-human participation and co-production [29, 30]. Transmedia storytelling presents an exciting avenue of transposing these theories to design applications. These perspectives can lead to transmedia storytelling that engages audiences outside academia with nature-related issues through alternative lenses, as is already being explored by some research projects [63–66]. They are inspiring pathways for explorations in *transmedia for change*.

The way the message is crafted, the story it tells, and the media used, are essential elements in the success or failure of the communication exchange. However, these aspects are normally not the focus of the papers analyzed. Likewise, projects that we can consider using interactive storytelling or transmedia strategies don't study the impact of these communication choices. Future work in climate change related interaction should consider the impact of the different aspects of the narrative construction and their efficacy. Interactions related with this pressing topic have multiple challenges to overcome and engaging, participatory and impactful digital experiences are a versatile and stimulating entry point into the climate dialogue.

# References

1. Wuebbles, D.J., Fahey, D.W., Hibbard, K.A., Dokken, D.J., Stewart, B.C., Maycock, T.K.: Climate science special report: fourth National Climate Assessment. U.S. Global Change Research Program (2017). https://doi.org/10.7930/J0J964J6
2. IPCC: Special Report on Global Warming of 1.5C (2018)
3. UNEP: Single-Use Plastic: A Roadmap for Sustainability (2018)
4. Climate Outreach: Climate Visuals. https://climatevisuals.org/. Accessed 01 Oct 2020
5. Leiserowitz, A., Maibach, E., Rosenthal, S., Kotcher, J.: Climate Change in the American Mind, November 2019 (2019)
6. European Commission: Citizen support for climate action—Climate Action. https://ec.eur opa.eu/clima/citizens/support_en. Accessed 09 Apr 2020
7. Knight, V.: 'Climate Grief': Fears About the Planet's Future Weigh on Americans' Mental Health—Kaiser Health News. https://khn.org/news/climate-grief-fears-about-the-planets-fut ure-weigh-on-americans-mental-health/. Accessed 09 Apr 2020
8. Clayton, S., Manning, C.M., Krygsman, K., Speiser, M.: Mental Health and Our Changing Climate: Impacts, Implications, and Guidance. American Psychological Association, and ecoAmerica. American Psychological Association, Washington, D.C. (2017)
9. Pratten, R.: Transmedia for Change. https://www.linkedin.com/pulse/transmedia-change-rob ert-pratten/
10. Corner, A., Lewandosky, S., Phillips, M., Roberts, O.: The Uncertainty Handbook. University of Bristol, Bristol (2015)
11. Corner, A., Shaw, C., Clarke, J.: Principles for effective communication and public engagement on climate change: A Handbook for IPCC authors. Climate Outreach, Oxford (2018)
12. Murray, J.H.: Research into interactive digital narrative: a kaleidoscopic view. In: Rouse, R., Koenitz, H., Haahr, M. (eds.) ICIDS 2018. LNCS, vol. 11318, pp. 3–17. Springer, Cham (2018). https://doi.org/10.1007/978-3-030-04028-4_1
13. Koenitz, H., Dubbelman, T., Knoller, N., Roth, C.: An integrated and iterative research direction for interactive digital narrative. In: Nack, F., Gordon, A.S. (eds.) ICIDS 2016. LNCS, vol. 10045, pp. 51–60. Springer, Cham (2016). https://doi.org/10.1007/978-3-319-48279-8_5

14. Ferreira, M., Coelho, M., Nisi, V., Nunes, N.: Climate change communication in HCI: a visual analysis of the past decade. Presented at the C&C 2021: Creativity and Cognition, June 2021. https://doi.org/10.1145/3450741.3466774
15. Wolfswinkel, J.F., Furtmueller, E., Wilderom, C.P.M.: Using grounded theory as a method for rigorously reviewing literature. Eur. J. Inf. Syst. **22**, 45–55 (2013). https://doi.org/10.1057/ejis.2011.51
16. Bruner, J.: Acts of Meaning. Harvard University Press, Cambridge (1990)
17. Spence, A., Pidgeon, N.: Psychology, climate change & sustainable behaviour. Environment (2009). https://doi.org/10.1080/00139150903337217
18. Moser, S.C.: More bad news: the risk of neglecting emotional responses to climate change information. In: Creating a Climate for Change (2009). https://doi.org/10.1017/cbo978051 1535871.006
19. Nisbet, M.C.: Framing science: a new paradigm in public engagement. In: Communicating Science: New Agendas in Communication (2009). https://doi.org/10.4324/9780203867631
20. Games for Change, Inc.: Games for Change. https://www.gamesforchange.org/. Accessed 14 Oct 2021
21. Nisbet, M.C.: Communicating Climate Change: Why Frames Matter (2009)
22. Pidgeon, N.: Climate change risk perception and communication: addressing a critical moment? Risk Anal. (2012).https://doi.org/10.1111/j.1539-6924.2012.01856.x
23. Maibach, E.W., Roser-Renouf, C., Leiserowitz, A.: Communication and marketing as climate change-intervention assets. A public health perspective. Am. J. Prev. Med. (2008). https://doi.org/10.1016/j.amepre.2008.08.016
24. Revkin, A.C.: Climate change as news: Challenges in communicating environmental science. In: Climate Change: What it Means for Us, Our Children, and Our Grandchildren, Second Edition (2014). https://doi.org/10.7551/mitpress/9178.003.0008
25. Javanshir, R., Carroll, B., Millard, D.: Structural patterns for transmedia storytelling. PLoS ONE **15**, e0225910 (2020). https://doi.org/10.1371/journal.pone.0225910
26. Jenkins, H.: Transmedia Storytelling 101. http://henryjenkins.org/blog/2007/03/transmedia_s torytelling_101.html. Accessed 17 June 2021
27. Jenkins, H.: Convergence Culture: Where Old and New Media Collide. New York University Press, New York and London (2006)
28. Pratten, R.: Getting Started in Transmedia Storytelling: A Practical Guide for Beginners (2015)
29. Bastian, M. (ed.): Participatory Research in More-than-Human Worlds. Routledge, Taylor & Francis Group, London, New York (2017)
30. Clarke, R., Heitlinger, S., Light, A., Forlano, L., Foth, M., DiSalvo, C.: More-than-human participation: design for sustainable smart city futures. Interactions **26**, 60–63 (2019). https://doi.org/10.1145/3319075
31. Tsekleves, E., Darby, A., Ahorlu, C., Pickup, R., de Souza, D., Boakye, D.: Challenges and opportunities in conducting and applying design research beyond global north to the global south. Presented at the Design Research Society Conference, 10 September 2020 (2020). https://doi.org/10.21606/drs.2020.145
32. Wong-Villacres, M., et al.: Decolonizing learning spaces for sociotechnical research and design. In: Conference Companion Publication of the 2020 on Computer Supported Cooperative Work and Social Computing, pp. 519–526. ACM, Virtual Event USA (2020). https://doi.org/10.1145/3406865.3418592
33. Clarke, R., Heitlinger, S., Foth, M., DiSalvo, C., Light, A., Forlano, L.: More-than-human urban futures: speculative participatory design to avoid ecocidal smart cities. In: Proceedings of the 15th Participatory Design Conference: Short Papers, Situated Actions, Workshops and Tutorial - Volume 2, pp. 1–4. ACM, Hasselt and Genk Belgium (2018). https://doi.org/10.1145/3210604.3210641

34. DiSalvo, C.: Critical making as materializing the politics of design. Inf. Soc. **30**, 96–105 (2014). https://doi.org/10.1080/01972243.2014.875770
35. DiSalvo, C., Dantec, C.A.L.: Civic design. Interactions **24**, 66–69 (2017). https://doi.org/10.1145/3137097
36. Le Dantec, C.A.: Design through collective action / collective action through design. Interactions **24**, 24–30 (2016). https://doi.org/10.1145/3018005
37. DiSalvo, C.: Community and conflict. Interactions **18**, 24–26 (2011). https://doi.org/10.1145/2029976.2029984
38. Lou, Y.: Designing interactions to counter threats to human survival. She Ji: J. Des. Econ. Innov. **4**, 342–354 (2018). https://doi.org/10.1016/j.sheji.2018.10.001
39. Blevis, E., et al.: Ecological perspectives in HCI: promise, problems, and potential. In: Proceedings of the 33rd Annual ACM Conference Extended Abstracts on Human Factors in Computing Systems, pp. 2401–2404. ACM, Seoul Republic of Korea (2015). https://doi.org/10.1145/2702613.2702634
40. Brynjarsdottir, H., Håkansson, M., Pierce, J., Baumer, E., DiSalvo, C., Sengers, P.: Sustainably unpersuaded: how persuasion narrows our vision of sustainability. In: Proceedings of the 2012 ACM annual conference on Human Factors in Computing Systems - CHI 2012, p. 947. ACM Press, Austin (2012). https://doi.org/10.1145/2207676.2208539
41. Dourish, P.: HCI and environmental sustainability: the politics of design and the design of politics. In: Proceedings of the 8th ACM Conference on Designing Interactive Systems - DIS 2010, p. 1. ACM Press, Aarhus (2010). https://doi.org/10.1145/1858171.1858173
42. Forlizzi, J.: Moving beyond user-centered design. Interactions **25**, 22–23 (2018). https://doi.org/10.1145/3239558
43. Fritsch, J., Loi, D., Light, A.: Designing at the end of the world. In: Companion Publication of the 2019 on Designing Interactive Systems Conference 2019 Companion, pp. 369–372. ACM, San Diego (2019). https://doi.org/10.1145/3301019.3319999
44. Hazas, M., Brush, A.J.B., Scott, J.: Sustainability does not begin with the individual. Interactions **19**, 14–17 (2012). https://doi.org/10.1145/2334184.2334189
45. Knowles, B., Bates, O., Håkansson, M.: This changes sustainable HCI. In: Proceedings of the 2018 CHI Conference on Human Factors in Computing Systems, pp. 1–12. ACM, Montreal (2018). https://doi.org/10.1145/3173574.3174045
46. Boehnert, J.: Anthropocene economics and design: heterodox economics for design transitions. She Ji: J. Des. Econ. Innov. **4**, 355–374 (2018). https://doi.org/10.1016/j.sheji.2018.10.002
47. Ceschin, F., Gaziulusoy, I.: Evolution of design for sustainability: From product design to design for system innovations and transitions. Des. Stud. **47**, 118–163 (2016). https://doi.org/10.1016/j.destud.2016.09.002
48. Kapadia, M., et al.: JUNGLE: an interactive visual platform for collaborative creation and consumption of nonlinear transmedia stories. In: Cardona-Rivera, R.E., Sullivan, A., Young, R.M. (eds.) ICIDS 2019. LNCS, vol. 11869, pp. 250–266. Springer, Cham (2019). https://doi.org/10.1007/978-3-030-33894-7_26
49. Kim, J., Lee, E., Thomas, T., Dombrowski, C.: Storytelling in new media: the case of alternate reality games, 2001–2009. First Monday (2009). https://doi.org/10.5210/fm.v14i6.2484
50. Smith, N., Bardzell, S., Bardzell, J.: Designing for cohabitation: naturecultures, hybrids, and decentering the human in design. In: Proceedings of the 2017 CHI Conference on Human Factors in Computing Systems, pp. 1714–1725. ACM, Denver (2017). https://doi.org/10.1145/3025453.3025948
51. Schalk, S.: Vox populi. In: Rouse, R., Koenitz, H., Haahr, M. (eds.) ICIDS 2018. LNCS, vol. 11318, pp. 408–411. Springer, Cham (2018). https://doi.org/10.1007/978-3-030-04028-4_48

52. Reitsma, L., Wessman, S., Nyström, S.: Spilltime: designing for the relationship between QS, CO2e and climate goals. Des. J. **22**, 1087–1100 (2019). https://doi.org/10.1080/14606925. 2019.1594976

53. Roth, C.: The 'Angstfabriek' experience: factoring fear into transformative interactive narrative design. In: Cardona-Rivera, R.E., Sullivan, A., Young, R.M. (eds.) ICIDS 2019. LNCS, vol. 11869, pp. 101–114. Springer, Cham (2019). https://doi.org/10.1007/978-3-030-33894-7_11

54. Sauvé, K., Bakker, S., Houben, S.: Econundrum: visualizing the climate impact of dietary choice through a shared data sculpture. In: Proceedings of the 2020 ACM Designing Interactive Systems Conference, pp. 1287–1300. ACM, Eindhoven (2020). https://doi.org/10.1145/3357236.3395509

55. Bertolotti, M., Catellani, P.: Effects of message framing in policy communication on climate change. Eur. J. Soc. Psychol. (2014). https://doi.org/10.1002/ejsp.2033

56. Tonkinwise, C.: Only a god can save us – or at least a good story: i love sustainability (because necessity no longer has agency). Des. Philos. Pap. **9**, 69–80 (2011). https://doi.org/10.2752/144871311X13968752924554

57. Project Drawdown: The Drawdown Review (2020)

58. Kobayashi, H.H.: Human–computer–biosphere interaction: beyond human - centric interaction. In: Streitz, N., Markopoulos, P. (eds.) DAPI 2014. LNCS, vol. 8530, pp. 349–358. Springer, Cham (2014). https://doi.org/10.1007/978-3-319-07788-8_33

59. Light, A., Powell, A., Shklovski, I.: Design for existential crisis in the anthropocene age. In: Proceedings of the 8th International Conference on Communities and Technologies, pp. 270–79 (2017). https://doi.org/10.1145/3083671.3083688

60. Mancini, C., Lehtonen, J.: The emerging nature of participation in multispecies interaction design. In: Proceedings of the 2018 on Designing Interactive Systems Conference 2018 - DIS 2018, pp. 907–918. ACM Press, Hong Kong (2018). https://doi.org/10.1145/3196709.3196785

61. Roudavski, S.: Multispecies cohabitation and future design. Presented at the Design Research Society Conference, 10 September 2020 (2020). https://doi.org/10.21606/drs.2020.402

62. Forlano, L.: Decentering the human in the design of collaborative cities. Des. Issues 42–54 (2016). https://doi.org/10.1162/DESI_a_00398

63. Dionisio, M., Nisi, V.: Leveraging transmedia storytelling to engage tourists in the understanding of the destination's local heritage. Multimed Tools Appl. (2021).https://doi.org/10.1007/s11042-021-10949-2

64. Mendes, J., Allison, L.: Bear 71. https://bear71vr.nfb.ca/. Accessed 17 June 2021

65. Bala, P., Dionisio, M., Oliveira, S., Andrade, T., Nisi, V.: Tell a Tail: leveraging XR for a transmedia on animal welfare. In: Nunes, N.J., Ma, L., Wang, M., Correia, N., Pan, Z. (eds.) ICEC 2020. LNCS, vol. 12523, pp. 223–239. Springer, Cham (2020). https://doi.org/10.1007/978-3-030-65736-9_19

66. Dionisio, M., Bala, P., Oliveira, S., Nisi, V.: Tale of T(r)ails: the design of an ar comic book for an animal welfare transmedia. In: Bosser, A.-G., Millard, D.E., Hargood, C. (eds.) ICIDS 2020. LNCS, vol. 12497, pp. 281–284. Springer, Cham (2020). https://doi.org/10.1007/978-3-030-62516-0_25

# User Evaluation of a Storytelling Application Assisting Visitors in Protected Nature Areas

Asim Hameed[1]([✉])(iD), Øyvind Sørdal Klungre[1]([✉]), Andrew Perkis[1](iD),
Gøran Bolme[2], and Andrew Brownridge[3](iD)

[1] Department of Electronic Systems, Norwegian University of Science
and Technology, 7491 Trondheim, Norway
{asim.hameed,oyvind.klungre}@ntnu.no
[2] iTrollheimen AS, 6657 Rindal, Norway
[3] Faculty of Social Sciences, Nord University, 7600 Levanger, Norway

**Abstract.** Storytelling has been part of human culture throughout history. Stories become profound when they are related to real places. In this paper we look at the use of location-based media and augmented reality to create storytelling experiences to assist visitors in a protected nature area. This was done in collaboration with an adventure tourism company to find alternatives to mountain signposts and take a technological approach promoting self-motivated tourism. Users (N = 30) tested a location-based AR application for mobile devices. Participants were split into two groups to test two variations of the application: a text-only variation was compared to an AR-based variation. Overall user experience for the two variations was evaluated using subjective measures. The results from our study indicate a higher immersion and a sense of flow in the AR-based variation of the application. Similarly, the AR-based variation also elicited higher desirability compared to the text-only variation.

**Keywords:** Location-based storytelling · Augmented reality · User evaluation · Field experiment

## 1 Introduction

The use of information technology, in specific digital media, has redefined our experience of tourism services [10,14]. Different technological tools are now available to encourage effective, self-motivated methods of engagement. One such example is technology-driven storytelling: a useful means of exploration, especially for those looking to expand upon their cultural, historical, and geographical awareness through meaning-making and self-learning [12,26]. Advancements in information & media technology have contributed to our meaning- and sense-making abilities by introducing new delivery mechanisms, media forms, and tools. The use of geo-referenced and immersive media applications within this context has a promising future for enriching tourism/adventure experiences. Of

© Springer Nature Switzerland AG 2021
A. Mitchell and M. Vosmeer (Eds.): ICIDS 2021, LNCS 13138, pp. 349–359, 2021.
https://doi.org/10.1007/978-3-030-92300-6_34

particular interest to us are locative or location-based media (LBM) and Augmented Reality (AR) technologies.

Often, we find cultural & adventure tourism best coincide at locations and geographical spaces that have legends, stories, and folklore associated with them. Norwegian folklore is full of stories about the Trolls that walk the spectacular Norwegian landscape. Trolls are intrinsically related to the environmental features of the landscape. We developed an application for a local tourism company interested in using this Norwegian mythical folklore to promote activities in a protected nature area. The aim of the project was to find alternatives to mountain signposts used for informing visitors. The application was designed to deliver a story-world blurring the line between reality and fiction. This work built upon an earlier prototype that was only tested in a lab setting [21]. This paper discusses findings from a real-world experiment performed to assess the user-perceived quality of the storytelling experience. The paper notes that works related to storytelling applications largely discuss technological perspectives while attempts at real-world user evaluations remain scarce. For this purpose, our study compared two instances of an application for its differences on overall user experience. Post-experience questionnaires documenting psychological, usability & eudaimonic aspects were used. In reference to this work, we question if AR-features improve the experiential quality compared to the text-only application.

## 2   Related Works

### 2.1   AR in Location-Based Experiences

Storytelling about places is an old, recognized tool to share personal experiences about places visited. But also, to imagine fictional locations like Calvino's descriptive explorations [4]. Paay et al. [28] immersed users in fiction with their non-goal oriented mobile guide for a city using LBM to weave fictional stories around existing physical, historical, and environmental features of the city. Informal post-experience interviews revealed users appreciated how their physical surroundings were associated to the story. LBM, or locative media, supplement spatial technologies with context-rich and site-specific information [11]. With computational advances we are now able to use bodily positions and spatial movements to provide location-based experiences for creating digitally pervasive worlds. M-View [7] is a context-aware system where media elements are triggered as users navigate the physical space. Based on their position, users prompt media instances depicting events that have occurred at the locations where they appear. Azuma [2] classifies AR storytelling as a subset of the broader location-based experiences that include ARGs (alternate-reality games), pervasive games, performance art, transmedia experiences, amongst others.

### 2.2   Immersive Media Experience (IMEx)

Immersive media technologies moves from real-world physical environment to fully virtual ones [25]. Immersive media experiences (IMEx) [13,29] emerge out of the confluence of its delivery mechanism (media), the information/experience dispensed (content), and the shape/structure of the content (form). User experience in immersive media manifests itself through concepts of immersion, presence, and immediacy [29]. Immersive media experiences (IMEx) include psychological and emotional determinants that bear influence on the user. For this purpose, subjective measures like questionnaires [22,24,32,33] have been a popular assessment method.

In gaming contexts [8,16,17] evaluations also include gameplay features in addition to experiential determinants. The choice of questionnaire used to assess user-perceived experience varies based on the sample size, purpose of study, and practical considerations, e.g. availability, ease of scoring, time to complete, etc. Various questionnaires assess gaming experience, however, many of them measure overlapping aspects. Such as flow-short & flow-state -scales [18,19] assess flow-related aspects, while engagement questionnaires like Game Engagement Questionnaire (GEngQ) [3] and Immersive Experience Questionnaire (IEQ) [20] evaluate engagement-related aspects of immersion and presence. For assessing other aspects of gaming, the Player Experience of Need Satisfaction (PENS) [30] and Game Experience Questionnaire (GEQ) [17] are widely used. PENS covers 5 aspects of gaming experience but this questionnaire is copyrighted [8]. This paper uses the GEQ [17], which has been a popular tool for gaming experience assessments and is also included in the ITU P. Game recommendation [31]. Moreoever, subjective quality ratings can also be collected using mean opinion scores (MOS).

## 3   Methods

### 3.1   Experiment Design

We conducted a field experiment in a natural environment. We chose a comparative between-subject design (N = 30) by investigating two different variations of a location-based storytelling application. To measure the effects on the overall user experience of the participating subjects, we manipulated between two independent variables (IV):

Condition 1: Story experience delivered through text only   *TB*; and,
Condition 2: Story experience delivered with AR-based virtual characters - *AR*.

**Lab-to-Nature:** The choice of a field experiment (as opposed to a lab experiment) was made to increase the ecological validity of the experiment. The experiment will replicate real-life use conditions for the application while manipulating between two variations (IV) to measure user experience (DV). Outside of lab conditions, participants are more likely to act natural and less likely to show demand characteristics [23]. However, the nature of a field experiment also presents limitations of having less control over extraneous variables, which makes it difficult to replicate the study in exactly the same way. Nonetheless, having a between-subject design in field is useful to achieve generalizability [1]: across situations—the extent to which we can generalize from the situation constructed by an experimenter to real-life situations; and across people.

## 3.2  Setup

**Location.** The experiment was designed along a trail that led from a car-park to an erected tipi on the edge of a lake. The trail is approximately 700-meter-long It was marked by six story points. The test required each participant to follow the trail from start to finish, stopping at the designated The area surrounding the trail is a wetland with a variety of vegetation.

**Story.** This storytelling experience follows the fantastical world of trolls residing in Trollheimen who are responsible for looking after mother nature. It is their job to modulate the seasons and manage the surroundings. They also inform and educate visiting humans on how to behave in Trollheimen.

**Application.** The application was developed in Unity (2019.3.4f1) using the Vuforia Engine (9.7.5). Six GPS coordinates were assigned along the physical trail. Coordinates are retrieved using the Bad Elf GPS (for Lightning Connector), with accuracy up to 2.5 m. All participants were given 5th Gen Apple iPads with 9.7 in. screens, $2048 \times 1536$ resolution, and 8-megapixel cameras. When a user passed any of the six implemented GPS points on the trail the application triggered a story event. Users received a notification as they approached a pre-defined location. Two variations of the application were used.

1. *TB*: This variation relies completely on reading, such that it would be similar to reading physical signposts. It provides information about the Trollheimen region (geography, flora, fauna, etc.) without the context of the troll stories. Information is received as notification at different points.
2. *AR*: This variation uses AR features as well as audio. Participants could locate virtual trolls through ground plane detection and screen touch. The information given in the text-only variation is complemented within a story line involving trolls. Voice overs were done in-house. The character models were digitally sculpted using Pixologic's ZBrush (2021), retopologized & UV mapped using Autodesk's Maya (2020), and textured using Adobe's Substance Painter (2020) & Photoshop (2021). Finally, they were exported using the FBX file format to be compatible with the Unity engine. The models were static.

## 3.3  Materials

The Game Experience Questionnaire (GEQ) [17] and AttrakDiff [15] were used. The GEQ [17] is a popular tool used frequently for assessments of gaming experience [6,27]. It satisfied the needs and requirements of our study and sample size.

GEQ has a 3-tier modular structure. This paper looks at 7 core aspects of the experience and two post-game aspects. Namely, Competence, Immersion, Flow, Tension, Challenge, Negative Affect, Positive Affect, Tiredness, and Return-to-Reality. We also used the Short AttrakDiff questionnaire [15], which divides user experience into pragmatic and hedonic qualities. It provides scores for pragmatic quality (PQ), hedonic quality from an identity (HQ-I) and a stimulation (HQ-S) point of view, as well as overall attractiveness (ATT). Users rank word pairs representing the worst and best on a range from $-3$ to $+3$.

### 3.4 Participants and Procedure

This between-subject study inducted 30 participants (11 male, 19 female, $\mu = 50.7 \pm 12.4$) split into two groups, each attempting only one condition. All participants filled out a pre-experiment consent form. Demographic data was also documented. Participants were casual users of smart devices and expressed basic competence. They were given a short tutorial on the features of the storytelling application. The experiment was performed following ITU-T guidelines in work item P.Game [31]. Test sessions took place over two days. *TB* was tested on the Day 1, followed by *AR* on Day 2. Both sessions were conducted at a similar time, i.e. early evening. Each group was given an introductory talk that included instructions on using the application. Participants were sent out individually to avoid crowding. Each concluded journey was immediately followed by a post-game questionnaire filled out on the same user device. All participants were native Norwegian speakers and some received help with translating questions.

## 4   Results

### 4.1   Game Experience Questionnaire (GEQ)

We find the means and standard deviations for the nine dependent variables in Table 1 for both conditions. A multivariate analysis of variance (MANOVA) was conducted to determine significant differences between the two categorical conditions when considered for the dependent variables, i.e. dimensions of the GEQ. Our investigation of the two independent variables, TB & AR, achieved a statistically significant result: $F(9, 20) = 3.382$, $p = 0.011$, Wilk's $\lambda = 0.397$, $\eta^2 p = 0.603$. Further univariate ANOVAs for the nine dimensions of the GEQ across the two conditions, TB & AR, show the following between-subject effects:

- Competence: $F(1, 28) = 0.078$, $p = 0.782$, $\eta^2 p = 0.003$
- Immersion: $F(1, 28) = 10.655$, $p = 0.003$, $\eta^2 p = 0.276$
- Flow: $F(1, 28) = 13.162$, $p = 0.001$, $\eta^2 p = 0.320$
- Tension: $F(1, 28) = 0.323$, $p = 0.574$, $\eta^2 p = 0.011$
- Challenge: $F(1, 28) = 1.142$, $p = 0.294$, $\eta^2 p = 0.039$
- Negative Aspects: $F(1, 28) = 0.137$, $p = 0.714$, $\eta^2 p = 0.005$

**Table 1.** The mean and standard deviation for the nine dimensions of the GEQ corresponding to both conditions.

| GEQ aspects | | | | |
|---|---|---|---|---|
| Item | Condition | Mean ($\mu$) | Std. dev | N |
| Competence | TB | 3.57 | 0.54 | 15 |
| | AR | 3.51 | 0.75 | 15 |
| Immersion | TB | 3.31 | 0.36 | 15 |
| | AR | 3.96 | 0.68 | 15 |
| Flow | TB | 2.60 | 0.69 | 15 |
| | AR | 3.52 | 0.70 | 15 |
| Tension | TB | 1.22 | 0.35 | 15 |
| | AR | 1.31 | 0.50 | 15 |
| Challenge | TB | 1.64 | 0.49 | 15 |
| | AR | 1.83 | 0.47 | 15 |
| Negative Aspects | TB | 1.40 | 0.43 | 15 |
| | AR | 1.33 | 0.55 | 15 |
| Positives Aspects | TB | 3.90 | 0.50 | 15 |
| | AR | 4.15 | 0.67 | 15 |
| Tiredness | TB | 1.63 | 0.92 | 15 |
| | AR | 1.43 | 0.59 | 15 |
| Return to Reality | TB | 1.62 | 0.62 | 15 |
| | AR | 2.02 | 0.48 | 15 |

– Positive Aspects: $F(1, 28) = 1.388$, $p = 0.249$, $\eta^2 p = 0.047$
– Tiredness: $F(1, 28) = 0.504$, $p = 0.484$, $\eta^2 p = 0.0018$
– Return to Reality: $F(1, 28) = 3.944$, $p = 0.057$, $\eta^2 p = 0.123$

The addition of AR-based features had a significant effect only on two dimensions of the GEQ. Namely, *immersion* with a $p$-value of 0.003, and *flow* with a $p$-value of 0.001. *Immersion* scores improved from condition-TB ($\mu = 3.31$, SD $= 0.36$) to condition-AR ($\mu = 3.96$, SD $= 0.68$). While that for *flow* also increased from condition-TB ($\mu = 2.60$, SD $= 0.69$) to condition-AR ($\mu = 3.52$, SD $= 0.70$). No significant differences were observed in the remaining seven variables (Fig. 1). An adjusted alpha-value ($p < 0.025$) was used to account for multiple ANOVAs. Min & Max scores can be seen in Fig. 2. The score deviation is markedly noticeable towards the maximum. Participants reported a higher immersion and flow in story experience when delivered using AR-based media.

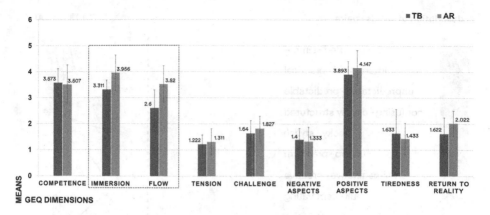

**Fig. 1.** A comparison of combined means for the nine GEQ dimensions under both conditions TB & AR

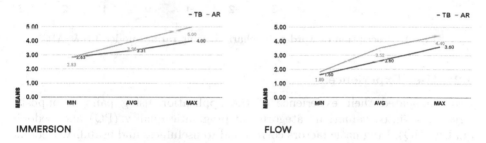

**Fig. 2.** Min & Max for *immersion* and *flow* under TB & AR

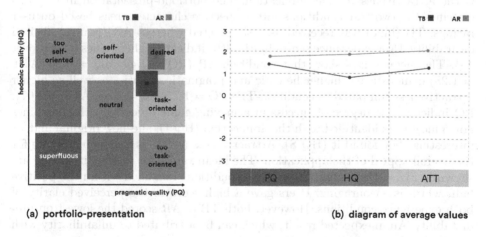

(a) portfolio-presentation

(b) diagram of average values

**Fig. 3.** Portfolio chart & average values chart for TB & AR (Color figure online)

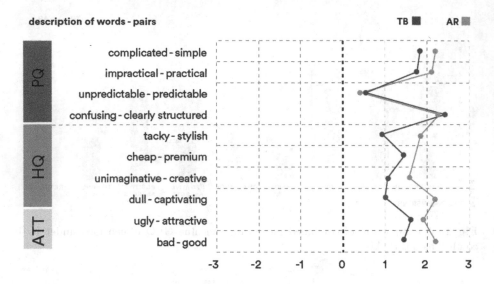

**Fig. 4.** Description of word-pairs chart showing ratings under TB & AR

## 4.2 User Experience

Users indicated their experience of the application using pairs of opposite adjectives—into evaluation categories of pragmatic quality (PQ) and hedonic quality (HQ). Pragmatic factors correspond to usefulness and usability. Hedonic factors cater to emotional needs, like curiosity and identification. The resultant is the attractiveness of the application. The portfolio-presentation in Fig. 3(a) classifies the two test conditions into respective character areas based on user ratings. TB (blue) was received as task-oriented whereas AR (orange) elicited desirability. User experience scores in Fig. 3(b) indicate higher values for AR over TB. The mean values show that condition-AR (PQ = 1.44, HQ = 0.86, ATT = 1.28) demonstrated higher hedonic and pragmatic qualities as well as higher attractiveness compared to condition-TB (PQ = 1.77, HQ = 1.85, ATT = 2.07). PQ indicates the degree of success in achieving game objectives. HQ combines how much users identified with the application (HQ-I), and how original and/or interesting they found it (HQ-S). Attractiveness (ATT) is a combined score for the overall appeal of the application. The mean values for word-pair scoring are shown in Fig. 4. User scores under both conditions remained within the positive half, which is encouraging. Users gave a high score to the perceived clarity of both experience conditions. However, both TB & AR scored the lowest on predictability. An unexpected result, which can be attributed to unfamiliarity with the application.

## 5    Discussion

In this paper, we investigated a location-based storytelling application. Our application used an off-the-shelf commercial tablet in a user study with 30 participants. We compared two variations, AR-based vs. text-based, for nine experiential dimensions of the GEQ. We also evaluated the overall desirability of the applications. The results for AR-based storytelling experience scored higher overall across GEQ aspects. However, statistically significance was only noticed for immersion and flow aspects. Condition-AR also scored higher on overall appeal and usability on the AttrakDiff. One clear outcome was that adding virtual characters make it captivating for the users. The higher ratings across the AttrakDiff survey confirm that AR features positively influenced user experience. The results are encouraging overall for as far as prototypes are concerned. Further prototypes would benefit greatly from revisions in light of similar user studies [5,9]. Judging by the results, improvements can be made to the interface, like adding navigation so users could locate where different information/content instances were situated. This can contribute to the improvement of predictability. The addition of interactive features, and content, would improve upon the engagement aspects of the application and also make it more captivating. Both conditions score fairly low in terms of the challenge they posed, which could be addressed by incorporating gamification elements such as badges, timer, & coins.

## 6  Conclusion

A notable outcome from this work has been the implementation of user evaluation in a field experiment. Most user studies are conducted under lab conditions, which risks the production of unnatural behavior due to the artificial setting, i.e. low ecological validity. With a field experiment it becomes possible to generalize findings to a real-life setting. Such evaluations give us a better understanding of our products. In this case, the application was used by everyday users in a real-world setting of a natural environment. The results confirm that AR features are a successful replacement for physical signposts. Future works include making improvements to the application. Character development and animation is currently underway. Additionally increased interactivity features are being introduced to the application, e.g. conversations with the virtual trolls. The inclusion of video and image formats are also implemented. Further user testing will follow before the commercial release.

## References

1. Aronson, E., Wilson, T.D., Akert, R.M.: Social Psychology, 7th edn. Upper Saddle River (2010)
2. Azuma, R.: 11 location-based mixed and augmented reality storytelling (2015)
3. Brockmyer, J.H., Fox, C.M., Curtiss, K.A., McBroom, E., Burkhart, K.M., Pidruzny, J.N.: The development of the game engagement questionnaire: a measure of engagement in video game-playing. J. Exp. Soc. Psychol. **45**(4), 624–634 (2009)
4. Calvino, I.: Italo Calvino on "invisible cities". Columbia: J. Lit. Art 37–42 (1983)
5. Carrigy, T., Naliuka, K., Paterson, N., Haahr, M.: Design and evaluation of player experience of a location-based mobile game. In: Proceedings of the 6th Nordic Conference on Human-Computer Interaction: Extending Boundaries, pp. 92–101 (2010)

6. Chertoff, D.B., Goldiez, B., LaViola, J.J.: Virtual experience test: a virtual environment evaluation questionnaire. In: 2010 IEEE Virtual Reality Conference (VR), pp. 103–110. IEEE (2010)
7. Crow, D., Pan, P., Kam, L., Davenport, G.: M-views: a system for location-based storytelling. In: ACM UbiComp (2003)
8. Denisova, A., Nordin, A.I., Cairns, P.: The convergence of player experience questionnaires. In: Proceedings of the 2016 Annual Symposium on Computer-Human Interaction in Play, pp. 33–37 (2016)
9. Dionisio, M., et al.: Evaluation of Yasmine's adventures: exploring the sociocultural potential of location aware multimedia stories. In: Schoenau-Fog, H., Bruni, L.E., Louchart, S., Baceviciute, S. (eds.) ICIDS 2015. LNCS, vol. 9445, pp. 251–258. Springer, Cham (2015). https://doi.org/10.1007/978-3-319-27036-4_24
10. Dionisio, M., Nisi, V., Correia, N.: Leveraging on transmedia entertainment-education to offer tourists a meaningful experience. In: Nunes, N., Oakley, I., Nisi, V. (eds.) ICIDS 2017. LNCS, vol. 10690, pp. 359–362. Springer, Cham (2017). https://doi.org/10.1007/978-3-319-71027-3_43
11. Farman, J., et al.: Location-based media. In: Dialogues on Mobile Communication, pp. 161–177. Routledge (2016)
12. Haahr, M.: Reconciling immersion and presence: locative game mechanics and narrative techniques for cultural heritage. Virtual Creativity 8(1), 23–37 (2018)
13. Hameed, A., Irshad, S., Perkis, A.: Towards a quality framework for immersive media experiences: a holistic approach. In: Cardona-Rivera, R.E., Sullivan, A., Young, R.M. (eds.) ICIDS 2019. LNCS, vol. 11869, pp. 389–394. Springer, Cham (2019). https://doi.org/10.1007/978-3-030-33894-7_41
14. Han, D.-I.D., Weber, J., Bastiaansen, M., Mitas, O., Lub, X.: Virtual and augmented reality technologies to enhance the visitor experience in cultural tourism. In: tom Dieck, M.C., Jung, T. (eds.) Augmented Reality and Virtual Reality. PI, pp. 113–128. Springer, Cham (2019). https://doi.org/10.1007/978-3-030-06246-0_9
15. Hassenzahl, M., Burmester, M., Koller, F.: AttrakDiff: a questionnaire to measure perceived hedonic and pragmatic quality. In: Szwillus, G., Ziegler, J. (eds.) Human Computer 2003, pp. 187–196. Springer, Heidelberg (2003). https://doi.org/10.1007/978-3-322-80058-9_19
16. Högberg, J., Hamari, J., Wästlund, E.: Gameful experience questionnaire (GAMEFULQUEST): an instrument for measuring the perceived gamefulness of system use. User Model. User-Adap. Inter. 29(3), 619–660 (2019)
17. IJsselsteijn, W.A., de Kort, Y.A., Poels, K.: The game experience questionnaire. Eindhoven: Technische Universiteit Eindhoven 46(1) (2013)
18. Jackson, S.A., Eklund, R.C.: Assessing flow in physical activity: the flow state scale-2 and dispositional flow scale-2. J. Sport Exerc. Psychol. 24(2), 133–150 (2002)
19. Jackson, S.A., Martin, A.J., Eklund, R.C.: Long and short measures of flow: the construct validity of the FSS-2, DFS-2, and new brief counterparts. J. Sport Exerc. Psychol. 30(5), 561–587 (2008)
20. Jennett, C., et al.: Measuring and defining the experience of immersion in games. Int. J. Hum. Comput. Stud. 66(9), 641–661 (2008)
21. Klungre, Ø.S., Hameed, A., Perkis, A.: Narrative's impact on quality of experience in digital storytelling. In: SA 2019: SIGGRAPH ASIA Art Gallery/Art Papers (2019)
22. Lessiter, J., Freeman, J., Keogh, E., Davidoff, J.: A cross-media presence questionnaire: the ITC-sense of presence inventory. Presence: Teleoper. Virtual Environ. 10(3), 282–297 (2001)

23. List, J.A.: Field experiments: a bridge between lab and naturally occurring data. BE J. Econ. Anal. Policy **5**(2) (2007)
24. Lombard, M., Ditton, T.B., Weinstein, L.: Measuring presence: the temple presence inventory. In: Proceedings of the 12th Annual International Workshop on Presence, pp. 1–15 (2009)
25. Milgram, P., Takemura, H., Utsumi, A., Kishino, F.: Augmented reality: a class of displays on the reality-virtuality continuum. In: Telemanipulator and Telepresence Technologies, vol. 2351, pp. 282–292. International Society for Optics and Photonics (1995)
26. Moscardo, G.: Stories and design in tourism. Ann. Tourism Res. **83**, 102950 (2020)
27. Norman, K.L.: GEQ (game engagement/experience questionnaire): a review of two papers. Interact. Comput. **25**(4), 278–283 (2013)
28. Paay, J., et al.: Location-based storytelling in the urban environment. In: Proceedings of the 20th Australasian Conference on Computer-Human Interaction: Designing for Habitus and Habitat, pp. 122–129 (2008)
29. Perkis, A., et al.: QUALINET white paper on definitions of immersive media experience (IMEx). arXiv preprint arXiv:2007.07032 (2020)
30. Ryan, R.M., Rigby, C.S., Przybylski, A.: The motivational pull of video games: a self-determination theory approach. Motiv. Emot. **30**(4), 344 360 (2006)
31. Schmidt, S., Zadtootaghaj, S., Möller, S., Metzger, F., Hirth, M., Suznjevic, M.: Subjective evaluation methods for gaming quality (p. game). CH-Geneva (2018)
32. Schubert, T.W.: The sense of presence in virtual environments: a three-component scale measuring spatial presence, involvement, and realness. Z. für Medienpsychologie **15**(2), 69–71 (2003)
33. Witmer, B.G., Singer, M.J.: Measuring presence in virtual environments: a presence questionnaire. Presence **7**(3), 225–240 (1998)

# The Magic of the In-Between: Mental Resilience Through Interactive Narrative

Sarah Harmon[1]($\boxtimes$) ⓘ, Hazel Gale[2], and Elitsa Dermendzhiyska[2]

[1] Bowdoin College, Brunswick, ME 04011, USA
sharmon@bowdoin.edu
[2] Mind Monsters Games, 140 Nuttall Street, London N1 5LJ, UK
hazel@mindmonsters.co.uk

**Abstract.** We present the latest iteration of *Betwixt*, an interactive narrative that combines therapeutic techniques with fantasy storytelling to help everyday users strengthen their mental resilience. In this paper, we highlight several features relevant to interactive narrative that appear to differentiate *Betwixt* from other interactive narratives for mental health based on preliminary user feedback. Future work will seek to build on the core *Betwixt* design and strengthen understanding of how to best strengthen mental resilience via digital intervention.

**Keywords:** Mental health · Digital interventions · Human-chatbot storytelling

## 1 Introduction

Many interactive narratives exist that are related to mental health. *Depression Quest* [13] and *Paper Cages* [8], for instance, are examples of simple games about dealing with depression and anxiety. The purpose of these games is, for the most part, awareness and simulation of these conditions. As such, they do not actually provide substantial resources for users in need of mental health support.

*Adventures with Anxiety* is a more complex interactive story that ultimately encourages the user to work in tandem with their anxiety [5]. A website containing links to mental health resources is presented at the conclusion of the game. Prior work [14] has suggested that *Adventures with Anxiety* is an example of an interactive narrative with transformative potential to "open our hearts and change who we are" [11].

During gameplay, *Adventures with Anxiety* breaks the fourth wall, stating that "building a healthy relationship with your emotions isn't as simple as clicking buttons on a screen". While it provides more support than a simulation game like *Paper Cages*, it recognizes that real life for its user will be harder than playing the game itself. *Adventures with Anxiety* thus points to the next level of interactive narrative for mental health support: one that could help users reliably build mental resilience over time.

© Springer Nature Switzerland AG 2021
A. Mitchell and M. Vosmeer (Eds.): ICIDS 2021, LNCS 13138, pp. 360–364, 2021.
https://doi.org/10.1007/978-3-030-92300-6_35

One example of a mental health app that aspires to be in this domain is *eQuoo* [10], which advertises as an interactive storytelling game that teaches the user about emotional fitness. This is a decision-based game where the user clicks through a tutorial session teaching them concepts, and then makes choices in an imaginary scenario.

Although it doesn't similarly express it outright, *eQuoo* falls prey to the same limitations *Adventures with Anxiety* warned its players about. Users can simply click through the story, selecting one of three choices at a time. The app also doesn't take any time to connect with the user, and pours out a continuous stream of information and gameplay. While it does include gamification elements which show promise for engagement [10], this type of design may not lead to long-term engagement to benefit users [4], or may even simultaneously distract users from thinking more deeply about their real-life problems [1].

We created *Betwixt* as an experiment to determine if interactive narrative could help users strengthen mental resilience in an engaging, constructive, and collaborative way over the long term. In the following sections, we will describe several elements of the *Betwixt* design and discuss some preliminary feedback from users as it relates to our design goals.

## 2  What Makes *Betwixt* Different

*Betwixt* is experienced by completing a sequence of *dreams*, which are similar to interactive book chapters. During a dream, one can interact with their surroundings and, at times, with a chatbot. Conversing with the chatbot provides opportunities for understanding the fantasy world, listening to stories, and self-reflection. Between dreams, users unlock optional quests that allow them to explore journal prompts and a library of guided meditations, among other resources.

*Betwixt* draws from research and therapeutic practices relating to cognitive behavior therapy, self-determination theory, narrative identity, and more. Most significantly, we seek to support mental resilience. To develop and sustain individual resilience, emotional literacy [15] and emotion regulation [19,20] are key. Self-reflection as well as self-expression have been found to facilitate resilience, emotional literacy, and well-being, but certain additional factors may be necessary, such as self-insight and positive core self-evaluations [6,9,17]. Most recently, Tabibnia proposed a tripartite model for resilience: down-regulating the negative, up-regulating the positive, and transcending the self [18].

Each of these factors were important to *Betwixt*'s design. Dreams and quests encourage self-expression and self-reflection. Positive psychology techniques are used to encourage self-discovery of what brings joy, connection, and purpose to each user [16]. Mindfulness exercises are also incorporated, which are not only associated with transcending the self but have been associated with decreased depressive symptoms by way of enhancement of self-insight [12].

For effective self-reflection, one must be able to focus on, understand, and reinterpret their negative emotions and experiences. Additionally, this reinterpretation process is less likely to fail (i.e., lead to rumination and the escalation of negative affect) when done from a *self-distanced* perspective [2,3]. In this case, self-distancing means that the person in question is able to view themselves from the perspective of an observer during their analysis.

*Betwixt* provides gradual transitions for users to slowly adjust into and out of the dreams. Headphones are encouraged as audio and calmly-paced text are used to enhance immersion with the fantasy world, helping the user to relax and focus. The overall experience was designed to maximize the potential for users to self-reflect from an observer's distance (via dreams), while also actively involving them in a collaborative telling of their own story. *Betwixt* maintains an immersive atmosphere until a resolution point is reached, at which point the user likely still has questions about the story to keep them interested in returning. Users gain further agency as they continue, which is intended to have an empowering effect each time they close the app and return to reality.

Here, we consider three findings relevant to interactive narratives for mental resilience: (1) the power of immersive yet self-distanced interactive storytelling for focus and self-reflection, (2) the value of collaborative conversation, and (3) support for healthy long-term engagement. Preliminary results were gathered via a survey of 40 *Betwixt* users. Users were asked to volunteer feedback about the overall experience to support the further development of the game but were not required, incentivized, or otherwise compelled to do so (2% response rate).

## 3   Results

### 3.1   Immersive Self-distanced Storytelling for Self-reflection

Users highlighted the importance of providing a means to immerse in the experience and relax first prior to being able to reach a desired mental state. This sense of immersion and focus was described as being achieved via "deliberate pacing of the text, the fantastic sound/music, and the excellent writing and story". Multiple users mentioned the overall idea of "storytelling through self-reflection" and "self-reflection as a conversation" to be "incredibly powerful", leading to a sense of connection and immersion that they had not observed in other apps for mental health and meditation.

### 3.2   Collaborative Conversation

Another praised aspect was the app's ability to "listen" as opposed to (1) "preach" or (2) dismiss the user's needs or concerns. In so doing, *Betwixt* frames self-reflection and reframing as a collaborative conversation, and encourages self-expression. Users found *Betwixt* to support a healthy balance between guiding (just enough to prevent a lack of connection or "freezing up") and "allowing your own mind and personal experiences to fill in the blanks to find meaning".

It is possible that these combined capacities of *Betwixt* encourage a *human-computer therapeutic alliance*. Traditionally, the term *therapeutic alliance* is applied in the context between a human patient and a human therapist. When such an alliance is established, the therapist is seen as a positive collaborator that helps the client achieve their goals, as opposed to, say, an authority figure or preacher of what the patient should do.

Thus far, we note that users have appeared to refer to the chatbot in the experience as a collaborative helper that is able to ask "deep questions without feeling intrusive". While a therapeutic bond has been previously shown to be possible in a chatbot application [7], more research is needed to assess the strength of a possible therapeutic alliance during usage of *Betwixt* and identify significant contributing factors for this type of alliance to occur.

### 3.3    Healthy Long-Term Engagement

*Betwixt* was designed with the intent that users should be able to build resilience at their own pace over the long term. Our survey revealed that the app would likely be used occasionally and/or when needed, as opposed to being an unhealthy presence in a user's life. Below are a few examples of how users described the ideal frequency for working through the *Betwixt* content:

- "A **bi-weekly basis** for stories I to III, engaging with a story and extra info in one session, and the meditation on a later day."
- "**Once or twice a week... right before bed, usually by reading the main chapter** then moving into the extra info/meditation."
- "**One dream a day** with their respective reading and meditation for five days in a row."
- "**One dream roughly every other night for about two weeks...** corresponding **meditations on the days in between.**"

One user also indicated that *Betwixt* fit best as a "20–30 break". Taken together, these findings are promising for future mental health apps that wish to secure regular user engagement while preventing addiction.

## 4    Discussion

We have described several of *Betwixt*'s features that appear to differentiate it from other interactive narratives for mental health support. In its current state, *Betwixt* appeals best to individuals with roughly half an hour available searching for a relaxing and self-reflective experience. Preliminary feedback suggests it appears to fulfill these needs, and does so in such a way that users can regularly learn from the app.

Our results point to features that enhance the power of interactive storytelling for mental resilience. Relaxing immersive elements and opportunities for personal, self-distanced reflection that relate to the setting appear to support healthy, consistent engagement in the self-reflection process rather than "clicking through" the experience. Collaborative brainstorming and reframing with an app that can "listen" and support self-expression and self-connection, rather than preach or dismiss, was also deemed valuable by users. Future work will continue to build on our understanding of how to best design interactive narratives like *Betwixt* to assist the general population in strengthening mental resilience.

# References

1. de Alva, F.E.M., Wadley, G., Lederman, R.: It feels different from real life: users' opinions of mobile applications for mental health. In: Proceedings of the Annual Meeting of the Australian Special Interest Group for Computer Human Interaction, pp. 598–602 (2015)
2. Ayduk, Ö., Kross, E.: Analyzing negative experiences without ruminating: the role of self-distancing in enabling adaptive self-reflection. Soc. Pers. Psychol. Compass 4(10), 841–854 (2010)
3. Ayduk, Ö., Kross, E.: From a distance: implications of spontaneous self-distancing for adaptive self-reflection. J. Pers. Soc. Psychol. 98(5), 809 (2010)
4. Baumel, A., Muench, F., Edan, S., Kane, J.M.: Objective user engagement with mental health apps: systematic search and panel-based usage analysis. J. Med. Internet Res. 21(9), e14567 (2019)
5. Case, N.: Adventures with anxiety (2019)
6. Cowden, R.G., Meyer-Weitz, A.: Self-reflection and self-insight predict resilience and stress in competitive tennis. Soc. Behav. Personal. Int. J. 44(7), 1133–1149 (2016)
7. Darcy, A., Daniels, J., Salinger, D., Wicks, P., Robinson, A., et al.: Evidence of human-level bonds established with a digital conversational agent: cross-sectional, retrospective observational study. JMIR Formative Res. 5(5), e27868 (2021)
8. Gameworks, P.: Paper cages (2019)
9. Greenberg, L.S.: Emotion-focused therapy. Clin. Psychol. Psychother.: Int. J. Theory Pract. 11(1), 3–16 (2004)
10. Litvin, S., Saunders, R., Maier, M.A., Lüttke, S.: Gamification as an approach to improve resilience and reduce attrition in mobile mental health interventions: a randomized controlled trial. PloS One 15(9), e0237220 (2020)
11. Murray, J.H.: Hamlet on the Holodeck: The Future of Narrative in Cyberspace. MIT Press (2017)
12. Nakajima, M., Takano, K., Tanno, Y.: Mindfulness relates to decreased depressive symptoms via enhancement of self-insight. Mindfulness 10(5), 894–902 (2019)
13. Quinn, Z., Lindsey, P., Schankler, I.: Depression quest: an interactive (non) fiction about living with depression. DepressionQuest.com (2013). http://www.depressionquest.com
14. Roth, C., Mekler, E.D., Bowman, N.: Transformative experience through interactive narrative. In: ICIDS 2020 International Conference on Interactive Digital Storytelling (2020)
15. Schneider, T.R., Lyons, J.B., Khazon, S.: Emotional intelligence and resilience. Pers. Individ. Differ. 55(8), 909–914 (2013)
16. Seligman, M.E.P., Csikszentmihalyi, M.: Positive psychology: an introduction. In: Csikszentmihalyi, M. (ed.) Flow and the Foundations of Positive Psychology, pp. 279–298. Springer, Dordrecht (2014). https://doi.org/10.1007/978-94-017-9088-8_18
17. Stein, D., Grant, A.M.: Disentangling the relationships among self-reflection, insight, and subjective well-being: the role of dysfunctional attitudes and core self-evaluations. J. Psychol. 148(5), 505–522 (2014)
18. Tabibnia, G.: An affective neuroscience model of boosting resilience in adults. Neurosci. Biobehav. Rev. 115, 321–350 (2020)
19. Troy, A.S., Mauss, I.B.: Resilience in the face of stress: emotion regulation as a protective factor. Resilience Mental Health: Challenges Across Lifespan 1(2), 30–44 (2011)
20. Tugade, M.M., Fredrickson, B.L.: Regulation of positive emotions: emotion regulation strategies that promote resilience. J. Happiness Stud. 8(3), 311–333 (2007)

# A Transmedia Narrative Framework for Pediatric Hearing Counseling

Nele Kadastik$^{(\boxtimes)}$ and Luis Emilio Bruni$^{(\boxtimes)}$

Department of Architecture, Design, and Media Technology,
Aalborg University Copenhagen, Copenhagen, Denmark
{neka,leb}@create.aau.dk

**Abstract.** To help fill the gap in pediatric communication tools and support child-centered care in pediatric hearing care, we designed and evaluated a novel narrative transmedia tool for facilitating communication with children during pediatric audiology and speech- and language therapy appointments. The digital tool integrates methods from narrative and play therapy, and applies a novel transmedia narrative framework using 360-degree video and smartphone-based Virtual Reality (VR). The tool was evaluated in three case studies. The findings suggest that the tool was effective in engaging the children in conversation about their hearing, supporting the specialists in exploring the functional impacts of the children's hearing loss. Through co-participatory design, implementation and evaluation with hearing care specialists, it became clear that such a multi-platform transmedia tool, combining interactive digital narrative and emerging narratives, represents a promising avenue for facilitating child-centered communication during pediatric hearing care appointments.

**Keywords:** Patient-centered care · Transmedia narrative · VR · Emerging narrative · Pediatric hearing care · Narrative therapy · Play therapy · Communication

## 1  Introduction

In adult and pediatric health care, communication and person-centredness serve as the basic elements for health literacy, but also as the main indicators of the quality of care received by children and their families [3, 38]. However, rather than focusing on promoting more effective child and care provider communication, and addressing the child's individual needs for treatment, new pediatric digital tools have been much more concerned with diagnostic or physical rehabilitative uses. To help fill this gap in current applications and to support child-centered care in pediatric health care, we designed and tested a novel narrative transmedia tool for enhancing child and care provider communication for pediatric audiology and speech- and language therapy appointments.

© Springer Nature Switzerland AG 2021
A. Mitchell and M. Vosmeer (Eds.): ICIDS 2021, LNCS 13138, pp. 365–378, 2021.
https://doi.org/10.1007/978-3-030-92300-6_36

Pediatric hearing care can be considered a collaborative process through which the child, the parent(s), the therapist, the child's teacher(s), and the audiologist, all must work together to support the child in the treatment process. It is therefore crucial that in this process the child's voice and needs are being heard and addressed, as the inability to meet them can have serious effects on the child's well-being, their speech- and language, and their psycho-social development. The digital application, designed together with hearing care professionals, integrates methods from narrative and play therapy, and uses a tablet computer, a smartphone, and a smartphone-based VR headset to help facilitate more effective child and care provider communication. By applying a novel transmedia narrative framework, the tool aims to support the goals and objectives of the appointment, while promoting the child's self-advocacy and self-efficacy skills through the child's active participation and engagement during the appointment.

## 2   From Narrative and Play Therapy to Digital Tools

When designing new technological solutions and tools in healthcare, designers and developers frequently rely on the translation of existing clinical and therapeutic methods, "[I]t is vital to understand the conventional practices and processes in the therapies when developing technology-based interventions and translating this in-depth understanding in the technology design" [18,30]. This is particularly pertinent when designing novel tools for pediatric populations.

Stemming from person- and family-centered practices, the concept of Child-Centered Care (CCC) relies on effective communication between the child and the care provider, recognizing the child as a responsible and active participant in their own care [10]. In pediatric therapy and counseling, a child-centric approach is often realized using methods and techniques from narrative and play therapy [4,15,29]. Through the language of play, play therapy allows the therapist to utilize the process of projection through which internal events are attributed to (play) objects and characters [17]. On the other hand, narrative therapy refers to an approach where the patient's stories are used in the treatment process to "re-author one' s own story", in which the externalizing process supports the patient in deconstructing problem-saturated stories, allowing them to be shaped into new narratives through unique outcomes [8,13,24].

The critical relationship between hearing loss and speech- and language development is well recognized, which can perhaps also explain why in the past, narrative approaches in pediatric hearing counselling have been considered to be problematic due to their logocentric nature [11]. However, as it has been demonstrated more recently, through combining narrative approaches with play therapy, they can allow for the necessary flexibility and sensibility for adapting to the child's developmental level and in effect, help enhance the communication process [2]. Moreover, |9] draw attention to the importance of the body when involving children in story authoring tasks. While recognized as central to the experience of play, [9] suggest that "enactment, through imagination, leads the child to better, richer and more coherent storytelling".

When introducing technology-based solutions that rely on existing therapeutic interventions, it is also vital to consider the children's changing communication and play habits in the current digital age [14, 39].

## 2.1 Interactive Digital Narrative in Therapy

One of the new modes of digital communication and representation, incipiently being used in narrative therapy and counseling, is interactive digital narrative (IDN). As proposed by [28], IDN poses a number of advantages for health interventions, including, but not limited to, introducing a more flexible and engaging way for patients to engage with care providers, increased accessibility to materials, as well as possibilities for customisation and personalization that respond to the needs and preferences of the user [28].

As a therapeutic intervention tool, IDN has been investigated in different pediatric populations, including pediatric cancer patients [36] and in pediatric hearing counseling [2]. With respect to the use of IDN based tools in pediatric hearing care, [2] suggest that "given a specifically designed emergent narrative system, structured around specific counseling goals and supported by a context-specific adaptation of scaffolding conversations maps, digital interactive narrative tools can be potentially useful in engaging and facilitating communication with children during counseling and/or therapy sessions". While IDN in pediatric counseling can in many ways still be considered in its infancy, recent findings and growing interest suggests its potential for applying a more child-centric approach whilst helping to promote more active participation in the care process [2, 36, 37].

More recently, IDN has also been explored through the integration of immersive technologies. It has been proposed that VR as a narrative medium can support changing concepts of the self: "through novel utilization of the storytelling medium, a person finds themselves immersed and starts changing their self-concepts more quickly and easily than in reality" [12]. Research that has examined VR in pediatric psychology and speech- and language pathology, suggests that controlled VR environments can allow children to engage with background narratives more effectively [25], and provide means for training and building communication skills that can be generalized to real-world experiences [6]. Although little is still known about the potential of VR for diverse applications of IDN in health care, we suggest that it may potentially enhance narrative based counseling and therapy processes.

## 3 Design

The tool was designed for initial and follow-up pediatric hearing counseling appointments and integrates methods from narrative and play therapy, as well as elements from some of the few existing pediatric hearing counseling tools [19, 23] developed by the Ida Institute. The tool aims to introduce a narrative communication platform for facilitating more effective communication during the appointment. In this case, we define a narrative communication platform as a foundation for reciprocal conversation and emerging narratives, built around specific themes embedded in pre-constructed fictional or non-fictional narrative elements. While by emergent narrative we refer to a narrative that is not pre-scripted, or pre-defined but which emerges through the interaction in the given context, "in the style of improvisational drama, rather than the authored narratives in more widespread use" [1,20]. The core design of the narrative framework applies a transmedia approach [16], distributing three different stages of the counseling process across two different media, involving an application on a tablet-computer and 360-degree video scenarios in mobile-VR.

The tool was designed together with hearing care professionals with whom we outlined essential requirements, and the key considerations for the tool through a co-design approach. To ensure a family- and child-centered focus, we worked in close collaboration with specialists from the Ida Institute, a non-profit organization working with integrating person-centered care (PCC) in hearing care. We also reviewed relevant studies, materials, tools and articles that had previously addressed considerations for pediatric counseling applications outside of just diagnostic purposes [2,7,19,23,26,27,33]. Additionally, we conducted 10 structured and semi-structured qualitative interviews with hearing care professionals, including a senior audiologist, a small-children's speech and language consultant, a school children's speech and language consultant, and an experienced speech and language pathologist.

Based on our research, we identified key considerations for the tool as follows: (1) ease of use and clear instructions, (2) fun and engaging for the child, (3) focus on the functional impacts of hearing loss in everyday scenarios, (4) allow documenting concise and key takeaways, (5) allow for providing a handout or take-at-home resource for the patient, (6) take into account the time constraints of the appointment, (7) support facilitating troubleshooting skills and communication strategies. These elements served as the underlying pillars for the general frameworks and design.

Moreover, as the tool has a narrative focus, it was important to consider the adaptability of the tool for children of different ages and developmental levels. It has been suggested that children from around age 6 are only beginning to improve their narrative skills, with preteens typically expressing relatively high-level narrative skills [5]. However, as this clearly differs from child to child, the age-group for the tool was broadly defined for children aged between 5–13. Additionally, we conducted a number of usability tests throughout the design and development process. This included among others, early usability testing with participants recruited through convenience sampling, followed by usability testing with normal hearing children (NH) in the intended age group.

## 3.1 Design and Implementation of the Narrative System

A transmedia approach was adopted to enrich the narrative elements for supporting emergent narratives, to subsequently help establish the narrative communication platform, but also to promote active user participation and involvement throughout the session. As mentioned, the narrative framework distributes three different stages of the counseling process across two different media (see Sect. 3.2 Counseling Stages below). Making use of the specific affordances of the two different media, i.e. immersion in the case of VR, and children's gameplay possibilities on tablet computer [21], each stage in the two media introduces new types of content and narrative elements to support context-specific open-ended emergent narratives. Moreover, the tasks and questions in the tool take inspiration from, and integrate elements from existing pediatric hearing counseling tools [19,23].

Firstly, on the tablet computer, the user is introduced to initial narrative elements, the context and the character (See Fig. 1), and is thereafter asked to prioritize and evaluate different communication environments (school/kindergarten, home, playground) (See Fig. 2).

**Fig. 1.** Introduction on the tablet computer. On the left, screen capture of the start screen. On the right, character introduction.

The three environments were chosen based on their pertinence and relevance, as advised by our participating specialists. After the introductory part, the user is asked to select one specific communication environment (the setting) they would like to explore further. The guiding thread is to help the character (Sara), who suffers from hearing loss to identify potential issues and challenges in the chosen communication environment, to subsequently encourage exploring and defining specific communication strategies for that environment. In this initial stage, through the interactive tasks and questions, the system also obtains relevant information about the user to personalize the experience, support the selecting of the most relevant communication environment, and to provide post-session documentation for the specialist.

Subsequently, a 360-degree video scenario introduces the setting and the point of view. The user can then experience their previously selected environment through 'Sara's eyes', using a mobile-VR head-mounted display (HMD) (See Fig. 3). All three possible scenarios are produced as scripted 2–3 min long one-shot 360-degree videos. To elicit context-specific emergent narratives, each 360-degree video concurrently conveys a number of typical situations that a

**Fig. 2.** Screen capture of interactive tasks and questions in the app on the tablet computer. On the left, prioritization of the three different communication environments. On the right, evaluation of the prioritized communication environments. (Given the original context of the implementation and evaluation, the texts are in Danish language)

child with hearing loss (HL) might encounter on a day-to-day basis, corresponding to the specific communication environment. When designing these three scenarios, it was important to take into consideration the desired margin for user-interpretation, as well as the opportunities for achieving this using the 360-degree video narrative medium. It was hypothesized that allowing more freedom in the interpretation of the scenarios, instead of introducing explicit narratives, could better support the therapeutic goals of the system. Although the user was expected to freely explore the scenario, it was nevertheless important to support keeping the focus on the specific context of the chosen communication scenario. This was done through directing the user's attention in the scenario through concurrent scripted situations. These scenario-specific situations were established based on an analysis of relevant materials, information gathered from the conducted semi-structured interviews, and observational data from Ida Institute's ethnographic videos. To encourage the user in adopting the character's perspective during the experience, all 360-degree video scenarios include a first-person avatar perspective of the character's virtual body.

Returning to the tablet app, the user is encouraged to reflect on their VR-experience and use the introduced narrative elements in a play activity on the tablet computer (See Fig. 4). The play activity aims to elicit and support the sharing of emergent narratives to meet the embedded counseling goals. The design for the play activity presents the user with a modifiable 'canvas', where pre-arranged elements that loosely depict some of the situations, characters, and relevant objects from the selected 360-scenario, but also present the user with additional context-specific items e.g. hearing aids, an FM-system (the wireless device that helps enhance hearing aids), and other items. The user can interact with the elements by dragging them around on the canvas, adding new items from the menu, or removing them. Additionally, the system also includes a drawing function, which allows the user to draw missing objects, characters or other desired elements to support their narratives. Lastly, the system also features a

**Fig. 3.** Screen capture of one the 360-degree video scenarios, the school environment.

'tips' section, providing the user(s) with questions, suggestions and discussion topics for conversation scaffolding during the activity. After the activity the user(s) can save their creation and are awarded with a "thank you" animation.

### 3.2 Counseling Stages

The counseling stages for the specialist include: (1) the exploratory stage (2) the immersive stage (3) the reflection, strategy, and decision-making stage. In order to support structuring the session in accordance with the embedded goals, the tool comes with an additional tool guide. The tool guide acts as a supporting guide for the professional to navigate the system and provides suggestions for conversation scaffolding during each stage. The suggestions for conversation scaffolding [2] draw inspiration from the Ida Institute tools [19,23], and narrative scaffolding conversation maps for supporting externalizing, deconstruction, and unique outcomes, as adapted by [34,35], originally based on Vygotsky's seminal work [31,32].

The flow of the three stages go as follows: (1) In the *exploratory stage*, the specialist and the child can explore the impacts and potential challenges in the three communication environments presented, through the initially introduced narrative elements (context, characters, setting), and the interactive tasks and questions. By the end of the exploratory stage, the child's responses to the questions will be displayed, and the specialist can further examine them: identify discrepancies, potential ambivalence and attitudes relating to the different com-

**Fig. 4.** Play activity on the tablet computer. On the left, screen capture of the play activity, school environment. On the right, specialist, child and parent engaging in the play activity, playground.

munication environments. Thereafter, the specialist and the child can select a communication environment they would like to discuss and explore further.

**Fig. 5.** On the left, participant exploring one of the VR scenarios, specialist and parent observing what the child sees on the tablet. On the right, form for the specialist to fill in comments and observations from the session.

(2) In the second, *immersive stage*, the specialist can make use of the VR feature. While the child is experiencing the 360-degree video in VR, the specialist and the parent(s) can see on the tablet what the child sees in VR (See Fig. 5). The specialist can use the suggestions in the tool guide to guide the child in the environment, or let the child experience it more on their own. In combination with the previous stage, the immersive stage serves as the foundation for the subsequent stage, helping to establish a common narrative communication platform.

(3) During the *reflection, strategy and decision-making stage*, the objective is to involve the child in the collaborative problem-solving and strategy-building process through play and emergent storytelling (becoming a 'co-expert'). Later

in the process, the child's creation from the activity can be saved and shared with the child and the parent(s), providing a type of a hand-out, or take-home resource. The system also allows saving the child's responses, and provides the specialist a post-session form for filling in comments and observations from the session (see Fig. 5). This documentation and the hand-out can be used during follow-up sessions, for instance, as a conversation starter for discussing progress and strategies.

## 4   Evaluation

In order to develop a more in-depth understanding and assess potential benefits and limitations of this type of solution as part of a real-life pediatric hearing care setting, we conducted three case studies in which the tool was tested with 3 different HI-children 5–9 years old (Participant A 9 y/o, Participant B 5 y/o, and Participant C 5 y/o), by two speech- and language specialists (Specialist A and Specialist B). The chosen research methodology was an exploratory multiple-case study, in which the primary unit of analysis was the specialist-child couple. Both participating specialists had over 20-years of experience in the field of pediatric speech and language therapy. The three children participating in the study were all diagnosed with moderate to severe hearing loss and were all fitted with auditory devices.

The purpose of the evaluation can be considered threefold. Firstly, we were interested in knowing to what extent the tool, which integrates methods from narrative and play therapy into the proposed transmedia narrative framework, supports facilitating child-centric communication during the session. Secondly, we aimed to establish how the embedded structure of the system supports the professional in fulfilling the counseling-goals. Lastly, we were interested in investigating the feasibility and usability of such a tool, when used as part of real-life pediatric hearing care appointments.

Prior to the tests, we obtained informed consent from all participants of the study. It was agreed prior to the testing sessions that the tests would take place in environments that would feel familiar and safe for the children. Before each session, the specialist was introduced to the procedure, handed a physical tool guide, and given an overview on how to use the equipment. Granted the permission by the child, parents and the specialist, each session was filmed for subsequent video analysis. After each session, a semi-structured interview was conducted with the specialist. The qualitative data from the individual cases was gathered using a combination of qualitative data collection methods including direct-observation, video and audio recordings, unstructured pre-test interviews, and pre-test questionnaires, and post-test semi-structured interviews.

The analysis of the data is based on three primary areas of investigation: (1) the tool as a platform for effective communication, (2) effectiveness relating to the counseling goals, and (3) feasibility and usability. As the aim was to study each case firstly individually and then together to establish similarities, differences, and patterns across all three cases, we used a cross-case synthesis to synthesize evidence from these multiple cases [22]. As the last step in the analysis we involved a pediatric hearing care specialist as part of our *participatory analysis* approach.

The equipment used during all testing sessions included two Samsung Galaxy tablets, one Samsung S8 smartphone, a Samsung Gear VR head-mounted-display (HMD), and an external Wonderboom Bluetooth speaker. One of the Samsung tablets was used for the tablet-app and the second one was used to mirror the Samsung S8 smartphone's VR image during the VR experience, so the specialist and the parent(s) could follow what the child was seeing in VR. In case the child did not want to pair their hearing device(s) to the smartphone, an external Bluetooth speaker was used to amplify the sound during the VR experience.

## 4.1  Results

In all three cases, the tool supported uncovering essential information about the functional impacts of the children's hearing loss and served as an effective springboard for facilitating communication during the sessions. Introducing digital technology as part of the appointment, particularly the VR headset, helped engage the children and the parents from the start. Moreover, as all participants had previous experience with using tablet computers at home, adopting the tablet app felt intuitive for all the children.

During the first stage, both specialists used the character and the subsequent interactive tasks and questions to elicit conversation on important themes and issues relating to the three presented communication environments. However, it was especially with the younger children, Participant B and Participant C, that important information emerged in this phase. For example, when discussing Participant B's kindergarten environment, it was brought up by Participant B that he does not hear very well in the play-hut when other children are speaking. Participant B's mother then supported the specialist in further exploring this issue by asking, "Do you hear some of what they [the other children] are saying?" to which Participant B replied, "I do not hear anything at all". While with Participant C, it emerged that he was highly sensitive to the noise of slamming doors and the noise of rain falling when at the kindergarten.

The narrative framework embedded in the tool, partially relying on the 360-video VR scenarios, was observed as most effective with the older participant (Participant A, 9 y/o). In this case, it supported the child in sharing his perspective and helped the specialist in introducing new strategies. During the play activity, reflecting on the VR scenario to help the character cope better in the selected environment, Participant A selected the same type of hearing equipment and the same type of technology for the character as he himself had. When Participant A was asked why he gave the character an iPad, he replied that, it was so the character Sara would not have to focus on what was going on around her, and could get away from the surrounding noise. It was later suggested by the specialist that the child likely projected his own coping-strategies and perspectives on the character. This gave the specialist an opportunity to better understand the child's perspective and identify previously unknown issues. The specialist also used the narrative platform to introduce new strategies in a way that did not directly involve the child, "Sara is 9 years old. And she just got the phone. Does she know how to hold it so that she can hear better?" The fact that Participant A felt it was more of a game where he could also be the expert, encouraged him to participate in the strategy-building and decision-making process more actively, while allowing the specialist to steer the conversation naturally to the child's own habits. Specialist 1 assessed the role of the VR feature in establishing the narrative communication platform with Participant A as an essential part of the tool, "It was something he was captivated by. When he gets captivated by it, we can then also talk about it. Had he [Participant A] thought it was too boring or had not liked it, we also would not have been able to talk about it later". In this case, not only did the VR feature help make the session more exciting and engaging for the Participant A, but it also had direct implications for helping facilitate the conversation during the later phases.

On the other hand, in the case of Participant B and Participant C, the narrative framework did not work as well as intended. It was clear that both younger participants found it difficult to apprehend the VR experience, subsequently making it more challenging in terms of bridging the experience with the latter play activity on the tablet. Although both enjoyed exploring the functionalities of the system, they also needed much more support from the specialist in terms of contextualizing the play activity based on the previously presented information. Furthermore, despite the suggestions provided in the tool guide, and both specialists seeing the VR feature as a valuable addition to the tool, it was also clear that the specialists were new to this type of technology, and found it challenging to put to use in terms of serving the goals of the session. Therefore, to encourage further exploration, and for the VR experience not to become underutilized during the session, this feature would require either an instructional debriefing, or some other type of an embedded protocol for the specialist.

Nevertheless, the findings suggest that the tool offered a structured and time-framed approach for the specialists to explore the various impacts of the children's hearing loss. And while the tool was demonstrated as most effective for exploring the functional impacts, it was evident that it also provided ways for scaffolding psycho-social impacts. Both participating specialists were interested in adopting the tool in their practice.

# 5   Conclusion

The present study was designed to explore the possibilities and potential of a narrative transmedia counseling tool that integrates smartphone-based VR for encouraging a more child-centered approach during pediatric hearing care appointments. The communication tool was based on a transmedia-based emergent narrative system, and was directly tied to the counseling goals, integrating methods from narrative and play therapy. The tool was evaluated through three case studies in which two speech- and language specialists tested the tool with three children diagnosed with hearing loss. The findings suggest that the tool was most effective in supporting the specialists in exploring the functional impacts of the children's hearing loss, while allowing for scaffolding psycho-social impacts. In all cases, by establishing a communication platform based on context-specific themes and narrative elements, the tool provided a way for the children to actively engage in conversation about their individual perspectives, promoting the children's self-advocacy skills during the session.

While the novelty of the VR feature managed to equally engage all the partici-pants, the younger participants found the experience more difficult to apprehend. Hence, the narrative communication platform integrating the VR feature, was more effective and beneficial when used with the older child. In this case, the nar-rative communication platform provided a way to better understand the child's perspective but also offered an additional way for the specialist to introduce and collaboratively define new strategies without putting unnecessary pressure on the child. Nevertheless, for the VR feature not to become underutilized during the session, it would require an instructional debriefing, or some other type of an embedded protocol for guiding the child in the VR environment.

In this study, the tool was tested by two speech and language specialists, who have different roles and approaches in the pediatric hearing care process, therefore, it could also be interesting to establish the potential of the tool in a more clinical context, for instance, when used as part of an audiological assess-ment. Moreover, future work should focus on providing more opportunities for personalization i.e. adding more characters, the children being able to themselves choose the character's gender, age, hearing equipment. While the narrative sys-tem was considered most successful when used with an older child, the different elements of the tool showed high potential with younger children. The fact that the specialists participating in the study were interested in adopting the tool into their practice, further demonstrates the potentiality of this type of a solution as part of a pediatric hearing care session for enhancing child and care provider communication.

# References

1. Aylett, R.: Narrative in virtual environments towards emergent narrative. In: Pro-ceedings of AAAI Symposium on Narrative Intelligence (1999)
2. Baceviciute, S., Rützou Albæk, K.R., Arsovski, A., Bruni, L.E.: Digital interactive narrative tools for facilitating communication with children during counseling: a case for audiology. In: Oyarzun, D., Peinado, F., Young, R.M., Elizalde, A., Mén-dez, G. (eds.) ICIDS 2012. LNCS, vol. 7648, pp. 48–59. Springer, Heidelberg (2012). https://doi.org/10.1007/978-3-642-34851-8_5
3. Bell, J., Condren, M.: Communication strategies for empowering and protecting children. Pediatr. Pharm. Advocacy Group **21**(2), 176–184 (2016). https://doi.org/10.5863/1551-6776-21.2.176
4. Bennett, L.: Narrative methods and children: theoretical explanations and practice issues. J. Child Adolesc. Psychiatr. Nurs. **21**(1), 13–23 (2008). https://doi.org/10.1111/j.1744-6171.2008.00125.x

5. Bräne, A.: User Experience Design for Children: Developing and Testing a UX Framework (Dissertation) (2016). http://urn.kb.se/resolve?urn=urn:nbn:se:umu:diva-125935. Accessed 12 Oct 2021
6. Bryant, L., Brunner, M., Hemsley, B.: A review of virtual reality technologies in the field of communication disability: implications for practice and research. Disabil. Rehabil. Assist. Technol. **15**(4), 365–372 (2020). https://doi.org/10.1080/17483107.2018.1549276
7. Chakraborty, K., Bhide, A.: General principles for psychotherapeutic interventions in children and adolescents. Indian J. Psychiatry (2020). http://www.indianjpsychiatry.org/text.asp?2020/62/8/299/276107. Accessed 23 July 2020
8. Chow, E.O.: Narrative therapy an evaluated intervention to improve stroke survivors' social and emotional adaptation. Clin. Rehabil. **29**(4), 315–326 (2015). https://doi.org/10.1177/0269215514544039
9. Chu, S.L., Quek, F., Tanenbaum, T.J.: *Performative Authoring:* nurturing storytelling in children through imaginative enactment. In: Koenitz, H., Sezen, T.I., Ferri, G., Haahr, M., Sezen, D., Çatak, G. (eds.) ICIDS 2013. LNCS, vol. 8230, pp. 144–155. Springer, Cham (2013). https://doi.org/10.1007/978-3-319-02756-2_18
10. Coyne, I., Holmström, I., Söderbäck, M.: Centeredness in healthcare: a concept synthesis of family-centered care, person-centered care and child-centered care. J. Pediatr. Nurs. **42**, 45–56 (2018). https://doi.org/10.1016/j.pedn.2018.07.001
11. Furlonger, B.: Narrative therapy and children with hearing impairments. Am. Ann. Deaf **144**, 325–333 (1999)
12. Georgieva, I., Georgiev, G.: Reconstructing personal stories in virtual reality as a mechanism to recover the self. Int. J. Environ. Res. Public Health **17**(26), 5 (2019). https://doi.org/10.3390/ijerph17010026
13. Gonçalves, M., Matos, M., Santos, A.: Narrative therapy and the nature of "Innovative Moments" in the construction of change. J. Constructivist Psychol. **22**(1), 1–23 (2009). https://doi.org/10.1080/10720530802500748
14. Gottschalk, F.: Impacts of technology use on children: exploring literature on the brain, cognition and well-being (2019). https://www.oecd.org/officialdocuments/publicdisplaydocumentpdf/?cote=EDU/WKP%282019%293&docLanguage=En. Accessed 29 July 2021
15. Guterman, J., Martin, C.: Using puppets with aggressive children to externalize the problem in narrative therapy. In: Drewes, A., Schaefer, C. (eds) Play Therapy In Middle Childhood, pp. 135–151. American Psychological Association (2015). https://doi.org/10.1037/14776-008
16. Jenkins, H.: Convergence Culture: Where Old and New Media Collide. New York University Press (2006)
17. Jenny, E.: Projection. In: Goldstein, S., Naglieri, J.A. (eds.) Encyclopedia of Child Behavior and Development, pp. 1162–1163. Springer, Boston (2011)
18. Kraft, P., Yardley, L.: Current issues and new directions in Psychology and Health: what is the future of digital interventions for health behaviour change? Psychol. Health **24**(6), 615–618 (2009). https://doi.org/10.1080/08870440903068581
19. Living Well for Teens and Tweens Digital Pediatric Counseling Tool: Ida Institute (2018). https://idainstitute.com/tools/living_well_for_teens_and_tweens/. Accessed 12 Oct 2021
20. Louchart, S., Aylett, R.: Narrative theory and emergent interactive narrative. Int. J. Continuing Eng. Educ. Life Long Learn. **14**(6) (2004)
21. Lundtofte, T.E.: Young children's tablet computer play. Am. J. Play **12**(2), 216–232. (2020). https://www.journalofplay.org/sites/www.journalofplay.org/files/pdf-articles/AJP-12-2-Article5-Tablet.pdf. Accessed 12 Oct 2021

22. Mills, A.J., Durepos, G., Wiebe, E.: Encyclopedia of Case Study Research (vols. 1–0). SAGE Publications, Inc., Thousand Oaks (2010). https://doi.org/10.4135/9781412957397
23. My World Digital Pediatric Counseling Tool: Ida Institute (2018). https://idainstitute.com/tools/my_world/. Accessed 12 Oct 2021
24. O'Connor, T.: Narrative therapy. In: Leeming, D.A. (ed.) Encyclopedia of Psychology and Religion, pp. 1182–1185. Springer, Heidelberg (2014). https://doi.org/10.1007/978-1-4614-6086-2_455
25. Parsons, T.D., et al.: Virtual reality in pediatric psychology. Pediatrics 140(2), 86–91 (2017). https://doi.org/10.1542/peds.2016-1758I
26. Pattison, S., Harris, B.: Counselling children and young people: a review of the evidence for its effectiveness. Couns. Psychother. Res. 6, 233–237 (2006). https://doi.org/10.1080/14733140601022659
27. Round, J.L.: The need and uses of the Ida 'My World' counselling tool in paediatric rehabilitation for hearing-impaired children (2013). https://idainstitute.com/fileadmin/user_upload/Downloads/My%20World%20Tool%20Thesis%20Jessica%20Round.pdf. Accessed 10 Oct 2020
28. Si, M., Marsella, S., Miller, L.: Interactive stories for health interventions. In: Aylett, R., Lim, M.Y., Louchart, S., Petta, P., Riedl, M. (eds.) ICIDS 2010. LNCS, vol. 6432, pp. 291–292. Springer, Heidelberg (2010). https://doi.org/10.1007/978-3-642-16638-9_46
29. Sweeney, D.S., Landreth, G.L.: Child-centered play therapy. In: O'Connor, K.J., Braverman, L.D. (eds.) Play Therapy Theory and Practice: Comparing Theories and Techniques, pp. 123–162. Wiley (2009)
30. Tabbaa, L., Ang, C., Siriaraya, P., She, W., Prigerson, H.: A reflection on virtual reality design for psychological, cognitive and behavioral interventions: design needs, opportunities and challenges. Int. J. Hum.-Comput. Interact. 37(9), 815–866 (2020). https://doi.org/10.1080/10447318.2020.1848161
31. Vygotsky, L.S.: Mind in Society: The Development of Higher Psychological Processes. Harvard University Press, Cambridge (1978)
32. Vygotsky, L.S.: Thinking and speech. In: Rievery, R.W., Carton, A.S. (eds.) The Collected Works of L. S. Vygotsky, Volume 1: Problems of General Psychology, pp. 39–285. Plenum Press, New York (1987)
33. Westby, C.: Resource review: my world. Word Mouth 29(2), 12–13 (2017)
34. White, M.: Externalizing conversations revisited. In: Morgan, A., White, M. (eds.) Narrative Therapy with Children and Their Families, pp. 2–56. Dulwich Centre Publications, Adelaide (2006)
35. White, M.: Maps of Narrative Practice. W.W. Norton & Company, New York (2007)
36. Wilson, D.K., et al.: Exploring the role of digital storytelling in pediatric oncology patients' perspectives regarding diagnosis: a literature review. SAGE Open (2015). https://doi.org/10.1177/2158244015572099
37. Wyatt, T., Hauenstein, E.: Enhancing children's health through digital story. CIN: Comput. Inform. Nurs. 26(3), 142–148 (2008)
38. Wynia, M., Osborn, C.: Health literacy and communication quality in health care organizations. J. Health Commun. 15(sup2), 102–115 (2010). https://doi.org/10.1080/10810730.2010.499981
39. Zaman, B., Mifsud, C.: Young children's use of digital media and parental mediation. Cyberpsychol.: J. Psychosoc. Res. Cyberspace 11(3) (2017). https://doi.org/10.5817/CP2017-3-xx

# "What's Important to You, Max?": The Influence of Goals on Engagement in an Interactive Narrative for Adolescent Health Behavior Change

Megan Mott[1]([✉]), Bradford Mott[2], Jonathan Rowe[2], Elizabeth Ozer[3],
Alison Giovanelli[3], Mark Berna[3], Marianne Pugatch[3], Kathleen Tebb[3],
Carlos Penilla[3], and James Lester[2]

[1] University of North Carolina, Chapel Hill, Chapel Hill, NC, USA
meganm18@live.unc.edu
[2] North Carolina State University, Raleigh, NC, USA
[3] University of California, San Francisco, San Francisco, CA, USA

**Abstract.** Interactive narrative technologies for preventive health care offer significant potential for promoting health behavior change in adolescents. By improving adolescents' knowledge, personal efficacy, and self-regulatory skills these technologies hold great promise for realizing positive impacts on adolescent health. These potential benefits are enabled through story-centric learning experiences that provide opportunities for adolescents to practice strategies to reduce risky health behaviors in engaging game-based environments. A distinctive feature of interactive narrative that promotes engagement is players' ability to influence the story through the choices they make. In this paper, we present initial work investigating engagement in an interactive narrative that focuses on reducing adolescents' risky behaviors around alcohol use. Specifically, we consider how the short-term and long-term goals adolescents choose as being important to the protagonist character relates to their engagement with the interactive narrative. Leveraging interaction log data from a pilot study with 20 adolescents, we conduct a cluster-based analysis of the goals players selected. We then examine how engagement differs between the identified clusters. Results indicate that adolescents' choices for the protagonist's short-term and long-term goals can significantly impact their engagement with the interactive narrative.

**Keywords:** Interactive narrative · Health behavior change · Alcohol use

## 1 Introduction

Many adolescents engage in behaviors that increase morbidity and mortality during adolescence [1]. In the United States, automobile accidents and unintentional injuries are the most prominent causes of adolescent deaths, often occurring in conjunction with using alcohol or other substances [2]. The majority of adolescent health problems are amenable to behavior change interventions and a wide array of health information

© Springer Nature Switzerland AG 2021
A. Mitchell and M. Vosmeer (Eds.): ICIDS 2021, LNCS 13138, pp. 379–392, 2021.
https://doi.org/10.1007/978-3-030-92300-6_37

technologies are being explored to promote improved health outcomes in adolescents [3–8]. Given the popularity of digital games as a source of entertainment for adolescents, recent years have seen growing interest in leveraging games to help address health care challenges [e.g., 9–12]. Interactive narrative technologies enable the creation of rich, story-centric game experiences in which players are active participants shaping the events of an unfolding story [e.g., 13–17]. Designing game-based interactive narratives to enhance adolescents' knowledge, personal efficacy, and self-regulatory skills holds significant potential for bringing about positive impacts on adolescent health [8].

INSPIRE is a game-based interactive narrative for adolescent health behavior change that targets reducing risky behaviors in high school students (ages 14 to 18) [8]. INSPIRE features a storyline with gameplay that is grounded in social cognitive theory for behavior change [18]. By situating players in a prototypical high school party setting, INSPIRE provides players with relatable characters that model a broad range of behaviors to promote learning, challenging situations to practice strategies, and guidance in developing skills for reducing alcohol use [8]. INSPIRE aims to foster increased self-regulation through a variety of mechanisms, including setting and monitoring goals (both short-term and long-term) [8]. Our previous work on INSPIRE has shown that adolescents find it to be engaging, believable, and relevant to their lives [8].

This paper reports on an exploratory cluster-based analysis of how players' choices of short-term goals (i.e., what are the protagonist's goals for the evening) and long-term goals (i.e., what is important to the protagonist) influence their engagement with INSPIRE. Specifically, we investigate the following research questions:

*RQ1: What groupings of players automatically emerge based upon the short-term and long-term goals players select as being important to the protagonist?*
*RQ2: How does reported engagement with the interactive narrative differ between the identified groups of players?*

To answer these questions, we use data collected in a preliminary pilot study with 20 adolescents. We perform a cluster-based analysis using the short-term and long-term goals players selected. The clustering algorithm automatically determines the optimal number of clusters and partitioned players into a four-cluster group based on their selected short-term goals and a two-cluster group based on their selected long-term goals. We then explore how engagement differs between the clusters in these groups. Findings suggest that the choices adolescents make early in the game for the protagonist's short-term and long-term goals can influence their overall engagement with the game.

## 2   Related Work

Digital games have for many years been a staple in the lives of adolescents. With 97% of children and adolescents playing games at least one hour per day, there is increasing interest in understanding the benefits of playing video games [19]. This underscores the potential of games to serve as a beneficial platform for reaching adolescents. Traditional entertainment focused games such as "Life is Strange" (2015) by Dontnod Entertainment have appropriated interactive narrative techniques to enhance players' experiences. Interactive narrative technologies allow players to have deeper interactions with narratives through the choices they make which can directly impact the outcome of the story.

Mawhorter and colleagues introduced the choice poetics framework that examines how choices and their structure impact user experience with a narrative [20]. The presentation of choices can also influence players' narrative experience [21]. Choices can help increase players' agency, by enabling them to have greater responsibility over the unfolding story to generate meaningful outcomes [22].

In recent years there has been growing interest in the potential of digital games to promote health behavior change. Digital games for health have tackled a variety of issues including providing emotional support [9], preventing disease [23, 24], facilitating communication [25], and teaching healthcare professionals [10, 26]. Digital games for health have also been designed to promote health behavior change for adolescents. For example, "Escape from Diab" is an action-adventure game designed to reduce childhood obesity where the athletic Deejay and his friends must escape from Diab, a world where it is difficult to acquire healthy food [23]. A key challenge to achieving successful health behavior change is ensuring players remain engaged with the intervention. Researchers have started investigating techniques to address this issue by providing tasks to keep players on track as well as purposely selecting narrative content to maintain engagement [27]. INSPIRE utilizes a familiar narrative-centric game design as well as impactful choices to promote health behavior change for adolescents.

## 3   The INSPIRE Interactive Narrative

INSPIRE is designed as a health behavior change intervention to support adolescents in developing strategies for handling challenging situations involving alcohol use (Fig. 1) [8]. INSPIRE encourages adolescents to enhance their knowledge, personal efficacy, and self-regulatory skills as they navigate events in the game. The design of INSPIRE is grounded in social cognitive theory, and it emphasizes vicarious learning, mastery experiences, connecting to adolescents' lives, and scaffolding self-regulation [8]. Central to social cognitive theory are beliefs of personal efficacy: perceived self-efficacy, one's belief in their own ability to carry out actions to achieve desired outcomes, has been shown to be an important predictor of behavior. Those who believe they can carry out an activity tend to engage in those activities while avoiding activities in which they are less confident [28, 29]. In our previous work on INSPIRE, we provide an in-depth discussion of social cognitive theory and its linkage to the design and development of the interactive narrative [8]. Development of INSPIRE is still underway; however, the first episode is fully playable and is the subject of the work reported in this paper.

**Fig. 1.** The INSPIRE interactive narrative for adolescent health behavior change.

INSPIRE features a mystery involving a high school student named Max who discovers that his little sister is missing the morning after a small get together with his friends, which he was hosting at his house while his parents were away, turns into an out-of-control party. In the game, players "relive" the events of the night before. They experience issues dealing with peer pressure, social norms, and the consequences of alcohol use, while practicing strategies for reducing risky health behaviors. The narrative sees Max solve the mystery of where his sister has gone before Max's parents arrive home.

### 3.1 Backstory and Tutorial

The INSPIRE story opens with a short trailer that sets the stage for the events taking place in the game (Fig. 2). The trailer introduces Max, his little sister Mia, and his close friends Nikki and Jay who he invites over, while his parents are away for the weekend at his grandparents. Jay, in turn, asks his friend Hailey to join them. Hailey tells Jay that it sounds like fun and asks for the address. The introduction ends with a foreboding message about the night not going as planned.

**Fig. 2.** Screenshots from the INSPIRE backstory trailer that introduces adolescents to the game.

The interactive narrative is set in Max's house where players assume the role of Max, the story's protagonist. As INSPIRE begins, players see Max awakening to the aftermath of the events from the previous night upon receiving a text message from his parents letting him know that they will be home earlier than expected (Fig. 3).

After getting out of bed, a short gameplay tutorial introduces players to navigating Max around the house and interacting with objects in the environment. The tutorial guides Max to look for his little sister to let her know that their parents will be home early, but she is not in her room. After hearing a noise, he heads downstairs where Max, expecting to find his sister, is startled by a stranger in his kitchen. Max remembers seeing Mia downstairs early on during the previous night, which was shortly before the party spiraled out of control. However, Max cannot remember where he last saw her. At this point, players are transported back to the beginning of the night where they are tasked with reliving the events of the party.

**Fig. 3.** The INSPIRE protagonist awakening the morning after the party.

## 3.2 Goal Setting and Gameplay

As the events of the night begin, players are asked to identify what is important to Max. This is accomplished using an in-game goal-setting interface that supports adolescents' self-regulatory processes by allowing them to set short-term and long-term goals for the protagonist (Fig. 4). First, players are asked to identify what is important to Max by selecting three long-term goals from a set of eight potential goals (e.g., being a good friend). Second, players select three short-term goals for Max that apply to the events of the evening (e.g., stay in control). These goals are intended to help guide adolescents' problem solving in the game.

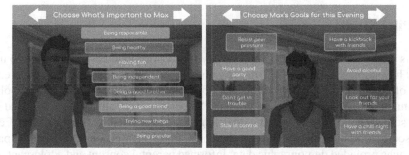

**Fig. 4.** Goal-setting interface in INSPIRE for long-term goals (left) and short-term goals (right).

As adolescents navigate the events of the night, they experience a series of problem scenarios in the interactive narrative that are realized through branching dialogue with non-player characters (Fig. 5, left). Players' interactions with non-player characters feature 2 to 4 dialogue responses, as well as a timer, that require adolescents to assess the situation and make choices under time pressure that affect the outcome of the story. The INSPIRE storyline features two types of branching narrative structures. The first type of choice has short-term impact on the story through the immediate reaction of non-player characters (e.g., Nikki responding enthusiastically to Max after he approves of her decision to invite additional guests), while the second type has long-term consequences on the outcome of the story (e.g., Nikki's excessive drinking resulting in accidentally breaking a porcelain vase). In addition to the two narrative structures, players are asked to monitor the protagonist's short-term goals when responding to difficult situations in the narrative by prompting them to consult the goals they chose prior to selecting a response to a non-player character (Fig. 5, right). INSPIRE concludes with a cutscene showing Mia heading back upstairs after briefly watching Max and his friends play a drinking game, setting the stage for the beginning of the second episode where players will assume the role of Hailey. The cutscene comes after navigating a series of problem scenarios that provide opportunities for players to observe models of healthy behaviors related to alcohol use, practice problem-solving strategies related to alcohol use, and analyze tradeoffs between different courses of action.

**Fig. 5.** Interfaces for players to select dialogue responses to non-player characters to advance the narrative: without goal monitoring (left) and with goal monitoring (right).

## 4 Pilot Study

In this work, we use data from a pilot study that was conducted with INSPIRE to understand how adolescents engage with the game [8]. A total of 20 adolescents between the ages of 14 and 19 (M = 16.63, SD = 1.36) from public and private high schools and community-based after school programs in San Francisco, California participated in the pilot study. The sample included a diverse group of participants from a range of ethnic and socioeconomic backgrounds as shown in Table 1 based on data from 19 participants who provided demographic data. Informed parental consent and adolescent assent was obtained from all participants in the pilot study under a human subjects approved protocol.

**Table 1.** Adolescents' demographic data.

| Gender | | Race | |
|---|---|---|---|
| Female | 53% (10) | Asian | 16% (3) |
| Male | 42% (8) | Hispanic or Latino | 37% (7) |
| Transmale | 5% (1) | Multiracial | 26% (5) |
| | | White | 21% (4) |

## 4.1 Procedure

Prior to interacting with INSPIRE participants completed an online pre-survey questionnaire to gather information about demographic variables such as age, gender identity, and race.[1] Next each participant individually interacted with INSPIRE on a Samsung Galaxy tablet, which took 20 min on average for them to finish. After completing the interactive narrative, participants were asked to respond to an online post-survey questionnaire about their interaction with INSPIRE.

## 4.2 Data

The pre-survey questionnaire asked participants about their video game playing experience, such as how frequently do you play video games. It also asked about alcohol use, such as have you used alcohol in the past 12 months. The post-survey questionnaire included 10 items from a narrative transportation measure [30], which included items such as "I could picture myself in the scene of the events presented in the narrative" and "The narrative affected me emotionally." These items were measured on a 7-point scale ranging from "Not at all" to "Very much." The post-survey also included 15 items from a user engagement measure for video gameplay that focused on satisfaction and perceived usability, which included items such as "The gaming experience was fun" and "The gaming experience was demanding" [31]. These items were measured on a 7-point Likert scale ranging from "Strongly disagree" to "Strongly agree."

Of the 19 participants who responded to the pre-survey, 5.3% reported playing games not at all, 36.8% rarely, 31.6% occasionally, 15.8% frequently, and 10.5% very frequently. Only 18 participants chose to report their alcohol use on the pre-survey with 61.1% indicating that they had used alcohol in the past 12 months and 33.3% reporting that they had at least one drink in the past 30 days. On the post-survey, adolescents reported a mean score of 4.16 (SD = 0.80) on the narrative transportation items measured on a 7-point scale, with the average item scores ranging from a high of 6.25 (SD = 1.16) on "I wanted to learn how the narrative ended" to a low of 2.95 (SD = 1.90) on "The events in the narrative are relevant to my everyday life." The mean score on the engagement measure was 4.93 (SD = 0.78) on a 7-point scale, with the average item scores ranging from a high of 5.65 (SD = 1.18) on "I felt interested in the game" to a low of 4.00 (SD = 1.52) on "I found the game confusing to use."

In addition to the data collected using the pre- and post-surveys, as participants interacted with INSPIRE the software recorded all of their interactions to log files on their tablet device. These interaction logs include records of all the events that occurred during the interactive narrative, such as navigating from one room to another, interacting with objects, selecting goals, and making dialogue choices. Across the 20 participants in the pilot study, over 70,000 events were recorded in the interaction logs.

---

[1] One participant did not complete the pre-survey questionnaire; however, they did complete the interactive narrative and post-survey questionnaire, so their data is included in the analysis.

# 5   Results

Using the data from the pilot study, we conducted a cluster-based analysis to examine groups of players based upon the short-term and long-term goals players select as being important to the protagonist (RQ1) as well as how engagement differs between the identified groups (RQ2).

## 5.1   Clustering by Long-Term Goals

Leveraging the interaction log data collected during the pilot study, we used a clustering technique to assign each participant to a cluster based on the long-term goals they selected as being important to the protagonist at the beginning of the interactive narrative. Specifically, we adopted SPSS's TwoStep Cluster Analysis algorithm to identify groupings of the adolescents using Bayesian Information Criterion (BIC) to automatically determine the optimal number of clusters [32]. The inputs to the clustering algorithm were the 8 binary variables (one for each potential long-term goal) indicating if the participant selected the corresponding long-term goal for the protagonist (Fig. 4, left). Through the clustering algorithm, 2 clusters were automatically identified, each of size 10: *LTC1* and *LTC2*. In determining the clusters, "Having fun" was identified as the most important variable by the clustering algorithm, while "Being independent" was least important (Fig. 6).

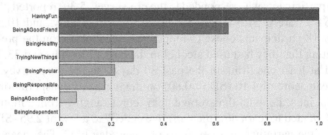

**Fig. 6.** Relative importance of long-term goals for identifying the two clusters.

In order to help interpret the derived clusters, a decision tree classifier was trained using the 8 binary variables as features and the assigned cluster as the class label. The decision tree was trained using Weka's J48 algorithm [33], which resulted in a decision tree of size 5 that partitions all of the participants into their assigned clusters (Fig. 7).

The decision tree leverages two long-term goals in deciding how to properly label each participant, including "Having fun" and "Trying new things." All but one of the participants is correctly classified by looking at whether "Having fun" was selected by the participant as a long-term goal for the protagonist (*LTC2*) or not (*LTC1*). To correctly label the remaining participant the "Trying new things" long-term goal is examined. The difference between these two clusters is further illustrated by the stacked column graph in Fig. 8, which shows "Having fun" and "Trying new things" as being selected by participants in *LTC2*, while "Being healthy" and "Being a good friend" are primarily associated with participants in *LTC1*. In short, *LTC1* consists of participants who did not

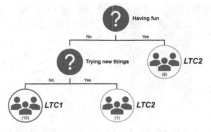

**Fig. 7.** Trained decision tree for predicting cluster assignment based on long-term goals.

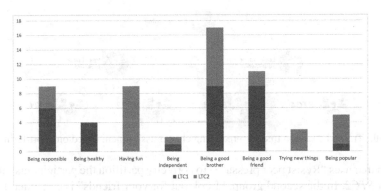

**Fig. 8.** Number of participants selecting each long-term goal across clusters *LTC1* and *LTC2*.

select "Having fun" as a goal for the protagonist, while *LTC2* consists of participants who selected "Having fun" or "Trying new things" as a goal.

### 5.2 Clustering by Short-Term Goals

Using the same clustering approach as presented in Sect. 5.1 above, we also identified clusters based on the short-term goals participants selected as being important to the protagonist. The inputs to the clustering algorithm consisted of 8 binary variables (one for each potential short-term goal) indicating if the participant selected the corresponding short-term goal (Fig. 4, right). Four clusters were automatically identified by the clustering algorithm: *STC1* with a size of 4, *STC2* with a size of 8, *STC3* with a size of 3, and *STC4* with a size of 5. In determining the clusters, the "Stay in control" goal was identified as the most important variable by the clustering algorithm, while the "Avoid alcohol" goal was least important (Fig. 9). Another decision tree classifier was trained using the 8 binary variables for the short-term goals as features and the assigned cluster as the class label. This resulted in a decision tree of size 7 that correctly classified all of the participants into their assigned short-term goal clusters (Fig. 10).

The decision tree uses three short-term goals in labeling each participant, including "Stay in control," "Resist peer pressure," and "Look out for your friends." At the top-level of the tree, "Stay in control" splits the participants into a group that is either in cluster *STC1* or *STC2* or a group that is in either clusters *STC3* or *STC4*. Within the first group the

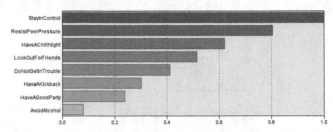

**Fig. 9.** Relative importance of the short-term goals for identifying the four clusters.

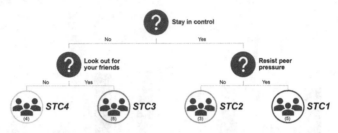

**Fig. 10.** Trained decision tree for predicting cluster assignment based on short-term goals.

decision tree uses "Resist peer pressure" to correctly partition the participants into either *STC1* or *STC2*. In the second group, "Look out for your friends" is consulted to decide between *STC3* or *STC4*. The stacked column graph in Fig. 11 shows the breakdown of short-term goals participants selected across the four clusters.

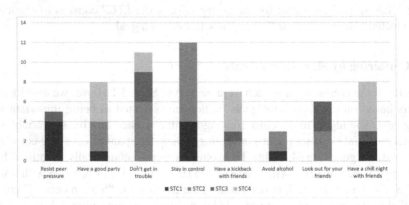

**Fig. 11.** Number of participants selecting each short-term goal across clusters.

Participants in cluster *STC1* wanted the protagonist to resist peer pressure and stay in control, while having a good time. Cluster *STC2* consisted of participants who wanted the protagonist to stay in control and not get in trouble, while looking out for friends and having a good time with limited alcohol use. Participants in cluster *STC3* wanted the protagonist to stay out of trouble and look out for friends, while resisting peer pressure and having a good time. Finally, cluster *STC4* was composed of participants who wanted the protagonist to have a good time, while not getting into trouble.

## 5.3 Engagement by Short-Term and Long-Term Clusters

To answer RQ2 we examined how engagement differed between the clusters identified based on the short-term goals and long-term goals using independent-samples t-tests. Prior to using the parametric tests in the analysis, normality was confirmed with the Shapiro-Wilk's test.

Participants' self-reported engagement ranged from 3.00 to 6.27 with a mean of 4.93 (SD = 0.78) on a 7-point scale. Looking at engagement based on short-term goals, participants in cluster *STC1* has an engagement mean score of 4.77 (SD = 0.67), *STC2* had a mean score of 4.84 (SD = 0.94), *STC3* had a mean score of 5.76 (SD = 0.45), and *STC4* had a mean score of 4.71 (SD = 0.53). A series of independent-samples t-tests confirmed that engagement scores were significantly different only between participants in clusters *STC3* and *STC4*, $t(6) = 2.854$, $p = 0.029$, indicating that adolescents in *STC3*, who did not select "Stay in control" but did select "Look out for your friends", reported higher engagement than adolescents in *STC4*, who did not selected "Stay in control" or "Look out for your friends" as a short-term goal for the protagonist.

Examining engagement based on long-term goals, participants in cluster *LTC1* reported engagement with a mean score of 5.33 (SD = 0.64), while participants in *LTC2* reported engagement with a mean score of 4.53 (SD = 0.72). An independent-samples t-test confirms that the engagement scores were significantly different between the two groups, $t(18) = 2.654$, $p = 0.016$, indicating that adolescents in *LTC1*, who did not select "Having fun" as a long-term goal for the protagonist, reported higher engagement than adolescents in *LTC2*, who selected "Having fun" or "Trying new things."

## 6 Discussion

Through the self-report questionnaires as well as our prior work on INSPIRE [8], preliminary evidence suggests that a diverse group of adolescents—with-respect-to race, gender, gaming experience, and alcohol use—found INSPIRE to be engaging. The storyline of the game appears to have successfully promoted adolescents' interest in the game as measured by items on both the narrative transportation and engagement scales, which will help drive continued use of the game. This will play an important role in supporting adolescents in developing mastery across a broad range of situations involving alcohol use and its effects.

Although adolescents overall reported being engaged with the game (M – 4.93, SD = 0.78 on a 7-point scale), the cluster analysis based on long-term goals identified a unique partitioning of players into two groups that reported a statistically significant difference in their engagement with the game. Deciding how to partition the players based on their selected long-term goals centered around the "Having fun" and "Trying new things" goals, while the "Being healthy" and "Being a good friend" goals were also identified as important. This suggests that one group of players (*LTC2*) approached the game wanting the protagonist to focus more on enjoyment and adventure, while the other group desired the protagonist to focus more on health and friends (*LTC1*). This later group reported significantly increased engagement with the game than the group focused on enjoyment and adventure.

Using the short-term goals that players selected as being important to the protagonist, the cluster analysis partitioned players into four unique groups. Two of these groups reported a statistically significant difference in their engagement with the game. Both of these two groups did not select "Stay in control" as a short-term goal, while one (*STC3*) selected "Lookout for your friends" and the other (*STC4*) did not. The analysis of the clusters based on short-term goals suggests that players who wanted the protagonist to look out for their friends were more engaged with the interactive narrative than players who wanted the protagonist to have a good time.

There are two limitations to the findings presented in this work. First, only 20 adolescents participated in the pilot study. This limited the available statistical power, inhibited some of the analysis we could conduct, and resulted in the sizes of the clusters based on short-term goals being somewhat small. Second, the pilot study focused on measuring adolescents' perceptions of (and engagement with) the interactive narrative since the primary objective of the pilot was to inform the continued development of the interactive narrative. The ultimate outcomes of changes in adolescents' self-efficacy and risky behaviors related to alcohol use have not been examined.

## 7  Conclusions

Game-based interactive narratives offer a promising approach for engaging adolescents in health behavior change. In these environments, adolescents are empowered to make active choices that provide opportunities to enhance their knowledge, improve their perceived self-efficacy, and develop their self-regulatory skills. In this work, we have utilized INSPIRE, an interactive narrative for adolescent health behavior change that targets the reduction of risky behaviors around alcohol use in high school students (ages 14 to 18), to investigate how the goals adolescents select as being important to the protagonist character relate to their engagement with the interactive narrative. A cluster-based analysis with data from a pilot study with 20 adolescents revealed that the short-term and long-term goals selected for the protagonist early in the game can have significant impacts on player engagement, suggesting that how players approach the goals of the protagonist in the interactive narrative influences their overall engagement.

This work suggests several promising directions for future work. First, it will be important to undertake extensive user studies to gain a clearer picture of how participants' individual differences impact their choices and engagement in the game. Second, investigations into the effects of incorporating interactive narratives for health behavior change into clinical settings need to be conducted. Finally, given the critical role engagement plays in achieving successful health behavior change, investigating AI-driven techniques for narrative generation that tailor narratives to individuals is particularly promising.

**Acknowledgements.** This research was primarily supported by the National Science Foundation through grants IIS-1344803 and IIS-1344670 and the National Cancer Institute through grant R01CA247705. Any opinions, findings, and conclusions expressed in this material are those of the authors and do not necessarily reflect the views of the National Science Foundation or the National Cancer Institute.

# References

1. Ozer, E., Irwin, C.: Adolescents and young adult health: from basic health status to clinical interventions. In: Lerner, L.M., Steinberg, L. (eds.) Handbook of Adolescent Psychology, 3rd edn. (2009)
2. Kann, L., et al.: Youth risk behavior surveillance. Morb. Mortal. Weekly Report-Surveill. Summ. **67**(8), 1–114 (2018)
3. Beale, I.L., Kato, P.M., Marin-Bowling, V.M., Guthrie, N., Cole, S.W.: Improvement in cancer-related knowledge following use of a psychoeducational video game for adolescents and young adults with cancer. J. Adolesc. Health **41**(3), 263–270 (2007)
4. Bickmore, T., Zhang, Z., Reichert, M., Julce, C., Jack, B.: Promotion of preconception care among adolescents and young adults by conversational agent. J. Adolesc. Health **67**(2), S45–S51 (2020)
5. Harris, S.K., et al.: Research on clinical preventive services for adolescents and young adults: where are we and where do we need to go? J. Adolesc. Health **60**(3), 249–260 (2017)
6. Majeed-Ariss, R., et al.: Apps and adolescents: a systematic review of adolescents' use of mobile phone and tablet apps that support personal management of their chronic or long-term physical conditions. J. Med. Internet Res. **17**(12) (2015)
7. Rowe, J.P., Lester, J.C.: Artificial intelligence for personalized preventive adolescent healthcare. J. Adolesc. Health **67**(2), S52–S58 (2020)
8. Ozer, E.M., et al.: Fostering engagement in health behavior change: iterative development of an interactive narrative environment to enhance adolescent preventive health services. J. Adolesc. Health **67**, S34–S44 (2020)
9. Bowman, A.: Creating a virtual support group in an interactive narrative: a companionship game for cancer patients. In: Rouse, R., Koenitz, H., Haahr, M. (eds.) ICIDS 2018. LNCS, vol. 11318, pp. 662–665. Springer, Cham (2018). https://doi.org/10.1007/978-3-030-04028-4_80
10. Christman, G.P., Schrager, S.M., Callahan, K.: Using interactive fiction to teach pediatricians-in-training about child abuse. In: Nunes, N., Oakley, I., Nisi, V. (eds.) ICIDS 2017. LNCS, vol. 10690, pp. 278–281. Springer, Cham (2017). https://doi.org/10.1007/978-3-319-71027-3_25
11. Jurdi, S., Montaner, J., Garcia-Sanjuan, F., Jaen, J., Nacher, V.: A systematic review of game technologies for pediatric patients. Comput. Biol. Med. **97**, 89–112 (2018)
12. Rodriguez, D.M., Teesson, M., Newton, N.C.: A systematic review of computerised serious educational games about alcohol and other drugs for adolescents. Drug Alcohol Rev. **33**(2), 129–135 (2014)
13. Ammanabrolu, P., Cheung, W., Tu, D., Broniec, W., Riedl, M.: Bringing stories alive: generating interactive fiction worlds. In: Proceedings of the AAAI Conference on Artificial Intelligence and Interactive Digital Entertainment, vol. 16, no. 1, pp. 3–9 (2020)
14. Kreminski, M., Wardrip-Fruin, N.: Throwing bottles at God: predictive text as a game mechanic in an AI-based narrative game. In: Rouse, R., Koenitz, H., Haahr, M. (eds.) ICIDS 2018. LNCS, vol. 11318, pp. 275–279. Springer, Cham (2018). https://doi.org/10.1007/978-3-030-04028-4_29
15. Miller, C., Dighe, M., Martens, C., Jhala, A.: Crafting interactive narrative games with adversarial planning agents from simulations. In: Bosser, A.-G., Millard, D.E., Hargood, C. (eds.) ICIDS 2020. LNCS, vol. 12497, pp. 44–57. Springer, Cham (2020). https://doi.org/10.1007/978-3-030-62516-0_4
16. Marc Cavazza, R., Young, M.: Introduction to interactive storytelling. In: Nakatsu, R., Rauterberg, M., Ciancarini, P. (eds.) Handbook of Digital Games and Entertainment Technologies, pp. 377–392. Springer, Singapore (2017). https://doi.org/10.1007/978-981-4560-50-4_55

17. Ware, S.G., Garcia, E.T., Shirvani, A., Farrell, R.: Multi-agent narrative experience management as story graph pruning. In: Proceedings of the AAAI Conference on Artificial Intelligence and Interactive Digital Entertainment, pp. 87–93 (2019)

18. Bandura, A.: Social cognitive theory for personal and social change by enabling media. In: Singhal, A., Cody, M.J., Rogers, E.M., Sabido, M. (eds.) Entertainment-Education and Social Change: History, Research, and Practice, pp. 75–96. Lawrence Erlbaum Associates Publishers, Mahwah (2004)

19. Granic, I., Lobel, A., Engels, R.C.: The benefits of playing video games. Am. Psychol. **69**(1), 66–78 (2014)

20. Mawhorter, P., Mateas, M., Wardrip-Fruin, N., Jhala, A.: Towards a theory of choice poetics. In: Proceedings of the 9th International Conference on the Foundations of Digital Game (2014)

21. Estupiñán, S., Maret, B., Andkjaer, K., Szilas, N.: A multidimensional classification of choice presentation in interactive narrative. In: Rouse, R., Koenitz, H., Haahr, M. (eds.) ICIDS 2018. LNCS, vol. 11318, pp. 149–153. Springer, Cham (2018). https://doi.org/10.1007/978-3-030-04028-4_12

22. Rezk, A.M., Haahr, M.: The case for invisibility: understanding and improving agency in Black Mirror's Bandersnatch and other interactive digital narrative works. In: Bosser, A.-G., Millard, D.E., Hargood, C. (eds.) ICIDS 2020. LNCS, vol. 12497, pp. 178–189. Springer, Cham (2020). https://doi.org/10.1007/978-3-030-62516-0_16

23. Thompson, D., et al.: Serious video games for health how behavioral science guided the development of a serious video game. Simul. Gaming **41**(4), 587–606 (2010)

24. Miller, L.C., Appleby, P.R., Anderson, A.N., Christensen, S., Marsella, S.: SOLVE-IT: socially optimized learning in virtual environments: a web delivered HIV prevention 3D game intervention for young at-risk MSM. J. Mob. Technol. Med. **1**(4S), 10 (2012)

25. Baceviciute, S., Albæk, K.R.R., Arsovski, A., Bruni, L.E.: Digital interactive narrative tools for facilitating communication with children during counseling: a case for audiology. In: Oyarzun, D., Federico Peinado, R., Young, M., Elizalde, A., Méndez, G. (eds.) ICIDS 2012. LNCS, vol. 7648, pp. 48–59. Springer, Heidelberg (2012). https://doi.org/10.1007/978-3-642-34851-8_5

26. Morningstar-Kywi, N., Kim, R.E.: Using interactive fiction to teach clinical decision-making in a PharmD curriculum. Med. Sci. Educ. **31**(2), 687–695 (2021)

27. Langxuan, Y., Bickmore, T., Montfort, N.: An interactive narrative system for narrative-based games for health. In: Intelligent Narrative Technologies 7: Papers from the 2014 Workshop, pp. 45–51 (2014)

28. Bandura, A.: Self-efficacy mechanism in human agency. Am. Psychol. **37**(2), 122–147 (1982)

29. Ozer, E.M., Bandura, A.: Mechanisms governing empowerment effects: a self-efficacy analysis. J. Pers. Soc. Psychol. **58**(3), 472–486 (1990)

30. Green, M.C., Brock, T.C.: The role of transportation in the persuasiveness of public narratives. J. Pers. Soc. Psychol. **79**(5), 701–721 (2000)

31. Wiebe, E.N., Lamb, A., Hardy, M., Sharek, D.: Measuring engagement in video game-based environments: investigation of the User Engagement Scale. Comput. Hum. Behav. **32**, 123–132 (2014)

32. Chiu, T., Fang, D., Chen, J., Wang, Y.: A robust and scalable clustering algorithm for mixed type attributes in large database environment. In: Proceedings of the 7th ACM SIGKDD International Conference on Knowledge Discovery and Data Mining, pp. 263–268 (2001)

33. Hall, M., Frank, E., Holmes, G., Pfahringer, B., Reutemann, P., Witten, I.H.: The WEKA data mining software: an update. ACM SIGKDD Explor. Newsl. **11**(1), 10–18 (2009)

# Transfordance: The Decentering Effect of Transformative Affordances in Virtual Reality in *The Hollow Reach*

John T. Murray[1]([✉]) [iD] and Mark C. Marino[2] [iD]

[1] Games and Interactive Media, University of Central Florida, Orlando, FL, USA
jtm@ucf.edu
[2] Writing Program, Humanities and Critical Code Studies Lab, University of Southern California, Los Angeles, CA, USA

**Abstract.** Virtual reality offers immense potential for subversive interactions to be the focus of stories. We argue that narrative framing is just as important as selecting meaningful user interactions in VR, and offer the portmanteau "transfordance" to describe how mechanics can decenter the normative embodied experience through narrative framing, and "transfordant design" to capture how they can be applied to expressive ends. We demonstrate the technique through a new virtual reality experience, *The Hollow Reach,* that centers traumatic recovery through experiences of mechanical and virtual prosthesis. In this demo, we use transfordant design in three meaning creation interactions: unreliable direct manipulation, gaze tendency, and voice (rather than speech).

**Keywords:** Virtual reality · Disability representation · Interaction mechanics

## 1 The Hollow Reach

When you look through the Virtual Reality (VR) lenses of *The Hollow Reach* (*THR*), the deck of a starship, reminiscent of Star Trek, stretches around you; at your side, an officer at attention. Your task: to complete a set of exercises to practice using your artificial limb. But the serene background of lightspeed is interrupted by your arrival to a new system. Appearing on the viewscreen is a disabled ship, drifting and identified as the Pelops. An enemy warship appears, the officer requests your orders. As a player, in any new interactive digital narrative (IDN), the question is the same: what can I do? The experience focuses on recovery from trauma through both mechanical and virtual prosthesis. A sequence of challenges connect interactions with characters, where they respond to the player's gaze or tone. The player's actions are also not reliable, departing from VR conventions. The player's speech content in dialogue choices is less important than the tone and gaze tendency when determining how characters respond.

The piece sets out to ask "How can we experience differently-abled bodies in an immersive medium?" What unique opportunities do VR IDNs offer to shape player expectations and understandings? This paper describes the design of *THR* and introduces

© Springer Nature Switzerland AG 2021
A. Mitchell and M. Vosmeer (Eds.): ICIDS 2021, LNCS 13138, pp. 393–398, 2021.
https://doi.org/10.1007/978-3-030-92300-6_38

the concepts and theories used in its development. The project is available for download[1] and runs on any OpenXR compatible headset.

## 1.1 VR Narratives

Participants have many ways of performing actions and navigating in simulated environments. Perhaps they interact by walking and talking in a cartoonish 3-D world, as in the AR adaptation of Façade or move through breathing in the scuba-inspired works of Char Davies, Osmose (1995) and Ephèmere (1998). However, most of these VR experiences map movement and other interaction onto a simulation of an able-bodied human moving through space, no matter how fantastic or infinite the virtual reality. Neither the virtual reality nor the embodied experience of it are equivalents to lived reality, so designers determine how to represent a boundless virtual space exists within a normative, embodied sensory experience.

Since the physical space around a VR user is limited, one technique is to constrain the visual environment. For example, in *I Expect You to Die* [1], an escape-room homage to the James Bond franchise, the player finds themself in tight places such as the interior of a car or an office. On the other hand, works such as *Virtual Virtual Reality* [2] and *The Under Presents* [3] offer innovative transportation mechanics, casting about as if fishing and dragging themselves. In *Hot Dogs, Horseshoes, and Hand Grenades* [4], players jog through the Weiner-filled realm by pumping their arms as if running.

While embodied movement is a necessary and obvious part of most VR experiences, we argue that designed interactions and input benefit from narrative framing. However, in our IDN, our goal was not to portray, but to decenter the normative sensory experience. We accomplished this by subverting existing interaction expectations, which led us to invent the term *transfordance*. Transfordance describes the interactions that decenter normative embodied experience for expressive purposes through narrative framing. Transfordance is a portmanteau of "transformative affordance." An affordance is "the relationship between a physical object and a person" [7]. Rather than just a sensorimotor substitution, a "transfordance" is an affordance, that evokes a re-assessment by the user of previous affordances. In other words, a transfordance decenters what was previously treated as "normal" affordances.

## 1.2 Physicality of Interaction

Traditional VR user interfaces design addresses specific tasks, such as selection, manipulation, transportation, or navigation [5]. Researchers have explored methods of improving VR interaction through the use of various forms of haptic feedback through reusable props [6] and small-scale props [7] as in haptic retargeting, through guiding images [8], and even guidance from the avatar's independent movement [9].

On the surface, the narrative framing of our scenario is most reminiscent of Janet Murray's [5] vision, especially as it includes a nod to the Holodeck from Star Trek. Indeed, Murray's term "dramatic agency" captures the importance of narrative significance of actions taken. Wardrip-Fruin and Mateas and others [10, 11] coined "operational logics"

---

[1] https://jtm.io/hollowreach/.

to describe the relationship between abstraction representations and concrete computational operations used by authors. Operational logics helps describe interactions with IDN, and to a certain extent, the *altered* interactions of transfordant design can be seen as a class of operational logics. We draw upon the work of Douglass [12], who writes of the way frustration can be written into the aesthetics of a game.

The term and our focus is on works that communicate difference from the dominant or normalized experience of reality. Here we learn from the work of Nonny de la Peña, who has placed audiences in war zones and, with Peggy Weill, in Guantanamo prison. Similarly, Be Another Lab's work [13] explores empathy through inter-subjective experiences. With respect to challenging the normative sensory experience, Arte Experience's "Notes on Blindness" adapts the audio recordings of John Hull in which he documents his loss of vision. The VR work re-imagines sight through visual analogues of other sensory information, capturing the heightened sensory experience, and inverting the usual hierarchy of able-bodied experience. We also draw on micha cárdenas' work, whose "Becoming Dragon" project of inhabiting an alternative subjectivity in a virtual world [14].

We argue the most important and subversive capacity of VR is altering the user's perception through experience. We call the incorporation and subversion of interaction "transfordant design." THR exemplifies this property through enforced limitations on and variations of the unmarked norms of everyday experience for expressive goals.

## 2 Narrative-Based Explorations

Direct manipulation is well studied in VR user interfaces [15], so our narrative centers on the experience of an unwieldy prosthesis. This frame was inspired by the use of VR to aid in rehabilitation of sensorimotor cognition [16]. To be clear, most VR systems can register at least some hand or arm movement. In *THR*, we narrate that exploration of a character's experiences with disability through the fiction of a prosthesis, as the main character must overcome physical and emotional traumatic loss of their arms through gaining acumen with prosthesis. At the start, we frame inability to control this virtual limb as the player character's lack of sensorimotor control.

### 2.1 Choices and Input Mechanics

Players in IDNs take actions such as making dialogue choices, using items, or navigating spaces. VR relies on gestures that imitate real-world interactions, such as grasping or pointing. Instead of pressing X, players can reach and grab an object by performing an embodied actions. The goal of *THR* is for players to experience a narrative of embodied otherness through the following mechanics:

**Destabilizing Bodies.** In the diegetic world of *THR*, the player's use of their limb does not directly relate to their controller position. After the first period of practice, they knock a coffee cup to the ground, shattering at once the cup and the illusion of the diegetic virtual world. The player is jolted into the "real world" of the game, a desolate, empty apartment. The loss of control is a false choice [17], such as used in *Depression Quest*

[18], that enacts a lack of player-character agency. The perceived limitation in agency becomes the means of delivering a non-normative subjective experience.

**Gaze as Input.** In *THR*, the player's head direction factors into the dialogue in subtle ways, signifying the player's attention to the world or a character. In *THR*, the environment is designed to distract from a character's gaze. The player's love interest, Jordan, commands the player to confront her emotional pain by meeting her gaze while also looking at (and examining) all that the player has so painfully lost physically and emotionally in order, of course, to overcome that loss. If the player chooses not to, the character observes and responds to that choice as if the player acted more explicitly.

**Voice as Input.** VR is considered a visual medium first. We require players to speak as part of character interaction. In a pivotal moment, Jordan asks the player whether they can explain why they cannot accept help. The prompts are short phrases inspired by Telltale's interface [19]. Player speech based on a prompt strikes a balance between parsing used in Façade and the method common in works by Telltale Games. Player's response is classified by Amazon Lex as either affirmative, negative, or other response. We believe this better connects players with the emotional consequences of the choices.

### 2.2 Transfordance in the Hollow Reach

The player's head position is considered a latent part of the experience of VR, since "looking around" is a fundamental capability. However, in *THR*, your gaze is an involuntary expression of attention, and as in social situations, a means of building or damaging relationships. For instance, confronting their hostile challenge of the alien commander or an offer of help from a loved one in their traumatized state. In other words, we treated gaze as an act. Another example is the player's inability to control the prosthetic limb, the subversion of direct control integrated into the player's character arc. Inability to control a prosthesis in VR becomes the narrative struggle with disability and pulls the player in through the control that is often taken for granted. This can be extended to speech. When our player character's love interest asks, "Why are you shutting me out?" the player must attempt some verbal defense. The response is determined not by recognizing words, but by the emotions recognized [20], using Arezina's technique [21]. Now, as in the case of the gaze and the prosthetic arm, the player must grapple with an input whose narrative implications are so overdetermined and entangled as to make it the dialogue equivalent of a prosthesis that cannot be manipulated with certainty. We frame the player's struggle to make themselves recognized by the system through the narrative as a struggle to communicate difficult and delicate emotional state. It is that tangled and tortured human condition of plays, novels, and games such as *Façade* built into the mechanic but rendered meaningful through the narrative.

Our demo highlights how a designed difference between desired interaction and user experience doesn't have to be either a failure of interface design nor a novel way to aestheticize frustration. *The Hollow Reach* demonstrates one way the gap can be narrated and rendered meaningful through transfordance. The player's negotiations of virtual reality are rendered narratively significant by being framed as a character's struggle to come to terms with physical reality. Transfordant design offers opportunities for further narrative exploration of the difference between hegemonic embodied experience and alternatives as a means of drawing the player into the story while they are drawn into the mechanisms of the game.

# References

1. Schell, J.: Making Great VR: Six Lessons Learned From I Expect You To Die. https://www.gamasutra.com/blogs/JesseSchell/20150626/247113/Making_Great_VR_Six_Lessons_Learned_From_I_Expect_You_To_Die.php. Accessed 18 July 2018
2. Virtual Virtual Reality. Tender Claws (2017)
3. The Under Presents. Tneder Claws (2019)
4. Hot Dogs, Horseshoes & Hand Grenades
5. LaViola, J.J., Jr., Kruijff, E., McMahan, R.P., Bowman, D., Poupyrev, I.P.: 3D User Interfaces: Theory and Practice. Addison-Wesley Professional, Boston (2017)
6. Azmandian, M., Hancock, M., Benko, H., Ofek, E., Wilson, A.D.: Haptic retargeting: dynamic repurposing of passive haptics for enhanced virtual reality experiences. In: Proceedings of the 2016 CHI Conference on Human Factors in Computing Systems, pp. 1968–1979 (2016)
7. Bergström, J., Mottelson, A., Knibbe, J.: Resized grasping in VR: estimating thresholds for object discrimination. In: Proceedings of the 32nd Annual ACM Symposium on User Interface Software and Technology, pp. 1175–1183 (2019)
8. Dürr, M., Weber, R., Pfeil, U., Reiterer, H.: EGuide: investigating different visual appearances and guidance techniques for egocentric guidance visualizations. In: Proceedings of the Fourteenth International Conference on Tangible, Embedded, and Embodied Interaction, pp. 311–322. Association for Computing Machinery, New York (2020). https://doi.org/10.1145/3374920.3374945
9. Gonzalez-Franco, M., Cohn, B., Ofek, E., Burin, D., Maselli, A.: The self-avatar follower effect in virtual reality. In: 2020 IEEE Conference on Virtual Reality and 3D User Interfaces (VR), pp. 18–25. IEEE (2020)
10. Mateas, M., Wardrip-Fruin, N.: Defining operational logics. In: Proceedings of the Digital Games Research Association, pp. 1–8 (2009)
11. Osborn, J.C., Wardrip-Fruin, N., Mateas, M.: Refining operational logics. In: Proceedings of the 12th International Conference on the Foundations of Digital Games, pp. 1–10. ACM, Hyannis Massachusetts (2017). https://doi.org/10.1145/3102071.3102107
12. Douglass, J.: Command Lines: Aesthetics and Technique in Interactive Fiction and New Media. ProQuest (2007)
13. Bertrand, P.: The machine to be another - embodied telepresence using human performers, 7
14. Cárdenas, M., Head, C., Margolis, T., Greco, K.: Becoming dragon: a mixed reality durational performance in second life. In: The Engineering Reality of Virtual Reality 2009, p. 723807. International Society for Optics and Photonics (2009). https://doi.org/10.1117/12.806260
15. Lilija, K., Kyllingsbæk, S., Hornbæk, K.: Correction of avatar hand movements supports learning of a motor skill. In: 2021 IEEE Virtual Reality and 3D User Interfaces (VR), pp. 1–8 (2021). https://doi.org/10.1109/VR50410.2021.00069
16. Tieri, G., Morone, G., Paolucci, S., Iosa, M.: Virtual reality in cognitive and motor rehabilitation: facts, fiction and fallacies. Expert Rev. Med. Dev. 15, 107–117 (2018). https://doi.org/10.1080/17434440.2018.1425613
17. Mawhorter, P., Zegura, C., Gray, A., Jhala, A., Mateas, M., Wardrip-Fruin, N.: Choice poetics by example. Arts. 7, 47 (2018). https://doi.org/10.3390/arts7030047
18. Quinn, Z.: Depression Quest (2013)

19. Maloney, M.: Out on a Limb: Practical Approaches to Branching Story (2017)
20. Mustaqeem, Kwon, S.: A CNN-assisted enhanced audio signal processing for speech emotion recognition. Sensors **20**, 183 (2019). https://doi.org/10.3390/s20010183
21. Arezina, K.: Live Speech Emotion Categorization. https://medium.com/nerd-for-tech/live-speech-emotion-categorization-7692933037ba. Accessed 15 Oct 2021

# Contextualization of Design Qualities in Interactive Story-Based Visualization Applied to Engineering

Jovana Plavšić[(✉)] [iD] and Ilija Mišković

Norman B. Keevil Institute of Mining Engineering, University of British Columbia, Vancouver, BC V6T 1Z4, Canada
plavsicj@ubc.mail.ca, eli.miskovic@ubc.ca

**Abstract.** Visualization is widely employed in the engineering industry to fulfill the increasing demand for robust data exploration and insight enhancement tools. It is valued for its ability to improve the performance and efficiency of various engineering tasks. Narrative visualization is a growing interdisciplinary field with a great potential for mission-critical, pressure-filled, and time-sensitive operations. Because of the novelty of the discipline, there is a lack of research focused on design strategies of story-based data representation in the engineering domain. Based on the existing visualization research, we identified four prominent design qualities: aesthetics, usability, novelty, and complexity; and examined them in the context of interactive story-focused engineering visualization. We concluded that: 1) Terminology needs to be re-evaluated in the new context; 2) All four design dimensions we analyzed are subjective and prone to personal interpretation; 3) All four design qualities can be both positive and negative, depending on the context; 4) Trade-off between design qualities has to be made; 5) There is a lack of completed case studies in the field. We hope this research will be beneficial for bridging the gap between storytellers, visualization designers, and engineers, as well as establishing design strategies for this emerging visualization form.

**Keywords:** Interactive digital narrative · Visualization · Engineering

## 1 Introduction

Growing data complexity and abundance, coupled with extreme performance requirements of pressure-filled, mission-critical, or other engineering-specific applications, increase the demand for robust data exploration tools. Visualization is the most widely employed technique for rapid knowledge extraction, insight enhancement, and information retention. It takes advantage of the human perceptual system to mitigate cognitive overload and ameliorate comprehension. It has been extensively used to aid engineers and scientists in a variety of tasks, such as design, simulation, monitoring and maintenance, remote collaboration, training, evaluation and optimization, risk modeling and assessment, decision-making, and presentation. Visualization techniques are constantly evolving to fulfill the requirements of their applied field and keep up with technological

© Springer Nature Switzerland AG 2021
A. Mitchell and M. Vosmeer (Eds.): ICIDS 2021, LNCS 13138, pp. 399–409, 2021.
https://doi.org/10.1007/978-3-030-92300-6_39

development. Narrative visualization is a growing discipline that amplifies visualization capabilities by framing data as a story [1]. Storytelling always had an important role in knowledge transfer [2]. Story-structured data communication improves memorability [3], comprehensibility, credibility, and involvement [4]. Narrative visualization is a communication tool that goes beyond conveying facts [5]. Wojtkowski and Wojtkowski argue that visual storytelling might be crucial for real-time and intuitive exploration of large, complex, and diverse data resources [6]. This narrative visualization capability is central to time-sensitive and analytics-based engineering applications. Examples of such use cases include extended reality (XR) immersive experiences, cyber-physical systems, and Internet of things (IoT) solutions.

Visualization in engineering and sciences is determined by its practical value and improvements in the performance of a system or a task [7, 8]. A significant body of work has been devoted to showing how different visualization aspects affect its overall efficiency. They include, for instance, aesthetics [9–13], complexity [14], and memorability [15]. The correlation between different design dimensions has been studied as well, for example, appearance and usability [16–19], complexity and aesthetics [20], and complexity and usability [21]. This collection of works provides strong empirical evidence and a theoretical foundation to support adequate visualization practices. However, there is a lack of research contributions focused on different design qualities of story-based data representation in engineering and sciences.

In this paper, the term visualization will be used broadly and as an umbrella term encompassing various subdisciplines (such as information and data visualization, and visual analytics). We provide an overview of prominent design qualities of narrative visualization. We discuss their effect on the visualization performance, i.e., the potential to improve the speed, accuracy, or efficiency of engineering operations. We focused on interactive applications because the human operator needs to be able to interactively and promptly exchange information with the physical or digital equipment, system, or environment. In the first part of this paper, we examined the relationship between digital narratives and engineering visualization. In the second part, we present concepts that received attention in the visualization research and examine them in the context of interactive story-focused engineering visualization. Based on the existing literature, we identified four prominent visualization qualities: aesthetics, usability, novelty, and complexity. Even though this is not a comprehensive list, we believe this research will benefit the visualization design process and help establish good visualization practices for interactive narratives in engineering.

## 2   Interactive Storytelling Concepts in the Context of Visualization for Industrial Purposes

Interactive narrative (IN) principles for serious applications significantly differ from those for the media or entertainment industries. Despite the promising potential that INs hold for scientific storytelling, the discipline has received little attention in the literature. Visualization is a non-traditional medium in which the understanding of narrative structure components is reshaped. Vosmeer and Schouten examined how narrativity, interactivity, and engagement are mutually reshaped when the same immersive technologies are applied to different domains [22]. They compared different disciplines in media entertainment (video games and cinematography). For industrial visualization, which is a disparate experience form, this means a further re-evaluation of established concepts. Ma et al. [4] emphasized the differences in key narrative elements (setting, character, and plot) of traditional and scientific storytelling. According to them, in traditional media, such as theatre, film, or gaming, the setting is treated as the physical or virtual environment in which the story is set, while in visualization it is the background information that provides context. Characters, which would normally be people or protagonists, are visual elements or data in visualization. Visualization's plot is the comparison, interaction, and evolution of visual elements.

In IN theory, the narrative progression is controlled by the author, observer, or both. Interactivity is determined by varying degrees of autonomy provided to the user. Wohlfart and Hauser proposed a model for different kinds of story consumption based on multiple levels of control between the author and the observer [23]. The example of full author-driven control is passive, non-interactive visualization; while the extreme opposite is liberal data exploration, dictated by the end-user. Segel and Heer explored the balance between author and reader-driven experiences through the identification of different genres of narrative visualization [24]. In evolving systems that employ robust analytics and learning techniques, visualization can also progress algorithmically. This type of storyline development takes data iterations as input. Algorithmic changes in visualization's narrative progression can be treated as an author-driven approach, as AI-generated work can be extrapolated to be human-generated [25].

## 3   Design Qualities of Narrative Visualization in Engineering

In the previous paragraph, we examined how basic concepts of IN theory, which are established in "old" storytelling media, should be reconsidered for engineering visualization applications. In this section, we will discuss different design dimensions of narrative visualization and how they impact the overall performance of visualization, which is particularly important for the engineering sector. Most of the visualization qualities have been already discussed in the literature. While Ghidini et al. focused on the analysis of design strategies of narrative visualization, taking narrative design space proposals as a starting point [1], we decided to take a different approach. We took publications in the field of visualization as the base premise for our research. The reason for this is that the IN theory focuses on the user and user experience, while the visualization theory's goals are targeted at improvements in system or task performance too. The latter is of great importance for engineering applications, which are the primary focus of this paper. We have identified four key qualities that are relevant for narrative visualization for engineering applications: aesthetics, usability, complexity, and novelty. Aesthetics and usability were included in the selection because their roles in visualization have been extensively discussed in the literature through theoretical and empirical research. Complexity and novelty were chosen because the engineering industries are facing rapid technological revolution and data expansion, which require adaptation from the users and visualization designers. The reader should note that this paper doesn't provide an extensive list of visualization qualities and it should be treated as a starting point for further research.

## 3.1 Aesthetics

Beauty can be used as a guiding principle in the practice of sciences and systems engineering [26]. The concept of aesthetics, its usage, and effect on storytelling and visualization has been extensively discussed in the literature. It has caused polarized opinions among visualization researchers. Iliinsky outlined this dichotomy, noting that beauty in visualization can be achieved through compelling graphical construction of visual elements, or as another opportunity to increase the utility of the visualization [27]. While merely decorative elements might not be in the interest of practitioners from engineering and sciences, they might appreciate aesthetics for its potential to add to the visualization's efficacy. For Krzywinski, form with function is beautiful [28]. Kyndrup argued that beauty is an independent quality and should, therefore, be assessed separately from the primary goals of the visualization [29]. He did, however, express the concern that too beautiful visualizations can disturb the viewer's attention and perception. Beauty is a subjective judgment that is difficult to quantify, so the appropriate level of beauty for visualizing data remains abstract. Benefits of aesthetics for data representation have been mostly addressed through its relationship with usability, which is the principal prerequisite for implementation of interactive experiences. Studies have shown a positive correlation between aesthetics and usability, a strong relationship between the perceived appearance and the usability of the interface [18, 30], and that users handle aesthetic visualizations more patiently and profoundly [17]. However, a recent study by Flangas et al. has failed to prove that aesthetic elements of the visual interface affect user performance or decision fatigue [31].

In interactive digital narrative (IDN) theory, aesthetics is understood through Murray's seminal model [32]. She proposed three aesthetic categories for interactive storytelling analysis: immersion, agency, and transformation, which will be briefly discussed in the context of narrative visualization.

Immersion is the sense of physical or mental absorption in content or medium, which is experienced by an interactor. It is a sensation and experiential pleasure of taking part in a synthetic reality in which the user's actions impact the immersive environment and follow its logic. Raja et al. showed that immersion in visualization results in better user performance, especially when viewing large datasets [33]. Aesthetic visualizations can facilitate a greater mental immersion into the data [9].

Agency denotes the user's ability to take meaningful action, which will happen in a dynamically responsive world. The changes should not be a result of arbitrary exploration of utilities, they rather have to reflect the user's intentions. While in IDN theory agency originally refers to user's responses within the domain of the digital environment, in narrative visualization the concept can be extended to the physical world, too. In some engineering applications (e.g., cyber-physical systems), the user can act as a bond within the real and the virtual world and send input to both ends of the system.

The beauty of narrative also comes from the transformational experience that can happen on multiple levels. Transformation can manifest through variations on the theme or role play. For narrative visualization, this can help the viewer gain a better understanding of data by providing insight in various forms (e.g., layering the data, providing different viewing angles, or using diverse graphic formats). Personal transformation is the ability of storytelling to change the viewer. It is crucial for the success of serious applications [34], such as engineering or scientific applications. In story-based visualization, personal transformation can be achieved through learning, knowledge discovery, and gaining a novel outlook on the subject matter.

## 3.2 Usability

Usability is tremendously important for interactive narrative visualizations, as it is a prerequisite for data exploration and message extraction. Lack of usability in engineering applications poses health, safety, malfunction, and error risks, which can have serious financial or fatal consequences. Usability has been widely evaluated as a dimension of user experience for IDNs [35]. From a human-computer interaction perspective, usability can be understood as the user's experience with both hardware and software. For an interactive experience, system usability is essential for its potential to influence efficacy, autonomy, and meet user expectations [34]. Roth and Koenitz identified usability as a subcategory of agency using Murray's model. Thus, it can be interpreted as an aesthetic experiential category of IDNs. We decided to treat the terms aesthetics and usability separately, as they bear different meanings in visualization research.

Usability can be interpreted as readability or visual literacy in visualization systems. It manifests as the user's ability to receive and disentangle content. As a visual exploration technique, visualization is prone to misinterpretation and mismatching between the creator's intent and the viewer's understanding.

Some limitations of hardware interaction arise from the user's unfamiliarity with the technology or adverse effects on the user (such as cyber or motion sickness). Failure to adequately interface with the software comes from the user's inability to navigate, operate, and manipulate the system and results in misapprehension, confusion, frustration, and task abandonment.

## 3.3 Novelty

In the context of story-based interactive visualization, novelty refers to perceived innovation and originality in different elements of the experience [35]. Novelty is powerful for narrative visualization because it triggers interest, facilitates learning, and elicits cognitive pleasure [36]. Unfamiliar or unexpected visualizations and interactions are more memorable to the user [37, 38]. A user study by Kolhoff and Nack [39] showed that novelty initiated the engagement of users with interactive narrative content. Cawthon and Moere compared various visualization methods and disproved the notion that familiar examples, which people are more exposed to, accustomed to, and trained to comprehend, result in high effectiveness [17].

Original visualization techniques can, however, be repelling if they aggravate the readability of the visual narrative. Novelty can negatively affect usability, which is a trade-off that has to be carefully considered for serious applications. According to the theory of preference-for-prototypes, people are biased towards the most familiar choices because they minimize the risk of the unknown [10, 40]. In time-sensitive and mission-critical engineering applications, decision-makers will want to avoid unpredicted scenarios and they might perform better in a well-known environment. It is easier to perform tasks in computer interfaces that take advantage of previously learned techniques [41]. This is particularly relevant to non-tech-savvy users, who will need to be trained to maneuver novel hardware or software solutions. Higgins and Howell explained that a stimulus that is excessively novel triggers a displeasure response and results in disengagement with the stimuli [42]. They also noted that the threshold for unpleasurable arousal is subjective and it differs between individuals. In the engineering environment, it will be important to determine how comfortable the users are with novelty and in which domains. It will be crucial to mitigating the possibility of an adverse reaction that can lead to negative feelings, errors, and task abandonment.

### 3.4 Complexity

The complexity of IN for the visual articulation of data is expressed as the degree of cognitive effort needed to extract and receive information, the quantity of content, or the number of options the narrative provides. We approached the complexity problem from two viewpoints: data complexity (e.g., types of data, layers of data, tasks to be performed), and narrative complexity (e.g., the number of decision points or autonomy levels).

First, we will consider the concept of data complexity. Presentation of complex and massive amounts of real-time information is extremely difficult, even when using visual media [43]. Data has to be organized and structured efficiently, so it doesn't overload the receiver. The complexity and scale of data are increasing, as insight gained from analytics is at the core of the Industry 4.0 revolution. For real-time engineering applications, this means that optimization techniques need to be employed to increase the visualization's efficiency and prevent bottlenecks. Some data complexity issues can be resolved using custom optimization techniques (e.g., limiting the polygon count and introducing different levels of detail in a virtual environment for immersive applications), while others are dependent on new generations of robust technology (e.g., using 5G network to instantaneously send and process data from the physical to the virtual world, and vice versa). Excessive intricacy can be also solved by carefully designing and organizing information. The rule of the thumb is to manage it by layering and displaying only the necessary information at a time [44]. Even though additional visual information can increase the system performance and mental effort requirements, it can aid the knowledge-grasping process [41]. Preference for complexity or simplicity varies between individuals. Some people tend to enjoy cognitive effort [42] and they will enjoy performing complex tasks more than those in a lower need for cognition, who opt for simple tasks [45]. Personal preferences and mental capabilities of users need to be taken into account when designing narratives for interactive engineering visualization.

In this paragraph, we will discuss the complexity of the narrative. Using IDNs to comprehend complex phenomena has received more attention in recent years, and it is best seen through initiatives such as INDCOR[1]. Complexity provokes interest [20], so it

---

[1] https://indcor.eu/.

initiates involvement with the narrative and motivates users to spend more time engaging in it. In the context of IDNs, complexity is best correlated with interactivity. Creators have to balance the interactive complexity and the quality of the IDN artifact [35]. Giving the users too much freedom can result in unexpected behavior in which users can, for instance, navigate away from the area of interest. Complexity can also be related to autonomy, the independence to choose from a series of options without the feeling of being pulled in a single direction [34]. The number and the quality of available options to influence the narrative has to satisfy the user's expectations and meet the author's intent. Too much content or available options result in increased anxiety [46]. Limitations are also necessary for designing a usable system, as complex systems and interfaces are harder to use [47].

## 4   Discussion and Conclusion

The goal of this paper was to examine design qualities relevant for visualization research and evaluate them in the context of interactive narrative visualization for engineering applications. Our motivation was to aid practitioners in the design process by setting up a theoretical foundation based on existing literature. We identified four design qualities (aesthetics, usability, novelty, and complexity) that are relevant for visualization research and which have a great potential for interactive story-based visualization in engineering. We discussed their interrelationships and influence on visualization efficiency (see Fig. 1). Our aim was not to create a comprehensive list, but rather to provoke critical thinking and provide a starting point for further development of this nascent field.

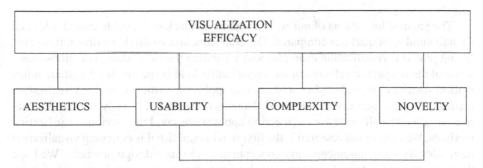

**Fig. 1.** Diagram presenting the four design qualities of interactive narrative visualization for engineering applications and their interrelationships.

As a result of our research, we concluded that:

1.  Terminology needs to be re-evaluated in the new context. In the first part of this paper, we discussed the idea of narrative visualization and identified the need to re-evaluate IN concepts in the new context. We further compared the shared concepts of aesthetics, usability, novelty, and complexity in visualization and IN research, and showed similarities and differences in their usage and understanding.

2.  All four design dimensions we analyzed are subjective and prone to personal inter-
    pretation. Different reactions, comfort levels, and preferences among users are asso-
    ciated with factors such as demographics, previous experiences, intellectuality, per-
    sonal taste, etc. Designing a good visualization is a complex process and while some
    guidelines exist, there is no guarantee that they will be successful in a particular
    context. More user studies will need to be conducted as the field develops.
3.  All four design qualities can be both positive and negative, depending on the con-
    text. Closely related to the first statement, presented concepts can be beneficial or
    disadvantageous as a result of a subjective judgment. There is a point beyond which
    subjects start experiencing negative effects and finding that threshold for every indi-
    vidual might be crucial. Also, different applications will require different design
    principles. Our research focused on the needs of the engineering industry, which can
    differ from those of other industries. Differences can be also made between different
    engineering subdisciplines and specific applications.
4.  Trade-off between design qualities has to be made. Design qualities can also posi-
    tively or negatively affect each other. Visualization designers will need to determine
    the end goal of visualization and give priority to features that best reflect the desired
    intent. This network of mutual relationships of visualization or story components
    will also vary with the application.
5.  There is a lack of completed case studies in the field. Despite the great potential
    of interactive storytelling for visualizing engineering data, the lack of completed
    case studies is evident. While work in the field of narrative visualization has been
    addressed in the literature, it only touches upon engineering applications. More
    practical visualization solutions are needed to expand our list and set up a theoretical
    foundation of the field.

The greatest limitations of our work come from a lack of available case studies and
a small number of qualities compared. Different conclusions might be drawn from analyzing practical visualization examples and expanding the list of design qualities. Also,
some of the research conducted in the visualization field is specific for 2D, static information visualization, and might not be directly applicable to more complex visualization
formats, and vice versa. We interpreted the term visualization broadly because interactive narrative visualization for engineering applications combines various visualization
methods. We believe our research is the first step to establish this emerging visualization
field, identify its requirements, and conceptualize adequate design practices. We hope
these results will help to bridge the gap between storytellers, visualization designers,
and engineers and expedite collaborative efforts to employ interactive narratives for
visualizing engineering data.

**Acknowledgements.** We acknowledge the support of the Natural Sciences and Engineering
Research Council of Canada (NSERC) [GR012389].

# References

1. Ghidini, E., Santos, C.Q., Manssour, I., Silveira, M.S.: Analyzing design strategies for narrative visualization. In: Proceedings of the XVI Brazilian Symposium on Human Factors in

Computing Systems, Joinville, Brazil, pp. 1–10. ACM (2017). https://doi.org/10.1145/316 0504.3160538

2. Koenitz, H.: An iterative approach towards interactive digital narrative – early results with the advanced stories authoring and presentation system. In: Chiu, D.K.W., Wang, M., Popescu, E., Li, Q., Lau, R. (eds.) ICWL 2012. LNCS, vol. 7697, pp. 59–68. Springer, Heidelberg (2014). https://doi.org/10.1007/978-3-662-43454-3_7

3. Haven, K.F.: Story Proof the Science Behind the Startling Power of Story. Libraries Unlimited, Westport (2007)

4. Ma, K.-L., Liao, I., Frazier, J., Hauser, H., Kostis, H.-N.: Scientific storytelling using visualization. IEEE Comput. Graph. Appl. 32, 12–19 (2012). https://doi.org/10.1109/MCG.2012.24

5. Ciuccarelli, P.: Turning visualisations into stories and "big pictures". In: Rendgen, S., Wiedemann, J. (eds.) Information Graphics, pp. 77–95. Taschen, Cologne, Köln (2012)

6. Wojtkowski, W., Wojtkowski, G.: Storytelling: its role in information visualization. Presented at the European Systems Science Congress (2002)

7. Card, S.K., Mackinlay, J.D., Shneiderman, B.: Readings in Information Visualization: Using Vision to Think. Morgan Kaufmann Publishers, San Francisco (1999)

8. Sack, W.: Aesthetics of information visualization. In: Lovejoy, M., Vesna, V., Paul, C. (eds.) Context Providers - Conditions of Meaning in Media Arts, pp. 123–149 (2011)

9. Filonik, D., Baur, D.: Measuring aesthetics for information visualization. In: 2009 13th International Conference Information Visualisation, Barcelona, Spain, pp. 579–584. IEEE (2009). https://doi.org/10.1109/IV.2009.94

10. Hekkert, P.: Design aesthetics: principles of pleasure in design. Psychol. Sci. 48, 157–172 (2006)

11. Philipsen, L., Kjærgaard, R.S. (eds.): The Aesthetics of Scientific Data Representation: More than Pretty Pictures. Routledge, New York (2017)

12. Quispel, A., Maes, A., Schilperoord, J.: Aesthetics and clarity in information visualization: the designer's perspective. Arts 7, 72 (2018). https://doi.org/10.3390/arts7040072

13. Ursyn, A.: Aesthetic expectations for information visualization. Int. J. Creative Interfaces Comput. Graph. 1, 19–39 (2010). https://doi.org/10.4018/jcicg.2010010103

14. Lima, M.: Visual Complexity: Mapping Patterns of Information. Princeton Architectural Press, New York (2011)

15. Borkin, M.A., et al.: What makes a visualization memorable? IEEE Trans. Visual. Comput. Graph. 19, 2306–2315 (2013). https://doi.org/10.1109/TVCG.2013.234

16. Cawthon, N., Moere, A.V.: A conceptual model for evaluating aesthetic effect within the user experience of information visualization. In: Tenth International Conference on Information Visualisation (IV 2006), London, England, pp. 374–382. IEEE (2006). https://doi.org/10.1109/IV.2006.4

17. Cawthon, N., Moere, A.: The effect of aesthetic on the usability of data visualization. In: Proceedings of the 11th International Conference on Information Visualisation, pp. 637–645. IEEE CS Press (2007)

18. Kurosu, M., Kashimura, K.: Apparent usability vs. inherent usability: experimental analysis on the determinants of the apparent usability. In: Conference Companion on Human Factors in Computing Systems - CHI 1995, Denver, Colorado, USA, pp. 292–293. ACM Press (1995). https://doi.org/10.1145/223355.223680

19. Norman, D.: Emotion & design: attractive things work better. Interactions 9, 36–42 (2002). https://doi.org/10.1145/543434.543435

20. Carbon, C.-C., Mchedlidze, T., Raab, M.H., Wächter, H.: The power of shape: how shape of node-link diagrams impacts aesthetic appreciation and triggers interest. i-Perception 9, 1–18 (2018). https://doi.org/10.1177/2041669518796851

21. Furnell, S.: Usability versus complexity – striking the balance in end-user security. Netw. Secur. **2010**, 13–17 (2010). https://doi.org/10.1016/S1353-4858(10)70147-1

22. Vosmeer, M., Schouten, B.: Interactive cinema: engagement and interaction. In: Mitchell, A., Fernández-Vara, C., Thue, D. (eds.) ICIDS 2014. LNCS, vol. 8832, pp. 140–147. Springer, Cham (2014). https://doi.org/10.1007/978-3-319-12337-0_14

23. Wohlfart, M., Hauser, H.: Story telling for presentation in volume visualization. In: Eurographics/IEEE-VGTC Symposium on Visualization, pp. 91–98 (2007). https://doi.org/10.2312/VISSYM/EUROVIS07/091-098

24. Segel, E., Heer, J.: Narrative visualization: telling stories with data. IEEE Trans. Visual. Comput. Graph. **16**, 1139–1148 (2010). https://doi.org/10.1109/TVCG.2010.179

25. Eshraghian, J.K.: Human ownership of artificial creativity. Nat. Mach. Intell. **2**, 157–160 (2020). https://doi.org/10.1038/s42256-020-0161-x

26. Devaney, K.: Beauty as a guiding principle for systems engineering. In: INCOSE International Symposium, vol. 26, pp. 1448–1462 (2016). https://doi.org/10.1002/j.2334-5837.2016.00238.x

27. Iliinsky, N.: On beauty. In: Steele, J., Iliinsky, N. (eds.) Beautiful Visualization, pp. 1–13. O'Reilly Media, Inc.

28. Krzywinski, M.: Scientific data visualization: aesthetic for diagrammatic clarity. In: Philipsen, L., Kjærgaard, R.S. (eds.) The Aesthetics of Scientific Data Representation More than Pretty Pictures, pp. 22–35. Routledge (2017)

29. Kyndrup, M.: "Facts" - and representational acts. In: Philipsen, L., Kjærgaard, R.S. (eds.) The Aesthetics of Scientific Data Representation More than Pretty Pictures, pp. 123–132. Routledge (2017)

30. Tractinsky, N., Katz, A.S., Ikar, D.: What is beautiful is usable. Interact. Comput. **13**, 127–145 (2000). https://doi.org/10.1016/S0953-5438(00)00031-X

31. Flangas, A., Tudor, A.R., Harris, F.C., Dascalu, S.: Preventing decision fatigue with aesthetically engaging information buttons. In: Yamamoto, S., Mori, H. (eds.) HCII 2021. LNCS, vol. 12765, pp. 28–39. Springer, Cham (2021). https://doi.org/10.1007/978-3-030-78321-1_3

32. Murray, J.H.: Hamlet on the Holodeck: The Future of Narrative in Cyberspace. MIT Press, Cambridge (1998)

33. Raja, D., Bowman, D., Lucas, J., North, C.: Exploring the benefits of immersion in abstract information visualization. In: Proceedings of the Immersive Projection Technology Workshop, pp. 61–69 (2004)

34. Roth, C., Koenitz, H.: Evaluating the user experience of interactive digital narrative. In: Proceedings of the 1st International Workshop on Multimedia Alternate Realities, Amsterdam, The Netherlands, pp. 31–36. ACM (2016). https://doi.org/10.1145/2983298.2983302

35. Revi, A.T., Millard, D.E., Middleton, S.E.: A systematic analysis of user experience dimensions for interactive digital narratives. In: Bosser, A.-G., Millard, D.E., Hargood, C. (eds.) ICIDS 2020. LNCS, vol. 12497, pp. 58–74. Springer, Cham (2020). https://doi.org/10.1007/978-3-030-62516-0_5

36. Biederman, I., Vessel, E.: Perceptual pleasure and the brain. Am. Sci. **94**, 247–253 (2006). https://doi.org/10.1511/2006.59.247

37. Gough, P.: From the analytical to the artistic: a review of literature on information visualization. Leonardo **50**, 47–52 (2017). https://doi.org/10.1162/LEON_a_00959

38. Larsen, B.A., Schoenau-Fog, H.: "Well, That was Quick" – towards storyworld adaptivity that reacts to players as people. In: Cardona-Rivera, R.E., Sullivan, A., Young, R.M. (eds.) ICIDS 2019. LNCS, vol. 11869, pp. 204–213. Springer, Cham (2019). https://doi.org/10.1007/978-3-030-33894-7_22

39. Kolhoff, L., Nack, F.: How relevant is your choice? In: Cardona-Rivera, R.E., Sullivan, A., Young, R.M. (eds.) ICIDS 2019. LNCS, vol. 11869, pp. 73–85. Springer, Cham (2019). https://doi.org/10.1007/978-3-030-33894-7_9

40. Whitfield, T.W.A.: Beyond prototypicality: toward a categorical-motivation model of aesthetics. Empir. Stud. Arts **18**, 1–11 (2000). https://doi.org/10.2190/KM3A-G1NV-Y5ER-MR2V
41. Ware, C.: Information Visualization: Perception for Design. Elsevier [u.a.], Amsterdam (2009)
42. Higgins, M., Howell, P.: Interpretive play and the player psychology of optimal arousal regulation. In: Bosser, A.-G., Millard, D.E., Hargood, C. (eds.) ICIDS 2020. LNCS, vol. 12497, pp. 243–257. Springer, Cham (2020). https://doi.org/10.1007/978-3-030-62516-0_22
43. Gershon, N., Page, W.: What storytelling can do for information visualization. Commun. ACM. **44**, 31–37 (2001). https://doi.org/10.1145/381641.381653
44. Shneiderman, B.: The eyes have it: a task by data type taxonomy for information visualizations. In: Proceedings 1996 IEEE Symposium on Visual Languages, Boulder, CO, USA, pp. 336–343. IEEE Computer Society Press (1996). https://doi.org/10.1109/VL.1996.545307
45. Cacioppo, J.T., Petty, R.E.: The need for cognition. J. Pers. Soc. Psychol. **42**, 116–131 (1982). https://doi.org/10.1037/0022-3514.42.1.116
46. Hick, W.E.: On the rate of gain of information. Q. J. Exp. Psychol. **4**, 11–26 (1952). https://doi.org/10.1080/17470215208416600
47. Paul, C.L., Rohrer, R., Nebesh, B.: A "Design First" approach to visualization innovation. IEEE Comput. Grap. Appl. **35**, 12–18 (2015). https://doi.org/10.1109/MCG.2015.7

# Encouraging Self-expression and Debate in *RecovR*: A Research-Creation Project to Build a Ludo-Narrative Model for a Sustainable Impact on Cultural Diversity and Inclusivity

Hélène Sellier[✉]

Studio The Seed Crew, Labège, France

**Abstract.** The paper introduces *RecovR*, a research-creation project whose aim is to develop a ludo-narrative model that would enable to have a sustainable impact on cultural diversity and inclusivity. The preliminary conclusions concerning the necessity of creating a space for debate and the poetics of chaos that could make it possible are discussed.

**Keywords:** Narrative design · Research-creation · Games for change · Expressive game

Dating back from the 2000's Art Game trend [1] and amplified with the expansion of the Indie Games at the end of the decade [2] as well as the rise of accessible authoring tools such as Unity [3] and Twine [4] (which gave birth to different artistic endeavours such as Serious Games [5], Games for Change or Queer Games [6]), there is a growing wave of games that tackle social issues concerning cultural diversity and the inclusion of varied identities by delivering a message or painting a personal experience. Thanks to their ludo-narrative structure, they aim to change society by raising awareness about existing problems, questioning social norms or empowering marginalized individuals. The idea of a discourse embedded in the game was famously theorized by Ian Bogost in his book *Persuasive Games* [7] and his conclusion infiltrated the industry, leading to debates such as the ludo-narrative dissonance debate [8].

The video games which emerged from this background often give a specific opinion or share a particular perspective on the social issues they discuss. However, the socio-cultural fabric is made of a variety of points of view and a multiplicity of ways to deal with them (stereotypes as a cognitive model, internalized self-prejudices, cognitive dissonance, etc.). For example, even within groups of people invested in the same issue (such as gender equality or disability), there are several conflicting views [9, 10].

To depict issues regarding cultural diversity, inclusiveness of different identities and social diversity, it seems adequate to find a way to allow "a genuine polyphony of fully valid voices" [11] than adopting a single teaching stance, a moralizing discourse, or a dominating perspective. This essay presents a research project, undertaken by the team

A. Mitchell and M. Vosmeer (Eds.): ICIDS 2021, LNCS 13138, pp. 410–415, 2021.
https://doi.org/10.1007/978-3-030-92300-6_40

of the indie game studio The Seed Crew, which aims to conceptualize and build a ludo-narrative model that enables the expression of different feelings and thoughts on multi-factorial and sensitive issues. Based on the idea that a consensus can emerge from the dissensus [12] it intends to bring people together and to foster social interconnectedness.

Following the recent developments of Game Studies as well as the evolution of the concerns in the professional world, a solution might be found with the approaches that emphasize the role of the player in the construction of the game's meaning. The project is thus grounded in several frameworks: firstly, Post-classical Narratology theories that focus on the reader's interpretation [13, 14]; secondly, Play Studies that posit the importance of the player's experience [15] and their applications, such as Expressive Games [16]; lastly, Narrative Design since this creative discipline focuses on the user's involvement [17].

In this essay, I will begin by describing the methodology of the project, then I will explain its current state and conclude by establishing the plan for further research.

To obtain a ludo-narrative model which is both conceptually interesting and pragmatically viable, methods from the field of research-creation [18, 19] are used. The project links theory, which is actualized in scientific publications and communications, and practice, which leads to the development of *RecovR*[1]. This video game, intended to be a tool for professional training, is divided into several modules, each related to a social issue (sexism, ableism – i.e. prejudices and discriminations against people with disabilities…) and made up of several episodes. According to Chapman and Sawchuck's categorization [20], the whole project falls mainly under the practices of "research-for-creation" and "research-from-creation".

On one hand, reading and interpreting scientific literature on media culture, game studies, social psychology, sociology, and cultural studies allows us to conceptualize a part of the game. Since most of the fictional situations in the game are based on facts taken from research papers, it could be said that the project also falls under the category that Chapman and Sawchuck call "creative presentation of research". However, individually, each topic is not our area of scientific expertise, so we don't define this feature as fundamentally part of our work.

On the other hand, the game is created in order to generate data that can be analyzed. Indeed, we designed the game to test several hypotheses regarding the narrativity and the expressive potential of video games, such as the power of seriality to encourage dialogue between the players. When finished, at least partially, the production can thus be analyzed in different ways (formal analysis, user experience…) to establish tentative results. Indeed, our work is an iterative process in which a phase of scientific discovery leads to a time of creation which, in return, introduces a stage of theorization.

As of June 2021, the first module of the game, focusing on sexism in the business world, was developed in a bit more than a year and is published. It was designed to enable the player's expression of themselves in several ways. In the following paragraphs, I will focus on the main features: each episode basically consists of four parts.

Playing Charlie, a young woman recently hired, the user is first invited to explore a 3D environment depicting an open office space. They can choose to listen to rumors which

---

[1] Visual presentations of the game can be found at those addresses: https://www.theseedcrew.com/ and https://www.youtube.com/watch?v=Yco9mtjN08Y (retrieved the 25th October 2021).

are spread all around. Some "barks" [21] are sexist comments which pollute the shared space; others are only quick pictures of everyday life. Similar to a kind of wandering [22] this type of play is completely optional and embraces the necessary random aspect of learning [23]. The player can choose how many complex and potentially disturbing situations they want to face.

Each exploration phase is followed by a phase of mandatory dialogue depicted in 2D in which the player can learn about the life of Charlie's colleagues, the challenges she faces, and the adversity of corporate life. Using curiosity, surprise, and suspense effects [14] as well as techniques particular to branching narratives (such as narrative puzzles or hidden paths), those moments aim to immerse the player in the fictional world by creating a narrative tension. If the user doesn't have the choice to endure the situation (be it a neutral, mundane, comment or a sexist microaggression), they can decide how they handle their response. Based on the two main behaviours identified by the research in psychology about sexism [24] and inspired by the Jakobson's functions of language [25], the dialogue options allow the player to either confront the Non-Player Characters (passionately or rationally) or dodge their observation (being vague or using humor). Since there is no right or wrong way to answer, but only different consequences that depend on the interlocutor's personality and occupation, this feature allows the player to freely express themself and to experiment their opinions.

If the narrative structure makes room for the player's voice, their avatar also has her own views. The text of every interface is diegetic: for example, the beginning and the ending menu are written like a personal journal in which Charlie sums up what happened to her but also expresses her feelings toward her colleagues' sexist comments. These moments invite the player to discover another interior life and assume that empathy can lead to a growing awareness of someone else's problems [26, 27]. Since the player-character is not only an interface allowing fictional immersion, but also a tool encouraging a reflexive attitude [28], we decided to harness the potential of this ambivalence to design moments of conflicting point of views. In the exploration or the dialogue phases, the player can push a red button each time they think the character's comment is sexist. The player is thus invited to adopt an analytical thinking. If their reasoning matches with Charlie's, her interpretation of the situation is unlocked in the ending screen. The player is encouraged to express their opinion, but they also face another consideration of the interpersonal situation.

The game expects the player to be alternatively immersed in the story and critical of its implications, but it also provides an emotional outlet. In each episode, there is a turn-based combat phase in which the player has to perform different QTEs (Quick Time Events), such as pushing frantically and repeatedly on one button or, on the contrary, aim at the right time in the right place. On one hand, this feature corresponds to the fundamental autotelic and non-productive characteristics of games [29] since it doesn't help learning about sexism and reconnects with the idea of play as fun. However, if the player wants to invest themself in an interpretation, this part of the game is also meaningful on several levels. Symbolically, the combat phase corresponds to the psychological fight Charlie endures when she can't take it anymore and thus is very different aesthetically. The combat stances coincide with the dialogue options, and there are correspondences between the player's movement and the meaning of the chosen attitude. For example, the passionate and confronting answer is linked with the successive hits. This feature encourages the player to verbally express their feelings, be it as a mumble for themself or an exclamation of triumph, when playing in a group.

The game was created to be played in two main contexts: either alone as a self-examination experience or with other people as a shared experience. However, in each case, the episodic format tends to stimulate the dialogue after the moments of play, since the users ponder upon the past fictional events and imagine what will happen next [30]. The seriality of the project thus aims to create an environment for the players to collectively talk about sexism and to give them the opportunity to gather around this social issue to find suitable and sustainable solutions in their interpersonal context.

*RecovR* confronts the player to various beliefs and behaviors, the NPCs prejudices, their avatar's views, and their own judgment. The game also urges the player to alternate between several opposite attitudes: immersion and reflexivity, empathy and self-expression, cathartic fun and analytical gaze... The ideal experience unsettles the player, who is constantly invited to interpret the game, to give their own perception and understanding of the fictional events.

Our current hypothesis is the following: To create a deep and sustainable impact on social issues such as sexism and ableism, games need to be catalysts for human relations, they need to let the players express their own feelings and thoughts on multifactorial and sensitive issues. For a game to foster exchange between diverse points of view, a solution seems to be to not try to impose a unique scope, but rather to create an experience based on tensions between diametrically opposed poles. Rather than focusing on designing harmony and consensus, we may seek to draft a chaotic structure and trust the player to take into their own hands the process to make sense of it.

This line of thought is close to the vibrant field of contemporary research on narrative structures which leave interpretative room for the players. More particularly, it is inspired by Rémi Cayatte's work [31] in which, focusing on procedural narratives, he argues that the expressive power of video games resides precisely in the moments when the player takes in charge the operating of the content of the game to inject meaning in the gaps in the ludo-narrative structure.

The preliminary conclusions obtained thanks to the conception of the first module of *RecovR* and the subsequent formal analysis of the created object form a knowledge which we need to question and build upon. Firstly, the complementary ideas of a balanced experience between converse elements and a breeding ground for debate will be tested in another module: the second part of *RecovR* will tackle the discriminations linked with the experience of disability and focus the discussion on the issue of ableism. Secondly, we have set up a series of user tests, in which a close observation of play will be followed by semi-directive interviews in order to determine if the theoretical hypotheses are verified in concrete uses. Thirdly, by communicating provisional results [32], we hope to enrich our understanding of the link between interpersonal communication and sustainable social impact through video gaming practices thanks to the feedback of the scientific and professional communities.

# References

1. Sharp, J.: Works of Game: On the Aesthetics of Games and Art. MIT Press, Cambridge (2015)
2. Sharp, J.: Independent game. In: Lowood, H., Guins, R. (eds.) Debuggin Game History: A Critical Lexicon. MIT Press, Cambridge (2016)
3. Nicoll, B., Keogh, B.: The Unity Game Engine and the Circuits of Cultural Software. Palgrave Macmillan, London (2019)
4. Anthropy, A.: Rise of the Videogame Zinesters: How Freaks, Normals, Amateurs, Artists, Dreamers, Drop-outs, Queers, Housewives, and People Like You Are Taking Back an Art Form. Seven Stories Press, New York (2012)
5. Alvarez, J., Djaouti, D.: Introduction au Serious Game. Questions théoriques, Paris (2012)
6. Ruberg, B., Shaw, A. (eds.): Queer Game Studies. University of Minnesota Press, Minneapolis (2017)
7. Bogost, I.: Persuasive Games. The MIT Press, Cambridge (2007)
8. Séraphine, F.: Ludonarrative dissonance: Is storytelling about reaching harmony? (2016). http://www.fredericseraphine.com
9. Freedman, E.: No Turning Back: The History of Feminism and the Future of Women. Ballantine Books, New York City (2003)
10. Goodley, D.: Disability Studies An Interdisciplinary Introduction. Sage Publications Limited, Thousand Oaks (2011)
11. Bakhtin, M.M.: Problems of Dostoevsky's Poetics. University of Minnesota Press, Minneapolis (1984)
12. Heraclite: Fragments. Seuil, Paris (1998)
13. Eco, U.: Lector in Fabula. Editions Grasset et Fasquelle, Paris (1979)
14. Baroni, R.: La Tension Narrative. Seuil, Paris (2007)
15. Sicart, M.: Against procedurality. Game Stud. 11(3) (2011)
16. Genvo, S.: Comprendre et développer le potentiel expressif. Hermès, La Revue 62(1) (2012)
17. Posey, J.: Narrative design. In: Despain, W. (ed.) Professional Techniques for Video Game Writing. AK Peters/CRC Press, Natik (2008)
18. Gosselin, P.: La recherche en pratique artistique. In: Le Cogiec, E., Gosselin, P. (eds.) La recherche création. Pour une compréhension de la recherche en pratique artistique. Presses de l'Université du Québec, Québec (2006)
19. Paquin, L.-C., Noury, C.: Définir la recherche-création ou cartographier ses pratiques? In: Association francophone pour le savoir (2018)
20. Chapman, O., Sawchuck, K.: Research-creation: intervention, analysis and "Family Resemblances". Canadian J. Commun. 37 (2012)
21. Beaulieu, S.: How a character says hello: Writing Barks for video games (2020). https://sarah-beaulieu.com
22. Flawinne, V.: L'œil vidéoludique et le nouveau flâneur. Mémoire de master, Université de Liège (2007)
23. Lavigne, M.: Les instrumentalisations du jeu numérique. Une approche critique de l'emploi contemporain de la notion de jeu au travers de ses manifestations numériques à vocation non distractives. Mémoire d'habilitation à diriger les recherches, Université de Limoges (2020)
24. Melotte, P.: Les femmes face au sexisme: confrontation ou évitement? Étude des processus émotionnels et cognitifs lors d'interactions comprenant une remarque sexiste. Thèse de doctorat, Université Libre de Bruxelles (2017)
25. Jakobson, R.: Essais de linguistique générale. Éditions de Minuit, Paris (1963)
26. Zanna, O.: Le corps dans la relation aux autres. Pour une éducation à l'empathie. Presses universitaires de Rennes, Rennes (2015)

27. Immordino-Yang, M.H.: Emotion, sociality, and the brain's default mode network: insights for educational practice and policy. Policy Insights Behav. Brain Sci. **3**(2) (2016)
28. Barnabé, F., Delbouille, J.: Aux frontières de la fiction: l'avatar comme opérateur de réflexivité. Sciences du jeu **9** (2018)
29. Huizinga, J.: Homo Ludens: essai sur la fonction sociale du jeu. Gallimard, Paris (1951)
30. Goudmand, A.: Récits en partage. Expériences de la sérialité narrative en culture médiatique. Thèse de doctorat, Université Paris Sciences et Lettres (2018)
31. Cayatte, R.: L'émotion comme moteur de jeu: mettre des mots sur une expressivité vidéoludique. Conference Les langages du jeu vidéo: codes, discours et images en jeu, Université de Lausanne (2019)
32. Bouchardon, S.: La Valeur heuristique de la littérature numérique. Mémoire d'habilitation à diriger des recherches, Université de Technologie de Compiègne (2012)

# Supporting Interactive Storytelling with Block-Based Narrative Programming

Andy Smith[1]([⊠]) [iD], Danielle Boulden[1] [iD], Bradford Mott[1] [iD],
Aleata Hubbard-Cheuoua[2] [iD], James Minogue[1], Kevin Oliver[1] [iD],
and Cathy Ringstaff[2] [iD]

[1] North Carolina State University, Raleigh, NC 27695, USA
{pmsmith4,dmboulde,bwmott,jminogu,kmoliver}@ncsu.edu
[2] WestEd, San Francisco, CA 94107, USA
{ahubbar,cringst}@wested.org

**Abstract.** Recent years have seen growing interest in utilizing digital storytelling, where students create short narratives around a topic, as a means of creating motivating problem-solving activities in K-12 education. At the same time, there is increasing awareness of the need to engage students as young as elementary school in complex topics such as physical science and computational thinking. Building on previous research investigating block-based programming activities for storytelling, we present an approach to block-based programming for interactive digital storytelling to engage upper elementary students (ages 9 to 10) in computational thinking and narrative skill development. We describe both the learning environment that combines block-based narrative programming with a rich, interactive visualization engine designed to produce animations of student generated stories, as well as an analysis of students using the system to create narratives. Student generated stories are evaluated from both a story quality perspective as well as from their ability to communicate and demonstrate computational thinking and physical science concepts and practices. We also explore student behaviors during the story creation process and discuss potential improvements for future interventions.

**Keywords:** Narrative-centered learning · Block-based programming

## 1 Introduction

Recent years have seen growing evidence that engaging students in digital storytelling activities is an effective tool for promoting meaningful learning across a variety of subjects [1–3]. While these activities have been shown to facilitate positive outcomes such as creative exploration of scientific phenomena [4, 5], studies have also shown that the benefits of digital storytelling can vary greatly between individual students. This highlights a critical need for a better understanding of how to effectively support students as they create and present stories.

Another barrier to large-scale adoption of digital storytelling activities in classrooms is lack of perceived alignment with existing curricular goals, specifically in areas such as

A. Mitchell and M. Vosmeer (Eds.): ICIDS 2021, LNCS 13138, pp. 416–424, 2021.
https://doi.org/10.1007/978-3-030-92300-6_41

computational thinking and physical science [6]. At the elementary level, many teachers have limited, if any, instructional time allocated to these topics, and may see digital storytelling activities as an inefficient use of that limited resource. However, there is a growing recognition of the similarities between the digital storytelling process and computational thinking and science competencies [7, 8]. Additionally, teachers who often lack significant training in science and computational thinking may be more comfortable supporting a more familiar task such as narrative construction.

To address these challenges, we have developed the INFUSECS narrative-centered learning environment, to engage students in deep, meaningful physical science and computational thinking learning through the creation of interactive narratives. INFUSECS utilizes a custom-built narrative programming environment, where students utilize a block-based programming interface to create, revise, and visualize interactive narratives. Building on research exploring design best practices for block-based programming for younger learners [9, 10], we created a learning environment to enable upper elementary students o create rich interactive narratives while also engaging with concepts and competencies from physical science and computational thinking. In this paper, we use INFUSECS to specifically focus on two research questions:

**RQ1**: How effectively are students able to use block-based programming to create interactive narratives, when evaluated from a story quality perspective?
**RQ2**: How do students exhibit knowledge of physical science and computational thinking concepts through their created interactive narratives?

To answer these research questions, we conducted a pilot study with students in the southeastern United States as part of an after school program. Initial results show students were able to effectively use the tool to create stories, while also demonstrating evidence of computational thinking concepts such as debugging and sequential execution. However, not all student generated stories met all story quality criteria, and all students struggled to integrated physical science concepts into their narratives.

## 2 Related Work

Narrative experiences offer an exceptionally promising tool for engaging students in computationally-rich problem solving. By leveraging narrative's unique ability to help us understand the world around us [11] and communicate conceptual understanding to others [12], storytelling has significant potential well beyond the traditional educational context of language arts. Specifically, digital storytelling has shown great potential to leverage the creativity and effectiveness of narrative for domains such as science [1, 13] through activities such as creating a multimedia presentation of a story. Other digital storytelling activities have shown positive effects for both cognitive measures of visual memory and writing skills [14], affective measures such as student engagement [2], and improved 21st century skills such as problem solving, argumentation, and cooperation [15].

However, the benefits of digital storytelling interventions are dependent on the ability of the student to construct a narrative. This has led to a broad range of research into how to best design and support digital storytelling interventions for students of a variety of age ranges, including approaches that seek to leverage the synergies between storytelling and computational thinking through block-based programming. A modified version of the popular Scratch environment was used to enable students to create animated stories involving placing and moving sprites, as well as including audio clips and other events responsive to user inputs [16]. Other research has investigated using block-based programming in non-traditional methods such as a tangible, sticker-based block language used as part of an interactive storybook [17], or as a method for introducing computational thinking strategies into English language learning [8]. This work extends these efforts by designing and investigating story quality and demonstration of conceptual knowledge using a block-based programming environment focused primarily on interactive storytelling augmented by rich visualizations.

## 3   Narrative-Centered Learning Environment

This study builds on a previous version of INFUSECS, which featured a block-based programming interface built with Google's Blockly framework that focused on the creation of text-based teleplays. The current version of INFUSECS is a WebGL-based application built with the Unity 3D game engine. In addition to supporting interactive multimedia content and simulation activities, this version also supports a greatly expanded narrative programming interface. The interface consists of two main parts: a custom block-based programming interface developed for the Unity 3D game engine, and an interactive visualization engine. Figure 1 below shows a short example story and the accompanying visualization.

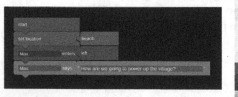

**Fig. 1.** Screenshots of a sample narrative displayed in INFUSECS's block-based editor and visualization of a line of dialog.

The narrative programming interface of INFUSECS utilizes four types of blocks designed to enable key aspects of digital storytelling including setting the location of the scene, arranging characters, enabling dialogue between characters, and supporting branching stories based on choices made by the viewer of the story. The custom blocks leverage design principles from previous research on block-based programming environments for upper elementary students [16, 18–20]. Specifically, the custom narrative blocks utilize distinct colors for each category to leverage visual affordances in the appearance of the blocks. Stories are executed sequentially starting from a *Start* block, avoiding event-driven programming. *Dialogue* and *Stage Direction* blocks utilize drop downs for character names and a starter story is provided to the students to encourage customization and editing rather than a purely generative activity. Finally, the language on the blocks is designed to limit complicated syntax and vocabulary.

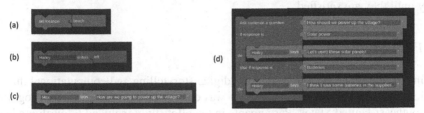

**Fig. 2.** Custom blocks for the INFUSECS narrative programming interface.

The set of custom blocks are separated into four categories corresponding to the main features of visual interactive narratives: describing a scene, moving characters in and out of the scene, character dialogue (including narration), and branching.

The *Scene* blocks, shown in Fig. 2a, allows students to set the location where the events in the narrative take place. Location blocks are defined before the activity to fit with the motivating scenario framing a particular digital storytelling activity, and to align with art assets for the visualization system described below. This also allows INFUSECS to utilize type-checking, and prevent students from attaching incompatible blocks, i.e. text fields, a feature also afforded by the color-coding scheme of blocks.

The *Stage Direction* blocks allow for students to move characters in and out of the scene of their story. The *Enter* block, shown in Fig. 2b, allows students to select which character is entering the scene, with fixed location blocks that can be attached similar to the locations for the *Scene* block. The other *Stage Direction* block currently implemented is the *Exit* block, where students can specify a character to leave the scene.

The *Dialogue* blocks, shown in Fig. 2c, are the core blocks of the storytelling system, as the majority of the content in the student-generated stories is dialogue between characters or statements by the narrator. A line of dialogue is generated through the combination of a *Character* block and a *Text* block. The name property of the *Character* block is filled with a list of characters that have been previously introduced to the student earlier in the activity. Additionally, a *Narrator* option can be chosen to provide narration for the story.

The *Ask Audience* block, Fig. 2d, is designed to allow students to incorporate branching into their narratives, while also providing them an opportunity to experiment with computational thinking concepts like conditionals and flow control. The *Ask Audience* block contains three properties that must be defined by learners. The first property is the question that will be asked to the audience, and then the two possible responses the audience can respond with to the question. Below each response, students can then place story blocks that will execute if that choice is selected.

At any point in the story authoring process, students can press a run button at the top of the editor to play an animation of their story. First, the block-based representation is converted into Ink script (https://www.inklestudios.com/ink/), a narrative scripting language developed primarily for game applications. Next, the generated ink script is passed to the visualization engine, which displays it using graphical assets in Unity. The visualization pauses after each dialogue utterance to give the audience time to read the story, and advances when a button is pressed. At the completion of the visualization, the student returns to the narrative editor where they can continue to iterate and revise their story until they are satisfied.

## 4   Pilot Study

To understand how INFUSECS supports digital storytelling and computational thinking in elementary classrooms, a pilot study was conducted at an after-school program in the southeast United States. Participants in the pilot study included 6 fourth grade students ages 9–10, including 4 males and 2 females. Four of the students were Black or African-American, one was White, and one was Multiracial. The 6 students worked independently, and students reported a range of previous experience with block-based coding environments with 1 student reporting no prior experience, 2 students reporting some prior experience, and 3 students reporting that they frequently used block-based coding environments.

The pilot study took place over 4 days, with approximately 30–45 min spent each day. Students and coordinators for the after-school program were together in person, while research staff observed remotely using video conferencing software. The first day students were given a brief introduction to the activity, completed a demographic survey, and watched an introductory video introducing the motivating scenario of a group of scientists who were shipwrecked on a remote tropical island. On the second day, students were presented with the task of solving how the scientists would power their makeshift village and engaged with physical science content focusing on types of energy and energy conversion. After completing the science content, students were given a planning worksheet to assist them with planning their story. On the third day, students completed their planning worksheet and began creating their stories using the narrative programming interface, and on the fourth day the students spent the entire time period working on their stories.

For all students, a brief starter story was provided in the block-based programming interface, which provided an example of each type of block. The learning environment logged detailed trace logs of student actions in the environment, as well as logging their story workspace each time the story was visualized.

All 6 students were able to use the system to create short narratives in the allotted time. Each student effectively used at least one of each type of block with stories ranging from 12–26 "lines of code" (i.e. two connected components of a *Dialogue* block counting as 1 "line"), consisting mostly of narration and dialogue between characters. Overall student stories averaged 17.3 total blocks (M = 17.3, s.d. = 5.64), 4 scene blocks per story (M = 4, s.d. = 1.78), 4.2 *Stage Direction* blocks per story (M = 4.2, s.d. = 1.94), 1.8 *Ask Audience* blocks (M = 1.8, s.d. = 0.98), and 7.3 *Dialogue* blocks (M = 7.3, s.d. = 1.97). Additionally, students used an average of 3.33 characters in their story. This represents a large increase compared to previous versions of the system containing a similar set of story blocks but lacking the visualization functionality of the current system [21].

We also evaluated the student stories based on a set of story quality metrics, as well as for evidence of curricular competencies from both physical science and computational thinking. We first investigate the research question:

**RQ1:** How effectively are students able to use block-based programming to create interactive narratives, when evaluated from a story quality perspective?

To measure story quality, we devised a scoring rubric to evaluate the students' stories based on the Common Core State Standards (http://www.corestandards.org/) for 4th grade English Language Arts Writing. Common Core State Standards are a set of standards for various subjects such as writing and mathematics that have been adopted by many states in the United States. Students' stories were evaluated based on six criteria in alignment with the standards and one additional criterion we added specifically focusing on how branching was utilized in the story to facilitate its organization and development. These criteria are described in Table 1 below. Each criterion was rated on a 0–2 scale, with 0 as having little to no evidence, 1 as having some evidence, and 2 as having sufficient evidence of the given criteria.

**Table 1.** Story evaluation criteria.

| Criteria | Description |
|---|---|
| Criteria 1 | Establishes a situation that introduces reader to characters/setting |
| Criteria 2 | Presents/establishes an organized event that unfolds naturally (including a distinct beginning, middle, and end) |
| Criteria 3 | Includes dialogue and description that develops experiences and events or shows the responses of characters to situations |
| Criteria 4 | Uses a variety of transitional words and phrases to manage the sequence of events |
| Criteria 5 | Uses concrete words and phrases and sensory details to convey experiences and events precisely |
| Criteria 6 | Provide a conclusion that follows from the narrated experiences or events |
| Criteria 7 | Integrates branching to organize and develop the story |

Analysis of student narratives using these criteria is shown below in Table 2. Overall, the custom blocks facilitated Criteria 1, 2, and 3 for all students. Student stories performed worst on Criteria 5 and 6. Summing across all criteria yielded an average of 6.67 per story, with a high score of 12 and a low score of 4.

**RQ2:** How do students exhibit knowledge of physical science and computational thinking concepts through their created interactive narratives?

To evaluate physical science content, we used frequency counts to measure how many science concepts from the physical content were referenced in their stories. Overall, the number of science concepts students utilized in their stories ranged from 0 to 3 with four of the students not integrating any science concepts in their stories.

**Table 2.** Story evaluation scores.

| Student | Criteria 1 | Criteria 2 | Criteria 3 | Criteria 4 | Criteria 5 | Criteria 6 | Criteria 7 |
|---------|-----------|-----------|-----------|-----------|-----------|-----------|-----------|
| Student 1 | 1 | 1 | 1 | 1 | 0 | 1 | 1 |
| Student 2 | 2 | 2 | 2 | 2 | 1 | 1 | 2 |
| Student 3 | 1 | 1 | 2 | 2 | 1 | 0 | 2 |
| Student 4 | 1 | 0 | 1 | 1 | 0 | 0 | 1 |
| Student 5 | 1 | 1 | 1 | 1 | 0 | 0 | 1 |
| Student 6 | 1 | 1 | 1 | 0 | 0 | 0 | 1 |

For computational thinking we looked at both the final story, as well as behaviors exhibited while creating the story. Using the K-12 Computer Science Framework (https://k12cs.org/) we identified concepts and practices that overlap with the story creation process. In addition to the concept of *Creating Computational Artifacts,* students also exhibited evidence of *troubleshooting/debugging* behaviors through the iterative running and modifying of their stories as they were created. Overall, the 6 students averaged 42 runs of their story (minimum = 12, maximum = 61). Students showed evidence of understanding *control structures* and *sequential execution* of their stories through their usage of the *Ask Audience* block. Multiple students stored segments of code on the workspace not connected to the *Start* block, showing evidence of their understanding of the single thread of execution.

## 5 Discussion

Overall, the INFUSECS learning environment enabled students to create interactive narratives incorporating features such as dialog, setting changes, and branching. Compared to a previous version of the system, the new system with a revised set of custom blocks and a story visualization system appears to have effectively supported longer, higher quality stories, as well as encouraged desirable debugging and troubleshooting behaviors. This was particularly noticeable in the students' improved understanding and usage of the *Ask Audience* block to incorporate branching into their narratives.

A noticeable shortcoming was the lack of physical science content included in the stories. Discussions with students suggested adding props representing the science content to the block palette may encourage their inclusion in the resulting narratives. Similarly, more explicitly including science concepts in the planning process may also encourage their usage in the resulting narratives. From a computational thinking perspective, further analysis of the students' debugging and troubleshooting behaviors could help ensure that the visualization functionality is being used in a productive manner, rather than a distracting one. Inclusion of more complex command structures, such as loops or event-based execution, could provide more opportunities for students to demonstrate richer understanding. Finally, including more traditional assessments (i.e. validated survey measures) could help determine if lack of understanding, or a shortcoming of the interface is responsible for the omission of concepts included in the narratives.

Finally, there are two key limitations to these findings. First, we acknowledge the small sample size makes it difficult to generalize the findings too broadly. Secondly, while researchers were able to observe the activities via video conferencing, lack of in person observations due to the ongoing pandemic makes qualitative analysis of the story creation process more difficult.

## 6   Conclusion and Future Work

As evidence of the transformative potential of digital storytelling continues to grow, so does the need for understanding how to effectively integrate and support digital storytelling in different educational contexts. The structured format and intuitive design of block-based programming environments provides a promising modality for both enabling rich interactive narrative creation, while at the same time providing an intriguing activity for integrating computational problem solving in a variety of subjects.

With this as motivation, we investigated student story creation utilizing block-based programming. Findings show that the custom story blocks enabled upper elementary students to create structured narratives, incorporating traditional storytelling concepts such as dialogue between characters and branching based on viewer input. Analysis of student stories highlighted how the storytelling activity can be used by students to demonstrate their conceptual understanding of physical science and computational thinking concepts and practices.

Future iterations of the learning environment will focus on revising the set of storytelling blocks, with a focus on encouraging students to communicate more science and computational thinking concepts and practices. This focus will also extend to the visualization portion of the environment, allowing for richer interactions to be authored by the students. We will also investigate how to improve storytelling through a more robust and structured planning phase as well as additional support to augment the story creation and revision process.

**Acknowledgments.** This research was supported by the National Science Foundation under Grants DRL-1921495 and DRL-1921503. Any opinions, findings, and conclusions expressed in this material are those of the authors and do not necessarily reflect the views of the National Science Foundation.

## References

1. Robin, B.R.: Digital storytelling: a powerful technology tool for the 21st century classroom. Theory Into Pract. **47**, 220–228 (2008). https://doi.org/10.1080/00405840802153916
2. Smeda, N., Dakich, E., Sharda, N.: The effectiveness of digital storytelling in the classrooms: a comprehensive study. Smart Learn. Environ. **1**(1), 1–21 (2014). https://doi.org/10.1186/s40 561-014-0006-3
3. Yang, Y.T.C., Wu, W.C.I.: Digital storytelling for enhancing student academic achievement, critical thinking, and learning motivation: a year-long experimental study. Comput. Educ. **59**, 339–352 (2012). https://doi.org/10.1016/j.compedu.2011.12.012
4. Henriksen, D.: Full STEAM ahead: creativity in excellent STEM teaching practices. STEAM J. **1**, 1–9 (2014). https://doi.org/10.5642/steam.20140102.15

5. Henriksen, D., Mishra, P., Fisser, P.: Infusing creativity and technology in 21st century education: a systemic view for change. Educ. Technol. Soc. **19**, 27–37 (2016)
6. Tan, M., Lee, S.-S., Hung, D.W.L.: Digital storytelling and the nature of knowledge. Educ. Inf. Technol. **19**(3), 623–635 (2013). https://doi.org/10.1007/s10639-013-9280-x
7. Lee, I., et al.: Computational Thinking for Youth in Practice (2011)
8. Parsazadeh, N., Cheng, P.Y., Wu, T.T., Huang, Y.M.: Integrating computational thinking concept into digital storytelling to improve learners' motivation and performance. J. Educ. Comput. Res. **59**, 470–495 (2021). https://doi.org/10.1177/0735633120967315
9. Hill, C., Dwyer, H.A., Martinez, T., Harlow, D., Franklin, D.: Floors and flexibility: designing a programming environment for 4th-6th grade classrooms. In: Proceedings of the 46th ACM Technical Symposium on Computer Science Education (SIGCSE), pp. 546–551 (2015). https://doi.org/10.1145/2676723.2677275
10. Weintrop, D., Hansen, A.K., Harlow, D.B., Franklin, D.: Starting from scratch: outcomes of early computer science learning experiences implications for what comes next. In: Proceedings of the 2018 ACM Conference on International Computing Education Research (ICER), pp. 142–150 (2018). https://doi.org/10.1145/3230977.3230988
11. Bruner, J.: Acts of Meaning. Harvard University Press, Cambridge (1990)
12. Avraamidou, L., Osborne, J.: The role of narrative in communicating science. Int. J. Sci. Educ. **31**, 1683–1707 (2009). https://doi.org/10.1080/09500690802380695
13. Robin, B.R.: The power of digital storytelling to support teaching and learning. Digit. Educ. Rev. 17–29 (2016). https://doi.org/10.1344/der.2016.30.17-29
14. Sarica, H.Ç., Usluel, Y.K.: The effect of digital storytelling on visual memory and writing skills. Comput. Educ. **94**, 298–309 (2016). https://doi.org/10.1016/j.compedu.2015.11.016
15. Niemi, H., Multisilta, J.: Digital storytelling promoting twenty-first century skills and student engagement. Technol. Pedagog. Educ. **25**, 451–468 (2016). https://doi.org/10.1080/1475939X.2015.1074610
16. Franklin, D., et al.: Using upper-elementary student performance to understand conceptual sequencing in a blocks-based curriculum. In: Proceedings of the Conference on Integrating Technology into Computer Science Education, ITiCSE, pp. 231–236 (2017). https://doi.org/10.1145/3017680.3017760
17. Horn, M.S., AlSulaiman, S., Koh, J.: Translating Roberto to Omar: computational literacy, stickerbooks, and cultural forms. In: Proceedings of the 12th International Conference on Interaction Design and Children, pp. 120–127 (2013). https://doi.org/10.1145/2485760.2485773
18. Franklin, D., Hill, C., Dwyer, H.A., Hansen, A.K., Iveland, A., Harlow, D.B.: Initialization in scratch: seeking knowledge transfer. In: Proceedings of the 47th ACM Technical Symposium on Computing Science Education, SIGCSE 2016, pp. 217–222 (2016). https://doi.org/10.1145/2839509.2844569
19. Weintrop, D., Wilensky, U.: Using commutative assessments to compare conceptual understanding in blocks-based and text-based programs. In: Proceedings of the 11th Annual International Conference on International Computing Education Research (ICER 2015), pp. 101–110 (2015). https://doi.org/10.1145/2787622.2787721
20. Dwyer, H., Hill, C., Hansen, A., Iveland, A., Franklin, D., Harlow, D.: Fourth grade students reading block-based programs: predictions, visual cues, and affordances. In: Proceedings of the 2015 ACM Conference on International Computing Education Research (ICER), pp. 111–120 (2015). https://doi.org/10.1145/2787622.2787729
21. Smith, A., et al.: Toward a block-based programming approach to interactive storytelling for upper elementary students. In: Bosser, A.-G., Millard, D.E., Hargood, C. (eds.) ICIDS 2020. LNCS, vol. 12497, pp. 111–119. Springer, Cham (2020). https://doi.org/10.1007/978-3-030-62516-0_10

# Climate Influence: Implicit Game-Based Interactive Storytelling for Climate Action Purpose

Zijing Song[1], Yating Sun[2], Vincent Ruijters[3], and Ray Lc[1(✉)] ⓘ

[1] School of Creative Media, City University of Hong Kong, Kowloon Tong, Hong Kong
LC@raylc.org
[2] Academy of Art University, San Francisco, USA
[3] Tokyo, Japan

**Abstract.** People have emotionally ingrained perspectives when it comes to climate action, making it difficult to argue against climate change denial using arguments like data and policy. Stories and games, however, engage audiences on a subconscious level, working to promote causes that align with readers' innate motivations. In creating visual narratives, we realized that interactive games in exhibit form can promote values that align with pro-climate actions of seeing long-term consequences, individual responsibility, and caring for others. We created a Tamagotchi device to narrate the caretaking theme to align audiences to climate action without policy argument. We found that audiences understood the game as showing caretaking in environmental contexts as opposed to intervention on resource depletion, interacting with the instrument on a human purposive level instead of the physical level of resource and policy.

**Keywords:** Climate action · Serious games · Implicit storytelling · Tamagotchi

## 1 Introduction

Despite the mass of scientific evidence on climate change [16], a gap remains between public awareness [17] and actions that people take. People often see climate change as distant and impersonal [11, 21], making it difficult to capture the attention and affect the actions of people using logical arguments, especially climate change skeptics distrustful of science. Climate change communication requires motivating strategies to cultivate long-term actions, using storytelling and interactive experiences designed for specific social goals [10] from a pro-environment mindset [3].

Stories have the potential to make climate change real, so that audiences may have greater emotional connection [12]. Previous work has shown that collaborative storytelling provides platforms for behavioral change [8, 10]. However, our previous narrative designs are Pavlovian [7] in the sense that they equate certain types of goals like future-looking orientation and individual responsibility with a positive outcome but do not ask

---

V. Ruijters—Independent Artist.

A. Mitchell and M. Vosmeer (Eds.): ICIDS 2021, LNCS 13138, pp. 425–429, 2021.
https://doi.org/10.1007/978-3-030-92300-6_42

the reader to take actions interactively. However, players are reinforced or punished in an operant conditioning context in an interactive environment like games [18], thus directly promoting certain actions. Games place players in scenarios and prompt them to analyze situations from different perspectives [20]. These scenarios enable the target audience to resonate with their physical situations and worldviews and create an emotional relationship with characters in the game [20]. In particular, analyzing risks inherent in climate change [19] and adapting to future climate change scenarios [13] have utilized serious games, whereas explicit forms of entertainment involving saving worlds from environmental catastrophe have populated efforts to influence climate action in players [5, 9, 15]. However, these games with explicit climate change goals can alienate those who don't align with climate action goals, so a more effective design would involve implicit forms of storytelling based on psychological goals rather than directly adding climate change themes into games [1]. To apply these operant interactive strategies that reinforce pro-climate behaviors, we created a game that uses the Tamagotchi to carry forth the care-taking metaphor to a climate change issue that is not explicitly told to players.

**Fig. 1.** (**Left**) Comic magazine *Drizzle* as narrative influence for pro-climate action. (**Right**) The serious game *Chikyuchi* promotes climate action by aligning players with pro-climate goal.

## 2   Designed Intervention

To understand the effect of storytelling on audiences, we designed five stories based on Booker's [2] story structure for particular human phenomena that lead to climate change, including immediate gratification, the idea that individual effort doesn't matter, myopia, etc. One story from the collection is *New Revolia*, which uses the plot of shipwreck on the Antarctic ocean to narrate the idea that distributing resources with others leads to self benefits (Fig. 1), a pro-climate action goal. While visual narratives can frame stories that promote actions consistent with climate action, they cannot reinforce behaviors that actively lead to pro-climate choices. To create an immersive experience that reinforces audience behavior to align with climate action goals, we created and exhibited a game that reinforces the notion of "caring for environment" without explicitly revealing the concept. The game uses a metaphor to reinforce players who take care of an avatar that implicitly represents the Amazon forest.

The main avatar in the Chikyuchi game anthropomorphizes a natural resource (trees of the Amazon) that is declining at the rate of a hectare a minute in reality, leading to increased surface temperature and reduced rainfall [14]. The Chikyuchi is connected to the deforestation API, reporting the actual size decreasing 2 km$^2$ with every second in the statistics menu. Chikyuchi is determined by its health and mood (1 to 4 hearts). Health is always low due to the situation of deforestation. Although users are able to temporarily cheer up the Chikyuchis with thematically related food and games, increasing their mood status, it won't change their critical health status. Chikyuchi also periodically chats about each crisis by interrupting the game. It does this by using text generated with the transformer language model GPT-2 pretrained on tweets containing the words "deforestation" and "global warming" over a 3 day period (temperature = 0.8 during generation, 6500 epochs training). The text generated are implicit forms of persuasion rather than directly lobbying for climate action.

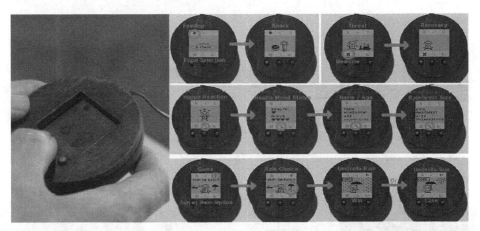

**Fig. 2.** (**Left**) Game Device. (**Top Right**) Feeding and threat interactions. (**Middle Right**) Info flow: name, age, health, declining rainforest size. (**Bottom Right**) The umbrella/sunglasses game play flow (the player must guess whether the next day will be sunny or raining).

There are three lower buttons (select, execute and cancel) that allow participants to make in-game decisions (Fig. 2). Participants could interact with the virtual pet through six functions: food, clean defecation, play game, medicine, information and attention. Each in-game decision affects Chikyuchi's mood in the short term but does not improve its health. For example, playing a guessing game with the weather about whether it should bring an umbrella (it'll rain) or sunglasses (it'll be sunny) can raise its mood if the guesses are correct. The random weather outcome also implicitly informs us about climate change. The stats menu gives the current health, mood, age, and size of Chikyuchi. In summary, Chikyuchi uses the interactive gaming paradigm to promote care-taking behavior from players in relation to climate change [4].

To allow engagement with Chikyuchi, we created an installation consisting of a live video-feed for real-time interaction of audiences in Tokyo and Hong Kong, two game devices, photos that hint at the climate topic, and a rusted bronze cast of Chikyuchi that represents destroyed natural resources as dead virtual pets. The interaction with Tamagotchi [6] is shown as a live video feed that brings people together to develop a common practice of caring across different places in the world.

## 3  Results and Discussion

To see how Chikyuchi affects visitors (18 to 35 years old), we surveyed audiences at the *Constructing Contexts* exhibit in Hong Kong (2021) following 15 min of game play each. One survey focused on the effectiveness of the installation (n = 23, 12 female), while another emphasized audience perception (n = 15, 7 female, 7 male, 1 other). Players found that the exhibit communicated the process of caretaking significantly more effectively than the physical layer of resource depletion (Fig. 3) (Wilcoxon p = 0.00011). All other effects were not significantly different from each other, although the amount of information learned was perceived to be low compared to other ratings like awareness of climate change generated from the intervention.

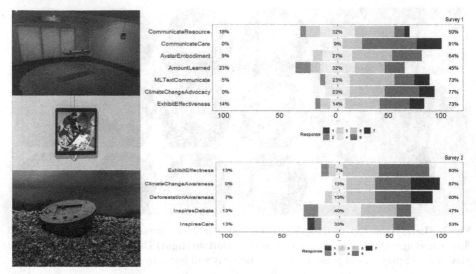

**Fig. 3. (Top Left)** Exhibition. **(Middle Left)** Real-time audience interaction. **(Bottom Left)** Bronze cast showing Chikyuchi's decline. **(Right)** Survey of effectiveness of intervention and of audience perception. (To see text of survey questions used: sites.google.com/view/chsu/app).

We studied the use of implicit influences in purposive interactive storytelling for climate communication. Narrative interactive games are proposed to reinforce the mental connection that alters climate awareness in the long run and take pro-climate actions. Indeed, evaluation showed audiences understood the caretaking aspect of the game significantly more than the actual information about resources conveyed. Future work would involve evaluating audience perception of comics for climate action to compare between interactive and non-interactive strategies for climate influence.

## References

1. Abraham, B., Jayemanne, D.: Where are all the climate change games? Locating digital games' response to climate change. 21 (2017)

2. Booker, C.: The Seven Basic PLOTS: Why We Tell Stories. A&C Black (2004)
3. Boykoff, M.: Creative (Climate) Communications: Productive Pathways for Science, Policy and Society. Cambridge University Press, Cambridge (2019)
4. Caillois, R., Barash, M.: Man, Play, and Games. University of Illinois Press, Urbana (2001)
5. Chen, Y., Bodicherla, D., Scott, B., Whittinghill, D.: Meltdown: a serious game for environmental awareness on climate change, pp. 388–394. Association for the Advancement of Computing in Education (AACE) (2014)
6. Clyde, A.: Electronic pets. Emerg. Libr. 25(5), 34–36 (1998)
7. Domjan, M.: Pavlovian conditioning: a functional perspective. Annu. Rev. Psychol. 56(1), 179–206 (2005)
8. Farinella, M.: The potential of comics in science communication. J. Sci. Commun. 17(1), Y01 (2018)
9. Fox, J., McKnight, J., Sun, Y., Maung, D., Crawfis, R.: Using a serious game to communicate risk and minimize psychological distance regarding environmental pollution. Telemat. Inform. 46, 101320 (2020)
10. Lc, R., Mizuno, D.: Designing for narrative influence: speculative storytelling for social good in times of public health and climate crises. In: Extended Abstracts of the 2021 CHI Conference on Human Factors in Computing Systems, pp. 1–13. Association for Computing Machinery, New York (2021)
11. Leiserowitz, A.: Climate change risk perception and policy preferences: the role of affect, imagery, and values. Clim. Change 77(1), 45–72 (2006)
12. Moezzi, M., Janda, K.B., Rotmann, S.: Using stories, narratives, and storytelling in energy and climate change research. Energy Res. Soc. Sci. 31, 1–10 (2017)
13. Neset, T.-S., Andersson, L., Uhrqvist, O., Navarra, C.: Serious gaming for climate adaptation—assessing the potential and challenges of a digital serious game for urban climate adaptation. Sustainability 12(5), 1789 (2020)
14. Nobre, P., Malagutti, M., Urbano, D.F., de Almeida, R.A.F., Giarolla, E.: Amazon deforestation and climate change in a coupled model simulation. J. Clim. 22(21), 5686–5697 (2009)
15. Onencan, A., Van de Walle, B., Enserink, B., Chelang'a, J., Kulei, F.: WeShareIt game: strategic foresight for climate-change induced disaster risk reduction. Procedia Eng. 159, 307–315 (2016)
16. Pachauri, R.K., Allen, M.R., Barros, V.R., et al.: Climate Change 2014: Synthesis Report. Contribution of Working Groups I, II and III to the Fifth Assessment Report of the Intergovernmental Panel on Climate Change. IPCC, Geneva, Switzerland (2014)
17. Rhodes, E., Axsen, J., Jaccard, M.: Exploring citizen support for different types of climate policy. Ecol. Econ. 137, 56–69 (2017)
18. Staddon, J.E.R., Cerutti, D.T.: Operant conditioning. Annu. Rev. Psychol. 54(1), 115–144 (2003)
19. Undorf, S., Tett, S.F.B., Hagg, J., et al.: Understanding interdependent climate change risks using a serious game. Bull. Am. Meteor. Soc. 101(8), E1279–E1300 (2020)
20. Villar, M.E.: Community engagement and co-creation of strategic health and environmental communication: collaborative storytelling and game-building. J. Sci. Commun. 20(01), C08 (2021)
21. Weber, E.U.: Experience-based and description-based perceptions of long-term risk: why global warming does not scare us (Yet). Clim. Change 77(1), 103–120 (2006)

# VR for Diversity: *Amelia's Dream*

Mirjam Vosmeer[✉]

Amsterdam University of Applied Sciences, Postbus 1025,
1000 BA Amsterdam, The Netherlands
m.s.vosmeer@hva.nl

**Abstract.** This demo is the first outcome of the research project *VR for Diversity*. The theoretical backgrounds for the project are shortly discussed and the concept for *Amelia's Dream* is presented. *Amelia's Dream* is a VR experience that is filmed using volumetric video capture technology, in which a young woman shares some of her dreams and concerns, relating to issues of gender equality. Focusing on how parasocial and physical interaction may impact the persuasive effects of VR, the research plan shortly elaborates on how the installation will be used for experimental studies into the possibilities of VR as a perspective shifter.

**Keywords:** VR · Media effects · Persuasion · Narrative interaction

## 1 Introduction

The VR experience that is demonstrated here is the first outcome of the *VR for Diversity* research project. The goal of *VR for Diversity* is to investigate the 'perspective shifting' affordances of VR by testing whether an interactive VR installation can have a positive impact on users' knowledge and attitude towards a topic. Our ambitions with the VR production *Amelia's Dream* are threefold: 1. it will be used for research into the effects of interactive virtual reality, 2. it enables the producers to experiment with the possibilities of volumetric video capture technology, 3. it will be presented to a general public at demo sessions and festivals, to inform them about the topic of gender equality. With this research project, we continue our investigations into interactive cinema and storytelling for VR [17–23].

## 2 The Concept: *Amelia's Dream*

*Amelia's Dream* is a VR experience that is filmed using volumetric video capture technology [6], in which the user enters the dream of a young woman. She will tease them a bit and have fun with her visitors, but also share some of her dreams and concerns. These concerns relate to issues of gender equality in contemporary society, focusing on how female politicians are confronted with online hate messages, how tools and articles are designed based on male standards and physique, and how female performers are often confronted with body shaming. To visualize her stories, the protagonist Amelia will be featured flying an airplane, reading online hate messages and performing as a ballerina.

© Springer Nature Switzerland AG 2021
A. Mitchell and M. Vosmeer (Eds.): ICIDS 2021, LNCS 13138, pp. 430–434, 2021.
https://doi.org/10.1007/978-3-030-92300-6_43

Volumetric video capture technology enables the producer to experiment with the size of the character in relation to the user: while Amelia will sometimes appear to be of 'normal' size, she will also be featured in a much larger scale as her face appears behind a window, or much smaller when she performs as a miniature ballerina.

## 3  VR as a Perspective Shifter

Since the re-introduction of VR in 2014 there has been considerable attention to the possible positive effects of the medium, with many initiatives investigating the ways VR may be used to contribute to a better world. Big companies founded projects such as VR for Impact [24] and VR for Good [25] in which all kinds of installations were presented that explored the possibilities of VR to change attitudes or behavior among the audience. By 2021, a whole range of VR productions have been presented, that according to the Digital Catapult report on *Immersive Content Formats for Future Audiences* [1], can be included in the category 'VR as Perspective Shifter'. In most productions that fall into the category the user enters someone else's life circumstances, either via the simulation of inhabiting their body or by 'meeting' them. The result the creators aim for in their audience is a shift in perspective. This could be an invitation to reflect on a particular theme, contributing to a shift in world view, an increase in understanding, the fostering of empathy for a particular group of people, or simply a change in opinion or better understanding of an issue.

However, after analyzing a representative sample of 150 non-fiction VR titles released between 2012 and 2018, Bevan et al. [2] stated that the degree to which VR is capable of evoking emotional engagement and how audience members respond to content is far from clear. The authors claim that the biggest current challenge for VR content producers therefore is to recognize that providing an immersive 360° environment may in itself not be sufficient to make a viewer feel present in a story. The Digital Catapult report seems to underwrite this insight. It describes how in most of the installations that aim to work as a perspective shifter, the user rarely has any agency beyond looking around.

## 4  Interaction in VR

The early promise of VR was that it would allow audiences to experience and connect to reality in ways beyond what could be achieved with traditional two-dimensional film. In this vision, audiences would no longer be limited to being passive observers of the story; they could be embodied and feel present within the story world, potentially taking a much more active, interactive role. Bevan et al. [2] state that perhaps the greatest surprise of their exploration of non-fiction VR was that the amount of content that attempts to directly fulfill this ambition is actually very small. They conclude that in their sample the role of the viewer in VR was still mainly passive and observant, instead of actively participatory. Rose [12] has also pointed out that the potential for embodied interaction has not yet been widely adopted for non-fiction VR. She therefore claims that the possibility of VR as a medium that would enable the user to 'do something' within the mediated world, instead of simply watching a troubling situation, could be exactly the distinctive feature that would allow us to think of VR as an experiential medium.

The term parasocial interaction is also defined as the 'pseudointerpersonal interaction' that occurs between mediated performers and their audiences [5, 7]. Mateer points out that the way viewers connect to characters in VR can be defined as social presence [10]. Cummings and Bailenson [3] state that the relationship between the immersive quality of a mediated environment and the level of (social) presence experienced by the user is often predicated on the assumption that greater system immersion causes greater user presence, which, in turn, enhances the applied effectiveness of the mediated environment. In their meta-analysis, they point out that immersive features such as the possibility to take action may be an important factor for users to perceive themselves as being located within a virtual space. In an overview of the literature around design for user engagement in virtual environments Sutcliffe points out that interactive features such as sliders, responsive objects and pop-up features allow the user to explore and control the virtual world and to become more "present" or immersed [16]. Hudson et al. [9] showed that immersion mediates the effects of interaction between users and the virtual environments with satisfaction and loyalty, supporting the notion that designing virtual environments with interactive features will lead to more immersive experiences. Based upon these insights, we hypothesize that physical and parasocial interaction can be expected to heighten the 'effectiveness' of a virtual environment.

## 5 Research Plan

With this installation, we aim to study a number of different concepts. During the experiments, the VR experience will be presented in two different versions: version A will be interactive, requiring the user to perform little tasks to move the narrative forward, such as opening a box to see the miniature ballerina, starting a sequence by pushing a button, or moving objects to facilitate the protagonist. In version B, the scenes will progress in the exact same way, but without user interaction. In this A-B test set up we intend to evaluate the user experience on the following dimensions, using scales that are based on the work of Roth and Koenitz [13]: social presence; spatial presence, agency/effectance, autonomy (perceived action possibilities), curiosity, enjoyment, satisfaction, (cognitive/emotional), empathy, affect and character believability. By comparing the outcomes for A and B, we hope to determine the impact of physical interaction in VR.

A second aim for our research is to verify the impact of eye gaze and attention: in some fragments the protagonist will look straight into the camera while sharing her stories, while in other fragments she will look in a different direction, for instance at her own reflection in a mirror. With this part of our research, we follow up on the work of Hartmann and Goldhoorn on the viewers' experience of parasocial interaction [8] and explorations into eye-gaze-based interaction for immersive virtual reality by [11]. The attention of the user will be operationalized by measuring head movement, which will enable us to determine whether mutual eye-gaze and shared attention leads to better story recall.

The third aim for our research is related to the persuasive impact of interactive VR. In their study into VR, presence and attitude change, Tussyadiah et al. [15] substantiate the persuasive role of the medium, suggesting that the subjective experience of presence in VR can translate into real world attitude and induce behavioral change. With previous explorations into the persuasive effects of VR in the context of marketing and advertising in mind [14, 26], we intend to establish the user's knowledge and attitude towards issues of gender equality, before and after experiencing *Amelia's Dream*, to verify whether an interactive VR experience may have a persuasive effect on its users. For this goal we intend to implement items from the questionnaire as presented by Faddoul and Chatterjee [4].

**Acknowledgements.** The research project *VR for Diversity* is led by the Amsterdam University of Applied Sciences, runs from October 2020 until October 2022 and is funded by SIA RAAK. The consortium consists of: Amsterdam University of Applied Sciences, Utrecht University of the Arts, Vrije Universiteit, WeMakeVR, IJsfontein, &Samhoud media, UC 360, The Virtual Dutchmen, Submarine Channel, VR Days Europe, Bostheater, VR Amsterdam, Interactieve Producenten Nederland, Federatie Dutch Creative Industries and ARDIN.

# References

1. Allen, C., Tucker, D.: Immersive content formats for future audiences. Digital Catapult (2019)
2. Bevan, C., et al.: Behind the curtain of the "Ultimate Empathy Machine": on the composition of virtual reality nonfiction experiences. In: Proceedings of the 2019 CHI Conference on Human Factors in Computing Systems (506) (2019)
3. Cummings, J.J., Bailenson, J.N.: How immersive is enough? A meta-analysis of the effect of immersive technology on user presence. Media Psychol. **19**(2), 272–309 (2016)
4. Faddoul, G., Chatterjee, S.: A quantitative measurement model for persuasive technologies using storytelling via a virtual narrator. Int. J. Hum.–Comput. Interact. **36**(17) (2020)
5. Giles, D.: Parasocial interaction: a review of the literature and a model for future research. Media Psychol. **4**, 279–305 (2002)
6. Hackl, C.: What is volumetric video and why it matters to the enterprise (2020). https://www.forbes.com/sites/cathyhackl/2020/09/27/what-is-volumetric-video--why-it-matters-to-the-enterprise/. Accessed 14 Sept 2021
7. Hartmann, T.: Parasocial interactions and paracommunication with new media characters. Mediated Interpersonal Commun. **177**, 199 (2008)
8. Hartmann, T., Goldhoorn, C.: Horton and Wohl revisited: exploring viewers' experience of parasocial interaction. J. Commun. **61**(6), 1104–1121 (2011)
9. Hudson, S., Matson-Barkat, S., Pallamin, N., Jegou, G.: With or without you? Interaction and immersion in a virtual reality experience. J. Bus. Res. **100**, 459–468 (2019)
10. Mateer, J.: Directing for Cinematic Virtual Reality: how the traditional film director's craft applies to immersive environments and notions of presence. J. Media Pract. **18**(1), 14–25 (2017)
11. Piumsomboon, T., Lee, G., Lindeman, R.W., Billinghurst, M.: Exploring natural eye-gaze-based interaction for immersive virtual reality. In: 2017 IEEE Symposium on 3D User Interfaces (3DUI), pp. 36–39. IEEE (2017)
12. Rose, M.: The immersive turn: hype and hope in the emergence of virtual reality as a nonfiction platform. Stud. Documentary Film **12**(2), 132–149 (2018)
13. Roth, C., Koenitz, H.: Evaluating the user experience of interactive digital narrative. In: Proceedings of the 1st International Workshop on Multimedia Alternate Realities, pp. 31–36 (2016)

14. Tussyadiah, I.P., Wang, D., Jia, C.H.: Exploring the persuasive power of virtual reality imagery for destination marketing (2016)

15. Tussyadiah, I.P., Wang, D., Jung, T.H., tom Dieck, M.C.: Virtual reality, presence, and attitude change: empirical evidence from tourism. Tourism Manag. **66**, 140–154 (2018)

16. Sutcliffe, A.: Designing for user experience and engagement. In: O'Brien, H., Cairns, P. (eds.) Why Engagement Matters, pp. 105–126. Springer, Cham (2016). https://doi.org/10.1007/978-3-319-27446-1_5

17. Verouden, N., Vosmeer, M., Sandovar, A.: Sleep tight johnny idaho a multicultural exploration into virtual reality. In: Rouse, R., Koenitz, H., Haahr, M. (eds.) Interactive Storytelling: 11th International Conference on Interactive Digital Storytelling, ICIDS 2018, pp. 356–358. Springer, Cham (2018). https://doi.org/10.1007/978-3-030-04028-4_41

18. Vosmeer, M., Sandovar, A., Schouten, B.: From literary novel to radio drama to VR project: the thousand autumns of Jacob de Zoet. In: Rouse, R., Koenitz, H., Haahr, M. (eds.) Interactive Storytelling: 11th International Conference on Interactive Digital Storytelling, ICIDS 2018, pp. 392–400. Springer, Cham (2018). https://doi.org/10.1007/978-3-030-04028-4_46

19. Vosmeer, M., Sandovar, A.: Circus noel: a case study into interaction and interface design for cinematic VR. In: Clua, E., Roque, L., Lugmayr, A., Tuomi, P. (eds.) Entertainment Computing – ICEC 2018, pp. 223–227. Springer, Cham (2018). https://doi.org/10.1007/978-3-319-99426-0_21

20. Vosmeer, M., Roth, C., Koenitz, H.: Who are you? Voice-over perspective in surround video. In: Nunes, N., Oakley, I., Nisi, V. (eds.) ICIDS 2017. LNCS, vol. 10690, pp. 221–232. Springer, Cham (2017). https://doi.org/10.1007/978-3-319-71027-3_18

21. Vosmeer, M., Schouten, B.: Project orpheus: a research study into 360° cinematic VR. In: Proceedings of the 2017 ACM International Conference on Interactive Experiences for TV and Online Video 2017, pp. 85–90. ACM (2017)

22. Vosmeer, M., Roth, C., Schouten, B.: Interaction in surround video: the effect of auditory feedback on enjoyment. In: Schoenau-Fog, H., Bruni, L.E., Louchart, S., Baceviciute, S. (eds.) ICIDS 2015. LNCS, vol. 9445, pp. 202–210. Springer, Cham (2015). https://doi.org/10.1007/978-3-319-27036-4_19

23. Vosmeer, M., Schouten, B.: Interactive cinema: engagement and interaction. In: Mitchell, A., Fernández-Vara, C., Thue, D. (eds.) ICIDS 2014. LNCS, vol. 8832, pp. 140–147. Springer, Cham (2014). https://doi.org/10.1007/978-3-319-12337-0_14

24. VR for Impact. https://vr4impact.com/. Accessed 26 July 2021

25. VR for Good. https://www.oculus.com/vr-for-good/. Accessed 26 July 2021

26. Wu, D., Lin, J.: Ways of seeing matter: the impact of a naturally mapped perceptual system on the persuasive effects of immersive virtual reality advertising. Commun. Res. Rep. **35**(5), 434–444 (2018)

# Exploring Narrative Novelties in VR

Mirjam Vosmeer[1]([⊠]) and Christian Roth[2]

[1] Amsterdam University of Applied Sciences, Postbus 1025,
1000 BA Amsterdam, The Netherlands
m.s.vosmeer@hva.nl

[2] HKU University of the Arts, Postbox 1520, 3500 BM Utrecht, The Netherlands
christian.roth@hku.nl

**Abstract.** Initial expectations about the interactive affordances of VR were often inspired by science fiction and technological fantasies rather than based on actual technical possibilities. In these futuristic accounts of VR, interactors would have the opportunity to fully engage with the characters that inhabit the story world, in ways that would feel so natural that it would be indistinguishable from reality. In 'real' reality however, the actual production of VR has turned out to be considerably more complicated. To provide a realistic impression of the actual possibilities of VR, this study presents four widely acclaimed contemporary VR experiences (*Wolves in the Walls, The Line, Down the Rabbit Hole* and *A Fisherman's Tale*) and reviews them from a media theory and communication science perspective. We discuss whether and how the concepts identification, parasocial interaction, 'breaking the fourth wall' and spatial and narrative presence can still be applied to these VR case studies, eventually aiming to contribute some rudimentary insights into the range of possible media conventions that narrative VR may contain.

**Keywords:** Virtual reality · Parasocial interaction · Identification · Fourth wall · Narrative engagement · Character involvement

## 1 Introduction

It was not that long ago that the most recent revival of virtual reality – now generally referred to as the third wave of VR [2] - managed to thrill the tech world and even the most critical platforms uninhibitedly expressed their high expectations for the new medium. Technology magazine *Wired*, for instance, declared early in 2014 that the first Oculus Rift demos did not only give rise to grand anticipations about the way VR would revolutionize video game play, but that the format was also highly probable to dramatically change the way we watch movies [40].

The possibility of unlimited interaction was one of the features that visionaries openly fantasized about. Cinematic VR would not only allow the viewer to walk around in movies, but also provide the opportunity to fully interact with the characters inhabiting the story world, thus creating one's own unique story by taking part in narrative fiction in a way that would ultimately be indistinguishable from real life.

Looking back though, while these assumptions often seem to have been based on pre-existing ideas and technological fantasies about VR, rather than on actual technical possibilities, these statements certainly influenced the public opinion and expectations about the medium. Graves [14] pointed out how the fictional representations of VR as a wondrous technology affected how the public perceived the medium and warned that since these fictional accounts on the possibilities of VR were often strongly positive, the public may become disappointed with their actual experiences of VR.

Janet Murray [30] stated that one of the most striking responses to 'the advent of digital modes of representation in the second half of the 20th century' has been the anticipation – framed sometimes as a hope, sometimes as a fear – that digitally generated forms will someday be indistinguishable from reality. By default, these expectations include the possibility to interact and communicate with the inhabitants of digital realities in a seemingly infinite domain of interactive narrativity. She pointed out that this attitude of omnipotent representational powers leading to a replacement of the real world with the virtual world has led non-scientists to overestimate the present and future of VR experiences.

In the current study, we therefore aim to take a closer look at the actual possibilities that 'real' contemporary VR offers in terms of interactive narrative and character inter-action. Rather than be inspired by over-enthusiastic technological predictions, future fantasies or science fiction, we intend to stick to what is actually available to the general public and can be experienced with increasingly affordable and obtainable headsets. We aim to present a selection of contemporary VR cases that feature a range of interesting narrative novelties that may eventually inspire new perspectives for the design and creation of interactive digital narratives.

## 2 Theoretical Considerations

In futuristic accounts of VR, interactors would have the opportunity to fully engage with the characters that inhabit the story world, in a seemingly boundless interactive narrative, with characters responding in ways that would feel so natural that it would be indistinguishable from reality. Lombard and Ditton [25] proposed to use the term 'perceptual illusion of non-mediation' for this level of technology that reaches a maximum level of immersion, eventually leading to a situation in which interactors are no longer aware of the fact that there is technology involved. In 'real' reality however, this level of technological perfection is still mostly a theoretical thought experiment, as the actual production of 'flawless' VR has turned out to be considerably more complicated [38].

One of the first industry accounts exploring the nature of the relation between users of VR technology and the characters that may be encountered in virtual environments was published on the blog of the Oculus Story Studio [4]. In his report, Matt Burdette described the uncomfortable sensation that was detected during the making of their early works such as *Henry* [17] and *Lost* [26]. Burdette describes how the team noticed that in previous versions of these experiences, the team had noticed a distinct lack of connection to the characters and the environment, and in turn, the story. Because of the ghost-like feeling that one may have with this lack of acknowledgement and the sensation of having no tangible relationship with your surroundings despite feeling present in the world, Burdette coined the 'Swayze Effect' in a reference to the movie classic *Ghost*. With *Henry*, the team discovered that by having the character 'lock eyes' with the user - by looking right into the camera and seemingly acknowledging their existence - this effect could be partially eliminated.

Since then, it has become clear that interactors in VR may develop dramatically different connections to the characters and the virtual environment they inhabit than they would with characters in traditional 'flat' media. As of yet however, research and theory on this specific aspect of VR is still scarce.

### 2.1 Identification

Mainly referring to traditional media such as cinema and television shows, the possibility to connect or interact with characters and the way audience members react to these characters has been studied from different perspectives. A first perspective is identification, described by Livingstone [24] as 'imagining being in someone else's shoes and seeing the world through his or her eyes'. In his extensive theoretical discussion of the topic, Cohen defined identification as 'an imaginative process through which an audience member assumes the identity, goals, and perspective of a character' [6]. The author defines identification as a mechanism through which audience members experience mediated events from the inside, as if the events were actually happening to them. On first glance, both descriptions seem to fit quite well to what users experience in cinematic VR, when they are invited to take the perspective of someone else's world as recorded by the 360° camera, as was for instance described by Chris Milk: "It's a machine, but inside of it, it feels like real life. And you feel present with the world you are inside, and you feel present with the people that you are inside of it with." [32]. Another aspect of the broader notion of identification with mediated characters has been explored within the field of video game studies. Hefner, Klimmt and Vorderer [16] discussed identification with game characters as a mechanism for computer game enjoyment and specifically proposed game interactivity as an important facilitator of strong identification.

### 2.2 Parasocial Interaction

A second perspective that is considered with relations between viewers and media characters is parasocial interaction (PSI). The concept of parasocial interaction refers to audience members interacting with media personae as they would in face-to-face interactions [22]. This concept was first discussed in reference to television personalities by Horton and Wohl, who proposed to consider individual audience members as actively relating to media performers in a psychological perspective, "as if they were involved in an active face-to-face exchange rather than in passive observation" [in 15]. Livingston [23] clarified that compared to identification, PSI adds an interactional component to the relation between viewers and media personae that the former is lacking. However, as Konijn and Hoorn [22] pointed out, the term parasocial interaction was coined in a period when the audience was considered to passively consume mass media. Cohen [6] argued that PSI applies to media figures who directly address the viewer, such as newscasters and presenters, while Giles [13] proposed to differentiate between media figures who are direct representations of real people such as newscasters, and dramatic characters played by actors and fantasy figures such as game characters.

### 2.3 The Fourth Wall

When dramatic characters and fantasy figures directly address the viewer, this is often referred to as 'breaking the fourth wall' [8, 21, 34, 39]. The fourth wall is a term borrowed from dramatic theory, first proposed by Denis Diderot [in 3] that considers the theatrical stage as having three walls (two sides and a rear) and an invisible fourth-wall boundary between the actors and the audience. Breaking the fourth wall thus refers to eliminating this imaginary divide between performer and audience, for instance by having actors in a film or television show look straight into the camera and acknowledge the viewer. Connecting the concept of the fourth wall back to parasocial relationships, Auter [1] described how participants who watched a television show in which the fourth wall was broken, scored significantly higher on a PSI scale than participants that viewed the same show in which the breaks were edited out. Conway [7] discussed the concept of the fourth wall in relation to video games, firstly stating that a direct acknowledgement of the player by the game is a clear fourth wall break in the most conventional sense. In games, breaking the fourth wall can also be seen as an action that may contract the magic circle or even place the player outside of it. However, games also have an inherent potential to not only break a fourth wall, but instead expand it, or relocate it entirely behind the player. Conway pursues his argument by stating that the concept of breaking the fourth wall therefore is actually insufficient to describe all of the possibilities of interaction between the user and the game world. Rather than referring to the breaking of the fourth wall, he suggests viewing these instances from a perspective of 'wall moving' [7].

### 2.4 Spatial Presence and Narrative Engagement

Another concept that is closely related to the way users interact with and react to characters in a virtual story world is presence, which is often connected to narrative engagement. Pressgrove and Bowman [31] suggested to distinguish presence and narrative engagement by associating the former with 'being in a mediated place' and the latter with 'being in a mediated story'. Ma [27] argued that spatial presence is more of a response to the media system, whereas narrative engagement is an emotional and cognitive reaction to the narrative content itself. In VR, the topic of presence is often connected to the concept of embodiment. The term 'sense of embodiment' refers to 'the ensemble of sensations that arise in conjunction with being inside, having, and controlling a body especially in relation to virtual reality' [21, pp. 374–375]. Mel Slater [35, 36] presented evidence that the experience of a virtual body may be a critical component of the sense of being in the virtual location.

## 3   Case Studies

For our current exploration, we have selected four contemporary VR case studies that feature different examples of interactive storytelling. All four are available in the Oculus

Store, can be viewed with the Oculus Quest headset and were released between 2019 and 2021. And importantly, they all have been praised by the international VR community as featuring innovative insights into narrative, gameplay and immersion, either by authors on VR review sites or by juries of VR and new media festivals. After shortly describing the VR experiences, we will discuss whether and how the concepts of identification, parasocial interaction, 'breaking the fourth wall' and presence can be accounted for in the selected sample.

## 3.1  Down the Rabbit Hole (2020)

Since its first publication in 1865, Lewis Carroll's *Alice's Adventures in Wonderland* [5] has inspired numerous movies, plays, exhibitions and other kinds of performances and retellings. The story has proved to be effectively convertible to a horror video game in *American McGee's Alice* [28] and *Alice Madness Returns* [29] and unsurprisingly, Wonderland also turned out to be an intriguing setting for a VR experience. With *Down the Rabbit Hole* [9], producer Cortopia Studios has chosen to explore the narrative affordances of VR by presenting a story-driven puzzle game in which the player needs to unravel riddles and solve puzzles to guide the protagonist through an extensive rabbit hole. While it is technically a third-person game, the first-person interaction consists of engaging with the rabbit hole itself. Positioned as a giant in the midst of the rabbit hole that is visible all around like a vertical 360° dollhouse diorama, players not only control the protagonist, but also need to manipulate the environment itself to be able to detect hidden objects and solve certain puzzles. The manipulation of the rabbit hole can be achieved by grabbing the tree roots that stick out of the walls and 'physically' moving the environment around, or upwards or downwards, to drag the viewpoint to the desired position. This mechanic enables the user to move the narrative forward by proceeding to the next scene, but it can also be used to turn the cylinder in an opposite direction and take another look at previous scenes with achievements that are already accounted for. Other game mechanics and narrative interventions include short scenes in which the player needs to solve puzzles in a first-person perspective and a reassuring voice-over that will sometimes reflect on these assignments.

## 3.2  The Line (2020)

*The Line* [23] is a short VR app that received acclaim for being a well put-together experience for newcomers to virtual reality, receiving the 'Best VR Immersive Experience' prize at the 76th Venice International Film Festival and a Primetime Emmy award for 'Outstanding Innovation in Interactive Programming'. The experience tells a love story of two miniature puppets named Rosa and Pedro who live in a toy train city that is a scale-model of 1940s São Paulo, presented to the user as a room-scale world-diorama. Laganaro explained in a press primer that his goal with *The Line* was to create a film that would only work in VR and that needs the user to exist [18]. What makes this interactive experience interesting is that all the user's movements in the physical world are equivalent in the virtual world. While the position of the user is outside of the story world, they can interact with the world and the characters and are physically responsible for the progress of the characters through the story, without having to solve puzzles or take part in other game-related actions. This way, *The Line* shows that it is possible to tell an interactive story to a user who is not involved with a body or a character, but still be very active and emotionally engaged in the narrative.

### 3.3   A Fisherman's Tale (2019)

*A Fisherman's Tale* [10] is a single-player adventure game built around a series of escape rooms, with the player taking up the role of Bob, a puppet fisherman who finds himself locked in his lighthouse. In the center of the first room sits a model of the lighthouse, with a tiny version of the fisherman inside, who mimics all his movements. Moreover, looking outside through the window, the player notices a giant version of Bob, who moves simultaneously as well. This technique of placing a smaller copy of an image within itself, often suggesting an infinitely recurring sequence, is known in Western art history as *mise en abyme* [19], and *A Fisherman's Tale* may be the first time that this principle was applied in VR. To move forward in the game the player needs to solve relatively simple puzzles that often make use of the fact that items laying around in the lighthouse have smaller or larger copies as well, which proves to be an important game mechanic for object interaction. According to Feltham [11] in a review on UploadVR, '*A Fisherman's tale* might be the first to achieve a perfect storm of gameplay, immersion and narrative in a single experience.'

### 3.4   Wolves in the Walls (2019)

Awarded a Primetime Emmy for Outstanding Innovation in Interactive Media in 2019, *Wolves in the Walls* [41] is a 40-min long interactive storytelling experience by Fable Studio, based on the children's book of the same name by author Neil Gaiman and illustrator Dave McKean [12]. In *Wolves in the Walls*, the interactor plays the role of an imaginary friend of Lucy's, an eight-year-old girl who suddenly hears strange scratching and wolves' noises coming from behind the walls of her family home. Since the story world is mediated through Lucy's imagination, everything unnatural is artistically possible, which allows for dream-like transitions and art styles. Together, the player and Lucy investigate the noises and meet the family members, who don't buy into Lucy's story about the wolves. Eventually, however, Lucy's suspicions prove to have been right all along and in a hectic final sequence, the family needs to flee the house. During the whole experience, Lucy is the only character who acknowledges the interactor, chatting and gesturing and constantly locking eyes. This VR experience features a whole range of remarkable interactive elements that serve to heighten the sensation of spatial presence as well as deepen the narrative engagement. Following up with Lucy's requests, the user is equipped with a pair of drawn hands to take pictures with a virtual in-game camera, write on walls, shine an in-game flashlight to explore dark area's and even fill jars in the kitchen with jam.

## 4   Discussion

A first essential difference between the definitions by Livingstone and Cohen for identification with characters in traditional media and the process of identification in VR seems to be the level of psychological engagement that is required from the user. Identification with a television character is based on a psychological attachment between the viewer and a character, but rather than leading to interaction with the character, it leads to imagining *being* the character. Precisely this last psychological process is partly superfluous in 360° VR, as the technology facilitates the step between watching a fictional character and imagining being in the shoes of that character. In the four cases that are presented in the current overview, this particular mode of relating to a character in VR is developed in a number of different ways.

*Down the Rabbit Hole* features a number of short scenes in which the gameplay shifts from the usual third person to a first-person perspective, in which the player temporarily takes up the role of the protagonist and is accordingly addressed by the other characters in the story world. In the biggest part of the experience, though, the role of the user is quite suitably described by Tekaia [37]: "You assume the role of what is essentially a disembodied spirit floating in the center of the rabbit hole, with its curved subterranean walls encircling you on all sides." And while *Down the Rabbit Hole* does not offer any surprising new insights into interactive storytelling, the particular narrative novelty of this experience lies in the fact that the traditional fourth wall is provoked in an intriguing way: not by breaking it but by transforming it into an interactive mobile cylinder.

In *The Line*, identification with the characters does not happen by taking up their role, since the user is placed outside of the story world as a spectator who nonetheless needs to perform certain actions to move the story forward. This mechanic, that in itself already causes a certain commitment to the characters and their love story, places the user in an interesting lacuna between presence and narrative engagement: while they are not taking part in the story world, at the moment of play they are no longer in the 'real' reality either, as they are surrounded by the spatial reality of the virtual room in which the diorama is placed. Near the end of the experience, the producers have inserted a small innovative interaction when Pedro the puppet falls out of the diorama and 'contacts' the user with gestures and facial expressions, begging them to help him get up again. Here, a fourth wall is broken, with the user and the protagonist engaging in an active parasocial relationship, temporarily taking part in the same performance and working together to progress the narrative towards a happy ending.

While the gameplay is fairly simplistic and the narrative comes across as a classic children's story, the fusion of experience and interactivity in *A Fisherman's Tale* show what VR as a narrative medium may be capable of in terms of providing new possibilities of interactive storytelling and character involvement. The user takes up the role of fisherman Bob in a more or less classical first-person perspective, but by adding the sensation of simultaneously being confronted with a giant and a miniature *doppelgänger,* and at the same time being able to interact with the objects in their worlds, the sense of embodiment in this experience is considerably stretched. While the use of a narrator's voice over ensures that users keep a clear cognitive distance between themselves and the protagonist, the sense of spatial presence that is heightened by the use of *mise en abyme* causes a distinct and surprisingly physical sense of engagement.

In *Wolves in the Walls* Lucy's imagination permeates the experience and the resulting dissonance between what is imagined and what could be real evokes a sense of curiosity and engagement. Furthermore, sharing and actively living Lucy's fantasies creates a bond with her and the player, leading to empathic immersion and social presence. The player's role undergoes an important transformation when Lucy draws them a pair of hands, thereby granting agency to interact with the world. By taking pictures, shining light in dark places or writing notes on the walls, they are from that moment on fully involved in the narrative, not by guiding or controlling the protagonist, but by actively cooperating with her. This coherence of narrative and gameplay mechanics creates what could be understood as ludonarrative harmony and supports the player's meaning-making process [33]. Remarkably, in this experience the role of the player sometimes resembles the ghost-like feeling that was described by Burdette [4], when the player's existence is not acknowledged by the other family members in the house. But the fact that Lucy is constantly talking to them, interacting and actively seeking the player's assistance and collaboration, and the distinct ability to interact with the surroundings, together create a sense of spatial presence as well as narrative engagement that show how the establishment of media conventions for VR is still in constant development.

## 5  Conclusions

A characteristic that the four reviewed case studies have in common, is the fact that while they all make use of technologically advanced interaction techniques, providing remarkable insights into the creative possibilities of the medium, their narrative content is mostly targeted at a children's audience and derived from children's books. And while the reviewed cases are to a certain level emotionally engaging, they mostly seem to serve as an exercise into what the medium eventually will be able to contain. However, the concerns that were formulated in early reviews on the medium, and that were mostly informed by future fantasies or science fiction, are not expected to easily become reality.

In her essay *Virtual/reality: how to tell the difference*, Janet Murray states that when users enter a well-crafted VR experience, they will suspend disbelief and get lost in it, the same way as they do in movies or video games. However, after taking the headset off, a viewer returns to the one reality we all live in, where we are responsible for our actions. The author points out that it is not hard now to tell the difference between the real and the virtual, 'and it will not get any harder in the future because that is not how a medium of technology develops' [30, p. 11]. She suggests viewing VR as an emerging medium within an evolving community that is beginning to develop the media conventions to support sustained interaction and immersion. With the current discussion of four selected VR case studies, showing how the application of theoretical conventions such as identification, parasocial interaction and 'breaking the fourth wall' may slightly shift when used for VR, we hope to have contributed some rudimentary insights into the range of possible media conventions that narrative virtual reality may contain.

**Acknowledgement.** This study is part of the VR for Diversity research project at the Amsterdam University of Applied Sciences, funded by SIA RAAK.

## References

1. Auter, P.J.: Psychometric: TV that talks back: an experimental validation of a parasocial interaction scale. J. Broadcast. Electron. Media **36**(2), 173–181 (1992)

2. Belisle, B., Roquet, P.: Guest Editors' Introduction: Virtual reality: immersion and empathy (2020)
3. Bell, E.: Theories of Performance. Sage, Los Angeles (2008)
4. Burdette, M.: The Swayze Effect (2015). https://storystudio.oculus.com/en-us/blog/the-swa yze-effect/. Accessed 26 July 2021
5. Carroll, L.: Alice's Adventures in Wonderland. Macmillan & Co. (1865)
6. Cohen, J.: Defining identification: a theoretical look at the identification of audiences with media characters. Mass Commun. Soc. 4(3), 245–264 (2001)
7. Conway, S.: A circular wall? Reformulating the fourth wall for video games. J. Gaming Virtual Worlds 2(2), 145–155 (2010)
8. Collins, K.: Breaking the fourth wall? User-generated sonic content in virtual worlds. In: The Oxford Handbook of Virtuality, pp. 351–363. Oxford University Press, Oxford (2014)
9. Down the Rabbit Hole, Cortopia Studio's (2020)
10. Feltham, J.: (2019). https://uploadvr.com/fishermans-tale-review/. Accessed 26 July 2021
11. A Fisherman's Tale. Vertigo Games (2019)
12. Gaiman, N., McKean, D., Friend, B.: The Wolves in the Walls. HarperCollins, New York (2003)
13. Giles, D.C.: Parasocial interaction: a review of the literature and a model for future research. Media Psychol. 4(3), 279–305 (2002)
14. Graves, E.: Media influence on expectations of virtual reality. Refractory 30 (2018)
15. Hartmann, T.: Parasocial interactions and paracommunication with new media characters. Mediated Interpersonal Commun. 177, 199 (2008)
16. Hefner, D., Klimmt, C., Vorderer, P.: Identification with the player character as determinant of video game enjoyment. In: Ma, L., Rauterberg, M., Nakatsu, R. (eds.) ICEC 2007. LNCS, vol. 4740, pp. 39–48. Springer, Heidelberg (2007). https://doi.org/10.1007/978-3-540-74873-1_6
17. Henry. Oculus Story Studio (2015)
18. IndieSamAdonis (2021). https://indiesamadonis.com/2021/04/13/the-line-vr-review-the-pup pets-of-sao-paulo-help-us-fall-in-love-with-vr/
19. Jefferson, A.: Mise en abyme and the Prophetic in Narrative. Style 196–208 (1983)
20. Kilteni, K., Groten, R., Slater, M.: The sense of embodiment in virtual reality. Presence: Teleoper. Virtual Environ. 21, 373–387 (2012)
21. Ko, D., Ryu, H., Kim, J.: Making new narrative structures with actor's eye-contact in cinematic virtual reality (CVR). In: Rouse, R., Koenitz, H., Haahr, M. (eds.) ICIDS 2018. LNCS, vol. 11318, pp. 343–347. Springer, Cham (2018). https://doi.org/10.1007/978-3-030-04028-4_38
22. Konijn, E.A., Hoorn, J.F.: Parasocial interaction and beyond: media personae and affective bonding. In: The International Encyclopedia of Media Effects, pp. 1–15 (2017)
23. The Line, Arvore Immersive Games Inc. (2020)
24. Livingstone, S.M.: Making Sense of Television: The Psychology of Audience Interpretation. Routledge, New York (1998)
25. Lombard, M., Ditton, T.: At the heart of it all: the concept of presence. J. Comput.-Mediated Commun. 3(2) (1997)
26. Lost. Oculus Story Studio (2016)
27. Ma, Z.: Effects of immersive stories on prosocial attitudes and willingness to help: testing psychological mechanisms. Media Psychol. 23(6), 865–890 (2020)
28. McGee, American: American McGee's Alice. Electronic Arts (2000)
29. McGee, American: Alice: Madness Returns. Electronic Arts (2011)
30. Murray, J.H.: Virtual/reality: how to tell the difference. J. Vis. Cult. 19(1), 11–27 (2020)
31. Pressgrove, G., Bowman, N.D.: From immersion to intention? Exploring advances in prosocial storytelling. J. Philanthropy Market. 26(2), e1689 (2021)
32. Rose, M.: The immersive turn: hype and hope in the emergence of virtual reality as a nonfiction platform. Stud. Documentary Film 12(2), 132–149 (2018)

33. Roth, C., van Nuenen, T., Koenitz, H.: Ludonarrative hermeneutics: a way out and the narrative paradox. In: Rouse, R., Koenitz, H., Haahr, M. (eds.) Interactive Storytelling, ICIDS 2018, pp. 93–106. Springer, Cham (2018). https://doi.org/10.1007/978-3-030-04028-4_7
34. Shafer, D.M., Carbonara, C.P., Korpi, M.F.: Exploring enjoyment of cinematic narratives in virtual reality: a comparison study. Int. J. Virtual Real. 18(1), 1–18 (2018)
35. Slater, M: A Note on Presence Terminology (2003). https://www.researchgate.net/public ation/242608507_A_Note_on_Presence_Terminology
36. Slater, M.: Immersion and the illusion of presence in virtual reality. Br. J. Psychol. 109(3), 431–433 (2018)
37. Tekaia, P.: Down the Rabbit Hole review (2020). https://adventuregamers.com/articles/view/ 40467. Accessed 30 July 2021
38. Vosmeer, M., Schouten, B.: Project Orpheus a research study into 360 cinematic VR. In: Proceedings of the 2017 ACM International Conference on Interactive Experiences for TV and Online Video, pp. 85–90 (2017)
39. Vosmeer, M., Roth, C., Koenitz, H.: Who are you? Voice-over perspective in surround video. In: Nunes, N., Oakley, I., Nisi, V. (eds.) ICIDS 2017. LNCS, vol. 10690, pp. 221–232. Springer, Cham (2017). https://doi.org/10.1007/978-3-319-71027-3_18
40. Watercutter, A.: Oculus is awesome for games, but it's the future of movies. Wired (2014). http://www.wired.com/2014/01/oculus-movies/. Accessed 26 July 2021
41. Wolves in the Walls, Fable Studio Inc. (2019)
42. Zibrek, K., Kokkinara, E., McDonnell, R.: The effect of realistic appearance of virtual characters in immersive environments-does the character's personality play a role? IEEE Trans. Visual Comput. Graph. 24(4), 1681–1690 (2018)

# The Interactive Narrative Research Discipline and Contemporary Practice

# A Preliminary Survey on Story Interestingness: Focusing on Cognitive and Emotional Interest

Byung-Chull Bae[1](✉), Suji Jang[1], Youngjune Kim[2], and Seyoung Park[2]

[1] School of Games, Hongik University, Sejong, South Korea
byuc@hongik.ac.kr, c0192001@g.hongik.ac.kr
[2] Language AI Lab, NCSoft, Seongnam, South Korea
{youngjune,park30}@ncsoft.com

**Abstract.** Story interestingness is of great importance in narrative understanding and generation. In this paper, based on the outlined literature review, we present our incipient framework for measuring story interestingness, consisting of two factors - cognitive interest and emotional interest. The cognitive factors include four components - goal, novelty, inference, and schema violation. The emotional aspects contain four elements - empathy, external emotions, humor, and outcome valence.

**Keywords:** Story interest · Cognitive interest · Emotional interest

## 1 Introduction

Storytelling has diverse roles. Through storytelling activities, we can learn languages and develop our literacy skills, including reading and writing [20]. Language and literacy learning is particularly effective in digital and online storytelling [28,38]. Storytelling research is also widely conducted for entertainment and other purposes such as transmedia storytelling [14], empathy building through collaborative storytelling [37] and Game AI [30].

In video games and interactive storytelling, interactivity is a key motivational factor for the player to continue playing [26,32]. Rigby and Ryan [32] introduce the Player Experience of Need Satisfaction (PENS) model to understand better the relationship between the players' motivation and their well-being due to game playing. In the PENS model, three core desires - competence, autonomy (i.e., choice and violation), and relatedness (i.e., companionship) - are suggested as motivations for game playing, bringing the player immersion. Similarly, in the interactive digital narrative, agency (i.e., "the user's ability to control aspects of the narrative") must make sense and be meaningful for user satisfaction [26]. Due to the time and space limit, we focus on linear narrative in this paper, leaving out interactivity as future work.

Narrative understanding entails a "mental mechanism" including cognitive and emotional processes [24,44], and interestingness is of great importance both

© Springer Nature Switzerland AG 2021
A. Mitchell and M. Vosmeer (Eds.): ICIDS 2021, LNCS 13138, pp. 447–453, 2021.
https://doi.org/10.1007/978-3-030-92300-6_45

in narrative understanding [11,31] and narrative generation [1,2,19]. This paper presents our initial analysis toward a framework of measuring story interest based on Kintsch's suggestion - interest from cognition and emotion [18].

## 2    Two Factors of Story Interestingness

Interest is a motivation for the reader to continue to read a story. Following the early studies of story interest [18,34], some studies focus on the cognitive aspect of story interest such as goal importance or goal attainment difficulty [15], and inferences [17]; others center around emotional aspects such as the taxonomy of the emotions as literary responses [27] and narrative empathy [16]. Since cognition and emotion are inherently intertwined with each other, many approaches to story interest involve both cognitive and affective properties together [6,8,11–13,36].

Narrative metrics are difficult to define. There may not be "correct answers" to evaluating how good a story is. Yet measuring story interestingness is different from measuring story quality. Based on Kintsch's notion of story interestingness, we propose our initial framework for story interest as in Fig. 1, consisting of two factors - cognition (comprehension) and (aesthetic) emotions.

### 2.1    Cognitive Factors

– **Protagonist's goal**: The protagonist's desire moves forward a story. Protagonists struggle to achieve their own goals or desires, while antagonists continuously attempt to thwart them. As a result, conflicts occur. To make a story interesting, the protagonist's goal needs to be important and hard to achieve [15]. A good logline, which can draw the audience's interest or attention, often involves a protagonist's desires or goals in a single sentence, possibly including irony in it [40].

– **Novelty**: Novelty is pivotal in narrative intelligence, which includes the capacities of "emploting (or editing), characterization, narration, genreation, and thematization" [29]. High-novelty, along with other dimensions such as complexity and comprehensibility, is a practical factor of story interest [36].

– **Predictive Inference**: Making inference about 'what will happen next' or 'how it has happened' influences the interestingness of a story, where the reader's background knowledge and the degree of uncertainty affects the inference processes [17,18]. Uncertainty is a necessary condition of suspense, despite debating concern of the paradox of suspense [9,46]. Postdictability [18] refers to grouping all the pieces as a consistent whole, including inferences and the story outcome, which is related to an important narrative device - foreshadowing [5].

– **Schema Violation**: The reader can use schema to understand a story, where a schema refers to "a data structure for representing the generic concepts stored in memory" [33]. The schema violation resulting from unexpectedness or incongruity can lead to story interest [22,34]. Furthermore, the violated unexpectedness or incongruity requires proper resolution, possibly with consistency and novelty. These schema violation factors are closely connected with surprise as an aesthetic emotion.

## 2.2 Emotional Factors

– **Empathy**: Storytelling is beneficial to developing empathy [23] - either "cognitive (mental perspective-taking)" or "emotional (the vicarious sharing of emotions)" [39]. In narrative, empathy differs from sympathy as it is also associated with "positive feelings of happiness, satisfaction, elation, triumph, and sexual arousal", which plays a key role in the reader's pleasure of reading a story" [16]. Empathy concerning story characters comprises sympathy, emotion memories, and identification with character's goals and plans as *internal* emotions [27]. Empathy is also crucial to designing immersive storytelling on the virtual reality (VR) platform [3,7].

– **External Emotions**: Curiosity, suspense, and surprise are *external* emotions of literary response which are related to story schema - e.g., curiosity and suspense as resulting from "assimilation to schema" and surprise as resulting from "accommodation of schema, from dishabituation, new connection, insights" [27]. These external emotions can be controlled by the narrative structure [6] and connected to the cognitive factors of interest (goals, novelty, inference, and schema violation).

– **Humor**: Humor is a positive aesthetic emotion, often accompanying with other positively emotional properties such as playfulness and amusement [35]. Experiencing humor is personal and requires subjective evaluation of the audience as the humor performer's intentions can be appreciated differently [10,43]. Humor theories in general address three dimensions - relief, incongruity, and superiority [25,42]. As the proper resolution of incongruity is important to surprise, incongruity and appropriate resolution are vital to humor. Including humor as a key emotional factor of story interest might be controversial, as humor is a sufficient condition rather than a necessary one. Our framework particularly focuses on humor as an attractive property of characters - protagonists, helpers, or even villains.

– **Outcome Valence**: Story outcome (goodness or badness; happy-ending or sad-ending) is an underlying cause of story liking [13]. Outcome valence is also linked with proper resolution of the unexpectedness and incongruity, which are mentioned in the cognitive aspects of story interestingness.

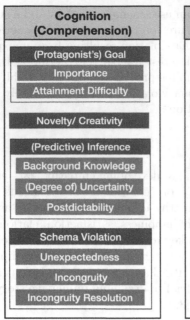
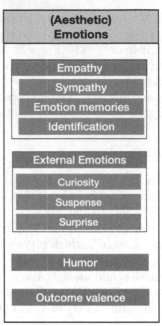

**Fig. 1.** Two factors of story interestingness - cognition and emotions

## 2.3  Discussion

In addition to the cognitive and emotional factors of story interestingness, another two aspects can be explored - interactivity and narrative factors. First, as mentioned earlier in the Introduction section with the PENS model [32], interactive narrative allows the reader to feel more immersive in a story world by giving a sense of control to the reader. Thus appropriate indicators such as choice ranges and choice variabilities for measuring interactive narrative experiences will be necessary [41].

Second, the suggested cognitive and emotional factors of story interestingness are related to story understanding to some extent. Narrative factors - such as plot structure, character types, narrative devices (e.g., temporal devices such as flashback and foreshadowing [4,45]), story conventions and cliché [21] - can be explored further.

## 3  Conclusion

In this paper we explore the two factors of story interestingness - cognitive interest and emotional interest. Based on the outlined literature review, we present our incipient framework for measuring story interestingness. The proposed framework consists of two factors - cognitive factors mainly for comprehension (goal, novelty, inference, schema violation) and emotional factors (empathy, external emotions, humor, outcome valence).

Our work is in its early stage and has limitations, such as a lack of computational metrics for measuring story interest. We plan to extend our current framework with two further steps. First, we intend to analyze the factors of story interestingness from the narrative theories perspective, centering around plot and characters. Second, we will investigate computational approaches to the proposed cognitive, emotional, and narrative factors, detailing the presented framework.

**Acknowledgements.** This work was supported by NCSOFT NLP Center. This work was also supported in part by Institute for Information & communications Technology Promotion (IITP) grant funded by the Korea government (MSIT) (No. 2017-0-01772, Development of QA systems for Video Story Understanding to pass the Video Turing Test) and the National Research Foundation of Korea (NRF) grant (2021R1A2C1012377).

# References

1. Alabdulkarim, A., Li, S., Peng, X.: Automatic story generation: challenges and attempts. In: Proceedings of the Third Workshop on Narrative Understanding, pp. 72–83. Association for Computational Linguistics, Virtual (2021). https://doi.org/10.18653/v1/2021.nuse-1.8

2. Alhussain, A., Azmi, A.: Automatic story generation: a survey of approaches. ACM Comput. Surv. **54**, 1–38 (2021). https://doi.org/10.1145/3453156

3. Bae, B.C., Jang, S.J., Ahn, D.K., Seo, G.: A VR interactive story using POV and flashback for empathy. In: 2019 IEEE Conference on Virtual Reality and 3D User Interfaces (VR), pp. 844–845 (2019). https://doi.org/10.1109/VR.2019.8797899

4. Bae, B.-C., Young, R.M.: A use of flashback and foreshadowing for surprise arousal in narrative using a plan-based approach. In: Spierling, U., Szilas, N. (eds.) ICIDS 2008. LNCS, vol. 5334, pp. 156–167. Springer, Heidelberg (2008). https://doi.org/10.1007/978-3-540-89454-4_22

5. Behrooz, M., Robertson, J., Jhala, A.: Story quality as a matter of perception: using word embeddings to estimate cognitive interest. In: Proceedings of the AAAI Conference on Artificial Intelligence and Interactive Digital Entertainment, vol. 15, no. 1, pp. 3–9 (2019). https://ojs.aaai.org/index.php/AIIDE/article/view/5217

6. Brewer, W.F., Lichtenstein, E.H.: Stories are to entertain: a structural-affect theory of stories. J. Pragmat. **6**(5), 473–486 (1982). https://doi.org/10.1016/0378-2166(82)90021-2

7. Cummings, J.J., Tsay-Vogel, M., Cahill, T.J., Zhang, L.: Effects of immersive storytelling on affective, cognitive, and associative empathy: the mediating role of presence. New Media Soc. (2021). https://doi.org/10.1177/1461444820986816

8. Dijkstra, K., Zwaan, R.A., Graesser, A.C., Magliano, J.P.: Character and reader emotions in literary texts. Poetics **23**(1), 139–157 (1995). https://doi.org/10.1016/0304-422X(94)00009-U

9. Gerrig, R.J.: Is there a paradox of suspense? A reply to Yanal. Br. J. Aesthetics **37**(2), 168–174 (1997). https://doi.org/10.1093/bjaesthetics/37.2.168

10. Gordon, M.: What makes humor aesthetic. Int. J. Human. Soc. Sci. **2**(1), 62–70 (2012)

11. Hidi, S., Baird, W.: Interestingness–a neglected variable in discourse processing. Cogn. Sci. **10**(2), 179–194 (1986). https://doi.org/10.1016/S0364-0213(86)80003-9

12. Hoeken, H., Vliet, M.: Suspense, curiosity, and surprise: How discourse structure influences the affective and cognitive processing of a story. Poetics **27**, 277–286 (2000). https://doi.org/10.1016/S0304-422X(99)00021-2

13. Iran-Nejad, A.: Cognitive and affective causes of interest and liking. J. Educ. Psychol. **79**, 120–130 (1987)

14. Jenkins, H.: Transmedia storytelling and entertainment: an annotated syllabus. Continuum **24**(6), 943–958 (2010). https://doi.org/10.1080/10304312.2010.510599

15. Jose, P.E.: Story interestingness: goal importance or goal attainment difficulty? Paper presented at the Annual Meeting of the American Education Research Association (1984)

16. Keen, S.: Empathy and the Novel. Oxford University Press, Oxford (2007)

17. Kim, S.I.: Causal bridging inference: a cause of story interestingness. Br. J. Psychol. **90**(1), 57–71 (1999). https://doi.org/10.1348/000712699161260

18. Kintsch, W.: Learning from text, levels of comprehension, or: why anyone would read a story anyway. Poetics **9**(1–3), 87–98 (1980)

19. Kybartas, B., Bidarra, R.: A survey on story generation techniques for authoring computational narratives. IEEE Trans. Comput. Intell. AI Games **9**(3), 239–253 (2017). https://doi.org/10.1109/TCIAIG.2016.2546063

20. Lucarevschi, C.R.: The role of storytelling on language learning: a literature review (2016)

21. MacDowell, J.: Happy Endings in Hollywood Cinema. Edinburgh University Press, Edinburgh (2014)

22. Mandler, G.: The structure of value: accounting for taste. CHIP report, Center for Human Information Processing, Department of Psychology, University of California, San Diego (1981)

23. Manney, P.: Empathy in the time of technology: how storytelling is the key to empathy. J. Evol. Technol. **19**(1), 51–61 (2008)

24. Matravers, D.: Fiction and Narrative, 1st edn. Oxford University Press, Oxford (2014)

25. Meyer, J.C.: Humor as a double-edged sword: four functions of humor in communication. Commun. Theory **10**(3), 310–331 (2000). https://doi.org/10.1111/j.1468-2885.2000.tb00194.x

26. Miller, C.: Digital Storytelling: A Creator's Guide to Interactive Entertainment, 4th edn. CRC Press, Boco Raton (2019)

27. Oatley, K.: A taxonomy of the emotions of literary response and a theory of identification in fictional narrative. Poetics **23**(1–2), 53–74 (1995). https://doi.org/10.1016/0304-422X(94)P4296-S

28. Rahimi, M., Yadollahi, S.: Effects of offline vs. online digital storytelling on the development of EFL learners' literacy skills. Cogent Educ. **4**(1), 1285531 (2017). https://doi.org/10.1080/2331186X.2017.1285531

29. Randall, W.: Narrative intelligence and the novelty of our lives. J. Aging Stud. **13**, 11–28 (1999). https://doi.org/10.1016/S0890-4065(99)80003-6

30. Riedl, M., Thue, D., Bulitko, V.: Game AI as storytelling. In: González-Calero, P.A., Gómez-Martín, M.A. (eds.) Artificial Intelligence for Computer Games, pp. 125–150. Springer, New York (2011). https://doi.org/10.1007/978-1-4419-8188-2_6

31. Riedl, M.O.: Computational narrative intelligence: a human-centered goal for artificial intelligence (2016)

32. Rigby, S., Ryan, R.: Glued to Games: How Video Games Draw Us in and Hold Us Spellbound. New directions in media, Praeger (2011)

33. Rumelhart, D.E.: Understanding Understanding. Taylor & Francis, Milton Park (2013)
34. Schank, R.C.: Interestingness: controlling inferences. Artif. Intell. **12**, 273–297 (1979)
35. Schindler, I., et al.: Measuring aesthetic emotions: a review of the literature and a new assessment tool. PLOS ONE **12**(6), 1–45 (2017). https://doi.org/10.1371/journal.pone.0178899
36. Silvia, P.: Looking past pleasure: anger, confusion, disgust, pride, surprise, and other unusual aesthetic emotions. Psychol. Aesthetics Creativity Arts **3**, 48–51 (2009). https://doi.org/10.1037/a0014632
37. Skaraas, S.B., Gomez, J., Jaccheri, L.: Playing with empathy through a collaborative storytelling game. In: Clua, E., Roque, L., Lugmayr, A., Tuomi, P. (eds.) ICEC 2018. LNCS, vol. 11112, pp. 254–259. Springer, Cham (2018). https://doi.org/10.1007/978-3-319-99426-0_26
38. Smeda, N., Dakich, E., Sharda, N.: The effectiveness of digital storytelling in the classrooms: a comprehensive study. Smart Learn. Environ. **1**(1), 1–21 (2014). https://doi.org/10.1186/s40561-014-0006-3
39. Smith, A.: Cognitive empathy and emotional empathy in human behavior and evolution. Psychol. Rec. **56**(1), 3–21 (2006). https://doi.org/10.1007/BF03395534
40. Snyder, B.: Save the Cat!: The Last Book on Screenwriting You'll Ever Need. Cinema/Writing, M. Wiese Productions (2005)
41. Szilas, N., Ilea, I.: Objective metrics for interactive narrative. In: Mitchell, A., Fernández-Vara, C., Thue, D. (eds.) ICIDS 2014. LNCS, vol. 8832, pp. 91–102. Springer, Cham (2014). https://doi.org/10.1007/978-3-319-12337-0_9
42. Vandaele, J.: Humor mechanisms in film comedy: incongruity and superiority. Poetics Today **23**(2), 221–249 (2002). https://doi.org/10.1215/03335372-23-2-221
43. Vandaele, J.: Narrative humor (i): enter perspective. Poetics Today **31**, 721–785 (2010). https://doi.org/10.2307/25835337
44. Worth, S.E.: Narrative understanding and understanding narrative. Contemp. Aesthetics **2**(2), 9 (2004)
45. Wu, H.Y., Young, M., Christie, M.: A cognitive-based model of flashbacks for computational narratives, vol. 12, pp. 239–245 (2016). https://ojs.aaai.org/index.php/AIIDE/article/view/12873
46. Yanal, R.J.: The paradox of suspense. Br. J. Aesthetics **36**(2), 146–159 (1996)

# Imagining the Other for Interactive Digital Narrative Design Learning in Real Time in Sherlock

Colette Daiute[1] , Daniel Cox[2] , and John T. Murray[3](✉)

[1] The City University of New York, New York, NY, USA
cdaiute@gc.cuny.edu
[2] Texts and Technology, University of Central Florida, Orlando, FL, USA
[3] Games and Interactive Media, University of Central Florida, Orlando, FL, USA
jtm@ucf.edu

**Abstract.** Collaboration is at the heart of Interactive Digital Narrative (IDN), yet IDN designers and players rarely encounter one another's subjective experiences around an IDN. Making that communication explicit can enhance beginning IDN design students' understanding of the inherently collaborative quality of IDN and the importance of digital tools. Researching such collaboration presents many challenges, ranging from ensuring participants have tools to facilitate sharing and feedback to providing researchers data for relevant analysis. We describe our design for a real-time collaborative IDN education design workshop, "Imagining the Other." The workshop protocol involves students learning the basics of Twine authoring, designing IDNs, playing a peer's IDN, and sharing comments for the ongoing design process in real-time. To run the workshop in a scalable way, we extended an existing web-based research platform, Sherlock, to support synchronous editing and data collection from novice authors exchanging feedback. The platform modifications support practice-based research by surfacing the numerous interactions in this social learning process for analysis. We evaluated the system feasibility by an initial pilot study with undergraduates new to IDN and analyzing the comments and content produced using an existing narrative coding scheme, showing preliminary evidence of the intended insight. The primary contribution is an integrated methodology and guidelines for subsequent large-scale studies exploring the social-relational merits of IDN education within an innovative research platform.

**Keywords:** IDN design education · Peer collaboration · Online research platforms · Sherlock · Cultural diversity

## 1 Introduction to Imaging the Other

Research in interactive digital narratives has traditionally focused on the individual: either the experience of an existing interactive narrative, or the process of authoring a new one. In this paper, we introduce the Imagining the Other in Interactive Digital Narrative Design Education project (Imagining the Other for short) and its goals of

© Springer Nature Switzerland AG 2021
A. Mitchell and M. Vosmeer (Eds.): ICIDS 2021, LNCS 13138, pp. 454–461, 2021.
https://doi.org/10.1007/978-3-030-92300-6_46

foregrounding the importance of collaboration between designers and players and for making the study of collaborative behaviors scalable and seamless. We also define the term *authoring-other exchange* to describe the process where authors gain knowledge through IDN authoring and sharing reflections in real time (synchronously) while using the same tool and exchanging feedback. We are particularly interested in examining how peers of similar and different sociocultural affiliations exchange viewpoints through such feedback. This paper presents the design considerations, architecture and preliminary findings of a pilot conducted on an online media research platform modified to facilitate the workshop.

This paper is organized as follows. First, in this section, we describe the background of the Imaging the Other project and its connection to previous research. Next, we describe extensions we developed for an existing media research platform and, specifically, the Twine module created for it. We then introduce the *Imagining the Other* workshop series, describe the coding schema used for analysis, and provide a sample analysis and insights from a preliminary pilot study. Finally, we discuss the implications for future research directions.

## 1.1  Background

A prior study in a physical lab setting showed how exchanging the designer–player roles was productive to show how novice peers were able to incorporate feedback into their authoring process [1]. However, the methods of using unmodified tools proved too cumbersome to implement for educational practice and research. Imagining the Other focuses on scaling such research because of the importance of studying how peers of similar sociocultural backgrounds (ethnicity, gender, language) work when acting as authors and audience members. In the new design, peers not only learn an authoring tool for the first time but are also providing and receiving feedback synchronously with another player-author in alternating turns. This real time learning, designing, and playing process, we argue, has the potential to illustrate the inherently social nature of IDN and the ways in which different social interactions impact development of the interactive narrative. To better study these interactions, we also needed a practice-based research tool to accommodate hundreds of students across a large urban university system. We turned to Sherlock, an existing media research tool [2] that previously supported collecting, analyzing and visualizing research data on IDN traversals through a web interface. We extended the platform with a Twine module that enables participants to both author stories and exchange feedback through a Sherlock web client. In addition to collecting the data, we further identified the need to manage participant participation through scheduling and communication in order to minimize errors and drop outs.

## 1.2  Existing Research

Previous work on studying novice authors includes work by Alex Mitchell et al. which focused on supporting authors in creating specific types of narrative structures through a new writing tool, HyperDyn [3]. Creating new authoring tools in order to improve the authoring experience is one approach to understanding authoring process. Another is to manage the social interactions of authors in a community of collaboration. Rouse provides an example of one such research project, offering guidelines for how to shape and encourage collaboration among larger groups [4]. Recently, Millard et al. call for additional research on the authoring process itself as they report on interviewing 20 different digital interactive authors about the process [5]. Our approach focuses on the initial introduction to authoring for interactive digital narratives but shares many of the concerns with understanding the nature of authoring through observation and tool-building, and further argue that the community needs to collaborate on shared platforms to enable additional research in this area.

## 2    Extending Sherlock to Support IDN Authoring and Research

The Imagining the Other project required supporting multi-user interaction on Twine. The previous work identified several challenges in how the study was conducted, including physical steps required to share the output of one participant with the other. Twine supports exporting a project as HTML, but sharing the file requires participants to understand and employ another method, such as email or other channel, and be able to identify the recipient. This proved challenging, as participants would need to receive additional instructions and could lose work due to user error. Internally, Twine saves story data using local browser storage, which is available to other JavaScript applications running from the same domain. With this knowledge, we developed code to watch for changes and record the saved browser data as a story was edited.

### 2.1    Sherlock

Sherlock is a media-user research tool created to study reactions to audio-visual stimuli [2]. It was initially designed to collate and study parallel streams of data alongside a representation of the experience content. These data streams included facial expressions, think-aloud notes, and biometric signals based on player interactions with Telltale Game's *The Wolf Among Us* [6]. The analytic interface ran on a web-based client that retrieved data from a server which maintained the data in a mongodb database. It has been expanded to support multiple research users, projects, and to broaden its scope beyond annotating screen recordings of graphical adventure games to support authoring and feedback directly. This necessitated expanding the platform beyond just analyzing data to conducting the workshop sessions remotely. This included enrolling participants, assisting with the scheduling of pairs, and managing the web-based study sessions, which we describe more in Sect. 3.

### 2.2    Twine Module for Sherlock

Twine was designed for a single author to create interactive stories and publish them as a web page. Recording and transferring Twine data required participant action in the default version of Twine, such as exporting the work as an HTML file, slowing down the overall process. In the current version of Twine, there is also no support for recording events or histories of edits made to the story. These two limitations of the open-source tool necessitated modifications both to the Twine authoring tool itself as well as additional support for recording data to study.

For the Imagining the Other project, we developed a special module for Sherlock that wraps and adds features to Twine. We record events generated by the Twine editor, such as creating, editing, and deleting passages, from a modified version of Twine inside an inline frame element and share it through the server with the partner, including the story content typically stored in the session storage. This allows us to save timestamped snapshots of the story, which effectively transforms Twine from a single-user tool into a multi-user environment, and further allowed partners to annotate passages using their titles with their comments as they played the story. Using the existing API within Sherlock, this data is sent to the server and stored in the database and published to other clients.

In addition to embedding both the Twine interface and runtime into the Sherlock web application, we implemented additional logic in JavaScript to manage the overall protocol of the study, such as advancing to the next step and changing the mode of the interface as well as publishing events and data to the server. This automation enabled participants to remain in sync during the session. These features were critical for making the real-time exchange of comments available to the peers and supporting the authoring-other exchange process.

## 3 Integrating Social Research Methodology in the Sherlock Research Platform

The Imagining the Other project arises out of two previous research avenues and includes an initial pilot study showing the utility of combining Sherlock and the developed Twine module to convene a workshop with students new to IDN authoring. A previous project included using an unmodified version of Twine where participants exchanged feedback using audio and through an in-person session changing physical rooms as they changed roles from author to player and back again [1]. The challenges identified in the previous work motivated the development of both the platform and for modifying Twine described in Sect. 2.2. These features were necessary not only for the participants to exchange views, but also to conduct the workshop series and study the resulting data. We describe the workshop protocol along with the complexity and richness of the endeavor in this section.

### 3.1 Imagining the Other Workshop Series

As part of the Imagining the Other project, we study narrative pedagogy and authoring behavior through observing and prompting the exchange of views by authors in a practice-based workshop context. The design for the workshop involves each participant viewing a basic Twine tutorial, followed by being directed to a participation pane, with the instructions to "[t]hink of a story idea and use the Twine tools you learned to begin designing an IDN" as the beginning of a nine step process each lasting fifteen minutes, shown in Fig. 1. After the 15-min initial authoring session, participants are presented with their partner's design. For this player reflection step, the prompt is "Share with your partner what you are thinking and feeling as you play their emerging design". On the next authoring turn, each participant is prompted to "Consider your player's reflections and continue your IDN design."

**Fig. 1.** Pilot Workshop Steps (2.5 h total length)

To evaluate the feasibility of the series, we applied a coding schema to the data produced by the workshop sessions. These data included authored Twine content, the comments from the author and their partner, and how the author acted on the comments across several design-play-edit turns. In the next subsection, we describe the data analysis categories as they were implemented from the pilot and a sample analysis in the following subsection.

### 3.2 Coding Scheme

We applied coding across three strands of analysis: the IDN designs of players, their experience reflections, and a measure of the final IDN design in the study. These strands were chosen based on previous research [7] with sociocultural relational narrative research and based on existing IDN pedagogy studies. In examining the IDN design of players, the major narrative elements were WORLD, CHARACTER, EVENT, and PSYCHO-LOGICAL STATE, providing categories of the story content in a way relating to other measures. These design structure measures draw on decision tree analysis and combine connection density (branches/non-terminal passages/leaves (terminal), connection tree depth, and the length of the path from the first passage to the farthest leaf). They provide a quantified assessment to connect with player experience reflections.

Player experience reflections account for the nature of designer-player interactions and subsequently the impact of different kinds of comments to the IDN element and structural design measure. Major player experience reflection categories include IDN FEATURE ("Give me more choices"); PSYCHOLOGICAL STATES ("I was expecting something different"; "I really liked that you started with 'Where Am I?'"; "Did it shock you too?"; EVALUATION ("Good beginning"); CO-DESIGN ("Try adding another room"); and NARRATIVE GENRE ("This is like a story I once read"). Although expressive units may include several smaller narrative elements (such as a character name), this analysis focuses on the social pragmatic function of each propositional unit. For example, the player reflection "I don't know where Mama is" emphasizes player cognition overall, even though character and location words are embedded. This decision is based on the theoretical premise player experience is what the designer will pick up on, which will be testable in the subsequent larger study [8]. These player experience categories were applied to the real time recording and immediate availability to the designer who could then use them when editing and continuing their IDN design–interaction dynamics the Sherlock platform facilitates.

The strands of analysis (IDN elements, final IDN design structure, and player experience reflections) accounted for all the data in the pilot testing, even as the workshop process and platform underwent changes, as appropriate for a pilot run of such a complex system. We also explored how features of the authoring-exchange platform, unavailable offline, might suggest dynamic analysis categories linking all three strands of the data. Because of the time stamps in the research panel shown in Fig. 2, we explored possible intra-dyad creative synergies at those moments, as detailed in the next subsection.

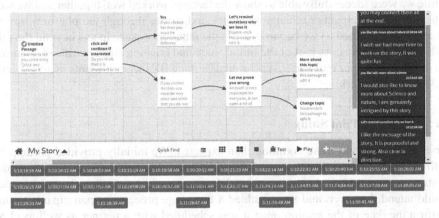

**Fig. 2.** Researcher view in Sherlock Twine Module

## 3.3 Sample Analysis

The following sample analysis is based on a pilot participant dyad, which indicates the dynamic pattern we label "intersubjective design pivots." During an authoring turn, one participant began a story about Patsy as a "kind hearted[sic] girl who loved nothing more than reading her books and spending time with her farm animals." The author then added characters, some character development, setting, and different branches: (A) "Patsy quickly walks past the man and mummbles[sic] a 'hit me baby one more time' britney spears song, a song she had heard from a cd[sic] she found in the ancient ruins of Nueva York" and (B) "The man hands Patsy 30,000 PSD", and cons her, resulting in the content of "Patsy Walks[sic] home in dismay, and decides to commits suicide [but first] she has to kill her mother." Upon seeing the darker of the two branches, the partner commented how the outcome "was unexpected" and continued how they "did not expect for Patsy to be a killer or something like that." On the next authoring turn, the original author produced a relatively dramatic shift in the story. In a new branch, "Patsy Goes[sic] to the top of the cliff just as the sun is setting" and "tells her mother to make a wish and count to three." Patsy then "watched[sic] her mother hit the pointy edges of the rocks and come to a stop, about 300 m above the ground." As a result of the comments from the partner, Patsy's mother, instead of being killed in the original branch, survives the encounter based on immediate feedback.

The relatively strong emotional reflection to the darker branch in the Patsy initial story, and the subsequent design offering of a non-lethal choice, reifies our emphasis on the potential power of the player's sharing of emotions and cognitions [9]. This "intersubjective design pivot", we argue, is a key finding and central to ongoing research using Sherlock and the application of the coding schema.

# 4 Limitations and Future Work

While we were successfully able to show the features worked well together and we were able to have participants exchange feedback and stories through the platform, several issues were identified as we began to scale the number of participants beyond the pilot and add new features. As part of the initial study and ongoing work, we also recognized the uniqueness of our multi-user synchronous remote IDN work presents many potential areas for future work.

## 4.1 Issues with Pilot Study

First, no-shows were more common than expected. We initially provided participants with a custom link to join a session and could observe through the logs whether participants were currently on the session page. We were not able to confirm that a participant would attend, however, and so we added a two-stage process for participants to both confirm the date of the session once it was scheduled with a partner as well as check in one hour prior to the session start time, which was sent via email from the server. This information would allow us to further automate the rescheduling or canceling of sessions based on whether both partners were present.

Another issue we found was that some participants would either miss the video or continue to be confused as to how to create Twine works. One way we could address this would be to include an interactive tutorial on creating a passage and sending a link to both participants to confirm they understand the basics as well as to review the primary authoring features of Twine before the session.

Finally, while we were able to export data from the database for analysis using our coding schemes in ATLAS.ti [10], certain changes in content depended on the unique structure of linked nodes in Twine. We learned further support for navigating the parallel datasets in Sherlock with program features to assist researchers conducting analysis across a larger set of data without manually we needed to help with copying the content or coding back and forth. A solution for this issue could take the form of including content annotation features directly into Sherlock, or simply highlighting the sequence of changes instead of simply presenting snapshots of the story state in the Researcher view.

## 4.2 Future Work

This work represents the only multi-user synchronous remote IDN research that we are aware of, and so we encountered several issues relating to logistics and conducting the study itself that could be further improved through appropriate platform support. Sherlock is an open-source platform, and this study was only possible due to the availability of Twine as an open-source platform for both authoring and publishing interactive digital narratives through HTML. Other platforms would be worth examining using similar techniques, though, including Unity and Ink, and in the future, XR content authoring tools such as that found in Facebook Horizons [11].

One thing we have found is that there is an urgent need to attend to the needs of researchers studying the authoring tools and the use of the authoring tools. The complexity of the content and the availability of open-source versions of many of the tools provides an opportunity to collect detailed data that would allow understanding of how collaborative IDN authoring can be used for various ends, such to offer insights for IDN authoring pedagogy and for the field to elaborate the social justice potential of IDN design, such as creating and supporting creation with someone of a very different background and identity.

**Acknowledgments.** The authors thank Jack J. Wright for developing the design structuremeasure and Fedor Marchenko for assistance with early phases of the pilot.

# References

1. Daiute, C., Duncan, R.O., Marchenko, F.: Meta-communication between designers and players of interactive digital narratives. In: Rouse, R., Koenitz, H., Haahr, M. (eds.) ICIDS 2018. LNCS, vol. 11318, pp. 134–142. Springer, Cham (2018). https://doi.org/10.1007/978-3-030-04028-4_10
2. Murray, J.T.: Telltale hearts: encoding cinematic choice-based adventure games (2018). https://escholarship.org/uc/item/1n02n02z
3. Mitchell, A., McGee, K.: Designing hypertext tools to facilitate authoring multiple points-of-view stories. In: Proceedings of the 20th ACM conference on Hypertext and hypermedia - HT '09. pp. 309. ACM Press, Torino (2009). https://doi.org/10.1145/1557914.1557966
4. Rouse, R.: Someone else's story: an ethical approach to interactive narrative design for cultural heritage. In: Cardona-Rivera, R.E., Sullivan, A., Young, R.M. (eds.) ICIDS 2019. LNCS, vol. 11869, pp. 47–60. Springer, Cham (2019). https://doi.org/10.1007/978-3-030-33894-7_6
5. Kitromili, S., Jordan, J., Millard, D.E.: What authors think about hypertext authoring. In: Proceedings of the 31st ACM Conference on Hypertext and Social Media, pp. 9–16. ACM, Virtual Event USA (2020). https://doi.org/10.1145/3372923.3404798
6. Telltale Games: The Wolf Among Us. (2013)
7. Daiute, C.: Narrative Inquiry: A Dynamic Approach. Sage Publications (2013)
8. Koenitz, H., Dubbelman, T., Knoller, N., Roth, C.: An integrated and iterative research direction for interactive digital narrative. In: Nack, F., Gordon, A.S. (eds.) ICIDS 2016. LNCS, vol. 10045, pp. 51–60. Springer, Cham (2016). https://doi.org/10.1007/978-3-319-48279-8_5
9. Murray, J., Mateas, M., Wardrip-Fruin, N.: Proposal for analyzing player emotions in an interactive narrative using story intention graphs. In: Proceedings of the 2017 International Conference on the Foundations of Digital Games (2017)
10. Atlas.ti. Scientific Software Development GmbH
11. Murray, J.T., Johnson, E.K.: XR Content Authoring Challenges: The Creator-Developer Divide. CRC Press (2021). https://doi.org/10.1201/9781003052838-16

# A Proposed Curriculum for an Introductory Course on Interactive Digital Narratives in Virtual Reality

Joshua A. Fisher[1]([✉]) [iD] and Janíce Tisha Samuels[2] [iD]

[1] Department of Interactive Arts and Media, Columbia College Chicago, 600 S Michigan, Chicago, IL 60605, USA
jofisher@colum.edu
[2] National Youth Art Movement, 200 East Randolph Street, Suite 5100-38, Chicago, IL 60601, USA
janice@nationalyouthartmovement.org

**Abstract.** Immersive Media programs of study are being developed and enacted at many higher education institutions. It is proposed that a course on Interactive Digital Narratives (IDN) in Virtual Reality (VR) can familiarize undergraduate students of diverse backgrounds with the foundational technical, design, and development tenets of immersive storytelling. Course curriculum balances IDN design and immersive storytelling strategies with VR project management, user experience and interface design, spatial audio, digital scenography, introductory programming, and rudimentary artificial intelligence. The course connects technical and media affordances to theories of IDN to provide an introductory understanding of IDN in VR. The proposed course ran in the spring of 2021 at a small liberal arts college. The paper presents the course's 15-week curriculum. An evaluation that includes student work, insights lessons, and resources is provided.

**Keywords:** Virtual Reality · Interactive Digital Narratives · Curriculum design

## 1 Teaching an Emerging Practice

Teaching an emerging practice such as Interactive Digital Narratives (IDN) is a challenge [1–3]. Teaching students how to implement that narrative form within the emerging medium of Virtual Reality (VR) makes achieving pedagogical goals more difficult. In the domain of IDN, theories and taxonomies seek standardization, and tools for composition are always changing along with design strategies [3–6]. In Immersive Media, the technologies and production tools are ever evolving [7]. Further, as a media of attraction, VR draws on interdisciplinary practices to produce experiences [8]. These shifting sands, experimentation, and diverse media traditions make it challenging to build a pedagogical foundation for students that will help them become immersive storytellers. Yet, as noted by the Association for Research in Digital Interactive Narratives (ARDIN) committee, there is need for effective curricula [9]. Through integration of theory and hands-on skill

© Springer Nature Switzerland AG 2021
A. Mitchell and M. Vosmeer (Eds.): ICIDS 2021, LNCS 13138, pp. 462–477, 2021.
https://doi.org/10.1007/978-3-030-92300-6_47

building, the main objective for the proposed course was for students to become adept at developing IDN experiences for VR.

In academia, the desire to standardize IDN language, design strategies, and theories has been emphasized by Hartmut Koenitz and other members of ARDIN [1, 2, 4, 10, 11]. The authors of a recent presentation by the Immersive Research Learning Network (IRLN), "The State of XR and Immersive Learning Outlook 2021" expressed a desire for more immersive storytelling in XR curricula as a credible pathway toward standardization [12]. Yet, as of this writing, in the archived proceedings of the IRLN there is not a single article proposing a curriculum for a course that teaches IDN for VR [13].

The VR audience, which grew by 60% in 2020 (headset purchases) [14], is a testament to industry's need for capable developers, designers, and storytellers. To prepare undergraduate students to succeed in these areas, this paper proposes a 15-week curriculum for an introductory course on creating IDNs in VR. Note that by introductory, we do not mean that this course is suitable for first-year students. Instead, we propose this as an introduction to the practice of crafting IDNs in VR. The course was evaluated by an informal midterm evaluation and an end-of-the-semester formal evaluation. Due to the small sample size, the results are preliminary and should not be generalized. Lessons, outcomes, and insights for future research and curriculum development follow.

## 2 The Course

As part of a new Immersive Media BA and minor program at Columbia College Chicago, a series of intensive courses were being developed to replace two survey courses. The two survey courses introduced students to immersive media generally, from augmented to mixed reality and projection mapping to immersive theater. They provided no technical training or theory. To give form to the discipline as part of the degree program, the proposed course was designed and developed. The course goals were: (1) Develop an understanding of the design and development techniques for VR experiences (Virtual Environment Design, Unity programming, Spatial Audio, VR UI, VR UX, and Interaction Design), (2) Construct a VR experience with best practice and artist-led techniques, (3) Understand IDN story structures and implement them in a VR experience (4) Articulate and receive clear feedback through usability studies.

With the establishment of the Immersive Media program. It was deemed critical that theory and practice be well-balanced and blended within its curricula. As discussed in previous work on IDN pedagogy, the creation of IDNs requires a "practice-based education" [1]. Accordingly, the course was scheduled to meet once a week for three hours to accommodate both direct instruction (lectures) and practice-based learning.

The course time was broken into 3 one-hour sections. In the first five weeks, two hours were spent on lectures on IDNs in VR. One hour was spent on design, coding, or development activities. In the second five weeks, time was split evenly between lecture and studio activities. In the final five weeks, students spent class time doing work on their VR IDNs and working through usability studies to produce the final experience.

The topics covered in the course were C# programming in Unity, locomotion, spatial audio, virtual environment design and digital scenography, interaction design, VR UI and UX, usability tests and feedback, IDN story structures and writing strategies. Critically, each of these topics needed to scaffold effectively over 15 weeks for students to produce a compelling portfolio piece [15].

## 2.1 The Course Structure

Students iterated on their VR IDN over the course of the semester. During the first 7 weeks of the semester, students focused on building their concept, diegetic material, and a usable late-stage alpha or early-beta version of their IDN. For the midterm, due at the end of the first 7 weeks, students were required to turn in this rudimentary build for usability testing and feedback. Over the final 8 weeks, students iterated two more times before turning in their final experience with a cinematic trailer for their portfolio. The entire course structure is in Table 1 below. Longer explanations of content follow.

**Table 1.** IDN in VR Course Schedule. Classes were broken up into lectures, instructor-led activities, and studio time. Subjects and practices would often meld from one class to the next.

| Weeks | Material Covered |
| --- | --- |
| 1–2 | IDN Overview |
| 3 | IDN Writing Strategies, Narrative and Character Development |
| 4–6 | Basic Interaction Design and Locomotion |
| 6–7 | Virtual Environment and Digital Scenography |
| 8–9 | Rudimentary AI and Custom Narrative Game Mechanics [16] |
| 9–12 | User Interface and User Experience Design |
| 12–15 | Dedicated Studio Time and Usability Studies |

**Interactive Digital Narrative Overview.** Early lectures on IDN surveyed the field's history [17], what differentiates IDN from traditional narrative[18], dramatic agency[19], and canonical IDN works suggested by Hartmut Koenitz and Mirjam Palosaari Eladhari [4]: namely Façade [20], afternoon, a story[21], and Save the Date [22]. Further, VR IDNs from SideQuest were assigned. A list of these follows this section. Marie-laure Ryan's work on textual architectures is also presented by Week 3 [23]. These architectures were then used in the next weeks to begin producing IDNs. With only 15 weeks, the goal was to get students building as quickly as possible.

**Interactive Digital Narrative Writing Strategies.** Ryan's story structures [24], were used as worksheets and templates. Specifically, the Vector with Side Branches structure was presented as a plot to travel through in a Spatial Storyworld Architecture [24, 25]. This encouraged the students to think of each of the vector's branches as a different VR space. As Asim Hameed and Andrew Perkis discuss, from each space come moments for dramatic agency and storytelling [26]. Following the suggestion of Colette Daiute and Hartmut Koenitz, students were led in character development exercises [3]. These Non-Player Characters (NPC) became nodes for branching dialogue and the narrative within the VR spaces. Concepts of worldbuilding were introduced along with immersion [18, 25] and Sense of Presence (SoP) [27–29]. Students created their storyworld, the spaces within that world, and what interactions would increase and maintain immersion and SoP. These were then reviewed and critiqued by peers in class before being revised.

**Basic Interaction and Locomotion Design.** VR IDNs that achieve immersion, support an SoP for interactors that enforces an affective experience [30], and provides them dramatic agency requires consistent, transparent, and meaningful interactions [18, 23, 31, 32]. At this point in the semester, students were taught to code and design basic interactions. Tutorials were foundational and implemented in Unity. Advanced narrative game mechanics were discussed in a later module. Students were taught the importance of interaction design, both as being meaningful to the narrative [19] and as an opportunity for joy and play [33] to support immersion. Video tutorials for designing foundational grabbing and pointing interactions were provided along with Unity Packages of pre-coded and designed scenes. A 3rd party interaction framework was provided later in the semester to help students develop and design faster.

Locomotion Design is critical for creating immersion and for exploring an IDN with a Spatial Storyworld architecture [33–36]. Simultaneously, locomotion in VR is an issue of accessibility wherein an interactor's natural mode of locomotion must be considered [37]. Students are taught to implement multiple forms of locomotion including (1) impossible space architectures [38], (2) joystick, (3) teleportation, (4) flight, (5) climbing, (6) and vehicle or platform based [39].

**Virtual Environment Design and Digital Scenography.** For the course's prescribed story architecture, Virtual Environment (VE) Design and Digital Scenography were taught to achieve spatial immersion, a focus on game spaces [33] that tell stories. Level design material was based on the work of Miriam Bellard of Rockstar North [40] and others [41–43]. There is a fair amount of semantic overlap between narrative in games, experience, and level design. Students were taught to collapse these concepts into a form of digital scenography. Digital Scenography is the practice of using the design and composition of space to tell stories and support immersion [26, 44]. These practices included how to use light [45], compose spatial sound [46], and the use of color to direct user attention [47, 48]. Activities on how to create these environments—the technical processes and conceptual work—were done in class and for homework.

**Rudimentary Artificial Intelligence and Narrative Game Mechanics.** In VR, worlds enforce immersion and a sense of social presence when there are NPCs [49]. NPCs reinforce narrative immersion, and their behavior within the world lends social presence. Beyond the NPCs, movement of animals, machines, objects, and more can give interactor's a sense of embodied scale [50], scenographic energy [51], and help direct their attention [52]. Impressing upon interactors that there is emergent behavior in the space enforces the narrative immersion [25, 53].

Narrative game mechanics were introduced. As defined by Teun Dubbelman, "Narrative game mechanics invite agents, including the player, to perform actions that support the construction of engaging stories and fictional worlds in the embodied mind of the player." [16] These mechanics go beyond the foundational interactions discussed earlier in the semester. Given the unique nature of each IDN, materials and resources for these mechanics were produced through one-on-one instruction with peer review.

**VR User Interface and User Experience Considerations.** Students were taught best practices for User Interfaces (UI) and User Experience (UX) back-to-back. They reviewed the material from Oculus Quest [31] and from LiminalVR [54]. LiminalVR's collected research on the psychological impacts of immersive design choices is valuable for IDN work. As in previous work on IDN curricula, engagement with the psychological impacts of interactions is required [3]. Their research covers the impacts of motion, color, lighting, music, sound, interactivity, ludic interactions, flow, and cognitive load. Student's familiarity with these concepts helps them achieve immersion and SoP.

Students were encouraged to make as many interactions narrative game mechanics as they could. An effective UX is necessary for an IDN [11, 55]. For example, one student created a teleportation interaction that looked like a rope that was, in some way, connected to the character's story and the world. This was to encourage UI and UX that achieve Jay Bolter's transparency in service of immersion [56–58]. For example, one student's story involved a bully being turned into a gecko who then must converse with bugs. To begin the game, the interactor must open a box. After opening the box, insects scurry around inside, their movement encouraging the user to lean in. When the user leans in, an interaction is triggered that leads to a scene change that starts the narrative.

Usability studies for iterative design were presented. Due to the pandemic, students created their VR experiences in isolation. This made conducting usability studies difficult. Students were taught two procedures: usability interviews [59] and the think-aloud method [60]. For the latter, students would record their playthroughs and speak through their thoughts and interactions. The student designers of those experiences then summarized their peers' thoughts into action items for iteration. VR UX issues of fatigue, simulator sickness, and accessibility were also addressed with solutions.

## 2.2 Proposed Experiences

Students may not have had the opportunity to experience VR. Accordingly, they need to become familiar with how people tell stories with the medium. The following are suggested experiences. They are available on SideQuest and the Oculus store.

- Vanishing Grace [61]: A narrative puzzle game that uses spatial exploration, two different modes of locomotion, rich voice acting, and interactions that are both ludic and narratological. It is also a case study in limiting scope, standardizing interactions in the world, and designing meaningful spaces.
- Moss [62]: A 3$^{rd}$ Person VR adventure experience that upsets expectations for VR narratives. The interactor plays a god-like character that directs Quill, a young mouse. The spaces are lush, but more importantly, Moss is a case study in how to build a social sense of presence for the interactor with a character. When the interactor is not active, Quill will look up at them and respond to their inactivity. This interaction helps to teach the importance of character development and social presence and their impacts on immersion.

- The Book of Isabel [63]: An exploratory walking simulator through a traumatized girl's mind. Interactors walk through memories and hear Isabel discuss the event and her recovery. With limited interactions but an emotional story, the experience is a good template for students with limited programming experience. Further, it was produced by a graduating undergraduate at the Academy of Art and Design St. Joost. This makes it a motivating example for students.
- A Fisherman's Tale [64]: This VR experience is a puzzle game that plays with perception. It uses recursion and chains of interactions to create a world wherein the interactor is controlling an avatar, that is controlling another avatar, and so on. It is a case study in using non-Euclidean space in VR to create compelling spaces for interactions. For students, it helps to inspire creative ideas outside of their familiar game worlds and their natural reactions.
- Shadow Point [65]: Another VR puzzle experience wherein diegetic content helps interactors solve puzzles to find a missing woman. Each world provides a new kind of interaction to appropriately script the interactor for future scenarios. It is a good case study on connecting ludic elements and creating narrative game mechanics.
- Last Labyrinth [66]: A true VR IDN with multiple endings that utilizes puzzles and social presence to achieve immersion. Interactors communicate with Katia, who is unintelligible, to escape a labyrinth of horrific traps. Much like in Moss, the bond created with Katia is used to raise the emotional stakes and is instructive for students in producing SoP. Further, limited interactions—nodding and shaking the head; using a laser pointer—demonstrate to students that they do not need complex interaction designs to create an active and rich IDN in VR.

## 2.3 Teaching Challenges

As alluded, there are challenges to producing the proposed curriculum. They stem from the evolving IDN and Immersive Media spaces, as well as students' literacy in both. In the instance of a course covering an emerging field, especially one developed for a new program, it can be challenging to ascertain incoming students' technical capacity, visual or digital design skills, and general background in the material [67, 68]. Self-reporting through pre-course surveys can be inaccurate [69]. Students may come from different traditions entirely if the course is an elective. Preparing effective material, both in providing enough rigor for the most skilled and accessible for the least, is difficult. This is especially true of programming and experience with development engines like Unity.

Access to hardware and experiences is an issue. The Oculus Quest was used in the case study and may be an affordable option. However, the recent announcement that ads would become part of VR experiences may not make the Quest acceptable [70]. Further, students may, and did, resist being forced into the Facebook ecosystem. Lastly, if an instructor were to require students to purchase all the suggested experiences, they would be spending $115 (as of writing). Finding a solution for renting or sharing VR experiences would offset this financial burden and increase accessibility.

An additional challenge is physical space. Some students will be able to work and create their VR experiences in large apartments. Others may only have access to a small bedroom or dorm. For the sake of equity, a common space should be provided to students somewhere on campus where they can experiment. Additionally, a VR emulator should be made available to all students. The emulator will speed development for all students regardless of the size of their physical space.

## 3   The Case Study

This course ran at Columbia College Chicago in the spring of 2021 within the Department of Interactive Arts and Media. Eight students participated in the course. The students self-selected into or chose to substitute an elective on interactive storytelling with the proposed course. The students came from the following programs: one from Creative Writing, one from Programming, one from Interaction Design, one from Cinema and Television, and four from Game Design. Two of the students were seniors who graduated. One student failed to complete the course.

Each student was provided with an Oculus Quest that they could use for the entirety of the semester. Further, they had access to lecture and tutorial videos hosted for asynchronous access on the college's learning management system, Canvas. Lastly, students had access to either tutors or the instructor via Microsoft Teams.

### 3.1   Evaluation Instruments

To evaluate the course's effectiveness, a midterm informal course evaluation was given with the same 5-point Likert-scale questions (one being the worst and five being the best) as the final formal course evaluation. In both instances, students were encouraged to explain or reflect on their chosen value. Six of the eight students completed all the evaluation instruments. The student who did not complete the course did not engage with any of the evaluations. The evaluation questions were broken up into two sections—a set on the course and another on the instructor. Only the questions about the course are discussed. Note that for the midterm evaluation, the tense of the questions was set to the present perfect continuous tense (i.e., I have been intellectually challenged by the course). They were: (Q1) I was intellectually challenged by the course, (Q2) I was encouraged to take learning seriously and to think critically in this course, (Q3) Class requirements and activities were useful learning tools to support the achievement of course goals, and (Q4) Overall, the course was well organized.

### 3.2   Evaluation Results

Before continuing to discuss the results, it must be noted that due to the small sample size, that these results cannot be generalized. They should be viewed as preliminary. During the midterm evaluation, the average score for the midterm evaluations was 4.6 of 5. A selection of written responses (A1,2,3) to these questions (Q1,2,3) are below.

- Q1 (4.8/5): (A1) I want more discussion of the VR experiences and best practices. (A2) Some of the videos are less useful than others. I would prefer having a smaller core of videos that best demonstrate learning concepts and then having a list of extra videos we can choose to watch for more inspiration.

- Q2 (4.5/5): (A1) The lectures on immersion and presence felt rushed. (A2) If I had known this course was about storytelling and not games I might not have taken it (A3) Too much focus on narrative and not VR. (A4) The lectures are a little heavy, however, the classes always provide interesting and useful content that I think will help me in the future.
- Q3 (4.2/5): (A1) Slower tutorials please! (A2) There are not enough tutorials for my story. (A3) Class playthroughs for feedback are long and boring. (A4) The C# programming is very difficult. Provide more documentation.
- Q4 (4.9/5): N/A

In response to this feedback, a number of course corrections were made as the course transitioned from the lecture-heavy first half to the production-based second half. In response to Q1 A1, students were asked to come to class with video recordings of an experience playthrough they felt was effective. Reflecting on the problems, solutions, and recommendations discussed at the conclusion of each playthrough, students then discussed how to design similar aspects for their own experiences. In response to Q2 A1 and A2, the ludology and narratology discussion was presented along with an activity that encouraged students to consider the connection between play and narrative. Students were encouraged to build ludic elements into their IDN. In response to Q1 A2 and Q3 A1, 2, and 4, templates were developed for various interactions, dialogue, IDN transitions, locomotion, and spatial audio. Walkthroughs were presented in class and as recorded videos. Before studio time, quick one-on-one meetings with students were held to clarify processes and overcome obstacles. In response to Q3 A3, class playthroughs for feedback were turned into asynchronous sessions for the students to complete independently during class time.

For the final evaluation, the average score for the questions improved to a five out of five. The high score is not representative of a perfect course.

- Q1 (5/5): (A1) The class was tough, but it felt worth it to learn. (A2) This course certainly wasn't for the faint of heart. It was incredibly challenging, but also very fulfilling. (A3) In the future I think it is very important to do some pre-evaluation on the skill level and knowledge of the students. This course was incredibly challenging, and I felt way in over my head. (A4) Students need to know the level of work before signing up.
- Q2 (5/5): (A1) When I joined the course I was told that as long as I followed tutorials I would be able to have a finished project enough to do well. This was not the case for me. (A2) In studio collab, I feel that since the project would not be my own, I would not feel as motivated as I did in this class.
- Q3 (5/5): (A1) I had to put in probably 20 h a week on this course. Students need to know and be prepared for the level of work they are signing up for. (A2) My experience in this course was probably different from other students in the course, simply because I had no previous experience with game design or Unity, as well as very very basic understanding of C#. (A3) I'm really really proud of myself for sticking with it and producing the final product.
- Q4 (5/5): (A1) Teach the class about SideQuest earlier. (A2) Once we started to build our world the guidance and tutorials didn't feel like enough. (A3) Presenting the

students with tools and things they can utilize to build their worlds would be beneficial before starting to get into the conception phase. If I knew how difficult some of the world & interaction building be I would probably start with something a whole lot simpler for myself.

The responses to the questions during the final evaluation indicate several changes for the future course. As indicated by all respondents, the class was difficult and required a major investment outside of course time. The college where the class was run expects students to spend 9 h outside of class on material. Clearly, as discussed in Q3 A1, some students did more than double that amount of work. And, as in Q1, some students felt wholly unprepared for the scope of work required to complete an IDN in VR. In response to these challenges, future courses will provide a wide range of design and code templates to ease the production demands for students. Plug-and-play templates might be the most effective even if it reduces the diversity of IDNs created. Options like Quill [71], the VR illustration and animation tool, might be more accessible and are frequently used for sequential narratives.

In response to questions and responses about the production demands (Q2 A1, Q4 A2 and A3), an established 3rd party framework for interactions will be implemented in the future course earlier in the semester. There are several 3rd party frameworks that can be implemented in Unity for the Oculus Quest (VR Easy [72], VRTK [73], and NewtonVR [74] to name a few). These templates provide a breadth of interactions with comprehensive documentation. The future course will utilize The VR Interaction Framework produced by Bearded Ninja Games [75]. The framework has documentation and tutorials for grabbing, grabbable events, climbing, teleportation, joystick locomotion, ziplines, platform movement, buttons, switches, levers, inventory management, tools, damageable items, drawing, UI elements, and more.

As discussed by Q1 A1, Q2 A1 and A3 during the midterm evaluation and Q4 A1-3 in the final evaluation, a stronger connection between technical practices in VR and IDN storytelling needs to be established earlier on in the semester. Not only will this help with project scope (Q4 A3), but it may result in interactions that have stronger dramatic agency and connection to the narrative. IDNs in VR should be presented as case studies that students can emulate using provided frameworks and templates.

## 4  Outcomes, Insights, and Resources

Of the eight students who enrolled in the class, five students produced complete IDN VR experiences that earned top marks. To earn the top grade, students had to present an experience that was bug free, had a complete narrative arc with a beginning middle and end, that achieved immersion and SoP as reported by peers, created at least five areas for the story, included interactions that provided dramatic agency, and had to have completed most of the action items from the usability studies. Students presented their final experiences through a trailer and in an in-class playthrough.

Of the seven students who completed the course, the top grades were given to one student from the Creative Writing program and two from the Game Design program. These students produced the most comprehensive and longest experiences (20 or more minutes long). These experiences also had multiple branching dialogue options that expanded the storyworld, and in one case, changed the outcome of the story.

## 4.1  Select Student Work

The best student work is presented here with summaries of their narratives as well as stills. Links to their trailers are also provided.

**Corbit.** *Corbit*, in Fig. 1, "takes place in a whimsical world in the center of the earth, where every cog has their purpose in the machine. *Corbit* aims to explore existential and environmental concepts in a fun, hopeful and engaging way." The interactor embodies a Cog, part of a system of cogs and gears, that help to keep earth alive while humanity causes damage. Over the course of five spaces, interactors learn who they are in this world and what their role is, how humans are destroying the earth, and what they can do to fix it. In conclusion, the interactor learns that their work is Sisyphean—that the machine is made for the earth, not humans, and will exist long after they are gone. *Corbit* uses digital scenography melded with UI elements to maintain immersion while supporting the user's SoP. The narrative is grounded within contemporary issues and anxieties which works to support SoP and engagement. *Corbit* effectively utilized the antechamber VR design method [76] to script the interactor before the experience began. Not only did the student capably weave diegetic information into the antechamber, but the interactions they scripted in the space modified the world.

**Fig. 1.** From left to right: (1) The interactor rides a platform through the world of the machine. It is a sprawling space of massive scale intentionally designed for immersion. (2) NPCs in the space provide branching dialogue options and diegetic information. (3) UI to access the IDN content is rendered in world on screens or consoles that do not break immersion. (4) Scenographic clues are given to encourage user interactions that impact the world. The trailer is here: https://youtu.be/QRdEI5mdfss

**The Spotted Journey.** In this experience, shown in Fig. 2, the interactor inhabits the role of a bully who is transformed into a gecko for their immoral acts. The student loosely based the narrative off a myth about the goddess Demeter's punishment for a man that mocked her as she ate and drank. The interactor must do good deeds while collecting crystals from rooms within their own house. Once the interactor is transformed into a gecko, the bugs and small creatures within the space take the opportunity to scold them for their bad behavior (when large). *The Spotted Journey* relies strongly on scale and climbing locomotion to make the player feel small and feckless. As the interactor goes from room to room, the climbing challenges require larger body movements. Such movements have a beneficial impact on SoP. NPCs are quick to let the interactor know how rude they were when they were a fully-sized human inhabiting the space with them.

**Fig. 2.** From left to right: (1) When the experience starts, the interactor is a young child. They are then scaled down into a gecko for the experience. (2) Interactors are made to traverse large rooms to encourage feelings of helplessness. (3) Interactors must climb on furniture to get magical crystals and do good deeds. (4) At the end of the experience, if the interactor has chosen the right dialogue options, NPCs that travel with them throughout the experience are present when they are turned back into humans. The trailer is here: https://youtu.be/X-LLmQ3bkZk

**System Security.** Presented in Fig. 3, in this VR experience, the interactor is a character that is a program inside of a larger system. Their role is to stop viruses from sneaking into the system and causing havoc. A mix between *Paper's Please* and *Tron, System Security* forces the player to make difficult choices regarding who gets to enter the system and who gets deleted. Over the course of the experience, the interactor befriends a coworker. The interactor learns that this new friend may have a virus inside of them. After plugging into their friend's head and discovering that they are infected, the interactor is forced to delete their friend. *System Security* effectively used worldbuilding and characters to create a sense of narrative immersion. The difficult choices interactors had to make increased the stakes of their dramatic agency. In the end, the interactor is not actually able to change the world in which they inhabit.

These three experiences present the range of IDNs developed. Each had their own unique world, story, and narrative game mechanics. Not presented were the following: one, interactors play as a worm in a community of migratory worms moving from one rotting food to another; two, the interactor plays a piece of patch work cloth in an oppressive tailor shop run by an oligarchy of pure fabrics; three, the interactor is a discarded robot searching for their old human owners; and four, where the interactor is an overworked factory caterpillar looking to overthrow their oppressive spider bosses.

### 4.2 Successes and Failures

The course was successful in introducing students to the world of IDNs in VR. It was also successful in helping students achieve the course goals. All but two of the students

**Fig. 3.** From left to right: (1) In the antechamber space, interactors are introduced to the world and are taught how to scan "bytes" to see if they are infected or not. (2) The interactor's bedroom showcases the dystopian and dark world of the narrative. The billboard says, "Remember their Names". (3) The main interactions occur in the security hall where bytes are scanned. In the background, an infected byte is escorted away. The interactor hears the byte get deleted in the distance. (4) Inside of their befriended colleague's head, the interactor learns that they are infected and witnesses their friend execute a fellow byte. The trailer is here: https://youtu.be/jXitKdS3o4w

produced a playable IDN in VR. Almost every student met the challenges of the course, learned a variety of different technical skills, and became more literate in the VR design and development space. Given that a creative writer, with no prior Unity experience, produced the most comprehensive and emotionally satisfying experience is a testament to how scaffolding, templates, and direction can help novices achieve their goals. Templates and resources from the course are available here: https://github.com/jadlerfisher/IDN-in-VR-Resources. These resources will allow students to focus more on their stories than their technical implementation.

This course's failures fall into two domains. The first domain is connected to IDN and VR Literacy. Students were introduced to the free experiences available on SideQuest too late in the semester. This delayed learning and then implementing conventions. Further, not connecting these same experiences to technical demos made it difficult for students to connect their own IDNs to VR affordances. In short, teaching narrative game mechanics came too late. The second domain of failures connects to the scope and variety of work required to complete a comprehensive and compelling experience. There was simply too much for a single student. They often felt overwhelmed. Templates and tutorials were produced on an ad hoc basis to meet needs and skill levels for various narrative game mechanics. Additionally, introducing the user study prototype pair protocol discussed by Koenitz and colleagues would have been beneficial both from a research perspective and to produce better stories [1]. Lastly, only one student produced an IDN wherein dramatic agency produced a new ending for the story. Most students produced branching narratives wherein all choices resulted in a common ending. So, while students did gain a working knowledge of IDN, the majority were unable to produce either IDNs with multiple endings or kaleidoscopic stories [77].

### 4.3  Looking Ahead

Establishing IDNs in VR, as a discipline, will require persistent community participation in the design and development of curricula. Interdisciplinary practitioners and scholars will need to continue to work together to institutionalize a set of practices to concretize the field's sands into a foundation. Sharing syllabi, curricula, and pedagogy can help standardize the discipline's language, history, and canon of experiences. This is critical and exciting work to prepare the next generation of immersive storytellers.

# References

1. Koenitz, H., Roth, C., Dubbleman, T., Knoller, N.: Interactive narrative design beyond the secret art status: a method to verify design conventions for interactive narrative. **6**, 107–119 (2018). https://doi.org/10.14195/2182
2. Dubbelman, T.: Teaching narrative design on the importance of narrative game mechanics. In: Suter, B., Bauer, R., Kocher, M. (eds.) Narrative Mechanics: Strategies and Meanings in Games and Real Life, pp. 79–89. Transcript Verlag, Bielefeld (2021)
3. Daiute, C., Koenitz, H.: What is shared? - A pedagogical perspective on interactive digital narrative and literary narrative. In: Nack, F., Gordon, A.S. (eds.) ICIDS 2016. LNCS, vol. 10045, pp. 407–410. Springer, Cham (2016). https://doi.org/10.1007/978-3-319-48279-8_37
4. Koenitz, H., Eladhari, M.P.: Challenges of IDN research and teaching. In: Cardona-Rivera, R.E., Sullivan, A., Young, R.M. (eds.) ICIDS 2019. LNCS, vol. 11869, pp. 26–39. Springer, Cham (2019). https://doi.org/10.1007/978-3-030-33894-7_4
5. Roth, C., Koenitz, H.: Towards creating a body of evidence-based interactive digital narrative design knowledge: approaches and challenges. In: AltMM 2017 - Proceedings of the 2nd International Workshop on Multimedia Alternate Realities, co-located with MM 2017, pp. 19–24 (2017). https://doi.org/10.1145/3132361.3133942
6. Shibolet, Y., Knoller, N., Koenitz, H.: A framework for classifying and describing authoring tools for interactive digital narrative. In: Rouse, R., Koenitz, H., Haahr, M. (eds.) ICIDS 2018. LNCS, vol. 11318, pp. 523–533. Springer, Cham (2018). https://doi.org/10.1007/978-3-030-04028-4_61
7. Murray, J.T., Johnson, E.K.: XR content authoring challenges: the creator-developer divide. In: Fisher, J.A. (ed.) Augmented and Mixed Reality for Communities, pp. 245–264. CRC Press, Boca Raton (2021)
8. Rouse, R.: Media of attraction: a media archeology approach to panoramas, kinematography, mixed reality and beyond. In: Nack, F., Gordon, A. (eds.) Interactive Storytelling. ICIDS 2016. LNCS, vol. 10045, pp. 97–107. Springer, Cham (2016).https://doi.org/10.1007/978-3-319-48279-8
9. Association for Research in Digital Interactive Narratives: Committees and Task Forces. https://ardin.online/committees/. Accessed 7 Sep 2021
10. Koenitz, H.: Design approaches for interactive digital narrative. In: Koenitz, H. (ed.) International Conference on Interactive Digital Storytelling, pp. 50–57. Springer, Cham, Nov 2015
11. Koenitz, H.: Five theses for interactive digital narrative. In: Fernández-Vara, C., Mitchell, A., Thue, D. (eds.) Interactive Storytelling: 7th International Conference on Interactive Digital Storytelling, pp. 134–139. Springer International Publishing, Singapore (2014). https://doi.org/10.1007/978-3-319-12337-0
12. Lee, M.J.W., Georgieva, M., Alexander, B., Craig, E., Richter, J.: State of XR & Immersive Learning 2021 Outlook Report. Immersive Learning Research Network, Walnut (2021)
13. Immersive Learning Research Network: Immersive Learning Research Network Digital Library.
14. Grand View Research: Virtual Reality Market Size, Share & Trends Analysis Report By Technology (Semi & Fully Immersive, Non-immersive), By Device (HMD, GTD), By Component (Hardware, Software), By Application, And Segment Forecasts, 2021–2028. San Francisco (2021)

15. Nurbekova, Z., Grinshkun, V., Aimicheva, G., Nurbekov, B., Tuenbaeva, K.: Project-based learning approach for teaching mobile application development using visualization technology. Int. J. Emerg. Technol. Learn. **15**, 130–143 (2020). https://doi.org/10.3991/IJET.V15I08.12335
16. Dubbelman, T.: Narrative game mechanics. In: Nack, F., Gordon, A.S. (eds.) ICIDS 2016. LNCS, vol. 10045, pp. 39–50. Springer, Cham (2016). https://doi.org/10.1007/978-3-319-48279-8_4
17. Carey, B.P.: The Architect of Forking Paths: Developing Key Writing Strategies for Interactive Writers (2018)
18. Murray, J.H.: Hamlet on the Holodeck: The Future of Narrative in Cyberspace. MIT Press, Cambridge (2017)
19. Murray, J.: Agency. In: Hamlet on the holodeck, pp. 159–189. MIT Press, Cambridge (2017)
20. Mateas, M., Stern, A.: Façade (2005)
21. Michael, J.: Afternoon, a story (1987)
22. Cornell, C.: Save the Date (2013). http://paperdino.com/save-the-date/
23. Ryan, M.L.: Interactive narrative, plot types, and interpersonal relations. In: Spierling, U., Szilas, N. (eds.) Interactive Storytelling. ICIDS 2008. Lecture Notes in Computer Science, vol. 5334, pp. 6–13. Springer, Berlin, Heidelberg (2008). https://doi.org/10.1007/978-3-540-89454-4_2
24. Ryan, M.: Toward an interactive narratology. In: Avatars of Story, pp. 97–125. University of Minnesota Press, Minneapolis (1997)
25. Ryan, M.-L.: The text as world: theories of immersion. In: Narrative as Virtual reality 2: Revisiting Immersion and Interactivity in Literature and Electronic Media, pp. 61–84. JHU Press, Baltimore (2015)
26. Hameed, A., Perkis, A.: Spatial storytelling: finding interdisciplinary immersion. In: Rouse, R., Koenitz, H., Haahr, M. (eds.) Interactive Storytelling. ICIDS 2018. LNCS, vol. 11318, pp. 323–332. Springer, Cham (2018). https://doi.org/10.1007/978-3-030-04028-4_35
27. Engberg, M., Bolter, J.D.: The aesthetics of reality media. J. Vis. Cult. **19**, 81–95 (2020). https://doi.org/10.1177/1470412920906264
28. Sundar, S.S., Kang, J., Oprean, D.: Being There in the Midst of the Story: How Immersive Journalism Affects Our Perceptions and Cognitions. Cyberpsychology, Behav. Soc. Netw. **20**(11), 672–682 (2017). https://doi.org/10.1089/cyber.2017.0271
29. Sallnäs, E.-L.: Effects of communication mode on social presence, virtual presence, and performance in collaborative virtual environments. Presence Teleoperators Virtual Environ. **14**, 434–449 (2005). https://doi.org/10.1162/105474605774785253
30. Quesnel, D., Riecke, B.E.: Awestruck: natural interaction with virtual reality on eliciting awe. In: 2017 IEEE Symposium on 3D User Interfaces (3DUI), pp. 205–206. IEEE (2017)
31. Facebook: Interactions | Oculus Developers. https://developer.oculus.com/learn/hands-design interactions/. Accessed 11 July 2021
32. Murray, J.H.: Inventing the Medium (2003)
33. Thon, J.: Immersion revisited: on the value of a contested concept. Extending Exp. Struct. Anal. Des. Comput. Game Play. Exp. 29–43 (2008)
34. Slater, M., Usoh, M., Steed, A.: Taking steps: the influence of a walking technique on presence in virtual reality. ACM Trans. Comput. Interact. **2**, 201–219 (1995)
35. Soler-Domínguez, J.L., de Juan, C., Contero, M., Alcañiz, M.: I walk, therefore I am: a multidimensional study on the influence of the locomotion method upon presence in virtual reality. J. Comput. Des. Eng. **7**, 577–590 (2020)
36. Nilsson, N.C., Serafin, S., Steinicke, F., Nordahl, R.: Natural walking in virtual reality: a review. Comput. Entertain. **16**, 1–22 (2018)
37. Boletsis, C.: The new era of virtual reality locomotion: a systematic literature review of techniques and a proposed typology. Multimodal Technol. Interact. **1**, 24 (2017)

38. Fisher, J.A., Garg, A., Singh, K.P., Wang, W.: Designing intentional impossible spaces in virtual reality narratives: a case study. In: Proceedings - IEEE Virtual Reality (2017). https://doi.org/10.1109/VR.2017.7892335

39. Di Luca, M., Seifi, H.: Locomotion vault: the extra mile in analyzing vr locomotion techniques. In: Conference Human Factors Computer System - Proceedings (2021). https://doi.org/10.1145/3411764.3445319

40. Bellard, M.: Environment Design as Spatial Cinematography: Theory and Practice. https://www.youtube.com/watch?v=L27Qb20AYmc&t=53s. Accessed 3 Jan 2021

41. Taylor, D.: Ten Principles of Good Level Design.

42. Feil, J., Scattergood, M.: Beginning Game Level Design. Thomson Course Technology, Boston (2005)

43. Blom, K.J., Beckhaus, S.: The design space of dynamic interactive virtual environments. Virtual Real. **18**(2), 101–116 (2013). https://doi.org/10.1007/s10055-013-0232-y

44. Howard, P.: What is Scenography? Routledge, Abingdon-on-Thames (2009)

45. Larionow, D.: Space, light and sound in performances of Leszek M'dzik's Scena Plastyczna KUL as the innovation in theatre design, vol. 1, pp. 1–3. Scenography International (2001)

46. Gruber, C.: Scenography of virtual sound-stages. Perform. Res. **18**, 1972013https://doi.org/10.1080/13528165.2013.818338

47. McKinney, J.: Empathy and exchange: audience experience of scenography. In: Kinesthetic Empathy in Creative and Cultural Practices, pp. 221–235 (2012)

48. McKinney, J.: The role of theatre design: towards a bibliographical and practical accomodation, vol. 1, pp. 1–13. Scenography International (1998)

49. Dzardanova, E., Kasapakis, V., Gavalas, D.: Affective impact of social presence in immersive 3D virtual worlds. In: 2017 IEEE Symposium on Computers and Communications (ISCC), pp. 6–11. IEEE (2017)

50. Kilteni, K., Groten, R., Slater, M.: The sense of embodiment in virtual reality. Presence Teleoperators Virtual Environ. **21**, 373–387 (2012). https://doi.org/10.1162/PRES_a_00124

51. Feng, C., Bartram, L., Riecke, B.E.: Evaluating affective features of 3D motionscapes. In: Proceedings of the ACM Symposium on Applied Perception, pp. 23–30. Association for Computing Machinery, New York, NY, USA (2014). https://doi.org/10.1145/2628257.2628264

52. Tagiuri, R.: Movement as a cue in person perception. In: David, H.P., Brengelmann, J.C. (eds.) Perspectives in Personality Research, pp. 175–195. Springer, Berlin, Heidelberg (1960). https://doi.org/10.1007/978-3-662-39598-1_9

53. Gorini, A., Capideville, C.S., De Leo, G., Mantovani, F., Riva, G.: The role of immersion and narrative in mediated presence: the virtual hospital experience. Cyberpsychol. Behav. Soc. Netw. **14**, 99–105 (2011)

54. LiminalVR: Home - Liminal VR. https://liminalvr.com/. Accessed 11 July 2021

55. Murray, J.: Hamlet on the Holodeck: The Future of Narrative in Cyberspace. The MIT Press, Cambridge (1998)

56. Bolter, J., Gromala, D.: Transparency and reflectivity: digital art and the aesthetics of interface design. Aesthetic Comput. **7** (2004)

57. Bolter, J.D., Grusin, R.: Introduction: the double logic of remediation. Remediat. Underst. New Media **2**, 3–15 (1999)

58. Bolter, J.: Transference and transparency: digital technology and the remediation of cinema. Intermédialités Hist. théorie des arts, des lettres des Tech. Hist. Theory Arts, Lit. Technol. 13–26 (2005)

59. Kuter, U., Yilmaz, C.: Survey methods: questionnaires and interviews. Choos. Human-Computer Interact. (HCI) Appropr. Res. Methods. (2001)

60. Desurvire, H., El-Nasr, M.S.: Methods for game user research: studying player behavior to enhance game design. IEEE Comput. Graph. Appl. **33**, 82–87 (2013)

61. Monte Perdido Studio: Vanishing Grace (2021). https://www.oculus.com/experiences/quest/4603898999650318/
62. Polyarc: Moss (2019). https://www.oculus.com/experiences/quest/1654565391314903/
63. Den Boef, A.: The Book of Isabel (2020). https://sidequestvr.com/app/1077/the-book-of-isabel
64. Innerspace VR: A Fisherman's Tale (2019). https://afishermanstale-game.com/
65. Coatsink Software: Shadow Point (2019). https://shadowpointgame.com/
66. Takahashi, H.: Last Labyrinth (2019). https://lastlabyrinth.jp/en/
67. Mills, K.A.: What learners "know" through digital media production: learning by design. e-Learning **7**, 223–236 (2010). https://doi.org/10.2304/elea.2010.7.3.223
68. Reyna, J., Hanham, J., Meier, P.C.: A framework for digital media literacies for teaching and learning in higher education. E-Learn. Digit. Media **15**, 176–190 (2018). https://doi.org/10.1177/2042753018784952
69. Lew, M.D.N., Alwis, W.A.M., Schmidt, H.G.: Accuracy of students' self-assessment and their beliefs about its utility. Assess. Eval. High. Educ. **35**, 135–156 (2010). https://doi.org/10.1080/02602930802687737
70. Zacks Equity Research: Facebook (FB) Plans to Put Ads on Oculus Quest VR Headset | Nasdaq. https://www.nasdaq.com/articles/facebook-fb-plans-to-put-ads-on-oculus-quest-vr-headset-2021-06-17. Accessed 9 July 2021
71. Facebook Technologies, L.: Quill. https://quill.fb.com/features/
72. AVR Works: VR Easy (2020)
73. Sysdia Solutions Ltd.: VRTK - Virtual Reality Toolkit - [VR Toolkit] (2019)
74. Bradner, K., et al.: Newton VR (2017). https://assetstore.unity.com/packages/tools/newtonvr-75712
75. Bearded Ninja Games: Virtual Reality Interaction Framework Wiki. https://wiki.beardedninjagames.com/. Accessed 6 Jan 2021
76. Ballantyne, J.: The Problem with Reality. https://www.oculus.com/story-studio/blog/the-problem-with-reality/. Accessed 7 July 2021
77. Murray, J.H.: Research into interactive digital narrative: a kaleidoscopic view through the kaleidoscope, and across the decades. In: Rouse, R., Koenitz, H., Haahr, M. (eds.) Interactive Storytelling. ICIDS 2018. LNCS, vol. 11318, pp. 1–16. Springer, Cham (2018). https://doi.org/10.1007/978-3-030-04028-4_1

# The Complexity Analysis Matrix

Noam Knoller[1](✉) 🆔, Christian Roth[2] 🆔, and Dennis Haak[3]

[1] Institute for Cultural Inquiry, Utrecht University, Muntstraat 2a, Utrecht, The Netherlands
[2] HKU University of the Arts, Nieuwekade 1, Utrecht, The Netherlands
christian.roth@hku.nl
[3] &Ranj Serious Games, Lloydstraat 21-M, 3024 Rotterdam, The Netherlands
dennis@ranj.com

**Abstract.** This paper outlines an approach to describing complexity representation in interactive narratives, in order to understand and evaluate how narrative serious games and similar forms might scaffold cognitive reduction of complexity. We adapt Yoon et al.'s media-agnostic framework for complexity learning to the interactive narrative context. Using the userly text model, we distinguish between first-order (observing) and second-order (enactive) subject positions and the distinct types of knowledge that they afford. The resulting matrix allows us to comparatively describe three components of a complexity triad - complexity in the (story)world, in the artefact and in subjective understanding. This makes it possible to assess and compare differences between the complexity representations within each component and thus evaluate complexity reduction as a function of the distance between the complexity representations within the artefact and within the subject. With this matrix, we begin to address the challenge of interactively narrating complexity as a problem of learning effectiveness, integrating insights from narratology, complexity theory and the learning sciences.

**Keywords:** Complexity · Representation · Cognitive reduction of complexity · Serious games · Userly text

## 1 Introduction

In recent years, there has been a growing interest in, as well as concern about, the societal challenge posed by the increasing complexity of the world and in the potential of digital mediation to address that challenge. In [1], the authors interviewed a variety of experts and drew stark conclusions about the severity of the challenge and the need to promote complexity thinking to address it, recommending the use of playable models, as well as calling for "new narratives". The examples discussed, however, were serious games, understood as simulations of complex dynamic systems. These were shown to have helped people recognise that certain issues were more complex than they had anticipated. Yet the report did not explain how playable models constituted new narratives. If playable simulations appeal to a logico-scientific rather than a narrative mode of thinking [2], they might fail to employ a crucial resource, since simulation without narrative lacks specific explanatory power [3, 4], and since narrative can organise knowledge into patterns that are more meaningful [2] and self-relevant [5].

© Springer Nature Switzerland AG 2021
A. Mitchell and M. Vosmeer (Eds.): ICIDS 2021, LNCS 13138, pp. 478–487, 2021.
https://doi.org/10.1007/978-3-030-92300-6_48

Popular authors [6, 7] have also been emphasising the crucial role of storytelling in society, pointing out that our ability, as humans, to collaborate in large numbers has always depended on our ability to imagine and share common stories and storyworlds. Narrative is more than an individual cognitive process, being, as cognitive narratologist David Herman has pointed out in [8], "anchored in collaborative discourse processes - how the mind is grounded in participants' relations with one another and with their surrounding social and material environment" (p. 320). In this he has endorsed folklorist and anthropologist Richard Bauman's analytic strategy [9], based on ethnographic studies of the performative aspects of oral storytelling, that took it to be constituted as an "indissoluble unity of text, narrated event and narrative event" (p. 7), in which story-world events (narrated events) are emergent in performance. Thus, cognitive narrative processes cannot fruitfully be understood to be uncoupled from their social and material environment, or indeed from their deep relation to the practices and communicative and social functions of storytelling. Complexity thinking, as a cognitive process, might require more than just individual shifts brought about by engagement with playable models. It is common stories and storyworlds that bind our individual experiences of the natural, social, cultural, or technological environment together into a meaningful shared experience.

Reviewing [1] and sharing the concerns it raised, Knoller [10] has therefore argued for a more explicitly narrative approach, and suggested that interactively narrating complexity may be more likely to further an understanding of complexity, and that this might be a challenge for Interactive Digital Storytelling and Narrative (IDS&N). Narrative *Userly Texts* [10, 11] in various forms - narrative serious games, interactive documentaries, digitally immersive theatre, as well as other forms - can develop to become the way humans make (common) sense of the world, and of being and acting within and upon it, through a developed narrative understanding of complex systems. Creators of such systems can draw on the affordances of digital media that distinguish them from pre-digital media [12]: the ability to store vast amounts of data, to disseminate narratives instantaneously around the world, to allow audiences to participate in the narrative experience as interactors and to try out different options. This may make it possible to represent, communicate, experience, and grasp complex systems, dynamics and processes, and to experience how to be agents within them (individually as well as collaboratively) in ways that are distinct from preceding media.

This has led Knoller [10] to reframe the societal challenge for IDS&N as the potential to design and employ narrative userly texts as semiotic scaffolds for a cognitive reduction of complexity (p. 107) - a step further than the realisation, scaffolded by playable models, that something is complex [1]. This potential, as well as the urgency of the societal challenge, have gained further recognition with the creation of the EU-funded INDCOR network [13], whose aim is "the interdisciplinary study of the potential interactive digital narrative has as a means to addressing complexity as a societal challenge by representing, experiencing and comprehending complex phenomena".

Given the potential, urgency, and institutional recognition, it is both necessary and possible to concentrate efforts on looking for evidence for the effectiveness of such an approach. In this paper, we begin to address this by focusing on the conceptual challenge of describing complexity. Such description is necessary as a preliminary step to operationalising and measuring the effectiveness of a narrative userly text in achieving a cognitive reduction of complexity. Our approach combines insights from narratology, complexity theory and the learning sciences and emerging in the context of an empirical study of an existing serious game [14], which is still ongoing.

How do we begin to break down complexity? What needs to be described and measured in order to provide evidence for effectiveness, grounded in a theory of how interactive digital storytelling functions and how its narrative artefacts are structured?

In answering the first question, we have to consider the three components of the complexity triad [15] which describes a communicative process: (i) environment/world complexity: the primary complexity of a represented phenomenon; (ii) the secondary complexity of the representation within a mediating artefact; (iii) the tertiary complexity of the interactor's subjective representation of the primary complexity, scaffolded by interaction with the secondary complexity.

In the next section, we present a framework that is used in the learning sciences to measure the effectiveness of learning about complex systems. We then explain what a narrative userly text is and what needs to be described to empirically study its effectiveness in achieving a cognitive reduction of complexity. We conclude by describing our extended complexity analysis matrix.

## 2    Cognitive Reduction of Complexity in the Learning Sciences: The Learning Progression Framework

While the potential of games for learning, in general, has been widely discussed [16] and many serious games for learning have been created, their effectiveness in achieving learning goals has rarely been evaluated [17]. To ground our description of complexities in an empirical discipline that regularly evaluates the effectiveness of cognitive learning processes, we turned to an existing model from the learning sciences. We adapted and extended a model that was originally used to evaluate the learning outcomes of high school biology students in the US who studied ecological systems, and specifically their ability to describe the complexity of such systems.

The Learning Progression Framework, proposed by Susan Yoon and colleagues [18], operationalises the cognitive reduction of complexity as a learning process. The model breaks the complexity of a system down to six complex system ideas. Yoon et al.'s analysis of a number of studies has furthermore led them to hypothesise that the cognitive challenge the six different ideas pose to learners is not equal, and can be ordered in the following ascending order, or learning progression:

(i)  **Scaling effects.** Three components are considered:

    a.   the relative scale of outcomes (small actions can lead to large effects);
    b.   the cascading, ripple or $2^{nd}$ order effects of an action, beyond a local effect;
    c.   the time scale: changes can be immediate, delayed or develop over a period.

(ii)  **Networked interactions.** Three components are considered:

a. interdependency among parts in the system;
b. nonlinearity of interactions, with feedback;
c. emergent patterns form at the system level, i.e. on top of the components.

(iii) **Multiple causes.** Multiple actions can contribute to an outcome or effect.
(iv) **Dynamic processes.** Processes refer to the dynamism of the mechanisms that underlie the phenomena or, to how the system works or is thought to work. The system is an ongoing, dynamic process and continues to be in a state of flux. The parts adapt or evolve, and continue to do so accordingly.
(v) **Order.** Control is decentralised to multiple parts, the system is self-organized or 'bottom-up', emerging spontaneously.
(vi) **Non-determinism.** The way in which a variable operates or affects other variables is unpredictable. Surprising patterns might emerge over time.

To measure the level of learners' understanding, for each of the six complex-systems ideas, Yoon further used a four-level scale of complexity that she had developed and validated earlier [19], ranging from "completely clockwork" to "completely complex". "Clockwork" describes systems as linear, single-cause, non-networked, centralised, static or. "Complex" describes systems as nonlinear, networked, multiple-cause, dynamic, decentralised, or non-deterministic. This results in a general 6 by 4 matrix that can be used to describe:

(i) The six complexity dimensions of any complex system S. These correspond to the *primary* complexity in the complexity triad mentioned in the introduction.
(ii) Responses by learners to questions asking them to describe a complex system S. These correspond to the *tertiary* complexity in the complexity triad.

Measuring the distance between the two descriptions can be considered as an approximation of the cognitive reduction of the complexity of system S: the smaller the distance, the more effective the cognitive reduction.

Alert readers will have noticed that a component of the complexity triad is missing: (ii) The *secondary* complexity, that of the mediating artefact, the userly text.

The learning progression framework is media agnostic. It is not interested in the media specificity of the learning materials or methods, and does not discuss whether the media used have anything to do with how complexity is being represented or understood. But the mediatic complexity of artefacts is significant. Interactive Digital Narrative artefacts have not yet been studied to the extent that we possess a wealth of empirical evidence to support any theory about how they might function, or a validated methodology according to which such evidence might be collected and assessed so that it can then be used to inform theory and even provide design guidelines.

While it allows for a comparison primary and tertiary complexity and thus for a measurement of learning outcomes, the original framework cannot provide us with insight into how this evident effectiveness is scaffolded by mediating artefacts. In the next section we will discuss the Userly Text model, how it addresses the mediation and scaffolding of complexity, and how this leads us to extend the framework.

# 3 Narrative Userly Texts for Complexity

## 3.1 The Userly Text Model

To understand how digital artefacts can function as complex semiotic scaffolds, Knoller [10] has suggested "an understanding of their textuality that incorporates not just the way they organize information but also the way they structure the processes of reception". The term *userly text*, is meant "to connote Roland Barthes's distinction in S/Z between readerly and writerly texts" (pp. 106–7). Barthes's writerly texts differ from readerly texts in that they require cognitive effort [20]. *Userly* texts require not merely mental-cognitive but also embodied-cognitive engagement – *userly performance*. In addition, "a userly text is any object that can be used" [10], and thus the term is not necessarily specific to narrative artefacts but to any form of interactive storytelling that uses the digital medium.

The *userly text* model distinguishes between two constructs: the *encoded storyworld* and the *interaction model*. Userly performance potentially entails a hermeneutic (interpretive) engagement with both, through proceduralised participation, which is structured by the userly text, implemented as a computer system "in which the perception of the content and point of the work is premised on the simultaneous reflexive perception of the user's (embodied) activity" [10].

**The Encoded Storyworld.** This construct has three levels of abstraction: (1) The most basic elements are the units of diegetic materials (locations, agents, and events) and form (units of media, either remediated assets such as media files or digitally native units of code). (2) A middle level establishes Discourse Relations between elements: causality, temporal order, spatial location, formal relations such as symmetry, colour or rhyming, semantic relations, statistical pattern matching and so on. (3) Discursive strategies build on the relations of the second level. The *narrative* strategy, which emphasises causal and spatiotemporal relations between events involving agents in locations, is one possibility, but other storytelling strategies are available. In film, for example, materials may be organised along the linear temporal dimension according to the discursive strategy of narrative form (establishing relations of space, time, and causality), or thematically, or alphabetically, or according to formal-abstract qualities such as rhythm and composition, or to construct a rhetorical argument [21].

**The Interaction Model.** The second construct manifests as the hardware user-input and user-output components of the system, as well as software driving the hardware and interpreting its operations to produce affordances for interaction, and software that models the user(s) and interpreting their operation, and thus translating userly performance to encoded-storyworld terms. The authoring of an interactive digital storytelling experience also entails the authoring of the interaction model. The interface, which mediates the semiotic and affective feedback loops between the encoded storyworld and the user's body-mind, is very much part of the userly text. The creator of such an experience is authoring a complex system of communicative exchanges. Authoring an interaction model entails – even if implicitly - a choice of hardware platform that determines which information can be communicated between the human system (and which parts of the human body are treated as the human system's interface) and the computer system(s).

Authoring the interaction model also entails structuring the software procedures that model the possibilities of interaction that define and constrain the potentials of userly performance.

## 3.2 Userly Performance and Complexity: Skill, Repetition, and the Hermeneutic Spiral

Userly performance is the specific mode of reception that userly texts afford. It is this procedural, embodied-cognitive activity that can activate the potential of narrative userly texts to offer scaffolding for cognitively reducing complexity.

The term userly *performance* welds together senses of the performative or performantial [22] in both the performing arts and sociology. Artistic performance connotes the execution of a score or a script, and it requires skill, which is developed through repetition. The skill involved in userly performance is not merely sensorimotor in nature, but can also be hermeneutic, connoting the artistic sense of performance as interpretation (which can also develop further into expressive interpretation).

Narrative userly texts can be structured to encourage replay, and thus a *hermeneutic spiral*: a process of gradually accumulated double-interpretation, in which the interactor needs to make sense both of the encoded storyworld and of the interaction model, as well as of both the current plot they are performing and the relation of this plot-performance to other plot-performances. Whereas traditional narratology speaks of a narrative circle [23], and traditional hermeneutics of a hermeneutic circle [24] moving between parts and the whole text, the metaphor of the spiral reflects the fact that userly texts appear as materially different every time they are "read" (in the semiotic sense, which is extended here to refer to the performance of interactive reception). As has also been theorised in Koenitz's SPP model [25], plots, as well their performances, exist in the system as potentials, requiring instantiation contingent on input from a user and further procedural processing, enacting a variability of performed instantiations.[1] This flexible variability of outputs is constitutive of the userly text. A hermeneutic spiral might allow interpretation to connect the different performances and outputs together into a meaningful subjective, enactive representation of systemic complexity.

**First- and Second-Order Subject Positions: Observation vs. Enaction.** The distinction between the encoded storyworld and the interaction model foregrounds a distinction within narrative userly texts for complexity between first-order and second-order complex representations of complex systems, which entail different subject positions.

---

[1] The encoded storyworld is similar to Koenitz' *protostory* [25], and differs in its internal abstractions, since the userly text model attempts to also account, through the added strategic abstraction level, for the instantiation of non-narrative discursive strategies and for the potential of a text to shift between different discursive strategies (for example, from chronological recitation to stream of consciousness) in response to patterns of user input. This aspect is particularly relevant for complexity representation in a post-PC landscape because it allows for a description of how different interaction models might be coupled with one encoded storyworld, not just within a single artefact (shifting strategies, but now of interaction), but also across distinct artefacts (as could be the case in a transmedial implementation).

The distinction between first-order and second-order systems emerged in cybernetics when Heinz von Foerster needed to extend cybernetic language from its engineering and natural-scientific origins to account for reflexivity [26], and thus for cognition. In the words of organisational scientist Christophe Bredillet [27], "[C]omplexity is not only an intrinsic characteristic of a system under inquiry. It is also a matter of 'naming', of the way we think about it" and it involves a shift "from an observer 'independent' to an observer 'dependent' mode of inquiry, from first-order to second-order complexity" (p. 74). Anthony Giddens, although not drawing upon complex-theoretical neo-cybernetics, offers quite a homologous description of what social scientific theory does [28]: whereas in the natural sciences, "scientists construct theories about a 'given' world... the social sciences operate within a double hermeneutic[2], involving two-way ties with the actions and institutions they choose to study" (pp. 30–31). Arguing for a narrative approach to organisational complexity, Tsoukas and Hatch [29] observe that "in narrative mode, the researcher making claims about systems is in full view – his/her goals and desires are reflected in his/her language. It is thus that second-order complexity is engaged – the complexity (subjectivity) of the researcher (i.e. narrator) attempting to understand complexity is revealed and made available for analysis" (p. 989).

Second-order complexity can be engaged also in userly performance. Since userly performance can become, with skill, a deliberate enactment guided by interpretation, the subject position of the interactor may, depending on the design of the interaction model, be constructed as a second-order position in relation to the (first-order complex) diegesis. The encoded storyworld can be regarded as a first-order cybernetic representation of a complex storyworld. The interaction model, which organises the process of interactive reception, then determines the second-order cybernetic subject position in relation to that first-order representation. It can position the interactor outside of the represented system, allowing them to function as an external *observer* with the agency to manipulate the system's representation, or switch between multiple perspectives, but without affecting the diegesis. Alternatively, it can position the interactor as a fully performative participating agent within the diegesis, whose interpretation of the system, when expressed through narratively *enactive* userly performance, can affect the first-order system, enacting their own reflexive subjectivity as a second-order complexity.

### 3.3 Extending Yoon et al.'s Framework to Narrative Userly Texts

Considering the above, the original framework proposed by Yoon et al. needs to be extended to account for some additional complexities that narrative userly texts can represent. The original framework, accounting for natural-scientific complex systems, addresses learners only as observers. How do we account for the enactive position and the second-order consequences made possible by narrative userly texts?

**Observation vs. Enactment: Declarative and Procedural Types of Knowledge.**
With enactment, narrative userly texts can afford additional modes of instruction, such as

---

[2] See [30, 31] for different takes on double hermeneutics in games and [32] for an extended discussion of double hermeneutic circles and spirals.

complex skills training, and represent complexities using additional types of knowledge [33]. The original framework considers only *declarative* knowledge, knowledge *about* a complex system, observational knowledge that can be described and reproduced using statements in language. Enactment, however, also concerns the *procedural* knowledge type, knowledge *how*, knowledge-in-use, which a learner may be able to successfully apply despite not being able to consciously verbalise.

The implications of the userly text model for extending the original framework are ultimately not limited to the description of the secondary complexity in the triad, that of the mediating userly text itself. Depending on the type of system and the mode of instruction, the description of the tertiary, subjective complexity might need to incorporate skills, understood as procedural knowledge. Likewise, the description of the primary complexity, the one to be reduced, requires an extension to describe the subjective and reflexive roles of agents within the complex system - particularly when interactively narrating complex systems involving human agents.

# 4   Conclusion: The Complexity Analysis Matrix

After examining the limitations of the original matrix and the requirements to extend it, we decided to split each of the six ideas between first-order complexity and second-order effects, both of which can then independently be described as completely clockwork, somewhat clockwork, somewhat complex or completely complex. This results in a double-matrix of 6 complexity dimensions (in total – 12 dimension) by 4 levels of complexity. The matrix can be used, if necessary, for each of the components of the complexity triad. It can initially be used to describe the primary complexity of the phenomenon. This may be useful as a benchmark to then critique or validate the quality of a userly text as a representation of the primary complexity[3]. Once that is established, it becomes possible to create a specific coding matrix for a narrative userly text to evaluate the tertiary, subjective complexity, and thus to measure its effectiveness in achieving a cognitive reduction of complexity. This can be achieved by finding correlations between (1) the design features that distinguish A/B versions, (2) the actual performance of the learner (measurable, for example by the system or through observation), (3) the subjective experience of the learner (using either objective measures or self-reporting), (4) the resulting declarative knowledge outcomes (using common testing methods), and (5) the procedural knowledge outcomes (measurable using a post-test separate simulation or role playing assessment task) – all of which can then be described in terms of both first- and second-order complexity understanding, on a 4-level scale.

**Acknowledgments.** This research was supported by a grant from the Dutch Creative Industries Fund.

---

[3] Visit [14] for further resources, including a filled-out matrix describing the serious training game Mission Zhobia [34].

# References

1. Rajeski, D., Chaplin, H., Olson, R.: Addressing complexity with playable models. Paper, Science and Technology Innovation Program. Wilson Center, Washington DC (2015)
2. Bruner, J.: The narrative construal of reality. In: Bruner, J. (ed.) The Culture of Education. Harvard University Press, Cambridge (1996)
3. Hayles, N. K.: Making the cut: the interplay of narrative and system, or what systems theory can't see. In: Cultural Critique, 30: The Politics of Systems and Environments, Part 1 (Spring 1995), pp. 71–100. University of Minnesota Press (1995)
4. Walsh, R.: Narrative theory at the limit. In: Middeke, M., Reinfandt, C. (eds.) Theory Matters: The Place of Theory in Literature and Cultural Studies, pp. 265–279. Palgrave-Macmillan, London (2016)
5. Ricoeur, P.: Time and Narrative. University of Chicago Press, Chicago (1984–1988)
6. Gottschal, J.: The Storytelling Animal. Houghton Miffling, Boston (2012)
7. Harari, Y.N.: Sapiens, a Brief History of Humankind. Harvill Secker, London (2014)
8. Herman, D.: Storytelling and the sciences of mind: cognitive narratology, discursive psychology, and narratives in face-to-face interaction. Narrative **15**(3), 306–334 (2007)
9. Bauman, R.: Story, Performance, and Event: Contextual Studies of Oral Narrative. Cambridge University Press, Cambridge (1986)
10. Knoller, N.: Complexity and the userly text. In: Grishakova, M., Poulaki, M. (eds.) Narrative Complexity: Cognition, Embodiment, Evolution, pp. 98–120. Nebraska University Press, Lincoln (2019)
11. Knoller, N.: The expressive space of IDS-as-art. In: Oyarzun, D., Peinado, F., Young, R.M., Elizalde, A., Méndez, G. (eds.) ICIDS 2012. LNCS, vol. 7648, pp. 30–41. Springer, Heidelberg (2012). https://doi.org/10.1007/978-3-642-34851-8_3
12. Murray, J.H.: Inventing the Medium. MIT Press, Cambridge and London (2012)
13. INDCOR – COST Action CA18230 – Interactive Narrative Design for Complexity Representations. https://www.indcor.eu. Accessed 15 Oct 2021
14. Mission Zhobia: Validating a Narrative Game for Complexity. https://www.userly.tech/research/zhobia/. Accessed 5 Oct 2020
15. Knoller, N.: The complexity triad and two+ systemic models of IDS/N (2020). https://doi.org/10.13140/RG.2.2.14721.58729. Accessed 07 July 2021
16. Gee, J.P.: What Video Games Have to Teach Us About Literacy and Learning. Palgrave Macmillan, New York (2003)
17. van't Riet, J., Meeuwes, A.C., van der Voorden, L., Jansz, J.: Investigating the effects of a persuasive digital game on immersion, identification, and willingness to help. Basic Appl. Soc. Psychol. **40**(4), 180–194 (2018)
18. Yoon, S.A., Goh, S.-E., Yang, Z.: Toward a learning progression of complex systems understanding. Complicity: Int. J. Complexity Educ. **16**(1), 1–19 (2019)
19. Yoon, S.A.: An evolutionary approach to harnessing complex systems thinking in the science and technology classroom. Int. J. Sci. Educ. **30**(1), 1–32 (2008)
20. Barthes, R.: S/Z. Hill and Wang, New York (1974)
21. Bordwell, D., Thompson, K.: Film Art: and Introduction, 5th edn. McGraw-Hill, New York (1997)
22. Ryan, M.L.: Multivariate narrative. In: Schreibman, S., Siemens, R., Unsworth, J (eds.) A Companion to Digital Humanities. Blackwell, Oxford (2004). http://www.digitalhumanities.org/companion/. Accessed 30 July 2021
23. Bal, M.: Narratology, 2nd edn. University of Toronto Press, Toronto, Buffalo and London (2004)
24. Gadamer, H.G.: Truth and Method. Crossroads, New York (1985)

25. Koenitz, H.: Towards a specific theory of interactive digital narrative. In: Koenitz, H., Ferri, G., Hahr, M., Sezen, D., Sezen, T.İ. (eds.) Interactive Digital Narrative - History, Theory and Practice, pp. 91–105. Routledge, New York and London (2015)
26. Clarke, B.: Heinz von Foerster's demons - the emergence of second-order systems theory. In: Clarke, B., Hansen, M.B.N. (eds.) Emergence and Embodiment: New Essays on Second-Order Systems Theory, pp. 34–61. Duke University Press, Durham and London (2009)
27. Bredillet, C.: A discourse on the non-method. In: Drouin, N., Muller, R., Sankaran, S. (eds.) Novel Approaches to Organizational Project Management Research: Translational and Transformational [Volume 29: Advances in Organization Studies], pp. 56–94, Copenhagen Business School (2013)
28. Giddens, A.: Social Theory and Modern Sociology. Stanford University Press, Stanford (1987)
29. Tsoukas, H., Hatch, M.J.: Complex thinking, complex practice: the case for a narrative approach to organizational complexity. Hum. Relat. **54**(8), 979–1013 (2001)
30. Karhulahti, V. M.: Double fine adventure and the double hermeneutic videogame. In: Fun and Games' 2012, Toulouse, France—4–6 September 2012, pp. 19–26. ACM (2012)
31. Roth, C., van Nuenen, T., Koenitz, H.: Ludonarrative hermeneutics: *a way out* and the narrative paradox. In: Rouse, R., Koenitz, H., Haahr, M. (eds.) ICIDS 2018. LNCS, vol. 11318, pp. 93–106. Springer, Cham (2018). https://doi.org/10.1007/978-3-030-04028-4_7
32. Knoller, N.: How hermeneutic spirals may reduce complexity to narrative schemata - expanding on "complexity and the userly text" (2021). https://hal.archives-ouvertes.fr/hal-03254233. Accessed 15 Oct 2021
33. de Jong, T., Fergusson-Hessler, M.G.M: Types and qualities of knowledge. Educ. Psychol. **31**(2), 105–113 (1996)
34. &Ranj: Mission Zhobia - Winning the Peace [online game]. PeaceNexus (2017)

# Interactive Digital Narratives (IDN) as Representations of Complexity: Lineage, Opportunities and Future Work

Hartmut Koenitz[1]([✉]) [iD], Jonathan Barbara[2] [iD], and Mirjam Palosaari Eladhari[3] [iD]

[1] Södertörn University, Huddinge, Sweden
hartmut.koenitz@sh.se
[2] Saint Martin's Institute of Higher Education, Hamrun, Malta
jbarbara@stmartins.edu
[3] Stockholm University, Stockholm, Sweden
mirjam@dsv.su.se

**Abstract.** In this overview paper, we consider interactive digital narratives (IDN) as a means to represent and enable understanding of complex topics both at the public level (e.g. global warming, the COVID-19 pandemic, migration, or e-mobility) and at the personal level (trauma and other mental health issues, interpersonal relationships). We discuss scholarly approaches to complexity, limitations of traditional media to represent complex issues, and describe the potential of IDN in this regard and what aspects need further work in research and beyond, which serve as the starting point for the EU COST action INDCOR.

**Keywords:** Representation of complexity · Interactive Digital Narratives (IDN) · Journalism · SPP model · IDN design · Education · Evaluation · Business models

## 1 Introduction

Interactive digital narratives (IDN) have advantages in representing complexity in comparison to traditional, fixed media due to the specific affordances of the digital medium as defined by Janet Murray (procedural, participatory, spatial, encyclopedic) [1]. This means that IDN can use the ability of the computer to hold practically limitless amounts of data while enabling audiences as participants to influence the progression and outcome of narrative experiences. These interactors [1] can see the effects of decisions and revisit them in replay, they can choose between different viewpoints, and in principle even add their own perspectives and discuss their insights with others, all within the same IDN artifact. Taken together, these aspects describe the potential of IDN for an enhanced understanding of complex issues. However, more work is needed to investigate how exactly audiences gain an enhanced understanding through the experience of IDN artifacts. This means to conceptualize complexity, to consider design approaches, to develop evaluation methods and investigate the best application of such works in order

© Springer Nature Switzerland AG 2021
A. Mitchell and M. Vosmeer (Eds.): ICIDS 2021, LNCS 13138, pp. 488–498, 2021.
https://doi.org/10.1007/978-3-030-92300-6_49

to have societal impact. This is the interdisciplinary endeavor of the COST Action IND-COR[1]. In this overview paper, we will focus on conceptual aspects, describe the history of complexity and its representations, the need for new narratives, provide a conceptual framing and suggest focal points for future work.

## 2    Lineage – Complexity in Scholarly Enquiry

Complexity as a concern for scholarly enquiry emerged in the natural sciences from the realization that the Newtonian, mechanistic way of considering the universe is not sufficient to explain the complex world around us - an insight reflected at least since Einstein's Relativity theory [2], further developed in quantum physics (most famously explained in Schrödinger's 'cat' thought experiment [3]), and more generally applied in approaches such as cybernetics [4, 5], system theory [6–8] and chaos theory [9–11]. An interactive map of complexity sciences is provided by Castellani [12]. What these perspectives share is the insight that many phenomena cannot be explained with simple linear one-to-one mappings of cause and effect, that combinatorics, unpredictability and randomness are important factors. This understanding is at the heart of research on complexity. Accordingly, [13] defines complexity as resulting "from the inter-relationship, inter-action and inter-connectivity of elements within a system and between a system and its environment" (p. 1). In addition, the behavior across time of such systems [14] is a crucial aspect when the focus is on systemic change.

Complexity as an academic field is an umbrella term for a number of different perspectives and approaches, e.g. in the guise of complexity sciences concerned with problems in Physics and other natural sciences [14, 15] or as complexity theory (for an overview see [16]). One exemplar approach in complexity theory resulted from a multi-disciplinary collaboration pursuing lines of enquiry characterized by emergent complex behaviors of multi-level systems [13]. Concrete applications of complexity sciences include weather forecasts [17], the analysis of ecological systems [18] and accident investigations [19]. Resilience theory in ecology is based on complexity science [20] while complexity science is being suggested as an alternative approach to traditional economics [21], especially for forecasting [22] as well as a crucial element in order to reach the goals of the UN 2030 Agenda [23].

However, the recognition of complexity is not limited to the natural sciences. Many developments in the 20th century in the social sciences can be understood similarly as ways to acknowledge and analyze complexity. In this vein we can for example understand approaches such as psychoanalysis [24], feminism [25], system theory applied to society [26], queer theory [27], critical race theory [28] and intersectionality [29]. The latter, a method of analysis that takes discrimination as a combination of multiple factors, including gender, race, age, class, sexuality, physical appearance, nationality and ability, is clearly an example of complexity - in this instance of the complex societal combinatorics behind oppression and discrimination. Earlier, the advent of psychoanalysis was predicated on the complex relationship between the conscious and the unconscious [30], while feminism [31] and queer theory [27] investigate the complexity of gender relations

---

[1] https://indcor.eu.

and gender roles [32, 33]. Critical race theory started with legal scholars investigating the complex relationship between discrimination and laws in the United States [28]. Concrete applications of these approaches are in national and internal policies and laws to support equality, diversity, and assure equity, but also in movements such as Black Lives Matter [34] and Fridays for Future [35]. Another important application is found in psychotherapy [36].

Equally, complexity is integral to many humanities approaches. For example, post-structuralism has left behind the fixed structural analysis of literary texts and other phenomena [37], while phenomenology [38] concerns itself with the relationship between body and mind, leading to recent discussions on embodiment [39]. Postmodernism [40] is the recognition that the unifying grand narratives of old (nation, religion, class etc.) no longer represent a complex reality [41]. These aspects are captured in concepts such as amalgam, dispositive and heterotopia. Complexity is thus an issue that all academic disciplines have been concerned with for a considerable time.

## 3 Depictions of Complexity

The arts were equally affected by the scientific developments at the turn of the last century, but also by societal changes due to increased industrialization, mass culture and world events such as both world wars, the Great Depression and the holocaust. Different art movements found new approaches to express the complexity of contemporary human experience. Examples in this vein include surrealism (meant to express the unconscious), gothic novels and magic realism (expressing the supernatural), abstract art and 'new music' (expressing sentiments rather than depicting objects) postmodern literature (expressing the multiplicity of meanings), the theatre of the absurd (expressing the complex relationship between cultural veneer and human nature) as well as participatory forms such as Happenings [42] and participatory theater which put the complex relationship between planned event and emerging participation front and center. Later examples include cybernetic art [43] and system art.

### 3.1 Reduction as Non-fiction Approach to Complexity

Non-fiction forms of expression have so far struggled to find ways to express complexity. Instead, documentary filmmaking and modern journalism established practices to improve the truthfulness and objectivity of reporting – for example, by clearly distinguishing opinion from "objective" reporting, by attempting to minimize the impact of the documentary filmmaker (cf. in the 'cinema verite' movement [44]) and by improving ways of verifying the depicted content through fact-checking. More recently, linked sources, multimedia content, infographics and interactive databases became standard. However, even with these additions, non-fiction forms are still focused on linear communication, on reducing the complexity so it can be expressed with the established means of the newspaper article and the TV broadcast. A concrete instance of this overarching issue is in what Widholm and Appelgren [45] have termed the "data journalism paradox", the difficulty of connecting the individual perspectives enabled by interactive forms of narratives with journalistic practices predicated on collective representations.

## 3.2 Representing Complexity in Postmodern Societies

In democratic societies, journalism and other forms of non-fiction communication (e.g. documentary films, textbooks) have a crucial role to help citizens understand the world around them and make informed decisions in their private lives and as political actors. Indeed, Habermas understood citizens as informed newspaper readers [46]. However, with the increasing complexity of many contemporary issues (e.g. economic globalization, global warming, migration, pandemics, terrorism), political decision making has equally become more complex and as part of this development, the fixed coordinate systems in the political sphere (left/right. conservative/progressive etc.) have become a more complex, dynamic space, in which novel parties emerge and old parties shift positions. In modern times, democracy was predicated on fixed ideological positions in competition with one another, yet in the contemporary postmodern world, more ideologically flexible approaches towards complex challenges have taken over.

This situation is a challenge to traditional forms of journalism with its dominant forms of the newspaper article and the TV broadcast. These fixed forms are structurally disadvantaged when it comes to representing the dynamic systems underlying complex issues. In other words: journalism still mostly relies on modern forms in a postmodern world. We can see Lyotard's insight of postmodernity as a "crisis of representation" [40] in this way, as a warning about the limits of modernist representation. Certainly, truth and objective reporting remain important values, but when there are no longer a limited number of ideologically delimited 'truths', but instead a complex space of possible solutions, then we need new ways to report, inform, and educate with the ultimate aim to establish and support systemic thinking as a standard way to approach issues as Rejeski et al. remind us in a research report for the Wilson center [47].

Systemic thinking, the ability to understand the dynamic nature of many contemporary phenomena, is necessary to understand both the challenges and the possible approaches towards complex issues. So far however, systemic thinking has only taken a limited hold in the representation of politics, both from political actors and from journalists. One aspect of this crisis is a disconnect between actual political decision making and an often outdated, simplistic ideological frame narrative, in which the same political actors are caught in. Germany's chancellor Angela Merkel is a relevant example, as a pragmatic, contemporary political actor chained to the outdated ideological framing of her conservative CDU party, which forced her to agree to 20 laws restricting asylum in Germany after her famous decision to let one million refugees into the country in 2015. In the terms of our discussion, while Merkel was able to calm down her party and conservative voter base after her decision[2], she was unable to create a new, complex narrative in order to supersede the established, conservative anti-migrant stance of her party. In the absence of successful strategies for representations of complexity, purveyors of simplistic narratives feed many people's longing for the simple, modernist narratives of old, as we had to learn through the successes of the Brexit campaign, Donald Trump's 2016 election win as well as the populist parties in many western democracies.

The search for representations of complexity that educate citizens in systemic thinking and thus enable understanding of complex topics is a crucial contribution to

---

[2] https://qz.com/1076820/german-election-how-angela-merkel-took-in-one-million-refugees-and-avoided-a-populist-upset/.

strengthen democracy. Systemic thinking has to become the norm and unduly simplistic narratives have to be branded as inadequate and thus problematic, regardless from which ideological side they come from.

## 4   New Narratives for Complexity

The challenge of representing complexity [48] has seen the use of narrative, for example to represent organization studies [49], and complex urban spaces [50]. However, whenever we use narrative to represent complexity, we need to be aware of the limitations of traditional fixed forms in this regard. In perspectives influenced by literary theory, there is a prevailing misunderstanding of the dynamic nature of narrative as confined to reception. Scholars rooted in this school of thinking (as well as many of the practitioners they have trained) often ignore the fact that with IDN we have dynamic artifacts as well as dynamic reception. The latter is certainly also complex, and interacts with the dynamic artifact, but the reader/viewer of fixed narrative objects like the novel or the movie can only speculate about the progression and outcome, they cannot influence them and make plans, execute them and see the results of this action. Planning, execution and resulting consequences as well as replay is what sets IDN apart from fixed narratives and these qualities are crucial for enabling an understanding of the dynamic nature of complex issues. Indeed, scholars working on complexity have pointed out that "complexity needs new narratives" [47]. The characteristics of IDN match these requirements, enabling multiple perspectives, continuous feedback, choices and consequences, emergence, and replay. What IDN offers are representations of complex dynamic systems combined with a central human form of communication - narrative.

### 4.1   Understanding IDN: The SPP Model

To understand the new narratives of IDN, a model is necessary that emphasizes the specificity of interactive narratives. Koenitz' SPP model (system, process, product) [51] does that, understanding a dynamic system as the central element, and describing the interactive process which results in instantiated narrative products. The SPP model includes the notion of a protostory - a space of potential narratives combining fixed and dynamic elements. This kind of narrative design can feature complexity in the form of an underlying network of rules and contrasting claims, implementing for example the initial conditions and backstories in cultural heritage [52], or the rules of a particular political system. The engagement of the interactor with the dynamic system of the protostory in the process moves the narrative forward, facilitating the personal interpretation of the narrative experience. The SPP model has been related to three separate aspects of complexity [53], that of environment (the real-world complexity implemented in the protostory), of representation (the complexity of the artifact) and of message (the complexity of interpretation and interactors' actions resulting in recorded playthroughs and retellings [54]) and is a basis of INDCOR's effort in creating a shared vocabulary [53]. IDN afford multilinear and multi-perspective narratives (including conflicting views) that trigger choices and evoke audience's reflections. through their 'double hermeneutic' of interpreting both the current narrative trace and their opportunities for interaction [55, 56]. The increase in comprehension during this activity can be described as a transformation in the interactor [1] as they become aware of alternatives, of choices not taken, even during a single playthrough experience and even more so through replay [57].

## 4.2 Example IDN Complexity Applications

A range of applications demonstrate the potential for IDN as representations of complexity on the societal as well as personal levels. For example, the complex issue of Somali piracy is explored in the interactive documentary *The Last Hijack Interactive* [58] where the interactor can explore different perspectives surrounding a particular hijacking incident. Interviews with the victims, perpetrators and their respective lawyers shed light on what leads to such behavior. The complex economy of the illegal drug trade in the Netherlands is the subject of another IDN called *The Industry* [59], Here, interactors explore what drug-related activities happened around their own zip code, learn about the shallow organization structure and follow audio interviews with different players in the industry, virtually visiting them in their own offices, restaurants, homes, etc. Complexity also features in many narrative-focused video games. For example, *Papers, Please* [60] explores the conditions of life in totalitarian regimes. Here, the interactor is in the role of an involuntary border control officer, in charge of admitting or rejecting visitors, under pressure of constantly changing instructions and retributions in case of errors, responsible for their family's survival and also facing the fact that some visitors are actual terrorists who will commit murders if let in. Likewise, *The Sims* [61] brings to the fore aspects of the complexity of life in late capitalism, including earning a living, reaching life objectives, finding a partner and raising a family. The interactive drama *Façade* [62] explores the complexity of a relationship at the breaking point, essentially putting the interactor into the role of a therapist, while *PromWeek* [63] explores the complex social dynamics surrounding a high school prom.

## 5   The Problem Space of Complexity and IDN

So far, we have established IDN as a means to represent complexity and described several examples. However, in order to make IDN a standard feature of democratic discourse and education, more work is needed. When it comes to implementing IDNs for public representations of complexity, additional factors need to be taken into account, including established forms of media production and dissemination, as well as education and design approaches. In addition to understanding IDN conceptually, we need to engage with the questions of creation and distribution, as well as how to educate creators and audiences about IDN and where to place it in the existing ecology of media forms. The following diagram (Fig. 1) is an attempt to represent this problem space and the following aspects:

1.  There are scientific ways to handle complexity, but these need to be translated to make them understandable to general audiences.
2.  IDN has the potential to do that, once we understand its specific affordances, in particular its ability to represent dynamic systems
3.  In order to use IDN as a tool in society to understand complexity, audience education is needed

4. For journalism to seriously pick up IDN, journalists need training in the new form, while new workflows as well as business models need to be established
5. Research has an important role in supporting the development and adoption of IDN.

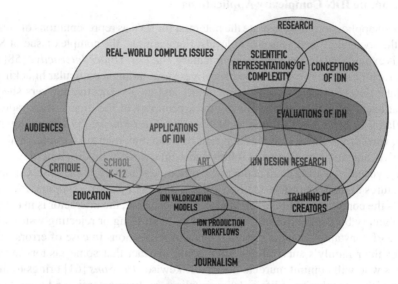

**Fig. 1.** The problem space of IDN and complexity

The problem space highlights aspects that need scholarly attention, in particular the design of IDNs (approach, methods and building blocks), evaluation to verify effectiveness, professional training of creators as well as the education of both adult audiences as well as school-age children.

In terms of design, an adequate paradigm is system building [64], improving upon 'Newtonian mechanics' in game design, as exemplified in the popular MDA model (mechanics, dynamics, aesthetics) [65] as well as Brenda Romero's pronouncement of the mechanics as the message [66]. Conversely, narrative design has often been misunderstood in a mechanical way, as the combination of fixed narrative forms with interactivity (i.e. cinematic cutscenes in games). With the dynamic systems of IDN, new challenges arise, as the creator is now the designer of a procedural and participatory system. IDN design thus means to accommodate audiences' new role as interactors as well as the unpredictability that is introduced by unexpected combinatorics and interactors' behavior [67]. In addition, IDN design means to consider the different aspects of complexity as shown in Fig. 1. The development of specific evaluation methods to verify the effectiveness of IDN complexity designs (e.g. the further development of Roth's toolbox [68]) is an important aspect of IDN design research.

The implementation of a system building paradigm in actual production, especially when it comes to integrating into the workflows of journalism organizations pose considerable challenges. Some steps in this regard have been taken, for example, in the

JOLT project[3] which investigated the combination of game design and journalism and collected resources on the topic. Of particular concern in this regard is the tendency documented in the project to see journalistic 'interactives' mostly as add-ons to 'normal journalistic activity', as a means to drive subscribers to newspapers' websites. Instead, IDN design needs to become a standard journalistic activity which requires (re-)training of journalists as IDN system builders. Else, there is a danger that interactive forms are relegated to a position of cheap gimmick, a possible development Bogost et al. have been warning about for newsgames [69] (also see [70]). In this regard IDN, with its focus on narrative, has the potential to bridge the divide between games and traditional news stories. Furthermore, as a multi-linear and multivariate form, IDN can also address shortcomings of newsgames, in particular a forced "quick closure and a problematic binary (good versus bad behavior)" [71] as well as a tendency of 'wanting to win'. Instead, IDN can focus on complexity. As there is also an ethical dimension in terms of representing complexity as a contribution for public discourse, the development of a code of conduct, similar to the ones for journalism, is an important topic for further investigation. Another necessary aspect is the consideration of how the production of IDN complexity products will be financed - possible solutions include public funding as a service akin to public broadcasting, but also business models similar to the ones used by commercial video games or commercial newspapers. Finally, the education of audiences about IDN is an area in need of attention. IDN can be used in schools to teach about complex subjects, but there is also the need for high-profile critique (similar to film critics) educating adult audiences about IDN.

# 6 Conclusion

In this paper, we traced the lineage of complexity and discussed the need for complexity representations in democratic societies. Then, we explained the potential of IDN in representing complexity, applying the SPP model and its emphasis on dynamic systems and interactive processes. After describing a range of examples, we discuss the problem space of IDN and complexity, identifying areas for future work in order to realize the potential of IDN as a means to help citizens in understanding the many complex issues we are faced with - from global warming to issues of personal mental health.

**Acknowledgments.** The authors acknowledge the support of the EU COST Association in the form of the COST Action 18230 INDCOR (Interactive Narrative Design for COmplexity Representations). https://indcor.eu.

# References

1. Murray, J.H.: Hamlet on the Holodeck: the Future of Narrative in Cyberspace. Free Press, New York (1997)
2. Einstein, A.: Die Grundlage der allgemeinen relativitätstheorie. Analen Phys. **49**, 769–822 (1916)

---

[3] https://edspace.american.edu/jolt/.

3. Schrödinger, E.: Die Gegenwärtige situation in der quantenmechanik. Die Naturwissenschaften **48**, 807–812 (1935)
4. Wiener, N.: Cybernetics or Control and Communication in the Animal and the Machine. MIT Press, Cambridge (1948)
5. van Dijkum, C.: From cybernetics to the science of complexity. Kybernetes (1997)
6. Bertalanffy, L.V.: Zu einer allgemeinen systemlehre. Blätter deutsche Philos. **3**, 139–164 (1945)
7. Bertalanffy, L.V.: General System Theory. George Braziller, New York (1969)
8. Walby, S.: Complexity theory, systems theory, and multiple intersecting social inequalities. Philos. Soc. Sci. **37**, 449–470 (2007)
9. Lorenz, E.N.: Deterministic nonperiodic flow. J. Atmos. Sci. **20**, 130–141 (1963)
10. Cambel, A.B.: Applied Chaos Theory: A Paradigm for Complexity. Elsevier, Amsterdam (1993)
11. Alligood, K.T., Sauer, T.D., Yorke, J.A., Crawford, J.D.: Chaos: an introduction to dynamical systems. Phys. Today **50**, 67 (1997)
12. Castellani, B.: Map of the Complexity Sciences, pp. 928–940. Art and Science Factory (2018)
13. Chan, S.: Complex adaptive systems. Presented at the ESD. 83 Research Seminar in Engineering Systems (2001)
14. Mathews, K.M., White, M.C., Long, R.G.: Why study the complexity sciences in the social sciences? Hum. Relat. **52**, 439–462 (1999)
15. Mitleton-Kelly, E., Land, F.: Complexity \& information systems. Blackwell Encycl. Manag. **11**, 41 (2004)
16. Turner, J.R., Baker, R.M.: Complexity theory: an overview with potential applications for the social sciences. Systems **7**, 4 (2019)
17. Mihailović, D.T., Mimić, G., Arsenić, I.: Climate predictions: The chaos and complexity in climate models. Adv. Meteorol. **2014** (2014)
18. Biggs, R., de Vos, A., Preiser, R., Clements, H., Maciejewski, K., Schlüter, M.: The Routledge Handbook of Research Methods for Social-Ecological Systems. Taylor \& Francis (2021)
19. Dekker, S., Cilliers, P., Hofmeyr, J.-H.: The complexity of failure: implications of complexity theory for safety investigations. Saf. Sci. **49**, 939–945 (2011)
20. Folkeis, C.: How much disturbance can a system withstand? With roots in ecology and complexity science, resilience theory offers new ways to turn crises into catalysts for innovation. SEED Global Reset (2010)
21. Chen, P.: From complexity science to complexity economics. In: Alternative Approaches to Economic Theory, pp. 19–55. Routledge (2019)
22. Speigel, I.: Adopting and improving a new forecasting paradigm. Intelligence and National Security. 1–17 (2021)
23. Gentili, P.L.: Why is Complexity Science valuable for reaching the goals of the UN 2030 Agenda? Rendiconti Lincei. Sci. Fisiche Nat. **32**(1), 117–134 (2021). https://doi.org/10.1007/s12210-020-00972-0
24. Freud, S.: Das Ich und das Es. Internationaler Psycho-analytischer Verlag (1923)
25. Friedan, B.: The Feminine Mystique. W. W. Norton (1963)
26. Luhmann, N.: Soziale Systeme: Grundriss einer allgemeinen Theorie. Suhrkamp (1984)
27. Watson, K.: Queer theory. Group Anal. **38**, 67–81 (2005)
28. Delgado, R., Stefancic, J.: Critical Race Theory. New York University Press (2017)
29. Crenshaw, K.: On Intersectionality. New Press (2012)
30. Bateman, A., Holmes, J.: Introduction to Psychoanalysis: Contemporary Theory and Practice. Routledge, London (2002)
31. Allen, K.R., Jaramillo-Sierra, A.L.: Feminist theory and research on family relationships: pluralism and complexity. Sex Roles **73**, 93–99 (2015)

32. Haraway, D.: Situated knowledges: the science question in feminism and the privilege of partial perspective. Fem. Stud. **14**, 575 (1988)
33. Butler, J.: Gender Trouble. Routledge, London, New York (1999)
34. Chase, G.: The early history of the black lives matter movement, and the implications thereof. Nev. LJ **18**, 1091 (2017)
35. Spannring, R., Hawke, S.: Anthropocene challenges for youth research: understanding agency and change through complex, adaptive systems. J. Youth Stud., 1–17 (2021). https://doi.org/10.1080/13676261.2021.1929886
36. Coburn, W.J.: Attitudes in psychoanalytic complexity: an alternative to postmodernism in psychoanalysis. In: Beyond Postmodernism, pp. 195–212. Routledge (2013)
37. Dillon, M.: Poststructuralism, complexity and poetics. Theory Cult. Soc. **17**, 1–26 (2000)
38. Husserl, E.: The Idea of Phenomenology. Springer, Heidelberg (1964)
39. Csordas, T.J.: Embodiment and cultural phenomenology. na (1999)
40. Lyotard, J.-F.: The Postmodern Condition. University of Minnesota Press, Minneapolis (1984)
41. Cilliers, P.: Problems with representation. In: Complexity and Postmodernism, pp. 68–98. Routledge (2002)
42. Kaprow, A.: "Happenings" in the New York scene. In: The New Media Reader, pp. 1–6. MIT Press (2003)
43. Ascott, R.: The cybernetic stance: my process and purpose. Leonardo **1**, 105 (1968)
44. Mamber, S.: Cinema Verite in America: Studies in Uncontrolled Documentary. Lightning Source (1974)
45. Widholm, A., Appelgren, E.: A softer kind of hard news? Data journalism and the digital renewal of public service news in Sweden. New Media Soc. 1461444820975411 (2020)
46. Habermas, J., Lennox, S., Lennox, F.: The public sphere: an encyclopedia article (1964). New German Critique 49–55 (1974)
47. Rejeski, D., Chaplin, H., Olson, R.: Addressing Complexity with Playable Models. Wilson Center (2015)
48. Rosen, R.: On complex systems. Eur. J. Oper. Res. **30**, 129–134 (1987)
49. Luhman, J.T., Boje, D.M.: What is complexity science? A possible answer from narrative research. Emerg. J. Complexity Issues Organ. Manag. **3**, 158–168 (2001)
50. Uprichard, E., Byrne, D.: Representing complex places: a narrative approach. Environ. Plan A **38**, 665–676 (2006)
51. Koenitz, H.: Towards a specific theory of interactive digital narrative. In: Interactive Digital Narrative: History, Theory, and Practice. New York (2015)
52. Vanoverschelde, F.: No Story without a backstory: the role and importance of the backstory in an augmented reality application for cultural heritage. Presented at the Proceedings of the 8th International Workshop on Narrative and Hypertext (2019)
53. Koenitz, H., Eladhari, M.P., Louchart, S., Nack, F.: INDCOR white paper 1: a shared vocabulary for IDN (Interactive Digital Narratives) (2020)
54. Eladhari, M.P.: Re-tellings: the fourth layer of narrative as an instrument for critique. In: Rouse, R., Koenitz, H., Haahr, M. (eds.) ICIDS 2018. LNCS, vol. 11318, pp. 65–78. Springer, Cham (2018). https://doi.org/10.1007/978-3-030-04028-4_5
55. Karhulahti, V.-M.: Double fine adventure and the double hermeneutic videogame. Presented at the Foundations of Digital Games, New York, New York, USA (2012)
56. Roth, C., van Nuenen, T., Koenitz, H.: Ludonarrative hermeneutics: a way out and the narrative paradox. In: Rouse, R., Koenitz, H., Haahr, M. (eds.) ICIDS 2018. LNCS, vol. 11318, pp. 93–106. Springer, Cham (2018). https://doi.org/10.1007/978-3-030-04028-4_7
57. Mateas, M.: A preliminary poetics for interactive drama and games. Digit. Creat. **12**, 140–152 (2001)
58. Duijn, M., Wolting, F.: Co-director documentary. In: Pallotta, T. (ed.) Co-Director Documentary: Last Hijack Interactive (2014)

59. Duijn, M.: The industry (2018). https://theindustryinteractive.com/
60. Pope, L.: Papers, Please (2013)
61. Wright, W.: The sims [video game] (2000)
62. Mateas, M., Stern, A.: Procedural authorship: a case-study of the interactive drama façade. Presented at the Digital Arts and Culture 2007 (2005)
63. McCoy, J., Treanor, M., Samuel, B., Mateas, M., Wardrip-Fruin, N.: Prom week: social physics as gameplay. ACM, Bordeaux (2011)
64. Koenitz, H., Eladhari, M.P.: Teaching game system building as an artistic practice. Presented at the Teaching Games: Pedagogical Approaches: DiGRA 2019 Pre-Conference Workshop (2019)
65. Hunicke, R., LeBlanc, M., Zubek, R.: MDA: a formal approach to game design and game research. Presented at the Proceedings of the AAAI Workshop on Challenges in Game AI (2004)
66. Brathwaite, B., Sharp, J.: The mechanic is the message: a post mortem in progress. In: Ethics and Game Design: Teaching Values Through Play, pp. 311–329. IGI Global (2010)
67. Bossomaier, T.R.J., Green, D.G.: Complex Systems. Cambridge University Press, Cambridge (2000)
68. Roth, C.: Experiencing Interactive Storytelling (2016). https://research.vu.nl/en/publications/experiencing-interactive-storytelling
69. Bogost, I., Ferrari, S., Schweizer, B.: Newsgames. Journalism at play (2010)
70. Treanor, M., Mateas, M.: Newsgames: procedural rhetoric meets political cartoons (2009)
71. Plewe, C., Fürsich, E.: Are newsgames better journalism? Empathy, information and representation in games on refugees and migrants. Journal. Stud. **19**, 2470–2487 (2018)

# Toward Narrative Instruments

Max Kreminski[✉] and Michael Mateas

University of California, Santa Cruz, Santa Cruz, CA 95060, USA
{mkremins,mmateas}@ucsc.edu

**Abstract.** Interactive narrative systems are often embedded in games: works of *playable media* that enable players to participate in or experience a story through game mechanics. But play practices directed toward the expressive creation of story seem to challenge a games-centric understanding of narrative play. Consequently, we propose that some interactive narrative systems can be better understood as a different form of playable media: *narrative instruments*, analogous to musical instruments in their provision of support for authorship-oriented forms of play.

**Keywords:** Emergent narrative · Retellings · IDN theory

## 1 Narrative Instruments

Recently, several parallel developments in the study of interactive emergent narrative (IEN) games have suggested that some players view these games primarily as expressive tools for the creation of new stories [15], rather than as devices for experiencing or participating in a partly pre-authored story or "multiform plot" [22, p. 347]. The study of retellings [7], or player-created stories about gameplay experiences, has highlighted play practices in which players make use of IEN games as tools for expressive story-making, while extensively embellishing the resulting stories by adding detail not modeled by the game itself [14, 21] or even ironically commenting on the flaws or limitations of the game as a storytelling tool within the resulting retellings [33]. Ryan's work on simulation-driven IEN [26] has drawn a distinction between emergent narrative (a particular telling or representation of a series of game events) and the raw narrative *material* produced by simulation directly, which is only transformed into narrative by a process of *curation*—often undertaken by the player. And several recent IEN play experiences [11–13, 29] have been explicitly designed with the goal of supporting player storytelling practices.

In light of these developments, new design perspectives may be warranted to help us create IEN play experiences that prioritize the use of IEN systems for player storytelling. To this end, we propose that some IEN systems may be better viewed not quite as narrative *games* but as another form of playable narrative media, namely as narrative *instruments*. Like musical instruments, narrative instruments require a player to operate them; afford certain expressive possibilities through their design while discouraging others; may be played more

© Springer Nature Switzerland AG 2021
A. Mitchell and M. Vosmeer (Eds.): ICIDS 2021, LNCS 13138, pp. 499–508, 2021.
https://doi.org/10.1007/978-3-030-92300-6_50

virtuosically by more practiced players; may be played solely for the player's own enjoyment, or for a wider audience; are often played as part of a larger ensemble, in concert with other instruments; and may be modified or creatively misused by their players to achieve novel or unexpected effects.

Why instruments? We take inspiration in the use of this analogy from several other scholars who have tried to characterize what makes instruments special— distinguishing them from tools on one side and from toys on the other. Writing in the context of creativity support tools [31], or computational tools intended to support human creative practices, Nakakoji [23] contends that some creativity support systems may be better characterized as instruments. For Nakakoji, a creativity support system may be more of an instrument than a tool if it is often used playfully and if its designers prioritize the creation of a particular user experience over maximal efficiency. Tanaka [34] further unpacks the distinction between instruments and tools, suggesting that musical instruments succeed not by maximizing the efficiency of musical creation, but by contributing a particular desirable "personality" or "voice" to the music they are used to create:

> The term tool implies that an apparatus takes on a specific task, utilitarian in nature, carried out in an efficient manner. A tool can be improved to be more efficient, can take on new features to help in realizing its task, and can even take on other, new tasks not part of the original design specification. In the ideal case, a tool expands the limits of what it can do. It should be easy to use, and be accessible to a wide range of naive users. Limitations or defaults are seen as aspects that can be improved upon.
> A musical instrument's raison-d'etre, on the other hand, is not at all utilitarian. It is not meant to carry out a single well defined task in the way that a tool is. Instead, a musical instrument often changes context, withstanding changes of musical style played on it while maintaining its identity. A tool gets better as it attains perfection in realizing its tasks. The evolution of an instrument is less driven by practical concerns, and is motivated instead by the quality of sound the instrument produces. In this regard, it is not so necessary for an instrument to be perfect as much as it is important for it to display distinguishing characteristics, or "personality". What might be considered imperfections or limitations from the perspective of tool design often contribute to a "voice" of a musical instrument.

This argument for instruments as succeeding or failing on the basis of the characteristic voice they provide may help to explain why games that exhibit strong, recurring narrative texture across multiple playthroughs—such as the recurring "gradual rise followed by sudden precipitous decline" arc of many *Dwarf Fortress* stories—do not disqualify these games from use by players as story-making tools. What might be a weakness from a perspective that privileges a tool's *generality*—the way that these stories bend characteristically toward disaster—may actually represent a key desirable attribute of *Dwarf Fortress* as an instrument. From the narrative instruments perspective, the perceptibility of an instrument's grain in the stories that it is used to create marks not a failure of generality, but a success of voice.

Moreover, Wardrip-Fruin has written extensively about the instrument metaphor in the context of what he calls *textual instruments* [36]: playable "systems for language to inhabit" that facilitate textual performance by a human operator, who uses these systems to arrange and rearrange text in expressive and playful ways.[1] Wardrip-Fruin finds it useful to distinguish instruments not just from games, but also from the less rules-oriented form of playable media known as toys. For Wardrip-Fruin, the key distinguishing feature of instruments is that they "seek a lyric engagement"—they invite expressive use, and are meant to be used for expression first and foremost. It is here that instruments cease to resemble toys, which might or might not be used for expressive purposes— whereas if you pick up an instrument, the odds are good that you have some sort of expressive use in mind.

For the remainder of this paper, we will position our definition of instruments between Tanaka's and Wardrip-Fruin's. We argue that both a characteristic voice and a primarily lyric mode of engagement are key distinguishing features of instruments as playable media. We do not intend to assert that narrative instruments must necessarily be used for live performance, nor do we intend to assert that narrative instrument play must be targeted at an audience other than the players themselves—indeed, musical instruments themselves need not be played in live performance or for an audience. However, we do hope that the term "instrument" carries some of the connotations of how musical instruments are used socially: for instance, that learning to play an instrument may take some time; that instrument-play may be a deeply skilled and socially valued activity; that instruments are often played alongside other instruments; and that instruments are often modified by their players with specific expressive goals in mind.

## 2    Case Studies

To explore the implications of treating IEN systems as narrative instruments, consider the following brief case studies of narrative instruments in action.

### 2.1    Bad News

*Bad News* [30] is a computationally supported immersive theater experience that involves two highly-trained human performers (an "actor" and a "wizard") and a third untrained participant. The participant is tasked with entering a fictional small American town generated by the Talk of the Town simulation engine [27], locating the next of kin of a simulated character who has recently died, and informing them of the bad news. As the participant makes their way

---

[1] Though the systems Wardrip-Fruin highlights here are *textual*, they are not *narrative*; therefore we depart from his term in attempting to characterize the class of instrumental playable systems that produce *narrative structure* as narrative, rather than textual, instruments.

through the simulated world, they may speak to any of the simulated characters they encounter; during a conversation with the participant, these characters are embodied by the actor, who improvises a personality and dialogue for each character based on the character's role and traits within the simulation. During conversation, the wizard provides the actor with a live feed of relevant information about the identity of the character they are playing and the state of the simulated storyworld—including the network of social relationships and the history of the town's development—with the goal of subtly directing the participant toward discovery of narratively charged situations currently active within the town.

The *Bad News* performers make use of at least three distinct narrative instruments: the Talk of the Town simulation, which is run at the start of a performance to generate the storyworld in which the performance will take place; the "wizard console", a command line-based sifting tool used to investigate the storyworld, operated backstage by the wizard during a performance; and the actor interface operated by the actor, which allows them to quickly access information about the character they are currently playing and chat with the wizard to request additional information as needed. These instruments were designed to be played in concert, and each has a crucial role in enabling *Bad News* to be performed.

The importance of the wizard in this performance context stems from the fact that leaving a simulation to run (regardless of the simulation's narrative potency) does not in and of itself produce compelling narrative directly. Instead, some agent—often a human, as in the case of *Bad News*—is required to sift through the storyworld state to surface and narrativize the interesting situations that emerge. Since improvisationally performing as a character based on a relatively limited amount of background information requires the actor's full attention, the wizard is needed to perform this narrativization function. This division of labor suggests that a wide variety of new narrative authorship play experiences may be enabled by a willingness to examine and divide up the tasks that existing tabletop roleplaying games (for instance) tend to bundle up within a single player role. Additionally, it is interesting to examine the *Bad News* performance team as something like a touring narrative band. Due to the high degree of skill involved in performing the actor and wizard roles, almost all past performances of *Bad News* have featured the same two highly-trained individuals (Ben Samuel and James Ryan) in the actor and wizard roles respectively. This performance crew has traveled the world to perform *Bad News* at a diverse array of venues, and they have become renowned, virtuosic operators of their narrative instruments in the process.

## 2.2   Dwarf Fortress

*Dwarf Fortress* [2] offers several distinct narrative instruments—namely the world simulation, Fortress Mode, and Adventurer Mode—packaged within a single piece of software. Each of these instruments presents the player with different story-making affordances: the world simulation can be run for variable lengths of time to produce worlds with different depths of backstory as narrative starting points, while the Fortress and Adventurer mode allow the player to take up different roles in guiding the narrative evolution of an already-generated world. The popular third-party tool Legends Viewer [16] is another narrative instrument with different affordances again, intended to be played in concert with the first three; some players use Legends Viewer to sift stories from worlds generated in a totally nonineractive context, while others use it to get additional perspective on a world in which they have actively interfered. Dwarf Grandpa [8] is a sort of narrative effects pedal for Legends Viewer: an add-on that shapes its affordances to aid in the creation of stories with a particular tone, centered on the doings of certain sorts of vampires. And of course, players who intend to construct retellings can also make use of conventional text, image, audio and video capture and editing tools to stitch their stories together. *Dwarf Fortress* has attracted a number of virtuosic retellers, many of whom employ elaborate assemblages of narrative instruments to do their work: Kruggsmash uses a wide variety of instruments (including mods, custom tilesets, drawing tools, and video editing software) to produce his video retellings [17]; Tim Denee used a different set of instruments to produce his *Dwarf Fortress* comics [5,6]; and the lengthy episodic multimedia *Dwarf Fortress* retelling *Matul Remrit* [32] was produced by a sort of four-person narrative jam band that made use of many different narrative instruments in concert to weave an elaborate story through text, screenshots, video, and audio.

## 2.3   Blaseball

*Blaseball* [35] is a live narrative idlegame driven by a simulation of a surrealist fantasy baseball league. Uncommonly for an emergent narrative game, *Blaseball* provides a single simulation instance that is shared between all players, rather than spinning up a new simulation instance for each game or playthrough. Every week of real time represents a single "season" of storyworld time, with a season consisting of approximately 1000 simulated baseball games between different pairs of teams. Characters in the storyworld are procedurally generated baseball players, frequently with humorous names (e.g., "Jessica Telephone", "Gerund Pantheocide"), and have a mix of visible and hidden numerical "stats" that run the gamut from the practical (e.g., "baserunning") to the absurd (e.g., "Shakespearianism"). The simulation juxtaposes typical baseball game events (like a simulated baseball player scoring a run or striking out) with much stranger events (such as players being incinerated by "rogue umpires", swapped to the opposing team mid-game due to "weather conditions", or trapped in giant peanut shells).

Additionally, members of the game's fan community are given the chance to earn virtual money by betting on the outcomes of simulated games, which they can then spend to increase the likelihood that their favored team will receive certain "blessings" at the start of the next season; to temporarily change the rules of baseball as they apply to specific simulated teams; or to pursue various kinds of collective community progression in the game's overarching metanarrative. The blessings and metanarrative options available in the end-of-season election, as well as some scripted metanarrative event sequences, are crafted in near-realtime by the game's developers, and influenced heavily by the stories that fans have woven around the various simulated characters. These user-created stories, meanwhile, often extrapolate dramatically from the information actually modeled in the simulated storyworld. Familial, romantic, friendship, rivalry, and other significant relationships between characters (for instance) make no appearance in the simulation mechanics, but have been documented in extensive and remarkably consistent detail by the fan community, for instance via the Players pages [3] on the fan-maintained Blaseball Wiki.

At the heart of this communal improvisatory process, the *Blaseball* simulation functions as the narrative equivalent of a programmable drum machine, providing a repetitive but time-varying narrative backbone that is occasionally adjusted by the game's developers as they introduce new systems and units of content to the ongoing simulation. The *Blaseball* fan community structures their narrative improvisations around this backbone, using it to achieve a degree of coordination between a large number of narrative co-constructors operating in a largely decentralized and bottom-up fashion. This coordination, while apparently successful overall, also has its limits; as the *Blaseball* fanbase has grown, some prominent *Blaseball* fans who have taken active roles in the communal construction of narrative have noted that the sheer number of co-authors has resulted in a diminished sense of individual ability to meaningfully contribute to the shared narrative consensus.[2] With too many improvisers in the same band, it becomes impossible to avoid accidentally contradicting another's improvisations, and the overall result begins to sound less like music and more like cacophony. Promoting the creation of a larger number of smaller bands, each with their own narrative drum machines, might be a design goal worth pursuing for narrative instrument designers going forward.

## 2.4   Tabletop Roleplaying Groups

Tabletop roleplaying groups are often skilled in the appropriation of systems as narrative instruments. Many groups are prone to modifying officially published rulesets and books of material through house-ruling; building up custom rulesets through bricolage, or accumulation of favorite rules, subsystems, and content from a variety of different roleplaying systems; and sometimes even designing their own systems to flesh out the aspects of the collaboratively constructed narrative that they would like to explore further. Additionally, they may make use of story-making games like *Microscope* [25], *The Quiet Year* [1], or the Engine of the Ages system in *The Book of Ages* [28] as worldbuilding tools in a larger story-making pipeline [9]; for instance, a tabletop roleplaying group in which one of the authors is a participant has made extensive use of these games to establish setting and background for later exploration via more conventional character-oriented roleplaying systems. These processes could also be augmented by the use

---

[2]  As related to us by Cat Manning, a high-profile member of the *Blaseball* fan community who has also worked together with the *Blaseball* team on systemic and narrative design directions for the game.

of digital tools like Imaginarium [10] to define and use new, simple constraint-based procedural content generators (for things like encounters with enemies, NPCs, and so on) as the course of the story demands. In this way, tabletop roleplaying groups focused on storytelling may serve as natural testing grounds for new kinds of narrative instruments. TTRPG groups can perhaps be viewed as the narrative equivalent of garage bands: their members gather to co-construct narrative on an ongoing basis largely due to enjoyment of the process, but they may occasionally produce narrative artifacts that are suitable for consumption by a wider audience.

In addition, the importance of a characteristic voice to the success or failure of an instrument may help to explain why later and more restricted story-making tabletop games (such as *Fiasco* [4], *Microscope*, and *The Quiet Year*) have proven more successful as narrative instruments than the apparently more general story-making tools presented by games like the earlier *Universalis* [19]. In its aspirations to generality, *Universalis* attempts to avoid fixing any part of the storyworld or narrative structure in place, instead leaving everything up to the players—in sharp contrast to later systems, which all impart a certain distinctive texture on the stories they are used to construct.

# 3   Discussion and Conclusion

All of these case studies demonstrate the active use of IEN systems by players with the explicit goal of crafting stories: in other words, the use of IEN systems as narrative instruments. In the context of Louchart and Aylett's taxonomy of user roles in emergent narrative [18], the systems with which we are concerned primarily position the user as an *author* of narrative, rather than a spectator or participant.

From a narrative instruments perspective, non-interactive emergent narrative systems that position the user as a spectator (such as non-interactive story generators like *Tale-Spin* [20]) resemble the narrative equivalent of windchimes: they produce a kind of pretty but uncomplicated ambient background narrativity that fades in and out of the spectator's awareness, with most generated stories or events failing to arouse much interest because of their great similarity to one another. These narrative generation systems are at an inherent disadvantage due to their need to compete for attention with stories that a human author had some role in crafting; unlike participatory or authorship-focused emergent narrative experiences, they can't easily trade on the interactor's sense of involvement to make the stories they produce seem special. Nevertheless, low-stakes ambient narrativity is worth exploring further, especially in concert with other forms of narrativity that may demand or benefit from more active player involvement.

The play-pleasures of participatory IEN are more like the pleasures of going to a concert. At the lower end of involvement, you might listen more or less passively. But you might also dance, mosh, headbang, or otherwise move along with the music; sing along with familiar lyrics; participate in call-and-response rituals led by the band; call for the performance of specific songs from the band's own back catalog, or for covers of songs by other bands; capture images or video of key moments in the show, as a sharable souvenir; exchange shouted dialogue with the band members between songs; or generally "vibe with" the band in a wide variety of ways. The band, in turn, rarely ignores the audience completely: instead, they pay attention to the energy of the crowd, allowing it to bleed into the music in various ways, and engage with the audience in ways that foster a sense of involvement or participation without ceding the stage entirely.

And then there are the play-pleasures of authorship, which are most closely analogous to the play-pleasures of making music yourself. It is here that we want to particularly focus our attention. Both spectatorship and participation have formed the groundwork for a number of compelling emergent narrative experiences—but what we are most interested in is exposing more people to the joys of *making narrative*, and in expanding the set of instruments available for casual narrative play. Existing story-making tabletop games have begun to map out the contours of this design space, but the prominence and growth of IEN-driven retelling practices also indicates player demand for narrative instruments that leverage digital computation to provide forms of creativity support that would not be possible or feasible without it.

The narrative instruments framing perhaps helps to clarify why participation tends to bleed into spectatorship at one end of the involvement spectrum and into authorship at the other. Some bands are much more interactive or responsive toward the audience than others, and in extreme cases a band may either ignore the audience completely (leading to an experience that resembles spectatorship) or permit the audience to play a significant role in determining the tone and flow of the concert (leading to an experience that resembles authorship). Moreover, nothing can stop a sufficiently dedicated member of the narrative avant-garde from grabbing a set of narrative windchimes and operating them in some unexpected way, leveraging a system designed for spectatorship as an unlikely narrative instrument to produce an experience of authorship for themselves. But narrative instruments, like musical instruments, are nevertheless designed to be used in certain ways—and the design of narrative instruments to afford novel forms of narrative expression has as many nuances and complexities as the design of musical instruments to afford novel forms of musical expression.[3]

More broadly, we find the idea of narrative instruments compelling. As an explanatory framework, it helps us make sense of several recent IEN projects that challenge our traditional design categories, but that nevertheless seem to be compelling to players. As a design metaphor, it suggests future directions for the development of new IEN systems. And as a provocative genre label, it centers play practices and experiences that had previously been treated as marginal in interactive narrative research communities. Altogether, we believe

---

[3] In fact, there exists an entire academic conference—New Interfaces for Musical Expression (NIME)—dedicated to the development of experiential new musical instruments. Parrish's New Interfaces for Textual Expression project [24] extends the NIME ethos to the development of textual instruments, much like those called for by Wardrip-Fruin in his own writing on the subject.

that the creation of narrative instruments represents an ambitious new potential goal for our research community—one that we are excited to develop further.

# References

1. Alder, A.: The Quiet Year (2013). https://buriedwithoutceremony.com/the-quiet-year
2. Bay 12 Games: Dwarf Fortress (2006). https://bay12games.com/dwarves
3. Blaseball Wiki contributors: Category: Players - Blaseball Wiki (2020). https://www.blaseball.wiki/w/Category:Players
4. Bully Pulpit Games: Fiasco (2009). https://bullypulpitgames.com/games/fiasco
5. Denee, T.: Bronzemurder. https://www.timdenee.com/bronzemurder
6. Denee, T.: Oilfurnace. https://www.timdenee.com/oilfurnace
7. Eladhari, M.P.: Re-tellings: the fourth layer of narrative as an instrument for critique. In: Rouse, R., Koenitz, H., Haahr, M. (eds.) ICIDS 2018. LNCS, vol. 11318, pp. 65–78. Springer, Cham (2018). https://doi.org/10.1007/978-3-030-04028-4_5
8. Garbe, J.: Simulation of history and recursive narrative scaffolding (2018). http://project.jacobgarbe.com/simulation-of-history-and-recursive-narrative-scaffolding
9. Guzdial, M., et al.: Tabletop roleplaying games as procedural content generators. In: International Conference on the Foundations of Digital Games (2020)
10. Horswill, I.: A declarative PCG tool for casual users. In: Proceedings of the AAAI Conference on Artificial Intelligence and Interactive Digital Entertainment, vol. 16, pp. 81–87 (2020)
11. Kreminski, M., et al.: Cozy Mystery Construction Kit: prototyping toward an AI-assisted collaborative storytelling mystery game. In: Proceedings of the 14th International Conference on the Foundations of Digital Games (2019)
12. Kreminski, M., Dickinson, M., Mateas, M., Wardrip-Fruin, N.: Why are we like this?: Exploring writing mechanics for an AI-augmented storytelling game. In: Electronic Literature Organization Conference (2020)
13. Kreminski, M., Dickinson, M., Mateas, M., Wardrip-Fruin, N.: Why are we like this?: The AI architecture of a co-creative storytelling game. In: International Conference on the Foundations of Digital Games (2020)
14. Kreminski, M., Samuel, B., Melcer, E., Wardrip-Fruin, N.: Evaluating AI-based games through retellings. In: Proceedings of the AAAI Conference on Artificial Intelligence and Interactive Digital Entertainment, vol. 15, pp. 45–51 (2019)
15. Kreminski, M., Wardrip-Fruin, N.: Generative games as storytelling partners. In: Proceedings of the 14th International Conference on the Foundations of Digital Games (2019)
16. Kromtec: Legends Viewer (2015). https://github.com/Kromtec/LegendsViewer
17. Kruggsmash: Kruggsmash - YouTube. https://www.youtube.com/user/kruggsmash
18. Louchart, S., Aylett, R.: The emergent narrative theoretical investigation. In: Narrative and Interactive Learning Environments Conference, pp. 21–28 (2004)
19. Mazza, R., Holmes, M.: Universalis: The Game of Unlimited Stories (2002)
20. Meehan, J.R.: TALE-SPIN, an interactive program that writes stories. In: International Joint Conference on Artificial Intelligence (1977)
21. Murnane, E.: Emergent narrative: stories of play, playing with stories. Ph.D. thesis, University of Central Florida (2018)

22. Murray, J.H.: Hamlet on the Holodeck: The Future of Narrative in Cyberspace. MIT Press, Cambridge (1997)
23. Nakakoji, K.: Meanings of tools, support, and uses for creative design processes. In: International Design Research Symposium, vol. 6, pp. 156–165 (2006)
24. Parrish, A.: New interfaces for textual expression. Master's thesis, New York University (2008)
25. Robbins, B.: Microscope: a fractal role-playing game of epic histories (2011). https://lamemage.com/microscope
26. Ryan, J.: Curating simulated storyworlds. Ph.D. thesis, University of California, Santa Cruz (2018)
27. Ryan, J., Mateas, M.: Simulating character knowledge phenomena in talk of the town. In: Game AI Pro 360, pp. 135–150. CRC Press (2019)
28. Ryder-Hanrahan, G.: The Book of Ages (2018). https://site.pelgranepress.com/index.php/the-book-of-ages
29. Samuel, B., Mateas, M., Wardrip-Fruin, N.: The design of *Writing Buddy*: a mixed-initiative approach towards computational story collaboration. In: Nack, F., Gordon, A.S. (eds.) ICIDS 2016. LNCS, vol. 10045, pp. 388–396. Springer, Cham (2016). https://doi.org/10.1007/978-3-319-48279-8_34
30. Samuel, B., Ryan, J., Summerville, A.J., Mateas, M., Wardrip-Fruin, N.: *Bad News*: an experiment in computationally assisted performance. In: Nack, F., Gordon, A.S. (eds.) ICIDS 2016. LNCS, vol. 10045, pp. 108–120. Springer, Cham (2016). https://doi.org/10.1007/978-3-319-48279-8_10
31. Shneiderman, B.: Creativity support tools: accelerating discovery and innovation. Commun. ACM 50(12), 20–32 (2007)
32. Snow, K., Kavallines, G., Ferkol, T., McClure, A.: Matul remrit (2013). http://www.bravemule.com/matulremrit
33. Sych, S.: When the fourth layer meets the fourth wall: the case for critical game retellings. In: Bosser, A.-G., Millard, D.E., Hargood, C. (eds.) ICIDS 2020. LNCS, vol. 12497, pp. 203–211. Springer, Cham (2020). https://doi.org/10.1007/978-3-030-62516-0_18
34. Tanaka, A.: Interaction, experience and the future of music. In: O'Hara, K., Brown, B. (eds.) Consuming Music Together. Computer Supported Cooperative Work, vol. 35, pp. 267–288. Springer, Dordrecht (2006). https://doi.org/10.1007/1-4020-4097-0_13
35. The Game Band: Blaseball (2020). https://www.blaseball.com/
36. Wardrip-Fruin, N.: Playable media and textual instruments. Dichtung Digital (2005)

# Hypertext as a Lens into Interactive Digital Narrative

David E. Millard[1]([email]) [ID] and Charlie Hargood[2] [ID]

[1] University of Southampton, Southampton, UK
dem@soton.ac.uk
[2] Bournemouth University, Poole, UK
chargood@bournemouth.ac.uk

**Abstract.** Interactive Narrative is blessed with a myriad of forms, this richness makes it hard to compare IDN systems or to develop general theories and tools as each example can seem like a special case. We take the approach of using hypertext as a method of inquiry to explore the similarities of different IDN forms. Using the Interactive Process Model to scope our analysis we systematically examine IDN from the perspective of hypertext structure. We show that hypertext can coherently explain the transition functions (the parts of the system that manages narrative state) across calligraphic, sculptural (storylets), adaptive, database driven, parser, and game narratives. In doing so we define a Hypertext Lens, made of layers of lexia state, story state, world model, and story engine. We also show how sculptural systems, parser fiction, and game narratives make use of interaction and presentation engines that complement and build upon these structures. Rather than trying to reconcile hypertext and IDN our approach instead presents hypertext as a useful thought pattern for approaching IDN that can bridge the gap between IDN forms and clarify their relationships to one another. Our analysis clearly shows a fluidity of form, encourages experimentation, and provides a mechanism through which theory can be applied widely.

**Keywords:** Calligraphic hypertext · Sculptural hypertext · Adaptive hypertext · Storylets · Parser fiction · Database narrative · Narrative games

## 1 Introduction

Interactive Digital Narrative (IDN) has its foundations in both early text adventure games and the hypertext fiction of the 80s and 90s. Hypertext is therefore often seen as a precursor to modern IDN systems, or (as manifest in popular tools such as Twine) as a particular subset of IDN, based on textual nodes and navigational links. However, Hypertext research has continued over the last few decades, with many contributions around hypertext models, applications, usage in the wild, tools and standards. This knowledge could be a valuable resource

© Springer Nature Switzerland AG 2021
A. Mitchell and M. Vosmeer (Eds.): ICIDS 2021, LNCS 13138, pp. 509–524, 2021.
https://doi.org/10.1007/978-3-030-92300-6_51

to the IDN community if the relationship between Hypertext and modern IDN systems could be defined more clearly.

Rather than try to rationalise IDN as Hypertext, or vice-versa, in this paper we instead consider "Hypertext as Method", an approach that uses Hypertext as a method of inquiry to understand different types of systems [5]. In this way Hypertext acts as a lens through which we can understand the common hypertextuality of different IDN systems, creating an analytical tool which can show how IDN forms are related to one another.

We also use Thue's Interactive Process Model [43] as a way to scope the lens and understand the boundaries of that hypertextuality. Rather than setting out hypertext as a restrictive view of IDN, we thus hope that this approach is a liberating one that could help us to understand how, through this common hypertextuality, theories developed for one form of IDN might translate to others.

## 2    Background

Hypertext has its roots in the work of its pioneers, Doug Engelbart who created NLS/Augment and considered hypertext as 'augmenting man's intellect' [14], and Ted Nelson and his conceptual system Xanadu, that imagined a global 'Permascroll' with digital technologies to seamlessly navigate and explore [34]. In both cases the central idea was to allow readers to navigate between text (or other media) by traversing navigational structures (such as links or trails). By the 1980s there were many digital implementations available such as IBIS, Intermedia, NoteCards, Hyperties, and ZOG [11], and by the end of the 1990s hypertext was an established research area, with distinct sub-communities working both on hypertext as a knowledge tool and hypertext as digital literature [45].

There were also attempts, working across both sub-communities, to formalise hypertext and create agreed models so that systems might interoperate [12,13]. This led to an appreciation that there were different domains of hypertext, sets of models and behaviour focused on a particular task. *Navigational hypertext* based around nodes (containing media) connected via navigable links, *spatial hypertext* focused on spatial structures like lists or sets that could be dynamically arranged and identified by a spatial parser, and *taxonomic hypertexts* where conceptual hierarchies are arranged into alternative views that can be traversed [31].

In the last two decades Hypertext has gone feral, adopted and adapted by thousands of Internet communities [44], it has spawned studies in folksonomies and semantic graphs [27], been applied to the expanding web and social networks [4,22], as well as the real world via both augmented and mixed reality [17,42], and it continues to struggle with its own form and poetics [8,35].

Interactive Digital Narratives share some of this early history, with key works published in early hypertext systems such as Notecards, and dedicated platforms such as Storyspace [7]. However, a mirror heritage in parser-based games, and a focus on high level narrative and content rather than low level associative structure, has given IDN research its own flavour, and ultimately a distinct community. Popular free platforms have been established such as Twine and Inform, encouraging a wider audience and experimentation that has driven craft knowledge [15]. In the last decade advances in game development frameworks has resulted in an explosion of independent narrative games, unconstrained by traditional forms, that are pushing IDN in a myriad of directions [16,33,38].

Not surprising then, that many in the IDN community consider hypertext to be either something from the history books or at best a tiny subset of what IDN can be. Millard attempts to reconcile the two, seeing 'literary hypertext as a subset of games, but narrative games as fundamentally hypertextual.' [32] But what does this *hypertextuality* actually mean?

Atzenbeck and Nürnberg suggest the approach that we use in this paper. They argue that Hypertext is a method of inquiry; a way of thinking about systems that can provide new insights [5]. They identify three hypertext perspectives: first class structure, context dependent structure, and open ended structure, and point out that 'other fields may adopt features of some of these perspectives, but the primacy the hypertext literature places upon them is distinguishing.' They tend towards viewing hypertext as a knowledge tool, but in this paper we explore the other hypertext tradition, hypertext as digital literature.

We also draw on Thue's model of an interactive narrative process [43], this views IDN systems as three functions that control respectively observation (what the reader sees), action (what the reader does), and transitions (how those actions change narrative state). Our approach is to use the hypertext lens to analyse the transition functions of different IDN forms, arguing that the hypertext focus on structure helps to understand and contextualise those forms. By examining the observation and action functions we can also scope the lens, and see what important elements lie beyond the hypertextual analysis.

## 3   Hypertext as a Lens

In this section we systematically examine a series of IDN forms, looking at how a hypertext lens might help explain how they function and how they are similar or distinct to one another. We do this by exploring the way in which IDNs are *structured*, using hypertext terms and structural models.

### 3.1   Linking, Adaptation, and Guard Fields

When we use the term hypertext, most people will think of the navigational domain of hypertext, defined with nodes and links. Where these are explicitly defined this has also been called *Calligraphic Hypertext*, as the links are drawn deliberately between nodes to create navigational paths between them [6]. Links are emblematic of hypertext systems, so much so that Halasz referred to the 'Tyranny of the Link' to complain about the extent to which they exclude other types of structures (such as trails, or virtual documents) [19].

This *hyperstructure* is concerned with defining the possible states of the hypertext, and the ways in which a reader might move between them. It is therefore a way of describing the *transition function* of a system. In calligraphic hypertext it is tempting to think of the nodes of the hypertext as states, and the links as the transitions. But this confuses what is displayed on screen with the state of the story (the salient parts of the reader's understanding of the hypertext as modelled by the system). The story state only changes *after* the reader has read the lexia[1] within a node. It is therefore the lexia that represent transitions between states of the story.

In calligraphic hypertext this distinction may seem moot, as there is a one-to-one mapping between the lexia and the possible states of the story (the lexia the reader has just read is sufficient to model their position in the story). However, *Adaptive Hypertext* breaks this strict connection. In adaptive hypertext additional rules dynamically adjust the lexia or the links or both [10]. The changes were classified by Brusilovsky into multiple methods (for example, removing content or links vs. changing presentation) [9]. These rules mean that in adaptive hypertext the current lexia is no longer sufficient to model the state of the story, and instead adaptive hypertext systems include some form of user model that is combined at runtime with the calligraphic hypertext model. The user model might be set up in advance (for example, selecting a learning preference in an educational hypertext system) and/or can be dynamically adjusted at runtime (for example, to track what the reader has already seen). The later means for example, that while calligraphic hypertexts can have circular structure, they cannot distinguish between repeat visits to a lexia (each visit returns to the same state), while an adaptive hypertext can do this (return visits can be different states).

StorySpace is an adaptive hypertext system, as it uses *guard fields* to control whether links are available or not [7]. Twine is also an example of an adaptive hypertext system where the author can define variables that are modified during reading [15]; both content and links within Twine can then be made dependent on these variables to achieve many of the effects set out by Brusilovsky.

Strict calligraphic hypertexts could therefore be defined as those where *lexia state* is sufficient to model the reader's position in a story, whereas adaptive hypertext systems - whilst still mostly calligraphic - require both lexia state and additional *story state* that can modify the presence and appearance of both content and structure[2].

---

[1] Although we use the term *lexia* this need not be textual content, and in fact our emphasis on lexia representing state changes means that it is their purpose within the overall narrative that is important rather than their form, making our use of the term very similar to Mateas' notion of 'dramatic beats' [30].

[2] The adaptive hypertext literature refers to a user model, as an amalgam of user preferences and current reading state, but in IDN non-diegetic user preferences (from outside of the user's interaction with the hypertext, e.g. age or expertise level) are less important, so we adopt the term story state to describe the same concept.

## 3.2    Sculptural Hypertext and Storylets

Sculptural Hypertexts are those that use purely story state to manage the progression of the narrative. The lexia state is ignored. You can imagine that in a sculptural hypertext all nodes are potentially connected (which is why it is irrelevant which lexia you have just read), but at runtime the story state is used to sculpt away most of the connections [6]. For example, one node might assert that the reader has now 'met Alice' while another states that it is only available if 'met Alice' has been asserted.

The notion of Storylets emerged separately in the interactive fiction community [26]. Storylets are effectively the building blocks of a sculptural hypertext, they contain the lexia itself, as well as the conditions that govern whether it is available, and the behaviour that modifies the story state when the lexia is read. A collection of storylets *is* a sculptural hypertext (in the interactive fiction community these have also been referred to as quality-based stories [41]).

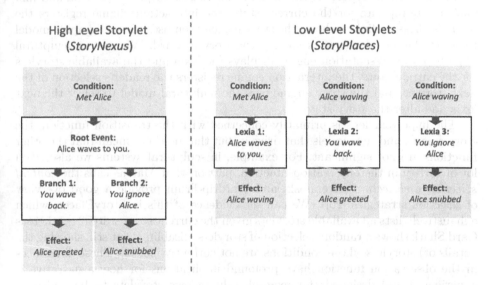

**Fig. 1.** One high level Storylet captures the behaviour of three low level Storylets.

In the hypertext literature these building blocks have been conceptualised as a 'context-sourced link' (i.e. a link where the source is a story state rather than a node) [46], meaning that storylets can be modelled consistently alongside calligraphic hypertexts. Storylets also exist at different levels of complexity. For example, in StoryPlaces [21] each storylet is a single lexia with conditions and effects, this low level approach is powerful but makes authoring branching structures difficult[3]; whereas in StoryNexus [1] the storylet is made up of a root event

---

[3] Sculptural Hypertext is a good fit for locative literature systems like StoryPlaces, because location can be modelled as just another condition.

(a starting lexia) followed by branches with different effects. This difference is shown in Fig. 1. StoryPlaces then is a strict sculptural hypertext - using only story state, whereas StoryNexus, although primarily sculptural, adds additional lexia state to make authoring branching choices and consequences simpler.

### 3.3    Story Engines and Database Narratives

Hypertext systems are more than a hypertext model, they also require a runtime system to apply those models and manage state. As described previously Thue's model of an interactive narrative process deconstructs this system into a transition, observation, and action function [43]. We have already described the transition function in IDN as typically being fulfilled by a *story engine*, and we can say that in most IDN systems the observation function is fulfilled by some sort of *presentation engine*, and the action function by some sort of *interaction engine* (although in practice they may be implemented together).

In calligraphic hypertext the presentation engine displays the lexia and link anchors appropriate for the current state, the interaction engine registers the reader's clicks on link anchors, the story engine then uses the calligraphic model to select the next lexia, thus moving the story forward. Whereas in sculptural hypertext the presentation engine displays the lexia and the available storylets for the current state, the interaction engine registers the reader's selection of the next storylet, and the story engine uses the sculptural model to select the next lexia and alter the story state.

The hypertext lens is primarily concerned with the transition function, the story engine, and the models that drive it, but that does not mean that the other functions are not significant. For example, in sculptural systems we also see a lot of variety in the observation function, part of what Mateas calls the *content selection architecture* (Kreminski and Wardrip-Fruin provide a good overview of selection strategies [26]). We can see evidence of this in StoryPlaces, which exhaustively lists all available storylets given the current story state [21], whereas Card Shark shows a random selection of storylets, disabling (but still showing the details of) storylets whose conditions are not currently met [6]. These differences in the observation function have profound implications for how a narrative is experienced and designed (for example, this allows storylets to be added to Card Shark that can never be reached, but which influence the player when they appear in the selection as players do not know that they are unreachable).

In Sam Barlow's *Her Story* and *Telling Lies* the action function is not to click on links or select storylets, but to type search terms into a database of video. Gasque et al. call this approach 'database narratives' [16]. From the hypertext perspective database narratives are effectively a form of sculptural hypertext, but where the player rather than the system manages the transition function, in other words, database narratives require no story engine. Despite this, the underlying story model, used to design and plan the narrative, is still sculptural. But when lexia (or in this case video) is seen, it only changes the story state if the player themselves makes note of what new elements have been revealed. In the absence of a story engine Barlow uses the limitation of only returning the first 5 items (a modification of the observation function) in order to manage progression through the story [16].

## 3.4 Parsers, Narrative Games and World Models

Like sculptural hypertexts, parser fiction uses story state to manage its narrative, only here the interaction engine relies on interpreted typed commands rather than clickable links. These parser fictions often take the form of a traditional text adventure and express the story state in terms of a *world model*, a schema or super structure that provides a framework for a coherent (and more complete) description of the story world. This allows authors to express themselves at a higher level than a set of variables - for example, in Inform we declare a set of rooms and their relationships, objects and their locations within rooms, and scenes in which story unfolds. There is then a grammar for interacting with this world model (moving between rooms, picking up and inspecting objects, etc.) The query interface of database narratives can also be considered as a simple grammar, but the superstructure of the world model makes a more complex grammar possible, as valid actions can be defined against whole classes of objects. Parser fiction also often uses a different presentation engine to traditional hypertext, as it doesn't show you explicit choices and instead expects your choices to be made diegetically by interacting with the world model [28].

While parser based adventure games adopt new interaction and presentation engines, narrative games can take this even further. Whilst still built on a story engine (and often a world model) their interactions can include rich ludonarrative mechanics [2], with elements of the story being delivered through a variety of channels, such as cutscenes, scripted events/character barks, log entries, interactive dialog, and environmental storytelling (reminiscent of transmedia [23]).

The element of environmental storytelling means that, like database narratives, narrative games and parsers do not necessarily track and manage all of the state through their story engines, and that there is the possibility that the transition function is shared between player and machine. To some extent then, all three forms are epistemic, not in Ryan's motivational sense (in that players are "driven by the need to know") [40] but rather they are at least partially driven by *what* the player knows.

As we have considered these different forms of IDN - Calligraphic, Adaptive, Sculptural, Database, Parsers, and Games - we have moved through and then beyond the hypertext lens. Particularly in these last two forms, where there is increased importance of the observation and action functions as ways of delivering story and managing the experience. Thus a design theory of narrative games cannot be solely based on hypertext, but these hypertextual models can be used to understand the transition function - the story engine and underlying structural models for such experiences. Hypertext models can therefore be used as analytical tools to understand how narrative games work, and hypertext systems can be used as authoring tools for much of their narrative structure.

## 4   Discussion

Through our hypertextual description of IDN forms we have developed a simple layer model of the Hypertext Lens (shown in Fig. 2).

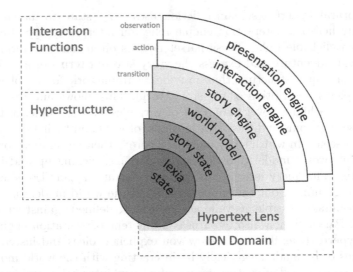

**Fig. 2.** The hypertext lens as applied to the layers of IDN

Central to this is a finite state model where each lexia that the reader encounters represents a transition between states of the narrative. Note that lexia represent transitions, not states (see Sect. 3.1). However, it is possible that narratives are managed solely via *lexia state*, in which case there is a one-to-one correlation between the lexia state and the state of the narrative (e.g. the state might be: 'You have just read Page 1'). Calligraphic Hypertext exists at this level, reading a lexia in the hypertext transitions you to a matching state, and links in that lexia represent the next possible lexia and state transitions. Authors are effectively directly writing the narrative state graph. Because of this one-to-one match Calligraphic Hypertext is easy to understand and is therefore one of the most accessible forms of IDN, although if the narrative is very open (meaning that the reader has many choices) then the density of the state graph can become high, and the hypertext becomes difficult to author and visualise.

A way to solve this problem is to model *story state* explicitly, and to use this and not lexia state to model the narrative. Figure 3 shows a simple story sequence modelled as a calligraphic hypertext (using only lexia state) and as a sculptural hypertext (using only story state). Lexia still act as transitions between story states (e.g. reading 'You take the key.' leads to the state: 'has key') but now, assuming that not all of the information in the lexia will affect the onward story[4], different lexia can transition you to the *same* story states,

---

[4] In our example we are not interested in modelling the state of the guard.

which simplifies the state graph (in Fig. 3, Original Story, states 2 and 3 in the calligraphic model have been consolidated into one state in the sculptural model). This is the basis of Sculptural Hypertext, which exclusively uses story state to manage the reader's progress.

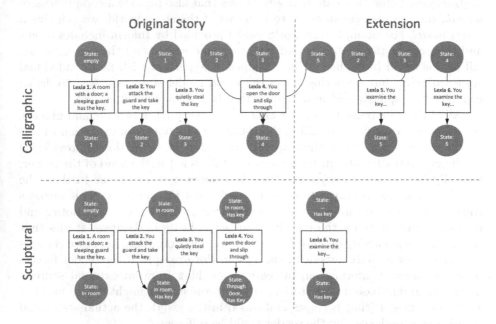

**Fig. 3.** Calligraphic Hypertext relies on Lexia State and authors directly write the state model, whereas Sculptural Hypertext uses Story State and users write at a higher level

Sculptural Hypertext has a further advantage. Authors writing calligraphic hypertext have no choice but to use the whole of the state information when creating transitions, because the states of the story are collapsed down into a single piece of information (the current lexia). For example, if I want to add a lexia where the reader can 'examine the key' to the calligraphic system (Fig. 3, Extension) then I have to create transitions from all states where the reader has that key (states 2, 3, and 4), in addition I will need two versions of the lexia, one if they examine it in the room (state 5), and another for after the door (state 6) in order to present the correct set of onward transitions. However, in a sculptural system I can define the transition based on partial story state. I can do this by creating a single storylet that transitions from any state where 'has key' is set, this will then be available from all states in the underlying state model where this is true. Sculptural hypertext authors are not therefore directly authoring the state graph, but working at a higher level of abstraction (effectively they are creating parallel story state models that each track a different aspect of the story and can be checked and altered independently, e.g. a state model for the key, another for the room). This is what makes sculptural hypertext so powerful, but also more complex to conceptualise and design.

Adaptive Hypertext (which is what most node/link systems actually represent) is a way to balance this power and complexity, here we use lexia state to model the bulk of the hypertext, but story state to simplify that graph when needed (e.g. using guard fields [7]). Parser-based fiction also uses story state abstractions. Often these are text adventures that also provide a comprehensive schema to help manage story state in terms of the story world, we call this a *world model*. For example, the world model provided by Inform includes rooms and their connections, objects and inventory, and scenes and their progression. All of this could be replicated in a sculptural hypertext with many individual state variables, but authoring using the world model is an easy way to define complex state quickly and in a manner that is familiar to writers [36].

All of these systems use a *story engine* [3] to keep track of state and manage the available transitions (fulfilling the transition function). An exception to this are database-driven stories, these operate using story state but do not provide the machinery to track state. Instead the story state is left in the head of the reader, typically in the form of keywords that they might wish to pursue further (the transition function is undertaken by the reader, not the machine). This weakens the connection between lexia and state changes, as the reader must notice and remember that state for the transition to occur. Lexia in database stories thus represent the *possibility* of state transitions. In addition, there are state changes that can occur entirely outside of the system (for example, if the reader forgets a crucial piece of information, or learns something from an external source). Therefore in database driven stories, although the author might design an ideal story state model (that becomes embedded in the lexia), the actual states and transitions experienced by the reader could be different.

Hypertext works well to examine these inner layers of the model. However, there are clearly limits to its ability to describe IDNs. For a start (and following Adam's terminology [3]) there are a wide variety of interaction engines (fulfilling the action function) and presentation engines (fulfilling the observation function), and it is possible to play with these in order to get specific effects. Calligraphic hypertexts convey subtle information about choices via the placement of link anchors. Sculptural hypertexts typically list available lexia and use explicit names or prompts to provide clues to the reader. Parsers often don't present story options at all, but provide a set of actions and a grammar to interact with the world model by typing commands. Database narratives provide a search interface where the users type keywords directly.

Variations in interaction and presentation engines are at the very edges of the Hypertext space, what Bernstein calls 'Strange Hypertexts' [6], and at their extremes result in the sophisticated action functions we see in games - where the interaction engine constitutes a complex set of mechanics[5]. Similarly hypertext says very little about the presentation engine that is used to translate lexia and player options to the screen. In this the Hypertext Lens outlined above matches the classic Dexter Model of hypertext [18], which separates systems into different

---

[5] Even in calligraphic hypertext, the observation and interaction engines convey meaning, e.g. Mason and Bernstein's work on the poetics of contemporary link usage [29].

layers, and places hypertext in a central 'Storage Layer'. The Lens we have set out (lexia state, story state, world model, and story engine) correspond to this 'Storage Layer'. Whereas interaction engines are part of the 'Runtime Layer' and presentation engines part of the 'Within Component Layer', both of which Dexter considers to be outside of the core hypertext design.

The Hypertext Lens does not therefore cover the entirety of IDN systems. However, it helps to explain what Millard called a 'core hypertextuality' in narrative games [32], evidenced in attempts to characterise Bandersnatch as a Gauntlet [37] or to map the structure of The Walking Dead [24]. We go beyond this claim and have begun to unpack this hypertextuality and to relate it to different IDN forms. Thue's model of an interactive narrative process helps to explain that the Hypertext Lens describes the transition function of IDN, whereas games design better covers the observation and action functions. This means that when those functions are relatively simple the hypertext lens is a more complete description than when they are complex. While the explanatory power of the lens is focused on the interactive narrative elements of games, it does not follow that it is limited to games where narrative is seen as a minor element, just that its scope is limited within those games. In these cases the lens provides clarity precisely because it allows you to focus on one part of a more complex medium.

The Hypertext Lens also reveals the fluidity of IDN forms. This might inspire us to consider IDNs that mix forms together. For example, we might imagine database stories with some sculptural elements, sculptural stories with a more robust world model, or calligraphic stories that include some free text query and therefore push some story state outside of the story engine. We have also seen how hypertext can help explain complex IDNs that already mix up these forms. This is true even in the case of commercial narrative games, for example Supergiant's narrative roguelike *Hades* could be seen as a sculptural hypertext using large grain storylets with calligraphic internal structure, coupled with a presentation engine that selects storylets based on a priority selection strategy.

Understanding the hypertextual commonalities of these forms also enables them to benefit from theories and craft knowledge developed elsewhere. Database narratives may seem like unknown design spaces, but much of the craft knowledge from storylets could be applied to them (e.g. by utilising sculptural patterns in their design [20]). Understanding whether the narrative model of a game is more calligraphic or sculptural enables us to apply the right narrative design principles, and to pick an appropriate IDN tool in which to write the script.

Hypertext is a structure-centric view of IDN (after all, Atzenbeck argued that a focus on structure was the defining perspective of hypertext [5]), and while it does not fully capture all of the elements it does allow us to think about the structures separately from the other parts of the experience. Thus it has real value as a *thought pattern*, a way of approaching IDN that sits alongside similar analytical models such as SPP [25] or the Double-Hermeneutic Circle [39] and can be used both descriptively for analysis and prescriptively for design.

# 5 Conclusion

In this paper we have adopted Atzenbeck's approach of using Hypertext as a Method of Inquiry in order to analyse IDN forms through a hypertext lens. We have also used Thue's Interactive Process Model as a means to scope that lens, and have shown that it helps to deconstruct the transition function of IDN systems (how the system manages narrative state). In doing so we have revealed how different IDN forms relate to one another. Calligraphic hypertext purely uses lexia states and transitions (resulting in a one to one mapping between lexia and narrative state), sculptural hypertext (a set of storylets) purely uses story states and transitions, and adaptive hypertexts mix the two, using lexia state to manage most of the narrative, with story state employed to simplify overly complex sections. In all three cases a story engine manages the transition function. The lens also shows that database IDNs are sculptural in nature, but instead of a story engine the transition function occurs within the mind of the reader; and it reveals parser fiction as structurally sculptural but defined against a world model (which makes authoring complex state easier). Throughout, we have given small or abstract examples of the lens in action, and in future work we hope to use the lens to explore specific IDN works in more detail.

The hypertext lens is a thought pattern that puts structure first, it thus moves the focus away from the presentation and interaction engines that fulfil the observation and action functions (how narrative and choices are presented, and the ways in which the reader/player interacts with them). In calligraphic and adaptive hypertext these are relatively simple, and the lens provides an almost complete picture, but in sculptural systems a more complex presentation engine makes decisions about which storylets to reveal next, and in parser fiction a more sophisticated interaction engine manages a complex grammar made possible by the world model. In narrative games there is a high level of experimentation with presentation and interaction engines - with multiple channels reminiscent of transmedia, and complex mechanics that yield only to game design theory. Nevertheless, the hypertext lens continues to usefully highlight the structures within the transition function and the activity of the game's story engine.

This coherent hypertextual view of IDN suggests a fluidity of forms, with the potential for theory to be applied consistently across them. When new ideas emerge (such as database narratives) if they can be explained in terms of existing hypertext models they immediately benefit from design theory that already exists. Hybrid approaches that seem at first esoteric and strange (for example, the located and contextual nodes of StoryPlaces) can be explained in terms of what has gone before. It also implies a core set of narrative design skills that could be taught, and would be relevant across many different forms.

Finally it is worth acknowledging that the hypertext lens is a technical deconstruction of IDN, it does not tell us how to write dramatic plots, how to manage agency effectively, or how to build believable characters, but it does explain the structural narrative architecture of IDN forms and reveals the fluidity between them. This comprehensive explanation of a part of IDN is valuable. If we understand the hypertextual similarities between IDNs then when we see best practice in one form we can translate it to another, even though the lens doesn't tell you what that best practice itself might be. We hope that by using hypertext to set out a coherent view of IDN forms, and by describing a lens that can be used in future to analyse new works and approaches, that we will empower the next generation of writers, designers, and tool developers to explore these other questions, and in doing so, develop answers that can be applied widely.

**Acknowledgements.** The authors would like to thank David Thue and Joey Jones for providing feedback on an earlier draft of this paper.

# References

1. Storynexus: Reference guide, version 1.04. Technical report, Failbetter Games (2012). http://wiki.failbettergames.com/start
2. Aarseth, E.. A narrative theory of games. In: Proceedings of the International Conference on the Foundations of Digital Games, FDG '12, pp. 129–133. Association for Computing Machinery, New York (2012). https://doi.org/10.1145/2282338. 2282365
3. Adams, E.: Fundamentals of Game Design, 3rd edn. New Riders Publishing, New York (2014)
4. Anderson, M., Carr, L., Millard, D.E.: There and here: patterns of content transclusion in wikipedia. In: Proceedings of the 28th ACM Conference on Hypertext and Social Media, pp. 115–124 (2017)
5. Atzenbeck, C., Nürnberg, P.J.: Hypertext as method. In: Proceedings of the 30th ACM Conference on Hypertext and Social Media, HT '19, pp. 29–38. Association for Computing Machinery, New York (2019). https://doi.org/10.1145/3342220. 3343669
6. Bernstein, M.: Card shark and thespis: Exotic tools for hypertext narrative. In: Proceedings of the 12th ACM Conference on Hypertext and Hypermedia, HYPERTEXT '01, pp. 41–50. Association for Computing Machinery, New York (2001). https://doi.org/10.1145/504216.504233
7. Bernstein, M.: Storyspace 1. In: Proceedings of the Thirteenth ACM Conference on Hypertext and Hypermedia, HYPERTEXT '02, pp. 172–181. Association for Computing Machinery, New York (2002). https://doi.org/10.1145/513338.513383
8. Bernstein, M.: On hypertext narrative. In: Proceedings of the 20th ACM Conference on Hypertext and Hypermedia, pp. 5–14 (2009)
9. Brusilovsky, P.: Adaptive hypermedia. User Model. User-Adap. Inter. **11**(1), 87–110 (2001)
10. Brusilovsky, P., Kobsa, A., Vassileva, J.: Adaptive Hypertext and Hypermedia. Springer, Heidelberg (1998). https://doi.org/10.1007/978-94-017-0617-9
11. Conklin, J.: Hypertext: an introduction and survey. Computer **20**, 17–41 (1987). https://doi.org/10.1109/MC.1987.1663693
12. Davis, H.C., et al.: Interoperability between hypermedia systems: the standardisation work of the OHSWG. In: Proceedings of the Tenth ACM Conference on Hypertext and Hypermedia: Returning to Our Diverse Roots: Returning to Our Diverse Roots, HYPERTEXT '99, pp. 201–202. Association for Computing Machinery, New York (1999). https://doi.org/10.1145/294469.294904

13. Davis, H., Reich, S., Millard, D.: A proposal for a common navigational hypertext protocol. Technical report, Dept. of Electronics and Computer Science, University of Southampton (1997)
14. Engelbart, D.C.: Augmenting human intellect: a conceptual framework. Menlo Park, CA (1962)
15. Ford, M.: Writing Interactive Fiction with Twine. Que Publishing, Seattle (2016)
16. Gasque, T.M., Tang, K., Rittenhouse, B., Murray, J.: Gated story structure and dramatic agency in Sam Barlow's *Telling Lies*. In: Bosser, A.-G., Millard, D.E., Hargood, C. (eds.) ICIDS 2020. LNCS, vol. 12497, pp. 314–326. Springer, Cham (2020). https://doi.org/10.1007/978-3-030-62516-0_28
17. Grønbæk, K., Kristensen, J.F., Ørbæk, P., Eriksen, M.A.: "Physical hypermedia" organising collections of mixed physical and digital material. In: Proceedings of the Fourteenth ACM Conference on Hypertext and Hypermedia, pp. 10–19 (2003)
18. Halasz, F., Schwartz, M., Grønbæk, K., Trigg, R.H.: The dexter hypertext reference model. Commun. ACM **37**(2), 30–39 (1994). https://doi.org/10.1145/175235.175237
19. Halasz, F.G.: "Seven issues": revisited, hypertext'91 closing plenary. In: Proceedings of Third ACM Conference on Hypertext (Hypertext'91) (1991)
20. Hargood, C., Hunt, V., Weal, M., Millard, D.: Patterns of sculptural hypertext in location based narratives. In: HT'16: Proceedings of the 27th ACM Conference on Hypertext and Social Media, pp. 61–70. ACM (2016). https://eprints.soton.ac.uk/390748/
21. Hargood, C., Weal, M., Millard, D.: The storyplaces platform: building a web-based locative hypertext system. In: HT '18 Proceedings of the 29th ACM Conference on Hypertext and Social Media, pp. 128–135. ACM (2018). https://eprints.soton.ac.uk/421122/
22. Helic, D., Strohmaier, M., Granitzer, M., Scherer, R.: Models of human navigation in information networks based on decentralized search. In: Proceedings of the 24th ACM Conference on Hypertext and Social Media, pp. 89–98 (2013)
23. Javanshir, R., Millard, D., Carroll, E.: Structural patterns for transmedia storytelling. PLoS ONE **15**(1) (2020). https://eprints.soton.ac.uk/438130/
24. Killham, E.: Here's a chart of every choice in the walking dead: season 1 (image) (2013). https://venturebeat.com/2013/03/31/the-walking-dead-season-one-plot-graph/
25. Koenitz, H.: Towards a theoretical framework for interactive digital narrative. In: Aylett, R., Lim, M.Y., Louchart, S., Petta, P., Riedl, M. (eds.) ICIDS 2010. LNCS, vol. 6432, pp. 176–185. Springer, Heidelberg (2010). https://doi.org/10.1007/978-3-642-16638-9_22
26. Kreminski, M., Wardrip-Fruin, N.: Sketching a map of the storylets design space. In: Rouse, R., Koenitz, H., Haahr, M. (eds.) ICIDS 2018. LNCS, vol. 11318, pp. 160–164. Springer, Cham (2018). https://doi.org/10.1007/978-3-030-04028-4_14
27. Marlow, C., Naaman, M., Boyd, D., Davis, M.: HT06, tagging paper, taxonomy, flickr, academic article, to read. In: Proceedings of the Seventeenth Conference on Hypertext and Hypermedia, pp. 31–40 (2006)
28. Mason, S.: On games and links: extending the vocabulary of agency and immersion in interactive narratives. In: Koenitz, H., Sezen, T.I., Ferri, G., Haahr, M., Sezen, D., Ç atak, G. (eds.) ICIDS 2013. LNCS, vol. 8230, pp. 25–34. Springer, Cham (2013). https://doi.org/10.1007/978-3-319-02756-2_3

29. Mason, S., Bernstein, M.: On links: exercises in style. In: Proceedings of the 30th ACM Conference on Hypertext and Social Media, HT '19, pp. 103–110. Association for Computing Machinery, New York (2019). https://doi.org/10.1145/3342220. 3343665

30. Mateas, M., Stern, A.: Structuring content in the façade interactive drama architecture. In: Proceedings of the First AAAI Conference on Artificial Intelligence and Interactive Digital Entertainment, AIIDE'05, pp. 93–98. AAAI Press (2005)

31. Millard, D.E., Moreau, L., Davis, H.C., Reich, S.: FOHM: a fundamental open hypertext model for investigating interoperability between hypertext domains. In: Proceedings of the Eleventh ACM on Hypertext and Hypermedia, HYPERTEXT '00, pp. 93–102. Association for Computing Machinery, New York (2000). https://doi.org/10.1145/336296.336334

32. Millard, D.: Games/hypertext. In: ACM Conference on Hypertext and Social Media (13/07/20 - 15/07/20), pp. 123–126 (2020). https://eprints.soton.ac.uk/442652/

33. Di Pastena, A., Jansen, D., de Lint, B., Moss, A.: The link out. In: Rouse, R., Koenitz, H., Haahr, M. (eds.) ICIDS 2018. LNCS, vol. 11318, pp. 206–216. Springer, Cham (2018). https://doi.org/10.1007/978-3-030-04028-4_21

34. Nelson, T.H., et al.: Literary machines: The report on, and of, project Xanadu, concerning word processing, electronic publishing, hypertext, thinkertoys, tomorrow's intellectual revolution, and certain other topics including knowledge, education and freedom (1981)

35. Pisarski, M.: New plots for hypertext? Towards poetics of a hypertext node. In: Proceedings of the 22nd ACM Conference on Hypertext and Hypermedia, pp. 313–318 (2011)

36. Reed, A.A.: Telling stories with maps and rules: using the interactive fiction language "inform 7" in a creative writing workshop. In: Creative Writing in the Digital Age: Theory, Practice, and Pedagogy, pp. 141–152 (2015)

37. Rezk, A.M., Haahr, M.: The case for invisibility: understanding and improving agency in black mirror's bandersnatch and other interactive digital narrative works. In: Bosser, A.-G., Millard, D.E., Hargood, C. (eds.) ICIDS 2020. LNCS, vol. 12497, pp. 178–189. Springer, Cham (2020). https://doi.org/10.1007/978-3-030-62516-0_16

38. Roth, C., Koenitz, H.: Bandersnatch, yea or nay? Reception and user experience of an interactive digital narrative video. In: Proceedings of the 2019 ACM International Conference on Interactive Experiences for TV and Online Video, pp. 247–254 (2019)

39. Roth, C., van Nuenen, T., Koenitz, H.: Ludonarrative hermeneutics: A Way Out and the narrative paradox. In: Rouse, R., Koenitz, H., Haahr, M. (eds.) ICIDS 2018. LNCS, vol. 11318, pp. 93–106. Springer, Cham (2018). https://doi.org/10.1007/978-3-030-04028-4_7

40. Ryan, M.-L.: Interactive narrative, plot types, and interpersonal relations. In: Spierling, U., Szilas, N. (eds.) ICIDS 2008. LNCS, vol. 5334, pp. 6–13. Springer, Heidelberg (2008). https://doi.org/10.1007/978-3-540-89454-4_2

41. Short, E.: Beyond branching: quality-based, salience-based, and waypoint narrative structure (2016). https://emshort.blog/2016/04/12/beyond-branching-quality-based-and-salience-based-narrative-structures/

42. Sinclair, P., Martinez, K., Millard, D.E., Weal, M.J.: Links in the palm of your hand: tangible hypermedia using augmented reality. In: Proceedings of the Thirteenth ACM Conference on Hypertext and Hypermedia, pp. 127–136 (2002)

43. Thue, D.: What might an action do? Toward a grounded view of actions in interactive storytelling. In: Bosser, A.-G., Millard, D.E., Hargood, C. (eds.) ICIDS 2020. LNCS, vol. 12497, pp. 212–220. Springer, Cham (2020). https://doi.org/10.1007/978-3-030-62516-0_19

44. Walker, J.: Feral hypertext: when hypertext literature escapes control. In: Proceedings of the Sixteenth ACM Conference on Hypertext and Hypermedia, pp. 46–53 (2005)

45. Wardrip-Fruin, N.: What hypertext is. In: Proceedings of the Fifteenth ACM Conference on Hypertext and Hypermedia, HYPERTEXT '04, pp. 126–127. Association for Computing Machinery, New York (2004). https://doi.org/10.1145/1012807.1012844

46. Weal, M.J., Millard, D.E., Michaelides, D.T., Roure, D.C.D.: Building narrative structures using context based linking. In: In Hypertext '01. Proceedings of the Twelfth ACM Conference on Hypertext, Aarhus, Denmark. (01/08/01), pp. 37–38 (2001), https://eprints.soton.ac.uk/256136/

# A Pilot Study on Analyzing Critical Retellings Using Digital Humanities Tools

Tonguc Ibrahim Sezen(✉) (iD) and Digdem Sezen(✉) (iD)

Teesside University, Campus Heart, Southfield Rd, Middlesbrough TS1 3BX, UK
{t.sezen,d.sezen}@tees.ac.uk

**Abstract.** This paper presents the early findings of a pilot study on the analysis of longform video essays as critical retellings of video game narratives. Using web-based reading and analysis environment Voyant, the study explores the indicators of how players critically approach and discuss game narrative design.

**Keywords:** Retelling · Video essay · Game narrative · Digital humanities

## 1 Introduction

Videogames, as multi-faceted drillable texts with an intrinsic multiplicity, provide fertile ground for diverse forms of paratextual retellings interpreting and investigating them. Retellings not only report on the games' stories but also reflect how players interact with the narrative design in action. They open new ways of analyzing video games' complexity [1], play a significant role in understanding how videogame narratives work [2, 3], and reveal players' emotions, reactions, and thought processes during play [4]. Recent studies utilizing retellings in game research have been fruitful in revealing aspects of the relationships between player experiences and narrative design. The broad spectrum of retelling forms diversifies the focus, scale, and methodological approaches of these studies [10–12]. In this poster we present the findings of a pilot study on the utilization of distance reading techniques for evaluating a subset of retellings, longform video essays. For this plot study we have chosen a long form essay on the video game *The Last of Us Part II* (here-after *TLoU Part II*) [9].

## 2 Longform Video Essays

Steven Sych [5] suggests the concept of "critical retellings" which he describes a subset of retellings that do not directly track the success of a narrative system but instead take a deliberately critical stand towards it. Critical retellings, according to Sych, provide commentary on the flaws in a game's system, tend to be more anecdotal, target an experienced and knowing audience, use irony in their criticism, and explicitly reference and reflect on the mechanics of the narrative system. Sych's description emphasizes the role of subjectivity, self-reflexivity, and satirical position while experiencing games, and

© Springer Nature Switzerland AG 2021
A. Mitchell and M. Vosmeer (Eds.): ICIDS 2021, LNCS 13138, pp. 525–529, 2021.
https://doi.org/10.1007/978-3-030-92300-6_52

analyzing and interpreting narrative outcomes of game systems. While Sych describes critical retellings as short, sharp, ironical texts; the elaborate, personal, and creative longform video essays retell game experiences with a deliberately critical stand towards videogame systems as well. Considered one of the most prominent contemporary forms of non-scholarly videogame criticism [6, 7], longform video essays on video games can be seen as a variation of critical retellings. Not solely narrative products [8] instantiated in one uninterrupted play through, longform video essays shared on social media platforms provide in-depth discussions and interpretations exemplifying open scholarship in videogame studies [7].

Game vlogger Noah Caldwell-Gervais' video essays can be seen as examples of longform video essays as critical retellings. Compared to film critique Roger Ebert for legitimizing the form of videogames and demonstrating its potential [13], he produces in-depth, several hours long analyses and critiques of videogames. In his two-hour long video essay titled *How does the Last of Us Part 2 compare to the Last of Us Remastered?* Caldwell-Gervais [14] presents his experiences in playing both incarnations of the videogame series *TLoU* and discusses the connections between gameplay, narrative design, and the story. *TLoU* [15] and its sequel *TLoU Part II* [9], are action-adventure games set in a post-apocalyptic future. Featuring elements of the survival horror genre, they share a character-driven linear narrative design. *TLoU* was praised [16] for its representation of its protagonists Joel and Ellie, a hardened man, and a young girl, who throughout the game develop a father-daughter relationship, leading Joel to commit questionable acts of violence to protect Ellie at the end of the game. *TLoU Part II* starts with the murder of Joel by the daughter of one of his victims from the previous game, Abby, and then follows the crossing paths of now vengeful Ellie and Abby with their respected companions Dina and Lev, till a final confrontation. Both the choice of killing off Joel and making Abby a protagonist alongside a hostile Ellie in *TLoU Part II* has caused negative reactions in some fan communities [17]. Providing a nuanced reaction to *TLoU Part II*, Caldwell-Gervais' retelling [14] in comparison describes the narrative direction of the series as creatively unique and genuinely surprising, as it allows the player to discover the other side of the same story from the opponents' perspective. He argues that the designers expected the players to feel anger towards Abby, and at the same time allowed them to explore her perspective and invited them to re-evaluate the story of the previous game critically [14].

## 3   Analyzing Longform Video Essays with Voyant

Close captioning Caldwell-Gervais' video essay provides a text which is more than 26000 words long, which analysis can benefit from the usage of digital humanities tools. Eladhari [3] proposes the use of data mining methodologies in analyzing retellings to reveal shared and diverging aspects. The open-source, web-based text analytics and visualization tool Voyant [18], may prove useful in such an analysis. It is an entry level tool for text mining but also one of the longest supported tools to be used in continuous research. Voyant provides word frequency and collocate data to reveal word and topic trends, possible contexts of words usage, and clusters. It can analyze multiple texts withing a short time. A Voyant analysis of the closed caption transcription of Caldwell-Gervais' essay's sections on *TLoU Part II*, provides details of how he approached and discussed the game's narrative design. Caldwell-Gervais' top-five repeating phrases are variations of "*TLoU Part II* is", which reflects his descriptive attitude. The most repeated words after ignoring common English words, mainly focus on the protagonists, with Ellie (104), Abby (68), Joel (56), and Lev (34) being in top-ten. The rest of his most repeated words reflect his discussions on game time, with "moment" (33) and "time" (26), and the core themes of the story, with "violence" (34) and "revenge" (31). "Game" (92) and "player" (31) are in the list as unavoidable terms to be used in a text on videogames. Character names use frequency of Caldwell-Gervais (see Fig. 1), reveals which characters he focuses and prioritize in his retelling. He focuses on each main character and discusses them in connection with each other. His discussion of Lev, Abby's companion character, stands out in his retelling since Lev plays a major role in the personal story of Abby and thus potentially shapes her image for the players.

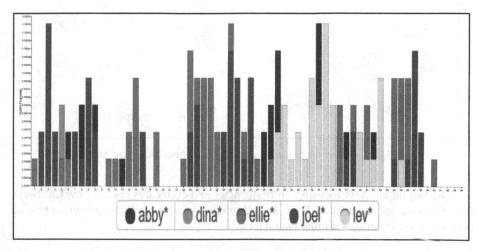

**Fig. 1.** Character names use frequency in Caldwell-Gervais' text

Another way of investigating how Caldwell-Gervais approached the game narrative is identifying their collocates. Yet, collocates of terms related to the narrative design such as character, plot, and story reveal little, with most of these being common English words. Common collocates of character names is reveals more (see Fig. 2). Collocates in Caldwell-Gervais' text reveals a connected understanding of characters. Companion characters' names are juxtaposed with verbs and concepts reflecting their roles in the story, such as Dina with "discussed" and "abandoned", Lev with "say" and "respect". In this regard Ellie and Dina are also linked with "revenge" while Abby and Lev are linked with "just". Ellie's relation with Joel's brother Owen and Abby's sanctuary, the "aquarium" where she spends her private moments, are visible as collocates too. The disconnection between Abby and Joel is also noteworthy and can be read as a reflection of Caldwell-Gervais focusing on the relationship between Joel and Ellie, and not Abby killing Joel.

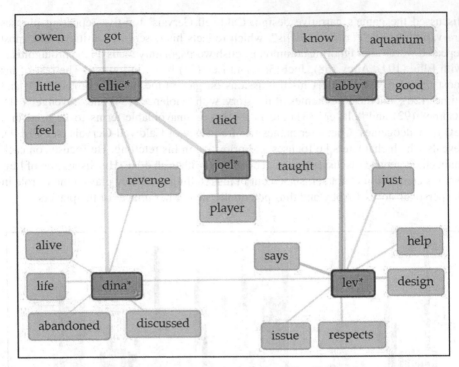

**Fig. 2.** Collocates of character names in Caldwell-Gervais' text.

The Voyant analysis focusing on frequencies and collocates reveals how Caldwell-Gervais discusses the story of *TLoU Part II* gradually in his retelling and shows how he constructs his arguments around characters.

## 4    Conclusion

As detailed, informed, and critical discussions of videogames, longform video essays hold the potential to provide an in-depth record of players' meaning-making processes. Digital humanities tools may prove useful in analyzing how such retellings are constructed by their authors. The Voyant analysis provided a look on how Caldwell-Gervais perceives game characters and their relationships. Further comparative research on a larger sample size is required to understand further advantages of this methodology and may reveal situatedness of game narrative perception. Inclusion of social aspects of shared retellings such as comments and discussion threads may also prove useful. Using custom categories in text mining such as gameplay and narrative design and using further tools focusing on networks formed around retellings may provide deeper insights on how videogame narratives are perceived and discussed among players as well.

## References

1.  Fernandez-Vara, C.: Introduction to Game Analysis. Routledge, New York (2014)

2. Mukherje, S.: Videogames as minor literature: reading videogame stories through paratexts. GRAMMA J. Theory Crit. **23**, 60–75 (2016)
3. Eladhari, M.P.: Re-tellings: the fourth layer of narrative as an instrument for critique. In: Rouse, R., Koenitz, H., Haahr, M. (eds.) ICIDS 2018. LNCS, vol. 11318, pp. 65–78. Springer, Cham (2018). https://doi.org/10.1007/978-3-030-04028-4_5
4. Kerttula, T.: What an eccentric performance: storytelling in online let's plays. Games Cult. **14**(3), 236–255 (2016)
5. Sych, S.: When the fourth layer meets the fourth wall: the case for critical game retellings. In: Bosser, A.-G., Millard, D.E., Hargood, C. (eds.) ICIDS 2020. LNCS, vol. 12497, pp. 203–211. Springer, Cham (2020). https://doi.org/10.1007/978-3-030-62516-0_18
6. Cramer, M.: How We Talk About Games. https://www.youtube.com/watch?v=JVN9h-5UHMk&t=3438s. Accessed 5 June 2021
7. Saklofske, J.: Gaming the Publishing Industry: Exploring Diverse Open Scholarship Models in Digital Games Studies. https://popjournal.ca/issue02/saklofske. Accessed 5 June 2021
8. Koenitz, H.: Towards a specific theory of interactive digital narrative. In: Koenitz, H., Ferri, G., Haahr, M., Sezen, D., Sezen, T.I. (eds.) Interactive Digital Narrative: History, Theory and Practice, pp 91–105. Routledge, New York (2015)
9. Naughty Dog: The Last of Us Part II. Sony Interactive Entertainment (2020)
10. Kreminski, M., Samuel, B., Melcer, E., Wardrip-Fruin, N.: Evaluating AI-based games through retellings. In: Proceedings of Fifteenth AAAI Conference on Artificial Intelligence and Interactive Digital Entertainment, pp 45–51. The AAAI Press, Palo Alto (2019)
11. Toh, W.: The player experience of bioshock: a theory of ludonarrative relationships. In: Ensslin, A., Balteiro, I. (eds.) Approaches to Videogame Discourse: Lexis, Interaction, Textuality, pp 247–268. Bloomsbury Academic, New York (2019)
12. Roth, C., van Nuenen, T., Koenitz, H.: Ludonarrative hermeneutics: a way out and the narrative paradox. In: Rouse, R., Koenitz, H., Haahr, M. (eds.) Interactive Storytelling. ICIDS 2018. LNCS, vol. 11318, pp. 93–106. Springer, Cham (2018). https://doi.org/10.1007/978-3-030-04028-4_7
13. Good, N.: This Oregon-Based Vlogger Might Be the Closest Thing Video Games Have to Roger Ebert. https://www.wweek.com/technology/2020/05/20/this-oregon-based-vlogger-might-be-the-closest-thing-video-games-has-to-roger-ebert/. Accessed 5 June 2021
14. Caldwell-Gervais, N.: How does the Last of Us Part 2 compare to the Last of Us Remastered? https://www.youtube.com/watch?v=Bat38vErWr4. Accessed 5 June 2021
15. Dog, N.: The Last of Us. Sony Interactive Entertainment (2013)
16. Anyó, L., Colom, À.: Emotional ambivalence in the last of us. emotion in video games, between narrative complexity and player loyalty. L'Atalante: Revista de estudios cinematográficos **31**, 85–101 (2021)
17. Vargas, J.A.: AngryJoeShow: The Last of Us Part II - Angry Review. https://www.youtube.com/watch?v=_-sTlYUeT8o&t=3s. Accessed 5 June 2021
18. Sinclair, S., Rockwell, G.: Voyant Tools. http://voyant-tools.org/. Accessed 5 June 2021

# Author Index

Printed in the United States
by Baker & Taylor Publisher Services

Printed in the United States
by Baker & Taylor Publisher Services